Springer Series on Cultural Computing

Cultural Computing is an exciting, emerging field of Human Computer Interaction, which covers the cultural impact of computing and the technological influences and requirements for the support of cultural innovation. Using support technologies such as artificial intelligence, machine learning, location-based systems, mixed/virtual/augmented reality, cloud computing, pervasive technologies and human-data interaction, researchers can explore the differences across a variety of cultures and cultural production to provide the knowledge and skills necessary to overcome cultural issues and expand human creativity.

This series presents monographs, edited collections and advanced textbooks on the current research and knowledge of a broad range of topics including creativity support systems, creative computing, digital communities, the interactive arts, cultural heritage, digital culture and intercultural collaboration.

This Series is abstracted/indexed in Scopus.

Fotis Liarokapis · Maria Shehade ·
Andreas Aristidou · Yiorgos Chrysanthou
Editors

Interactive Media for Cultural Heritage

Springer

Editors
Fotis Liarokapis
CYENS Centre of Excellence
Nicosia, Cyprus

Maria Shehade
CYENS Centre of Excellence and Cyprus University of Technology
Nicosia, Cyprus

Andreas Aristidou
University of Cyprus
Nicosia, Cyprus

Yiorgos Chrysanthou
CYENS Centre of Excellence
Nicosia, Cyprus

ISSN 2195-9056 ISSN 2195-9064 (electronic)
Springer Series on Cultural Computing
ISBN 978-3-031-61017-2 ISBN 978-3-031-61018-9 (eBook)
https://doi.org/10.1007/978-3-031-61018-9

This Springer imprint is published by the registered company Springer Nature Switzerland AG
The registered company address is: Gewerbestrasse 11, 6330 Cham, Switzerland

Introduction

In an era where digital technologies continually redefine our interactions with the world, the field of cultural heritage stands at a transformative crossroads. Digital technologies, particularly interactive media, are reshaping how we preserve, interpret, and engage with cultural artefacts and historical narratives. This edited volume seeks to serve as a comprehensive reference for the latest advancements in the application of interactive media to digital cultural heritage research. By examining a wide array of methodologies—from visual data acquisition to immersive extended reality experiences—this volume aims to provide a multifaceted understanding of how interactive media can enhance the preservation, presentation, and exploration of cultural heritage.

Interactive media, with its capacity for creating engaging, immersive, and dynamic experiences, offers unprecedented opportunities for cultural heritage preservation and dissemination. These technologies enable us to transcend traditional boundaries, making cultural heritage accessible to a global audience. Whether through virtual reconstructions of ancient sites or augmented reality applications that bring history to life, interactive media fosters a deeper connection between the public and cultural heritage, enhancing both education and enjoyment.

The integration of interactive media into cultural heritage is not merely about adopting new tools; it represents a paradigm shift in how we approach the preservation and interpretation of our past. These technologies facilitate interdisciplinary collaboration, bringing together experts from fields as diverse as archaeology, computer science, history, and digital humanities. This collaborative spirit is essential for addressing the complex challenges of cultural heritage preservation in the digital age. By leveraging the strengths of multiple disciplines, we can develop more robust and innovative solutions that ensure the longevity and accessibility of cultural heritage for future generations.

Moreover, interactive media plays a crucial role in addressing the evolving needs and expectations of contemporary audiences. In a world where digital engagement is ubiquitous, cultural institutions must adapt to remain relevant and impactful. Interactive media provides the tools to create personalized, engaging, and educational experiences that resonate with diverse audiences. Through the use of gamification, immersive storytelling, and interactive exhibits, cultural heritage institutions can attract and engage a wider public, fostering a greater appreciation for our shared cultural legacy.

This book aims to highlight these transformative potentials, offering insights and case studies that illustrate the dynamic interplay between technology and cultural heritage. It also seeks to address the growing need for interdisciplinary approaches that leverage these technologies to enhance the accessibility, understanding, and appreciation of cultural heritage. By bringing together contributions from leading researchers and practitioners, the volume highlights the diverse and innovative ways in which interactive media is being employed to preserve and animate the past for present and future generations.

Volume Overview

Interactive Media for Cultural Heritage is structured in four parts, each dedicated to exploring different types of interactive media and applications within the realm of cultural heritage. These parts collectively provide a comprehensive overview of the state-of-the-art in the field, featuring both theoretical discussions and practical case studies. By including examples from diverse geographical locations, the volume ensures an international perspective, thereby enriching the discourse with varied cultural contexts and practices. This interdisciplinary approach not only fosters cross-fertilization of ideas but also encourages collaboration among different research communities, bridging gaps and creating new synergies between the fields of computer science and cultural heritage.

Part I, entitled *Cutting-Edge Applications of Extended Reality in Cultural Heritage Preservation*, delves into the integration of extended reality technologies in cultural heritage preservation. The six chapters of this part explore various applications, including mixed-reality installations in museums, innovative technologies for archaeological sites, human-centered extended reality experimentations, immersive acoustics, olfactory memory mapping, and virtual tour systems. These contributions highlight how extended reality has the potential to revolutionize the way we experience and interact with cultural heritage, making it more accessible and engaging for diverse audiences.

In Part II, entitled *Cultural Heritage Preservation and Exploration Through Emerging Digital Technologies*, the focus shifts to emerging digital technologies that facilitate the preservation and exploration of cultural heritage. The seven chapters cover a wide spectrum of topics, from digital surrogates of modern architecture and 3D digital fabrication to photogrammetric computer vision, digital cultural heritage twins, motion labelling and recognition, virtual restoration, and multispectral imaging. These studies emphasize novel interaction modalities, best practices, and future perspectives, demonstrating the versatility and importance of digital technologies in preserving and understanding cultural artefacts.

Part III is dedicated to *Interactive and Immersive Experiences for Storytelling in Cultural Heritage.* Storytelling is a powerful tool for cultural heritage engagement, and this part examines how interactive and immersive experiences can enhance narrative forms. The five chapters investigate gameplay elements, interactive narratives, digital interactions in children's museums, cultural heritage space design, and human animatronics in museum experiences. By exploring these innovative approaches, the part demonstrates the potential of interactive media in creating engaging and meaningful cultural heritage narratives.

The final Part IV, entitled *Innovative Approaches to Interactive Cultural Heritage Visualization*, focuses on the visualization of cultural heritage through innovative interactive media. The four chapters discuss multimodal presentations of traditional crafts, associative principles in virtual collections, best practices for interactive kiosk design, and applications of real-time graphics systems. These contributions highlight the importance of visualization in making cultural heritage accessible and engaging, providing practical insights into designing effective interactive experiences.

Presentation of the Chapters in this Volume

Part I: *Cutting-Edge Applications of Extended Reality in Cultural Heritage Preservation* explores the innovative use of extended reality (XR) technologies in cultural heritage. Through case studies and theoretical insights, it highlights approaches that merge digital tools with user-centered design to preserve and present cultural heritage in engaging, multisensory ways. Chapter 1, "Conveying Intangible Cultural Heritage Via Mixed-Reality Installations in Museums: Reflections from Three Case Studies", by Vosinakis and Koutsabasis examines three mixed-reality (MR) installations in museums across Greece, focusing on industrial craftsmanship and intangible heritage. By analyzing design processes, interaction methods, and user engagement, it provides actionable insights for creating impactful and educational museum experiences. Chapter 2, "Creating Innovative Technologies for Archaeological Sites: Augmented—Mixed Reality Educational Platform at the Spartan Sanctuary of Apollon Amyklaios", by Vlizos et al., showcases an AR/MR platform developed for the Sanctuary of Apollon Amyklaios in Sparta. It explores how 3D mapping, modelling, and metadata schemes enhance archaeological documentation and create immersive educational tools, bridging research and public engagement. In Chap. 3 "From Headsets to Mindsets: A Taxonomy for Human-Centred Extended Reality Experimentations for Cultural Heritage", Lameras et al. Introduce a taxonomy for XR applications, providing guidance on the design of interactive and meaningful cultural heritage experiences. It outlines strategies to align technology with user needs, emphasizing participation and significance-building in XR environments. Chapter 4 "Immersive Acoustics in Cultural Heritage Applications", by Harvey et al., investigates the role of sound in cultural heritage through a case study of the Panagia Angeloktisti Byzantine church in Cyprus. It highlights methods for integrating spatialized sound with visual elements to create authentic and emotionally engaging heritage experiences. In Chap. 5, "Mapping Olfactory Memories: Digital Maps as an Interactive Medium for Olfactory Cultural Heritage", Pastra et al. explore the potential of digital maps to document and share olfactory cultural heritage. The chapter discusses interdisciplinary challenges and proposes strategies for visualizing olfactory data to foster community connections and multisensory engagement. Finally, Chap. 6 "User Acceptance of 720-Degree Virtual Tour Systems for Online Museum Experiences: Effects of Immersion, Interaction, and Personal Innovativeness" by Li et al., studies factors influencing the acceptance of 720° virtual tours in online museum settings. It identifies key design elements, such as immersion and interaction, that enhance user experience and provides recommendations for improving accessibility and engagement. The chapters of this part highlight the transformative potential of XR technologies in cultural heritage, emphasizing innovative approaches to enhance accessibility, engagement, and multisensory storytelling. These insights serve as a foundation for advancing XR's role in preserving and sharing cultural heritage.

Part II: *Cultural Heritage Preservation and Exploration Through Emerging Digital Technologies* underscores the transformative impact of digital technologies in the preservation, reconstruction, and engagement with cultural heritage. By leveraging tools like virtual reality, 3D printing, photogrammetry, and artificial intelligence, these chapters explore how tangible and intangible heritage can be digitized, enhanced, and made more accessible. Chapter 7, "Immersed in Architecture's Digital Surrogates" by Artopoulos et al., emphasizes the role of immersive technologies in revitalizing the preservation and understanding of modern architectural heritage. Through the integration of archival content, virtual reality, and community-driven participation, the chapter highlights how immersive 3D real-time visualization provides a richer and more accessible approach to architectural history. In Chap. 8 "From Physical to Digital and Back: Novel Modalities for Interaction with Cultural Heritage Through 3D Digital Fabrication", Samaroudi and Rodriguez Echavarria explore the integration of 3D fabrication technologies. The study points to how tactile engagement through replicas transforms heritage interactions, fostering deeper connections between communities and heritage. Chapter 9, "Photogrammetric Computer Vision—Good Practices and Pitfalls" by Georgopoulos and Tapinaki provides an overview of photogrammetry's evolution through computer vision algorithms. While automation and democratization have broadened accessibility, the chapter warns against pitfalls for non-expert users, offering illustrated guidelines for achieving reliable results, highlighting best practices and practical considerations for using photogrammetry in heritage documentation. Introducing the concept of "Digital Cultural Heritage Twins," the next Chap. 10 by Zarri bridges the physical and conceptual dimensions of heritage. It advocates for a dual representation system: one capturing measurable physical traits and another embodying symbolic and emotional narratives. The case study demonstrates how narrative knowledge representation can enrich our understanding of iconic works, such as Da Vinci's "hidden painting" beneath the Mona Lisa, enabling immersive exploration of complex heritage narratives. Chapter 11, "Motion Labelling and

Recognition: A Case Study on the Zeibekiko Dance" by Skublewska-Paszkowska et al., focuses on the intangible cultural heritage of folk dance, using Zeibekiko as a case study for applying motion capture and recognition technologies. The chapter highlights potential applications, such as indexing dance patterns across cultures and developing e-learning tools for teaching traditional dances. In Chap. 12 "Virtual Restoration of Archaeological Artifacts", Shimshoni and Tal address the challenges of restoring ancient artifacts in digital formats, exploring tasks such as reassembly, re-colorization, and document enhancement. By emphasizing the scarcity of archaeological datasets and the limitations of general-purpose algorithms, the chapter presents specialized methods and innovations for achieving realistic restorations of eroded and fragmented artifacts. Finally, in Chap. 13 "Low-Barrier-to-Entry Multispectral Imaging: Enhancing Understanding of and Furthering Access of Cultural Heritage Artifacts", Decker et al. focus on the creation of an affordable and user-friendly multispectral imaging system (MISHA), highlighting its application in capturing and visualizing artifacts to enhance accessibility and understanding. Through case studies, the chapter illustrates how this system democratizes access to advanced imaging techniques, enabling diverse professionals to uncover hidden details in historical artifacts. From fostering participatory approaches and tactile engagements to enhancing visualization and accessibility, the digital tools presented in this part allow for nuanced and multifaceted explorations of heritage, also highlighting the importance of specialized methodologies, underscoring the need for tailored approaches in cultural heritage research and practice.

Part III: *Interactive and Immersive Experiences for Storytelling in Cultural Heritage* highlights the transformative role of interactive and immersive technologies in enriching storytelling practices for cultural heritage. By focusing on innovative applications such as gamification, virtual agents, interactive installations, immersive performances, and animatronics, these chapters demonstrate how digital tools can bridge the gap between cultural heritage content and audiences, creating more engaging, educational, and entertaining experiences. Chapter 14, "Gameplay Elements in Digital Cultural Heritage Applications", by Rizvic et al., explores how gamification and interactive storytelling can create an edutainment factor in cultural heritage applications. By employing virtual reality to immerse users in historical events, traditions, and settings, the chapter highlights how gameplay elements can enhance learning and overcome challenges like the narrative paradox. Chapter 15, "Virtual Agents and Interactive Digital Narrative in XR Experiences for Cultural Heritage", by Katifori et al., examines the role of virtual guides (VGs) in immersive extended reality (XR) applications. By critiquing current design approaches, it advocates for more engaging and interpretive narrative designs that utilize virtual agents to enrich cultural heritage storytelling in immersive virtual and augmented reality contexts. In Chap. 16, "Delving Into Fairy Tales: Designing for Digital Interactions in a Children's Museum", Shehade et al. focus on interactive installations for young audiences. By analyzing two installations, the chapter explores how interactive technologies can foster fantasy and imagination in museum settings, particularly in the context of fairy tales. Similarly, Chap. 17 "ReInHeriting Cultural Heritage Spaces", by Papapetrou et al., discusses two interdisciplinary immersive performances developed under the Horizon 2020 ReInHerit project. These performances used cultural heritage sites as dynamic backdrops, encouraging audience participation and demonstrating the potential of interactive media for performance design and community engagement. Chap. 18, "Human Animatronics in Museum Experience: Casa Parlante—The Living Museum", by Paschou and Papaioannou, presents findings from a study on visitor engagement with human-resembling animatronics in a museum in Corfu, Greece. It reveals how animatronics captivate audiences by enriching the museum narrative and fostering both cognitive and emotional engagement. Together, these chapters of this part emphasize the power of interactive and immersive experiences to reimagine cultural heritage storytelling and deepen connections between heritage content and diverse audiences.

The chapters in Part IV: *Innovative Approaches to Interactive Cultural Heritage Visualization*, collectively explore how innovative visual technologies are being leveraged to enhance the presentation, interpretation, and engagement with cultural heritage. By examining multimodal presentations, interactive media design principles, interactive kiosks, and real-time graphics systems, these chapters provide a comprehensive overview of the cutting-edge techniques used to visualize and experience cultural heritage. Chapter 19, "Multimodal Presentations of the Tangible and Intangible Dimensions of Traditional Crafts" by Partarakis et al., discusses the integration of digital assets and semantic annotations to capture the rich socio-historic context of traditional crafts. The authors argue that using personalized storytelling, AR, augmented physical artifacts, MR exhibitions, and web-based presentations can significantly enhance cultural experiences, boosting interest and tourism. In Chap. 20, "Re-Mediating Interaction with Online Art Collections" Bertrand et al. critique current digital cultural participation models. The chapter introduces an interactive recommender system that employs a 'creative curating' approach, diverging from typical algorithmic curation to foster user-driven exploration and aesthetic choice in online art collections. Chapter 21, by Potenziani et al., "Designing and Developing Interactive Kiosks for Cultural Heritage: Best Practices and Common Issues," provides practical guidance on creating interactive kiosks. These kiosks enhance visitor engagement and complement digital heritage projects by displaying complex 2D and 3D data and implementing advanced interaction paradigms. The authors highlight strategies, tools, and past examples to aid developers in this process. Chapter 21, "Interactive Tangible and Intangible Heritage Applications Built on Real-Time Graphics Systems", by Anderson et al., explores the use of modern virtual environment infrastructure, such as game engines, in creating diverse cultural heritage applications. Through various case studies, the chapter showcases the effectiveness of real-time computer graphics technology in developing interactive museum exhibits, games, and mobile apps, demonstrating their utility in both tangible and intangible heritage contexts. By delving into these innovative approaches, this part underscores the transformative potential of interactive media in making cultural heritage more accessible, engaging, and immersive. The insights provided not only highlight current advancements but also pave the way for future developments in cultural heritage visualization.

Through all the aforementioned chapters, *Interactive Media for Cultural Heritage* presents a collection of theoretical insights and practical case studies that illustrate the transformative potential of interactive media in the field of cultural heritage. By showcasing the diverse ways in which digital technologies can enhance the preservation, interpretation, and engagement with cultural heritage, this volume aims to inspire further innovation and collaboration amongst academics, researchers, and practitioners from computer science and cultural heritage. The interdisciplinary approach adopted in this book not only bridges the gap between technology and humanities but also paves the way for future collaborations and research endeavours, ensuring a dynamic and evolving landscape for cultural heritage preservation.

The case studies and theoretical discussions within this volume highlight the myriad applications of interactive media, from extended reality experiences that bring history to life, to digital surrogates that offer new ways of engaging with architectural heritage. These examples demonstrate the capacity of interactive media to provide deeper, more immersive experiences that transcend traditional methods of cultural heritage dissemination, emphasizing at the same time the importance of user-centred design. The integration of technologies such as augmented reality, virtual reality, and mixed reality into cultural heritage projects opens up new avenues for exploration and learning, making cultural heritage more accessible and engaging to diverse audiences.

As we continue to navigate the digital age, the insights and innovations presented in this book will undoubtedly play a crucial role in shaping the future of cultural heritage preservation and engagement. It is our hope that this book will serve as a valuable resource and point of reference for those engaged in this dynamic and interdisciplinary field, to create more engaging, accessible, and meaningful cultural heritage experiences for all.

Nicosia, Cyprus
2024

Fotis Liarokapis
Maria Shehade
Andreas Aristidou
Yiorgos Chrysanthou

Acknowledgements The editors of this volume are affiliated with the CYENS Centre of Excellence, Cyprus. CYENS Centre of Excellence has received funding from the European Union's Horizon 2020 Research and Innovation Programme under Grant Agreement No. 739578 and the Government of the Republic of Cyprus through the Deputy Ministry of Research, Innovation and Digital Policy.

Contents

Part I Cutting-Edge Applications of Extended Reality in Cultural Heritage Preservation

1 Conveying Intangible Cultural Heritage Via Mixed-Reality Installations in Museums: Reflections from Three Case Studies 3
Spyros Vosinakis and Panayiotis Koutsabasis

2 Creating Innovative Technologies for Archaeological Sites: Augmented—Mixed Reality Educational Platform at the Spartan Sanctuary of Apollon Amyklaios 27
Stavros Vlizos, Konstantinos Kotsopoulos, and Sarantos Kapidakis

3 From Headsets to Mindsets: A Taxonomy for Human-Centred Extended Reality Experimentations for Cultural Heritage 59
Petros Lameras, Sylvester Arnab, Jacqueline Cawston, Alex Masters, Michael Loizou, and Panagiotis Petridis

4 Immersive Acoustics in Cultural Heritage Applications 75
Carlo Harvey, Mattia Colombo, Benjamin West, Jassim Happa, and Islah Ali-MacLachlan

5 Mapping Olfactory Memories: Digital Maps as an Interactive Medium for Olfactory Cultural Heritage 107
Katerina Pastra, Margarita Kokla, Eleni Tomai, Fotis Liarokapis, Maria Bezerianou, Athanasia Darra, Kostas Cheliotis, and Marinos Kavouras

6 User Acceptance of 720° Virtual Tour Systems for Online Museum Experiences: Effects of Immersion, Interaction, and Personal Innovativeness 129
Yue Li, Jiachen Liang, Enhao Yang, and Hai-Ning Liang

Part II Cultural Heritage Preservation and Exploration Through Emerging Digital Technologies

7 Immersed in Digital Surrogates: Reconstructing Difficult Heritage of Modern Architecture 157
Georgios Artopoulos, Nicolas Loucas, and Popi Iacovou

8 From Physical to Digital and Back: Novel Modalities for Interaction with Cultural Heritage Through 3D Digital Fabrication 179
Myrsini Samaroudi and Karina Rodriguez Echavarria

9 Photogrammetric Computer Vision—Good Practices and Pitfalls 201
Andreas Georgopoulos and Sevasti Tapinaki

10 Digital Cultural Heritage Twins: New Tools for a Complete Fruition of the Cultural Heritage Entities 227
Gian Piero Zarri

11 Motion Labeling and Recognition: A Case Study on the Zeibekiko Dance 251
Maria Skublewska-Paszkowska, Pawel Powroznik, Marilena Lemonari, and Andreas Aristidou

12 Virtual Restoration of Archaeological Artifacts 267
Ilan Shimshoni and Ayellet Tal

13 Low-Barrier-to-Entry Multispectral Imaging: Enhancing Understanding of and Furthering Access to Cultural Heritage Artifacts 291
Juilee Decker, David W. Messinger, and Roger L. Easton Jr.

Part III Interactive and Immersive Experiences for Storytelling in Cultural Heritage

14 Gameplay Elements in Digital Cultural Heritage Applications 313
Selma Rizvic, Bojan Mijatovic, Ivona Ivkovic-Kihic, and Dusanka Boskovic

15 Virtual Agents and Interactive Digital Narrative in XR Experiences for Cultural Heritage. Designing for Engagement 335
Akrivi Katifori, Angeliki Chysanthi, Androniki Agelada, Maria Vayanou, and Vlasios Kasapakis

16 Delving into Fairy Tales: Designing for Digital Interactions in a Children's Museum 359
Maria Shehade, Theopisti Stylianou-Lambert, Panagiotis Kyriakou, Fotos Frangoudes, Maria Pavlou, Stefanos Papadas, and Kleanthis Neokleous

17 Reinheriting Cultural Heritage Spaces: Performance Design and Practice ... 381
Andreas Papapetrou, Fotos Frangoudes, Alexis Polydorou, Stefanos Papadas, Maria Shehade, Niki Kyriakou, and Kleanthis Neokleous

18 Human Animatronics in Museum Experience: *Casa Parlante—The Living Museum*, Corfu, Greece ... 407
Sofia Paschou and Georgios Papaioannou

Part IV Innovative Approaches to Interactive Cultural Heritage Visualization

19 Multimodal Presentations of the Tangible and Intangible Dimensions of Traditional Crafts ... 425
Nikolaos Partarakis, Paraskevi Doulgeraki, Efrosyni Karouzaki, Emmanouil Zidianakis, and Xenophon Zabulis

20 Re-mediating Interaction with Online Art Collections: How Creative Curating Can Enhance Discovery Through Recommendations Towards a New Model of Cultural Participation ... 449
Stéphanie Bertrand, George Papagiannakis, George Margetis, Stavroula Ntoa, Nikolaos Partarakis, Xenophon Zabulis, and Constantine Stephanidis

21 Designing and Developing Interactive Kiosks for Cultural Heritage: Best Practices and Common Issues ... 473
Marco Potenziani, Marco Callieri, and Paolo Cignoni

22 Interactive Tangible and Intangible Heritage Applications Built on Real-Time Graphics Systems: Heritage Experiences in Desktop CG, Virtual and Augmented Reality ... 499
Eike Falk Anderson, Valery Adzhiev, Paul Cheetham, Glyn Hadley, David John, Catja Larsson, Ana-Maria-Cristina Ureche, and Mario Romero

Contributors

Valery Adzhiev The National Centre for Computer Animation, Bournemouth University, Poole, UK

Androniki Agelada Department of Cultural Technology and Communication, University of the Aegean, Lesvos, Greece

Islah Ali-MacLachlan College of Computing, STEAMhouse, Birmingham City University, Birmingham, UK

Eike Falk Anderson The National Centre for Computer Animation, Bournemouth University, Poole, UK

Andreas Aristidou Department of Computer Science, University of Cyprus, Nicosia, Cyprus

Sylvester Arnab Coventry University, Coventry, UK

Georgios Artopoulos The Cyprus Institute, Nicosia, Cyprus

Stéphanie Bertrand Foundation for Research and Technology Hellas, Heraklion, Greece

Maria Bezerianou School of Rural, Surveying and Geoinformatics Engineering, National Technical University of Athens, Athens, Greece

Dusanka Boskovic Faculty of Electrical Engineering, University of Sarajevo, Sarajevo, Bosnia and Herzegovina

Marco Callieri ISTI, CNR, Pisa, Italy

Jacqueline Cawston Coventry University, Coventry, UK

Paul Cheetham Department of Archaeology and Anthropology, Bournemouth University, Poole, UK

Kostas Cheliotis School of Rural, Surveying and Geoinformatics Engineering, National Technical University of Athens, Athens, Greece

Angeliki Chysanthi Department of Cultural Technology and Communication, University of the Aegean, Lesvos, Greece

Paolo Cignoni ISTI, CNR, Pisa, Italy

Mattia Colombo College of Computing, STEAMhouse, Birmingham City University, Birmingham, UK

Athanasia Darra School of Rural, Surveying and Geoinformatics Engineering, National Technical University of Athens, Athens, Greece

Juilee Decker Rochester Institute of Technology, Rochester, NY, USA

Paraskevi Doulgeraki Foundation for Research and Technology Hellas, Institute of Computer Science, Heraklion, Crete, Greece

Roger L. Easton Jr. Rochester Institute of Technology, Rochester, NY, USA

Fotos Frangoudes CYENS Centre of Excellence, Nicosia, Cyprus

Andreas Georgopoulos Laboratory of Photogrammetry, School of Rural, Surveying and Geoinformatics Engineering, National Technical University of Athens, Zografou, Greece

Glyn Hadley Department of Creative Technology, Bournemouth University, Poole, UK

Jassim Happa Department of Information Security, Royal Holloway, University of London, Egham, UK

Carlo Harvey School of Digital Arts, Manchester Metropolitan University, Manchester, UK

Popi Iacovou University of Cyprus, Nicosia, Cyprus

Ivona Ivkovic-Kihic Faculty of Electrical Engineering, University of Sarajevo, Sarajevo, Bosnia and Herzegovina;
Graz University of Technology, Graz, Austria

David John Department of Creative Technology, Bournemouth University, Poole, UK

Sarantos Kapidakis University of Western Attica, Aigaleo, Greece

Efrosyni Karouzaki Foundation for Research and Technology Hellas, Institute of Computer Science, Heraklion, Crete, Greece

Vlasios Kasapakis Department of Cultural Technology and Communication, University of the Aegean, Lesvos, Greece

Akrivi Katifori Department of Informatics and Telecommunications, National and Kapodistrian University of Athens, Athens, Greece

Marinos Kavouras School of Rural, Surveying and Geoinformatics Engineering, National Technical University of Athens, Athens, Greece

Margarita Kokla School of Rural, Surveying and Geoinformatics Engineering, National Technical University of Athens, Athens, Greece

Konstantinos Kotsopoulos University of Patras, Patras, Greece

Panayiotis Koutsabasis Department of Product and Systems Design Engineering, University of the Aegean, Ermoupoli, Greece

Niki Kyriakou CYENS Centre of Excellence, Nicosia, Cyprus

Panagiotis Kyriakou CYENS Centre of Excellence, Nicosia, Cyprus

Petros Lameras Coventry University, Coventry, UK

Catja Larsson Bournemouth University, Poole, UK

Marilena Lemonari Department of Computer Science, University of Cyprus, Nicosia, Cyprus

Yue Li Department of Computing, School of Advanced Technology, Xi'an Jiaotong-Liverpool University, Suzhou, China

Hai-Ning Liang Department of Computing, School of Advanced Technology, Xi'an Jiaotong-Liverpool University, Suzhou, China

Jiachen Liang School of Advanced Technology, Xi'an Jiaotong-Liverpool University, Suzhou, China

Fotis Liarokapis Extended Experiences MRG, CYENS - Centre of Excellence, Nicosia, Cyprus

Michael Loizou University of Plymouth, Plymouth, UK

Nicolas Loucas The Cyprus Institute, Nicosia, Cyprus

George Margetis Foundation for Research and Technology Hellas, Heraklion, Greece

Alex Masters Coventry University, Coventry, UK

David W. Messinger Rochester Institute of Technology, Rochester, NY, USA

Bojan Mijatovic Sarajevo School of Science and Technology, Sarajevo, Bosnia and Herzegovina

Kleanthis Neokleous CYENS Centre of Excellence, Nicosia, Cyprus

Stavroula Ntoa Foundation for Research and Technology Hellas, Heraklion, Greece

Stefanos Papadas CYENS Centre of Excellence, Nicosia, Cyprus

George Papagiannakis Foundation for Research and Technology Hellas, Heraklion, Greece

Georgios Papaioannou Museology Research Laboratory, Ionian University, Corfu, Greece

Andreas Papapetrou CYENS Centre of Excellence, Nicosia, Cyprus

Nikolaos Partarakis Foundation for Research and Technology Hellas, Institute of Computer Science, Heraklion, Crete, Greece

Sofia Paschou Museology Research Laboratory, Ionian University, Corfu, Greece

Katerina Pastra Institute for Language and Speech Processing, ATHENA Research Center, Athens, Greece

Maria Pavlou CYENS Centre of Excellence, Nicosia, Cyprus

Panagiotis Petridis Aston University, Birmingham, UK

Alexis Polydorou CYENS Centre of Excellence, Nicosia, Cyprus

Marco Potenziani ISTI, CNR, Pisa, Italy

Pawel Powroznik Department of Computer Science, Lublin University of Technology, Lublin, Poland

Selma Rizvic Faculty of Electrical Engineering, University of Sarajevo, Sarajevo, Bosnia and Herzegovina

Karina Rodriguez Echavarria School of Architecture, Technology and Engineering, University of Brighton, Brighton, UK

Mario Romero Department of Computational Science and Technology, KTH Royal Institute of Technology, Stockholm, Sweden;
Department of Science and Technology, Linköping University, Linköping, Sweden

Myrsini Samaroudi School of Architecture, Technology and Engineering, University of Brighton, Brighton, UK

Maria Shehade CYENS Centre of Excellence, Nicosia, Cyprus;
Cyprus University of Technology, Limassol, Cyprus

Ilan Shimshoni The University of Haifa, Haifa, Israel

Maria Skublewska-Paszkowska Department of Computer Science, Lublin University of Technology, Lublin, Poland

Constantine Stephanidis Foundation for Research and Technology Hellas, Heraklion, Greece

Theopisti Stylianou-Lambert CYENS Centre of Excellence, Nicosia, Cyprus;
Cyprus University of Technology, Limassol, Cyprus

Ayellet Tal Technion, Haifa, Israel

Sevasti Tapinaki Laboratory of Photogrammetry, School of Rural, Surveying and Geoinformatics Engineering, National Technical University of Athens, Zografou, Greece

Eleni Tomai School of Rural, Surveying and Geoinformatics Engineering, National Technical University of Athens, Athens, Greece

Ana-Maria-Cristina Ureche Bournemouth University, Poole, UK

Maria Vayanou Department of Informatics and Telecommunications, National and Kapodistrian University of Athens, Athens, Greece

Stavros Vlizos Ionian University, Corfu, Greece;
Amykles Research Project, Sparta, Greece

Spyros Vosinakis Department of Product and Systems Design Engineering, University of the Aegean, Ermoupoli, Greece

Benjamin West College of Computing, STEAMhouse, Birmingham City University, Birmingham, UK

Enhao Yang School of Advanced Technology, Xi'an Jiaotong-Liverpool University, Suzhou, China

Xenophon Zabulis Foundation for Research and Technology Hellas, Institute of Computer Science, Heraklion, Crete, Greece

Gian Piero Zarri STIH Laboratory, Sorbonne University, Paris, France

Emmanouil Zidianakis Foundation for Research and Technology Hellas, Institute of Computer Science, Heraklion, Crete, Greece

Part I
Cutting-Edge Applications of Extended Reality in Cultural Heritage Preservation

Chapter 1
Conveying Intangible Cultural Heritage Via Mixed-Reality Installations in Museums: Reflections from Three Case Studies

Spyros Vosinakis and Panayiotis Koutsabasis

Abstract Mixed reality (MR) is considered an effective medium for enriching museums with digital content, enhancing the visiting experience with interactive and playful elements and contextualizing the exhibits and the physical space. Especially in the case of intangible heritage, where human practices and traditions cannot be easily expressed by inanimate objects alone, targeted MR installations may provide an additional source of communication and dissemination with active user involvement. However, the wide variety of approaches, paradigms and technologies that have been developed so far create a large design space with little feedback on the impact of each design choice on visitor experience and learning effectiveness. This chapter reflects on the design, implementation, and user evaluation of three Mixed-Reality installations in respective museums in the Aegean region in Greece, highlighting intangible cultural heritage, and more specifically industrial and craftsmanship heritage. The installations utilize methods from interaction design following iterative evaluation cycles, from concept creation to final system development, both in the laboratory and the museums' settings, and inform on the suitability of the adopted processes. The three MR design approaches range in terms of technological configuration and affordances, interaction metaphors and user's perspective, users' collaboration, gamification, education, and entertainment. Based on the results of the field studies and the intermediate user evaluation cycles, we present how user experience can align with the conceptual design inspired by specific nuances of the presented intangible cultural heritage, focusing on local craftsmanship, industrial heritage, and the working culture of the people in these places. In addition, the chapter provides design recommendations for other researchers, practitioners, and professionals working in similar museum and heritage contexts.

S. Vosinakis (✉) · P. Koutsabasis
Department of Product and Systems Design Engineering, University of the Aegean, Ermoupoli, Greece
e-mail: spyrosv@aegean.gr

P. Koutsabasis
e-mail: kgp@aegean.gr

F. Liarokapis et al. (eds.), *Interactive Media for Cultural Heritage*, Springer Series on Cultural Computing, https://doi.org/10.1007/978-3-031-61018-9_1

Keywords Mixed reality · Interactive installations · Museums · User experience · Intangible cultural heritage · Industrial heritage

1.1 Introduction

The appropriate design and use of technology in museums can provide an engaging means of sharing knowledge and information, facilitate museum-visitor communication and improve the visitor experience. Interactive technologies such as virtual and augmented reality, kinesthetic and gesture-based interactions, voice and multi-touch interfaces, and others, have been developed in various combinations that arouse the interest and engagement of visitors, who may gain information and knowledge, stimulate emotions, bring up memories, and more generally contribute to unique user experiences (UX). This is one of the main goals of modern museums and exhibition spaces.

Many museums promote the idea of intangible cultural heritage (ICH) that has its roots in the emergence of a holistic approach to documentation, restoration, and promotion of culture. In contrast to tangible cultural heritage that refers to physical artifacts and structures created by human beings, such as buildings, monuments, documents, and artworks, ICH encompasses non-physical attributes passed down through generations. These include the practices, expressions, knowledge, and skills that communities, groups, and sometimes individuals recognize as part of their heritage. Preserving and highlighting intangible cultural heritage is crucial for maintaining cultural diversity and ensuring the transmission of traditions, knowledge, and expressions from generation to generation (Idris et al. 2016). Tangible, and intangible heritage are inevitably connected but not always distinguishable; cultural expressions are almost always associated with tangible elements, such as clothes, tools, buildings, or places. To understand the importance and meaning of the first, one needs to consider the latter and vice versa (Bouchenaki 2003).

Two important aspects of ICH are industrial heritage and traditional craftsmanship. The first refers to the history of industrial technology, the organization of production, the people, factories, places, architecture, as well as related customs and social activities (Douet 2016). The latter refers to the skills and knowledge involved in craftsmanship, craft products themselves and on encouraging artisans to continue to produce craft and to pass their skills and knowledge onto others, particularly within their own communities. According to UNESCO it is "perhaps the most tangible manifestation of intangible cultural heritage".

The use of smart artifacts and interactive installations in museums can be a promising means for communicating aspects of tangible and intangible heritage to younger generations. The concept of "hybrid" museum artifacts, combining physical and digital representations has emerged over the last two decades (Bannon et al. 2005). Initially, these installations involved physical objects responding to movement and triggering digital media. Later approaches emphasized user interaction with tangible elements, offering a more engaging and natural experience than common touchscreen interfaces (Dimitropoulos et al. 2017; Gkiti et al. 2018; Hornecker and Bur 2006). New sensor and projection technologies have enabled personalized narratives, audiovisual content, tactile, and olfactory sensations, creating "phygital" heritage experiences (Chu et al. 2016; Ioakeim et al. 2020; Koutsabasis and Vosinakis 2018; Price et al. 2016). These installations have shown to benefit museum visitors by offering personalized and constructive learning experiences, encouraging collaboration, and engaging diverse preferences.

The above-mentioned approaches fall in the area of Mixed Reality (MR) in the sense that they effectively blend physical and digital elements in a unified interaction space. Although there is no universally agreed upon definition for MR (Speicher et al. 2019), in this Chapter we are using the term in an inclusive way, to describe museum visiting experiences that may incorporate various types of visualization and interaction technologies to achieve this goal (Bekele et al. 2018). MR systems remain a relatively new area for designers and heritage professionals, with limited guidelines available, creating a large and unexplored design space. In agreement to Hornecker and Stifter (2006), we argue that the emphasis in designing these installations should be on interactivity, personalized content, and optimizing the visitor experience. Factors like information design, presentation, navigation, and environment settings are crucial for designing virtual environments for cultural heritage (Ibrahim and Ali 2018). Integrating real and virtual concepts and combining different interaction paradigms, such as tangible interfaces and virtual reality, can enhance the museum experience for a diverse audience (Pietroni 2019).

This chapter reflects on three MR installations developed for respective museums in the Aegean region in Greece, highlighting intangible cultural heritage and heritage of craftsmanship, in terms of the R&D project Mouseion Topos (i.e., Museums' place), which promotes industrial heritage and heritage of craftsmanship of three Aegean islands with the design of interactive and playful technologies. For each island and museum an MR installation was developed (Nikolakopoulou et al. 2022a, b; Vosinakis et al. 2021), as well as a mobile location-based game (Koutsabasis et al. 2022). For each MR system, we present (a) the aspects of ICH of concern, (b) the design and development approach followed, and (c) the empirical evaluation of the UX of museum visitors. The chapter discusses lessons learnt and makes recommendations for other researchers, practitioners, and professionals working in similar museum and heritage contexts.

1.2 A Physical Interactive Crane for Playful Tasks in a Digital Marble Quarry

1.2.1 Intangible Cultural Heritage of Tinian Marble Craftsmanship

The Museum of Marble Crafts in Pyrgos, Tinos, Cyclades, exhibits the Tinian marble craftsmanship, which constitutes intangible cultural heritage of humanity since 2015. The exhibits present the technology, techniques, crafts, artefacts, and expertise around Tinian marble (Fig. 1.1). Based on these, the museum aims to inform the visitors about the social and economic context from which the craftspeople of Pyrgos advanced their knowledge and businesses, contributing to the cultural legacy of their place. This legacy is also natural. Tinos is an island 'resting on marble veins', and therefore, Tinian quarries are not excluded from the museum's exhibits. Moreover, quarries complement marble craftsmanship, including workers' methods and know-how and rare pieces of pre-industrial machinery. The museum is located at the village of Pyrgos, which is the birthplace of many Tinian marble crafts artists and workers, and it is full of marble works and monuments.

The MR installation focuses on the marble extraction process and the use of the old crane in the quarries of Tinos. This subject is presented in the museum with two landmark exhibits. The first is about the "Karageorgy's company at Vathi", a historic Tinian quarry business located at the island's northwest coast and is exhibited at the middle of the museum's visit. The exhibit concerns the workings process in the mining business: from marble extraction at the quarry's spring to transportation of marble blocks at the quarry's dock. The second exhibit is a pre-industrial marble lifting machine that dominates the museum's entrance. This historic crane, known as 'biga', belonged to the company. It is an impressive piece of machinery, restored from the quarry's dock, but it is neither operational nor explanatory about its functionality. The exhibit provides information mainly about its restoration process and usage inside the quarry. Thus, visitors do not have the opportunity to interact with the 'biga' and learn more about its operation. Our design approach attempts to enhance this gap in the visiting experience by engaging visitors in a playful learning environment.

1.2.2 System Design and Development

The MR installation serves two purposes. First, to make visitors get to know the basic functionality of the marble-lifting crane and understand how to operate it. And secondly, to explain how the quarry workers worked together to extract the marble. That is, to present the roles, the form of communication (gestural signals between workers) and the operational flow.

Fig. 1.1 Left, up: the biga (crane) at the entrance of the museum of marble crafts. Left, down: View of the interior of the museum, section of 'works at the quarry'. Right, up: View of a house in the village of Pyrgos with lintels made of marble works of art. Right, down: A bus stop made of marble in the village (!), a creation and contribution by local artists

The system combines a physical object as an input device and a real time digital representation that presents a virtual quarry environment on screen (Fig. 1.2). The user is required to operate the crane to transport a volume of marble from the quarry to a wagon, which will eventually direct it to the port to be loaded onto the ship. To achieve this goal, the user must use the physical controller that has an abstract simplified form of a small-scale crane and analogous ways of operating it. Possible actions include: turning a crank forward or backward, changing gears, and pulling the crane's side ropes to the left or right. Gear shifting determines the effect of turning the crank. In one position the crank raises or lowers the boom, and in the second position it raises or lowers the hook to which the marble volume will be attached. Finally, pulling the strings causes the boom to rotate left or right. These commands are translated into corresponding actions of workers in a virtual crane that is depicted in the 3D environment, and which presents in a fairly high degree of detail the real crane that is exhibited at the entrance of the museum. The virtual crane is controlled by four digital workers who perform the user's actions depending on the input they receive: two perform crank rotation and gear changes, and two others pull the side ropes.

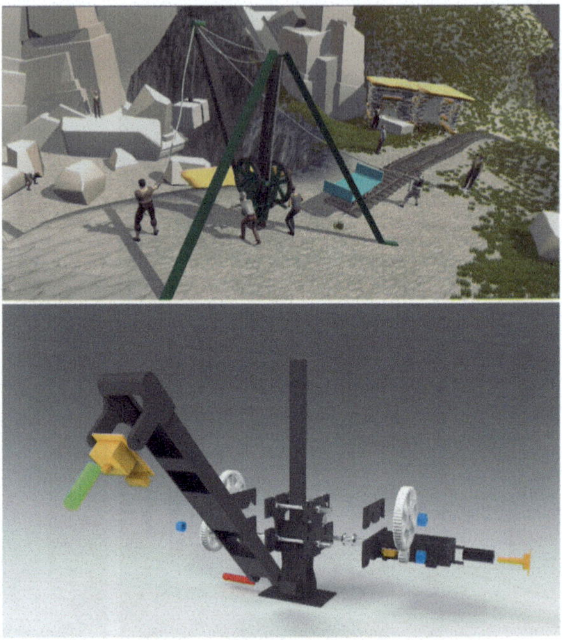

Fig. 1.2 Up: screenshot of the digital environment, workers operating the crane. Down: detailed assembly model of the physical controller

The scenario given to the user has two phases. The user is first asked to bring the crane hook over the marble block so that the workers can tie it, and then transfer the block to the wagon. A worker provides instructions to the user using signals (e.g., turn left, change gears, raise the boom, etc.). The user challenge is to monitor the signals and correctly operate the crane. The system gives the user the freedom to follow a different course of action than the one indicated by the signals, as long as they do not lead the crane to a critical situation that causes the risk of an accident. In such a case part of the control is blocked and users are only allowed to move to the opposite direction until they exit the critical state.

Several technologies were used to implement the system. The hardware controller was created through 3D printing, augmented with sensors and a micro-controller to interpret, and transmit the user's actions. The quarry area and constructions were modelled loosely based on the map of the real quarry business exhibited in the museum. The animations of the crane operators and other workers of the quarry were created through motion capture and post-processing. The final application was developed in Unity and is displayed on a large screen inside the museum.

1.2.3 Empirical Evaluation

A series of formative evaluations of the MR installation feedthrough the design process during project development. In this section we provide an overview of the final evaluation that was in the form of a field study in the museum with visitors.

1.2.3.1 Method

A field study of the user experience of visitors' use of the interactive crane MR installation was conducted at the first days of its operation at the museum of Tinian Marble Crafts. A total of 64 visitors interacted with the hybrid interactive installation at the Museum of Marble Crafts in Tinos in twelve (12) days during July (mean: 6.3 visitors per day), according to installation's data logs. We collected empirical data with the following means:

- An online version of the UEQ (User Experience Questionnaire) (Schrepp et al. 2017) could be completed by visitors by scanning a QR code on the posters nearby.
- The learning effect of the experience was measured with the participation of two groups of visitors (test group vs control group) who filled-in a learning questionnaire after their visit to the museum.
- We additionally identified UX issues from our observations and notes.

1.2.3.2 Results

From the total 64 visitors who interacted with the installation (Fig. 1.3), fifty-seven (57) completed the game, while seven (7) users quitted. The visitor UX was very positive according to the UEQ for all dimensions of attractiveness, perspicuity, efficiency, dependability, stimulation, and novelty (Fig. 1.4). According to Schrepp (2023) values greater than +0.8 present a very positive experience for users. A total of 31 users voluntarily participated in the testing of the learning effect. Regarding this aspect, we found that visitors who used the MR app (test group) performed better that those who did not (control group). The t-test's p-value 0.037 (<0.05) represents statistical significance. This indicates that visitors who interact with the hybrid installation present a significant learning effect on aspects of marble crafts conveyed, compared to those that do not select to try this interactive experience. Lastly, we collected several UX issues from observation that we noted down for further work on possible improvement of the interactive crane installation, such as: to improve user guidance, to add an introductory tutorial, to possibly provide explanations about the operation of the crane.

Fig. 1.3 Left: Museum visitors near the biga (crane), reading the informative sign. Right: Visitors playing the game of loading marbles with the interactive biga at the MR installation

Fig. 1.4 UEQ results from field testing of the MR interactive crane installation

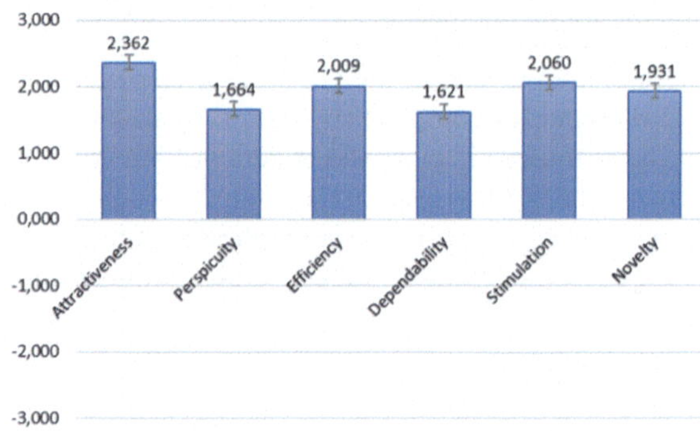

1.3 An In-Situ Journey to the Past Operation of an Olive Oil Factory

1.3.1 Intangible Cultural Heritage of Olive Oil Industrial Production in Greece and the Mediterranean Diet

The island of Lesvos in Greece is well-known for its large production of olive oil from ancient years. Olive oil is a principal ingredient of the Mediterranean Diet that is inscribed on the UNESCO Representative List of the Intangible Cultural Heritage of Humanity in 2013. The Museum of Industrial Oil Production is in the old communal oil press of Aghia Paraskevi, being a 'museum of itself' (Fig. 1.5). In the main building, which used to be the factory, the machinery and the tools are still in their original placement; some are operational and can be demonstrated on demand.

The museum gives a very good overview of the machinery, tools, clothing, and objects of that time. Visitors may observe and admire the place and the machinery, but they may not understand the full operation of the factory. Therefore, the main concept

Fig. 1.5 Left, up: A house in the Aghia Paraskevi settlement in Lesvos Island. Right, up: A bird's eye view of the settlement. Left, down: View of the interior main hall of the museum of industrial oil production. Right, down: A close-up view of the presses in the museum

of the MR installation was to provide visitors with a journey to the past, allowing them to observe the workings of the old factory on a screen while associating the digital events with the tangible elements that are still around them: the building, the machinery, and the props.

1.3.2 System Design and Development

The MR interactive installation implemented in the Museum of Industrial Oil production informs users about the workings, the machinery and the tools used in the past for producing olive oil (Fig. 1.6). The machines are present in their physical form in the former factory and some of them are operational. However, the dynamics are missing: which were the roles of the workers, how did they coordinate, which tools did they use and how, what was the use of the industrial machines, which were the

Fig. 1.6 A view of the digital model of the factory and the workers during cooperation

basic production stages? The MR system contributes towards these ends by showing a 'journey to the past' on top of the physical environment.

The installation consists of a rotating monitor placed in a fixed position near the entrance of the factory. Users can rotate it using designated handles around two axes. It can turn around the vertical axis to the left or right covering an area of 270°. Respectively, it can be turned up or down by around 10 degrees. Through this monitor users can view an older version of the same physical space (as an operating factory) with the workers executing their roles. The mixed reality effect is generated by aligning the digital content to the physical one, so users can point it to any area of the factory and view through the monitor the reconstructed digital version from the same point of view.

The MR installation presents an overview of the oil production process in the factory. It shows a digital version of the factory and the containing machines and tools and demonstrates through animated characters the various stages of the process. It is split into three main parts presented sequentially: the milling of the olives, the loading of the olive pulp into the press, and the final production of the oil. In each stage users can observe the animated process and listen to audio narration explaining the details and purpose of each task. During the presentation of the tasks, the important terminology is highlighted as floating labels that appear above workers, tools, or machines, aiming to enhance memory and learning and to connect the audio description to the actual elements of the physical space.

The development of the interactive installation involved many technologies and processes. The building interior has been scanned using a laser scanner in 10 scanning positions resulting into a large accurate point cloud. A 3D model of the building has been reconstructed based on the scanned data. The model was textured using old photographs and videos. The machines and their moving parts have been modelled and placed in their final positions. The digital characters representing the factory workers have been modelled in low poly based on photos and descriptions. Their animation has been created using motion capture and post-processing. The prototype of the installation has been designed in CAD (Computer-Aided Design). Four out of five parts of the main construction have been created using additive manufacturing. The final assembled system included a touchscreen monitor, an ESP23 microcontroller and two analogue potentiometers. The software running on the installation has been developed in Unity game engine.

1.3.3 Empirical Evaluation

A series of formative evaluations of the MR installation feedthrough the design process during project development. In this section we provide an overview of the final evaluation that was in the form of a field study in the museum with visitors.

1.3.3.1 Method

The field evaluation of the user experience was conducted in the museum during a period of over two months. We performed several observation sessions and retrospective interviews with visitors during that period, and we asked users to provide their views voluntarily into the UEQ. We also collected several comments for further work and improvements.

1.3.3.2 Results

A total of 126 visitors answered the UEQ voluntarily, after interacting with the system (Fig. 1.7). Visitor responses indicate that their UX was very positive (all UX dimensions were rated positively, above 0.8) (Fig. 1.8). This was also evident from many visitor reactions to the installation. For example, we often observed parents with children to interact together with the installation in ways where children manipulated the screen and parents engaged in explaining what is depicted on the screen concerning the museum's surrounding exhibits, i.e., the machines, tools, equipment, and parts of the building. We found that the interactive experience was positive and satisfying for visitors, while the installation served its purpose, i.e., to augment and complete the central space of the museum and its main exhibits.

Fig. 1.7 Museum visitors interacting with the MR installation about olive oil production

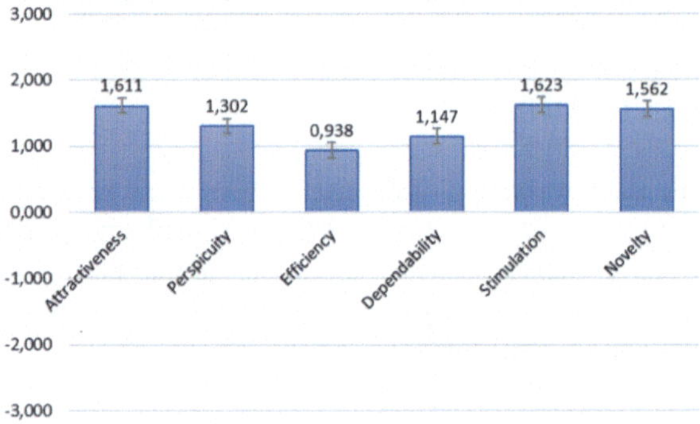

Fig. 1.8 Results of the UEQ for the MR installation of olive oil production

1.4 Interactive Storytelling with Projection Mapping About Mastic Villages

1.4.1 Intangible Cultural Heritage of Mastic

Mastic is a unique resin with numerous medicinal and cooking properties. The mastic tree (scientific name: Pistacia Lentiscus var. Chia) is an evergreen shrub, that may be found in many places of the world, however it can slowly generate mastic only in the southern part of Chios Island, Greece. This striking fact is explained to some extend by the microclimate of the area, and mainly to the know-how of cultivation by the local community who produce mastic from the ancient times. The know-how of mastic cultivation is inscribed in the Representative List of Intangible Cultural Heritage of Humanity by UNESCO. The Mastic Museum highlights the sustainability of the mastic tree and its traditional cultivation, processing, and industrialization. Also, it integrates mastic's significance into the broader social, economic, historical, architectural, and cultural scenery of Chios (Fig. 1.9).

Fig. 1.9 Left, up: mastic trees surrounding the museum of Mastic. Left, down: A close-up view at mastic resin. Right, up: View of an alley at a mastic village. Right, down: A close-up view of a non-interactive model of a typical mastic village at the museum of Mastic

Architecture, as an element of culture defined by landscape and human activities and, in our case, it stands as the pivotal axis affected by both the mastic people's cultivating habits (buildings and house floors dedicated for these habits) and the structural reinforcements made by the various regimes (fortified urban evolution of the mastic villages). The scale model of the mastic village is one of the central exhibits of the museum along with models of rooms of a typical house of the area. In cooperation with the museum curators, we decided to work on a concept of an interactive scale model onto which visitors would trigger projections to unrestrictedly unravel all the relevant information of the surrounding exhibits that encompass the two-faceted story.

1.4.2 System Design and Development

The MR interactive installation in the Mastic Museum communicates important aspects related to the mastic villages of Chios following a spatial augmented reality approach (projection mapping). It presents the evolution of the villages based on a series of historical periods, as well as the mastic cultivation process during each

Fig. 1.10 The final installation at Chios Mastic Museum

season of the year. The museum already contains some exhibits that present facts about the villages, their evolution over various historic periods and their role in mastic production. The installation integrates these elements in an interactive way by combining a physical scale model of the village, animated digital content presented on top of it that enlivens its history, tangible elements that trigger digital content, and small touchscreen devices that offer additional information (Fig. 1.10).

The MR installation uses the village scale model as a reference point to project a two-faceted story. One facet depicts the troubled years of Chios, the Genoese and Ottoman regimes, and the historic cooperative mastic exploitation that advanced the industrialization of the island. The other facet shows the repeated seasonal occupation of the villagers to cultivate mastic and their main activities and representative tools for each season. Therefore, the storytelling axis runs along two independent speedways: a linear timeline spanning four important historical periods for the island, and a circular one repeating around the four seasons of the year. The installation contains two independent "stations" located in opposite corners of the scale model, each of which controls the respective timeline and lens.

Visitors interact through tangible objects, four for each station. These physical objects represent respective stages of the timeline: architectural elements or conquerors' symbols in one station and seasonal cultivating tools in the other. The placement of a tangible object on a designated placeholder of the station triggers an audiovisual story that is presented on the scale model and narrated.

1.4.3 Empirical Evaluation

A series of formative evaluations of the MR installation feedthrough the design process during project development. In this section we provide an overview of the final evaluation that was in the form of a field study in the museum with visitors.

1.4.3.1 Method

A field study of visitor interactive experience with the MR installation was conducted at the first days of its operation at the museum of Mastic. We employed the similar approach to the previous study, specifically: we provided an online link to UEQ was available for visitors to complete in a voluntary basis (56 questionnaires collected), we conducted a learning effect study between two groups of visitors (test vs control group, 15 visitors each), and we made several observations during user interaction.

1.4.3.2 Results

The visitor UX was very positive according to the UEQ responses, especially to the emotional aspects of the experience (Figs. 1.11 and 1.12). This was also evident from many visitor reactions to the installation. All the visitors were thrilled by the vibrant illustrations, the audio narration, and the surrounding sounds presented by the installation. They eagerly explored all eight stories and, as they noticed the alternating sequence of stories between stations, it fostered better communication among them. They started signaling to each other about who would place the next tangible asset, even though they were positioned on opposite sides of the installation. Another observation was that many visitors walked around the installation to closely examine the projections inside the model's building blocks due to the spatial affordances of projection mapping. Regarding the learning effect, we found that the test group performed better than the control group, however we did not find a statistically significant effect (t-test: p-value $= 0.073 > 0.05$).

1.5 Reflection and Discussion

The case studies presented three mixed reality museum installations for communicating intangible cultural heritage to visitors. They all share that they employ a hybrid physical/digital approach and that their content is related to human craftsmanship and traditions of the past. They have also important differences in terms of the technologies used and the ways knowledge is presented and communicated to users.

Fig. 1.11 Left: A museum visitor interacts with the MR installation. Right: Visitors observing the storytelling about the history of mastic

Fig. 1.12 UEQ results from field testing of the MR installation of mastic cultivation history and local architecture

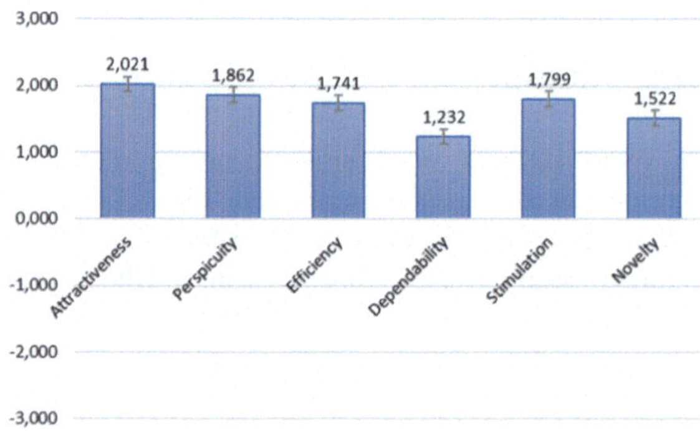

All three MR installations have been developed using a combination of modern technologies (Table 1.1). These involve: *3D printing* for creating constructions enhanced with microcontrollers and sensors (case studies 1 and 2), and the scale model for case study 3; *motion capture* for creating the natural movement, tool usage and coordination of workers in the case studies 1, 2; *laser scanning* for producing an accurate model of the factory in Lesvos; *projection mapping* for aligning the digital content to the village scale model; *NFC tags and readers* for recognizing the tangible objects of case study 3.

The ICH elements presented in the installation also vary between the three case studies. The knowledge and facts about the associated ICH of the installations are communicated through the form of digital objects and scenery (worker appearance, tools, quarry), animations (worker communication signals, machinery operation, processes), the form of physical elements (tangible objects and village scale model of case study 3, crane controller), and the operation of physical constructions, i.e., the handling of the physical crane controller. Each of the three case studies utilizes a combination of these elements to convey the designated message to the public.

Table 1.1 Mixed reality installations and intangible cultural heritage

	Case study 1 (Tinos)	Case study 2 (Lesvos)	Case study 3 (Chios)
Associated ICH	Marble extraction and processing	Industrial oil production	Mastic cultivation
Technologies involved	3D Printing, motion capture, sensors and microcontrollers	3D Printing, motion capture, sensors and microcontrollers, laser scanning	3D Printing, projection mapping, NFC tags/readers
Cultural elements	Worker appearance, tools, crane operation, physical crane controller, worker communication signals, extraction process, quarry overview	Worker appearance, tools, machinery operation, oil production process	Tangible objects (tools and symbols), mastic cultivation process, architectural elements, evolution and expansion of the village through time
Presentation	Challenge/mini-game	Animated process and narrative	Multiple animation clips (mini-documentaries)
Interactivity	Operate physical controller, accomplish task	Turn monitor towards target areas	Pickup and place tangible objects to trigger animations
Mixed reality elements	Physical actions on scale object control digital crane	Digital content aligned with physical space	Digital content augments/ reshapes scale model

The system setup, presentation, and interactivity of the three installations have also some noteworthy differences. The first case study is presented as a challenge or mini-game, where the user has to accomplish a given task. The mixed reality environment is generated by the combination of physical control of a small-scale crane and the associated digital response of a crane representation being used by digital workers. In the second case study, users are observing the digital presentation by controlling the rotation of a monitor that acts as a window to the past. The alignment of the digital view on top of the physical environment generates a mixed reality effect. Finally, in the third case study users select tangible objects to trigger respective videos. The physical scale model is augmented and 'reshaped' (in the sense that part of its architecture is hidden or extended during the stories) while the content is being presented.

1.5.1 Motion Capture and Digital Characters

Motion is sometimes a critical element of intangible heritage and needs to be carefully recorded, documented and preserved, e.g., dances, rituals, craftsmanship (Alivizatou-Barakou et al. 2017; Kico et al. 2018). In our installations we had to digitize the motion of workers using tools, operating machinery, or even communicating with each other, extending previous approaches that rested on digital characters in virtual worlds (Vosinakis et al. 2017).

It is not always easy to capture human motion on site, e.g., while operating the actual crane in Tinos, or while carrying baskets with pulp to the press in the old oil factory. High precision motion capture is usually done in dedicated studios and while wearing the appropriate equipment. In our case we used the mocap studio of our lab to capture the movement. However, in cases where the human motion was linked to the usage of an external object, such as holding a tool, or the operation of a machine with specific restrictions, such as the crane, or even worse the coordination of two workers, such as carrying oil baskets, it is difficult to achieve the desired quality without postprocessing. In our case, we used some constructed props of the same dimensions to capture human motion while holding tools or using machinery, but still the results were not always natural. Therefore, we needed to edit the motion after it was captured and, in some cases, to add inverse kinematics to the hands of the digital workers, to be able to align properly the human limb movements to the machinery operation.

Designers of future MR applications of intangible cultural heritage should carefully study the human motion to be digitized and the associated parameters (i.e., use of tools, collaborative actions) and test available capture technologies beforehand. An interesting challenge would be to try and test tools and methods for capturing human motion on site using transferrable motion capture technologies without significant loss of accuracy or naturalness (Hou et al. 2022). Possible solutions include inertial motion capture systems (Morris and Rodriguez-Amat 2022), or even using multiple cameras and deep learning techniques (Kim et al. 2023).

1.5.2 Level of Abstraction

Presenting cultural heritage elements through digital applications, especially in mixed and virtual reality involves varying levels of abstraction to enhance user experience, interpretation, and learning. These levels of abstraction range from highly detailed and realistic 3D reconstructions to more simplified or symbolic representations that capture the essence of cultural heritage elements while facilitating interaction and engagement in virtual environments.

The selection of an appropriate level of abstraction is a key consideration for application designers. This pertains to content presentation and user interaction, balancing accuracy with simplicity for non-experts. Educators often simplify objects to convey important characteristics while omitting distracting details, aiding understanding, and concept mastery. Conversely, archaeologists and curators prioritize precise object presentation to facilitate new interpretations. The challenge in this case lies in preserving important details in digital representations without critically increasing the complexity. An interesting theoretical discussion about virtual reconstruction and the reliability of the content is presented in the work of Not et al.

(2019). Similarly, human processes and user interactions with tools can be simplified, acknowledging that public users may not handle complex tools as experts do. Thus, a simplified version can offer effective engagement and experiential understanding, provided that users recognize the abstraction and still can perceive the analogies with the actual task and usage.

A careful analysis of the associated cultural elements, educational goals and usability aspects of the interactive application should guide the selection of appropriate levels of abstraction of digital and physical content and user interactions.

1.5.3 Narrative, Playfulness, and Challenge

A critical design decision for MR installations in cultural heritage is the content presentation. Will the content be presented in a linear way, or will the user be involved somehow? Will the presentation be storified and enhanced with dramatic elements or will it have a more flat and academic style? In our three case studies we followed different approaches that led to some interesting observations.

In the marble quarry installation, the content was interactive, and the information emerged mostly through the user actions and the response of the environment. The user adopts a role and learns about the process of carrying marble blocks by trying to complete the challenge given. So, they gradually unveil information about tying, lifting and releasing the blocks. At the same time, they also learn the main principles of the operation of the crane, both by observing the physical crane-controller and also by using it and noticing the effects of their actions. Although the installation was positively rated in terms of user experience, as the evaluation results imply, some users asked for further explanations about the operation of the crane and the workings in the quarry. Users were absorbed by the challenging nature of the installation, but it is not clear if they had the chance to carefully inspect and reflect on the presented cultural environment.

In the oil factory installation, there is no user participation. The information is presented through character animations, audio narrations and textual annotations. No story is involved; the whole process of oil production is presented linearly in three phases. The user can control the field of view and simply observes the animated characters, listening to the narration and looking at labels that name the various elements, tools and worker roles of the scene. In this case, users need to bring their attention to the content and to the surrounding physical space in order to understand the presented process and recognize the role of the associated physical elements. Thus, its approach is mostly didactic, leaving no room for user action and experimentation. This was sometimes regarded as a limitation, especially for younger visitors.

Finally, in the third installation about the Mastic villages of Chios, the content is again presented in a non-interactive way, but users get to choose the animated content. The options are organized in two layers, the history and the mastic production, and each of the videos is quite independent from the others, so there is no need to watch them in a sequential order. Furthermore, the installation included some strong dramatic elements, such as a pirate attack to the village, or Chios massacre, enhanced with appropriate music and effects. In this case, the use of tangible objects as content selector, and the fact that visitors could be split in two control spaces and had the freedom to choose the subject of presentation, made the experience more playful and fun, even for younger ages.

Based on our observation, it seems that the inclusion of interaction and challenges makes the experience more engaging, but on the other hand it is difficult to draw users' attention to the educative elements. Keeping users interested and engaged in a linear presentation is quite more difficult, but it is also easier to fit in more content for visitors who are really interested in learning more about the topic. So, the first option might be more appropriate for younger audiences that are more familiar with digital games, while the second is more suited to engaged museum visitors ('ant' visitors) that are attracted by the subject and have the desire to expand their knowledge. Still, the use of 'wow' elements, such as the metaphor of 'viewing the past' in the case of the oil production and the live projection mapping in the case of mastic villages, can attract younger audiences, at least for a while. As noted by other researchers, there is a notable need for further studies to identify the impact of gamification in shaping the experience and perception of cultural heritage (Pietroni and Ferdani 2021).

1.5.4 Reference to Real World Objects and Exhibits

Museum installations are typically not isolated experiences, but part of larger exhibitions, situated within a context that shapes the experience, including space, decoration, and surrounding elements. These installations aim to connect their content with real-world materials, either within or outside the museum. Users are expected not only to engage with the installation itself but also to expand their understanding and curiosity about related museum content. Thus, these installations often serve to contextualize and communicate the significance of tangible exhibits, bridging their history and importance (Marques et al. 2023).

Some critical design choices revolve around how interactive installations relate to physical objects or places depicted. The challenge lies in creating a meaningful connection between these two realms. Can visitors establish a lasting link between digital interaction and physical elements? Can they recognize the digital version after seeing the real object, or vice versa? Is it feasible for users to simultaneously interact with the installation and observe the actual reference object? Each case study presents a distinct relationship with the real object(s) of focus.

In the case of the marble crane, the actual object has been seen by the visitors before the interaction. It is dominating the entrance of the museum, so all visitors can get a first look at it. The digital representation is quite simplified, but with the same colors and proportions. Given that the users get to interact with its digital version, it would be interesting to study whether they wish to visit the real object again, after the experience, to observe some elements critical for its functionality (such as the gear-switching mechanism) that might have gone unnoticed.

In the olive oil production factory MR installation, the object of reference is there, all around the installation. The factory space that is represented in the app is surrounding the user, the machinery is also there and only the workers, and their actions are missing. Given also that the view is aligned with the physical space, users can easily link the digital content to the actual space and objects. The installation communicates the feeling that the old factory 'comes to life' through the monitor. The evaluation results indicate that users did indeed associate the physical content with the digital process presented in the installation, and it helped them pay closer attention to the physical factory and its elements.

Finally, in the Chios mastic MR installation, the actual object is a village and users observe a scale model of it. They have a holistic view looking at it mostly from the top and at a much smaller scale. In the real-world village they will never have a similar view (unless they look at it from a helicopter or the camera of a drone), and they will probably notice other things, such as architectural details, that are not visible in the scale model. So, the digital representation and the actual visit provide complementary views, and it is expected that visitors who have experienced the installation might experience the visit to the village with a more informed view and might pay more attention to architectural elements that are associated with the settlement's history and mastic cultivation routine. Again, further studies are needed to observe the effect that the installation has on village visitors and how the holistic presentation of its architecture will affect their attention and experience.

It is evident that the relationship between digital presentations of cultural heritage artifacts and their physical counterparts, and the impact of digital applications on users' attention towards actual objects, is an important topic in the field of cultural heritage preservation and presentation (Ray et al. 2013). More studies are needed to understand how an MR installation might shape the visitors' view of real-world objects of reference and enhance their understanding.

1.5.5 Design for Friends and Bystanders

Museum visits are usually done by pairs or groups. Therefore, when a visitor interacts with an installation there are probably one or more of their companions nearby. And there are also other bystanders looking at users interacting. As noted by other researchers, e.g., Hornecker (2010), museum installations must be designed taking into account the presence of other users nearby. If possible, the installations should afford the participation of more than one people, so that visitor's friends, children, or mates are joining the experience. It should also let other people view without interrupting the experience or making the user feel uncomfortable. In our case studies we adopted different strategies regarding the presence of friends and bystanders.

In the case of the interactive crane, we designed the controller and challenges having in mind that two users could collaborate to operate it. So, the crank operation and switching, and the string pulling for lateral rotations are functionally independent and can be operated by two users together. A different way of sharing the experience is to have one user observe and interpret the signals (orders given by other workers and feedback in case of a wrong action) looking at the screen and the other operating the controller. We observed that these design choices did actually work, as there were visitors that used the installation as a pair. However, given the quite small size of the crane controller, it was not always easy to stand side-by-side and use it.

In the case of the oil production factory the user is only controlling the view, so it is not possible to have two users operating together. However, the screen has been designed to be large enough so that more than one users can observe the content and probably try to associate the presented process to the actual space and machinery. Again, we observed couples or parents with children that observed the content together and commented about its relationship to the physical space.

Finally, in the augmented scale model of Chios mastic villages, we have intentionally designed two control areas in opposite sides. Therefore, a pair of users could split in these two areas and interact with the installation while looking at each other and being able to discuss on the content. Also, the content has been created in a way that is well perceived from any side, so that even bystanders can fully experience it. Indeed, this installation could attract a lot of observers from all sides, without seriously interrupting the flow of the experience.

1.6 Conclusions

This chapter reflected on the design, implementation, and user evaluation of three MR installations in respective museums in the Aegean region in Greece. The installations focused on the presentation of intangible cultural heritage, and more specifically industrial and craftsmanship heritage using novel and playful approaches. Each case study involved different ICH domains and technological setups, utilizing a wide range of technologies. From our involvement throughout the conceptualization, design and evaluation of these MR installations we have provided discussion on several design issues including: capturing human performance and assigning it to digital characters, deciding on the appropriate level of abstraction, choosing between predefined content and more dynamic and gamified approaches, providing appropriate references to real world objects and exhibits, and designing for friends and bystanders.

References

Alivizatou-Barakou M, Kitsikidis A, Tsalakanidou F et al (2017) Intangible cultural heritage and new technologies: challenges and opportunities for cultural preservation and development. Mix Rity Gamification Cult Herit 129–158

Bannon L, Benford S, Bowers J et al (2005) (2005) Hybrid design creates innovative museum experiences. Commun ACM 48:62–65

Bekele MK, Pierdicca R, Frontoni E et al (2018) A survey of augmented, virtual, and mixed reality for cultural heritage. J Comput Cult Herit (JOCCH) 11(2):1–36

Bouchenaki M (2003) The interdependency of the tangible and intangible cultural heritage. In: 14th ICOMOS general assembly and international symposium: 'place, memory, meaning preserving intangible values in monuments and sites', Victoria Falls, Zimbabwe, 2003, pp 27–31

Chu JH, Harley D, Kwan J et al (2016) Sensing history: contextualizing artifacts with sensory interactions and narrative design. In: Proceedings of the conference on designing interactive systems, Brisbane, Australia, 4–8 June 2016, pp 1294–1302

Dimitropoulos A, Dimitropoulos K, Kyriakou A et al (2017) The loom: interactive weaving through a tangible installation with digital feedback. Digital cultural heritage: final conference of the Marie Skłodowska-Curie initial training network for digital cultural heritage, ITN-DCH 2017, Olimje, Slovenia, May 23–25, 2017. Springer International Publishing, Revised Selected Papers, pp 199–210

Douet J (2016) Industrial heritage re-tooled: the TICCIH guide to industrial heritage conservation. Routledge

Gkiti C, Varia E, Zikoudi C et al (2018) I-Wall: a low-cost interactive wall for enhancing visitor experience and promoting industrial heritage in museums. Euro-mediterranean conference. Springer International Publishing, Cham, pp 90–100

Hornecker E, Buur J (2006) Getting a grip on tangible interaction: a framework on physical space and social interaction. In: Proceedings of the SIGCHI conference on human factors in computing systems, Montréal, QC, Canada, 22–27 April 2006, pp 437–446

Hornecker E, Stifter M (2006) Learning from interactive museum installations about interaction design for public settings. In: Proceedings of the 18th Australia conference on computer-human interaction: design: activities, artefacts and environments, Sydney, Australia, 20–24 November 2006, pp 135–142

Hornecker E (2010) Interactions around a contextually embedded system. In: Proceedings of the fourth international conference on tangible, embedded, and embodied interaction, pp 169–176

Hou Y, Kenderdine S, Picca D et al (2022) Digitizing intangible cultural heritage embodied: state of the art. J Comput Cult Herit (JOCCH) 15(3):1–20

Ibrahim N, Ali NM (2018) A conceptual framework for designing virtual heritage environment for cultural learning. J Comput Cult Herit 11:1–27

Idris MZ, Mustaffa NB, Yusoff SOS (2016) Preservation of intangible cultural heritage using advance digital technology: issues and challenges. Harmon J Arts Res Educ 16(1):1–13

Ioakeim N, Printezis P, Skarimpas C et al (2020) Kirini: an interactive projection-mapping installation for storytelling about mediterranean beekeeping heritage. In: Digital heritage progress in cultural heritage: documentation, preservation, and protection: 8th international conference, EuroMed 2020, November 2–5, 2020, revised selected papers 8. Springer International Publishing, pp 190–201

Kico I, Grammalidis N, Christidis Y et al (2018) Digitization and visualization of folk dances in cultural heritage: a review. Inventions 3(4):72

Kim JW, Choi JY, Ha EJ et al (2023) Human pose estimation using mediapipe pose and optimization method based on a humanoid model. Appl Sci 13(4):2700

Koutsabasis P, Vosinakis S (2018) Kinesthetic interactions in museums: conveying cultural heritage by making use of ancient tools and (re-) constructing artworks. Virtual Rity 22(2):103–118

Koutsabasis P, Partheniadis K, Gardeli A et al (2022) Co-designing the user experience of location-based games for a network of museums: involving cultural heritage professionals and local communities. Multimodal Technol Interact 6(5):36

Marques CG, Pedro JP, Araújo I (2023) A systematic literature review of gamification in/for cultural heritage: leveling up, going beyond. Heritage 6(8):5935–5951

Morris PI, Rodriguez-Amat JR (2022) Collaborative design in kinetic performance: safeguarding the uilleann pipes through inertial motion capture. Multimodal Technol Interact 6(11):97

Nikolakopoulou V, Printezis P, Maniatis V et al (2022) Conveying intangible cultural heritage in museums with interactive storytelling and projection mapping: the case of the mastic villages. Heritage 5(2):1024–1049

Nikolakopoulou V, Vosinakis S, Nikopoulos G et al (2022) Design and user experience of a hybrid mixed reality installation that promotes tinian marble crafts heritage. ACM J Comput Cult Herit 15(4):1–21

Nofal E, Reffat M, Vande Moere A (2017) Phygital heritage: an approach for heritage communication. In: Proceedings of the immersive learning research network conference, Coimbra, Portugal, 26–29 June 2017. Verlag der Technischen Universität Graz, Graz, Austria, pp 220–229

Not E, Cavada D, Maule S et al (2019) Digital augmentation of historical objects through tangible interaction. J Comput Cult Herit (JOCCH) 12(3):1–19

Pietroni E (2019) Experience design, virtual reality and media hybridization for the digital communication inside museums. Appl Syst Innov 2:35

Pietroni E, Ferdani D (2021) Virtual restoration and virtual reconstruction in cultural heritage: terminology, methodologies, visual representation techniques and cognitive models. Information 12(4):167

Price S, Sakr M, Jewitt C (2016) Exploring whole-body interaction and design for museums. Interact Comput 28:569–583

Ray CA, Van Der Vaart MJ (2013) Contextualizing collections: using virtual reality in archaeology exhibitions. Exhibitionist 32(2):73–79

Schrepp M, Thomaschewski J, Hinderks A (2017) Construction of a benchmark for the user experience questionnaire (UEQ). Int J Interact Multimed Artif Intell 4(4)

Schrepp M (2023) UEQ handbook. https://www.ueq-online.org/Material/Handbook.pdf. Last Accessed 27 Mar 2023

Speicher M, Hall BD, Nebeling M (2019) What is mixed reality? In: Proceedings of the 2019 CHI conference on human factors in computing systems, pp 1–15

Vosinakis S, Avradinis N, Koutsabasis P (2017) Dissemination of intangible cultural heritage using a multi-agent virtual world. In: Advances in digital cultural heritage: international workshop, Funchal, Madeira, Portugal, June 28, 2017, revised selected papers. Springer International Publishing, pp 197–207

Vosinakis S, Nikolakopoulou V, Nikopoulos G et al (2021) Designing mixed reality experiences that provide views to the past: reviving the operation of an industrial olive oil factory. In: Proceedings of the 25th pan-hellenic conference on informatics 2021, pp 39–44

Chapter 2
Creating Innovative Technologies for Archaeological Sites: Augmented—Mixed Reality Educational Platform at the Spartan Sanctuary of Apollon Amyklaios

Stavros Vlizos, Konstantinos Kotsopoulos, and Sarantos Kapidakis

Abstract In this article, we thoroughly describe and evaluate an innovative software platform for documenting an excavation of an archaeological site and the use of its findings in creating augmented and mixed reality educational applications. The excavation that contributed to the design of the platform and showcased its functionality is that of the archaeological site at the Sanctuary of Apollon in Amykles (Sparta, Greece). For the 3D mapping of the site and the 3D modeling of the structure of the findings, motion photogrammetry software was used including processing of terrestrial photos, aerial photos, and total station data. The platform consists of three systems, namely a central documentation platform (CDP) that support 3D, a system for creating educational narrative applications (END) in AR, and a system for creating mixed reality training modules (MRT). The development of a focused metadata scheme that supported the three systems of the platform played a significant role in the coherence and usage of the information and insights obtained by the 3D models and the archaeological documentation. The demonstration and evaluation of the platform that we present here show that it facilitates improvements in the workflow from the 3D digitization and documentation of an excavation to the exploitation of the findings and the entire excavation procedure through an educational approach utilizing AR and MR technologies.

S. Vlizos (✉)
Ionian University, Corfu, Greece
e-mail: vlizosst@ionio.gr

K. Kotsopoulos
University of Patras, Patras, Greece
e-mail: kkotsopoulos@upatras.gr

S. Kapidakis
University of Western Attica, Aigaleo, Greece
e-mail: sarantos@uniwa.gr

S. Vlizos
Amykles Research Project, Sparta, Greece

F. Liarokapis et al. (eds.), *Interactive Media for Cultural Heritage*, Springer Series on Cultural Computing, https://doi.org/10.1007/978-3-031-61018-9_2

Keywords Amyklaion · Documentation platform · Mixed reality educational application · Narrative-based educational application · Portable device application

2.1 Introduction

In recent years, the field of cultural heritage documentation and visualization has witnessed significant advancements through the utilization of new technologies (Saborido et al. 2018). This text presents a comprehensive overview of various studies and frameworks that employ 3D models, virtual reality (VR), and innovative software solutions to reconstruct, classify, manage, and visualize archaeological finds, cultural landscapes, and historical sites. These cutting-edge approaches not only enhance the work of cultural heritage professionals, but also foster interdisciplinary collaboration and engagement with the wider public (Liritzis et al. 2015). Through the synthesis of key research contributions, this text highlights the potential and significance of 3D technologies in the field of cultural heritage.

One notable framework described in the literature is the digital framework developed for the Superintendence of Pompeii, Italy (Apollonio et al. 2012). This framework leverages advanced 3D web-based repositories and semantic reality-based structures to create an information system that assists in the digital reconstruction, classification, management, and visualization of archaeological finds. By using 3D digital models as cognitive systems, this framework extends the concept of 2D GIS to 3D GIS, providing a scalable application for multiple users.

To address the specific needs of cultural heritage professionals, the AGATA software has been developed. AGATA allows specialists to interact in real time with high-resolution polygonal models and annotate raster and vectorial information directly onto them. This feature facilitates data organization and collaboration among researchers from different disciplines, as the annotations can be exported in a standard format for easy access (Soler et al. 2016).

Also, the emergence of virtual reality and immersive technologies has opened new possibilities for cultural heritage preservation and education (Cassidy et al. 2018). Ferdani and his partners describe a workflow for producing historically accurate 3D assets in interactive, immersive VR products. By focusing on the Forum of Augustus, they emphasize the importance of a multi- and interdisciplinary approach to ensure the fidelity of the 3D reconstructions. This tailored workflow showcases the potential of applied VR games and immersive experiences in bringing the past to life (Ferdani et al. 2020).

Expanding the definition of cultural heritage, a detailed survey of the ancient city of Sarmizegetusa has been presented. They propose the concept of a "digital replica" to capture not only the structures of the city, but also the surrounding natural environment, providing a comprehensive representation of the cultural landscape. The integration of photogrammetry and computer graphics enables the creation of a reproducible workflow that facilitates navigation and exploration of large three-dimensional datasets (Demetrescu et al. 2020).

In the realm of 3D reconstruction, a practical system for reconstructing large-scale objects has been introduced. This system utilizes a 3D scanner, guide rails, and a high-precision motion control system to align partial reconstructions and achieve accurate results. The effectiveness and performance of this method surpass similar approaches, making it a valuable tool for capturing intricate details (Bai et al. 2019).

For the LVR-Archaeological Park Xanten, digital media plays a pivotal role in educating visitors about the Roman city of Colonia Ulpia Traiana. The park employs a virtual reconstruction film displayed on large screens in the museum's permanent exhibition. This immersive experience offers visitors a detailed impression of the architectural appearance, spatial layout, and atmosphere of the ancient city, based on archaeological evidence (Quick 2018).

Finally, the advantages and methods of 3D approximations in cultural heritage presentations have been explored. This approach offers enhanced realism, interactivity, and presence compared to traditional methods. It enables diverse output formats, including gaming software and 3D simulations, which aid in the interpretation of archaeological contexts and facilitate engagement with a broader audience (Barratt 2021).

In conclusion, the integration of 3D technologies into cultural heritage documentation and visualization has revolutionized the field. From digital frameworks for reconstruction and management to VR applications and 3D approximations, these advancements offer new avenues for interdisciplinary collaboration, public engagement, and the comprehensive representation of cultural heritage. By harnessing the potential of 3D technologies, cultural heritage professionals can safeguard and share our rich historical and archaeological legacy for generations to come.

2.2 Innovative Technologies Experiences at the Archaeological Site of Amyklaion in Sparta, Greece

The ancient Sanctuary of Apollon Amyklaios, the most important religious center for the Lacedaemonians during antiquity, is located 5 km south of Sparta in the Peloponnese, Greece, situated on the hill of the church of Hagia Kyriaki (Vlizos 2017, 2020). Within the site, various monuments from different time periods can be found, with the noteworthy presence of the Throne of Apollon. This distinctive architectural monument of the late sixth century B.C.E., resembling a temple in the shape of a seat, was created to house the colossal cult statue of Apollon around which the annual Hyakinthia cultic festival took place, which paid homage to the local hero Hyakinthos and Apollon. The archaeological site encompasses a range of values for the local community and foreign visitors, and provides substantial scientific, historical, educational, aesthetic, local, and economic benefits to society, as well as to various associated groups such as neighboring settlements and the scientific community (Vlizos

2022). The location of the site stipulates a captivating multi-sensory experience, situated in a panoramic position that showcases abundant natural beauty. These distinctive features establish the hill as a significant archaeological, religious, and natural landmark, and it is crucial to convey these attributes directly and experientially to both the local community and visitors. All these challenges provide an opportunity to explore existing methods and develop innovative approaches to overcome obstacles commonly encountered by cultural heritage sites in general. The project "Digital platform for the development of educational applications focused on cultural heritage tourism with the use of augmented reality, mixed reality and gamification" (ACRONYM: AMREP—Augmented—Mixed Reality Educational Platform) was an opportunity to identify effective solutions related to these issues.[1]

The inspiration for this project at the archaeological site of Amyklaion in Sparta, Greece, is rooted in the site's rich historical and cultural heritage and the absence of any inspirational experiences for visitors. It aims to tackle the difficulties faced by cultural heritage sites by providing visitors with valuable information. The project aims to devise novel approaches to conquer typical obstacles in cultural heritage preservation and education, thereby providing substantial scientific, historical, educational, aesthetic, local, and economic advantages. The site's location offers a distinctive multi-sensory experience that combines archaeological, religious, and natural elements, making it crucial to convey these elements experientially to both the local community and visitors.

This paper presents a methodological approach for documenting archaeological excavations and utilizing the findings to create augmented and mixed reality educational applications. The case study focuses on the excavation of the Sanctuary of Apollon in Amykles. The methodology involves 3D mapping of the site and 3D modeling of the findings using motion photogrammetry software, which processes terrestrial and aerial photos from UAVs, along with GNSS RTK receiver and total station data (Moraitou et al. 2023; Zachos and Anagnostopoulos 2023). A key aspect of this approach is the development of a focused metadata scheme that supports the three systems of the platform, ensuring coherence and effective use of the information and insights obtained from the 3D models and archaeological documentation. The software platform comprises a central documentation platform (CDP) supporting 3D, a system for creating educational narrative applications (END) in AR, and a system for creating mixed reality training modules (MRT). This innovative approach significantly improves the workflow from 3D digitization and documentation of an excavation to the exploitation of the findings and the entire excavation process through educational applications utilizing AR and MR technologies.

A widely adopted approach in application architecture is the n-tier architecture (Patwardhan et al. 2016; Suzuki and Suzuki 2020). This proposed solution features

[1] The current research is based on the project "Digital platform for the development of educational applications focused on cultural heritage tourism with the use of augmented reality, mixed reality and gamification" (ACRONYM: AMREP—Augmented—Mixed Reality Educational Platform), which is co-financed by the European Union and Greek national funds through the Operational Program Competitiveness, Entrepreneurship and Innovation, under the call RESEARCH—CREATE—INNOVATE.

a three-tier structure, with each layer performing specific functions and communicating only with the layer directly beneath it. This architecture allows for independent maintenance and upgrading of each layer without affecting the overall system functionality.

The Presentation Layer, also known as the Application Layer, houses the educational application for mobile devices, the mixed reality application, and the content management applications. The mobile device application provides information about the archaeological site and its findings. The mixed reality application offers the capability for live presentations augmented with three-dimensional content and information in real space. Both applications, through beacons and GPS, deliver content based on the user's location. The management applications provide the ability for content documentation, user application design, and their continuous updating.

The Business Layer executes both the management processes of the user application elements, the users, and the content. Through an Application Programming Interface (API), the content and processes are offered to the respective applications. In the Database Layer, the file system stores multimedia material related to all subsystems of the Business Layer, while the metadata documenting the findings, the elements of the applications (structure and texts), and the user elements are stored in databases. A crucial factor for the successful implementation of such a project is the correct understanding of the project's objectives by the entire interdisciplinary project team, already at the needs analysis level.

2.3 Archaeological Information Management

The digital information can provide very valuable results, but in order to be accessible in the first place, it needs to be well defined and structured according to existing standards, such as CIDOC CRM (Deicke 2016; Klein et al. 2023). In this direction, the definition of the documentation schema that will describe in detail how to represent all the excavation information is critically important. This schema is normally case specific as it can be defined only after a careful study of the available information and its requirements.

Traditionally, the excavation findings have insofar been always documented in a shallow manner, as documentation mainly referred to their general characteristics, such as coloring, dimensions, provenance, chronology, and related images. Moreover, the inconsistent use (if any) of explicitly defined rules and/or controlled vocabularies as well as the arbitrarily of description patters, made excavations' documentation a time-consuming task that was prone to discrepancies and conflicts.

The iDig software is used for on-site recording of items, which imposes minimum ground rules on some of the data recorded, thus offering basic interoperability between the records and other excavations that are using the same software (Psarros et al. 2022). Thus, more rules are needed that will also concern both the selection of the values in the iDig and the documentation of the findings in other ways, as well as the transfer of the values from these to the final database.

2.3.1 Documentation Schema

Pre-existing database records were examined to understand the common practice of the previous cataloguers and to recognize whether it's sufficient or should be improved/expanded for the pre-existing and new requirements. The adoption of an existing, suitable format will facilitate a good understanding and observance of the metadata by the documenters and compatibility with already recorded data. As there are not many public examples of documentation from other similar excavations, we were unable to rely on other complete figures. Instead, we studied and improved the individual elements of the description and their values to meet the needs of documenting the items (Kapidakis 2019; Alma'aitah et al. 2020). Due to its limited use in archaeology, the use of an ontology or thesaurus is not recommended, as it would be difficult to train the cataloguers to use it. Neither general purpose classification systems, such as Dewey Decimal Classification or LCSH (O'Neill and Chan 2006), nor more specialized thesauri offer the resolution needed to categorize/classify items in any useful way (Getty 2021, 2022).

Combining the pre-existing documentation elements with the new needs (avoiding major changes that will make the previous records incompatible) and augmenting them with rules for their values, we reached the following schema. The proposed schema below is based on the format that was in use in the frame of the Amykles Research Project, with minor additions mentioned earlier. The type of values is briefly defined below (Table 2.1 Amykles Research Project Documentation Schema):

However, it is recommended that controlled values/records of authorities be used in the retained metadata, where possible, which will be either a fixed pre-defined or a list that grows during the course of excavation and documentation, as new cases arise. Using controlled vocabularies for metadata element values brings significant benefits, such as fewer errors in values, clarity in value meaning, easier machine processing and straightforward connection of the items that share the same controlled values. Therefore, it is recommended to use controlled vocabularies for items when possible. The vocabulary terms should be chosen so that this detail is sufficient to be useful in any application. But there are cases when this may not be enough, such as when:

A. There is more information, which is not necessary for the following applications; e.g., if we describe that an item is a "leg part", we may not care in the various applications to know which part it is, and there may not be a term for the specific part. If we want this clarification on the value to be recorded (probably for the sake of completeness—and if it is readily available), it should be recorded in another element, probably in related comments.
B. There is less information than it is needed to select a term from the controlled vocabulary. Then we cannot choose a term with certainty, and often choose one with uncertainty, e.g., we may not be sure if an item is a "fork". If the description was completed in free text, we would express our doubts (in the simplest case with a question mark) within that description. But when we have to choose a term from a dictionary, we choose the most appropriate one, and record our doubts as clarification in another item, probably in related comments.

Table 2.1 Amykles research project documentation schema

Item code	Item name	Item type	Required	Optional
A unique identifier/ number that each individual item receives upon its discovery. The code of each item is unique and is formed as follows, AM (for Amykles) "/" the initials of the category of each item, and the serial number, e.g., AM/ KG1044	Importance Level	Numbers 1–3, indicating the degree of interest and description for the item, according to excavation policy. The lowest value, 1, is for most discovered items, the next, 2, for the most interesting items (metal and bone, as per current policy), and a value of 3 for selected interesting items—we can give it higher values later, for items of particular importance	√	
	Category	Controlled Vocabulary. Initially we define 5 categories, but more can be added later	√	
	Type	Controlled vocabulary, different for each category. A total of 125 types were initially defined for the 5 categories, but more can be added as needed. In case the researcher is not sure about the type of an item (e.g., a vessel), he can record additional types in the "comments" element	√	
	Part	Controlled Vocabulary, describing whether the item is part of the original object (e.g., lip, body, handle, base, stem, etc.), by choosing one of the initially 12 common part names. This value can also be an integer (usually 1), indicating that the item is not a part but an entire object of the specific type. More details can be added as descriptive texts in the "Conservation" or "Description" elements, wherever they fit best	√	
	Material	[Used on metal items only] Controlled Vocabulary. Initially we define 4 common metal materials, but more can be added when needed	√	
	Texture	Descriptive text where the quality, composition, and contents of the clay of the item are described in detail. The texture of clay can be fine or coarse and it can contain various organic and inorganic materials		√

(continued)

Table 2.1 (continued)

Item code	Item name	Item type	Required	Optional
	Description	Descriptive text of the shape of each item (e.g., part of a ring-shaped base of a cup or part of a bottle rim, vertical rim). In the element of description, a comment is made on the shape (e.g., part of a ring-shaped base of a cup or part of a bottle rim, vertical coke rim) or the general form of the item (e.g., figurines, sparks, and other small findings). Generally, in the field of description we describe in a few words what we see at first glance at the item in front of us		√
	Decoration	Text detailing the decorative patterns an item can have whether it is metal or clay. A vase can be decorated both internally and externally		√
	Conservation	Text detailing the conservation level of each item, e.g., damage (cracks, peeling, sediments and in the case of metal slag) to what extent and in which parts of the item		√
	Conservation Level	Consist of an integer, in the range 1–5, corresponding to the conservation values of the item: BARELY IDENTIFIABLE, POOR, MODERATE, GOOD and EXCELLENT	√	
	Related item	The unique code of another item, if any, to which the item is related by construction. Additional related items, as well as their type of relationship can be recorded in the "Description" element		√
	General comments	Text for anything necessary to the study of each item as well as comments of any nature, general or on values of the controlled elements		√

(continued)

Table 2.1 (continued)

Item code	Item name	Item type	Required	Optional
	Clay1, Clay2, Clay3, Glaze1, Glaze2, Coating	Controlled Vocabulary: Munsell color scheme. These elements are used for the colors found in the corresponding place of the item. The colors are placed in order of importance to the corresponding elements. So, the value of each element (if any) will always be a single color from the Controlled Color Vocabulary of colors and not an array of multiple colors. If additional colors are found, or other comments about the colors and how they are applied, they will be reflected in the "Color Comments" item		√
	Color comments	Additional text describing the coloring of the item, as in the color elements the values are strictly standardized		√
	Height, length	Decimal number in meters, mainly drawn with a special tool called a caliper	√	
	Thickness	Decimal number in meters, the thickness of the wall, mainly drawn with a special tool called a caliper	√	
	Base height	The base height of the vase in meters	√	
	Diameter	Decimal number in meters, for vases is the diameter of the base, calculated with a special diagram (rim chart)	√	
	Rim diameter	Decimal number in meters, calculated with a special diagram (rim chart)	√	
	Layer	Controlled Vocabulary, based on the layers discovered in the excavation	√	
	Square	Controlled Vocabulary, based on excavation area division into squares	√	

(continued)

Table 2.1 (continued)

Item code	Item name	Item type	Required	Optional
	Excavation context	Text with a description of the discovery site of the item. It could also take values from a controlled vocabulary, but it has a wide variety of values, often depending on local characteristics. Alternatively, it is suggested to prefer values that have been used in the past, as long as they express the desired value, without being obligatory	√	
	X, Y, Z	For importance level is at least 2: x, y or z (height from sea level) position coordinates—decimal number. All 3 result from using GPS	√	
	Chronology	Controlled Vocabulary, from which the closest possible chronological period/date must be chosen. Initially we define 33 such well known periods forming a two-lever hierarchy, but more periods can be added later	√	
	Chronology comments	Text with additional data on the chronology of the item		√
	Year	Contains a representative (approximate) year, in integer form, with negative values for BC years. The year element should include a representative/typical date, at the year resolution level, from the chronological information of the item, to be used in time-based display of the items	√	
	Date found	"YYYY-MM-DD" format, with year, month, and day of the month	√	
	Excavation log	Format "YYYY/XX", calendar year, optional reference to a section of the log	√	
	Related bibliography	Text, in bibliography format		√
	Study status	Description of the scientific publications	√	
	Photos	Repetitive element: usually png/jpg/tiff files	√	

The above clarifications on the values of elements with a controlled vocabulary can be recorded either separately per element, or per groups of elements or all together, in metadata elements with content comments or other elements determined for this reason—depending on their frequency and importance—and are often described in free text. In our case, it is recommended that all clarifications on the values of the elements that are not free text be recorded in the "comments" element. It should be noted that, as is customary in the use of authorities, the values of controlled vocabularies can be increased with their appropriate approval process, if necessary, often by a suitably informed and responsible member of the team. Consequently, it is not essential to predict from the beginning all the terms that may be needed, but it is necessary to have a good understanding of the values and the relationships between them, and to have an idea of which terms express the different values that we want to register.

2.3.2 *Digitalization Initiatives and Shaping of Digitized Material*

Designing digitalization initiatives and shaping of digitized archaeological excavation material, as crucial as it is for unveiling new data and feeding archaeological study for a better understanding of the past, inherently involves the destruction of the area being excavated. This is because the course of excavation work irreversibly alters the geomorphology of the archaeological site through the artificial dissection of the overall area and the removal of soil, often to a considerable depth, until the sought-after evidence is systematically and fully revealed (Huisman 2012).

Given the above reality, it becomes evident that frequent and detailed photographic recording of the archaeological excavation is vital for its proper monitoring and documentation. For this purpose, the means or combination of means are chosen in advance that will meet the needs of each site.

Excavation Photography for the Needs of the Excavation Diary

In the case of Amyklaion, a combined use of an unmanned aircraft system (drone) and a DSLR camera has been chosen. The drone offers several advantages in this field as it can photograph the desired area vertically, under an adjustable viewing angle, or even horizontally with great stability without the need for a tripod as is the case with the camera, which would add unwanted elements to the photo. In addition, it has the ability to fly at a low altitude, for close shots with more detail, up to a high one, for photographing the entire area of an archaeological square of 5 × 5 m, sets of squares, or even the entire archaeological site.

The DSLR camera is mainly used to support the drone, as for the needs of this particular archaeological research it does not offer the same seamless user experience. In cases where the drone does not have the ability for clear shooting or safe access, such as when there are very strong winds, when the area to be photographed is extremely small, for example, a mobile find in situ, when a great depth and existence of masonry or other buildings are observed, or/and when there are trees or bushes in dense clusters, the use of a camera is alternatively chosen for photography.

During the first day of the excavation period, once the squares of the excavation area are defined, they are photographed to document their pristine/initial condition. A special scale, usually with a size of 0.50 m, is placed on the ground of each square, with an arrow pointing north. This ensures the accurate calculation of the actual dimensions from the photograph. A drone is used for capturing the photographs, flying at an altitude of approximately 5–30 m above the surface of each square or group of squares, with the camera facing downward at a 90° angle. This setup allows the excavation area to be viewed in a sectional perspective on the smartphone screen of the operator in real-time. Great attention is given to aligning the sides of each square as seen on the live image displayed on the smartphone's remote-control screen, using the sides of the screen as reference. This minimizes the need for extensive post-processing of the photographs in terms of their boundaries in the subsequent step.

Under these conditions, multiple photographs are taken, some from lower altitudes and some from higher ones, to adequately capture the excavation area. Whenever a new layer is excavated and before removing the next layer, the aforementioned process is repeated precisely, with the addition of taking some photographs at a 45° angle downward when a lateral view of the excavation area is required. As the depth increases with each layer and stationary features such as structures or walls are revealed, the timing of the photography also considers minimizing shadows on the excavation data. Therefore, this procedure is typically carried out before sunrise when the lighting is soft, and all details are well visible. The photographs are examined daily by the archaeologists to better understand the progress and development of the excavation work. Additionally, photographs from previous years may be utilized, or new ones are taken of already excavated squares when required for archaeological research.

At the end of the excavation period, a detailed photography session is conducted for the entire newly excavated area and its individual sections. Finally, the photographs are included in the excavation journal to visually depict the description of the squares and the overall excavation process.

Excavation Photography for 3D Modeling Purposes

With a view to developing digital applications (apps) for students, scholars, and "archaeological" tourists, specialized photography is frequently conducted alongside the progress of excavation work. This photography serves the purpose of capturing the overall excavation area, including the individual squares it contains, as well as providing detailed documentation of the excavation process from the square delineation phase to the final exposure of the natural ground. As the objective of the photography is to create 3D models, which requires the use of specialized image processing software, all parameters are adjusted according to the software's operational requirements. In this case, the software falls under the general category of photogrammetry and drone mapping software. Therefore, the selected method for capturing the necessary images is using an unmanned aerial vehicle system, commonly known as a drone. On the first day of the excavation period, as soon as the squares are delineated in the area, specific reference points/targets are placed on the ground around the squares. These points acquire georeferencing coordinates through a specialized surveying instrument called a Total Station, and they remain fixed throughout the entire excavation process. These reference points will be used by the software in the subsequent steps to accurately position dimensions within the 3D model. Subsequently, the squares are photographed to capture their undisturbed/initial state. The drone flies at an altitude of approximately 3–6 m above the surface of each square or group of squares. Initially, the camera is oriented at a 90° angle downward to provide a vertical view of the excavation area, and then at a 45° angle to capture an oblique view of the excavation. Photos are taken in a grid pattern to ensure complete coverage of the area to be modeled. Typically, about 500 photos are taken for a 5×10 m area, and a high degree of overlap, exceeding 70%, is required between the photos. After completing the excavation of each new layer and before removing the next layer, the aforementioned process is repeated precisely. As the depth increases with each layer and non-moveable features such as structures or walls are exposed, the time of photography must also be taken into consideration to minimize shading of the excavation data. Therefore, this process is usually carried out before sunrise when the lighting is gentle, and all details are clearly visible. Finally, the captured photographs, along with the necessary georeferencing information obtained from the fixed reference points, are stored daily on a computer. They are organized into folders based on the date of capture and prepared for transfer to the modeling/mapping software.

2.4 Documentation Platform for Findings in a Three-Dimensional Environment

The subsystem for documenting findings contains the objects discovered at the site, accompanied by corresponding descriptive and three-dimensional information. This subsystem provides visualization of the findings in a three-dimensional replica of the archaeological site, both at the object level and in combination. It constitutes an online tool for documenting findings in an archaeological site, both at the metadata level and at the level of depicting the points of discovery, extending to the three-dimensional representation of the objects in the space and time they were found (excavation phase). This allows for a more comprehensive understanding of where and how the objects were found, while simultaneously offering the potential for this content to be used in the development of educational applications.

Indicative screens of the software's functionality are presented in the following figures (Fig. 2.1 Initial Screen of the Findings Documentation Platform Fig. 2.2 Orthophotography of the excavation).

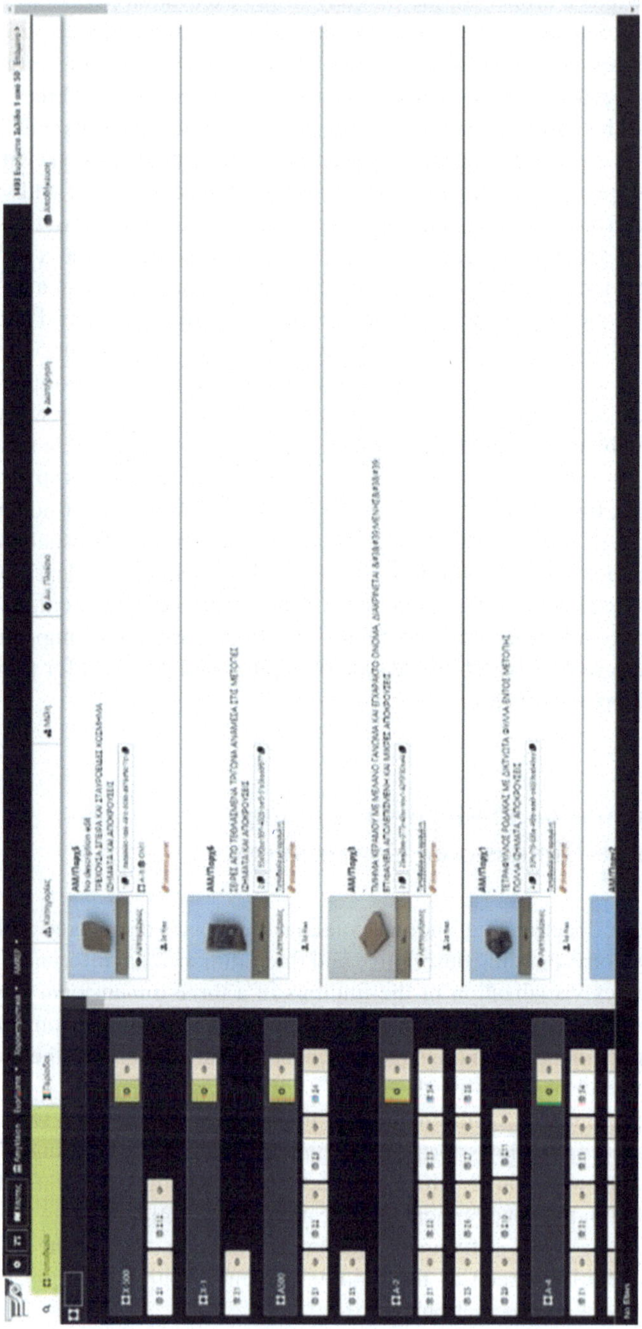

Fig. 2.1 Initial screen of the findings documentation platform

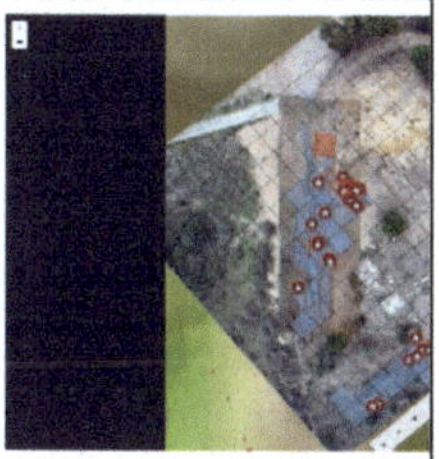		
Orthophotography of the excavation	*The editing of a finding point*	*Display of layers of a selected archaeological square.*

Fig. 2.2 Orthophotography of the excavation

2.5 Mixed Reality Application

The forefront of digital innovation at archaeological sites is marked by two interconnected systems: the 'Mixed Reality Educational Application Development Subsystem' and the 'Mixed Reality Application'. These systems represent a groundbreaking approach in the fusion of technology and cultural heritage education. The Mixed Reality Educational Application Development Subsystem is designed to facilitate the creation of immersive educational content by leveraging mixed reality (MR) technology to bring ancient history to life. It functions as a dynamic platform for developers and educators to craft interactive learning experiences by blending real-world archaeological environments with digital enhancements (Huang 2019). Complementing this, the Mixed Reality Application acts as the interface through which end-users, whether they are students, tourists, or researchers, engage with these enriched, interactive experiences. These systems not only revolutionize the way we interact with historical sites, but also deepen our understanding and appreciation of cultural heritage through a blend of tangible and virtual elements.

The core development environment for our Mixed Reality (MR) application was established using Unity in conjunction with the Mixed Reality Toolkit (MRTK) specifically tailored for Hololens 2 (Microsoft 2022). This integration is pivotal in crafting immersive MR experiences. MRTK, functioning as a versatile plugin within Unity, equips developers with a comprehensive suite of tools, components, and preconfigured assets, all meticulously designed to streamline MR development. This toolkit is adept at supporting a variety of MR platforms, yet it particularly excels with Hololens 2, offering specialized features and optimizations such as enhanced spatial awareness, sophisticated hand tracking, and precise eye-tracking capabilities.

In our application, MRTK's integration into Unity was instrumental in harnessing Hololens 2's spatial awareness features. This allowed for an acute recognition of the user's environment, enabling the precise placement and real-time localization of 3D models of the excavations. This was achieved by leveraging Microsoft Azure's Spatial Anchors technology, which anchors virtual content in the physical world, ensuring consistency and reliability in user interactions. Furthermore, the advanced full hand tracking capabilities of Hololens 2 were adeptly utilized within the Unity framework through MRTK. This enabled users to interact with the MR environment in a more natural and intuitive manner, allowing for gestures such as moving, enlarging, and pointing at virtual objects. The development of holographic user interface elements, including buttons, sliders, and panels, was undertaken to enhance user interaction and manage 3D components effectively within the MR space. Voice command functionality was also integrated, providing users with an alternative method of interaction, particularly useful in scenarios where hand gestures were impractical or ineffective. This feature proved invaluable in situations where users' hands were occupied, or in conditions where lighting constraints affected the clarity and visibility of holograms, making hand-based interactions challenging. Voice commands facilitated seamless navigation through menus and control over the application, thereby augmenting the overall user experience and accessibility of the MR system.

2.5.1 Mixed Reality Educational Application Development Subsystem

In this subsystem, the content creator selects the content they wish to display in the mixed reality application in the form of a presentation, defining the point at which each content will be activated and the desired time period which will be visible (start of display, duration of display, etc.). The subsystem is connected to the documentation subsystem from which the three-dimensional content will be drawn. The creator can specify the display of more than one type of content at each point (timeline) to present the excavation work that was carried out. Additionally, the ability is offered for this content to be activated/deactivated through the interaction modes offered by the HoloLens device.

Specifically, through the platform's environment for documenting findings in a three-dimensional environment, all the material that will be utilized in the application for creating the presentation is registered, which includes images, texts, three-dimensional models, etc. In the application for creating the presentation (Mixed Reality Educational Application Development Subsystem), the stages of the excavation are registered with the basic structural element being the archaeological layer of each excavation period, which the specialist analyzes the course of the excavation. In case there are findings in an archaeological layer, these findings are placed on the three-dimensional model.

The following steps were followed for the registration of the presentation data:

- The excavation was created.

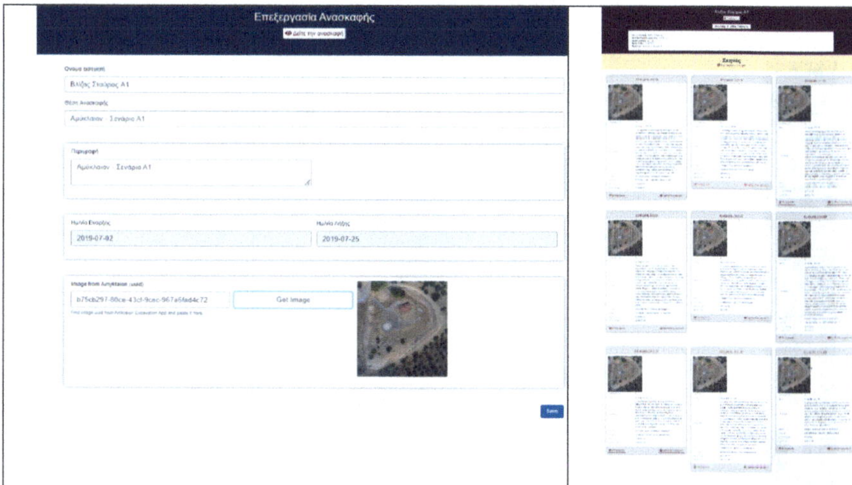

Excavation element editing

List of all scenes - archaeological layers.

Fig. 2.3 Registration of excavation elements

- The scenes of the excavation were created, to which the corresponding archaeological layer was added.
- The object groups were created.
- 3D objects were added to the corresponding object group.
- The presentation was created.

The following are indicative screens from elements of an excavation that were registered in the system (Figs. 2.3 and 2.4 Registration of excavation elements).

2.5.2 *Mixed Reality Application*

The use of mixed reality techniques integrated into the latest generation of mixed reality headsets is equipped with specialized systems and sensors aimed at detecting the user's position through environment recognition, allowing the display of three-dimensional flow and information in real time. Through the developed application, the selected content is displayed as the user moves around the Amyklaion area. The image that the user (archaeologist) sees, including augmentations and other information provided by the application, is transmitted in real time, through live display to other users who "watch" the tour via the internet (Fig. 2.5 Images seen by the HoloLens user—Fig. 2.6 Images seen by the HoloLens user).

The initial aim to display the information at the Amyklaion by placing the three-dimensional archaeological layers and findings, created a slight delay in the flow

Indicative archaeological layer - A1-square_2-7-19

Object group editing.

Fig. 2.4 Registration of excavation elements

By raising their left hand, the user selects whether to place the three-dimensional information in the space or load already saved presentations..	*Loading of presentation and navigation through the phases of the excavation.*

Fig. 2.5 Images seen by the HoloLens user

Placement of the archaeological layer in its position in the space.	*Placement of the archaeological layer in its position in the space.*

Fig. 2.6 Images seen by the HoloLens user

of the presentation, although it met the goals of the research. This period of time translates into less energy consumption of the HoloLens and less data consumption as well as staying in the field for a shorter period. This need led to the creation of a new option in the HoloLens application in which the archaeologist/specialist visits the space before the presentation and places all the three-dimensional data of the presentation in the archaeological space and saves their position using Microsoft

Azure's spatial anchors technology. In this way, during the presentation, the three-dimensional models automatically appear in the correct position and the flow of the presentation continues. It was necessary for the specialist to interact with the audience watching the presentation in real time, since the presentation through the mixed reality application aims at an audience which is outside the archaeological space. The ways in which this possibility was given were two: either with the device portal of the HoloLens, or with the Dynamics 365 Remote Assist service, which was chosen as the best solution.

The stages of development of the mixed reality application for the archaeological site of Amyklaion were the following:

- Preparation of presentations.
- Placement in the archaeological space of the three-dimensional models through the HoloLens application.
- Start of communication with the audience through Dynamics 365 Remote Assist.
- Start of presentation through the HoloLens application.

2.6 AR Application

For enriching the experience of a visitor in archaeological and cultural heritage sites, two crucial systems have developed: the 'Narrative-Based Educational Application Development Subsystem' and the 'Portable Device Application'. These systems effectively fuse storytelling with state-of-the-art technology to enhance the educational and experiential aspects of historical exploration. The Narrative-Based Educational Application Development Subsystem is specifically designed to create captivating, story-driven educational content. This subsystem enables developers and educators to craft engaging narratives around archaeological findings, thereby revolutionizing the way historical information is communicated and comprehended. The Portable Device Application complements this narrative approach by serving as a user-focused platform, delivering these rich, narrative-based experiences directly to handheld devices. This application is designed to be intuitive and accessible, ensuring that users, whether they are students, tourists, or history enthusiasts, can effortlessly navigate and become immersed in the stories of the past while walking through the archaeological site (Khan et al. 2022).

2.6.1 Narrative-Based Educational Application Development Subsystem

At the Amyklaion, the subsystem for developing digital applications (apps) for students, pupils, and "archaeological" tourists takes the form of a narrative with gamified elements, leveraging augmented reality technology and location detection

(GPS and beacons). This subsystem is connected to the documentation subsystem, thus providing the ability to create the content of the applications with real findings (Figs. 2.7 and 2.8). Composed of different entities, each application adapts to the way the user moves in the archaeological space, without indicating how to move, instead, allowing them to choose freely. For each type of content that the creator chooses to insert into the application, they can link an audio file and a virtual character that narrates the information about the content in question. Each content can also be linked to games (puzzle, questions, role-playing games, treasure hunt) that unlock as the user approaches a specific point of the archaeological site.

2.6.2 Portable Device Application

This tool presents to the users the applications developed by the corresponding subsystem and provides the required interaction and experience. The content of each application and the corresponding interactive tools are activated when the user approaches the area that concerns the specific content. The application receives the user's position both via GPS and via beacons installed in the space. When the visitor approaches a point, the narration automatically starts, three-dimensional findings and buildings in their original form are displayed (or requested to be discovered), and games related to the specific content are unlocked (Fig. 2.9). The application downloads the respective content from an application programming interface (API).

2.7 Pilot Study

2.7.1 Implementation

Quality control is a crucial element in the implementation of a project as it can influence its development (Formative Control) and highlight the acceptance of the project by the target audience (Report Audit). In the case of the Amyklaion and the AMREP project, the purpose of the quality control process, which is both formative and debriefing, was to:

- Ensure that systems are working as expected.
- Evaluate usability, suitability, and viability.
- Measure the acceptance of systems by potential users.
- Justify the reasons why they were proposed and developed.
- Measure the quality of the services offered.

To achieve the above objectives, a quality control process was followed, through which the necessary information was collected from both future users of the system and the specialized audience, who may be the key people for the promotion and

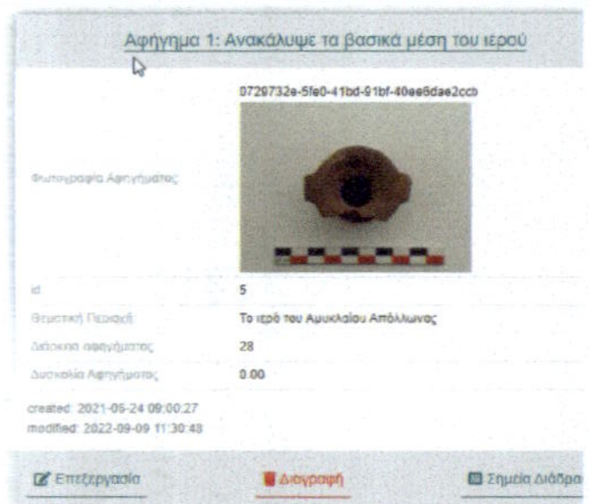	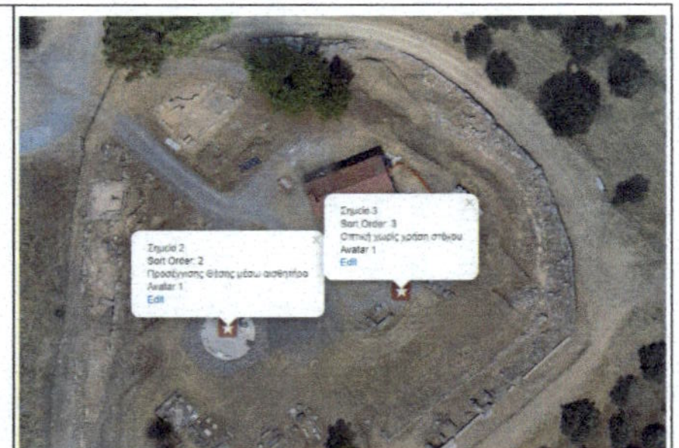
Narrative management screen.	*Overview of an example scenario in the educational application, containing points of interest and goals for the visitor/user.*

Fig. 2.7 The subsystem for developing digital applications

Mobile device application screen.

Mobile device application screen.

Recognition of the area where the augmentation will appear.

Fig. 2.8 Portable device application

Fig. 2.9 Screens with augmentation representing a sacrifice on the altar containing animation

sustainability of the project. The quality control methodology used was based on ISO 25022:2016 "Systems and software engineering—Systems and software quality requirements and evaluation (SQuaRE)—Measurement of Quality in Use" which replaced ISO/IEC 9126-4 "Quality in Use metrics". This standard specifies how to measure (question types, how to calculate results, etc.) characteristics of software applications as defined in ISO/IEC 25010.

The audit was conducted in three phases.

A. In the first phase and after the first prototype of the integrated system was delivered, selected users managed the systems (administrative systems, navigation, and mixed reality applications) following a usage scenario given to them. This scenario helped to test the largest percentage of systems functionality (at least 75%) with test content and to measure issues of effectiveness and efficiency for administrative environments and satisfaction for applications. The users who used the systems in Phase 1 were "internal", executives of the institutions, familiar with the internet with some, even minimal previous experience in accessing websites. The audit environment simulated real conditions and was conducted in the presence of control users.

B. In the second phase, after the installation of the applications for the site of Amyklaion was completed and the problems of functionality and usability were solved by the results of the first phase, selected users were invited to use the applications at the archaeological site. During the second phase, user satisfaction with the use of the mobile app and the mixed-reality application was measured.
C. In the third phase, an evaluation was carried out by real users, visitors of the site, who after using the app, were asked to answer satisfaction questionnaires.

Phase A Results

The results of the first evaluation phase are useful for drawing basic conclusions for project subsystems. Regarding management software, most users managed to complete the tasks they were given (Table 2.2 Results on the effectiveness and efficiency of management software). In a small number of cases, they asked for help from the evaluation administrators, and their relative efficiency toward experienced users who knew the operation of the system and performed the same tasks was satisfactory. From the mistakes made, the observation of the use of the system, and the feedback of users, significant improvements were made that were implemented in the systems. Results on user satisfaction for mobile app and mixed reality app were encouraging (Table 2.3 Phase A results on user satisfaction). The percentage of positive responses dominated most responses, whereas in some cases, some weaknesses were identified and addressed.

The results of the evaluation are presented in the table below. The results were satisfactory with regard to the effectiveness criterion.

Phase B Results

The objectives of the second phase were to evaluate the AMPEP subsystems addressed to end users within the archaeological site of Amyklaion with the scenarios developed by the project team.

Specifically, the following applications were evaluated.

- Mobile app: Use of the application with free choice of scripts implemented.
- Mixed reality app: Use of the application mixed with free choice of the implemented scripts.

The results of the second evaluation phase were very satisfactory, on the one hand, because they confirmed that the improvements and additions to the applications were in the right direction and on the other hand, because they were carried out at the archaeological site for which they were intended. The users who used the systems in the second phase were "internal", executives of the institutions, familiar with the internet with some, even minimal previous experience in accessing websites. Some problems regarding the content of the scripts in the browser application will be addressed after user observations and re-evaluated in Phase C by visitors to the

Table 2.2 Results on the effectiveness and efficiency of management software

Results on the effectiveness and efficiency of management software			
User efficiency (time to complete tasks compared to experienced users) highlighted problems in the management subsystems which are improving			
Back-end		Results (Target value)	
Operation	Weight	Effectiveness	Relative efficiency
Documentation software			
Login to the system	0,1	100% (75%)	70% (50%)
Insert a new finding	0,5	100% (75%)	48% (50%)
Insertion of a new excavation site layer	0,2	94% (75%)	63% (50%)
Placement of a find in a layer	0,2	92% (75%)	56% (50%)
Tour creation software			
Create a narrative	0,2	100% (75%)	56% (50%)
Insert initial point of interaction	0,4	100% (75%)	59% (50%)
Insertion of a new interaction point	0,4	92% (75%)	51% (50%)
MR presentation creation software			
Create an excavation	0,2	100% (75%)	58% (50%)
Create a presentation	0,2	100% (75%)	54% (50%)
Insert a new scene	0,3	91% (75%)	51% (50%)
Insert a new object	0,3	88% (75%)	52% (50%)

Table 2.3 Phase A results on user satisfaction

User satisfaction results	
User satisfaction was below the desired limits and improvements will be made which will be evaluated in future evaluations at the archaeological site	
Front-end	Results (Target value)
Operation	Satisfaction
Mobile app	
Satisfaction questionnaire	71,6% (80%)
Mixed reality app	
Satisfaction questionnaire	70,8% (80%)

Table 2.4 Phase B results on user satisfaction

User satisfaction results	
User satisfaction was higher than the desired limits, clearly better than the satisfaction of users who participated in Phase 1	
Front-end	Results (Target value)
Operation	Satisfaction
Mobile app	
Satisfaction questionnaire	85,6% (80%)
Mixed reality app	
Satisfaction questionnaire	86,8% (80%)

Table 2.5 Phase C results on user satisfaction

User satisfaction results	
User satisfaction was higher than the desired limits, reaching 94%	
Front-end	Results (Target value)
Mobile app	Satisfaction
Satisfaction questionnaire	94% (80%)

archaeological site. The observations for the mixed reality application mainly concern the method of hand handling that requires some familiarity but also problems related to this technology, such as changing weather conditions and the level of lighting that differs in different phases of the day.

The results of the evaluation have been completed in the table below (Table 2.4 Phase B results on user satisfaction).

Phase C Results

Users who used the systems in the final phase were real visitors to the archaeological site. The results of the final evaluation phase were encouraging, on the one hand, because they confirmed the results of Phase B, and on the other hand, because they were carried out at the archaeological site by real visitors. There were no problems when using the application, and all functions, GPS positioning, beacon tracking, and augmentations with the recognition of real space, worked infallibly.

The results of the evaluation have been completed in the table below (Table 2.5 Phase C results on user satisfaction).

2.7.2 Evaluation

The augmented reality (AR) application received overwhelmingly positive feedback from site visitors. Regarding the use of terminology, 53% of users rated it 4 out of 5, while 47% provided a perfect score. Notably, all feedbacks were positive.

Comparing these outcomes with the first and second phases of evaluation, a consistent pattern emerges that aligns with improvements made in the application. The organization of information, particularly the adjustments made to scenarios after the second evaluation phase, elicited positive responses. Here, 71% of participants provided a perfect rating, and the remaining respondents gave a 4 out of 5. The functionality of the application was also positively evaluated. A total of 65% of participants expressed a very positive opinion, with no recorded negative responses. The application's design received similarly encouraging feedback, with 88% (15 out of 17) of visitors providing the highest score, and the remaining two visitors scoring it 4 out of 5. These results parallel the positivity seen in the second evaluation phase. The application's response fluctuated, echoing the pattern from the second phase, with 82% of visitors reporting a very positive experience. The application ran seamlessly, free of delays, as all content was pre-downloaded. Moreover, positioning detection and beacon recognition outperformed their office counterparts due to the lack of signal obstacles. The augmentations impressively integrated with the existing buildings (Temple and Altar), contributing to the visitor experience. When queried whether they would reuse the application during future visits, 76% (13 out of 17) respondents gave a score of 5 out of 5, and the remaining four scored it 4 out of 5. This feedback demonstrates the application's utility during site visits and highlights a significant feature—the ability to dynamically add new navigation scenarios—which could be utilized to enhance the experience for repeat visitors. Moreover, 88% of participants responded affirmatively when asked if they would recommend the application to a friend. Combined with their overall satisfaction with the application, this highlights the app's appeal among the archaeological site's visitors.

After several updates were implemented in the mixed reality application, particularly the introduction of voice commands, there was a noticeable improvement in the application's terminology usage. This significantly enhanced the user experience, with 90% of users responding positively. This outcome is impressive considering the unique challenges associated with information architecture in such devices, which are often unfamiliar to users. In addition to improved terminology usage, the way information was organized in the application also improved significantly. The use of realistic scenarios derived from actual excavations, coupled with the in situ use of the device, contributed greatly to this improvement. The organization of information is crucial for a mixed reality application, especially when it is used as an educational tool. The application's functionality was also received very positively, with 80% of users rating it a perfect 5 out of 5 and the remaining 20% rating it 4 out of 5. These results marked a clear improvement from the initial phase, despite mixed reality devices performing better indoors and issues regarding unclear interaction points in the scenario content. The application's functionality significantly improved from the software enhancements implemented after the first evaluation phase, notably the addition of voice commands for object manipulation, such as the "come closer" command when a user looks at an object. The application's design was also favorably received in the second evaluation phase, with 90% of participants expressing a positive opinion. Compared to the first evaluation phase, there were more 5 out of 5 ratings, and no negative responses were recorded. Regarding the application's response to various operations, the participants' responses improved compared to the first evaluation phase, despite certain challenges with outdoor equipment use, such as space recognition with different lighting and device overheating due to high temperatures. The application's response was significantly improved by the addition of voice commands. A positive response was recorded from 90% of the participants.

2.8 Conclusions

In agreement with Dunleavy (Dunleavy and Dede 2014) and Pollalis (Pollalis et al. 2017), this paper has introduced a pioneering approach to integrating Mixed Reality (MR) and Augmented Reality (AR) technologies in the exploration of archaeological sites. Additionally, the findings indicate a notable potential in enhancing user engagement and learning. However, it is crucial to recognize the limitations and challenges inherent in our research and hypotheses.

Our hypotheses, exploring the effectiveness of MR and AR in archaeological education, were developed in the context of current technological advancements and historical pedagogy. While the initial discussion in this paper highlighted the positive aspects and potential of MR and AR applications in archaeology, a more comprehensive analysis should also encompass broader considerations. These include diverse user experiences, technological accessibility, and the implications of the digital divide. The varying impacts of MR and AR across different demographics, such as age groups and individuals with different levels of technological proficiency, merit further investigation. The outcomes of the MR and AR applications demonstrated encouraging signs of increased engagement and interest in archaeological content. Nonetheless, the scope of these evaluations was somewhat constrained. Future research should strive to encompass a broader array of metrics, including long-term information retention, shifts in attitudes toward cultural heritage, and comparative analyses with traditional educational methods. A significant limitation of the MR application is its reliance on advanced technology, which might not be universally accessible across all educational institutions or to every individual. This issue underscores the broader challenge of technological equity and underscores the necessity for inclusive solutions that cater to a wider audience. Moreover, the development and upkeep of MR applications demand considerable resources and expertise. The intricacies involved in content creation, regular updates, and maintaining historical accuracy necessitate sustained collaboration among technologists, historians, and educators.

Future research directions should aim at developing more accessible and scalable MR solutions. Potential avenues include the adoption of lower-cost technologies, the creation of user-friendly content development tools for educators, and forming partnerships with institutions that lack the requisite resources. Additionally, establishing a comprehensive combined evaluation framework that integrates both qualitative and quantitative metrics is vital for a deeper understanding of the impact and efficacy of MR and AR applications in education.

In conclusion, while the MR and AR applications proposed for archaeological education show considerable promise, it is imperative to approach their development and implementation with an awareness of their strengths and limitations. By recognizing and addressing these challenges, we can forge a path toward more effective, inclusive, and impactful educational technologies for future generations.

References

Abbas WZ, Talib AZ, Osman MA (2020) Opportunities and challenges in enhancing access to metadata of cultural heritage collections: a survey. Artif Intell Rev 53(5):3621–3646. https://doi.org/10.1007/s10462-019-09773-w

Apollonio FI, Gaiani M, Benedetti B (2012) 3D reality-based artefact models for the management of archaeological sites using 3D Gis: a framework starting from the case study of the Pompeii Archaeological area. J Archaeol Sci 39(5):1271–1287. https://doi.org/10.1016/j.jas.2011.12.034

Bai S, Shi J, Ge Q et al (2019) Scanning-based 3D reconstruction of large-scale objects. In: Proceedings of the 2019 international conference on robotics, intelligent control and artificial intelligence (RICAI'19), 20–22 September 2019, pp 584–589. Association for Computing Machinery, New York. https://doi.org/10.1145/3366194.3366298

Barratt PR (2021) Speculating the past: 3D reconstruction in archaeology. In: Champion EM (ed) Virtual heritage: a guide, pp 13–23. Ubiquity Press, London. https://doi.org/10.5334/bck.c

Cassidy B et al (2018) A virtual reality platform for analyzing remote archaeological sites. In: Proceedings of the 32nd international BCS human computer interaction conference, Belfast, UK, 4–6 July 2018. https://doi.org/10.14236/ewic/HCI2018.171

Deicke AJE (2016) CIDOC CRM-based modeling of archaeological catalogue data. In: Luca EWD, Bianchini P (eds) Proceedings of the first workshop on digital humanities and digital curation co-located with the 10th conference on metadata and semantics research (MTSR 2016), CEUR workshop proceedings, vol 1764. Göttingen. http://ceur-ws.org/Vol-1764/4.pdf

Demetrescu E, d'Annibale E, Ferdani D et al (2020) Digital replica of cultural landscapes: an experimental reality-based workflow to create realistic, interactive open world experiences. J Cult Herit 41:125–141. https://doi.org/10.1016/j.culher.2019.07.018

Dunleavy M, Dede C (2014) Augmented reality teaching and learning. In: Spector J, Merrill M, Elen J, Bishop M (eds) Handbook of research on educational communications and technology, pp 735–745. Springer, New York. https://doi.org/10.1007/978-1-4614-3185-5_59

Ferdani D, Fanini B, Piccioli M et al (2020) 3D reconstruction and validation of historical background for immersive VR applications and games: the case study of the Forum of Augustus in Rome. J Cult Herit 43:129–143. https://doi.org/10.1016/j.culher.2019.12.004

Getty (2021) Art & architecture thesaurus online (AAT). https://www.getty.edu/research/tools/vocabularies/aat. Last Accessed 10 Jan 2024

Getty (2022) Categories for the description of works of art (CDWA). https://www.getty.edu/research/publications/electronic_publications/cdwa/. Last Accessed 10 Jan 2024

Huang TC (2019) Seeing creativity in an augmented experiential learning environment. Univ Access Inf Soc 18:301–313. https://doi.org/10.1007/s10209-017-0592-2

Huisman DJ (2012) Deep impact: what happens when archaeological sites are built on? Conservation and Management of Archaeological Sites 14:60–71. https://doi.org/10.1179/1350503312Z.0000000006

Kapidakis S (2019) Correcting and redesigning metadata for the excavation of an archaeological site. In: Proceedings of the international conference on theory and practice of digital libraries (TPDL), Oslo, Norway, 9–13 September 2019. Lecture notes in computer science, vol 11799, pp 410–414. Springer, Oslo

Khan I, Melro A, Amaro AC et al (2022) Role of gamification in cultural heritage dissemination: a systematic review. In: Yang XS, Sherratt S, Dey N, Joshi A (eds) Proceedings of sixth international congress on information and communication technology. Lecture notes in networks and systems, vol 235, pp 393–400. Springer, Singapore. https://doi.org/10.1007/978-981-16-2377-6_37

Klein K, Wohde A, Gorelik AV at el (2023) AutArch: an AI-assisted workflow for object detection and automated recording in archaeological catalogues. https://arxiv.org/abs/2311.17978. Last Accessed 10 Jan 2024

Liritzis I, Al-Otaibi FM, Volonakis P et al (2015) Digital technologies and trends in cultural heritage. Mediter Archaeol Archaeom 15(3):313–332. https://doi.org/10.5281/zenodo.33832

Microsoft (2022) What is mixed reality toolkit 2. https://learn.microsoft.com/en-us/windows/mixed-reality/mrtk-unity/mrtk2/?view=mrtkunity-2022-05. Last Accessed 10 Jan 2024

Moraitou M, Konstantakis M, Chrysanthi A et al (2023) Supporting the conservation and restoration OpenLab of the acropolis of ancient Tiryns through data modelling and exploitation of digital media. Computers 12(5):96. https://doi.org/10.3390/computers12050096

O'Neill E, Chan LM (2006) A faceted LCSH based subject vocabulary. In: ALA annual conference, New Orleans, 24 June 2006. www.oclc.org/research/projects/fast/ala06-5f.ppt. Last Accessed 10 Jan 2024

Patwardhan A, Patwardhan R, Vartak S (2016) Self-contained cross-cutting pipeline software architecture. https://arxiv.org/abs/1606.07991. Last Accessed 10 Jan 2024

Pérez Saborido AE, Castanò F, Buono M (2018) Review on new technologies in art and archaeology: the Vesuvian cities. IOP Conf Ser Mater Sci Eng 364. https://doi.org/10.1088/1757-899X/364/1/012051

Pollalis C, Fahnbulleh W, Tynes J et al (2017) HoloMuse: enhancing engagement with archaeological artifacts through gesture-based interaction with holograms. In: TEI'17: proceedings of the eleventh international conference on tangible, embedded, and embodied interaction, pp 565–570. Association for Computing Machinery, New York. https://doi.org/10.1145/3024969.3025094

Psarros D, Stamatopoulos MI, Anagnostopoulos CN (2022) Information technology and archaeological excavations: a brief overview. Sci Cult 8(2):147–167. https://doi.org/10.5281/zenodo.6323149

Quick S (2018) Using digital media to mediate archaeology in the LVR-archaeological park Xanten/LVR-RömerMuseum. In: Hageneuer S (ed) Communicating the past in the digital age. Proceedings of the international conference on digital methods in teaching and learning in archaeology, 12–13 October 2018, pp 73–84. Ubiquity Press, London. https://doi.org/10.5334/bch.f

Soler F, Melero F, Luzon M (2016) A complete 3D information system for cultural heritage documentation. J Cult Herit 23:49–57. https://doi.org/10.1016/j.culher.2016.09.008

Suzuki T, Suzuki L (2020) On the benefit of 3-tier SOA architecture promoting information sharing among TMS systems and Brazilian e-Government web services: a CT-e case study. https://arxiv.org/abs/2005.13047v1. Last Accessed 10 Jan 2024

Vlizos S (2022) Ανάδειξη αρχαιολογικών χώρων και αγαθών: Προβληματισμοί και προτάσεις. In: Vlizos S (ed) Αρχαιολογία και Μουσεία: Η ενότητα της ελληνικής μνημειακής παράδοσης. Athens Archaeological Society, Athens, Πρακτικά Συνεδρίου στη μνήμη του Άγγελου Δεληβορριά, pp 201–219

Vlizos S (2017) Das Heiligtum und seine Beigaben: Bronzestatuetten vom Amyklaion. In: Frielinghaus H, Stroszeck J (eds) Kulte und Heiligtümer in Griechenland: Neue Funde und Forschungen. Beiträge zur Archäologie Griechenlands, vol 4, pp 71–95. Bibliopolis, Möhnesee

Vlizos S (2020) Metallwerkstätten, Produktion und Infrastruktur des Heiligtums: der Fall des spartanischen Amyklaions. In: Lo Monaco A (ed) Spending on the gods. Economy, financial resources and management in the sanctuaries in Greece. Annuario della Scuola Archeologica di Atene e delle Missioni Italiane in Oriente, Supplementum 4, pp 37–46. Athens.

Zachos A, Anagnostopoulos Ch-N (2023) Using terrestrial laser scanning, unmanned aerial vehicles and mixed reality methodologies for digital survey, 3D modelling and historical recreation of religious heritage monuments. https://arxiv.org/abs/2401.01380. Last Accessed 10 Jan 2024

Chapter 3
From Headsets to Mindsets: A Taxonomy for Human-Centred Extended Reality Experimentations for Cultural Heritage

Petros Lameras, Sylvester Arnab, Jacqueline Cawston, Alex Masters, Michael Loizou, and Panagiotis Petridis

Abstract Cultural heritage is undergoing a technological transformation that has an impact on how people experience, act and relate to cultural heritage found in galleries, libraries, archives and museums. There is a surge in the use of extended reality applications and tools that influence the way people experience virtual artefacts, crafts, traditions and historical stories. Extended reality is used as an umbrella term incorporating immersive experiences that utilise varying degrees of digital visualisation, encompassing virtual reality, augmented reality and mixed reality. Despite the hype around such technologies and the increasingly affordable and enhanced visual experiences they afford, there is still ambiguity in terms of the processes, strategies and human-centred design elements that drive innovation in using extended reality for cultural heritage applications. This chapter proposes a taxonomy that acts as a catalyst for designing features, elements and mechanics reflexively and purposefully for constituting the sense and significance of interaction, participation and meaning-making. The taxonomy could be significant in helping technologists, cultural heritage

P. Lameras (✉) · S. Arnab · J. Cawston · A. Masters
Coventry University, Coventry, UK
e-mail: ab3430@coventry.ac.uk

S. Arnab
e-mail: a8110@coventry.ac.uk

J. Cawston
e-mail: aa5237@coventry.ac.uk

A. Masters
e-mail: ac0187@coventry.ac.uk

M. Loizou
University of Plymouth, Plymouth, UK
e-mail: mchael.loizou@plymouth.ac.uk

P. Petridis
Aston University, Birmingham, UK
e-mail: p.petridis@aston.ac.uk

F. Liarokapis et al. (eds.), *Interactive Media for Cultural Heritage*, Springer Series on Cultural Computing, https://doi.org/10.1007/978-3-031-61018-9_3

specialists and educators harness a culture of change when designing and conveying cultural heritage experimentations through extended reality.

Keywords XR · Cultural heritage · Human-centred design · Taxonomy

3.1 Introduction

The advent of Extended Reality (XR) technologies encompassing Virtual Reality (VR), Augmented Reality (AR) and Mixed Reality (MR) proliferates trailblazing ways, processes and strategies for designing and utilising Cultural Heritage (CH) objects, artefacts, exhibitions and experiences found in Galleries, Libraries, Archives and Museums (GLAMS). There is a plethora of XR applications and tools for CH that are employed in GLAMS to encourage users to create and preserve memorable, educational and fun cultural experiences spanning from 2D, AR and VR to wearable and embodied 3D experiences (e.g., Liew et al. 2022; tom Dieck et al. 2018; Brigham 2017). The influx of a vast array of XR devices such as digital headsets and the exponential rise of computing power and Artificial Intelligence (AI) signals an unprecedented transformation of how visitors and users of cultural heritage sites are experiencing virtual, augmented and mixed reality for engaging in cultural activities.

For years, academic scholars and researchers have been examining the advantages and difficulties associated with employing XR in various cultural settings (e.g., Doolani et al. 2020; Okanovic et al. 2022; Schaper et al. 2018). These settings involve the use of distinct immersive technologies, both during and after visits, with a wide range of usage scenarios, requirements and goals that depend on the context, the user profiles, needs and interests. (e.g., Margetis et al. 2020). There is evidence that modern CH activities have evolved from static and monolithic activities, often sought to be completed during the visit, to multimodal and dynamic activities that are extended beyond the visit, by encouraging visitors to use AR applications for exploring cultural objects and distilling digital historical representations.

Despite this significant growth in the use of XR for improving visualisations and representations of digital cultural objects, content, and activities, research on human-centred and process-based paradigms for promoting elevated levels of discourse and meaning through XR is still under-developed (Banfi et al. 2023). It is key that the use of XR technologies in CH activities does not only represent technological advancements in reality-altering object visualisations and highly alluring content descriptions, but most importantly, considers aspects such as interactivity, storytelling, participation, personalisation, embodiment, ethics and user-centred frameworks for designing XR experiences (e.g., Doukianou et al. 2020; Steffen et al. 2019). This can enhance users' engagement with cultural content, leading to a sense of curiosity and motivation to continue interacting even after completing their visit (Rahaman et al. 2019; Maas and Hughes 2020). The focus on human-centred XR design can enrich XR interfaces as a means to provide rich-mediated constellations and meaning-making processes whilst engaging with CH activities. There is consensus that the slow uptake of XR is mainly due to a lack of consistency in hardware and software (Doolani et al. 2020) such as the tethering of devices to specific platforms (Jalo et al. 2022). However, there is less focus on the reasons of this lingering progress in terms of designing XR environments for enabling interaction, participation and meaning which may influence XR adoption in CH towards experiences that are meaningful, emotional and distinctive.

This chapter aims to provide a review of research evidence that draws on the design of XR technologies from a human-centred endeavour. The review acts as the basis for proposing a taxonomy for designing XR-based CH activities that are interactive, engaging, participatory and meaningful. The focus is not the technology and the linearity of features that underpin XR as a means to resemble and replicate CH, but rather to offer an account of rationalisation and contemplation of the different ways XR may be employed towards offering a more holistic and meaningful CH experience in its totality.

The chapter begins by exploring the various interpretations, understandings, challenges and possibilities related to XR from a 'headsets' perspective and their connection to technology, features and content. A rationale is then delineated as to the reasons for shifting design focus from technology and headsets to efforts for human-centred and participatory design, including interactivity and engagement, embodiment, participation, playful interventions, personalisation and storytelling, as portrayed in various frameworks and applications. Building on these design principles, we propose a human-centred taxonomy for designing CH experiences via XR as a means of aiding immersive technology designers, researchers and educators to create engaging and impactful experiences that go beyond devices, software and hardware.

3.2 XR for Cultural Heritage: A Headsets Perspective

When looking at XR through the lens of headsets, the main areas of interest are the technology, content creation, hardware and software that makes it possible to experience immersive and visually captivating CH digital content. There are different meanings, understandings and demarcations of XR along with associated technologies substantiated to form unified sets of virtual and augmented environments that describe how reality is generated or modified. As such, XR refers to combining VR, AR and MR for incorporating immersive experiences using varying degrees of reality and virtuality that are based on certain affordances embedded in the technology (Doolani et al. 2020; Steffen et al. 2019). XR can be perceived as an overarching term that subsumes AR, VR and MR used primarily by practitioners to describe a spectrum of contemporary forms of actuality for extending or replacing reality (Dalton 2021). Rauschnabel et al. (2022) proposed an XR classification model with AR and VR as two distinct sub-streams, which include their own attributes and properties. It differs from other definitions, where AR and VR are considered to have identical properties and located on the same continuum. AR can be understood as an overlay of the real world with digital content in real time, whereas VR transcends a user to a virtual location where they can manipulate objects and perform a series of actions. MR is an attempt to integrate the most prominent features of both AR and VR with the ultimate goal of allowing the user to interact in real time with both real and digital elements (Brigham 2017; Maas and Hughes 2020; Rokhsaritalemi et al. 2020).

XR is perceived as a spectrum of immersive technologies consisting of VR, AR and MR with distinctive properties and attributes that combine the physical and digital worlds. Contextualising this demarcation for CH, the authors are conscious that XR may be employed for creating a feeling of presence, engagement and participation, allowing users and visitors to explore and interact with objects, artefacts and sites in more engaging and meaningful ways. Boboc et al. (2022) argued that CH objects and artefacts are inaccessible or unpreserved due to their size and fragility. 3D reconstruction technologies merged with AR/VR may contribute to efficient digital accessibility and preservation of cultural objects through providing a high-level of detail and full-scale dimension of the space perception without requiring increased levels of knowledge from the end user. Digital touch screens, Internet of Things (IoT) and 3D printing are enmeshed with the 3D AR/VR application to determine the optimum restoration approach. The main shortcoming of this is the lack of guidelines for how to combine the complexity and fragility of cultural objects with the technological affordances of AR/VR for yielding a seamless experience.

To make the accessibility and presence of digital objects and installations more accessible to cultural sites, and to enable users to easily transition between the reality and virtuality of the cultural content, AR holographic projection systems can be utilised for the deployment of digital cultural content. Caggianese et al. (2018) presented a holographic projection system with spatial interaction techniques such as touchless interfaces for manipulating 3D cultural content. Gesture-based AR interfaces offer several advantages, they require minimal training time and may enhance accessibility due to the use of natural gestures familiar to users in their daily activities. Additionally, these interfaces improve safety by eliminating the need to physically touch the device. They can therefore potentially integrate with cultural sites without requiring any hardware configurations that might cause compatibility issues with pre-existing facilities.

To assist users and CH curators in the use of XR for digitising 3D CH content, predominantly found in galleries and museums, Rahaman et al. (2019) presented a methodology on 3D digitalisation for MR visualisation of CH assets based on open access software. Image modelling techniques, combined with HoloLens hardware and game engine processing, were incorporated in the workflow to produce 3D models that can be experienced in VR/AR. The methodology guided users to create 3D AR/VR models whilst understanding the technical workflow involved in overlaying virtual assets onto the real and virtual world view.

The generation of 3D CH models has drawn increased research attention for building new forms of onsite, online and hybrid visits in GLAMS and particularly in museums and their substrates, such as virtual museums. Banfi et al. (2023) argued that digitalisation of cultural content and its representation through AR/VR may facilitate new forms for communicating CH content that are simultaneously available onsite and online as demonstrated by recent efforts to develop a virtual museum from artefacts depicting ancient Rome. To assist visitors' efforts to focus on museum objects, Damala et al. (2016) detailed a study on the design process of creating 3D AR content for the Loupe thematic tour of a Greek gallery as part of a museum in Amsterdam. The study found that the AR application's highly descriptive 3D objects prompted visitors to revisit the real artefacts, encouraging reflection on their intricacies, importance and history. Pacheco et al. (2015) introduced an AR software architecture that integrates historical 3D reconstruction with geolocated historical resources and guidance components for narrative generation leading to conclusions that active exploration of a cultural environment may provide an enhanced spatial understanding of its collections, exhibitions and objects.

Functionality, device characteristics and ergonomics are prevailing in XR research investigations in relation to how they affect immersive experiences in CH sites and how they drive attitudes and behaviours after the site visit. Trunfio et al. (2022) explored the role of MR devices in enhancing the museum experience and influencing post-experience behaviour by examining their functionality and ergonomic impact. The study highlights the positive influence of MR devices on museum experiences and post-visit engagement. Usability, customisation, format, interaction and information retention are key factors that shape these experiences. Notably, valorisation and learning emerge as the critical drivers for post-experiences, long-term behaviours, museum attachments and the desire to revisit.

Although XR research and innovation from a headsets perspective is progressing at a fast pace and there have been technological developments that have contributed to the advancement of XR, resulting in mitigating barriers in acceptance and adoption, there are certain challenges that need to be addressed, especially in relation to hardware limitations, as XR headsets still require powerful hardware for maximum CH digital content rendering. XR devices remain expensive with issues around portability, which influences the size, manageability and usability of XR in physical cultural environments where there is often an array of artefacts across a length of physical space that visitors are required to walk through. As XR technology advances, there is a need for offering tailor-made, engaging and meaningful cultural experiences to the user by considering human-centred design aspects in line with, or ahead of, headset developments.

3.3 XR for Cultural Heritage: A Mindsets Perspective

Building on the empirical perspectives on human factors and user-centred design, we argue that multifaceted, multimodal and context-aware design strategies have the potential to leverage adoption of XR in CH through increasing interaction, engagement, participation, collaboration and situated learning. By adopting a mindsets perspective, we are synthesising evidence on what design features, strategies and paradigms are embraced for representing CH via XR. To remove barriers to engagement, it is vital to adopt a user-centred approach to designing and using XR technology. This facilitates user strategies and learning, creating enjoyable, memorable and sustainable experiences in vivid environments that effectively convey content with minimal obstacles and complexity.

Interactive digital story telling is at the forefront of human–computer interaction utilised through digital media platforms for the purpose of triggering interactivity and narrative. It may grant the user an active role in terms of influencing the flow of the story and its content. Okanovic et al. (2022) evaluated the impact of digital storytelling using edutainment levels and user experience metrics. The findings of the study revealed that natural interactions through motion sensor technology gestures can introduce distractions from the stories, highlighting the barriers technology can create. Podara et al. (2021) cast light on CH storytelling in relation to interactive documentary techniques using multimodal XR applications and tools. The analysis demonstrated the value of participative modes of engagement but less appropriateness when a certain story needs to be unfolded. Caution therefore should be placed in terms of whether it is appropriate to design interactions in XR-based storytelling, where the users select the direction of the story, or to design for a more passive storytelling pattern, having a pre-fixed narrative path. Informed decisions around this could be supported during the CH idea generation and user-requirements phases.

Rizvic et al. (2017) attempted to develop guidelines for interactive storytelling by involving stakeholders from multiple disciplines to test a digital storytelling application in terms of how it may be embedded in immersive technology for CH experimentations. The main elements that constituted the interactive digital storytelling guidelines were (1) multimedia narrative: the content should not have a unique flow, rather the user should be able to dynamically influence it; (2) Narration visualisation: a process-based design approach to how visualisation and visual components intertwine with narrative; (3) interactive narrative and its goals: creating a purpose for the narrative based on its content elements and capture the story's emotion and (4) interaction design: comprised of certain design elements such as the '*form*' for graphics design, '*behaviour*' for shaping users' attitudes towards the story and '*content*' created by immersive content experts, sound artists and animators. These elements may be applied in different phases of the XR design storytelling process from pre-production through to production and post-production. Fenu and Pittarello (2018) explored the impact on an iterative development process of an AR authoring tool and associated relationships between AR, storytelling and context for literary museums. Substantial connections emerged that shaped narrative experiences characterised using AR and location-based media via two pilot studies undertaken in the Svevo museum. Results from the pilot studies indicated the influence of context in the development of the story and how media and content could influence context and thereby lead to its fine-tuning.

The design of interactive XR experiences for cultural sites involves a multitude of considerations, processes and strategies for enhancing engagement through meaning making. XR-based interactive storytelling is an essential feature that enables users to unfold stories and drive meaning and emotional engagement. Multimodality can also be utilised as a set of concepts that highlight relationships between social contexts, the resources available in that context for meaning-making processes, and peoples' informed choices for the selected resources (e.g., Lameras and Papageorgiou 2020; Philippe et al. 2020). Liarokapis and Newman (2007) developed a multimodal MR interface that placed emphasis on user-centred interactions (e.g., marker-based tracking) for exploring superimposed information in 3D spaces and transferring virtual information between different locations of the same environment. Arrighi et al. (2021) experimented with multimodal affordances found in digital human reconstruction for VR storytelling. Body and facial motion captures were embedded in digital characters through AI-assisted technology and digital imaging restoration for enabling emotional engagement and meaningful learning within the virtual heritage site. Schaper et al. (2018) designed situated and embodied multimodal explorations and digital augmentations of CH sites through employing the *World-as-Support* (*WaS*) interaction design paradigm for offering increased levels of augmentation between the user and the context. Essentially, meaning-making processes are shaped by situated values and practices, with the world acting as a scaffold for these processes. This differs from the *Window-on-the-World* (WoW) paradigm, which layers stimuli around the user's physical surroundings in XR experiences, placing the focus on the device rather than the experience itself and the situational development within it. Schaper et al. (2018) argue that the WaS paradigm can assist in interaction design for CH sites for: (a) enabling users and visitors to focus on the on-screen experience for balancing CH content with the immersive experience; (b) providing opportunities for multimodal and multi-user engagement and collaborative tasks for discerning variation of meaning of cultural events and holistic understanding of the historical context and (c) allowing spatial, tangible and embodied interaction for delimiting emotional anchors, endorsing collaborative learning, and demarcating empathy, acceptance and presence (e.g., von der Pütten et al. 2012).

Another facet of WaS which is inextricably connected with the ecology of designing for meaning through context and situatedness is participation. Visitors' perception, exploration and understanding of a cultural heritage (CH) installation using XR technology shapes the significance and value of the cultural content. This, in turn, informs participatory discussions and interactions that contribute to the generation of personal meaning and the comprehensibility of the individual's experience. Heath et al. (2002) investigated how interactions among individuals shape participation and collaboration around installations in galleries and museums. They emphasised that reinvigorating the visitor experience involves augmenting tangible objects instead of simply replacing them with digital devices, fostering participation and collaboration.

It may be relatively rare to observe people in galleries and museums collaborating with each other in an AR/VR space, through wearing headsets, for exploring and making meaning together from discussions and constellations around exhibits and artefacts. Curiously, however, people that share common dexterities and passions on CH content and are simultaneously present within a museum site or installation can stimulate constructive discussions, deliberations and associations of the asymmetries observed in a prevailing object. This natural presence of people within the same gallery or museum setting can serve as a catalyst for meaningful dialogues and engagement in playful activities to collectively create meaning. Interaction design in XR cultural experiences has the potential to establish participatory scaffolds and situations that enable people to discover, learn and understand in a collaborative manner. For instance, the use of AR or VR in-game-like explorations by visitors can evoke curiosity, surprise and delight, thereby eliciting emotional responses and shaping social and cognitive contexts for the discovery and interpretation of augmented objects and artefacts.

Ciolfi and McLoughlin (2012) adopted interaction design from WaS to discern participatory memories of objects exhibited in a living history museum. Mobile AR was used to aid visitor interactions with the objects in the museum and for visitors to create their own content, reminiscing on their own life experiences. The installation fostered meaningful connections among diverse groups and deepened their engagement with museum objects. It also enhanced the visit by generating a wealth of user-generated content, particularly stories and reflections that contributed to form shared experiences of reflection and collaborative exchange. By incorporating carefully crafted participation mechanisms into the design of augmented and emotionally engaging experiences, which include additional narrative layers, creative stories, intriguing characters, meaningful conversations, and playful missions, users and visitors can establish subtle connections between the museum exhibits and the real-world cultural realms they originated from.

It is evidenced that the increased focus on participation and user engagement, embedded in human-centred design paradigms, as a means to enhance community inspiration and engagement in cultural heritage has raised questions in terms of how XR can enable such practices (e.g., Price et al. 2016; Ardito et al. 2018). Participatory practice in CH helps to democratise the process of collecting, curating and documenting CH data and activities that have historically been undertaken by CH specialists, academics and scientists. Visitors and users are now encouraged to contribute their own content to shape XR applications, enabling a more personalised and tailored approach to discovering and exploring cultural content. This fosters meaningful experiences that align with individual interests and needs. This entanglement between CH and immersive technologies brings to the fore interesting research questions around participation, personalisation and co-creation. For example, what are the experiences of and approaches to designing and enacting XR for co-creative and personalised cultural heritage practice? Shedding light to research questions that emphasise community-based and personalised processes, as delineated from users, will enable XR designers to consider a spectrum of needs, requirements and evaluation mechanisms that will couple XR features and mechanics to personalised experiences of co-creation and participation (e.g., Liew et al. 2022).

To address the challenge of evaluating participatory design applications using rich-mediated applications and tools such as games, Malinverni et al. (2016) suggested a multimodal analytical approach, grounded on empirical data from a serious game, based on a full body interaction for guiding design considerations and actions as well as for facilitating communication within the design teams in terms of aligning choices, requirements, content and aesthetics. The findings from the study triggered constellations and patterns around situated and embodied meaning making for intangible CH through (1) exploration of the space (e.g., could the system recognise and react to repetitive actions? could the system reward participation, collaboration and personalisation in the exploration paths?); (2) movements (e.g., how to facilitate the tracking of users' performance while promoting participation, exploration, and co-creation?); (3) focus of attention (e.g., what design strategies are employed for allowing users to gain interest in other users instead of focusing only on the environment? and what design strategies are commissioned to enable co-creation and creativity in the production of objects and artefacts?).

Tammaro (2016) tethered participation, collaboration and co-creation with the phenomenon of crowdsourcing for co-developing new forms of public engagement, enriching existing CH digital content and co-developing new CH resources through contributions of the crowd. Hannewijk et al. (2020) suggested a framework for helping to capture intangible cultural values through mobile crowdsourced cultural heritage but certainly the principles identified can be extended to designing for crowdsourced CH activities in XR. The most salient features for enabling XR-based crowdsourced activities can span from: (a) user-based tasks and missions; (b) enabling users to create profiles; (c) persuasive points, rewards and badges; (d) using a reputation system; (e) meaningful feedback through an array of visual representations; (f) enabling teamwork for communally exploring an object or collaborating on restoring a cultural artefact by adding missing pieces virtually through an AR application.

Despite the abundance of research evidence on user-centred design principles and how these could be instantiated to foster a more participatory and engaging CH experience, there are still few, if any, models, frameworks, or taxonomies that gather and enmesh design elements that guide users and designers in engendering meaningful, collaborative and participatory experiences of CH using XR.

3.4 A Taxonomy for Designing Human-Centred XR for Cultural Heritage

It is axiomatic that we should critically understand the plethora of XR experimentations, models and frameworks that have been analysed in the XR research domain, particularly for developing meaningful visitor experiences from interactions with CH content and resources in an immersive digital cultural setting. Human-centred design through XR for enhancing CH experiences, as we define it, is anchored in experience, which in turn leads to action. CH actions are guided and regulated by the XR system and by the CH specialists and curators for tracking the achievement of expected outcomes, prior to, concurrent with and retrospective to the actual visit. This process is key and central to the tenets of making decisions, modifying design aspects and calibrating processes of engagement, participation and interaction through the features, elements and mechanics offered by the XR system. What is apparent but not often made explicit in design frameworks for XR experimentations in CH is the critical importance of constructing a set of aspects, with associated variations, and how these are mapped to XR features, elements and mechanics for turning the experience into meaning (see proposed taxonomy in Table 3.1).

The taxonomy depicted in Table 3.1 enables XR designers to become aware and skilful in terms of forming the basis for actions and considerations to be taken in order to engender meaning, participation and engagement during XR-based CH activities. For example, *the role of the XR designer*, often flouted in design frameworks, is essential for establishing roles and patterns in the multiplicity of variables that define meaning in XR environments. The authors propose three roles as: creator, developer and facilitator representing the internal and external actions, the arena in which XR-based cultural activities are enacted, as interactions, engagement and co-creation that are transformed into meanings and behaviours. Storytelling, interaction, audio-visual, content and testing form the basis for actions or the mechanisms through which meaning and learning transformation is achieved. It is for this reason they are interpreted as mechanics because they may enable or constrain the processes of meaning-making based on the intended goals set out by the XR system and the user.

The role of the XR designer is central to the process of designing user-centred XR environments and the *role of the user or visitor* is relational to the role of the XR designer. The authors propose five roles as: explorer, learner, creator, collaborator and spectator to emphasise the inherent learning nature and knowledge construction as the overarching product gained from the interaction with the immersive CH content and the superimposed historical cultural objects. What is of particular interest is how such roles are manifested from the users themselves through creating interactions and navigations with objects and people for linking immersive action with meaning-making. Knowing what XR features to use and how these features can aid the purposes and aims of the user are critical skills for fostering a sense of self-direction and regulation for constructing meaning.

The *role of the XR system* resembles a multi-directional and multimodal mechanism for discerning the user's intentions and actions towards being more participatory, engaging, critical and creative. The roles proposed are augment, enhance, simulate, reconstruct and track as means to providing options or alternatives so that the outcomes of the actions better match the user's intended goals. Context-specific goals are a central function that needs to be supported by the XR application in order to maintain, initiate, adjust and transfer meaning in response to a specific situation that the user experiences. The authors propose that focusing on concurrent adjustments in augmentation, context and immersive content contributes to the direct and immediate impact of XR mechanics on participation, interaction and meaning-making.

The *level of interaction* is also multi-dimensional as it can be modified relatively easily during an XR-based CH activity. The variation of passive, active and reactive serves different meaning-making purposes and can be used in conjunction with the perceived role of the user. For example, if the user acts as a spectator, then the level of interaction will be passive, whereas when the user's role is that of an explorer

Table 3.1 A taxonomy for human-centred design in CH experimentations

Aspect	Variation	XR features, elements and mechanics
Role of XR designer	Creator, developer, facilitator	*Storytelling*: Developing narratives that support meaning-making *Interaction*: Designing multimodal interactions that encourage critical practice and reflection *Audio-visual*: Using audio and visual elements to evoke emotional, empathic and sensory responses *Content*: Designing multimodal content that can generate interactive, participatory and co-creative processes *Testing*: Evaluating the effectiveness of the XR experience and refine overall XR design to support meaning-making
Role of user/visitor	Explorer, learner, creator, collaborator, spectator	*User roles and perspectives*: Participating in CH activities that are aimed to explore, create, collaborate and observe *Creating interactions*: Constituting a sense of interaction and participation with virtual objects and virtual/real humans *Navigation and co-creation*: Navigating between the realms of real and virtual and transcending physical CH to virtual CH
Role of XR system	Augment, enhance, simulate, reconstruct, track	*Augment*: Supporting users to augment personal experiences with XR activities for meaning-making purposes *Contextualisation*: Linking contextual information to support user understanding and engagement *Track*: Tracking the experience for providing personalised feedback and performance triggers
Level of interaction	Passive, active, reactive	*User input and feedback*: Designing for interactions that provide users with opportunities for input and feedback *Gesture recognition*: for enabling more natural and intuitive interactions *Haptic feedback*: enhancing the sensory aspects of user engagement
Level of participation	Observational, experimental, interactive	*Participation mechanics*: Supporting different levels of participation (individual, shared, passive, interactive) *User-generated content*: Co-creation of multimodal content for collective meaning-making *Multimodal experiences*: Participatory multimodal experiences that evoke different levels of engagement and meaning making
Emotional anchors	Informative, educational, entertaining, engaging	*Games/Gamification*: Using game mechanics to make the experience more playful, collaborative and co-creative *Storytelling*: Crafting immersive stories that evoke emotional, participatory and cognitive responses *Emotional design*: Designing XR experiences that evoke specific emotions or moods

(continued)

Table 3.1 (continued)

Aspect	Variation	XR features, elements and mechanics
Decision making	Linear, branching, interactive, collaborative, adaptive	*Linear and branching narrative design*: Providing users with decision-making scenarios *Interactive and collaborative mechanics*: Supporting interactive and collective decision making *Adaptive mechanics*: Designing adaptive mechanics that adjust to user decisions and provide adaptive experiences
Tracking performance	Qualitative, quantitative, mixed methods,	*Analytics*: Tracking user engagement and performance *Performance metrics*: Defining performance metrics for measuring different levels of engagement, learning and XR impact in meaning-making *User-feedback*: Soliciting user feedback to gain insights into user engagement and meaning-making

then interaction becomes more active or reactive, especially when collaboration and feedback is the focus of attention. Modifications to features and mechanics such as gesture recognition and haptics may frame the level and purpose of the intended interaction and the levels of flexibility needed to support the user's intended use of the XR system.

The *level of participation* represents broad and in-depth interaction structures accumulated via observation, experimentation and interaction. Participation mechanics, user-generated content and multimodal XR experiences can provide the mechanisms for inferring different types of acquired knowledge for CH, which can be associated with a particular digital object or exhibition (explicit knowledge) and knowledge that cannot yet be described or verbalised and may be related to emotions and feelings (tacit knowledge). Both types of knowledge are important and the relationship between them is where we perceive XR plays an important role.

The authors hypothesised that emotions and feelings can be delimited and represented in XR in ways that can transform actions into meaning. Such *emotional anchors* can be informative, educational, entertaining, or engaging, and when applied, users may begin to see patterns across multiple experiences manifested in games, storytelling and emotional design for extracting principles of meaning. Similarly, emotional anchors can help to elicit tacit knowledge for bringing to the fore users' intentions and actions and in making connections between and among contents and processes that seem familiar.

Decision making is influenced by the emotional state of the users which in turn may affect levels of interaction and participation. Making decisions on what and how the XR-based cultural experience will be started, developed, and completed is essential for developing actions that are based on the user's prior knowledge, interests and needs. Such decisions can be linear, branched, collaborative, interactive and adaptive through scenarios and quests that include conceptions and preconceptions that users of different ages and backgrounds have for making the XR experience more adaptive and interactive. This contour considers decision-making as a developmental process that causes changes in thinking about what meaning is through the cultural representations and symbols depicted in the XR environment.

Tracking performance in XR can be a qualitative, quantitative, or mixed process that can be incrementally slow but may offer points of improvement both in terms of how design decisions can be modified to build XR iterations that meet user requirements and for observing shifts on users' meaning making levels and progress through analytics, visual performance metrics, levels of engagement and user-feedback.

The example of developing an XR experience for a historical site, such as an ancient city ruins, is conveyed for illustrating a practical implementation of the framework. The XR designer employs immersive storytelling, intuitive interactions and spatial reconstruction. The users assume roles such as 'historian' or 'explorer' with tailored research informed tasks, contributing interpretations through user-generated content. The XR system is designed to propagate immersion via 360° visuals, while decision points, gesture recognition and collaborative elements enhance user engagement. Emotional anchors such as audio-visual design and compelling storytelling evoke a sense of historical significance. The implementation includes analytics for tracking user engagement and regular user testing to refine the experience based on feedback, adhering to a human-centred design approach.

3.5 Conclusions

In this chapter, the authors introduced a human-centred taxonomy for designing CH activities using XR, including its subsets AR, VR and MR. Our argument is that an overly narrow focus on headsets, hardware and software can impede the process of meaning-making and learning. In some sense, the practice of learning constructively and thinking critically about CH objects, artefacts and content through using XR has remained epiphenomenal and yet the way XR environments are designed and manifested may influence roles, levels of interactions and participation, emotional qualities, decision-making and performance constituting the foundation for developing situated and meaningful experiences. We perceive that detailed empirical and interpretive studies on XR features that afford specific human-centred aspects around roles, participation, collaboration, emotional scaffolding, interactivity and performance monitoring can provide a unique yet complementary approach to understanding experiences of using XR and associated mechanics, by placing the users, their actions and conscious decision making at the forefront of investigations. The taxonomy presented in the study can be exploited by future research investigations as a means to empirically validate its applicability and to direct analytic attention towards the ways in which the proposed features are constituted through experimentations on actual usage and purposeful CH activity within an XR environment.

References

Ardito C, Buono P, Desolda G, Matera M (2018) From smart objects to smart experiences: an end-user development approach. Int J Hum Comput Stud 114:51–68. https://doi.org/10.1016/j.ijhcs.2017.12.002

Arrighi G, See ZS, Jones D (2021) Victoria Theatre virtual reality: a digital heritage case study and user experience design. Digit Appl Archaeol Cult Herit 21:e00176. https://doi.org/10.1016/j.daach.2021.e00176

Banfi F, Pontisso M, Paolillo FR, Roascio S, Spallino C, Stanga C (2023) Interactive and Immersive Digital Representation For Virtual Museum: VR and AR for semantic enrichment of Museo Nazionale Romano, Antiquarium di Lucrezia Romana and Antiquarium di Villa Dei Quintili. ISPRS Int J Geo Inf 12(2):28. https://doi.org/10.3390/ijgi12020028

Boboc RG, Băutu E, Gîrbacia F, Popovici N, Popovici D-M (2022) Augmented reality in cultural heritage: an overview of the last decade of applications. Appl Sci 12(19):Article 19. https://doi.org/10.3390/app12199859

Brigham TJ (2017) Reality check: basics of augmented, virtual, and mixed reality. Med Ref Serv Q 36(2):171–178. https://doi.org/10.1080/02763869.2017.1293987

Caggianese G, Gallo L, Neroni P (2018) Evaluation of spatial interaction techniques for virtual heritage applications: a case study of an interactive holographic projection. Future Gener Comput Syst 81:516–527. https://doi.org/10.1016/j.future.2017.07.047

Ciolfi L, McLoughlin M (2012) Designing for meaningful visitor engagement at a living history museum. In: Proceedings of the 7th nordic conference on human-computer interaction: making sense through design, pp 69–78. https://doi.org/10.1145/2399016.2399028

Dalton J (2021) Reality check: how immersive technologies can transform your business. Kogan Page Publishers

Damala A, Hornecker E, Van der Vaart MJ, van Dijk D, Ruthven I (2016) The loupe: tangible augmented reality for learning to look at ancient Greek art. Mediterr Archaeol Archaeom 16(5):73. https://doi.org/10.5281/zenodo.204970

Doolani S, Wessels C, Kanal V, Sevastopoulos C, Jaiswal A, Nambiappan H, Makedon F (2020) A review of extended reality (XR) technologies for manufacturing training. Technologies 8(4):Article 4. https://doi.org/10.3390/technologies8040077

Doukianou S, Daylamani-Zad D, Paraskevopoulos I (2020) Beyond virtual museums: adopting serious games and extended reality (XR) for user-centred cultural experiences. In: Liarokapis F, Voulodimos A, Doulamis N, Doulamis A (eds) Visual computing for cultural heritage, pp 283–299. Springer International Publishing. https://doi.org/10.1007/978-3-030-37191-3_15

Fenu C, Pittarello F (2018) Svevo tour: The design and the experimentation of an augmented reality application for engaging visitors of a literary museum. Int J Hum Comput Stud 114:20–35. https://doi.org/10.1016/j.ijhcs.2018.01.009

Hannewijk B, Vinella FL, Khan V-J, Lykourentzou I, Papangelis K, Masthoff J (2020) Capturing the city's heritage on-the-go: design requirements for mobile crowdsourced cultural heritage. Sustainability 12(6):2429. https://doi.org/10.3390/su12062429

Heath C, Luff P, Lehn DV, Hindmarsh J, Cleverly J (2002) Crafting participation: designing ecologies, configuring experience. Vis Commun 1(1):9–33. https://doi.org/10.1177/147035720200100102

Jalo H, Pirkkalainen H, Torro O, Pessot E, Zangiacomi A, Tepljakov A (2022) Extended reality technologies in small and medium-sized European industrial companies: level of awareness, diffusion and enablers of adoption. Virtual Rlty 26(4):1745–1761. https://doi.org/10.1007/s10055-022-00662-2

Lameras P, Papageorgiou V (2020) Experiences of multimodal teaching through a serious game: meanings, practices and discourses. In: Isaias P, Sampson DG, Ifenthaler D (eds) Technology supported innovations in school education, pp 175–193. Springer International Publishing. https://doi.org/10.1007/978-3-030-48194-0_10

Liarokapis F, Newman RM (2007) Design experiences of multimodal mixed reality interfaces. Proceedings of the 25th annual ACM international conference on design of communication, pp 34–41. https://doi.org/10.1145/1297144.1297152

Liew CL, Goulding A, Nichol M (2022) From shoeboxes to shared spaces: participatory cultural heritage via digital platforms. Inf Commun Soc 25(9):1293–1310. https://doi.org/10.1080/1369118X.2020.1851391

Maas MJ, Hughes JM (2020) Virtual, augmented and mixed reality in K–12 education: a review of the literature. Technol Pedagog Educ 29(2):231–249. https://doi.org/10.1080/1475939X.2020.1737210

Malinverni L, Mora-Guiard J, Pares N (2016) Towards methods for evaluating and communicating participatory design: a multimodal approach. Int J Hum Comput Stud 94:53–63. https://doi.org/10.1016/j.ijhcs.2016.03.004

Margetis G, Apostolakis KC, Ntoa S, Papagiannakis G, Stephanidis C (2020) X-reality museums: unifying the virtual and real world towards realistic virtual museums. Appl Sci 11(1):338. https://doi.org/10.3390/app11010338

Okanovic V, Ivkovic-Kihic I, Boskovic D, Mijatovic B, Prazina I, Skaljo E, Rizvic S (2022) Interaction in eXtended reality applications for cultural heritage. Appl Sci 12(3):1241. https://doi.org/10.3390/app12031241

Pacheco D, Wierenga S, Omedas P, Oliva LS, Wilbricht S, Billib S, Knoch H, Verschure PFMJ (2015) A location-based Augmented Reality system for the spatial interaction with historical datasets. 2015 Digit Herit 1:393–396. https://doi.org/10.1109/DigitalHeritage.2015.7413911

Philippe S, Souchet AD, Lameras P, Petridis P, Caporal J, Coldeboeuf G, Duzan H (2020) Multimodal teaching, learning and training in virtual reality: a review and case study. Virtual Rity & Intell Hardw 2(5):421–442. https://doi.org/10.1016/j.vrih.2020.07.008

Podara A, Giomelakis D, Nicolaou C, Matsiola M, Kotsakis R (2021) Digital storytelling in cultural heritage: audience engagement in the interactive documentary new life. Sustainability 13(3):1193. https://doi.org/10.3390/su13031193

Price S, Sakr M, Jewitt C (2016) Exploring whole-body interaction and design for museums. Interact Comput 28(5):569–583. https://doi.org/10.1093/iwc/iwv032

Rahaman H, Champion E, Bekele M (2019) From photo to 3D to mixed reality: a complete workflow for cultural heritage visualisation and experience. Digit Appl Archaeol Cult Herit 13:e00102. https://doi.org/10.1016/j.daach.2019.e00102

Rauschnabel PA, Felix R, Hinsch C, Shahab H, Alt F (2022) What is XR? Towards a framework for augmented and virtual reality. Comput Hum Behav 133:107289. https://doi.org/10.1016/j.chb.2022.107289

Rizvic S, Djapo N, Alispahic F, Hadzihalilovic B, Cengic FF, Imamovic A, Okanovic V, Boskovic D (2017) Guidelines for interactive digital storytelling presentations of cultural heritage. In: 2017 9th International conference on virtual worlds and games for serious applications (VS-Games), pp 253–259. https://doi.org/10.1109/VS-GAMES.2017.8056610

Rokhsaritalemi S, Sadeghi-Niaraki A, Choi S-M (2020) A review on mixed reality: current trends, challenges and prospects. Appl Sci 10(2):Article 2. https://doi.org/10.3390/app10020636

Schaper M-M, Santos M, Malinverni L, Zerbini Berro J, Pares N (2018) Learning about the past through situatedness, embodied exploration and digital augmentation of cultural heritage sites. Int J Hum Comput Stud 114:36–50. https://doi.org/10.1016/j.ijhcs.2018.01.003

Steffen JH, Gaskin JE, Meservy TO, Jenkins JL, Wolman I (2019) Framework of affordances for virtual reality and augmented reality. J Manag Inf Syst 36(3):683–729. https://doi.org/10.1080/07421222.2019.1628877

Tammaro AM (2016) Participatory approaches and innovation in galleries, libraries, archives, and museums. Int Inf & Libr Rev 48(1):37–44. https://doi.org/10.1080/10572317.2016.1146040

tom Dieck MC, Jung TH, tom Dieck D (2018) Enhancing art gallery visitors' learning experience using wearable augmented reality: generic learning outcomes perspective. Curr Issues Tour 21(17):2014–2034. https://doi.org/10.1080/13683500.2016.1224818

Trunfio M, Jung T, Campana S (2022) Mixed reality experiences in museums: exploring the impact of functional elements of the devices on visitors' immersive experiences and post-experience behaviours. Inf & Manag 59(8):103698. https://doi.org/10.1016/j.im.2022.103698
von der Pütten AM, Klatt J, Ten Broeke S, McCall R, Krämer NC, Wetzel R, Blum L, Oppermann L, Klatt J (2012) Subjective and behavioral presence measurement and interactivity in the collaborative augmented reality game TimeWarp. Interact Comput 24(4):317–325. https://doi.org/10.1016/j.intcom.2012.03.004

Chapter 4
Immersive Acoustics in Cultural Heritage Applications

Carlo Harvey, Mattia Colombo, Benjamin West, Jassim Happa, and Islah Ali-MacLachlan

Abstract This chapter embarks on a comprehensive exploration of immersive acoustics within the cultural heritage domain, a rapidly emerging field bridging technological innovation with historical preservation. While traditional efforts have frequently centred on visualising the histories of spaces and places, there is a growing recognition of the significance of sound in conveying historical authenticity and enriching cultural experiences. Sound enhances emotional connections and authenticity in cultural heritage experiences, fostering accessibility, interdisciplinary collaboration and educational value, while also benefiting tourism and the economy. In response to this trend, we present a standard methodology for auralising locations of historical significance. This methodology integrates the auditory dimension with visual representations, cultivating a multi-modal context that provides a more complete sensory experience of heritage sites. We delve into various common approaches to spatialised sound generation, acoustic rendering, auditory-visual cross-modal inter-actions and their application within historical settings. The distinguishing feature of this is the introduction of a case study on the Panagia Angeloktisti, a Byzantine church in Cyprus. Through this targeted investigation, we illuminate best practice approaches for applying immersive acoustics in cultural heritage environments. This includes a detailed analysis of the church's unique acoustic properties, the innovative

C. Harvey (✉)
School of Digital Arts, Manchester Metropolitan University, Manchester, UK
e-mail: c.harvey@mmu.ac.uk

M. Colombo · B. West · I. Ali-MacLachlan
College of Computing, STEAMhouse, Birmingham City University, Birmingham, UK
e-mail: mattia.colombo@bcu.ac.uk

B. West
e-mail: ben.west@bcu.ac.uk

I. Ali-MacLachlan
e-mail: islah.ali-maclachlan@bcu.ac.uk

J. Happa
Department of Information Security, Royal Holloway, University of London, Egham, UK
e-mail: Jassim.Happa@rhul.ac.uk

F. Liarokapis et al. (eds.), *Interactive Media for Cultural Heritage*, Springer Series on Cultural Computing, https://doi.org/10.1007/978-3-031-61018-9_4

technological solutions employed and the aural experience created for users. Furthermore, we consider challenges and limitations within the field, laying the groundwork for future inquiries. By synthesising insights from technology, art, psychology and history, we craft a cohesive narrative that emphasises the multifaceted nature of immersive acoustics in cultural heritage. This chapter contributes both a broad survey of the field and a specific, practical application through the Panagia Angeloktisti case study. This narrative underscores the transformative potential of integrating sound with visual components in cultural heritage applications and suggests fertile ground for future research direction, innovation and collaboration.

4.1 Introduction

Immersive acoustics has emerged as an interdisciplinary field that encompasses various applications ranging from entertainment to education, connecting users with an environment through auditory experiences. In recent years, this technology has increasingly been employed in cultural heritage applications, where it plays a pivotal role in providing an engaging and authentic connection to history and tradition.

Cultural heritage is a complex concept that includes the tangible and intangible aspects of culture, including art, architecture, traditions, landscapes and more. The integration of immersive acoustics with cultural heritage applications aims to create an engaging experience that connects visitors to the cultural context, allowing them to hear the past (Poupyrev et al. 2001).

The synthesis of acoustical modelling, signal processing and spatial audio offers novel opportunities for the immersive exploration of historical sites and cultural phenomena. Virtual and augmented reality environments can be enhanced with site-specific sounds that provide a spatially coherent experience, connecting the visitor with the surroundings in a multi-sensory manner (Serafin et al. 2018).

This chapter explores the intersection of immersive acoustics and cultural heritage applications, focusing on the technological requirements, methodologies, established best practices and a case study that demonstrates the transformative potential of sound in cultural experiences. It also highlights the challenges and ethical considerations involved in recreating and preserving cultural soundscapes.

4.1.1 Background

Immersive acoustics, which relies on spatial audio and advanced sound reproduction techniques, has evolved from early experimental stages into a mature field with applications in various domains. The roots of immersive acoustics can be traced back to the development of binaural recording and playback in the late twentieth century (Begault 1994).

The integration of immersive acoustics into the field of cultural heritage represents a convergence of technology and tradition. Historical spaces, artefacts and cultural practices carry unique acoustic signatures that can be captured, modelled and recreated through immersive sound technologies (Murphy et al. 2016). This enables audiences to engage with cultural heritage in an unprecedented way.

The application of immersive acoustics in cultural heritage requires a synergy of various technologies, including spatial sound reproduction, room acoustics simulation, audio signal processing and human auditory perception modelling. Techniques such as Wave Field Synthesis (WFS) and Ambisonics have become instrumental in creating spatially accurate sound fields (Daniel et al. 1998; Ahrens and Rabenstein 2015). WFS and Ambisonics are two advanced audio reproduction techniques that enable the creation of immersive soundscapes, allowing listeners to experience sound originating from various directions and distances, thus creating a three-dimensional auditory experience.

Wave Field Synthesis is a spatial audio rendering technique that uses an array of loudspeakers to create virtual acoustic environments. The principle behind WFS is to synthesise the sound field in a way that the sound waves emanating from the loudspeakers combine to form a desired sound field within the listening area. This is achieved by simulating the natural wavefronts of sound that would occur in a real environment. By controlling the phase and amplitude of the sound emitted from each speaker, WFS can accurately recreate the position and movement of sound sources in three-dimensional space, giving the listener the impression that the sound is emanating from a specific location in the room, even if there is no actual sound source at that point.

Ambisonics, on the other hand, is a full-sphere surround sound technique that, unlike traditional stereo or surround sound systems, does not target sound to be played back from specific locations or speakers. Instead, it captures and reproduces the entire sound field around a point, allowing for a more flexible and realistic audio experience. Ambisonic audio is encoded in a format that includes the sound's directionality and intensity from all directions. During playback, this format allows the sound to be decoded to any speaker layout, providing an immersive listening experience that can adapt to various playback systems. Ambisonics is particularly effective in virtual reality environments or installations where the listener's position and orientation can change, as it offers a consistent sound field irrespective of the listener's perspective. Both WFS and Ambisonics are instrumental in pushing the boundaries of spatial audio, offering more dynamic and realistic auditory experiences that enhance a range of applications from musical performances to virtual reality simulations, making them pivotal in the field of immersive acoustics.

The advancements in 3D sound generation have transcended beyond virtual and immersive environments, moving towards more comprehensive and computationally demanding methods. While the simulation of light and sound wave propagation at a physically accurate spatiotemporal quality remains a challenge in real-time, human perceptual and attentional limitations have become a subject of exploration and exploitation in various fields. This understanding has paved the way for new techniques in generating spatialised sound, taking into account perceptual and cross-modal influences (Hulusic et al. 2012).

Several museums, historical sites and cultural festivals around the world have successfully incorporated immersive acoustics to enhance visitor experiences. Notable examples include virtual recreations of historical concerts, soundscapes of ancient cities and interactive multimedia exhibits (Bekele et al. 2018; Atzeni et al. 2022).

The preservation and recreation of cultural soundscapes are not without challenges. Issues related to authenticity, accessibility, cultural sensitivity and intellectual property must be carefully addressed (Schafer, 1994; Manžuch 2017). Immersive acoustics in cultural heritage applications lays the groundwork for an in-depth exploration of how sound can bring history and culture to life, weaving technology, art and human perception into a cohesive and engaging narrative.

4.1.2 Objectives

The primary objectives of this chapter are to explore, analyse and articulate the multifaceted relationship between immersive acoustics and cultural heritage applications. The collective aim of these objectives is to offer readers a comprehensive and nuanced perspective on the subject, bridging gaps in understanding and laying the groundwork for future research, innovation and collaboration in the exciting intersection of immersive acoustics and cultural heritage. These objectives are further delineated as follows:

- Understanding the Evolution: To trace the historical development of immersive acoustics, considering the technological advancements and methodologies that have shaped its application broadly and in cultural heritage contexts.
- Exploring Application via Case Study: To examine the integration of immersive acoustics in various cultural heritage settings, including museums and historical sites, drawing insights from a contemporary case study.
- Analysing Technologies and Techniques: To provide a detailed analysis of the tools and techniques used in acoustic rendering, including spatialised sound generation and the limitations inherent in current technologies.
- Highlighting Challenges and Future Directions: To identify existing challenges and limitations within the field and to offer insights into emerging trends, potential solutions and future directions for research and practice in immersive acoustics within cultural heritage applications.

4.1.3 Contributions

The Panagia Angeloktisti, situated in Kiti, close to Larnaca in Cyprus, serves as the central focus of our study. This case study forms an integral part of our contribution to the broader discussion on immersive acoustics in cultural heritage applications.

Our investigation aims to illuminate the unique challenges and opportunities presented by the application of immersive acoustics in a historically significant environment. This is facilitated by conducting an in-depth analysis of the acoustic properties of the church, capturing its unique sonic fingerprint. This work develops and implements immersive audio techniques tailored to the specific architectural and cultural context of the church building and looks to evaluate the impact of immersive acoustics on visitors' experiences and engagement. This contribution leverages state-of-the-art techniques in spatialised sound generation, acoustic modelling and auditory perception studies and applies innovative methods to simulate and recreate the acoustics of the Byzantine church that can be readily translated by readers to other case studies.

4.1.4 Chapter Structure

This chapter provides a comprehensive exploration of immersive acoustics within the realm of cultural heritage. Below is a summary of the chapter's structure, designed to guide readers through our examination of immersive acoustics in this context:

- Introduction, Sect. 4.1: This is the current section and introduced the pivotal role of immersive acoustics in cultural heritage, outlining the chapter's objectives and contribution to the field.
- Theoretical Foundations of Immersive Acoustics, Sect. 4.2: Explores the essential principles of immersive acoustics, focusing on DSP and the creation of spatial audio and its implications for historical settings.
- Common Approaches to Immersive Acoustics, Sect. 4.3: Examines key methodologies like WFS and Ambisonics, demonstrating their practical application in authentic auditory environments.
- Visualising Histories: Challenges and Limitations, Sect. 4.4: Considers the challenges of integrating audio with visual elements in cultural heritage, emphasising the need for sensory balance.
- A Methodology to Acoustical Simulation Sect. 4.5: Provides a practical guide to acoustical simulation, from conceptualisation to execution, useful for practitioners and researchers.
- Future Research Directions and Conclusion, Sect. 4.6: Explores future research opportunities in immersive acoustics and underscores the ongoing importance of immersive acoustics in cultural heritage.

4.2 Theoretical Foundations of Immersive Acoustics

Immersive acoustics represents a growing and complex field interwoven with multiple disciplines, including physics, engineering, psychology and art. The underlying theory is anchored in understanding sound's behaviour in space, human perception of sound and the technologies that enable the creation of spatialised auditory experiences.

4.2.1 Overview of Immersive Acoustics

Immersive acoustics involves the recreation or simulation of sound in a manner that immerses the listener within a three-dimensional auditory environment. The goal is to create a lifelike auditory experience that corresponds to real or imagined spaces. The creation of spatial sound requires an understanding of the sound's physical properties, such as wave propagation, reflection, absorption and diffraction (Howard and Angus 2017). The acoustic environment's modelling is crucial in generating an immersive auditory experience (Kleiner et al. 1993). Technologies such as binaural recording, Ambisonics and Wave Field Synthesis (WFS) play a crucial role in creating immersive soundscapes (Rumsey 2001; Zotter and Frank 2019). These technologies enable the control and manipulation of sound within a three-dimensional space. The study of how humans perceive sound, including spatial hearing and the localisation of sound sources, is fundamental to immersive acoustics (Blauert 1996). Understanding the Human Auditory System (HAS) helps in creating auditory experiences that align with human perceptual abilities (Middlebrooks and Green 1991). Integrating sound with visual or other sensory modalities enhances the immersiveness of an experience (Stein and Meredith 1993). Research in auditory-visual cross-modal interactions has revealed how these modalities can influence and complement each other (Lewald 2002). The application of immersive acoustics in cultural heritage requires a sensitive approach that considers the authenticity, cultural significance and ethical implications of recreating historical soundscapes (Pujol and Champion 2012).

Various technologies exist that enable acoustic rendering. These technologies collectively contribute to the creation of immersive and authentic auditory experiences, both in cultural heritage settings and other applications. By leveraging these methods, researchers and practitioners can craft soundscapes that resonate with historical accuracy, perceptual authenticity and technological innovation. Acoustic rendering is the process of simulating sound behaviour within a specific environment, and various technologies have been developed to achieve this. Here are some of the key technologies:

- Digital Signal Processing (DSP): DSP plays a foundational role in acoustic rendering by allowing the manipulation of sound signals to recreate spatial characteristics, such as reflections and reverberations (Oppenheim and Schafer 2010).

- Ray Tracing: Ray tracing is a method that models how sound waves travel and interact with surfaces within an environment. By tracing the paths of individual sound rays, it provides a detailed simulation of sound propagation, reflections and diffractions (Savioja and Svensson 2015).
- Wave-Ray Hybrid Methods: These methods combine ray tracing with wave-based techniques, allowing for a more comprehensive and nuanced modelling of sound behaviour. Hybrid methods can capture both high-frequency reflections and low-frequency diffractions (Mehra et al. 2012).
- Wave Equation Solvers: Wave equation solvers numerically model the wave equation, providing an accurate and physically-based simulation of sound wave propagation. These solvers can capture complex wave phenomena, including diffraction and scattering (Bilbao 2004).
- Head-Related Transfer Functions (HRTFs): HRTFs are essential for binaural rendering, allowing the simulation of how sound is heard by each ear. By considering the individual listener's ear shape and head size, HRTFs enable the creation of highly realistic and personalised spatial sound experiences (Algazi et al. 2001).

4.2.2 Digital Signal Processing for Acoustic Rendering

Digital Signal Processing (DSP) is the science of analysing time-dependent physical processes. In the acoustics realm, it deals with analogue signals and digital signals, terms used to indicate a continuous variation of amplitude values in a physical process. Electricity utilised to drive loudspeakers is an example of an analogue signal, expressing continuous changes in voltage applied to magnets to displace the position of a cone. The cone displacement causes pressure differences in air particles, transforming such changes in voltage to changes in air pressure, which the human auditory system interprets as sound. Acoustic signals consist of one or multiple sound waves oscillating, where each wave is an oscillation of energy at regular intervals; the duration of each interval determines the wavelength λ and oscillations are measured as frequency, in Hertz (Hz).

On the other hand, a digital signal is a discrete representation of a continuous physical process, resulting in a sequence of measurement samples of an analogue signal expressed as amplitude values over time. Figure 4.1 shows the difference between a continuous signal and a discrete signal: digital signal is represented with stems to indicate its nature of quantised measurements over time, abscissa, as opposed to a continuous change in amplitude, ordinate. The discrete nature of a digital signal has inherent problems and advantages that relate to the time interval between measurements: a digital signal representing an analogue one will always be an approximation of the continuous process as the system may change its state between measurement intervals. The approximated nature of digital signals causes information loss, which is counteracted by theories shown later, but allows digital systems to store and process acoustical data efficiently.

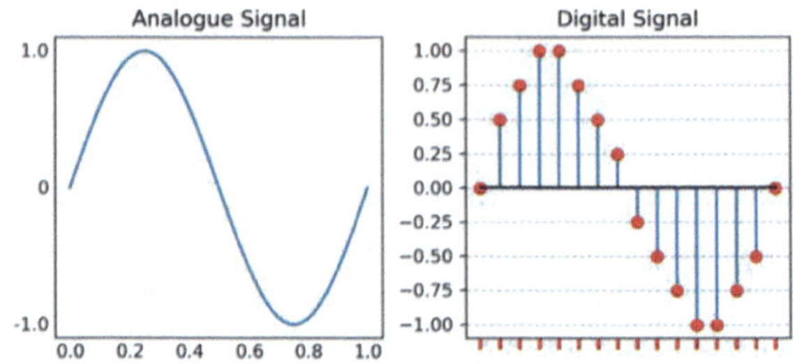

Fig. 4.1 Analogue and digital signal: left shows a continuous signal, and right shows discrete digital signal samples representing the continuous signal on the left

DSP applies to both, but in this book chapter, we will only focus on the branch of DSP that deals with digital signals. Digital systems like computers are used to process stored acoustical signals for several reasons, such as storing recordings of anechoic acoustic signals that simulation software can then process to generate realistic acoustic simulations, expressed as a processed digital signal.

4.2.2.1 Sampling and Resolution of Discrete Signals

Some of the fundamental problems that DSP addresses are the quantisation and measurement of continuous signals, performed by Analogue-to-Digital (A/D) converters, systems taking a continuous signal as input and outputting a series of digital numbers to represent said input.

The process of converting continuous signals to digital information involves taking measurements of the amplitude of a continuous signal at regular time intervals. There are two dimensions in which the analogue signal is measured during this process, the amplitude and time, respectively, the abscissa and the ordinate of Fig. 4.1.

Due to the physical limitations of digital technology, A/D converters can only take a finite number of measurements between time intervals, and they have limited accuracy in representing amplitude levels. In Fig. 4.1, it is possible to see how an A/D converter sees analogue signals: given an acoustic continuous signal as input, it takes amplitude samples at every time step, marked with red ticks, and measures using the available amplitude levels (the dotted horizontal lines). As a result, the process outputs a series of data points, the red dots, approximating the input, and the resolution and fidelity of the approximation depend on the time elapsed between time steps and the available amplitude level points. There are standards to ensure the reproduction and manipulation of acoustical signals in digital systems with an appropriate fidelity, such as the "Red Book" IEC 60908 standard, adopted for the Compact Disc music format, determining that digital signals must be represented by 44,100 measurement samples per second, at 16-bit amplitude resolution. 16-bit refers to the binary representation adopted by digital systems to store amplitude values, allowing $2^{16} = 65,535$ possible amplitude levels. The sampling frequency, the number of measurements per second, is calculated in Hertz (Hz), and it is a fundamental property of digital signals that must be taken into account for almost all types of audio manipulation and analysis involved in acoustical applications and it paramount to correct reconstructions of any acoustic information in any digital system.

To ensure the correct representation of an analogue, the Nyquist-Shannon sampling theorem determines that a wave must be sampled at least twice during each oscillation period. A periodic wave oscillating at 20 kHz, which is around the maxi-mum perceivable frequency in the human hearing range, would need to be sampled at least 40,000 per second; hence, the standard 44.1 sampling rate.

4.2.2.2 Analysis of Digital Signals

Acoustical signals are often analysed in the time domain, as varying sound pressure levels over time, or in the frequency domain. By considering acoustical signals as a Fourier series, a function composed of sinc or cosine primitives, the frequency domain representation determines how the power of an acoustical signal is distributed in a range of sine and cosine functions with wavelengths usually ranging from the minimum to the maximum perceivable frequencies of the human auditory system low to high frequencies. Time- and frequency-domain representations are often used for both analysis and manipulation of acoustical signals, often adopted in tasks like determining the effects of an environment in the perception of sound emitted by an object and arriving to a listener in said environment. In acoustics for interactive applications, engineers often adopt the Discrete-Time Fourier Transform (DTFT), a Fourier series for digital signals, which is one of the fundamental concepts in DSP. It takes a sequence, such as the signal represented in Fig. 4.1 and generates N complex numbers, representing power across N sinusoids. The DTFT transforms a signal x_n containing samples $x_0, x_1, \ldots, x_{N-1}$ into a series X_k of complex numbers $X_0, X_1, \ldots, X_{N-1}$. X_k is defined by.

$$X_k = \sum_{n=0}^{N-1} x_n \cdot e^{-\frac{i2\pi}{N}kn} \tag{4.1}$$

4.2.2.3 Binaural Room Impulse Responses

Common approaches to acoustic simulations involve the approximation of acoustic phenomena affecting a sound transmission occurring within a given environment between a sound source and a listener. To represent the result of such a simulation as a measurable process, where the environment is thought of as a dynamic system, Impulse Responses (IR) are used. IRs describe the effect that a system has on a sound transmission as a function of time. From DSP theory, there are several variations of IRs that the fields of immersive acoustics borrow to model several dynamic systems that affect how the human auditory system perceives soundscapes.

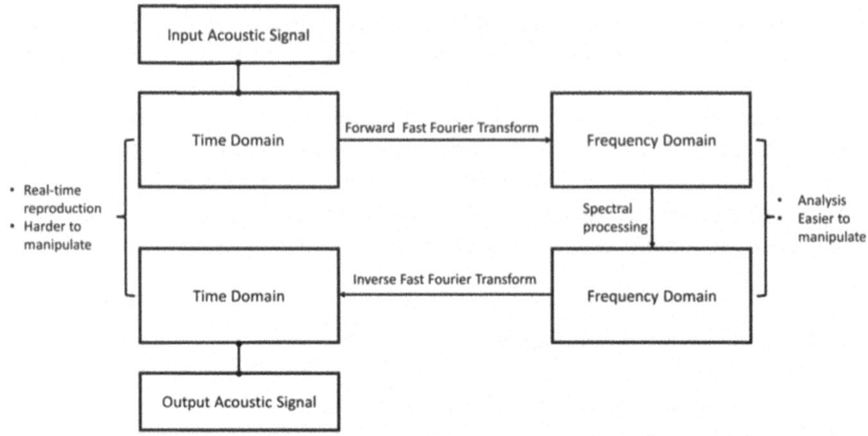

Fig. 4.2 A basic chain for signal processing aimed at analysing or manipulating signal in auralisation, visualisation or interactive applications. Analysis and processing of digital signals in the time domain is generally a hard task due to the complex nature of the function representing audio. The frequency-domain representation eases analysis and manipulation problems even with the added computational load of transforming between the two domains

Figure 4.2 shows how the auditory display is affected by interconnected systems associated with aspects of the soundscape. Time invariance is the fundamental property of these systems, making it possible to model their effect as an IR by observing their response to a Dirac-Delta function, which is a function whose value is zero except at the origin, where it is infinite. In practical terms, the Dirac-Delta function is an infinitely narrow spike of energy that is often used to excite the system and obtain a response across the frequency spectrum over time. In DSP terms, the function is simply represented as a finite sequence of numbers, the Finite Impulse Response (FIR), representing amplitude levels of the output of the system over time, given an input, commonly used to measure the effects of time-invariant linear systems like amplifiers or loudspeakers.

In the acoustic domain, the FIR adapts to several tasks, like modelling the acoustic fingerprint of a space with respect to a source and listener by observing, at the listener, a Dirac-Delta-like signal being emitted by the source. Such IR is differentiated from standard IRs and referred to as a Room Impulse Response (RIR); such distinction has emerged from the ongoing research in techniques and methods for measuring responses from real spaces, also due to the chaotic nature of room acoustics and real soundfields (Farina 2007). IRs, as well as measuring the acoustic fingerprint of spaces, can extend as far as measuring the effect of the human auditory system on the perception of the soundscape, and there are methods for modelling how anthropometric characteristics of the human body affect sounds arriving at both ears. Such IRs are defined as Binaural Room Impulse Responses: they extend RIRs by providing individual responses for both ears. BRIRs are a representation of Head-Related Transfer Functions (HRTFs), a function that describes how the anatomic

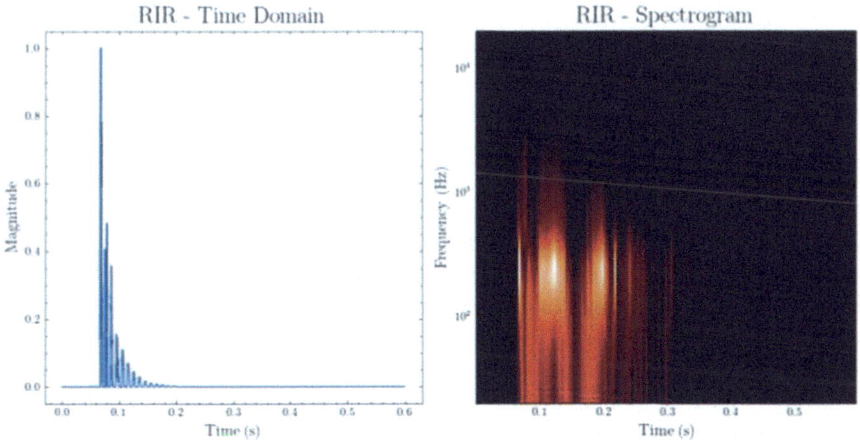

Fig. 4.3 Both time and frequency-domain, left and right respectively, representations of a Room Impulse Response (RIR). The time domain representation shows the magnitude of sound paths from a sound source to a receiver over time. The frequency domain representation shows how the energy of sound paths is distributed across the frequency spectrum over time, which is visualised with an infrared colourmap

features, rotation and position with respect to a sound source, affect the arrival of sound to the ears. Figure 4.3 is an example of a monaural RIR, shown both in the time and frequency domain.

4.2.3 Importance of Sound in Cultural Heritage

Sound is an essential aspect of cultural heritage, enhancing understanding, enriching experience and bridging time and space. Sound is not merely an accessory in cultural heritage but a vital and multi-functional element. Its integration within the representation and exploration of cultural heritage fosters a more profound connection to history, enhances learning, promotes inclusivity and contributes to cultural preservation and economic development. Integrating sound into the representation and preservation of cultural heritage provides several key benefits.

Sound evokes strong *emotional responses and connections*, helping visitors to connect with a place or time on a deeper level. Music, speech and ambient sounds can recreate the atmosphere of historical settings, making the experience more visceral and engaging (Ouzounian 2015; Seeger 2004; Brezina 2013; O'Connor, 2008). Through auralisation techniques, the acoustic properties of historical sites can be recreated or simulated. This adds *authenticity and immersion* to the representation of cultural heritage (Katz et al. 2020a). Sound provides an alternative means of enabling *accessibility* to cultural heritage for those with visual or auditory impairments or other disabilities. Audio guides and auditory displays can create inclusive experiences for a wider audience (Lim et al. 2021). In many cultures, oral traditions, music and soundscapes are integral to cultural identity and memory—*intangible heritage*. Preserving and representing these elements is crucial in maintaining the integrity and continuity of intangible cultural heritage (Selmanovic et al. 2018; Selmanović et al. 2020). The integration of sound in cultural heritage encourages *interdisciplinary collaboration* between historians, acousticians, artists and technologists. This promotes a more comprehensive and nuanced understanding of heritage sites (Scarre 2006). Sound enhances the *educational value* of these experiences by providing contextual auditory cues that complement visual information. This multisensory approach aids in learning and retention, particularly in educational programs related to history and culture (Howard et al. 2020; Ebrahimi et al. 2021). Innovative auditory experiences can attract more visitors to cultural heritage sites, contributing positively to local economies and the broader cultural *tourism and economic impact* (Kausar and Gunawan 2018).

4.3 Common Approaches to Immersive Acoustics

Achieving a convincing immersive acoustic experience is no trivial task, and various techniques and methodologies have been developed to address this complex challenge. These approaches must consider the spatial, temporal and perceptual aspects of sound, as well as the HAS's intricate response to auditory stimuli. Understanding these approaches is not only essential for the technical implementation of immersive soundscapes but also offers a pathway to appreciate the artistic and cultural possibilities that sound can unlock in the context of cultural heritage.

4.3.1 Spatial Audio Rendering Algorithms

Sound reproduction for immersive acoustics can be defined as a rendering problem concerning providing a listener with synthetic believable auditory stimuli that are perceived as if they belong to a specific space. Such a problem is often tackled by adopting a system that has complex scene and scene elements as input, and an acoustic signal as output.

Audio rendering refers to the process of affecting anechoic audio with acoustic phenomena approximated by simulations. It utilises generated IRs and takes into account the characteristics of a human listener from the perspectives of a sound-perceiving object in a virtual environment and a human receiver with psychoacoustic abilities.

One of the fundamental operations in audio rendering is the manipulation of anechoic audio with a filter encapsulating the acoustic effect of an environment to a sound transmission, expressed as an IR. Given anechoic audio expressed as a digital sequence x containing $x_0, x_1, \ldots, x_n$ elements, and an IR expressed as a digital sequence h containing $h_0, h_1, \ldots, h_n$, through the convolution operation $*$ we can obtain the resulting sequence y containing $y_0, y_1, \ldots, y_n$ samples, expressing the resulting signal with the applied IR. The following mathematical notation shows how a new function is created as a result of the convolution operation:

$$y[n] = x[n] * h[n] \tag{4.2}$$

In audio rendering terms, these functions will often represent an anechoic acoustic signal that is convolved with an IR to apply to create an auralised resulting signal. Given a signal X as a sample sequence of N points, and a filter h as a sample sequence of M points, the resulting full convolution y will be a sample sequence of $N + M - 1$ points. Each sample of the resulting y sequence is the sum of the products of both sequences:

$$(x * h)[n] = \sum_{m=0}^{M} x[n - m]h[m] \tag{4.3}$$

As shown in Fig. 4.4, frequency-domain representation makes specific problems easier to solve compared to the time-domain, and convolution is one example because of the summation required in the convolution process. This summation determines the computational complexity of the operation and grows with increasing M filter lengths. One key property of the convolution is that the product of the frequency-domain representation of a signal with the frequency-domain representation of a filter is the frequency-domain of their convolution. Essentially, the added complexity of summation is removed in the frequency domain at the cost of transforming the signals using the DTFT. Hence, audio rendering algorithms use the much faster Fast Fourier Transform (FFT) Convolution, commonly defined as:

$$(x * h)[n] = IDTFT_N(DTFT_N(x[n]) \cdot DTFT_N(h[n])) \tag{4.4}$$

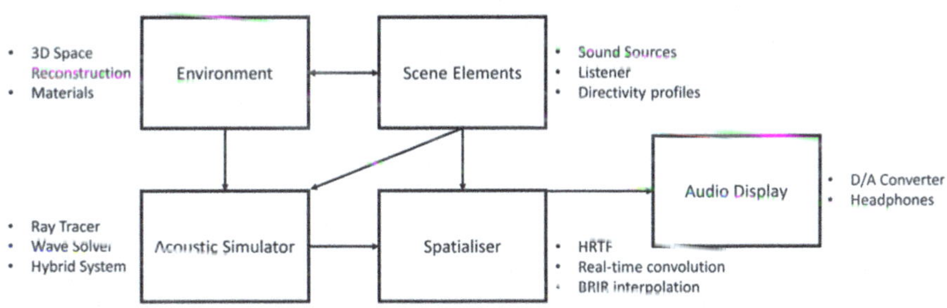

Fig. 4.4 An example chain of 3D reproduction based on acoustic simulators: an environment is fed into acoustic simulators to produce BRIRs. A spatialiser system consumes these to generate an audio signal considering the listener and scene elements

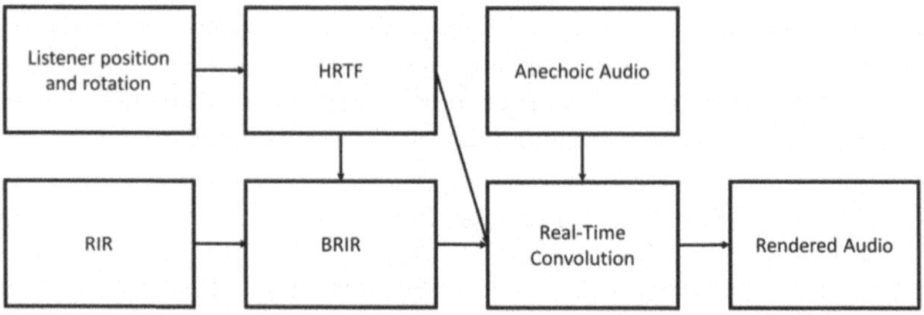

Fig. 4.5 Common spatial audio pipeline: the listener's position and rotation in the scene is used to sample an interpolated HRTF from the currently loaded bank, combined with the generated IR, the real-time convolution algorithm applies the BRIR to an anechoic audio signal. The result is an audio signal arriving at the listener, taking into account their position and rotation with respect to the sound-emitting object in the virtual environment

where $DTFT_N$ and $IDTFT_N$ are, respectively, the DTFT and the inverse DTFT of both the signal and the filter calculated over N frequency points. The Overlap-Add and the Overlap-Save are examples of real-time convolution algorithms often adopted in DSP to implement a wide range of audio effects. They are solutions to the problem of applying BRIR to long signals or to implementing interactive systems, where the listener is displayed rendered audio from a dynamic virtual environment. Thanks to the advances in such algorithms, it is now computationally feasible to manipulate anechoic audio signals with simulated acoustics on the fly, evoking a sense of immersion in the listener due to the auditory stimuli responding to changes in the dynamic environment at interactive rates.

The Overlap-Add algorithm adopts the divide-and-conquer approach towards an acoustic signal by segmenting an input digital sequence into multiple parts, processing the individual parts and assembling the resulting sequence to produce a whole manipulated sequence. The goal is to evaluate Eq. (4.4) over small chunks of audio, storing resulting convolved chunks into a queue from which samples are summed together into an output sequence.

Interactive audio rendering algorithms benefit from such systems as they enable on-the-fly convolution with live audio streams, which are generally implemented as a circular audio buffer. In the case of an immersive application, such audio buffers may be storing audio propagating from sound-emitting objects that interact with the user. As illustrated in Fig. 4.5, spatialiser systems or acoustic simulation systems provide filters in the forms of IRs that can be applied to audio chunks from the audio buffer.

4.3.2 Acoustic Modelling of Historical Spaces

Acoustic modelling of historical spaces is a complex and fascinating endeavour that aims to recreate the sonic environments of the past. This intricate process provides a bridge between the visual and auditory experience, enabling a richer and more authentic connection with history. Historical spaces often possess unique acoustic characteristics that have been shaped by their architecture, materials and usage. The resonance of a Gothic cathedral, the echoes within a Roman amphitheatre, or the bustling sounds of a mediaeval market square all play a vital role in defining the sonic signature of a place (Kutruff 2016). The acoustic modelling process begins with a detailed analysis of the physical space, including dimensions, acoustic materials and shape. Various methods can be employed to achieve this, such as ray tracing, which simulates the paths of sound rays as they bounce and reflect off surfaces (Vorländer et al. 2015); wave equation solvers that analyse the propagation of sound waves (Bilbao 2004); or head-related transfer functions (HRTFs) to simulate how sound is heard by a listener within the space (Algazi et al. 2001).

Once the physical properties are understood, historical context is integrated, including the potential sounds that would have been present, such as voices, music or ambient noise. The combination of the space's inherent acoustic properties with historically accurate sounds can create a vivid sonic representation of the past (Murphy et al. 2016). However, there are significant challenges in this process. Accurate acoustic modelling requires significant computational resources, and the results are often sensitive to small changes in parameters (Siltanen et al. 2007). Additionally, there may be limited information available about the historical usage of a space, leading to assumptions or approximations that can affect the authenticity of the simulation (Lokki and Pätynen 2020). Despite these challenges, acoustic modelling offers immense potential in cultural heritage applications. It can enhance museum exhibits, aid in architectural restoration and provide new ways to engage with history in educational settings (Richards-Rissetto et al. 2023).

4.4 Visualising Histories: Challenges and Limitations

The integration of visual and auditory elements in cultural heritage applications offers a multi-sensory gateway into history, but it's a path laden with challenges and limitations. This section delves into the complexities of visual dominance, the often-neglected importance of acoustic experience and the imperative need for a multi-modal approach.

4.4.1 Visual Dominance in Cultural Heritage Applications

The prominence of visual elements in cultural heritage is well-established, with images, videos and 3D renderings often being the focal point of exhibits and presentations (Ch'ng et al. 2013, 2022). This visual dominance has its roots in technological advancements that have facilitated stunning visual recreations of historical sites and objects. However, this focus on the visual has its downsides. Visual information can overwhelm other sensory experiences, leading to a loss of nuance and depth in the representation of history (Loomis et al. 2012; Lloyd-Esenkaya et al. 2020). The tendency to prioritise visuals can result in a one-dimensional experience that neglects the richness of historical soundscapes. While impressive visually, this approach can miss opportunities to engage visitors on a deeper, more immersive level.

The relative neglect of acoustic experience in cultural heritage applications has significant consequences. Sound plays a vital role in shaping our perception of space, time and culture (Blesser and Salter 2005). Whether it's the echo in a cathedral or the bustling noise of a market, sound provides context, ambience and emotion. Despite this, acoustic considerations often take a backseat to visual elements. This is partly due to technological challenges, as accurately simulating historical soundscapes is complex and computationally intensive (Siltanen et al. 2007). Additionally, there has been a lack of emphasis on the role of sound in conveying historical narratives (Murphy et al. 2016). The neglect of sound not only limits the depth of the historical experience but may also overlook significant cultural aspects. Different cultures place varying importance on sound, music and oral tradition. Ignoring these elements can lead to a lack of authenticity and cultural sensitivity (Katz et al. 2020b).

The limitations associated with visual dominance and the neglected importance of sound underscore the need for a more holistic, multi-modal approach. A multi-modal approach considers both visual and auditory elements, striving to create a more immersive and authentic representation of history (Begault 1994). Integrating sound with visuals not only enhances the realism but also aligns more closely with how humans naturally perceive their surroundings (Stanton and Spence 2020). Sound can guide attention, trigger memories and add emotional depth, transforming a visual exhibit into a living, breathing historical experience (Ghaleb et al. 2019). The development of tools and methodologies that enable seamless integration of visuals and sound is crucial for realising this vision. The case study of the Panagia Angeloktisti in Kiti, Cyprus, presented next, exemplifies how a multi-modal approach can revitalise and enrich cultural heritage applications.

4.4.2 Ethical Considerations and Safety of Using Audio in Cultural Heritage Contexts

The integration of audio in cultural heritage applications not only enhances the immersive experience but also introduces complex ethical considerations. One primary concern is cultural sensitivity, particularly when dealing with indigenous or traditional soundscapes. It is imperative to obtain consent from relevant communities before recording or replicating their auditory heritage. This approach ensures respect for intellectual property rights and acknowledges the cultural significance of these sounds. Furthermore, the portrayal of historical events or cultures through audio should strive for accuracy and respect, avoiding stereotypical or biased representations. Ethical considerations also extend to the selection and presentation of content, ensuring it does not inadvertently marginalise or misrepresent any group.

When employing immersive audio, safety is a paramount concern. Prolonged exposure to high sound levels can cause hearing damage, making it crucial to monitor and control audio levels within safe limits. The design of auditory experiences should consider the diverse range of visitors, including children, the elderly and those with heightened auditory sensitivity, to prevent any adverse effects. Additionally, the safety protocols should address the risks associated with immersive audio environments, such as disorientation or reduced awareness of the surroundings, which could pose physical hazards, especially in crowded or complex spatial settings.

To address these ethical and safety concerns, developers and researchers should adopt a comprehensive strategy that includes

- Community Engagement: Engage with communities or representatives to gain insights, obtain permissions and ensure that the audio content is culturally appropriate and respectful.
- Expert Consultation: Collaborate with ethicists, cultural historians and legal advisors to navigate the complexities of cultural representation and intellectual property rights.
- Safety Guidelines: Develop and adhere to strict safety guidelines that dictate the maximum sound levels and exposure durations, tailored to protect all visitor demographics.
- Accessibility and Inclusivity: Design auditory experiences that are accessible to a diverse audience, including provisions for those with sensory sensitivities or disabilities.
- Continuous Evaluation: Implement feedback mechanisms to continuously assess and refine the ethical and safety aspects of the audio experience, ensuring they adapt to evolving standards and community perspectives.

4.5 A Methodology to Acoustical Simulation

The ability to auralise historical sites is one of the fundamental objectives in the domain of acoustics for cultural heritage. As seen in Sect. 4.3, there are DSP techniques that allow the application of acoustic fingerprints onto audio recordings by treating the acoustics phenomena as measurable functions that can be convolved to digital signals, see Eq. (4.2). In higher-level terms, auralisation is the process of experiencing audio stimuli in a simulated soundscape, which can be perceiving an orchestra in a digital representation of a church, approximating how room acoustics affect the sound transmission between the orchestra and the listener in the virtual space. There are factors associated with this process that determine how well the resulting signal is able to fool the listener's auditory system into believing that the auralisation is real. Realism and presence are often a function of the performance of the components in the chain of the 3D audio reproduction system; see Fig. 4.5.

4.5.1 *Case Study: Auralising a Historical Site*

The Panagia Angeloktisti, translating to "Our Lady built by angels", is a historic Byzantine church situated in Kiti, a locale near Larnaca, Cyprus. The overview acoustics methodology was applied to a building that is a symbol and cultural reference of this era in Cyprus. The church is synthetically visualised in Fig. 4.6. Initially constructed as an early Christian basilica using wood, the church featured a semicircular stone bench known as a synthronon in the fifth century. Unfortunately, the majority of the original structure succumbed to a fire, leading to its reconstruction in stone during the sixth century. Following the rebuild, a striking gold mosaic was installed in the apse's semidome. In the twelfth century, a small chapel was added to the church's northern side, and between the late thirteenth and early fourteenth centuries, a Latin Chapel was constructed on the south side to cater to the Franks, who were the then rulers of Cyprus. A bell tower was introduced to the Latin Chapel in the early twentieth century but was later dismantled as it didn't align with the church's architectural ethos.

Byzantine churches in Cyprus, including Panagia Angeloktisti, are characterised by their small windows and compact, enclosed designs. The interior lighting of these churches was presumably intended to create a dramatic visual effect, encouraging a divine contemplation among the worshippers. It is suggested that the church's initial design aimed to manipulate light to create an immersive environment, especially after the addition of the gold mosaics in the altar area, with the upper sections receiving more light than the lower. Initially, this effect was achieved through natural daylight entering through doors and small windows. However, from the middle Byzantine period onward, natural light was increasingly replaced by artificial sources like oil lamps and candles, with doors remaining closed more frequently.

Fig. 4.6 Panagia Angeloktisti. Top, l–r: Outside shots of the 3D model of the church rendered at various moments in time over the course of the day. Bottom, l–r: Inside the church, visualised at different exposure values for a daylight scenario

4.5.2 Step-By-Step Approach to Auralisation

Methods for producing auralisation start from the creation of an environment, which is the first component of the system in Fig. 4.5 hosting the virtual sound-emitting objects, e.g. an orchestra, and the virtual sound-receiving objects, e.g. the listener. In computers, environments are generally represented using a broad range of computer graphics techniques, from simplistic Computer-Aided Design (CAD) to fully featured virtual worlds engineered in modern game engines. Such a statement blurs the definition of a virtual environment, as one could represent a room by creating a photorealistic 3D model or by simply drawing a cuboid. Research on acoustic simulations conducted over the last decades has expanded towards defining what is required from a virtual environment to produce a believable simulation. Combined with advances in real-space scanning technology and user-friendly 3D reconstruction software, it is now possible to create appropriate virtual environments for acoustic simulations without requiring expert computer graphics engineering knowledge.

Ray-based techniques, wave-ray hybrid techniques and wave-based techniques have emerged as prominent methods to generate impulse responses in the field of acoustics, each contributing to understanding how sound propagates within a given space. Ray-based techniques, rooted in geometric acoustics, simulate sound by tracing rays that emanate from a source and bounce off various surfaces within a space. This method creates echoes and reverberations contributing to the overall impulse response. Notably, it offers efficiency as it's computationally less demanding compared to wave-based techniques, making it suitable for real-time applications or large-scale spaces often found in cultural heritage contexts. The geometrical nature of ray-based methods allows for easier integration with existing architectural models or historical reconstructions, and the method's inherent flexibility makes it easily adjustable to different acoustic scenarios.

On the other hand, wave-ray hybrid techniques present a more complex picture, combining aspects of ray-based and wave-based methods. Rays are utilised to model the high-frequency components of the sound, while wave equations handle the low-frequency behaviour, attempting to capture the best attributes of both methods. However, the hybrid nature often means more computational resources are needed, and it might not always be the most suitable choice for cultural heritage applications where both high and low-frequency accuracy are not often the primary concern.

Wave-based techniques stand out for their precision, solving the wave equation to simulate how sound waves propagate through a space, accurately modelling diffraction, scattering and other complex wave phenomena. While highly accurate, wave-based techniques often require substantial computational resources, making them less suited for real-time or large-scale applications. Moreover, this level of detail may exceed what is necessary for conveying the historical or cultural experience.

Considering the landscape of immersive acoustics, ray-based techniques offer a compelling option for cultural heritage contexts. Their computational efficiency, relative simplicity and adaptability in handling various scenarios effectively capture the

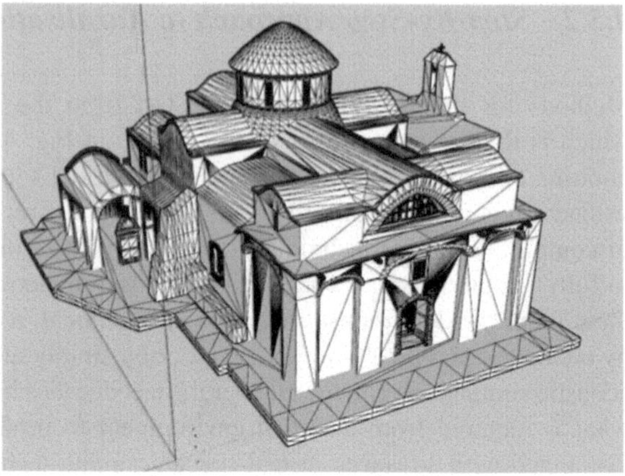

Fig. 4.7 A digital reconstruction of the Byzantine church of Panagia Angeloktisti, Kiti, Cyprus. The space was constructed in Autodesk Maya, imported to Sketchup as an OBJ file and exported to ODEON using the SU2ODEON plugin

essential acoustic characteristics of historical spaces. Unlike wave-based or hybrid methods, ray-based techniques can prioritise the aspects most relevant to the experience and understanding of cultural heritage, aligning well with the objectives and constraints often found in this field. Therefore, while the high accuracy of wave-based methods or the comprehensive nature of hybrid methods may have specific applications in areas of cultural heritage investigations, it is the ray-based techniques (such as those employed by acoustic simulation software such as ODEON) that generally stand out as the most appropriate choice for the unique challenges and opportunities presented within the context of cultural heritage.

4.5.2.1 Reconstruction of the Byzantine Church of Panagia Angeloktisti, Kiti, Cyprus

To produce a digital reconstruction of the site, the model shown in Fig. 4.7 was first constructed in Autodesk Maya. This was exported as a .obj file and imported into Sketchup, the preferred CAD system of ODEON.

4.5.3 3D Data Processing and Analysis

The selection of the toolset for running acoustic simulations and the audience who will be experiencing the resulting auralisations generate criteria for suitable 3D data to represent the environment. For the case study, ODEON was chosen to simulate the soundscape, a toolset that is based on Ray Tracing techniques, which has limited resolution around the low end of the frequency spectrum but allows a reasonable approximation of reverberation in the space. For this technique, representing smaller structures than 70 cm in the 3D reconstruction does not have a perceptual impact on the generated auralisation and can be pruned from the data to reduce computational load (Pelzer and Vorländer 2010). The model was simplified, reducing the number of surfaces from approximately 50,000 to approximately 20,000. The process of simplification plays a crucial role in acoustic modelling as it enables faster render times without substantially impacting the reverberation time calculation (Abd Jalil et al. 2019).

The successive step, following the generation of suitable 3D data, is the material tagging process, which consists of attributing acoustics characteristics to portions of the 3D, representing surfaces like brick walls, wood panelling or tiled floors. This is an essential determinant of perceptual aspects of the simulation as it determines how acoustics phenomena interact with the virtual environment, and it is agnostic to the nature of the acoustic simulation technique, whether it is Ray Tracing-based or a particle simulation. Ray Tracing was used in this case study, though most acoustic simulators, when modelling interactions between waves and surfaces, consider acoustic absorption and scattering characteristics of materials, often expressed as frequency-dependent coefficients (Colombo et al. 2021). Table 4.1 shows example acoustic absorption coefficients, divided by low and high density, targeting commonly used materials in game engines. Some acoustic simulation toolsets like ODEON have comprehensive databases of specific materials for bespoke use cases, which are often measured using impedance tubes (Dalmont 2001). As part of this process, the congregation was modelled as an audience brick (Nagy et al. 2010; Hammond et al. 2018) as shown in Fig. 4.8 using audience on wooden chairs, 1 per m^2 absorption coefficients (Meyer et al. 1964).

4.5.4 Running and Evaluating Acoustic Simulations

With a suitable 3D environment, tagged with acoustic materials, it is now possible to simulate how sound propagates from a sound-emitting object to a receiver. The next logical step is to ensure these source-receiver position pairs exist in the current environment. Figure 4.9 shows the position of the source and receiver in a section plane layout of the church. Figure 4.10 depicts the same source-receiver pair within the ODEON model. The goal of running an acoustic simulation is to produce RIRs, dependent on these position pairs, and it is crucial to ensure that the parameters of the generated RIR correctly express the acoustic effects approximated by the simulation. The number of samples in the IR has to enable the correct representation of the acoustic energy decay, as shown in Fig. 4.3, within 0.5 s the magnitude of the recorded response has fallen below an audible range, and it is no longer perceptually required to model its decay.

For the case study, we employed a Ray Tracing-based system, ODEON, that propagates a number of rays, from sources to listeners, calculates how surfaces with varying acoustic characteristics affect the energy of bouncing rays, and observes their final energy level at the listener. Such energy levels are logged in an IR response,

Table 4.1 Common acoustic absorption coefficients with ranges (low–high) of α absorption characteristics across the frequency bands for those material types. It should be noted that in cultural heritage contexts, building material types were often significantly different to modern construction materials and due care should be taken to appropriately tag surfaces with relevant and semantic types for the era of simulation

Material	Low α	High α
Glass and glazing		
Masonry walls		
Stud-work and lightweight walls		
Wood and wood panelling		
Floors		
Panels and doors		
Other		
Wall treatments and construction		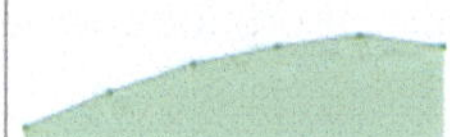
Ceilings		
Mineral wool and foams		
Audience and seating		

where the shortest paths will appear closer to the origin, at 0 s, and later reflections will appear later in time, according to the travelled distance.

There are several objective metrics that measure how well a RIR represents specific acoustic phenomena, such as reverberation, definition or clarity. In the case study, we obtain a real measurement using a speaker and a microphone (as discussed in Sect. 2.2.3); we replicate the source-listener position pair in the simulation and compare the reverberation time, using the T_{60} metric, which measures the time required for the acoustic energy to decay by 60 dB from the Dirac-Delta impulse signal.

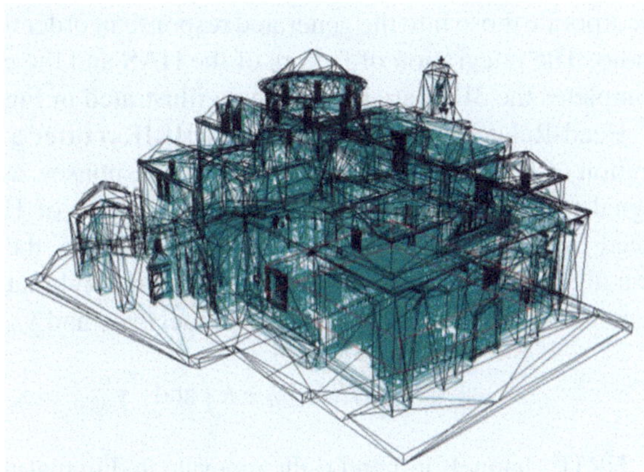

Fig. 4.8 A representation of the environment in the ODEON software, after simplification. The area used to denote the congregation is denoted in red

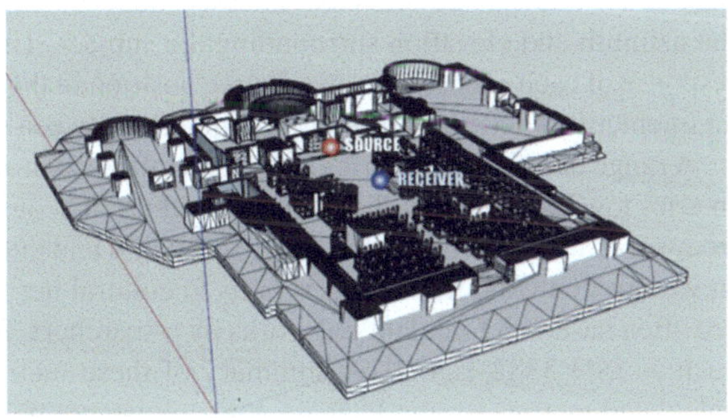

Fig. 4.9 Visualisations of source (red) and receiver (blue) positions superimposed on a section plane layout of the church

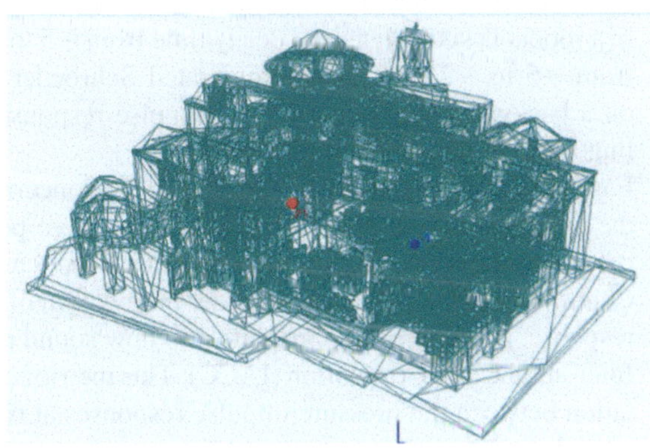

Fig. 4.10 Visualisations of source (red) and receiver (blue) positions in ODEON

4.5.5 *Implementation of Immersive Acoustics*

At this point, we have a system that generates RIRs based on a reconstructed environment and scene elements - though we need to consider factors of human listeners and incorporate those into the generated response in order to generate spatialised binaural audio. The integration of factors of the HAS and the convolution of anechoic audio completes the 3D spatial audio chain illustrated in Fig. 4.4.

Head-Related Impulse Responses (HRIRs) offer a compact solution to the integration of HAS features, much like room responses, as we can convolve a monaural signal to the frequency representation of a pair of HRIRs (one for each ear), the Head-Related Transfer Function (HRTFs). Hence, the discussed real-time convolution algorithms in Sect. 3.1 can be used, in combination with the h RIR signal, to generate binaural rendered audio channels y_{left} and y_{right} from a monaural signal x:

$$y_{left} = x * HRTF_{left} * h \quad \text{and} \quad \mathrm{y}_{\mathrm{right}} = \mathrm{x} * \mathrm{HRTF}_{\mathrm{right}} * \mathrm{h}. \tag{4.5}$$

HRTF channels left and right are evaluated in real-time, depending on the current position and rotation of the listener entity in the virtual environment, using a loaded bank or HRIRs that are often real measurements of subjects across a grid of points in the azimuth and elevation surrounding the subject. These measurements record the response of each ear canal from a source position in the surrounding sphere, allowing an interactive HRIR algorithm to interpolate between these measurements.

A range of objective metrics are commonly used in acoustic measurements. These metrics together offer a holistic understanding of acoustic properties of spaces, such as reverberation, clarity, strength, directionality and intelligibility, and can be applied in various contexts, from concert halls to cultural heritage sites. Their formulations are often based on foundational works by researchers, following standard definitions such as ISO 3382-1:2009. A summary of these metrics is provided here, and the calculated metrics for the Panagia Angeloktisti are provided in Table 4.2.

- Reverberation Time (T_{15}, T_{30}): These metrics measure how quickly sound decays in a room. T_{15} calculates the decay time from −5 to −20 dB, while T_{30} calculates from −5 to −35 dB on the integrated Schroeder curve. The method is based on a backward integration of the impulse response, providing insights into the lingering sound in space.
- Early Decay Time (EDT): This metric is concerned with the initial decay of the reverberant tail, emphasising the subjective perception of reverberation. It calculates the time for the sound to decay from 0 to −10 dB.
- Centre Time (Ts): It is the first-order momentum of the squared pressure impulse response, which provides insights into how sound pressure evolves over time.
- Inter-aural Cross Correlation (IACC): This metric calculates the normalised correlation between the pressure impulse responses at two ears, offering insights into spatial characteristics of the sound.
- Strength (G): Measuring the difference between the sound pressure level and the sound produced in a free field, this metric provides an understanding of how sound strength behaves in different environments.
- Clarity (C80, C50, C7): These metrics relate to the "transparency" of the music, depending on whether the clarity is associated with music or speech. They help in understanding the clarity of sound as experienced by listeners.

Table 4.2 Objective parameters for the Panagia Angeloktisti

Frequency band	(Hz)	63	125	250	500	1000	2000	4000	8000
EDT	(s)	4.81	4.75	3.85	1.81	1.51	1.25	1.04	0.62
T(15)	(s)	5.19	5.14	4.33	2.3	2.06	1.78	1.39	0.74
T(20)	(s)	5.22	5.17	4.37	2.37	2.14	1.87	1.46	0.78
T(30)	(s)	5.28	5.22	4.45	2.48	2.25	1.98	1.55	0.83
Ts	(ms)	318	313	249	110	89	72	61	37
SPL	(dB)	−9.9	−9.9	−11.1	−14.7	−15.5	−16.3	−16.8	−18.9
G	(dB)	21.1	21.1	19.9	16.3	15.5	14.7	14.2	12.1
C(7)	(dB)	−13.4	−13.2	−11.8	−7.6	−6.2	−5.3	−5.1	−3.8
C(50)	(dB)	−6.3	−6.2	−4.9	−0.7	0.6	1.7	2.3	4.8
C(80)	(dB)	−4.3	−4.2	−2.9	1.5	2.8	4	4.8	8
LF(80)		0.293	0.296	0.291	0.269	0.257	0.251	0.246	0.234
IACC		0.336	0.313	0.382	0.263	0.309	0.21	0.196	0.061
RASTI	0.56								
STI (Expected)	0.14								
EDT (Average)	1.66 s								
T (20 Average)	2.25 s								
T (30 Average)	2.37 s								
G (Average)	15.9 dB								
C (80 Average)	2.1 dB								
Ts (Average)	99 ms								
LF (80 Average)	0.278								
Arrival (early)	23 ms								

- Speech Transmission Index (STI) and Rapid Speech Transmission Index (RASTI): These parameters are based on the modulation transfer function and are used to describe intelligibility in spaces. STI offers a comprehensive measure, while RASTI simplifies the analysis.
- Lateral Efficiency (LE): It is the ratio between the late energy from lateral directions and total energy. It helps in understanding the directionality of sound.
- Lateral Fraction (LF): Similar to LE but includes early lateral reflections as well. It offers a more comprehensive view of sound reflections from various directions.

In Fig. 4.11, we present a comprehensive illustration of the acoustical modelling process that was employed for the Panagia Angeloktisti in Kiti, Cyprus, highlighting the transformation of sound from its original form to a spatial sound representation that evokes the unique sonic environment of the church.

The figure is divided into three main parts, each describing a different stage of the process. The first part of the figure focuses on the binaural room impulse response generated specifically for the Panagia Angeloktisti. This impulse response

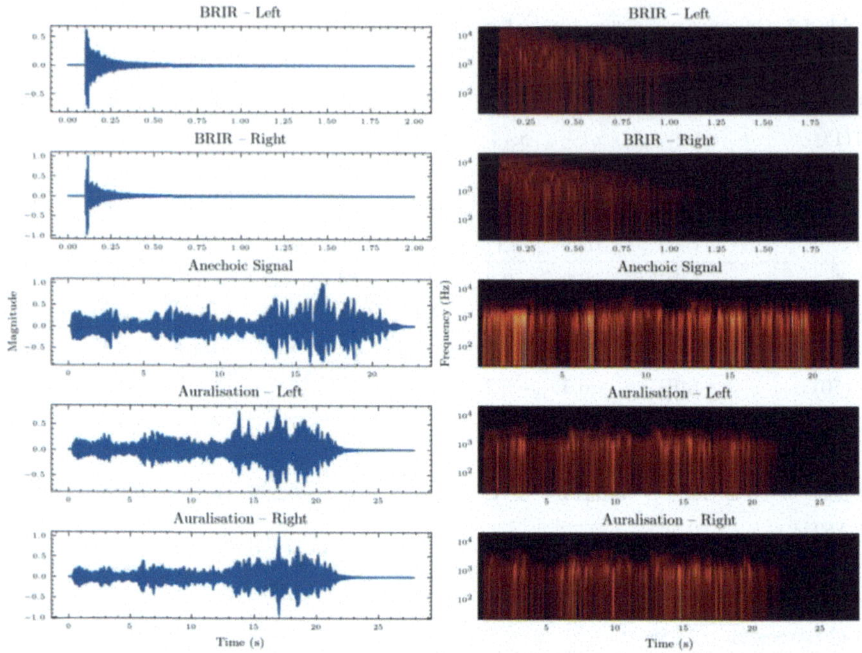

Fig. 4.11 Acoustical modelling Process for the Panagia Angeloktisti, Kiti, Cyprus. This illustration is divided into three main stages: (1, top) The impulse response of the church, depicted in both time and frequency domains, capturing the specific acoustic characteristics of the space; (2, middle) An anechoic sound waveform and its frequency spectrum, representing the initial sound source; (3, bottom) The convolution of the anechoic sound with the impulse response, resulting in a spatial sound that replicates the auditory experience inside the church

captures the acoustic characteristics of the church, including its reverberation, echoes, absorption and diffusion properties. It is presented in both the time and frequency domains.

The time-domain representation shows how sound waves reflect and interact within the space, whereas the frequency-domain representation helps to understand how different frequencies are affected by the architectural features of the church.

In the second part, the original anechoic sound is depicted as a waveform, representing the pure sound without any influence of the environment. This can be thought of as the "raw material" from which our immersive acoustic simulation will be crafted. Accompanying this, a corresponding frequency spectrum offers an insight into the sound's constituent frequencies, mirroring the representations of the BRIR.

Finally, the third part of the figure demonstrates the process of convolution, wherein the anechoic sound is combined with the impulse response. This mathematical operation effectively places the original sound into the Panagia Angeloktisti, giving rise to a spatial sound that carries with it the church's unique acoustical signature. This convolved sound is what a listener would experience when standing inside the church itself.

Together, these three stages illustrated in Fig. 4.11 provide a detailed and comprehensive view of the auralisation process that brings to life the rich acoustic heritage of the Panagia Angeloktisti. From the pristine clarity of an anechoic sound to the textured complexity of a spatial sound within a stone church, the figure helps to demystify the process and provides a tangible connection between mathematical modelling and our auditory experience of a historical space.

4.5.6 User Usability of Acoustics for Cultural Heritage

User usability ensures that the auditory experiences are accessible, engaging and beneficial for a broad audience. This section explores how users may typically interact with acoustic environments, focusing on their ease of use and the overall user experience. We delve into standard listening tests, particularly the MUltiple Stimuli with Hidden Reference and Anchor (MUSHRA), to evaluate the effectiveness and user engagement of these auditory experiences.

To assess the usability of immersive acoustic experiences, it is typical to employ standard listening tests like MUSHRA (ITU-R BS.1534), which is widely recognised for its robustness in evaluating intermediate audio quality. Common implementations exist for these procedures, such as webMUSHRA which supports other listening test methods, such as ITU-R BS.1116 and forced-choice procedures Schoeffler et al. (2018). These methods allow comparison of immersive acoustic renderings against a reference and an explicitly lower-quality anchor, providing insights into user perception and experience quality.

In the context of cultural heritage, MUSHRA can be adapted to evaluate how different acoustic renderings of historical sites or events are perceived by users. Participants are presented with multiple versions of an acoustic scenario, including the reference (high-quality rendering), various test conditions (different auralisation techniques) and the lower-quality anchor. During MUSHRA tests, users interact with a straightforward interface to rate the quality of each audio sample based on their experience. This interaction provides valuable data on the intuitiveness of the experience and the user's ability to discern and appreciate the nuances of immersive acoustic environments. The results from MUSHRA testing offer quantitative metrics on user satisfaction, preference and perceived audio quality. These metrics guide improvements in acoustic rendering techniques, ensuring they are user-centric and tailored to enhance the educational and experiential value of cultural heritage presentations.

By integrating standard listening tests like MUSHRA into the development and evaluation process of immersive acoustics, we can ensure that these technologies are not only technologically advanced but also user-friendly, engaging and accessible to a wide audience, thereby enhancing the overall impact of cultural heritage preservation and education.

4.6 Future Research Directions and Conclusion

The landscape of immersive acoustics within the cultural heritage domain is rich with opportunity and potential. Immersive acoustic technology is still in its infancy and continues to evolve at a rapid pace. Research must continue to invest in developing more realistic and intricate sound simulations. The quest for achieving real-time simulations with spatial and temporal quality that closely mimics the human auditory experience requires attention. Moreover, exploring novel algorithms for sound propagation and new techniques for binaural rendering will fuel the technological innovation needed for a more genuine immersion in historical contexts (Wang and Bocko 2023).

Cultural heritage is inherently diverse, spanning various regions, time periods and traditions. It dissects the tangible from the intangible too. Future research must broaden its scope to encompass this diversity, tapping into underrepresented cultures and histories. By integrating different storytelling techniques with immersive acoustics, new narratives can emerge, fostering a richer global understanding of human history. The potential applications of immersive acoustics in cultural heritage extend beyond museums and educational institutions; they have the power to revolutionise tourism, entertainment and even therapeutic interventions, using sound as a bridge to connect individuals to their cultural roots.

The complex task of authentically recreating historical environments requires expertise from various fields. Therefore, a commitment to interdisciplinary collaboration is paramount. Building bridges between these diverse domains will enable a more holistic approach, ensuring that both the technical aspects and the cultural nuances are accurately captured. Collaborative efforts can also facilitate the sharing of methodologies and insights, fostering a collective growth that transcends individual disciplines.

The future of immersive acoustics in cultural heritage applications is poised for growth, innovation and enrichment. Whether through technological advancements, embracing the diverse tapestry of global cultures or forging collaborative bonds across disciplines, the path forward is ripe with possibility. It beckons researchers, technologists, historians and artists alike to embark on a shared journey, one that promises to deepen our connection to the past and enrich our understanding of the human experience.

The exploration of immersive acoustics in cultural heritage applications has illuminated the profound possibilities and rich potential of this interdisciplinary field. This chapter has traversed a comprehensive landscape, unveiling the theoretical foundations of immersive acoustics and delineating the technologies that enable acoustic rendering. Through the specific case study of the Panagia Angeloktisti, practical insights and best practice methodologies were illuminated. From discussing the importance of sound in cultural heritage to the synergy between acoustics and visualisation, this exploration has striven to bridge technology and history, theory and practice. Furthermore, the section on future research directions has charted new terrains and called for innovation, diversification and collaboration. Immersive acoustics brings a multi-sensory dimension to cultural heritage that resonates with our intrinsic human nature. By recreating historical soundscapes, we do more than inform; we transport listeners back in time, offering an intimate and emotive connection with the past. This connection goes beyond mere entertainment or education. It's about empathy, understanding and cultural preservation. In a world where cultural identities are increasingly fluid and globalised, immersive acoustics stands as a powerful tool to preserve and celebrate human history and traditions.

References

Abd Jalil NA, Din NC, Keumala N,. Razak AS (2019) Effect of model simplification through manual reduction in number of surfaces on room acoustics simulation. J Des Built Environ 19(3):31–41

Ahrens J, Rabenstein R (2015) Sound field synthesis for audio presentation. In Physics. https://api.semanticscholar.org/CorpusID:195741607

Algazi V, Duda R, Thompson D, Avendano C (2001) The CIPIC HRTF database. In: Proceedings of the 2001 IEEE workshop on the applications of signal processing to audio and acoustics (Cat. No.01TH8575), pp 99–102. https://doi.org/10.1109/ASPAA.2001.969552

Atzeni M, Del Chiappa G, Mei Pung J (2022) Enhancing visit intention in heritage tourism: the role of object-based and existential authenticity in non-immersive virtual reality heritage experiences. Int J Tour Res 24(2):240–255. https://doi.org/10.1002/jtr.2497

Begault DR (1994) 3-D sound for virtual reality and multimedia. In: Physics. Cambridge. https://api.semanticscholar.org/CorpusID:13900357

Bekele MK, Pierdicca R, Frontoni E, Malinverni ES, Gain J (2018) A survey of augmented, virtual, and mixed reality for cultural heritage. J Comput Cult Herit 11(2). ISSN 1556-4673. https://doi.org/10.1145/3145534, https://doi.org/10.1145/3145534

Bilbao S (2004) Wave and scattering methods for numerical simulation. Wiley & Sons

Blauert J (1996) Spatial hearing: the psychophysics of human sound localization, p 10. The MIT Press. ISBN 9780262268684. https://doi.org/10.7551/mitpress/6391.001.0001

Blesser B, Salter L-R (2005) Spaces speak, are you listening? experiencing aural architecture

Brezina P (2013) Acoustics of historic spaces as a form of intangible cultural heritage. Antiquity 87(336):574–580. https://doi.org/10.1017/S0003598X00049139

Ch'ng E, Chapman H, Gaffney V, Wilson AS (2022) Visual heritage: digital approaches in heritage science. Springer

Ch'ng E, Gaffney VL, Chapman H (2013) Digital heritage: concluding thoughts. Visual heritage in the digital age, pp 349–361

Colombo M, Dolhasz A, Harvey C (2021) A texture superpixel approach to semantic material classification for acoustic geometry tagging. In: Extended abstracts of the 2021 CHI conference on human factors in computing systems, pp 1–7

Dalmont J-P (2001) Acoustic impedance measurement, part i: a review. J Sound Vib 243(3):427–439

Daniel J, Rault J-B, Polack J-D (1998) Ambisonics encoding of other audio formats for multiple listening conditions. J Audio Eng Soc

Ebrahimi F, Elahifar M et al (2021) Teaching speaking and listening skills through audio-lingual versus conventional methods of instruction: which method is more effective? Int J Linguist Lit Transl 4(11):72–81

Farina A (2007) Advancements in impulse response measurements by sine sweeps. In: Audio engineering society convention p 122. Audio Engineering Society

Ghaleb E, Popa M, Asteriadis S (2019) Multimodal and temporal perception of audio-visual cues for emotion recognition. In: 2019 8th International conference on affective computing and intelligent interaction (ACII), pp 552–558. IEEE

Hammond R, Hill AJ, Mapp P (2018) On the accuracy of audience implementations in acoustic computer modelling. In: Audio Engineering society convention p 145. Audio Engineering Society

Howard D, Angus J (2017) Acoustics and psychoacoustics, 5 edn. Routledge. https://doi.org/10.4324/9781315716879

Howard DM, Schofield J, Fletcher J, Baxter K, Iball G, Buckley S (2020) Synthesis of a vocal sound from the 3,000 year old mummy, Nesyamun 'True of voice'. Sci Rep 10(1):45000

Hulusic V, Harvey C, Debattista K, Tsingos N, Walker S, Howard D, Chalmers A (2012) Acoustic rendering and auditory–visual cross-modal perception and interaction. Comput Graph Forum 31(1):102–131. https://doi.org/10.1111/j.1467-8659.2011.02086.x

Katz BFG, Murphy D, Farina A (2002a) The past has ears (PHE): XR explorations of acoustic spaces as cultural heritage. In: Augmented reality, virtual reality, and computer graphics: 7th international conference, AVR 2020, Lecce, Italy, September 7–10, 2020, proceedings, part II, pp 91–98, Berlin, Heidelberg. Springer-Verlag. ISBN 978-3-030-58467-2. https://doi.org/10.1007/978-3-030-58468-97

Katz BFG, Murphy D, Farina A (2020b) Exploring cultural heritage through acoustic digital reconstructions. Phys Today 73(12):32–37. ISSN 0031-9228. https://doi.org/10.1063/PT.3.4633

Kausar DRK, Gunawan MP (2018) Managing heritage tourism in Toraja: strengthening local values and improving tourists' experiences. J Herit Tour 13(6):550–561

Kleiner M, Dalenbäck B-I, Svensson P (1993) Auralization-an overview. J Audio Eng Soc 41:861–875. https://api.semanticscholar.org/CorpusID:107179857

Kutruff H (2016) Room acoustics, 6 edn. CRC Press. ISBN 1482260433

Lewald J (2002) Vertical sound localization in blind humans. Neuropsychologia, 40:1868–1872. https://api.semanticscholar.org/CorpusID:13080549

Lim V, Khan S, Picinali L (2021) Towards a more accessible cultural heritage: challenges and opportunities in contextualisation using 3d sound narratives. Appl Sci 11(8):3336

Lloyd-Esenkaya T, Lloyd-Esenkaya V, O'Neill E, Proulx MJ (2020) Multisensory inclusive design with sensory substitution. Cogn Res Princ Implic 5:1–15

Lokki T, Pätynen J (2020) Auditory spatial impression in concert halls. Technol Binaural Underst 173–202

Loomis J, Klatzky R, Giudice N (2012) Sensory substitution of vision: importance of perceptual and cognitive processing, pp 162–191. CRC Press

Manžuch Z (2017) Ethical issues in digitization of cultural heritage. In: Governance of digital memories in the era of big data. https://api.semanticscholar.org/CorpusID:21719372

Mehra R, Raghuvanshi N, Savioja L, Lin MC, Manocha D (2012) An efficient GPU-based time domain solver for the acoustic wave equation. Appl Acoust 73:83–94. https://api.semanticscholar.org/CorpusID:9161141.

Meyer E, Kunstmann D, Kuttruff H (1964) Uber einige messungen zur schallabsorption von publikum. Acta Acust United Acust 14(2):119–124

Middlebrooks JC, Green DM (1991) Sound localization by human listeners. Annu Rev Psychol 42:135–59. https://api.semanticscholar.org/CorpusID:22801061

Murphy D, Shelley S, Foteinou A, Brereton J, Daffern H (2016) Acoustic heritage and audio creativity: the creative application of sound in the representation, understanding and experience of past environments. Internet Archaeol 11. https://doi.org/10.11141/ia.44.12

Nagy AB, Kotschy A, Gade AC, Johannessen H (2010) Room acoustical modelling differences and their consequences. In: INTER-NOISE and NOISE-CON congress and conference proceedings, number 8 in 2010, pp 3535–3542. Institute of Noise Control Engineering

O'Connor P (2008) The sound of silence: Valuing acoustics in heritage conservation. Geogr Res 46(3):361–373. https://doi.org/10.1111/j.1745-5871.2008.00529.x

Oppenheim A, Schafer R (2010) Discrete-time signal processing, 3rd edn. Prentice Hall, Upper Saddle River

Ouzounian, G (2015) Sound installation art: from spatial poetics to politics, aesthetics to ethics. In: Music, sound, and space: transformations of public and private experience, pp 73–89. Cambridge University Press

Pelzer S, Vorländer M (2010) Frequency-and time-dependent geometry for real-time auralizations. In: Proceedings of 20th international congress on acoustics, ICA, pp 1–7

Poupyrev I, Berry R, Billinghurst M, Kato H, Nakao K, Baldwin L, Kurumisawa J (2001) Augmented reality interface for electronic music performance. In: Proceedings of HCI. https://api.semanticscholar.org/CorpusID:7847478

Pujol L, Champion E (2012) Evaluating presence in cultural heritage projects. Int J Herit Stud 18(1):83–102. https://doi.org/10.1080/13527258.2011.577796

Richards-Rissetto H, Primeau KE, Witt DE, Goodwin G (2023) Multisensory experiences in archaeological landscapes—sound, vision, and movement in GIS and virtual reality. In: Capturing the senses: digital methods for sensory archaeologies, pp 179–210. Springer International Publishing, Cham

Rumsey F (2001) Spatial audio, 1 edn. Routledge. https://doi.org/10.4324/9780080498195

Savioja L, Svensson UP (2015) Overview of geometrical room acoustic modeling techniques. J Acoust Soc Am 138(2):708–730

Scarre C (2006) Archaeoacoustics

Schafer R (1994) The soundscape: our sonic environment and the tuning of the world. Destiny Books, Rochester Vermont

Schoeffler M, Bartoschek S, Stöter F-R, Roess M, Westphal S, Edler B, Herre J (2018) Web-Mushra—a comprehensive framework for web-based listening tests. J Open Res Softw. https://doi.org/10.5334/jors.187

Seeger A (2004) Why Suyásing: a musical anthropology of an Amazonian people. University of Illinois Press

Selmanovic E, Rizvic S, Harvey C, Boskovic D, Hulusic V, Chahin M, Sljivo S (2018) VR video storytelling for intangible cultural heritage preservation. In Sablatnig R, and Wimmer M (eds) Eurographics workshop on graphics and cultural heritage. The Eurographics Association. ISBN 978-3-03868-057-4. https://doi.org/10.2312/gch.20181341

Selmanović E, Rizvic S, Harvey C, Boskovic D, Hulusic V, Chahin M, Sljivo S (2020) Improving accessibility to intangible cultural heritage preservation using virtual reality. J Comput Cult Herit (JOCCH) 13(2):1–19

Serafin S, Geronazzo M, Erkut C, Nilsson NC, Nordahl R (2018) Sonic interactions in virtual reality: state of the art, current challenges, and future directions. IEEE Comput Graph Appl 38(2):31–43. https://doi.org/10.1109/MCG.2018.193142628

Siltanen S, Lokki T, Kiminki SP, Savioja L (2007) The room acoustic rendering equation. J Acoust Soc Am 122(3):1624. https://api.semanticscholar.org/CorpusID:22142911

Stanton TR, Spence C (2020) The influence of auditory cues on bodily and movement perception. Front Psychol 10:3001

Stein B, Meredith A (1993) The merging of the senses. The MIT Press. ISBN 9780262693011

Vorlander M, Schröder D, Pelzer S, Wefers F (2015) Virtual reality for architectural acoustics. J Build Perform Simul 8(1):15–25

Wang Y, Bocko M (2023) Universal global compact representation of head-related transfer functions with hemi-spherical harmonics and conformal mapping. J Acoust Soc Am 153(3 supplement):A126–A126

Zotter F, Frank M (2019) Ambisonics: a practical 3D audio theory for recording, studio production, sound reinforcement, and virtual reality. Springer Cham. https://api.semanticscholar.org/CorpusID:182231576

Chapter 5
Mapping Olfactory Memories: Digital Maps as an Interactive Medium for Olfactory Cultural Heritage

Katerina Pastra, Margarita Kokla, Eleni Tomai, Fotis Liarokapis, Maria Bezerianou, Athanasia Darra, Kostas Cheliotis, and Marinos Kavouras

Abstract Cultural heritage comprises not merely visual but multisensory experiences that individuals and communities share and which are related to specific sites and locations. Olfactory memories in particular are tightly connected to people, places and the physical 3D space and they are deeply ingrained in our emotion; they have a profound ability to connect people and communities through deeply shared experiences. The emerging field of Olfactory Cultural Heritage focuses on ways to capture, present and share olfactory experiences that are of value to a community. In this chapter, we suggest that digital maps can be employed to this end, functioning as a highly interactive medium. This requires that one goes beyond state of the art use of maps for documenting, delimiting and connecting heritage sites to their physical contexts, to employing maps as a communication tool; we identify the interdisciplinary challenges involved in large-scale collection, cartographic representation and visu-

---

K. Pastra (✉)
Institute for Language and Speech Processing, ATHENA Research Center, Athens, Greece
e-mail: kpastra@athenarc.gr

M. Kokla · E. Tomai · M. Bezerianou · A. Darra · K. Cheliotis · M. Kavouras
School of Rural, Surveying and Geoinformatics Engineering, National Technical University of Athens, Athens, Greece
e-mail: mkokla@survey.ntua.gr

E. Tomai
e-mail: etomai@mail.ntua.gr

M. Bezerianou
e-mail: bez@survey.ntua.gr

A. Darra
e-mail: adar@mail.ntua.gr

K. Cheliotis
e-mail: cheliotisk@mail.ntua.gr

M. Kavouras
e-mail: mkav@mail.ntua.gr

F. Liarokapis
Extended Experiences MRG, CYENS - Centre of Excellence, Nicosia, Cyprus
e-mail: f.liarokapis@cyens.org.cy

F. Liarokapis et al. (eds.), *Interactive Media for Cultural Heritage*, Springer Series on Cultural Computing, https://doi.org/10.1007/978-3-031-61018-9_5

alisation of olfactory memories and propose research directions that require joint efforts from a number of disciplines including Cartography, Language Science and Engineering, and Cognitive Science.

5.1 Introduction

Cultural heritage is much more than meets the eye; it goes beyond the visualscape to sound, smell, taste, and haptic experiences the combination of which constitutes the *cultural sensescape*: all these sensory experiences that individuals and communities share and which are related to specific sites and locations. Research has mainly focused on documenting, preserving, and protecting tangible and intangible cultural manifestations. The intangible ones are mainly documented through catalogues and inventories or through the use of videos, podcasts, and interviews. They mostly comprise memories of events and event/process-related traditions (e.g. traditional dances, recipes, crafts, and others). The rich sensory memories that accompany tangible and intangible cultural heritage and form themselves part of a community's intangible cultural heritage is a rather less documented and researched upon topic.

In this chapter, we will focus on olfactory memories in particular and the emerging field of Olfactory Cultural Heritage (see review in Bembibre and Strlič (2022)). Olfactory memories are tightly connected to people, places and to the physical 3D space and they are deeply ingrained in our emotion. They trigger recall even during infancy, when the olfactory system is much more robust than the visual, they assist in navigation and exploration of the world, and can be used to even recover from trauma (see review in Khamsi (2022)). They have a profound ability to connect people and communities through deeply shared experiences. Thus, preservation of olfactory memories contributes to the profiling of cultural spaces and actually enables a community to preserve the olfactory contemporary history of a place, observe the evolving smellscape (Porteous 1985; Henshaw 2013) and proceed to informed decision-making. However, given their intangible nature, *how could olfactory memories of cultural sites and locations be converted into actionable knowledge? How can one capture them at scale and present them to the wider public effectively?*

We suggest that **digital maps can be used as a highly interactive medium** to address these challenges. This requires that one goes beyond state of the art use of maps for documenting, delimiting and connecting heritage sites to their physical contexts, to employing *maps as a highly communicative tool*; *we identify the interdisciplinary challenges involved in large-scale collection, cartographic representation and visualisation of olfactory memories and propose research directions that require joint efforts from a number of disciplines* including Cartography, Language Science and Engineering, and Cognitive Science.

In what follows, we first introduce maps and their characteristics and uses in general and in Olfactory Cultural Heritage (OCH) in particular and then we elaborate on the idiosyncrasies of smell as a sensory experience through the lens of Cartography.

We focus on identifying and elaborating on the challenges posed for collecting, categorizing and visualizing olfactory memories from the perspective of cartographic representation and suggest methodological ways forward.

5.2 Olfactory Cultural Heritage and the Use of Maps

Three intersecting aspects of olfactory experiences have been identified as pillars of the emerging field of Olfactory Cultural Heritage (Bembibre and Strliĉ 2022):

- smells are (intangible) objects with cultural significance;
- smells are attributes of historic objects and spaces that carry valuable information on the identity of these objects, spaces, and the past and are therefore worthy of study and protection, and
- smells are associated with cultural practices significant for a certain community.

There has been an increasing number of official, systematic approaches that recognise smells as a vital part of cultural heritage (Bembibre and Strliĉ 2022). Indicatively, the Japanese Ministry for the Environment established in 2001 the "100 most fragrant spots" list which constitutes a community-led selection of aromas recognized as part of the country's heritage. In 2018, UNESCO acknowledged skills related to perfume in Grasse, France, the first olfactory entry to the list of intangible heritage, while in 2021, the City of Melbourne recognised a former Kraft Vegemite factory as a "site of local significance", partly because of the "distinctive odour" of the iconic Australian food which was produced there. In the same year, France passed a law protecting the "sensory heritage" of rural areas, including malodours. Furthermore, the smell of old books and historic libraries has been documented as a smellscape in a number of libraries and museums (including the Morgan Library and Museum, the Wren Library at St Paul's Cathedral and the Bodleian library).

Beyond the actual sensing of odorous, volatile compounds as emitted from entities, spaces, or as a result of an event, olfactory experiences may also be expressed verbally and/or visually in historical documents or other artwork (Ehrich et al. 2021; van Erp et al. 2023) or everyday communication channels. They form part of one's embodied experience of cultural heritage and the environment and they invoke other memories too (Bembibre and Strliĉ 2022). Natural language and image processing technologies are increasingly being employed for extraction of such olfactory experience-related information from text and images, especially in the context of digitised cultural heritage collections (Massri et al. 2022; Menini et al. 2022a, 2023; Shao et al. 2023).

5.2.1 The Role of Maps

Maps have a very long history going back to prehistoric times (Wolodtschenko and Forner 2007). They present spatial information at human perception scale; to this end, they scale down distances and sizes, abstract away physical features of geographical elements and represent landmarks through icons or symbols. Digital maps have become an everyday aid for modern man (Kavouras et al. 2021). Their availability through mobile phones, in particular, has enabled use anywhere and at any time. Navigation and spatial cognition related tasks are certainly among their basic uses: planning a route, finding the (shortest or best) way to a point of interest, being aware of one's location and spatial surroundings. Humans use maps—among others- to record spatial information so that the need for remembering such information is eliminated. In other words, maps function as memory aids, enabling cognitive offloading (Risko and Gilbert 2016), i.e., offloading of cognitive demands related to navigation and spatial reasoning.

From that perspective, maps capture space and time beyond here and now. They allow humans to "see" way beyond what they can actually see from their physical location, defying physical distance; they allow humans to "go" again and again to the places of interest, being ones that they visited in the past, or others that they intend to visit in the future. In a way, they function similarly to language, which goes beyond here and now, with the restriction that spatial reference is a *sine qua non* feature of the information they represent. Actually, any type of information with spatial reference can be represented through a digital map, including *verbal and quantitative data* mined from current or past media or acquired through crowdsourcing; characteristic examples include historical events, environmental information related to specific geographical areas, or even dominant emotions prevailing in specific places according to data mined from social media. Furthermore, diverse *sensory information* submitted by users themselves or extracted automatically, such as images or sounds of landmarks/places are commonly associated to digital maps. Of course, different types of maps are used for different types of data and different uses, the aim always being to serve user needs in the most efficient way through specific cartographic exemplars.

Cartography as a discipline itself has evolved radically; our information era fully exploits the concept of place, its features and characteristics through the plethora of location-based applications, the popularity of online cartographic tools, the diffusion of social networks, and the abundance of location-related data and content provided by humans (crowdsourcing). It is the era of Cybercartography (Taylor and Caquard 1997)

> the process of organization, presentation, analysis and communication of spatially referenced information on a wide variety of topics of interest and use to society in an interactive, dynamic, multimedia, multisensory and multidisciplinary format.

Actually, there have been more than 25 years since the inception of the term "Cybercartography"; *mapping* (process) and the *map* (product) make use of multimedia formats and new technologies (e.g. Augmented Reality, see review in Cheliotis et al. (2023)), they engage users as "creators" so that communities do not depend on external expertise (community ownership and control), and serve storytelling (geographic narrative) needs (Taylor 2019). Through the latter, digital maps cross over Cartography to Humanities and Social Sciences too and the notion of *deep mapping*, part of which considers digital maps a potentially ideal storyboard for spatial stories (Bodenhamer 2015). However, *cartographic representation of different sensory experiences* is still limited. The *use of maps as a memory aid for sensory experiences* is far from reaching its full potential; for olfactory information in particular, this has been considered extremely difficult due to the highly interdisciplinary nature of such task (Lauriault and Lindgaard 2006).

5.2.2 Maps in Cultural Heritage

Within the field of Cultural Heritage, Cartography and maps are important tools for documenting cultural heritage artefacts, for delimiting heritage sites, for connecting them to their physical contexts. Furthermore, as Avrami (2019) points out

> ...cultural mapping is a means of exploring people-place dynamics for multiple aims. It can generate new forms of knowledge about both tangible and intangible heritage within a community and provide new platforms for analysis and decision making. It can likewise serve as a vehicle for engaging populations in a dialogue about what they value within their community, and empower them to effectively create and re-create heritage.

Maps are used widely in cultural heritage archives to show the location of cultural heritage sites and communities,[1] and to record intangible cultural heritage, such as stories of individuals and communities (Caquard and Cartwright 2014). However, currently, cartographic representation is used *merely for pinning cultural heritage sites down on a map*. Typically, it comprises a world map with clickable parts that expand into tabs with textual, visual or audiovisual information with regards to the story or other cultural assets of a site. This information covers both content and metadata for the specific entry. The use of maps for featuring sensory, place-related human experience and what one could call "sensory cultural heritage" is largely unexplored. Additionally, hardly has sensory information found its way into maps beyond visual (images/videos) and auditory (sounds) memories .

In particular, there are currently two main approaches in mapping olfactory memories: a *sensory ethnographic* one and a *computational* one. In the first approach, *smellwalks* are required, during which experts or laymen walk in a region and log their olfactory experiences manually (Henshaw 2013; McLean 2020); these collective olfactory experiences are visualised then in smellmaps. In the second one, *smellmaps* visualise large-scale olfactory information mined automatically from social media (Quercia et al. 2021). Undoubtedly, both approaches contribute significantly to mapping olfactory memories. However, by definition, smellwalks are hard to perform at scale, due to high time and effort demands, while computational approaches achieve large-scale data collection but lack diversity and suffer from sparseness. More significantly though, both methodologies focus exclusively on *how to collect* rather than *how to best represent* such experiences through maps. In the context of odour nuisance analysis studies through use of olfactometry devices, maps have also been

[1] See for example the Maritime Cultural Heritage Maps, www.mapyourheritage.eu.

employed as a means to visualise olfactory-related findings (Kitson et al. 2019); still, these endeavours also use maps as a means of merely presenting information alongside its spatial reference, rather than as an interactive medium. The latter requires a cartographic perspective and an interdisciplinary endeavour so that the related challenges are both indicated and addressed. In the following sections, we will present in detail these challenges and methodologies to address them.

5.3 The Idiosyncrasies of Smell and Olfactory Memories Through Cartographic Lens

Collecting, representing and visualising olfactory memories is a very challenging task, for reasons that go way beyond one's awareness of a smell and are related to the transient nature of olfactory experiences and how people communicate their sensory memories. In this section, we will focus on identifying the idiosyncrasies of smells and olfactory memories employing an interdisciplinary perspective and cartographic lens.

5.3.1 Smells Beyond Here and Now: Smellmarks Without Spatiotemporal Borders

Smells *always have a source*, however, they travel with the wind/air and *spread out*. Thus, they expand, they cover some larger or shorter area. Their intensity is higher at/closer to their spatial source and tends to weaken as one moves further away from the source. The geographical location of a smell source, i.e., a place with distinct, reminiscent smell whose intensity may spread out, can be considered an *olfactory landmark* in cartographic terms, or what has been called *smellmark* (Porteous 1990). Hamburger and Nuhn (2023) point out the olfactory dimension of landmarks and their core role for navigation, wayfinding and spatial orientation. As landmarks do, smellmarks may also differ in size and type; for example they may comprise a block of buildings or a park expanding to several blocks, a specific store or a road intersection. However, contrary to traditional landmarks, smellmarks may also extend in space, the smell they emit may have a spatial range which -in essence- extends their boundaries. For example, some smellmarks may have a very localised reach (e.g., the smell of ground coffee beans within and outside a specific coffee shop), while others may cover a wide area (e.g., the smell of gas emitted by an oil refinery).

On the other hand, smells may also be *ephemeral* (e.g., gas from an old truck's exhaust), or more *permanent* (e.g., smells at the fish stalls of a permanent open market) depending on their source and on environmental conditions. Some smells appear *periodically*, such as the smell of ground coffee beans outside coffee shops in the morning, which does not persist when being at the same place at night. Other smells may *move around following a specific path/route*, as in the case of a mobile food canteen that changes locations. Maps can be used as a memory aid not only of the spatial range of smells but also of their *temporal signature*, allowing preservation of memories of the past, as well as ones that are contemporary but periodic or ephemeral. To this end and contrary to traditional landmarks, smellmarks need to be attributed a *temporal dimension* too. Furthermore, they need attribution of a *static versus mobile nature* to cover cases of smell sources that move around, creating *spatiotemporal, olfactory patterns*.

5.3.2 Smells Beyond Naming-Context Restrictions: Naturalistic Verbal Description

Naming an olfactory experience through language has been reported to be quite difficult (Olofsson and Gottfried 2015); unless one is an odour-expert (such as aroma maker, or wine tester), one feels challenged to name one's olfactory experiences, i.e., to go from a primary perceptual experience to a symbolic representation thereof. On the one hand, this difficulty may reflect limitations of the experimental conditions under which such information is elicited, i.e., outside of people's daily context (Majid 2021; Olofsson and Pierzchajlo 2021). This can be compensated through a variety of techniques that make the task feel more natural, easy or fun to participants; for example *naturalistic settings of elicitation* may be employed as in the case of smell-based navigation tasks or *games with a purpose* (Simperl et al. 2013), i.e., online games for indirect but entertaining and highly accurate elicitation of (usually semantic) data from humans. On the other hand, the naming difficulty is not evidenced *across cultures* (Majid 2021); *natural languages offer diverse ways for communicating one's experiences* and different ways may prevail in different languages and cultures. For example, in some western languages people tend to provide source-based descriptions of smells (e.g. "this smells like a lemon"), while in some asian languages, abstract naming terms are mostly used (e.g. "musty") (Majid et al. 2018; Majid 2021). Given such differences, asking people to identify (name) rather than describe an olfactory experience may be more or less difficult depending on one's native language and culture (Deroy 2022). In fact, asking people to *describe rather than identify or discriminate* a smell has been experimentally shown to be an easier task which leads to a larger variety of elicited verbal expressions (Poulton 2020).

In order to address requirements for a naturalistic context of olfactory experience elicitation and freedom for the speaker to express herself with diverse, shorter or longer verbal expressions, one may follow along the methodological lines of Vatakis and Pastra (2016). In particular, Vatakis and Pastra (2016) performed large scale elicitation of object descriptions and affordances; the experimental conditions were such, that made participants go out of their comfort zone and become creative in their responses, while at the same time being free to express themselves with no guidance or restrictions: they were presented with a small set of objects and where asked to name and describe these objects and their potential uses. It was only after the experiment had finished that the participants were informed that these objects were *lithic tools*, i.e., stones that millennia ago humans had carved into tools for achieving everyday tasks.[2] This created a condition in which participants were not familiar with the objects they were presented with; they could identify the material of the objects (i.e., stone), but beyond that they were free to describe and creatively report what these objects could be used for. Beyond being a unique in its kind and size verbal elicitation dataset, the output of this work provides evidence of the wealth of language when used for naming and description of object properties and uses. Among others, it was found that communication needs lead participants naturally to employing an extensive array of language mechanisms for describing objects and their uses, including not merely *direct references* (e.g., "it's a stone"), but also *indirect* ones (e.g. "it can be used as a plate"), *figurative language* (e.g., metaphors or similes, such as "it's like a knife"), *reasoning patterns* (e.g.,analogies, justifications, conditionals such as "if it was sharper, it could be used for cutting meat") and others. Similarly, in olfactory experience elicitation, one may employ (a) a "think aloud" verbal report protocol (Ericsson and Simon 1980) and (b) an experimental setup that requires communication about *unfamiliar or unidentified* smells, as well as *complex smells* (ones that comprise a synthesis of simple ones). It is expected, that in such experimental setup, elicitation of olfactory experiences will go beyond adjectives (e.g., "sweet") and direct references to the smell of the source-entity ("it is the smell of fish"), to indirect reference to the smell of another entity using an analogy (e.g., "these shoes smell like cheese that is off") and a wide range of other direct and indirect references, as well as reasoning patterns and figurative mechanisms.

Employing a non-restrictive verbal elicitation methodology, Cartography can make use of state of art natural language processing technology to harness the communicative power of language, semantically correlate different ways of verbally conveying the same memory and thus, organise olfactory memories into verbal categories *going beyond issues of familiarity or complexity of a smell* (see Sect. 5.4).

5.3.3 Smells Beyond Fine-Grained Schemas: Back to Smellmarks

In an attempt to encode and organise how people talk about olfactory experiences, a number of olfactory word lists, dictionaries (see Quercia et al. (2021)), metadata schemas and semantic data models have been developed and in many cases employed even for capturing how people express such information through images. For example, in the framework of the Odeuropa Project, a metadata schema is being developed addressing the need for curation of the *olfactory gaze*, i.e., visual elements referring

[2] The participants were controlled for knowledge of archaeology.

directly or indirectly to olfactory experiences and *verbal olfactory narratives* as found in digital libraries and databases of historical data and artwork (Ehrich et al. 2021; van Erp et al. 2023). The schema and the corresponding database comprise information on *olfactory gestures or events* (e.g., holding one's nose, cooking), *olfactory objects* (odorous substances, e.g., plants and artifacts such as perfume bottles), *fragrant spaces* (built or natural ones, e.g., parks) and *visual olfactory symbols or allegories* (e.g., sniffing a rose).

Along similar lines, in Lisena et al. (2022), a semantic annotation model (an ontology) has been developed for capturing information on historical smells, olfactory practices, and smellscapes in digital collections. Building upon CIDOC CRM,[3] the international standard for documenting cultural heritage information, this endeavour is *event-based*. Thus, it comprises *smell elements with associated attributes* (e.g. intensity, pleasantness, state etc.) and olfactory events including *smell emission* ones (i.e., events that generate smells, with specific agents involved, related to a specific smell source/olfactory object, at a specified time) and ones that capture *olfactory experience* (i.e., perception of the smell) with their own spatiotemporal dimensions, agents, emotions invoked and related olfactory gestures. Last, the *purpose* for which a smell may be used is also captured. *Smell transformation events* (e.g., opening a window) and *smell interaction events* (e.g. smells that result from mixing other smells) are included in the model. *Fragrant spaces* are included too, along with information on their type and/or geographical contiguity. In Tonelli and Menini (2021); Menini et al. (2022b), a FrameNet-based (Baker et al. 1998) event-centric semantic schema for olfactory experiences has been developed. The olfactory event frame comprises a number of semantic elements including *smell source* (something that produces the smell), *location of smell event* (if distinct from source), *smell carrier* (something that carries a smell produced by something else) if distinct from source, *qualities of smells* (e.g. intensity, duration, pleasantness, state), the *perceiver* or the *creator* of a smell, the *evoked odorant* (whatever evoked in perceiver's mind not present in the scene, e.g. through a simile), the *time of the smell event* (duration, point, frequency), the *circumstances* (state of the world that may affect the olfactory event), and the *effect of a smell* (event or emotion).

These semantic schemas are highly granular so that a wide range of questions by history and art researchers can be explored. However, in these approaches, *the same element may play different semantic roles in one or more olfactory events depending on verbal context*. For example, a "pine forest" may sometimes be a 'fragrant space', a 'smell source' (natural one), a 'smell carrier' (e.g., bearer of smell produced by something else, e.g. garbage thrown in the forest), the 'location of a smell emission event', or the 'location of an olfactory experience event'. At least for cartographic purposes, it is not clear what such *multiplicity of potential semantic roles for a single element* can serve. Furthermore, *sparseness* goes part and parcel with granularity regardless the methodology one employs for mining or collecting olfactory information. People may or may not be aware of the event(s) that generated the perceived smells or the exact smell-source or circumstances. In

[3] https://www.cidoc-crm.org.

olfactory memories mapping, such information may be inferred through analysis of the spatiotemporal and mobility-related characteristics of smellmarks when collected at scale and associated with information traditionally available in maps. Thus, for cartographic purposes, a *smellmark-centric* approach in capturing the semantics of olfactory memories -with the distinct features mentioned earlier in this section-is a simpler yet highly expressive approach.

5.3.4 Smells Across Cultures and the Subjectivity of Smells: Inclusiveness Is Key

Cultural differences may generally affect how people experience a place, in which locations they tend to go, which smells they notice, which landmarks they consider reminiscent with regards to smell and so on. As mentioned in Sect. 5.3.2, analyses of the different ways people talk about their olfactory experiences have pointed out cultural differences with e.g., western civilisations preferring reference to the source of the smell, while some eastern ones showing a high variability of abstract language terms for olfaction (Majid et al. 2018). Cartography can be used as a medium to interactively explore cultural effects in olfactory memory formulation, retention and recall, going beyond the use of language to talk about olfactory experiences to the spatiotemporal characteristics of such experiences across cultures, in multicultural communities and beyond.

Beyond cultural differences, there is no doubt that olfactory experiences may also be subjective; for example, smell sensitivity and/or smell pleasantness may differ substantially among people. Indeed, subjectivity lies mostly with the *intensity* of a smell (i.e., how intense it is in a specific location) and its *evaluation* (i.e., pleasant or unpleasant). Maps can be used to capture both aspects. With regards to intensity, maps can effectively visualise the spatial area covered by a smell, building on the hypothesis that the smell at the source is more intense and intensity decreases as one goes further away from the source, avoiding the subjective estimation of intensity values at any given point in space. With regards to evaluation of a smell, one needs to note that the cultural significance of a smell/smellmark stems from its *distinctiveness* for a community, rather than its pleasant or unpleasant feel; thus, maps can be used to collect both pleasant and unpleasant olfactory memories, providing also a quantification of the prevailing evaluation for each one of them, so that this information is truly actionable. On the other hand, smelling is also highly *adaptable*; one tends to adapt to smells that insist for some time in one's location. Thus, it is highly important for any methodology used to systematically collect olfactory memories to *monitor participants for inclusiveness* extending common diversity aspects (i.e., to balance the pool of participants with regards to age, sex, ethnicity/cultural background), to also include *familiarity of the participants with the mapped locations, so that both residents and visitors are included.*

5.4 Challenges in the Cartographic Representation of Olfactory Memories

In the previous section, we presented the idiosyncratic characteristics of olfactory experiences providing indications on how maps can be used to serve the requirements imposed. However, this is not trivial; the above characteristics pose a number of challenges for collecting, representing and visualising olfactory memories through maps. In this section, we will look into these challenges in more detail.

5.4.1 Crowdsourcing Olfactory Memories: Use of Spatiotemporal Smellmarks

As mentioned in Sect. 5.2.2, collection of olfactory experiences is currently undertaken mostly through smellwalks, i.e., a walk through a physical environment during which one makes olfactory observations with a research purpose (McLean 2020). These observations are either recorded on the spot, on site, or afterwards using a log. The Sensory Cities project of the Arts and Humanities Research Council in the UK has established an international research network on urban sensing (including olfactory sensing) and has developed a Sensory Think Kit with practical tips and methods for researching, designing, curating and representing the senses in the city, for making one's own sensory walk with no prior knowledge.[4] However, sensory walks are time and effort consuming and though entertaining for the 'walkers', hardly can they be employed for large scale collection of olfactory experiences. Furthermore, it has been reported that in many cases people do not report on what they perceive at the location during the walk, but they rather use the walk as a trigger to talk about their olfactory memories of the place (Henshaw 2013). Actually, instructions on which aspects of the olfactory experience to be logged do not systematically address the idiosyncrasies of smells especially from the mapping perspective (as elaborated in Sect. 5.3), thus resulting in descriptions that lack information on spatiotemporal aspects of the memories that could be effectively used in cartographic representation. Beyond this direct method for capturing the olfactory experience of people in specific sites and locations, indirect methods have also been used, such as mining olfactory descriptions and memories from text (e.g., travelogues, literature, messages) either manually (Dann and Jacobsen 2003) or automatically (Quercia et al. 2021). However, in such indirect sources, it is hard -if not impossible- for one to systematically collect the spatiotemporal aspects of olfactory experiences mentioned in the previous section given that one has no control over the information expressed in the mined resources. *So, how could one collect olfactory experiences at a large scale, while also capturing the idiosyncratic spatiotemporal characteristics of olfactory experiences?*

---

[4] http://sensorythinktank.com.

We suggest the use of a *crowdsourcing* methodology building on open-source cartographic platforms (such as the OpenStreetMap) to crowdsource smellmark tags from a large pool of people who reside or visit a location, monitoring always for inclusiveness and non-discrimination in the pool of participants, as well as for cultural diversity. More significantly, crowdsourcing should comprise acquisition of *smellmark tags*, i.e., landmarks that participants consider sources of significant smell(s). These might be existing landmarks on a map (e.g., an open food market), or ones that are not already tagged on the map (e.g., a specific street corner or building with a distinct, reminiscent smell). In the case of a new landmark, its category may also be denoted (e.g., "residential block of flats"). Furthermore, *smellmark spatial boundaries* should be elicited from participants, i.e., through denotation of the area around the smellmark in which the smell can be identified. The *temporal signature of the smellmark* is also essential for indication of the temporal period during which the smell is/was present, as well as indication of the mobility status of the smellmark. In other words, we suggest that olfactory memory acquisition should be *smellmark-centric* and should actually employ an *extended* definition of smellmarks, that will comprise not only spatial but also temporal and mobility-related attributes. Such approach can enable *clustering* of olfactory memories by smellmark and/or with regards to their spatiotemporal coverage, as well as identification of spatiotemporal patterns created by specific smells. In this way, maps can build on such clustering to organise the representation of olfactory memories according to cartographic criteria and can visualise the routes/paths or other spatial patterns created by smells. Using a common, open-source digital cartographic platform allows collection of olfactory memories both on the spot, i.e., while the participant is in a specific location that (s)he wishes to tag on the map, and/or when recalling olfactory memories while being at another place. The latter, olfactory memory recall, is not only appropriate but actually quite effective. It has been experimentally found to systematically go beyond 70% across age groups (Zach et al. 2018) and to be comparable in strength to auditory recall.

Crowdsourcing for olfactory mapping is certainly not a new suggestion; Henshaw (2013) reports on similar web-based endeavours, which have been criticised for assuming engagement of large crowds which is hard to achieve (Quercia et al. 2021). However, the previous endeavours did not go beyond asking people to "pin" their olfactory experiences down on a map. What one asks from the public to do is crucial for successful and effective use of crowdsourcing. Furthermore, projects like OpenStreetMap and participatory mapping, provide evidence of an established trend in the public globally, to engage in mapping activities especially when the latter has significant personal, social, or regional impact. Olfactory memory mapping does have such profound impact given that it allows one to visualise not only his/her personal memories but also to understand collective memories of artifacts, entities and spaces (see also Sect. 5.5).

5.4.2 *Cartographic Scaling of Olfactory Memories: Use of Verbal Categorization*

One of the most important features of maps is their ability for spatial scaling, i.e., for representing locations at different levels of spatial abstraction, or to put it simply, for representing locations with more or less visual detail. Users interact with digital maps employing different scales of the areas of interest (zooming in/out) according to their needs and intended use of the map. When doing so, location names on a map appear or hide, accordingly; for example, the names of smaller areas in a city appear when zooming in, while they disappear when zooming out and get replaced by the names of the larger areas in which they belong. For olfactory memory mapping, multiple representations of smells are needed so that by altering the scale of the map, *different smellscape resolutions* are available. *So, how could cartographic scaling of olfactory memories be achieved?*

We suggest that verbal categorisation can be employed for the task. *Scaling is a primary characteristic of natural language* too, though in language the scaling involved is not spatial but semantic. Natural language is used for verbal categorization of one's sensorimotor experiences and actually it does so employing varying levels of generalisation, i.e., words that denote more or less general categories of entities, actions, or features (Pastra 2013, 2014). Seminal work in verbal categorisation has identified three major levels of such abstraction, namely, *superordinate*, *basic level* and *subordinate* (e.g., "fruit", "apple", "green apple", respectively) (Rosch et al. 1976). Experimentation in this work focused exclusively on the verbal categorisation of entities, which is appropriate though for exploring categorisation in verbal expression of olfactory experiences given the common use of smell sources to describe smell. Further experimental exploration of verbal categorisation of perceptual features (e.g., "bitter") would be beneficial for one to see whether perceptual features follow a similar pattern in verbal categorisation. It is to be noted though that one should refrain from considering any adjective as one expressing a feature; for example, "fruity" may be used to describe a smell in a generic way, however it does so through reference to a general category of entities, that of "fruits". In contrast, "bitter" describes purely a perceptual experience with no reference to a category of entities or actions. As well noted in Deroy (2022), "fruity" invokes a number of sensory experiences with "fruits", including visual, olfactory, gustatory, and tactile, while "bitter" refers only to the gustatory one (and in many cases the olfactory one too).[5]

Thus, employing semantic scaling in mapping olfactory memories has the potential to provide one with *naming* of olfactory categories at different cartographic scales. Doing so is of course far from trivial. One needs to develop/employ natural language processing technology for:

[5] See Spence (2020) on the use of common terms for gustatory and olfactory experiences.

- *Semantic similarity matching* of verbally expressed olfactory experiences: as mentioned in Sect. 5.3, language has diverse ways to refer to the same sensory experience, which requires a semantic similarity metric for matching those olfactory memories that refer to the same experience though named differently (e.g. "banana-smell", and "sweet like a banana"). State of the art metrics (Chandrasekaran and Mago 2021) can be successfully employed for this task.
- *Classification of olfactory memories into verbal categorisation levels*: this process can actually identify the scale at which an olfactory memory has been named, and enable its correlation to cartographic scale. There are only a couple of attempts to identify categorisation levels algorithmically, the most recent of which is Mills et al. (2018). Research along these lines has the potential to open up new directions in language processing and especially in its relation to cartographic mapping.
- *Variable solving* of verbal references with missing/implied information (e.g., "this candle has the smell of the lemon"), where the actual smell reference is a variable, commonly shared by lemons and the specific candle (see related work in Pastra et al. (2011)). This requires common sense reasoning, i.e., employing reasoning methods and common sense knowledge of the world.
- *Identification of how olfactory memories relate to each other semantically*, i.e., identification of the semantic relations between memories that share either source or spatial coverage and/or temporal extension. Such memories may be semantically *equivalent* (though named at different levels of abstraction, e.g., "smell of pollution from cars", "smell of gas"), *complementary* (e.g. "smell of gas" and "smell of smoke") or *contradictory* (e.g., "smell of gas" vs. "flowery smell"). To this end, one may employ the COSMOROE cross-media semantic relations framework (Pastra 2008, 2015). The semantic relatedness among olfactory experiences in a specific spatial and/or temporal scale can provide actionable knowledge and guide decision making.

Such use of Natural Language Processing technology in combination with the naturalistic, olfactory memory elicitation method mentioned in Sect. 5.3 can actually address another state of the art challenge related to naming olfactory experiences, i.e., the need for a standardised or comparable odour-reference vocabulary (Bembibre and Strliĉ 2022).

5.4.3 *Visualizing Spatiotemporal Smellmarks: Use of Cross-Modal Associations*

Different practitioners and professionals have developed odor wheels and visual schemas for different purposes (e.g., the aroma wine wheel, the fragrance wheel by fragrance expert Michael Edwards, the coffee aroma wheel by the Specialty Coffee Association of America, and the odor wheel developed by St. Croix Sensory to encompass a broad range of environmental and product/material odours). Visualisation of an odour through colour has been a topic of increasing interest especially in the marketing communication field, where designers aspire to induce suitable odour expectations for the marketed products through colour cues (Spence 2020). In mapping olfactory memories, one encounters a similar need: *how to visualise olfactory information effectively on a map*. The aim is actually to go beyond linking a smell to its smellmark, to designing the visual attributes of the smellmark. For example, colour-coding by odour type is important for easier identification and discrimination of the olfactory information presented cartographically (Blackwell 1995; Stevenson and Oaten 2008).

Within Cognitive Science, there is significant experimental research on the cross-modal associations between odour and colour, and to a lesser extend between odour and shape; in this literature, studies have shown that people perform consistent, intuitive colour-odour associations (see review in Spence (2020)). *Odour naming accuracy/source identification*, *odour familiarity* and *odour pleasantness* have been found to affect such associations (Speed et al. 2023) that are commonly considered to be learned. However, experimental methodologies for studying such associations in non-food contexts have been criticised for lack of naturalistic elicitation conditions (i.e., olfactory stimuli used to elicit colour associations are usually presented out of context/in the lab), and for experimental designs that guide the participants to choose from a predefined set of colours the one that best associates with odours from a specific set too, limiting thus the participants in their choices (Spence 2020).

Taking this criticism into consideration, we suggest employment of a *free word-association paradigm* for exploring how people associate their olfactory memories with visual features (such as colour) for cartographical representation. Word association is an experimental method that has been used in psychology and psycholinguistics extensively for more than a hundred years (Boyd-Graber et al. 2005). It comprises a verbal cue - verbal response process, in which participants are required to freely respond with a word that first comes to mind when primed with another word. It is rooted to the assumption that lexical associations may reflect conceptual organisation in the human mind; the association strength between lexical concepts is measured through the number of people who have provided a specific association (Nelson et al. 2000). There have been quite a few large scale word association experiments the results of which are publicly available in the form of associative norms, including the Edinburgh Association Thesaurus (Kiss et al. 1973), and the University of South Florida Free Association Norms (Nelson et al. 2004)[6]. While such endeavours lack big data coverage, in the sense that experimentation cannot take place in such large scale to produce millions of associations, they do contain some odour-colour associations. Automatic prediction of word associations is a core task in Natural Language Processing too; there has been considerable research in automatically predicting word associations making use of large text corpora or large language models pretrained in such corpora, as in (Cattle and Ma 2017). In particular, the latest

[6] There is also the WordNet Evocation dataset (Hayashi 2016; Boyd-Graber et al. 2005), which has resulted from elicitation of associations by presenting users with specific pairs of words (to be precise: synonym sets); however, this methodology goes beyond the cue-response paradigm of free word association and comes closer to semantic similarity judgement approaches and thus, is beyond scope in this discussion.

advancements in developing large language models provide ample opportunities for one to employ cutting edge computational technology for predicting colour-odour associations.

Actually, the two approaches, i.e., experimental and computational are complementary: for example, experimentally elicited word association has the advantage that it goes beyond common language usage as reflected in verbal/textual resources. This is crucial for associations that involve sensory experiences, given language's tendency to omit common sense/easily inferred sensorimotor information (e.g., that the banana has a sweet smell) unless there are special conditions that require so (Pastra et al. 2011). Furthermore, experimental word-association captures unidirectional rather than bidirectional associations, as opposed to most automatic prediction methods. For mapping olfactory information, this assymetry is desired, given that map design is purely interested on visualisation features that are associated with odours, rather than the other way around or both, as in marketing communication (Spence 2020). On their own part, computational word-association approaches function within a language context, which is not the case in experimental conditions during which participants are primed with a cue word completely out of context, and thus free to interpret it as they consider appropriate (see criticism in (Cattle and Ma 2017)). Furthermore, not only the strongest association for a word but also alternative ones can efficiently be predicted in computational approaches as long as they are present in the data processed; this is not the case in experimental free association where participants are limited to one-word responses. Experimentation with letting the users free to provide responses with more than a word have yielded thought-chaining problems (e.g., it is not clear whether the second word provided is a response to the verbal cue or an association of the first uttered response) (De Deyne et al. 2016).

Regardless word association methodology, *odour naming as elicited from human participants* (see Sect. 5.4.2) is an important starting point, given the diversity of expressions one may use to communicate olfactory experiences (see Sect. 5.3). References to familiar and unfamiliar smells, simple and complex ones, are all important as verbal cues for eliciting or automatically predicting their colour (or other) associations. This also entails, that the free-word association paradigm will have to be extended beyond *word boundaries*, to phrases and larger verbal units as employed by humans for naming purposes.

Eliciting odour-colour associations purely verbally, comes with its own challenges of course. In de Valk et al. (2016) it has been shown that when people use abstract terms (i.e., terms with non-tangible reference) to express their olfactory experience (e.g., "sweet") they are not at all consistent with regards to the colours they associate with these experiences, while people who refer to olfactory experience using concrete terms, such as the source of the smell (e.g., "banana smell"), are absolutely consistent with the colour association for the olfactory experience (e.g., yellow, for the banana smell). Given that such verbal tendencies have been shown to be culture/language specific (see Sect. 5.3), software localization in odour-colour associations in map design may be required, i.e., customization of the digital map according to the users' linguistic/cultural preferences.

5.5 Potential Impact of Using Maps in Olfactory Cultural Heritage and Beyond

Olfactory memory mapping has a key-role in Cultural Heritage, not only for *preservation, but also for interactive presentation and communication* of the olfactory dimension of artifacts, processes, events, and locations. Digital maps are native media in galleries, libraries, archives and museums (GLAMs), as well as sites of any type, including archaeological, urban, and rural, which makes their use for capturing, representing and presenting olfactory information, a natural choice. On top of that, olfactory mapping has the potential to be employed within multisensory virtual reality applications (Apostolou and Liarokapis 2022) for *augmentation* of cultural sites allowing users to relive their memories, or acquire powerful sensory experiences that belong to the past or to another user group/community. Using maps for *reconstruction* or *preservation* of a community's olfactory past can lead to *deeper understanding* of a community's present in terms of socioeconomic activities and needs. Olfactory memory mapping can function as a *bonding mechanism for communities to embrace diversity and become inclusive*. Furthermore, multisensory maps can also function as an *enabling experience* for blind or partially-sighted people (Xiao et al. 2021); for instance, integrating olfactory memory maps with olfactory displays, i.e., interfaces that generate and diffuse odours to a user, opens up new possibilities to visual sensory deprived users. On the other hand, potential limitations in using maps as an interactive medium for Olfactory Cultural Heritage stem mostly from the effectiveness of large-scale collection, appropriate representation and intuitive visualisation of olfactory information; thus, identification of the challenges involved and adoption of robust methodologies for addressing them are key.

Beyond Cultural Heritage venues and related applications, olfactory mapping may have a profound impact on a diverse range of domains, including tourism, health, planning and architecture, education and training, and others. For example, *Smell Tourism* (Dann and Jacobsen 2003) is an application domain in which maps representing olfactory information can be used for the sensory experience not only of cultural assets, but also of entire regions; navigation in such regions through olfaction can contribute to a heightened sense of familiarity and emotional connection to a place. Furthermore, olfactory memories can "induce positive emotions, decrease negative mood states, disrupt cravings, and reduce physiological indices of stress, including systemic markers of inflammation" (Herz 2016); thus, *odour-induced well-being* is another application domain that extends beyond culture and tourism to well-being and the built environment (Xiao et al. 2021). Mapping olfactory memories opens up new directions in designing human-environment interaction spaces (Henshaw 2013) and human-computer interaction technologies (Obrist et al. 2014). Actually, *digital maps can play a vital role in representing everyday sensory (and olfactory in particular) experiences at different spatiotemporal scales, serving everyday cognitive offloading needs related to encoding, recollecting and learning from one's sensory experiences*. Thus, we consider olfactory memory mapping a research direction that holds great potential for both fundamental and applied research across a wide range of disciplines and with significant impact.

5.6 Conclusion

In this chapter, we looked into the challenges in employing maps as an *interactive medium* for collecting, representing and efficiently visualising olfactory memories. We have identified the idiosyncrasies of olfactory experiences and elaborated on the interdisciplinary endeavour required for addressing them, which leads one to extending or redefining cartographic practices and methodologies themselves. In particular, we introduced the notion of an *extended-smellmark* with spatial, temporal and mobility related attributes, and suggested a *smellmark-centric* crowdsourcing methodology for olfactory memory collection. Furthermore, we suggested a smellmark-centric representation of olfactory experiences and the use of verbal categorisation as a *semantic scaling process for achieving representation of olfactory experiences at multiple spatial resolutions*. Last, we pointed out the need for experimentally grounded cross-modal decisions in visualisation of olfactory memories on a map and suggested that a combination of a *word-association* experimental paradigm and computational approaches can be used to this end.

Acknowledgements Funding: This research is supported by the Hellenic Foundation for Research and Innovation (H.F.R.I.), under the "First Call for H.F.R.I. Research Projects to support Faculty members and Researchers and the procurement of high-cost research equipment" (CyberCarto Project, Number: HFRI-FM17-2661).This research was also partially supported by the European Union Horizon 2020 Research and Innovation Programme under Grant Agreement No 739578 and the Government of the Republic of Cyprus through the Deputy Ministry of Research, Innovation and Digital Policy. Conflict of interest/Competing interests: On behalf of all authors, the corresponding author states that there is no conflict of interest. Authors' contributions: All authors have contributed equally to this paper. Availability of Data: No datasets were generated during the current study.

References

Apostolou K, Liarokapis F (2022) A systematic review: the role of multisensory feedback in virtual reality. In: 2022 IEEE 2nd international conference on intelligent reality (ICIR), pp 39–42. https://doi.org/10.1109/ICIR55739.2022.00024

Avrami E (2019) Spatializing values in heritage conservation: the potential of cultural mapping. In: Avrami E, McDonald S, Mason R, Myers D (eds) Emerging approaches and research directions. Getty Publications, Values in Heritage Management, pp 35–49

Baker CF, Fillmore CJ, Lowe JB (1998) The Berkeley FrameNet project. In: 36th annual meeting of the association for computational linguistics and 17th international conference on computational linguistics, Volume 1, association for computational linguistics, Montreal, Quebec, Canada, pp 86–90. https://doi.org/10.3115/980845.980860

Bembibre C, Strliĉ M (2022) From smelly buildings to the scented past: an overview of olfactory heritage. Front Psychol 12. https://doi.org/10.3389/fpsyg.2021.718287

Blackwell L (1995) Visual cues and their effects on odour assessment. Nutr Food Sci 95(5):24–28. https://doi.org/10.1108/00346659510094008

Bodenhamer DJ (2015) Narrating space and place. In: Amd John Corrigan DJB, Bloomington T (eds), Deep maps and spatial narratives. Indiana University Press, pp 7–27

Boyd-Graber J, Fellbaum C, Osherson D, Schapire R (2005) Adding dense, weighted connections to wordnet. In: GWC 2006, Masaryk University, GWC 2006: 3rd international global wordnet conference, proceedings, pp 29–35, 3rd international global wordnet conference, GWC 2006; conference date: 22 Jan 2006 Through 26 Jan 2006

Caquard S, Cartwright W (2014) Narrative cartography: from mapping stories to the narrative of maps and mapping. Cartogr J 51(2):101–106. https://doi.org/10.1179/0008704114z.000000000130

Cattle A, Ma X (2017) Predicting word association strengths. In: Palmer M, Hwa R, Riedel S (eds) Proceedings of the 2017 conference on empirical methods in natural language processing, association for computational linguistics, Copenhagen, Denmark, pp 1283–1288. https://doi.org/10.18653/v1/D17-1132

Chandrasekaran D, Mago V (2021) Evolution of semantic similarity–a survey. ACM Comput Surv 54(2):1–37. https://doi.org/10.1145/3440755

Cheliotis K, Liarokapis F, Kokla M, Tomai E, Pastra K, Anastopoulou N, Bezerianou M, Darra A, Kavouras M (2023) A systematic review of application development in augmented reality navigation research. Cartography and geographic information science, pp 1–23. https://doi.org/10.1080/15230406.2023.2194032

Dann G, Jacobsen J (2003) Tourism smellscapes. Tour Geogr 5(1):3–25. https://doi.org/10.1080/1461668032000034033

De Deyne S, Perfors A, Navarro DJ (2016) Predicting human similarity judgments with distributional models: the value of word associations. In: Matsumoto Y, Prasad R (eds) Proceedings of the 26th international conference on computational linguistics (COLING): technical papers, The COLING 2016 organizing committee, Osaka, Japan, pp 1861–1870

Deroy O (2022) Olfactory abstraction: a communicative and metacognitive account. Philos Trans R Soc B: Biol Sci 378(1870). https://doi.org/10.1098/rstb.2021.0369

Ehrich S, Verbeek C, Zinnen M, Marx L, Bembibre C, Leemans I (2021) Nose-first. towards an olfactory gaze for digital art history. In: Carvalho S, Rocha Souza R (eds) Language, data and knowledge (LDK) workshops and tutorials 2021, CEUR-WS.org, CEUR Workshop Proceedings, pp 1–17

Ericsson KA, Simon HA (1980) Verbal reports as data. Psychol Rev 87(3):215–251. https://doi.org/10.1037/0033-295x.87.3.215

van Erp M, Tullett W, Christlein V, Ehrhart T, Hürriyetoğlu A, Leemans I, Lisena P, Menini S, Schwabe D, Tonelli S, Troncy R, Zinnen M (2023) More than the name of the rose: how to make computers read, see, and organize smells. Am Hist Rev 128(1):335–369. https://doi.org/10.1093/ahr/rhad141

Hamburger K, Nuhn E (2023) Cognitive landmark research beyond visual cues using giscience. Front Psychol 14. https://doi.org/10.3389/fpsyg.2023.1092715

Hayashi Y (2016) Predicting the evocation relation between lexicalized concepts. In: Matsumoto Y, Prasad R (eds) Proceedings of the 26th international conference on computational linguistics (COLING): technical papers, the COLING 2016 organizing committee, Osaka, Japan, pp 1657–1668

Henshaw V (2013) Urban smellscapes: understanding and designing city smell environments. Routledge

Herz R (2016) The role of odor-evoked memory in psychological and physiological health. Brain Sci 6(3). https://doi.org/10.3390/brainsci6030022

Kavouras M, Kokla M, Liarokapis F, Pastra K, Tomai E (2021) Comparative study of the interaction of digital natives with mainstream web mapping services. In: Lecture notes in computer science. Springer International Publishing, pp 337–350. https://doi.org/10.1007/978-3-030-78468-3_23

Khamsi R (2022) Unpicking the link between smell and memories. Nature 606(7915):S2–S4. https://doi.org/10.1038/d41586-022-01626-x

Kiss GR, Armstrong C, Milroy R, Piper J (1973) An associative thesaurus of English and its computer analysis. In: Aitkin AJ, Bailey RW, Hamilton-Smith N (eds) The computer and literary studies. University Press, Edinburgh, UK

Kitson J, Leiva M, Christman Z, Dalton P (2019) Evaluating urban odor with field olfactometry in Camden, NJ. Urban Sci 3(3). https://doi.org/10.3390/urbansci3030093

Lauriault TP, Lindgaard G (2006) Scented cybercartography: exploring possibilities. Cartographica: Int J Geograph Inf Geovisualization 41(1):73–92. https://doi.org/10.3138/w432-713u-3621-04n3

Lisena P, Schwabe D, van Erp M, Troncy R, Tullett W, Leemans I, Marx L, Ehrich SC (2022) Capturing the semantics of smell: the odeuropa data model for olfactory heritage information. In: The semantic web. Springer International Publishing, pp 387–405. https://doi.org/10.1007/978-3-031-06981-9_23

Majid A (2021) Human olfaction at the intersection of language, culture, and biology. Trends Cogn Sci 25(2):111–123. https://doi.org/10.1016/j.tics.2020.11.005

Majid A, Burenhult N, Stensmyr M, de Valk J, Hansson BS (2018) Olfactory language and abstraction across cultures. Philos Trans R Soc B: Biol Sci 373(1752). https://doi.org/10.1098/rstb.2017.0139

Massri MB, Novalija I, Mladenić D, Brank J, da Silva SG, Marrouch N, Murteira C, Hürriyetoğlu A, Šircelj B (2022) Harvesting context and mining emotions related to olfactory cultural heritage. Multimodal Technol Interact 6(7). https://doi.org/10.3390/mti6070057

McLean K (2020) Sensory mapping. In: Kobayashi A (ed) International encyclopedia of human geography, 2nd ed. Elsevier, Oxford, pp 153–168. https://doi.org/10.1016/B978-0-08-102295-5.10592-X

Menini S, Paccosi T, Tekiroğlu SS, Tonelli S (2022a) Building a multilingual taxonomy of olfactory terms with timestamps. In: Calzolari N, Béchet F, Blache P, Choukri K, Cieri C, Declerck T, Goggi S, Isahara H, Maegaard B, Mariani J, Mazo H, Odijk J, Piperidis S (eds) Proceedings of the 13th language resources and evaluation conference, european language resources association, Marseille, France, pp 4030–4039. https://aclanthology.org/2022.lrec-1.429

Menini S, Paccosi T, Tonelli S, Van Erp M, Leemans I, Lisena P, Troncy R, Tullett W, Hürriyetoğlu A, Dijkstra G, Gordijn F, Jürgens E, Koopman J, Ouwerkerk A, Steen S, Novalija I, Brank J, Mladenic D, Zidar A (2022b) A multilingual benchmark to capture olfactory situations over time. In: Proceedings of the 3rd workshop on computational approaches to historical language change, association for computational linguistics, Dublin, Ireland, pp 1–1. https://doi.org/10.18653/v1/2022.lchange-1.1

Menini S, Paccosi T, Tekiroğlu SS, Tonelli S (2023) Scent mining: Extracting olfactory events, smell sources and qualities. In: Degaetano-Ortlieb S, Kazantseva A, Reiter N, Szpakowicz S (eds) Proceedings of the 7th joint SIGHUM workshop on computational linguistics for cultural heritage, social sciences, humanities and literature, association for computational linguistics, Dubrovnik, Croatia, pp 135–140. https://doi.org/10.18653/v1/2023.latechclfl-1.15

Mills C, Bond F, Levow GA (2018) Automatic identification of basic-level categories. In: Bond F, Vossen P, Fellbaum C (eds) Proceedings of the 9th global wordnet conference, global wordnet association. Nanyang Technological University (NTU), Singapore, pp 298–305. https://aclanthology.org/2018.gwc-1.35

Nelson DL, Mcevoy CL, Dennis S (2000) What is free association and what does it measure? Mem Cogn 28(6):887–899. https://doi.org/10.3758/bf03209337

Nelson DL, McEvoy CL, Schreiber TA (2004) The university of south FL free association, rhyme, and word fragment norms. Behav Res Methods Instrum Comput 36(3):402–407. https://doi.org/10.3758/bf03195588

Obrist M, Tuch AN, Hornbaek K (2014) Opportunities for odor: experiences with smell and implications for technology. In: Proceedings of the SIGCHI conference on human factors in computing systems, association for computing machinery, New York, NY, USA, CHI '14, pp 2843–2852. https://doi.org/10.1145/2556288.2557008

Olofsson JK, Gottfried JA (2015) The muted sense: neurocognitive limitations of olfactory language. Trends Cogn Sci 19(6):314–321. https://doi.org/10.1016/j.tics.2015.04.007

Olofsson JK, Pierzchajlo S (2021) Olfactory language: context is everything. Trends Cogn Sci 25(6):419–420. https://doi.org/10.1016/j.tics.2021.02.004

Pastra K (2008) COSMOROE: a cross-media relations framework for modelling multimedia dialectics. Multimed Syst 14(5):299–323. https://doi.org/10.1007/s00530-008-0142-0

Pastra K (2013) Autonomous acquisition of sensorimotor experiences: any role for language? In: Newsletter on autonomous mental development, vol 10. IEEE Computational Intelligence Society

Pastra K (2014) Beware of the label! In: Newsletter on autonomous mental development, vol 11. IEEE Computational Intelligence Society

Pastra K (2015) Cosmoroe annotation guide. Tech Rep CSRI-TRS-150201, Cognitive Systems Research Institute

Pastra K, Balta E, Dimitrakis P, Karakatsiotis G (2011) Embodied language processing: a new generation of language technology. In: Proceedings of the 14th AAAI conference on language-action tools for cognitive artificial agents. AAAI Press, AAAIWS'11–14, pp 23—29

Porteous JD (1985) Smellscape. Prog Hum Geogr 9(3):356–378. https://doi.org/10.1177/030913258500900303

Porteous JD (1990) Landscapes of the Mind: Worlds of Sense and Metaphor. University of Toronto Press. http://www.jstor.org/stable/10.3138/j.ctvfrxgfs

Poulton T (2020) The smells we know and love: variation in codability and description strategy. Lang Cogn 12(3):501–525. https://doi.org/10.1017/langcog.2020.11

Quercia D, Schifanella R, Aiello LM, McLean K (2021) Smelly maps: the digital life of urban smellscapes. Proc Int AAAI Conf Web Soc Media 9(1):327–336. https://doi.org/10.1609/icwsm.v9i1.14621

Risko EF, Gilbert SJ (2016) Cognitive offloading. Trends Cogn Sci 20(9):676–688. https://doi.org/10.1016/j.tics.2016.07.002

Rosch E, Mervis CB, Gray WD, Johnson DM, Boyes-Braem P (1976) Basic objects in natural categories. Cogn Psychol 8(3):382–439

Shao Y, Sun J, Jiang Y, Li J (2023) Dual-grained text-image olfactory matching model with mutual promotion stages. In: Companion proceedings of the ACM web conference 2023, association for computing machinery, New York, NY, USA, WWW 2023 Companion, pp 669–67. https://doi.org/10.1145/3543873.3587649

Simperl E, Cuel R, Stein M (2013) Case study: games with a purpose for semantic content creation. Springer International Publishing, Cham, pp 67–89. https://doi.org/10.1007/978-3-031-79441-4_5

Speed LJ, de Valk J, Croijmans I, Huisman JLA, Majid A (2023) Odor-color associations are not mediated by concurrent verbalization. Cogn Sci 47(4).https://doi.org/10.1111/cogs.13266

Spence C (2020) Olfactory-colour crossmodal correspondences in art, science, and design. Cogn Res: Princ Implic 5(1). https://doi.org/10.1186/s41235-020-00246-1

Stevenson RJ, Oaten M (2008) The effect of appropriate and inappropriate stimulus color on odor discrimination. Percept Psychophys 70(4):640–646. https://doi.org/10.3758/pp.70.4.640

Taylor F (2019) Chapter 1—cybercartography revisited. In: Taylor F, Anonby E, Murasugi K (eds) Further developments in the theory and practice of cybercartography, modern cartography series, vol 7. Academic Press, pp 3–23. https://doi.org/10.1016/B978-0-444-64193-9.00001-4

Taylor F, Caquard S (1997) Cybercartography: maps and mapping in the information era. Cartogr: Int J Geogr Inf Geovisualization 41(1):1–6. https://doi.org/10.3138/U631-37K3-3NL6-4136

Tonelli S, Menini S (2021) FrameNet-like annotation of olfactory information in texts. In: Degaetano-Ortlieb S, Kazantseva A, Reiter N, Szpakowicz S (eds) Proceedings of the 5th joint

SIGHUM workshop on computational linguistics for cultural heritage, social sciences, humanities and literature, association for computational linguistics, pp 11–20. https://doi.org/10.18653/v1/2021.latechclfl-1.2
de Valk JM, Wnuk E, Huisman J, Majid A (2016) Odor–color associations differ with verbal descriptors for odors: a comparison of three linguistically diverse groups. Psychon Bull Rev 24(4):1171–1179. https://doi.org/10.3758/s13423-016-1179-2
Vatakis A, Pastra K (2016) A multimodal dataset of spontaneous speech and movement production on object affordances. Sci Data 3(1). https://doi.org/10.1038/sdata.2015.78
Wolodtschenko A, Forner T (2007) Prehistoric and early historic maps in Europe: conception of cd-atlas. E-Perimetron 2:114–116
Xiao J, Aletta F, Radicchi A, McLean K, Shiner LE, Verbeek C (2021) Recent advances in smellscape research for the built environment. Front Psychol 12. https://doi.org/10.3389/fpsyg.2021.700514
Zach P, Zimmelová P, Mrzílková J, Kutová M (2018) Difference in subjective accessibility of on demand recall of visual, taste, and olfactory memories. BioMed Res Int 2018:1–6. https://doi.org/10.1155/2018/1630437

Chapter 6
User Acceptance of 720° Virtual Tour Systems for Online Museum Experiences: Effects of Immersion, Interaction, and Personal Innovativeness

Yue Li, Jiachen Liang, Enhao Yang, and Hai-Ning Liang

Abstract As a type of immersive visual media technology, 720° virtual tours are developing rapidly and gaining popularity in various industries, such as online museum experiences. However, there is limited research on the user acceptance of 720° virtual tours. By reviewing the literature on technology acceptance theories, this study explores the factors affecting users' acceptance of 720° virtual tour systems based on the Unified Theory of Acceptance and the Use of Technology (UTAUT). We conducted a survey study and collected 150 responses. The analysis showed consistent results with UTAUT and confirmed the positive impacts of performance expectancy, effort expectancy, social influence, and facilitating conditions on behavioral intention. In addition, our study contributes to the understanding of technology acceptance of 720° virtual tour systems by introducing three constructs related to the technology and user characteristics: immersion, interaction, and personal innovativeness. Based on the research results, we propose some practical suggestions for the design and development of 720° virtual tour systems for future online museum experiences.

Y. Li · H.-N. Liang (✉)
Department of Computing, School of Advanced Technology, Xi'an Jiaotong-Liverpool University, Suzhou, China
e-mail: haining.liang@xjtlu.edu.cn

Y. Li
e-mail: yue.li@xjtlu.edu.cn

J. Liang · E. Yang
School of Advanced Technology, Xi'an Jiaotong-Liverpool University, Suzhou, China
e-mail: jiachen.liang21@student.xjtlu.edu.cn

E. Yang
e-mail: enhao.yang20@alumni.xjtlu.edu.cn

F. Liarokapis et al. (eds.), *Interactive Media for Cultural Heritage*, Springer Series on Cultural Computing, https://doi.org/10.1007/978-3-031-61018-9_6

6.1 Introduction

Virtual Reality (VR) allows immersive experiences and supports rich and natural interactions with the virtual environment (Violante et al. 2019; Nanjappan et al. 2018; Lu et al. 2023) When using VR, users are isolated from the real world and are able to interact with computer-generated, virtual content, usually through a head-mounted display (HMD) and hand-held controllers or hand gestures (Yu et al. 2018; Shi et al. 2023; Yu et al. 2021; Wang et al. 2023). As an emerging visual media technology, 720° virtual tour systems bring immersive experiences to users by providing a 720° viewing perspective of the digital content (Domański et al. 2017). It supports both immersive devices such as HMDs and 2D displays such as PCs and mobile devices. Compared to VR systems that often require significant resources and technical support in the design, development, and operations, a 720° virtual tour system is an alternative that shows a simpler development approach, lower creation cost, and wider application scenarios (Mabrook and Singer 2019; Wang and Wang 2021). 720° virtual tour systems have been increasingly applied in remote museum experiences (Kalving et al. 2022) and online education (Rupp et al. 2019).

Museums in China have been actively adopting 720° technologies for online experiences. A recent study showed hundreds of exhibitions curated and published online in China, most of which are based on panoramic technologies (Wang and Wang 2021). These authors discussed the advantages of 720° technologies in online virtual museum experiences, which can be summarized in four key aspects: (1) fast production regardless of the complexity of the exhibition layout, (2) flexible and customizable digital content creation, (3) effective copyright protection through watermarking and domain access control, and (4) rich presentation forms of exhibits and multimedia support. Researchers also identified that compared to onsite visits, 720° virtual tours enable the display of the museum exhibits with information fusion (Shan et al. 2021) and break the limitations of storage and time (Zhang and Xue 2023). In addition, social functions such as likes and sharing are afforded by 720° virtual tour systems deployed on the web, which contribute to users' effective social learning of cultural heritage (Li and Xiao 2021; Zhang and Xue 2023).

The potential benefits of a technology depend heavily on users' willingness to use it (Vallade et al. 2021). Previous work has shown efforts in the design, development, and evaluation of the usability of 720° virtual tour systems, especially in the field of education (Rupp et al. 2019; Sultan et al. 2019; Violante et al. 2019). However, user acceptance of 720° virtual tour systems is still not well understood. Many theories have been proposed to study technology acceptance and use, such as the Technology Acceptance Model (TAM) (Davis 1989) and the Unified Theory of Acceptance and Use of Technology (UTAUT) (Venkatesh et al. 2003). These theories and models have been applied and tested in various domains, usually with extended constructs. This chapter presents a study that attempts to fill the research gap by investigating the user acceptance of 720° virtual tour systems, with a particular focus on the theoretical frameworks for the use of immersive technologies.

This study aims to identify the main factors that affect the user acceptance of 720° virtual tour systems for online museum experiences. Considering the technology and user characteristics, we extended the UTAUT with three new constructs: immersion, interaction, and personal innovativeness. We collected 150 survey responses and tested the proposed research model. The results showed that users' behavioral intention is positively influenced by performance expectancy, effort expectancy, social influence, and facilitating conditions, as indicated in UTAUT. In addition, immersion and interaction positively influence performance expectancy and effort expectancy; personal innovativeness positively influences users' performance expectancy. Based on the results, we discuss implications and provide suggestions for the design of 720° virtual tour systems for online museum experiences.

The following sections are structured as follows. We first present a background of online museum experiences, 720° technologies, and the theoretical basis of technology acceptance. Next, we present our research model and introduce the research hypotheses. After explaining the data collection methods, we present the analysis results and show the validation of the hypotheses. The results and implications are then discussed, and a conclusion is drawn.

6.2 Background

6.2.1 Online Museum Experiences: From 2D to 3D

An online museum, sometimes referred to as a virtual museum, is defined as "a means to establish access, context, and outreach by using information technology" (Schweibenz 1998). It is an extension of the physical museum that presents content in any digital form, such as photographs of museum exhibits and 3D reconstructed collections.

Various forms of media have been used for online museum experiences. In the early days, online museum experiences primarily used images and sometimes videos to showcase museum exhibits, accompanied by text descriptions. These images and videos are often shown on 2D displays, presenting museum collections with a particular focus on the visual details. A recent growing trend in online museum experiences is to show collections in 3D (Perry et al. 2017), including reconstructions of the museum artifacts and the space around them.

Previous work has explored approaches to presenting immersive museum experiences. For example, (Bruno et al. 2010) adopted a large screen display with 3D glasses so that visitors can obtain stereoscopic views of the archaeological findings. Haydar et al. (2011) adopted a similar projection based approach with a large screen display, a head-mounted viewing device, and hand-held interaction devices for interactive visualizations of underwater archaeology. However, these are often included as part of a physical exhibition set up, but not for online museum experiences.

Researchers have also explored ways to present 3D museum collections through web-based approaches. For example, (Wojciechowski et al. 2004) introduced the ARCO system that supported the use of VR and Augmented Reality (AR) technologies to view reconstructed cultural objects. Specifically, they adopted AR markers and see-through HMDs for the triggering of the 3D models of museum collections and allowed users to use a standard mouse and keyboard to interact with the web interface menus and use other inputs such as touchscreens and physical marker manipulations to interact with the augmented 3D representations (Liarokapis 2007). The web-based approach is free from geographic constraints and offers the opportunity for a wider audience to visit museums online. However, although the use of novel technologies such as VR and AR can enable 3D views, these technologies have not been widely accepted nor applied in current online museum experiences. The main challenge lies in the need for specialized hardware, such as head-mounted displays.

720° virtual tour systems, on the other hand, have gained significant popularity in China. During the pandemic, the Ministry of Culture and Tourism of the People's Republic of China has jointly initiated 50 online exhibitions with numerous art galleries and museums nationwide (Ministry of Culture and Tourism of the People's Republic of China 2020), most of which adopted 720° technologies. These online exhibitions balance visual quality and accessibility, enabling the presentation of high-resolution virtual tours on standard devices such as personal computers and smartphones. While the exhibitions may not be as immersive and may offer limited interactivity compared to VR experiences, they effectively address the limitations of devices and ensure engagement with the public audience.

6.2.2 Virtual Reality and 720° Technologies

Immersive visual media technologies can simulate the surroundings of the museum objects and users, supporting them to feel a sense of being there in the 3D virtual environment (Ch'ng et al. 2020; Liu et al. 2021). In addition, interactions with digital content can be supported in these systems (Bruno et al. 2010). The sense of immersion and the interactive features differentiate VR and 720° virtual tour systems from online museum experiences based on traditional media and 2D displays.

Although 720° technologies are sometimes included in or referred to as VR technologies, we would like to make a distinction here. As defined by Brooks (1999), a VR experience is '*any in which the user is effectively immersed in a responsive virtual world*'. Specifically, the visual display is a completely simulated virtual world that blocks out the real world, and a VR system provides real-time rendering of the virtual environment based on users' dynamic control of their viewpoints and locations. Although web-based 720° virtual tours on PCs and mobile devices present immersive panoramas, given that users are not in a completely simulated virtual world, they are not true VR experiences.

720° technologies also differ from VR in content creation and the degree of control. Unlike VR, which may present artificial environments from 3D modeling,

720° virtual tour systems are usually based on panoramic views created from images of real physical spaces. Hu et al. (2017) described a technical framework of 3D virtual museum creation based on hybrid 3D data, which included panoramic images collected from laser scanning and some 3D modeling data to complement the scene. Based on high-resolution photos, this approach preserves visual details to a great extent. Achieving such high visual fidelity in VR requires a greater amount of data for 3D reconstruction. Recent advancements in hardware and software allow even faster creation of 720° panoramas. Tools such as PTGui[1] and Pano2VR[2] among others were used in some recent works (Cao et al. 2022; Shan et al. 2021; Wang and Wang 2021). These tools support panoramic image editing and stitching, as well as path planning for virtual navigation. By stitching images to create a panorama and integrating multiple panoramas into a path, a panoramic scene can be displayed, allowing users to move around and change viewing perspectives both horizontally and vertically (Violante et al. 2019). While 360° videos typically display a view from a fixed camera spot (such as in (Cai et al. 2018; Hayes and Yoo 2018; Kalving et al. 2022)), 720° systems allow users to travel between different teleport points. However, the control over navigation in 720° virtual tour systems is not as free as in VR. Users can only navigate among the preset camera positions, making continuous movements within the panoramic scene unsupported.

The web-based approach of 720° virtual tour systems makes online museum experiences accessible from a variety of devices, including mobile devices, personal computers, as well as VR HMDs. Accessing it using HMDs was found to have suffered from the lack of personal contact and missing multimodal contextual cues (Kalving et al. 2022). Still, thanks to the ubiquity of personal devices, 720° virtual tour systems are currently widely used in online museum experiences, such as historical sites (Li and Huang 2022; Li and Xiao 2021), indoor exhibition halls in museums (Hu et al. 2017; Shan et al. 2021), and outdoor archaeological sites (Sun et al. 2020). Extensive research has been conducted to show the design and implementation of panoramic virtual tour systems (Hayes and Yoo 2018; Hu et al. 2017; Lee and Tsai 2015). Nevertheless, the acceptance of technology and users' intention to use the systems are still not understood.

6.2.3 Technology Acceptance Theories

The theoretical studies of technology acceptance have a long history and there were models and theories being proposed from different perspectives. Examples include the Theory of Reasoned Action (TRA) (Fishbein and Ajzen 1977), the Motivational Model (MM) (Davis et al. 1992), the Theory of Planned Behavior (TPB) (Ajzen 1985), the Technology Acceptance Model (TAM) (Davis 1989) and TAM 2 (Venkatesh and Davis 2000), the Combined TAM and TPB (C-TAM-TPB) (Taylor

[1] https://ptgui.com/.

[2] https://ggnome.com/pano2vr/.

and Todd 1995), the Social Cognitive Theory (SCT) (Heffernan 1988), the Unified Theory of Acceptance and Use of Technology (UTAUT) (Venkatesh et al. 2003), and the UTAUT 2 (Venkatesh et al. 2012). In this section, we briefly review the key theories that have been widely adopted in existing works.

In the 1970s, (Fishbein and Ajzen 1977) proposed the Theory of Reasoned Action (TRA) and identified the effects of attitude and subjective norms on the intention to use. The TRA model has been widely considered as a general model for understanding the behavioral intention and users' behavior (Aleassa et al. 2011; Bhattacherjee and Lin 2015; Nor et al. 2008; Shih and Fang 2006). TRA assumes that each individual's use intention of a new technology is a personal rational process, without considering external influences. However, the interference of external factors can not be excluded or underestimated in practical applications, which limits the explanatory power of TRA for use behavior.

In the 1980s, (Davis 1989) proposed the Technology Acceptance Model (TAM), focusing on the relationship between attitude and intention in TRA. This model shows that individuals' attitude toward use is determined by two factors: perceived usefulness and perceived ease of use; their attitude and perceived usefulness jointly determine users' behavioral intention. TAM is one of the most known and applied theories of technology acceptance. In the 2000s, (Venkatesh and Davis 2000) revised TAM and proposed TAM 2. The revised model considered subjective norms in TRA, which were not considered in TAM. It included factors related to social influence and cognitive instrumental process and identified them as determinants of perceived usefulness. TAM 2 showed that perceived usefulness is the most important impact that influences behavioral intention (Venkatesh 2000).

Considering the effects of external variables and various theoretical models proposed for technology acceptance, (Venkatesh et al. 2003) proposed the Unified Theory of Acceptance and Use of Technology (UTAUT). Compared with previous models such as TAM, UTAUT demonstrated higher prediction power of users' behavioral intention (Lee et al. 2003; Wedlock and Trahan 2019). In addition, (Venkatesh et al. 2003) confirmed through empirical studies that behavioral intention has a direct effect on users' use behavior. UTAUT summarizes the factors that influence individual behavior into four core constructs: performance expectancy, effort expectancy, social influence, and facilitating conditions. In addition, four moderating variables were found to have significant effects: age, gender, experience, and voluntariness of use. In the 2010s, (Venkatesh et al. 2012) extended it to UTAUT 2 by adding three variables to the original UTAUT model: hedonic motivation, price value, and habit. It was found to have improved the variance explained in behavioral intention and use behavior.

Previous work has investigated the technology acceptance of immersive technologies in various domains, such as cultural heritage and tourism (Ch'ng et al. 2020; Haugstvedt and Krogstie 2012; Jung et al. 2018; Li et al. 2018; tom Dieck and Jung 2018), education and training (Barrett et al. 2023; Monteiro et al. 2022; Shen et al. 2019), and exercising (Xu et al. 2023b). Many of these studies extended the TAM or UTAUT by considering features of the technology and user characteristics. For example, (Barrett et al. 2023) considered the effects of immersion, interaction, and imagination on the intention to use VR for Chinese language education; users' personal innovativeness was considered in their use of AR applications for urban heritage tourism (tom Dieck and Jung 2018; Monteiro et al. 2022) studied the role of self-efficacy in the use of VR for practical learning. These factors were found to have a significant impact on the perceived usefulness (or performance expectancy) and perceived ease of use (or effort expectancy). While 720° virtual tour systems share similar technology characteristics, the impact of immersion and interaction on its acceptance has not been examined. Understanding the effects of technology features and user characteristics not only provides useful insights into the use of the technology but also helps guide the design of the information systems and user experiences.

6.3 Research Methodology

6.3.1 Research Model

In this study, we aim to explore the factors influencing user acceptance of 720° virtual tour systems for online museum experiences. After reviewing the related work, we propose our research model based on the UTAUT model (see Fig. 6.1). We did not choose UTAUT 2 because the 720° virtual tour systems for online museum experiences are usually free of charge, and it is not a system developed for habitual use. Thus, price value and habit are not relevant to the context of our study. In addition, previous work showed that the positive effects of hedonic motivation on behavioral intention were significant for immersive VR systems using a VR HMD (an HTC Vive) but not significant for desktop VR systems (Huang 2020). Given that 720° virtual tour systems are most likely to be viewed on PC and mobile devices, we opted to situate our study on the existing work and extend the original UTAUT model. In the next section, we explain the proposed hypotheses in detail.

6.3.2 Hypotheses

Our proposed research model includes nine constructs: Interaction (IN), Immersion (IM), Performance Expectancy (PE), Personal Innovativeness (PI), Effort Expectancy (EE), Social Influence (SI), Facilitating Conditions (FC), Behavioral Intention (BI), and Use Behavior (UB).

Immersion and Interaction. Immersion and interaction are the key features of immersive visual media technologies. Immersion is defined as the sense that users feel as if they are in a virtual environment when using a virtual technology (Witmer and Singer 1998). In contrast to the static image displays, 720° virtual tour systems enable real-time interactions that are instantly responsive to users' inputs. Previous research

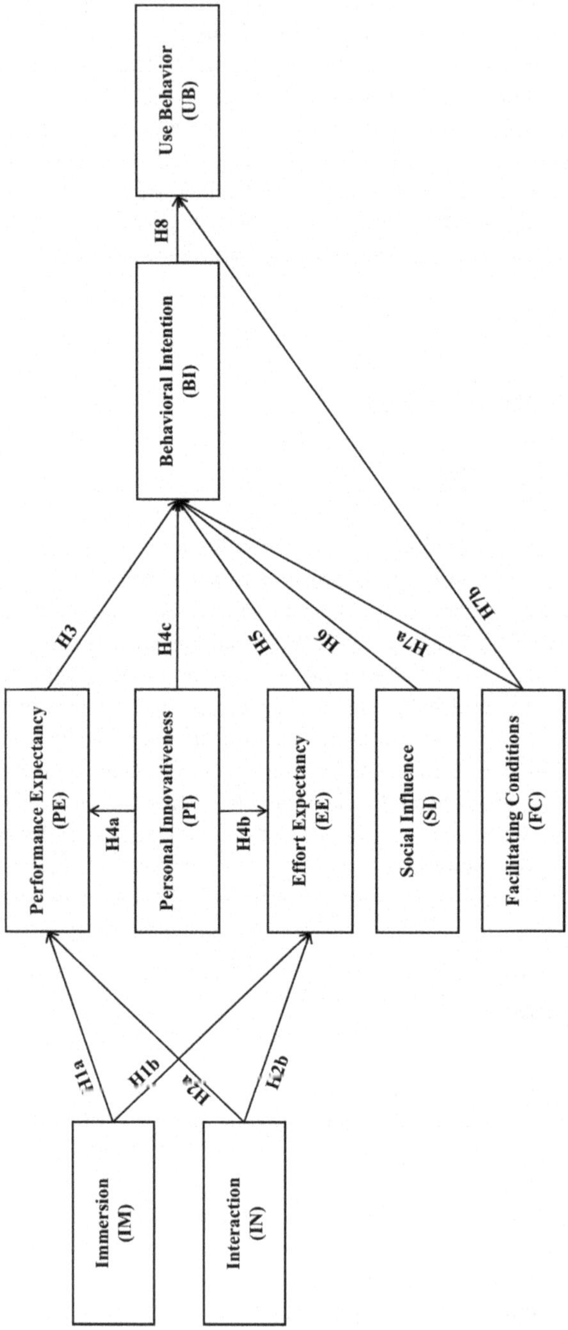

Fig. 6.1 Proposed research model

has examined the role of immersion and interaction on users' perceived usefulness and perceived ease of use (Barrett et al. 2023). These two factors correspond to the performance expectancy and effort expectancy constructs in UTAUT. Given the positive relationship shown in the literature, we hypothesize that

H1a: Immersion in 720° virtual tour systems has a positive impact on PE.

H1b: Immersion in 720° virtual tour systems has a positive impact on EE.

H2a: Interaction in 720° virtual tour systems has a positive impact on PE.

H2b: Interaction in 720° virtual tour systems has a positive impact on EE.

Performance Expectancy. PE reflects the usefulness, task completion efficiency, or the achievement of performance perceived by users. It is the most powerful predictor of users' behavioral intention (Venkatesh et al. 2003). In this study, the PE indicates that the use of 720° virtual tour systems meets their expectations of online museum experiences. For example, the system helps users obtain cultural and historical knowledge more efficiently during online museum visits. Therefore, we propose that

H3: PE has a positive impact on the BI to use 720° virtual tour systems.

Personal Innovativeness. PI is defined as an individual's willingness to accept any innovative technology and take the time to try it (Agarwal and Prasad 1998). It was shown to have a significant positive impact on perceived usefulness and perceived ease of use (Kim and Forsythe 2010; Lee et al. 2006; tom Dieck and Jung 2018). Previous work has also highlighted that personal innovativeness directly affects users' intention to use innovative information technologies (Fagan et al. 2012; Yi et al. 2006). Similarly, 720° virtual tour systems share novel characteristics of VR. We propose that

H4a: PI has a positive impact on the PE of 720° virtual tour systems.

H4b: PI has a positive impact on the EE of 720° virtual tour systems.

H4c: PI has a positive impact on the BI to use 720° virtual tour systems.

Effort Expectancy. EE is defined as the user's perception of the difficulty of using the system (Venkatesh et al. 2003). Prior research has shown that this factor strongly influences users' intention to use a technology (Matli and Ngoepe 2021; Rezaei and Ghofranfarid 2018; Venkatesh et al. 2003). Therefore, EE is considered the main predictor in the model, and we hypothesize that

H5: EE has a positive impact on the BI to use 720° virtual tour systems.

Social Influence. SI refers to the extent to which someone believes and adopts the opinions of others. Previous research has shown that social influence is a significant influencing factor of behavioral intention (Monteiro et al. 2022; Venkatesh et al. 2003). Thus, we propose that

H6: SI has a positive impact on the BI to use 720° virtual tour systems.

Facilitating Conditions. FC reflects the effect of users' knowledge and resources on their willingness to use a technology (Venkatesh et al. 2003). In previous studies, FC was considered to have a direct effect on users' intention to use, as well as the use behavior (Venkatesh et al. 2012). For 720° virtual tour systems, users may opt out of using the system if they feel a lack of guidance and instructions. Therefore, we hypothesize that

H7a: FC have a positive impact on the BI to use 720° virtual tour systems.

H7b: FC have a positive impact on the use behavior of 720° virtual tour systems.

Behavioral Intention. BI refers to a person's long-term plan and decision to adopt a technology. It is the key construct that has been adopted by most technology acceptance models (Venkatesh et al. 2003). Venkatesh et al. (2012) demonstrated that BI has a positive impact on use behavior. Thus, we propose that

H8: BI to use 720° virtual tour systems has a positive impact on the use behavior.

6.3.3 Data Collection and Analysis

An online survey study was conducted to collect users' responses to the identified constructs. The survey includes three parts: basic information about participant demographics, questionnaire items about the proposed constructs, and open-ended questions for comments and suggestions. Participants were asked to explore three 720° virtual tour systems for online museum experiences that are publicly available, including the *Palace Museum*,[3] *Suzhou Museum*,[4] and *ShaanXi History Museum*[5] (see Fig. 6.2). We selected them because they are national first-grade museums in China and thus have good quality control of the system usability and content. In addition, the three systems show a good coverage of online museum experiences about historical sites, indoor museum spaces, and archaeological sites. Figure 6.3 shows some example interactions supported in the 720° virtual tour systems.

The survey was distributed on Chinese social media using convenience and snowball sampling methods. The study followed the following procedure. First, we invited participants to read the information sheet and provide their consent. Following this, participants were asked to click on the links of the three 720° virtual tour systems and explore the online exhibitions. In order to obtain reliable evaluations, participants were required to confirm that they had completed the virtual tours before filling out the questionnaire. The questionnaire includes four questions about demographic information, including age, gender, device used, and technology familiarity. Participants were invited to evaluate their experiences and provide ratings for the measurement items, as shown in Table 6.1. They were instructed to rate on a Likert scale from 1

[3] https://pano.dpm.org.cn/.

[4] https://www.szmuseum.com/0pano/new/pano/index.html.

[5] http://hxmbh.sxhm.com:6868/pano/vrshow/showhxm.html?t=20210209142453245358.

Fig. 6.2 Screenshots of three 720° virtual tour systems for online museum experiences: The Palace Museum (top), Suzhou Museum (middle), and Shaanxi History Museum (bottom)

Fig. 6.3 Example interactions supported in the online museum experiences, including interactive labels, image and text descriptions, a close-up view of the mural, and a puzzle game

Table 6.1 Measurement items of the constructs and the factor loadings

Construct	Item	Description	Loading
IM	IM1	To what extent do you feel about the immersion of this system?	1.000
IN	IN1	To what extent do you feel about the interaction of this system?	1.000
PE	PE1	Using this system enables me to accomplish tasks more quickly	0.957
	PE2	Using this system can meet my requirements more effectively	0.976
	PE3	Using this system can meet my needs for obtaining information	0.944
PI	PI1	Compared with the people around me, I have a higher degree of innovativeness.	0.982
	PI2	I am willing to spend time and energy learning innovative technologies	0.978
EE	EE1	My interaction with this system would be clear and understandable	0.928
	EE2	It would be easy for me to become skillful at using this system	0.937
	EE3	Learning to operate this system is easy for me	0.918

(continued)

(strongly disagree) to 5 (strongly agree), and 'this system' in the statements refers to the 720° virtual tour systems. The final part of the questionnaire includes open-ended questions eliciting participants' comments about system limitations and suggestions for improvements. This study has been approve by the University Ethics Committee of Xi'an Jiaotong-Liverpool University.

Table 6.1 (continued)

Construct	Item	Description	Loading
SI	SI1	I care if people who are important to me think that I should use this system	0.956
	SI2	The publicity of the system in my surroundings will encourage me to try to use this system	0.962
FC	FC1	I have control over using this system	0.974
	FC2	I have the resources and knowledge necessary to use this system	0.952
	FC3	If I get guidance and instructions, I will use this system	0.917
BI	BI1	I am willing to use this system	0.846
	BI2	I intend to use this system in the next few months	0.838
	BI3	I am willing to recommend this system to people around me	0.818
UB	UB1	I am using this system	0.818
	UB2	I recommended my friend to use this system	0.821
	UB3	I will continue to use this system in the future	0.820

The survey data was analyzed using IBM SPSS Statistics and SmartPLS. We performed descriptive statistics on the demographics data and conducted structural equation model analysis to verify the research model and the proposed hypotheses.

6.4 Results

6.4.1 Participant Demographics

In total, we received 150 valid responses (85 females and 65 males). Participants aged between 18 and 35 (M = 23.19, SD = 2.68). More than half of the participants (55.33%) used PC when experiencing the 720° virtual tour systems, followed by smartphones (34.67%) and tablets (9.33%). On a 5-point Likert scale (5 = Very familiar), participants were familiar with the technology (M = 3.81, SD = 0.93). Overall, participants reported a high degree of interaction (M = 3.95, SD = 0.96) and immersion (M = 3.96, SD = 0.91) when using the 720° virtual tour systems.

6.4.2 Measurement Reliability and Validity

We analyzed the reliability and validity to examine the robustness of the measurement model. Specifically, we examined the Cronbach's alpha (CA) and composite reliability (CR) values for all constructs to test the internal reliability. For the convergent validity of the research models, we calculated the average variance extracted (AVE) of each construct for assessment. The results are shown in Table 6.2.

Comparing our results to the suggested thresholds (Fornell and Larcker 1981), the CA values for all constructs were above the standard value of 0.7 and ranged from 0.756 to 1.000, showing a high measurement reliability. The CR values were above the standard value of 0.7 and ranged from 0.757 to 1.000, which means that the constructs have high internal consistency. Overall, the measurement model shows a good reliability.

Table 6.2 Measurement validity and reliability results, showing the Cronbach's Alpha (CA), Composite Reliability (CR), and Average Variance Extracted (AVE)

Construct	CA	CR	AVE
Immersion	1.000	1.000	1.000
Interaction	1.000	1.000	1.000
Performance expectancy	0.956	0.957	0.919
Personal innovativeness	0.959	0.966	0.961
Effort expectancy	0.919	0.922	0.861
Social influence	0.912	0.916	0.919
Facilitating conditions	0.943	0.946	0.898
Behavioral intention	0.781	0.782	0.696
Use behavior	0.756	0.757	0.672

Table 6.3 Analysis results of discriminant validity

	EE	FC	IM	IN	PE	PI	SI
EE	**0.928**						
FC	0.925	**0.948**					
IM	0.872	0.880	**1.000**				
IN	0.851	0.787	0.682	**1.000**			
PE	0.923	0.947	0.892	0.733	**0.959**		
PI	0.811	0.918	0.892	0.681	0.893	**0.980**	
SI	0.865	0.923	0.899	0.752	0.896	0.942	**0.959**

In addition, the factor loadings of all measurement items were greater than the critical value of 0.7, ranging from 0.818 to 1.000 (see Table 6.1). The AVE values of all constructs were greater than the critical value of 0.5, ranging from 0.672 to 1.000. This indicates a high level of convergent validity of the measurement model.

For discriminant validity (Fornell and Larcker 1981), we examined the square root of AVE of each construct to check if it is greater than its correlation with other constructs (see Table 6.3). The results showed that all values on the diagonal were greater than the values in the same column and row; namely, the square root of AVE of the latent variables was greater than the correlation coefficient with all variables. Therefore, the measurement model shows acceptable discriminant validity.

6.4.3 *Structural Equation Modeling Analysis and Hypotheses Testing*

We adopted partial least squares (PLS) regression and bootstrap resampling method to conduct the structural equation modeling analysis. To evaluate the overall quality of the research model, we analyzed the coefficient of determination (R^2) to test the predictive power of the model and the predictive relevance (Q^2) to establish the predictive relevance of the endogenous constructs.

Coefficient of determination (R^2). The results showed that the R^2 of PE, EE, BI, and UB were 0.858, 0.883, 0.973, and 0.587, respectively, implying that the structural model has substantial ($R^2 > 0.75$) predictive power for PE, EE, and BI, and moderate ($R^2 > 0.5$) predictive power for UB (Hair et al. 2011).

Predicting relevance (Q^2). We also checked the value of Q^2 to examine the predicting relevance (Geisser 1974; Stone 1974). The results showed that the Q^2 of BI and UB were 0.663 and 0.381, respectively. Both values are greater than zero (Leguina 2015), indicating that the structural model has acceptable predictive relevance.

Hypotheses testing. Table 6.4 and Fig. 6.4 include the detailed statistics of the path coefficients and the hypotheses testing results. With the confirmation of significance

Table 6.4 Path coefficients (β) and hypotheses testing results

Hypothetical path	β	SD	t statistics	p value	Result
H1a: IM → PE	0.406	0.057	7.102	**0.000**	Supported
H1b: IM → EE	0.550	0.060	9.220	**0.000**	Supported
H2a: IN → PE	0.177	0.041	4.261	**0.000**	Supported
H2b: IN → EE	0.480	0.036	13.471	**0.000**	Supported
H3: PE → BI	0.278	0.042	6.555	**0.000**	Supported
H4a: PI → PE	0.411	0.066	6.234	**0.000**	Supported
H4b: PI → EE	−0.006	0.060	0.104	0.917	Not supported
H4c: PI → BI	−0.004	0.047	0.089	0.929	Not supported
H5: EE → BI	0.235	0.039	6.056	**0.000**	Supported
H6: SI → BI	0.138	0.051	2.715	**0.007**	Supported
H7a: FC → BI	0.369	0.048	7.624	**0.000**	Supported
H7b: FC → UB	0.080	0.232	0.346	0.729	Not supported
H8: BI → UB	0.688	0.224	3.069	**0.002**	Supported

of H1a ($\beta = 0.406$, $p<0.001$), H1b ($\beta = 0.550$, $p < 0.001$), H2a ($\beta = 0.177$, $p < 0.001$), and H2b ($\beta = 0.480$, $p<0.001$), it can be inferred that both immersion and interaction have significant positive effects on performance expectancy and effort expectancy. In addition, since H4a ($\beta = 0.411$, $p<0.001$) is supported and H4b ($\beta = -0.006$, n.s.) is rejected according to the results, personal innovativeness only has a significant positive impact on performance expectancy. The proposed H3 ($\beta = 0.278$, $p<0.001$), H5 ($\beta=0.235$, $p < 0.001$), H6 ($\beta = 0.138$, $p < 0.01$), and H7a ($\beta = 0.369$, $p<0.001$) were confirmed. Performance expectancy, effort expectancy, social influence, and facilitating conditions have a significant positive impact on behavioral intention. Besides, H8 is also supported ($\beta = 0.688$, $p < 0.01$), confirming that behavioral intention has a significant positive impact on use behavior.

6.5 Discussion

Our investigation of the technology acceptance of 720° virtual tour systems showed that users' behavioral intention is positively influenced by performance expectancy, effort expectancy, social influence, and facilitating conditions. Users' behavioral intention positively influences their use behavior. These are consistent with the UTAUT model. One exception was that facilitating conditions did not show a significant influence on use behavior of 720° virtual tour systems. This indicates that

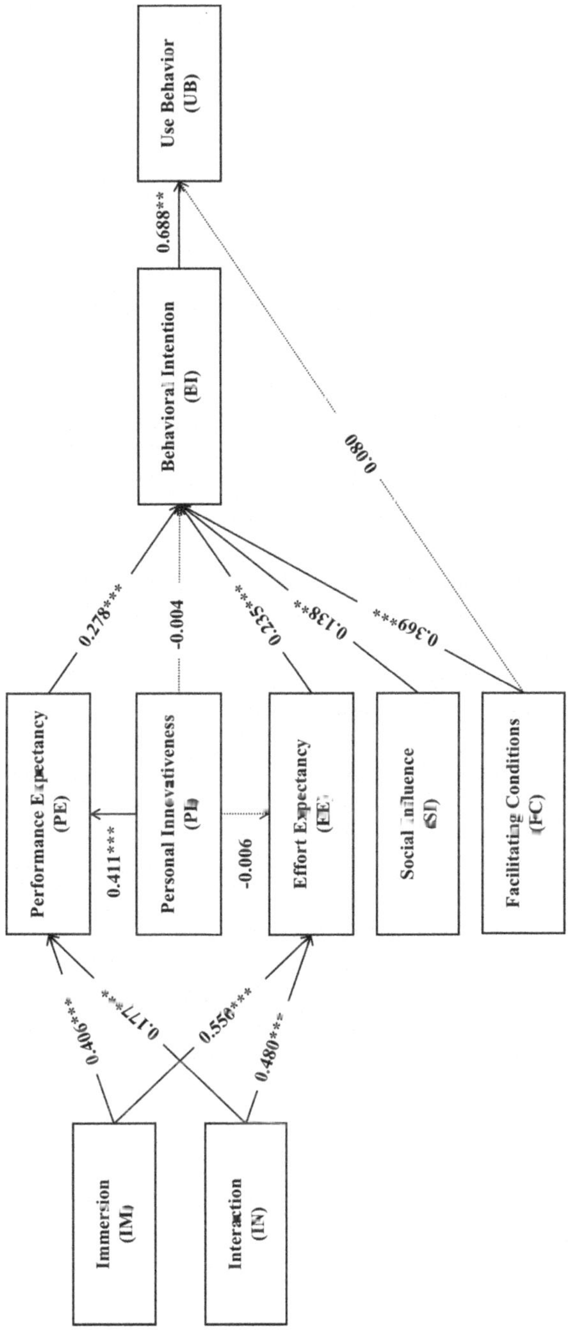

Fig. 6.4 Model validation results. Values on the path are coefficients (β). $^*p<0.05$; $^{**}p<0.01$; $^{***}p<0.001$. A dashed line indicates an insignificant path

while having facilitating conditions contributes to users' intention to use the system, it is insignificant when users are actually using it.

Based on UTAUT, we introduced three constructs related to technology and user characteristics in our research model, namely immersion, interaction, and personal innovativeness. Our results showed that immersion and interaction have positive impacts on performance expectancy and effort expectancy. Personal innovativeness has a positive impact on performance expectancy but shows no direct influence on effort expectancy or behavioral intention. Here, we discuss our findings in detail.

6.5.1 Immersion and Interaction in 720° Virtual Tour Systems

We examined the technology characteristics of 720° virtual tour systems, namely immersion and interaction, and found them to be significant antecedents of performance expectancy and effort expectancy. The positive effects of immersion indicate that the sense of being there in the virtual space facilitates users' expectations of their performance and effort. The higher the degree of immersion perceived by users, the more likely that users will find the system useful and easy to use. Immersion is arguably the greatest technology characteristic of 720° virtual tour systems. Thus, immersive experiences should be prioritized to increase users' intention to use the technology. Suggestions such as to '*improve the image clarity*' and '*avoid the lagging between the transitions*' were provided by participants for improving immersion.

Our results on the effect of interaction slightly differ from the findings in (Barrett et al. 2023). In their study, they found a significant effect of interaction on effort expectancy but not performance expectancy. In addition, the effect of effort expectancy on the intention to use was not significant. The authors discussed that their participants encountered some difficulties when interacting with the VR system. However, in our case, participants found the 720° virtual tour systems easy to use, and the impact of interaction on behavioral intention mediated by effort expectancy was found significant. When examining the suggestions left by participants in the open-ended questions, we found that they expected the system to be more interactive. For example, a participant commented that '*the interactive experience needs improvement*', and they hope to '*add more interactions to make the system more interesting*'. These have pointed to the need for rich interactive features to engage users in the future design of 720° virtual tour systems.

6.5.2 Personal Innovativeness in the Adoption of Novel Technologies

As a new construct introduced in our model, personal innovativeness was found to have a significant positive influence on performance expectancy. Users with a high degree of personal innovativeness are more likely to find the 720° virtual tour systems useful in obtaining cultural and historical knowledge. This will contribute to their intention to use it for online museum visits. While previous work showed a direct influence of personal innovativeness on behavioral intention (Fagan et al. 2012; Yi et al. 2006), our study showed that this effect is fully mediated by performance expectancy.

Our survey sample included a large number of responses from age groups that are relatively young. Previous work showed that teenagers and young adults are user groups who are willing to try out new things and learn new technologies (Xu et al. 2023a). Our participants reported that they found the system '*very easy to use*' and '*much cooler than the real museum*'. For cultural institutions that attempt to adopt 720° virtual tour systems for online museum experiences, it would be reasonable to target these user groups who are naturally keen to use novel technologies. This is in line with observations and findings in previous research on innovative technology use.

6.5.3 Implications for System Design and Development

Based on the above analysis and results, we suggest the following design guidelines for the design and development of 720° virtual tour systems in the future.

First, ensure image clarity and smooth transitions between 720° panoramic views. Our results showed that immersion has a strong effect on both performance expectancy and effort expectancy; thus, it should be prioritized for 720° virtual tour systems. Participants' responses in the questionnaire showed that immersion is closely related to the image quality and users' control over movements in the virtual environment, such as the smoothness in transitions between panoramas. These inform the design to improve users' immersion of the 720° virtual tour systems. This will contribute to users' performance expectancy and effort expectancy, and improve their intention to use the technology.

Second, design for interactive and playful narratives. Participants reported that they enjoyed the interactive experience in the online experience of Shaanxi History Museum: '*I like that I can play interactive games in the scene*'. The system (see Fig. 6.3) provided detailed information by placing interactive icons on top of the panoramic view. It also adopted some playful settings, such as letting users reassemble a stone gate from ruins through a puzzle game. These interactions have received positive feedback from participants. Designing such interactions with rich cultural knowledge and engaging gameplay will contribute to users' performance expectancy, effort expectancy, and intention to use the system.

Third, provide a comprehensive introduction to the historical and cultural background during the tour and make use of multimedia where appropriate. From the questionnaire results, we found that participants were concerned about gaining historical and cultural knowledge after using the 720° virtual tour systems. For example, several participants commented that they expected to have more detailed descriptions about the architecture, and suggested providing complementary images and texts, and audio guide systems. Therefore, future online museum experiences should provide users with a rich array of media to convey knowledge information that is comprehensive and understandable, to improve their performance expectancy and promote their behavioral intention to use this system.

Fourth, optimize the use for different user groups and provide necessary instructions. While most participants found the system easy to use, one participant pointed out the need to '*add some tutorial functions to help the elderly learn how to use the system*'. Similarly, another comment also highlighted the elderly user group: '*I hope to promote the system so that more people can use it, especially the elderly who cannot travel can use this system to feel that they are traveling*'. Given that effort expectancy has a significant positive impact on behavioral intention, designers should try to make the system easy to access and operate, catering to the needs of different user groups, similar to other applications like games (Xu et al. 2021). Although good designs are often easy to learn and intuitive, beginner guides and supporting instructions can be helpful to the adoption of novel technologies. This also addresses the positive influence of facilitating conditions on behavioral intention.

6.5.4 Limitations and Future Work

This research has some limitations. Although we collected a reasonable sample size, it showed a limited coverage of age groups. Most respondents are young adults aged between 18 and 35. Although the elderly were identified as a potential user group of 720° virtual tour systems, our sample did not include this age group. Future studies should attempt to reach a wider range of user groups. Second, our survey study was conducted online. As a result, it was difficult to strictly control the time users spent on the three 720° virtual tour systems. The differences in the amount of time they spent and the digital content they viewed and interacted with may have influenced their responses. Third, our current research did not consider all factors that may affect the use of 720° virtual tour systems for online museum experiences. We mainly explored factors related to the novel characteristics of the technology. Future work may explore factors that are specific to the museum learning context, such as interest, perceived enjoyment, and learning motivation. In addition, the three systems we selected were possibly created using different hardware, and our participants were using three different devices (PCs, smartphones, and tablets) with varying display sizes and resolutions. While this demonstrates broad device coverage for 720° virtual tour systems, the variance in the platform could elicit different experiences (Lu et al. 2023) and remains a limitation of our data. Finally, the effect of using 720° virtual tour systems should be more systematically evaluated by incorporating a control group, such as individuals participating in actual museum visits. Nevertheless, our study contributes to a deeper understanding of the effects of immersion, interaction, and personal innovativeness on the user acceptance of 720° virtual tour systems, providing insights into the design of future online museum experiences.

6.6 Conclusion

Providing high visual fidelity of museum exhibits with accessibility from standard devices, web-based 720° virtual tour systems have gained significant popularity in the past few years. They facilitate the online display of museum exhibitions and historical sites in high resolution, showcasing significant potential for delivering digitized museum experiences to a wide audience. This research validates a model extended from the Unified Theory of Acceptance and Use of Technology (UTAUT) to understand user acceptance of 720° virtual tour systems for online museum experiences. We introduced two constructs related to technology characteristics (immersion and interaction) and one construct about user characteristics (personal innovativeness). Through the data analysis of 150 online survey responses, we found that (1) immersion and interaction positively influence performance expectancy and effort expectancy; and (2) personal innovativeness has a positive impact on users' performance expectancy, but not effort expectancy or behavioral intention. The positive impacts of performance expectancy, effort expectation, social influence, and facilitating conditions on behavioral intention have also been confirmed. Overall, the proposed model demonstrates substantial predictive power for users' behavioral intention to use 720° virtual tour systems ($R^2 = 0.976$). Based on the findings and participants' suggestions, we suggest design guidelines focusing on the support for immersion and interaction in 720° virtual tour systems, the presentation of knowledge and information for online museum experiences, and the need for facilitating conditions to improve the ease of use for various user groups. Our work contributes to a deeper understanding of user acceptance of 720° virtual tour systems and reveals the significant effects of immersion, interaction, and personal innovativeness on its use for online museum experiences.

Acknowledgements The authors would like to thank all participants for their time and support. This work is supported by the National Natural Science Foundation of China (62207022) and the Natural Science Foundation of the Jiangsu Higher Education Institutions of China (22KJB520038).

References

Agarwal R, Prasad J (1998) A conceptual and operational definition of personal innovativeness in the domain of information technology. Inf Syst Res 9(2):204–215

Ajzen I (1985) From intentions to actions: a theory of planned behavior. In: Action control: From cognition to behavior. Springer, pp 11–39

Aleassa H, Pearson JM, McClurg S (2011) Investigating software piracy in Jordan: an extension of the theory of reasoned action. J Bus Ethics 98:663–676

Barrett A, Pack A, Guo Y, Wang N (2023) Technology acceptance model and multi-user virtual reality learning environments for Chinese language education. Interact Learn Environ 31(3):1665–1682

Bhattacherjee A, Lin CP (2015) A unified model of it continuance: three complementary perspectives and crossover effects. European J Inf Syst 24(4):364–373

Brooks FP (1999) What's real about virtual reality? IEEE Comput Graph Appl 19(6):16–27

Bruno F, Bruno S, De Sensi G, Luchi ML, Mancuso S, Muzzupappa M (2010) From 3d reconstruction to virtual reality: a complete methodology for digital archaeological exhibition. J Cult Herit 11(1):42–49

Cai S, Ch'ng E, Li Y (2018) A comparison of the capacities of VR and 360-degree video for coordinating memory in the experience of cultural heritage. In: 2018 3rd digital heritage international congress (DigitalHERITAGE) held jointly with 2018 24th international conference on virtual systems and multimedia (VSMM 2018). IEEE, pp 1–4

Cao K et al (2022) Development and design case function comparison of panoramic roaming system of virtual museum based on Pano2VR. Mob Inf Syst

Ch'ng E, Li Y, Cai S, Leow FT (2020) The effects of VR environments on the acceptance, experience, and expectations of cultural heritage learning. J Comput Cult Herit (JOCCH) 13(1):1–21

Davis FD (1989) Perceived usefulness, perceived ease of use, and user acceptance of information technology. MIS quarterly, pp 319–340

Davis FD, Bagozzi RP, Warshaw PR (1992) Extrinsic and intrinsic motivation to use computers in the workplace 1. J Appl Soc Psychol 22(14):1111–1132

tom Dieck MC, Jung T (2018) A theoretical model of mobile augmented reality acceptance in urban heritage tourism. Curr Issues Tour 21(2):154–174

Domański M, Stankiewicz O, Wegner K, Grajek T (2017) Immersive visual media-mpeg-i: 360 video, virtual navigation and beyond. In: 2017 International conference on systems, signals and image processing (IWSSIP). IEEE, pp 1–9

Fagan M, Kilmon C, Pandey V (2012) Exploring the adoption of a virtual reality simulation: The role of perceived ease of use, perceived usefulness and personal innovativeness. Campus-Wide Inf Syst 29(2):117–127

Fishbein M, Ajzen I (1977) Belief, attitude, intention, and behavior: an introduction to theory and research

Fornell C, Larcker DF (1981) Structural equation models with unobservable variables and measurement error: algebra and statistics

Geisser S (1974) A predictive approach to the random effect model. Biometrika 61(1):101–107

Hair JF, Ringle CM, Sarstedt M (2011) Pls-sem: indeed a silver bullet. J Mark Theory Pract 19(2):139–152

Haugstvedt AC, Krogstie J (2012) Mobile augmented reality for cultural heritage: a technology acceptance study. In: 2012 IEEE international symposium on mixed and augmented reality (ISMAR). IEEE, pp 247–255

Haydar M, Roussel D, Maïdi M, Otmane S, Mallem M (2011) Virtual and augmented reality for cultural computing and heritage: a case study of virtual exploration of underwater archaeological sites (preprint). Virtual Rity 15:311–327

Hayes J, Yoo K (2018) Virtual reality interactivity in a museum environment. In: Proceedings of the 24th ACM symposium on virtual reality software and technology, pp 1–2

Heffernan CJ (1988) Social foundations of thought and action: a social cognitive theory. Behav Change 5(1):37–38
Hu Q, Yu D, Wang S, Fu C, Ai M, Wang W (2017) Hybrid three-dimensional representation based on panoramic images and three-dimensional models for a virtual museum: Data collection, model, and visualization. Inf Vis 16(2):126–138
Huang FH (2020) Adapting UTAUT2 to assess user acceptance of an e-scooter virtual reality service. Virtual Rlty 24(4):635–643
Jung TH, Lee H, Chung N, tom Dieck MC, (2018) Cross-cultural differences in adopting mobile augmented reality at cultural heritage tourism sites. Int J Contemp Hosp Manag 30(3):1621–1645
Kalving M, Paananen S, Seppälä J, Colley A, Häkkilä J (2022) Comparing VR and desktop 360 video museum tours. In: Proceedings of the 21st international conference on mobile and ubiquitous multimedia, pp 282–284
Kim J, Forsythe S (2010) Factors affecting adoption of product virtualization technology for online consumer electronics shopping. Int J Retail Distrib Manag 38(3):190–204
Lee IC, Tsai F (2015) Applications of panoramic images: from 720 panorama to interior 3d models of augmented reality. Int Arch Photogramm Remote Sens Spat Inf Sci 40:189–192
Lee SM, Kim I, Rhee S, Trimi S (2006) The role of exogenous factors in technology acceptance: The case of object-oriented technology. Inf Manag 43(4):469–480
Lee Y, Kozar KA, Larsen KR (2003) The technology acceptance model: past, present, and future. Commun Assoc Inf Syst 12(1):50
Leguina A (2015) A primer on partial least squares structural equation modeling (pls-sem)
Li W, Huang X (2022) The interactive design and user experience of virtual museums: case study of the virtual palace museum. In: International conference on human-computer interaction. Springer, pp 400–409
Li W, Xiao JX (2021) User experience in digital museums: a case study of the palace museum in Beijing. In: International conference on human-computer interaction. Springer, pp 436–448
Li Y, Ch'ng E, Cai S, See S (2018) Multiuser interaction with hybrid VR and AR for cultural heritage objects. In: 2018 3rd digital heritage international congress (DigitalHERITAGE) held Jointly with 2018 24th international conference on virtual systems and multimedia (VSMM 2018). IEEE, pp 1–8
Liarokapis F (2007) An augmented reality interface for visualizing and interacting with virtual content. Virtual Rlty 11(1):23–43
Liu Y, Lin Y, Shi R, Luo Y, Liang HN (2021) RelicVR: a virtual reality game for active exploration of archaeological relics. In: Extended abstracts of the 2021 annual symposium on computer-human interaction in play, pp 326–332
Lu F, Nanjappan V, Parsons P, Yu L, Liang HN (2023) Effect of display platforms on spatial knowledge acquisition and engagement: an evaluation with 3d geometry visualizations. J Vis 26(3):667–686
Mabrook R, Singer JB (2019) Virtual reality, 360 video, and journalism studies: Conceptual approaches to immersive technologies. Jlsm Stud 20(14):2096–2112
Matli W, Ngoepe M (2021) Extending the unified theory of acceptance and use of technology with the problems of digital access to (re) connect the disconnected neets. Innov: European J Soc Sci Res 1–20
Ministry of Culture and Tourism of the People's Republic of China (2020) Design and application of virtual reality technology in the museum cloud display. http://culture.people.com.cn/GB/22226/431877/431878/index.html Accessed 18 Dec 2023
Monteiro D, Ma T, Li Y, Pan Z, Liang HN (2022) Cross-cultural factors influencing the adoption of virtual reality for practical learning. Universal Access in the Information Society, pp 1–14
Nanjappan V, Liang HN, Lu F, Papangelis K, Yue Y, Man KL (2018) User-elicited dual-hand interactions for manipulating 3d objects in virtual reality environments. Hum-Centric Comput Inf Sci 8(1):1–16
Nor KM, Shanab E, Pearson JM (2008) Internet banking acceptance in Malaysia based on the theory of reasoned action. JISTEM-J Inf Syst Technol Manag 5:03–14

Perry S, Roussou M, Economou M, Young H, Pujol L (2017) Moving beyond the virtual museum: Engaging visitors emotionally. In: 2017 23rd international conference on virtual system and multimedia (VSMM). IEEE, pp 1–8
Rezaei R, Ghofranfarid M (2018) Rural households' renewable energy usage intention in Iran: extending the unified theory of acceptance and use of technology. Renew Energy 122:382–391
Rupp MA, Odette KL, Kozachuk J, Michaelis JR, Smither JA, McConnell DS (2019) Investigating learning outcomes and subjective experiences in 360-degree videos. Comput Educ 128:256–268
Schweibenz W (1998) The"virtual museum": new perspectives for museums to present objects and information using the internet as a knowledge base and communication system. Isi 34:185–200
Shan T, Zhang A, Wang Q, Xing R, Xu Z (2021) Application of virtual panorama technology based on multi-source information fusion in high quality development of the yellow river. In: 2021 IEEE international conference on advances in electrical engineering and computer applications (AEECA). IEEE, pp 590–593
Cw S, Jt H, Ly P, Tc K (2019) Behavioural intentions of using virtual reality in learning: perspectives of acceptance of information technology and learning style. Virtual Rity 23:313–324
Shi R, Zhang J, Yue Y, Yu L, Liang HN (2023) Exploration of bare-hand mid-air pointing selection techniques for dense virtual reality environments. In: Extended abstracts of the 2023 CHI conference on human factors in computing systems, pp 1–7
Shih YY, Fang K (2006) Effects of network quality attributes on customer adoption intentions of internet banking. Total Qual Manag Bus Excel 17(1):61–77
Stone M (1974) Cross-validatory choice and assessment of statistical predictions. J R Stat Soc: Ser B (Methodological) 36(2):111–133
Sultan L, Abuznadah W, Al-Jifree H, Khan MA, Alsaywid B, Ashour F (2019) An experimental study on usefulness of virtual reality 360 in undergraduate medical education. Adv Med Educ Pract 907–916
Sun Y, Wang M, Zhang Y, Zhang C (2020) Application of the innovative design and digital technology in the construction of traditional village digital museum. In: 2020 international conference on innovation design and digital technology (ICIDDT), pp 354–357. https://doi.org/10.1109/ICIDDT52279.2020.00070
Taylor S, Todd PA (1995) Understanding information technology usage: a test of competing models. Inf Syst Res 6(2):144–176
Vallade JI, Kaufmann R, Frisby BN, Martin JC (2021) Technology acceptance model: investigating students' intentions toward adoption of immersive 360 videos for public speaking rehearsals. Commun Educ 70(2):127–145
Venkatesh V (2000) Determinants of perceived ease of use: integrating control, intrinsic motivation, and emotion into the technology acceptance model. Inf Syst Res 11(4):342–365
Venkatesh V, Davis FD (2000) A theoretical extension of the technology acceptance model: four longitudinal field studies. Manag Sci 46(2):186–204
Venkatesh V, Morris MG, Davis GB, Davis FD (2003) User acceptance of information technology: toward a unified view. MIS quarterly, pp 425–478
Venkatesh V, Thong JY, Xu X (2012) Consumer acceptance and use of information technology: extending the unified theory of acceptance and use of technology. MIS quarterly, pp 157–178
Violante MG, Vezzetti E, Piazzolla P (2019) Interactive virtual technologies in engineering education: why not 360° videos? Int J Interact Des Manuf (IJIDeM) 13(2):729–742
Wang C, Wang H (2021) On the status quo and application of online virtual art exhibition technologies. In: 2021 international conference on culture-oriented science and technology (ICCST). IEEE, pp 253–257
Wang Y, Li Y, Liang HN (2023) Comparative analysis of artefact interaction and manipulation techniques in VR Museums: a study of performance and user experience. In: 2023 IEEE international symposium on mixed and augmented reality (ISMAR). IEEE, pp 761–770
Wedlock BC, Trahan MP (2019) Revisiting the unified theory of acceptance and the use of technology (UTAUT) model and scale: an empirical evolution of educational technology. Res Issues Contemp Educ 4(1):6–20

Witmer BG, Singer MJ (1998) Measuring presence in virtual environments: a presence questionnaire. Presence 7(3):225–240

Wojciechowski R, Walczak K, White M, Cellary W (2004) Building virtual and augmented reality museum exhibitions. In: Proceedings of the ninth international conference on 3D Web technology, pp 135–144

Xu N, Li Y, Wei X, Xie L, Yu L, Liang HN (2023a) Cubemuseum ar: a tangible augmented reality interface for cultural heritage learning and museum gifting. Int J Hum–Comput Interact 1–29

Xu W, Liang HN, Yu K, Baghaei N (2021) Effect of gameplay uncertainty, display type, and age on virtual reality exergames. In: Proceedings of the 2021 CHI conference on human factors in computing systems, pp 1–14

Xu W, Liang HN, Yu K, Wen S, Baghaei N, Tu H (2023) Acceptance of virtual reality exergames among Chinese older adults. Int J Hum-Comput Interact 39(5):1134–1148

Yi MY, Fiedler KD, Park JS (2006) Understanding the role of individual innovativeness in the acceptance of it-based innovations: comparative analyses of models and measures. Decis Sci 37(3):393–426

Yu D, Liang HN, Lu F, Nanjappan V, Papangelis K, Wang W et al (2018) Target selection in head-mounted display virtual reality environments. J Univers Comput Sci 24(9):1217–1243

Yu D, Lu X, Shi R, Liang HN, Dingler T, Velloso E, Goncalves J (2021) Gaze-supported 3d object manipulation in virtual reality. In: Proceedings of the 2021 CHI conference on human factors in computing systems, pp 1–13

Zhang T, Xue W (2023) Design and application of virtual reality technology in the museum cloud display. In: Proceedings of the 2nd international conference on information, control and automation, ICICA 2022, 2–4 Dec 2022, Chongqing, China

Part II
Cultural Heritage Preservation and Exploration Through Emerging Digital Technologies

Chapter 7
Immersed in Digital Surrogates: Reconstructing Difficult Heritage of Modern Architecture

Georgios Artopoulos, Nicolas Loucas, and Popi Iacovou

Abstract This chapter presents how immersive technologies can be employed in exhibitions of architectural archives to activate static relationships between archival content and gallery visitors. It starts with a brief description of the evolving landscape of cultural heritage preservation, emphasising community-driven initiatives and participatory processes in safeguarding architecture. The chapter addresses two key aspects: a reevaluation of the preservation-worthy examples of architecture, particularly focusing on Modern architecture, and the implementation of a workflow to enhance Virtual Reality experiences with archival material and lived experiences of local custodians. It is argued that interacting with multiple types of knowledge through immersion contributes to a more comprehensive understanding of architectural history and facilitates public accessibility. This novel approach aims to enrich traditional documentation methods, presenting a case study that exemplifies the integration of immersive 3D real-time visualisation to convey the multifaceted narratives associated with architectural heritage, enriching more traditional means of representation of architecture, such as drawing, models, photographs and video.

Keywords Modern architecture heritage · Architectural exhibition · Inaccessible heritage

7.1 Introduction

Today, historic places can be of any form, such as built environments, architecture of the recent past, ecological zones, or any culturally valuable spatial construction. Scholarly research and international bodies are developing methods and new practices that offer local bearers and custodians of cultural heritage opportunities to

G. Artopoulos (✉) · N. Loucas
The Cyprus Institute, Nicosia, Cyprus
e-mail: g.artopoulos@cyi.ac.cy

P. Iacovou
University of Cyprus, Nicosia, Cyprus

F. Liarokapis et al. (eds.), *Interactive Media for Cultural Heritage*, Springer Series on Cultural Computing, https://doi.org/10.1007/978-3-031-61018-9_7

self-organise and define what needs to be safeguarded for future generations and to propose how heritage should be re-used by social groups and the society in a sustainable way for the future (COE 2005).

In this effort, communities increasingly generate new research enquiries and promote coordinated activities around new heritage topics that go beyond the existing definitions which are recognised by the local regulations, previously established practices or hegemonic views to heritage that are typically guided from the top down by authorities in the field (Laparelli and OMA 2018: 340). In this significant transformation in the field of community heritage, community-driven valorisation and bottom-up processes of safeguarding culturally valuable human products and expressions as examples of immaterial and tangible heritage are considered at the core of the discourse. Now policy makers are working closely with local stakeholders to co-develop sustainable management plans for heritage presentation and re-use through participatory and reflective processes.

Framed by this discussion, in this chapter is occupied with two main aspects that the authors consider relevant to said transformations. First it briefly reflects on the importance of reconsidering the chronological period of architecture that is usually considered as valuable and sensitive enough to be listed for preservation—at least by many authorities in the South-East Europe and Mediterranean. Then the chapter presents the technical details of a digital research that enriches Virtual Reality experiences of studying architectural heritage of the recent past with archival material and lived experiences of a building's past users (i.e. its local custodians). The authors argue that these two points contribute in a more holistic way to the current debate about Modern architecture (i.e. buildings designed respecting the principles and values of modernism, including Bauhaus, International Style and Brutalism, cf. Frampton 1992), than other forms of architectural representation. Addressing the debate about Modern architecture today is relevant to heritage studies and urban regeneration, as many examples of Modern architecture are typically considered by, arguably, the most conservative of authorities and policy makers as questionable of preservation value.

Specifically, the value of these buildings is debated due to the abundance of respective building stock, their construction material (e.g. concrete) that oftentimes is expensive to be conserved and restored, and their low quality of construction, which in combination with lack of maintenance for socio-economic reasons, results in very challenging situations of preservation (Bristol 1991). Other reasons include the standardisation and repetition of building parts and at the same time the lack of ornamentation (considered as examples of craftsmanship and local materiality, and therefore as cultural heritage), or simply due to subjective aesthetic criteria, e.g. valuing concrete as brutal.

Another aspect that challenges the valorization of said cases of architecture history is the lack of significant distance in time to allow for the foregrounding of critical historical views. At the same time though this very characteristic of Modern heritage, i.e. its proximity to the present, is offering us a unique opportunity to access surviving technical reports, visual documentations and press reports, as well as resident/stakeholder memories of their occupation. This rich information is an essential aspect of a valorisation process, as it enables researchers to access tacit knowledge, interpret meaningful points of view of the building, and oftentimes the vision of the building creator, in a multi-vocal way. Approaching local knowledge in a multi-vocal way recognises the coexistence of different perspectives and thus aims to bring into the fore alternative views of other people associated with a building's occupation, its construction process, or even its life after it was built, besides those of the architect and sole owners' views. Significantly, this approach may reveal new considerations about the role and value of these buildings in the continuum of architectural history that will render it important to be preserved. This proposed approach is expected to contribute to a more holistic understanding of a building, enriching more traditional means of documentation and representation of architecture, such as drawing, photographs and video. The chapter presents an example of how the authors integrate this lived knowledge with archival information to make it accessible to the public, via the exploitation of new capacities of digital tools, such as immersive 3D real-time visualisation.

7.2 Architectural Heritage of the Recent Past

Modern architecture and structures built in the recent past are increasingly attracting more attention by scholars, researchers, professionals and international bodies aiming to promote the value of their preservation for future generations, including networks and bodies like DoCoMoMo, Historic England, The Twentieth Century Society UK (Georgiou et al. 2023; Nonument 2023). This effort is not always and everywhere a straightforward process. Arguably, as the introduction of modern construction methods and the radical transformations this provoked, which culminated to the historical movements of Constructivism, Bauhaus and the international impact of Modernism, took place more than a century ago, today it becomes increasingly common for the city authorities and estates management to be having to deal with such kind of buildings (McCurry 2023; Victoria and Albert Museum 2023). This need has emerged recently not only through historical enquiries, as the distance from the historical period of their creation grows, but most importantly due to the abundance of Modern architecture examples in our cities, which have been largely developed, planned and urbanised according to the vision, principles and understanding of the post-war period. The great number of examples of industrial and residential blocks built during this period makes them a common subject of debate today whenever city authorities are engaged in urban regeneration and revitalisation operations, driven by market phenomena of urban gentrification, tourism or capital (Casiello et al. 2013).

In this challenging contemporary landscape for Modern architecture, human neglect and impact of severe climate anomalies have been foregrounded by experts internationally with the objective to raise awareness of policy makers, stakeholders and the public. These efforts aim to promote the value of examples of this architecture's historical period and to communicate that many of these buildings are also sensitive to external pressures and threatened by decay and loss. Significantly, this is even more true today in areas that have been through violent transformations because of conflict, political upheaval, or population movement (Domingo 2019).

This chapter makes a case for the capacity of immersive technology to contribute to this discourse. Specifically, it argues that VR-enabled digital methods can provide to the relevant policy makers new ways of addressing the challenge of valorising this type of architecture of the recent past. In the presented approach immersive technology is used as an instrument that would enable stakeholders to deeper understand the contemporary meanings and values people assign on these examples of Modern architecture, in addition to their historical aspects. In the scope of the research presented here, this expanded—in terms of inclusivity—process may offer to the communities fresh, neglected or overlooked examples of Modern architecture from the periphery of Europe that were not previously considered as worthy of preservation heritage by the authorities and experts.

7.3 A New Role for the Architectural Archive, A New Opportunity for Galleries and Exhibition Spaces

Recently a new museum definition was approved by the International Council of Museums (ICOM) Extraordinary General Assembly at the 26th General Conference (2022).[1] This new definition is aligned with some of the major changes in the role of museums, recognising the importance of inclusivity, community participation and sustainability. This new role of the museum and galleries paves the way for them to be managed as community and education environments that enable the interpretation of tangible and intangible cultural heritage. In this context, the integration of technology in the GLAM (Galleries, Libraries, Archives and Museums) sector changes modalities of visitor engagement. Through these new digital interfaces, new audiences are addressed who are willing to engage with the gallery in learning and exploration of knowledge. This shift of agency introduces new actors in the museum who can inform the collections of artefacts in archives, galleries and museums with their own knowledge. In this condition, digital technologies can empower these new actors to share their local knowledge aiming to enrich hegemonic narratives of the authorities with a multitude of voices and parallel historical accounts, including individuals' memories.

Typical approaches to exhibiting architecture archives limit the visitors' deep engagement with the building representations on display because they require prior knowledge of architecture language from them (e.g. in order for the visitors to be able to read technical drawings which represent the building exhibited). Oftentimes

[1] "A museum is a not-for-profit, permanent institution in the service of society that researches, collects, conserves, interprets and exhibits tangible and intangible heritage. Open to the public, accessible and inclusive, museums foster diversity and sustainability. They operate and communicate ethically, professionally and with the participation of communities, offering varied experiences for education, enjoyment, reflection and knowledge sharing." International Council of Museums (2022).

the meaning of the artefact on display within the context of the whole curation of the exhibition is left to be discovered through an open-ended, subjective interpretation process by the individual, who may end up looking at scaled models of buildings as if they were sculptures. Arguably, the process of engaging the visitor of an architecture exhibition with specific meanings requires a cognitive process that goes beyond the appreciation of the architect's masterful expression through specific representation means, e.g. the appreciation of the ingenuity of a sketch or drawing. This particular condition of the architecture exhibition calls for the introduction of media that enable the visualisation and communication of morphological aspects, functional parameters and experiential capacities of the exhibited architecture that go beyond the tools that the architect used to capture her idea and vision.

Brown and Szacka (2019) consider "how might the notion of environment (as media, physical settings, or systems) in relation to architecture be used as a lens through which to understand new forms of exhibition making?" While contemporary international architectural firms are drawing a distinction between exhibiting the material aspects of architectural structures and providing access to digital representations of their architectural edifices (AEX 2022), current approaches to curatorial practices explore more integrated modalities. Ram (2023) proclaims that "established histories can be […] re-interrogated through the lens of the current moment. By bringing the residues of the past into dialogue with the present, alternative narratives can be constructed and urgent new questions can be articulated". Going beyond the presentation of framed content from the archive (Goffman 1974), the aim of using time-based, digital media approaches is to strengthen the exhibition visitors' engagement with architecture through a creative and dynamic frame that offers opportunities for encountering the real-life conditions and complexity of the architecture on display. This complex need stems from the nature of architecture edifices (a built structure that is occupied by humans), the subsequent transformation of these edifices into places that stage human actions, that provide a space for memories to be constructed through events and human interactions, resulting in identities being assigned to them. Naturally, these social interactions in and with the built edifices that are represented in the drawings on display, along with the socio-cultural identities and meanings that people assign to them, change in time, together with the needs and lifestyle of the intended users of the building. During the last decade, "memory", "identity" and "heritage" enquiries have, to a degree, started taking over the interest that was formerly dedicated to "history, as a field". As Aleida Assmann, who coined the term 'cultural memory'—which is a particular kind of collective memory, stated, "it is only through this reframing of our enquiry that the connection between time, identity and memory in their three dimensions of the personal, the social and the cultural, has become more and more evident" (Assmann 2008). Our research expands on the premise of history exhibits, such as a historic architecture exhibition, as cultural and educational spaces that contribute new approaches to memory formation through digitally-enhanced engagement opportunities presented to their visitors.

As described above, when presenting in an exhibition the dynamic agency of buildings-as-places, a necessity emerges for media that can communicate dynamic views (Lester 2022) and visualising occupational patterns of the exhibited building.

Ultimately, this approach to the integration of digital tools in the curation of an architectural exhibition can help the visitors to better contextualise and reflect on the value of the exhibited (architecture) content for our contemporary societies.

7.4 Introducing Virtual Environments in the Architectural Exhibition

In the exhibition *Past-Forward: Stavros Economou Unarchived*, which took place at the State Gallery of Contemporary Art, Cyprus, (Iacovou et al. 2021) a cross-media approach was used as a mechanism of connecting threads of narratives among the archival content to offer the visitors new opportunities for reflection on the cultural values of the architecture presented. The visitors engaged with assemblages of relevant 'stories' about specific buildings (Iacovou and Artopoulos 2024) by means of a series of reconstructions of architecture via, among others, digital immersion tools. Relevant literature shows that today VR technology is used in gallery and museum spaces for reconstructing historical sites and monuments, for history interpretation and experience augmentation (Soto-Martin et al. 2020), as well as for educational purposes.

Virtual Reality (VR) can create a more engaging experience, one that enables the visitor to immerse in an event or place reconstruction, an experience that can lead to a deeper understanding of history than traditional exhibition approaches (Bucher 2017). The introduction of VR technology in galleries is supported by research about the opportunities offered by immersive visualisations in education (Hamilton et al. 2020). Presence through immersion refers to a feeling as if the visitor is "there" in the projected environment (Diemer et al. 2015). Presence is characterised by the capacity of the participant to recall details of the 3D virtual environment rather than simply 2D views of the point of interest (Slater 1999), i.e. images of the digital reconstruction of a building. This becomes possible by immersive technology that teleports the visitor in a projected, digital surrogate of the exhibited architecture and its surrounding environment affording bodily interactions with the building and its occupation through time. This experience of the visitor facilitates the concretization of information through multimodal interactions, such as auditory stimulation, proprioception by means of real-time movement in space through user input, stereoscopy and parallax with six degrees of freedom in movement.

Efforts in employing VR in cultural heritage have focused primarily on creating digital surrogates through activities that rely primarily on the 3D reconstruction of destroyed sites (Petrelli 2019). In the field of architecture and built heritage, researchers explore 3D documentation methods and interactive visualisation to study and provide remote access to monuments and heritage sites, while at the same time European initiatives are building online platforms that allow the public to visit remotely sites and observe artefacts from collections and archives in 3D environments. In this context, scholars, researchers and policy makers are following closely the development of novel methods that rely on digital representation tools for cultural heritage reconstructions and visualisation, especially of sites and monuments that are in risk of destruction (Europa Nostra 2018). VR can be used for raising public awareness about pressing challenges communities and cities are facing today through the visualisation of future conditions of built environment (Future Earth 2017). Specifically, technologies of immersion can be used for the dissemination of the cultural and architectural value of inaccessible monuments and sites that are already under threat by neglect and climate anomalies, with the purpose of mobilising communities for heritage preservation (Pinheiro and Ivanova 2018).

Poet and writer Octavio Paz talked about the museum collection and argued that

> A baked clay vessel. Don't put it in the glass display case full of rare objects. It would show up badly. Its beauty is allied with the liquid it contains and the thirst it quenches. Its beauty is corporeal: I see it, touch it, smell it, hear it. If it is empty, it must be filled; if it is full, it must be emptied. … It is not an object to contemplate, but one for pouring something to drink.[7]

A virtual environment affords exploring a variety of information-rich and visually realistic experiences through immersion. By doing so, it provides innovative ways of implementing what Paz was proclaiming in his remark above. Responding to this, and in the context of the discourse about the use of digital technology for public engagement towards heritage valorisation, the *Past-Forward: Stavros Economou Unarchived* employed new modalities of affect and engagement with architectural knowledge that go beyond the observation of 2D drawings and scaled models of buildings. Arguably, the coded nature of architectural drawings can constraint the extend of communication of the information that a non-expert audience can absorb from an exhibition visit. So, the aim of the proposed approach was to increase accessibility not only to the content of the archival material but also to its territorial-environmental context. Using VR, the architecture exhibition allowed visitors to virtually explore 3D reconstructions of buildings from the archive, projects that were never built or buildings that are inaccessible today.

Literature has been occupied with understanding how immersive encounters are experienced in physical space (Kenderdine 2016; Ciolfi 2015) and the ways through which bodily exploration of virtual environments can be further motivated to last longer when these immersive experiences are enriched with historical information and digital assets (Perry et al. 2017), e.g. scanned archival material and old photographs crowdsourced from private collections. Providing historical context to the visitors of the virtual space through these digital assets, creates new opportunities for understanding spatial and formal qualities of the exhibited architecture as well as of interpreting the archival material. Furthermore, these affordances of the virtual environment become more attractive for the visitors when they are enriched with specific stories and thus become more personalised, for example through the integration of sound recordings of memories recollected by a building's past users.

These new modes of engaging the visitors facilitated the aim of the curation to enable the public and non-expert audience to reflect on the significant role of architecture in the well-being of dwellers and city inhabitants. Addressing these

Fig. 7.1 S. Economou's Alasia sea recreation centre in Varoshia, a once cosmopolitan cityscape featuring high-rise buildings along the shoreline—an inaccessible time capsule of Modernism that is stuck in the UN Buffer Zone for the last 50 years (2021) (©the authors)

capacities of learning affordances of VR interfaces, the exhibition explored these new modalities by virtually reconstructing an inaccessible building from the archive, one of high significance for the local communities and visitors, the sea-side recreation centre Alasia (Fig. 7.1), which was named after the ancient city of Alasia (Engkomi) that was located near-by.

7.5 Method: Using Immersive Representations of Architectural Heritage to Reflect on Contested Environments

Spatially distributing personal stories and informal narratives in immersive visualisation can act as catalyst for engaging people with their historical built environment, cultures and difficult conditions of places that have been associated with competing identities and perplexing pasts (Artopoulos 2022). The exhibition aimed to utilise the affordances of VR (Hassapopoulou 2018) to engage the visitors in a discussion about an example that is characterised by highly recognised architectural qualities of Cypriot Modernism and is inaccessible since the division of the island in 1974. The building of Alasia is an example of heritage that relates to unsettling histories and memories (Macdonald 2007), as it is located in a controversial and sensitive site, in the militarised, UN-controlled buffer zone in Varoshia (Ministry of Foreign Affairs 2022). This is the infamous ghost city that still stands up, as a time shard from 1974 and the war. The design and architectural programme of the building that was built in 1952 was very innovative, as it was designed to address the needs of both local communities and tourists.

The layering of an architectural reconstruction with personal accounts of the building's history posed a big challenge to the curation of the information in the virtual space due to the difficult past of Varoshia (Michael 2020). One of the challenges that the introduction of an architectural experience associated with the difficult past of Varoshia in the gallery space of the exhibition had to address related to the visibility of the building of Alasia through the curated dissemination of historical information, such as the construction of the surrounding built environment, the transformation of the coastline, events documented in the press; a context that was provided to the visitor through the display of archival material that offered specific information and historical facts about the life in Varoshia at the time. The virtual experience of Alasia included personal accounts of the users of the space and how they appropriated it, stories about the everyday activities and events that were taking place. This draws directly on the emotional side of the visitors' experience of the exhibition, and the specific location of the VR installation in the gallery space was thus an important curatorial decision (Fig. 7.2). Acknowledging the affective experience of the visitors emerging through their exploration of the content of the exhibition (Smith and Campbell 2015), the Alasia VR installation was placed together with the exhibit of historical content informing the visitor of the transformation of the natural and built environment in the context of the value of architecture for the public, introducing the visitor to historical views of issues of local identity, designing for the community and learning from the past.

Curating material collected by the building's users, who still hold recollections of it before the division of the island, through open-ended questions, helped the research to focus on events that capture and communicate significant aspects of the architecture, its environment and the building becoming a landmark for the public. Accommodating fragments of memories from a variety of users, of different demographics, was a first step to enrich the sensorial abstraction of the virtual reconstruction (that is

Fig. 7.2 *Reconstructing Alasia* VR installation at the State Gallery of Contemporary Art (2021). Integrating the VR experience in the context of the exhibition included a physical model of the building and two video projections that displayed alternative views of the virtual environment without the need of wearing the VR goggles. (©the authors)

unavoidably experienced due to technical limitations of VR technologies today) with feelings that rely on empathy (Poole 2018). This helped the authors in making the information communicated through the VR to the visitors in a more direct way. The *Reconstructing Alasia* installation presented to the visitors historical and archival information about the context of the following points of reflection that were deemed relevant to the themes of the architecture exhibition:

- The life of the building as a heritage object that necessitates preservation;
- Reconstructing an immersive representation as a new medium of interpretation of content from architecture archives; and,
- Policies of urban development of coastal cities in relation to ongoing environmental transformations—coastal erosion threatening heritage buildings.

7.6 Setting up the Immersive Experience: A Workflow

The virtual life of the building of Alasia aimed to provide exhibition visitors new opportunities to experience, in an immersive way, the architecture of the exhibited archive as well as to explore the place this building created in the memories of its users which were spatially and temporally, contextualised in the rapidly transforming built environment of Famagusta between 1950 and 1970s. Below is presented the technical description of the production process of this VR-enabled exhibit which followed the steps listed:

- Archival research about the project, its geographical and architectural context (Fig. 7.3);
- Reconstruction of the urban fabric of Varoshia and the representation of its transformation;
- Dealing with uncertainty in data and historical information;
- Quality of representation of the building adapted to the particularities of immersive visualisation;
- Spatial distribution of archival material and historical information; and,
- Soundscape and memory documentations' location for enhancing immersion through spatialised audio technology.

One of the biggest challenges of creating visual experiences is how to convey the right atmosphere for the storytelling with the use of the senses available. By using visual and auditory channels, one can transmit specific feelings in an immersive context that delivers certain emotions to the visitors, which will allow them to connect with the respective narrative. The most common way of conveying emotions is with the use of an atmosphere, interrelated with the underlying narrative in the created experience. In the case of the presented VR installation, since Varoshia has been deemed inaccessible for almost fifty years, with a vibrant, popular past and an uncertain future, the lack of clarity is also the best way for these messages to be transmitted to the visitors.

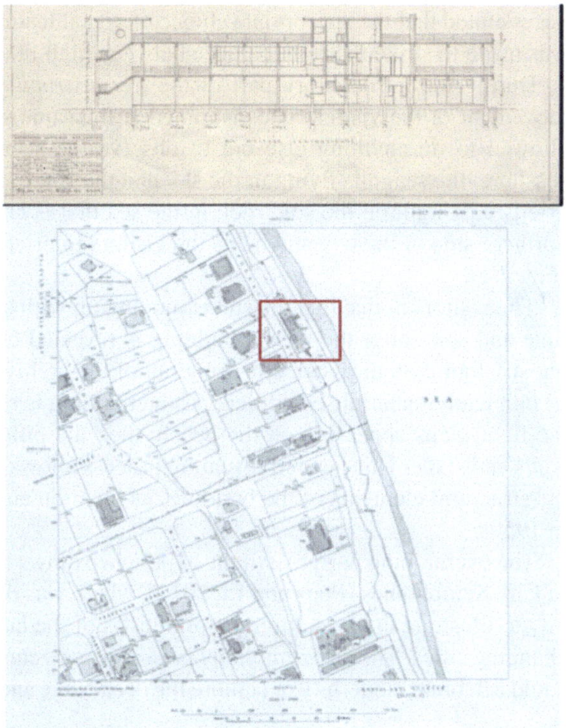

Fig. 7.3 Architectural drawings (top) and topographical survey of the site (bottom) from S. Economou's archive used for the accurate virtual reconstruction of the inaccessible site (©Economou Architects and Engineers)

Similarly, to a live action or an animated feature, an interactive and immersive experience needs to exploit these methods, based on the affordances provided. However, the difficulty in the latter case is that the users have the freedom of freely roaming the landscape and observe whichever direction they will. This means that the VR experience needs to depict numerous angles and objects but at the same time provide low latency to the users, so that they remain immersed. Low latency is arguably on the counter part of high visual fidelity. As, in the case presented, the feeling of immersion and presence was of the highest priority for the authors, the high fidelity of visual representation had to be compromised to have low latency and an acceptable frame rate by the untethered VR gear used in the exhibition, which was at least 30 frames per second (FPS).

The creation of the right atmosphere for the storytelling presented above played a crucial role in deciding whether the use of Unity's Universal Render Pipeline (URP) or the High-Definition Render Pipeline (HDRP) would be more appropriate. While URP was the logical path to follow for a VR experience, as it is much more lightweight in terms of features and subsequently computational intensity, the HDRP's environment, physically based sky, shadows, high dynamic range (HDR) options and other features provide a much more realistic and robust scene rendering. This decision necessitated that the appropriate choice of visual features and geometric complexity was made to strike the right balance between high fidelity and low latency.

During the introductory part of the *Reconstructing Alasia* VR experience, the movement of the visitors is constrained at the same spot and as such, they are not allowed to do anything else but to observe the scenery, to encounter the empty seashore, the seagulls flying in the sky and the sun rising behind a foggy horizon to briefly cast light on the sole rock in the sea that is characteristically located in the northern side of the bay and helps the visitors to orient themselves in the landscape (Fig. 7.4).

The visitors notice that the sun is moving up with a much faster pace than in real time and soon after the Alasia building is revealed before their eyes, initially as a ghostly figure on the sand, emerging out of the archival drawings and eventually as a completely materialised edifice. As the building is revealed, the users can observe the floor plans appearing on the beach, then the pillars and beams and eventually walls and slabs. This layered revealing process allows the visitor the time to observe the structural elements of the building, its location and orientation in the landscape in 1950s.

The overarching narrative of the experience draws inspiration from the film genre of City Symphonies (Penz and Lu 2011), which was developed as a genre in modernity to illustrate the forceful transformations of the built environment in the rapidly changing cities. The city symphony is an unusual genre; these films have no plot and could celebrate modernity or capture the decadence and the degradation of urban life.

Fig. 7.4 Screenshots from the VR experience; introduction to the atmosphere of the site through advanced visual processing methods of the 3D assets. (©the authors)

Their structure is borrowed from the movements and motifs of the hours of the day, rather than the dynamics of narrative pacing. Reconstructing Alasia was thus created using a *Dawn to Dusk* experience structure; using the method of a fast-forwarded sequence the feeling of time passing by is conveyed, covering 12 h of a day in 8 min of VR experience.

This was achieved by running a script to the sun light in the scene which changes the sun's Y rotation in time. In this script, an exposed field was set (i.e. to be easily adjustable from within Unity's interface, without having to reedit the code) for the speed of the rotation. In HDRP, the rotation of the sun light is linked with its position in the sky, which at the same time appears as an illuminated disc in the sky which also changes the colour of the scene accordingly. Objects eventually become clearer as the building of Alasia is revealed, the immediate environment is clear of fog, the sun is brightly shining and contextualised material is presented to the virtual visitors.

The visitors are allowed to freely roam around the building and on the beach. The method of achieving this is through 'Teleportation'—by squeezing either the left or right controller's trigger where a projectile line is drawn, the visitors can jump from one spot to the next, enabling a wide exploration of the area (Fig. 7.5). The teleportation control can be applied on whichever button, trigger, or joystick of the VR system's controller. In this case and given that the presented experience was designed to be displayed on the Oculus Quest 2, the best choice was to apply the teleportation controller situated where the user's index finger is resting, which the trigger button at the front of the controller. To be noted that this was decided after extensive user testing. This is an absolute necessity, since the available physical area in the gallery space was confined to a 3 × 3 m space, rendering the facility unaffordable to provide actual free roaming.

Archival and crowdsourced material, such as photographs of the building and its interior spaces, are placed in the virtual environment in the same location and angle as those from which they were originally taken (Fig. 7.6). Faintly lit arrows are projected on the ground where the hotspots are, to help the visitors have the correct orientation when teleporting to each respective hotspot. The arrows are rhythmically blinking and have an abstract shape (a basic triangle) to avoid any visual interference with the scene assets of the reconstruction. Once the visitors teleport on top of an

Fig. 7.5 Screenshot from the VR experience, teleportation enabled movement in the virtual environment to avoid triggering motion sickness to the visitors. (©the authors)

Fig. 7.6 Screenshot from the VR experience; archival and crowdsourced material placed in the virtual environment to trigger the visitor
spatial exploration and learning about the history of the site. (©the authors)

arrow, a trigger is activated, revealing the relative historical photograph respectively. In this case, collisions and colliders, an essential feature of Unity, were used for triggering events such as activating and deactivating objects (i.e. making them visible or invisible), turning on and off music and sound effects, ending a scene or starting a new one, etc.

Fog that surrounds the building was used to add an atmospheric perspective to the immersive experience and to contribute to the affective representation of the growth of the cityscape because of the construction of tall buildings in the narrow plots that started appearing along of the coastline of Varoshia (Fig. 7.7). This visual effect that allowed the authors to control the visibility of the horizon and provide a more realistic sense of depth was complemented with a building construction works soundscape functioning as an ambient environment to better contextualise Alasia in the landscape. The Fog effect is an option featured in both URP and HDRP, however it is much more accurate and provides to the author a lot more control parameters when using HDRP.

As the sun rapidly sets behind the building of Alasia, shadows of the emerged cityline start to appear on the sand, growing longer second-by-second to offer to the visitor a more vivid sense of the passage of time and eventually to cover the building in shadow as the landscape goes dark and the day ends. Using archival material and old photographs embedded in Polaroid frames were placed on the tables around the

Fig. 7.7 Screenshots from the VR experience; integration of atmospheres in the virtual environment to support immersion in the history of the site. (©the authors)

Fig. 7.8 Screenshot from the VR experience; introducing archival material in the virtual storyline. Furniture and objects (representing archival content, such as historical photographs, crowdsourced family photographs, maps and more) were placed in the building and used as proxies to the memories of old visitors of the building for the exhibition visitors to seek for and discover through their virtual exploration of the site. These realistic assets also addressed the need to introduce a visually and aesthetically-rich representation means in the visually abstract representation of the architecture, which was due to the graphical limitations that were imposed by real-time rendering. (©the authors)

two sitting areas the building featured a café on the ground floor and a restaurant on the first floor (Fig. 7.8).

As the visitor explores the building, wandering around its rooms, she starts hearing peoples' voices. Approaching one of the tables with photographs laid on it, narrations fade in, telling the stories of the people who lived and visited the Alasia building before 1974 (Fig. 7.9). The sound files start playing with the use of a 'box volume' asset (in Unity 3D), which are activated once they are collided with. As the visitor moves between the tables, the sound volumes start overlapping with each other, and once they are activated, the visitors can listen stories coming from more than one tables in variety of volume and direction because of the effect of spatial (or 3D) sound.

One of the technical challenges facing this part of the VR experience was the way that the volume of the environment outside the building would lower once the visitor enters the interior space of the Alasia building. This was achieved again with the use of separate 'trigger volumes' (Unity 3D asset) at every possible opening area of the walkable interior space (windows, doors, etc.) (Fig. 7.10), to dim the ambient soundscape that included children playing, sea waves, seagulls and more.

As introduced above, one of the main objectives of the authors was to offer to the visitor opportunities to draw links between the history of this culturally and architecturally important building and issues that our cities are still facing today, such as deterioration of concrete constructions by exposure to harsh climate and by neglect. This heritage threatening condition of inaccessible assets like the Alasia Recreation Centre was communicated to the visitors through the animated transformation of the surrounding environment of the building. Specifically, at the beginning of the

Fig. 7.9 Reconstructing human memories in virtual environments. Drawing inspiration from archival photographs (as depicted by the picture on the left side), the authors reconstructed 'moments' of the history of the building in the virtual environment to introduce the exhibition visitors to the contested past of the site that remains inaccessible 50 years after the war of 1974 ([left]:@Economou Architects & Engineers, [right]:©the authors)

Fig. 7.10 Unity 3D 'trigger volumes' placement in the restaurant area of the Alasia building. (©the authors)

experience, as the visitors gaze over the coastline from one of the eastern verandas of the building, they can clearly observe the distance of the waterfront from the building. By the end of the duration of the experience, as the sun is about to set, users discover that the sea level is much higher than before, hitting on the building's respective side, almost covering the steps of the staircase that leads to the ground floor. Similarly to the way the sunlight was controlled, a script was applied to the water plane, which enabled it to gradually rise within the 8 min-long duration of the VR experience. This transformation of the environment during the VR experience was a curatorial decision to trigger reflections on the impact of climate change to our built environment and was spatially associated with archival material on display in the cabinet and tables surrounding the *Reconstructing Alasia* booth in the gallery space.

7.7 Results

Drawing from the relevant literature (Konstantakis and Caridakis 2020) about the combined utilisation of experimental and analytical methods, the authors complemented the VR interaction in the exhibition with a questionnaire for measuring User Experience (Artopoulos and Louca 2022). More than 50 visitors responded to a user experience survey that was provided to them after the interaction session with the VR installation in the gallery space. The users were asked to respond via the Likert scale and written feedback to a series of questions to share their level of immersion and quality of experience. The questionnaire also included open ended questions to allow participants to communicate their experience in detail. Points of consideration in the survey referred to the visitors' appreciation of heritage in their everyday, the visual appearance of reconstructions in the VR, engagement with the projected narratives and embodiment in virtual space, media assets type and spatial interpretation in the virtual location. Starting with the demographics of the valid responders, 59% of the participants registered as female, 45% were of Cypriot nationality, with other visitors coming from Italy, Russia, Denmark, France and Greece (in numerical order), while the majority of the interviewees (43%) belonged to the range 25–34 years of age.

Specifically, regarding prior experience of the visitors, 53% of the valid responders were experienced with videogames and 40% had previous experiences of VR. We evaluated the experience provided by our application, with 92% of the responders considering the experience interesting and 81% not physically tiring. 62% of the participants felt that the immersion would be weaker if the visualisation of the Alasia building was less realistic. The survey asked about the richness of the historic content and information that is provided in the virtual environment, and 64% of the participants agreed or strongly agreed that the virtual objects seemed to belong to the historically accurate space of the building. It is worth mentioning here that there were several visitors of the exhibition who had memories and experiences of Varoshia and the Alasia building, hence the value of that question was relevant to the authors.

More questions focused on the aims and objectives of the application, in assessing the quality of visualisation, as well as understanding the visitors' response to the interaction design and the user interface of the application. 62% of the responders would like to learn more about the building by means of a VR visit, whereas 87% of the participants would like to interact with more objects in the VR and be able to explore the whole neighbourhood. There were also a few unexpected results of the survey regarding the interface and interaction technology, as only 34% of the participants would prefer to experience the virtual visit with friends, while 41% were neither positive nor negative to this. Further to this, just 38% of the visitors would like to leave comments in the application. These somehow unforeseen results are attributed to the limitations of the VR interfaces today that are still weak in provoking people to engage in more responsive, dialectic activities in the virtual environment.

The visitors' responses provided to the authors with an insight into their experience of the exhibition, the value of the virtual reconstruction of built heritage as a research tool and its potential to be further developed in the future as an educational tool. For example, 87% of the responders noticed the presence of the high-rise buildings in the coastline, which was one of the authors aims for connecting the VR visit with the archival content of the exhibition and the curation of this material in the space of the gallery.

7.7.1 Limitations and Future Directions

Significantly, what became evident from the user experience survey was the limited interaction of the visitors within space, in terms of their capacity to interact with virtual objects to be found in the spaces of the building. Arguably, this would require a more engaged training of the visitor of the gallery before they would be able to use properly the VR gear and explore the installation. The authors avoided to include sophisticated interactions in the VR though due to the logistics of the exhibition (based on the capacity of invigilators), as well as because of the long duration that each visitor would have to dedicate on the VR experience, should there be more extended interaction with objects located in the building. Another limitation of the installation concerned the extent to which a large number of high-resolution, digitised historical assets from the archive would become accessible within the virtual environment for observation. The authors' intention to rely solely on wireless VR gear necessitated the display of a limited number of visual assets to maintain high frame rates of rendering the 3D content and to offer a smooth visual experience to the visitor. Finally, responders expected to be able to interact with other human avatars in the virtual environment, but this was well outside the objectives of this research.

The authors are working in a direction that is more aligned with the objectives of this research, focusing on enriching the VR experience with further archival material and crowdsourced assets (e.g. photographs) while planning to continue interviewing visitors of the Alasia that are still alive to expand the point of view and voices represented in the VR installation. The goal of this future work is to transform the presented virtual environment of the reconstruction of Alasia into a living virtual archive of architectural histories.

7.8 Instead of a Conclusion

The chapter presented the Reconstructing Alasia, a VR museum installation that used advanced digital representation tools, immersive visualisation and storytelling, to promote the cultural value of 'difficult heritage' of the still divided island of Cyprus, as well as to provoke reflections about the purpose of safeguarding buildings that are not yet listed as monuments, but which carry significant social meanings and cultural values.

These objectives created a virtual place of exploration of 'difficult' histories, challenging subjects and contested experiences of the local communities. Digital technologies can act as catalyst for engaging people with their urban environment and cultures. The presented work goes beyond the 3D representation of heritage buildings and explores interactive visualisation for user interpretation, for engagement and eventually for raising awareness about inaccessible or neglected architecture as cultural heritage. The virtual reconstruction of the Modern heritage building of Alasia aims to provide exhibition visitors opportunities to experience, in an immersive way, the architecture and the place it created in the memories of its users, spatially and temporally, contextualised in the rapidly transforming built environment of the cosmopolitan city of Famagusta between 1950 and 1970s.

The chapter addressed the question about the opportunities provided by using immersive technology to (re)mediate multi-layered narratives about buildings. Through the analysis of a VR installation, it presented possible ways for this mediated immersion in architectural reconstructions to enrich and expand the role of the archive. This VR experience became an assemblage that integrates architectural and environmental materialities (Latour 2003), which obtain socio-cultural relevance through an embodied/spatial experience of interacting with heterogenous assets, such as photographs, voices, soundscapes, 3D reconstructions and maps. Presence in a spatialized reconstruction of historical material from Economou's archive offered to the exhibition visitors a new way of framing (Goffman 1974) the relevant architectural context. This enabled the restaging of the context of the time when the reconstructed historical building was occupied, helping in this way the visitors of the exhibition to conceptualise and interpret another part of its history that could not be communicated through technical drawings.

Ultimately, the VR experience aimed at bringing *other* voices to the fore, beyond the opinions of experts and professionals, and which animate the virtual reconstruction of the building with what is missing—the people, the birds, the wind and sea soundscapes (Hruby 2019). These are memories relating to the life of the building, an insight that enriches the understanding of architecture through the perspective of its users. In this context, the exhibited VR experience explored the affordances of VR in engaging the gallery visitors in new, dynamic learning opportunities that go beyond the formal methods of architectural historiography. This approach was further put in practice during the operation of the exhibition *Past-Forward: Stavros Economou Unarchived* which invited diverse communities in a series of curated events featuring guided tours, talks, roundtable discussions, film screenings and educational activities exploring a number of themes which arose from the content on show, and which relate to the contemporary Cypriot city. Roundtable discussions addressed the topics of 'City, Citizens and Climate Crisis', 'Re-appropriating Modern Architecture', 'The Architectural Archive: Creative Practices of Documenting, Collecting, Displaying', 'Digital Tools and Practices of Engagement with Modern Architecture Heritage' and 'Women in Architecture'. Through these staged dialogues amongst citizens, diverse communities, professionals, academics and artists, the content of the exhibition material was discussed in relation to current environmental, spatial, political and social urgencies of the contemporary city.

Acknowledgements This research was supported by the Ministry of Education Culture, Sport and Youth—Cultural Services, with the support of the University of Cyprus, The Cyprus Institute, Neapolis University Pafos, Cyprus Architects Association, Cyprus Scientific and Technical Chamber, and the Pancyprian Organisation of Freelance Architects and Civil Engineers. Concept, Coordination, Text & Production of the *Reconstructing Alasia*: Georgios Artopoulos; Interactivity design & VR application: Nicolas Louca; 3D modelling: Nestoras Skantzouris; Performance, concept: Julie Gregoriou, Popi Iacovou; text: Julie Gregoriou, Alekos Michaelides, Eva Kalomire, Mara Constantinou; performers: Mara Constantinou, Julie Gregoriou, Maria Poyiadji, Giorgos Evagorou, Michalis Kazakas; interviewees: Andreas Morfites, Nitsa Patsalide, Lia Mousoupetrou, Christodoulos Pitsires, Chrystalla Stamatare, Maro Lissandridou, Silea Hadjihambi-Hapipi; Sound design: Constantinos Lemesios.

References

Architecture Exhibitions International (AEX) (2022) The living archive of a studio. https://www.architecture-exhibitions.com/en/het-nieuwe-instituut/mvrdvhni. Last Accessed 10 Nov 2022

Artopoulos G, Loucas N (2022) VR in the museum: reconstructing difficult heritage of modern architecture. In: At the conference the art museum in the digital age, at Belvedere Research Center, Vienna, Austria

Artopoulos G (2022) Practices of digital immersion for the study of built heritage as a promoter of equity in urban sites challenged by difficult pasts. In: Benardou A, Droumpouki AM (eds) Difficult pasts and immersive experiences, pp 123–144. Routledge, UK. https://doi.org/10.4324/9781003200659-8

Assmann J (2008) Communicative and cultural memory. In: Erll A, Nünning A (eds) Cultural memory studies. An international and interdisciplinary handbook, pp 109–118. Berlin

Bristol KG (1991) The Pruitt-Igoe myth. J Arch Educ 44(3):163–171. https://doi.org/10.1080/10464883.1991.11102687

Brown A, Szacka L-C (2019) The architecture exhibition as environment. Arch Theory Rev 23(1):1–4. https://doi.org/10.1080/13264826.2019.1616369

Bucher J (2017) Storytelling for virtual reality: methods and principles for crafting immersive narratives. Routledge, New York and Oxon

Casiello S, Pane A, Russo V (2013) Modernist boroughs: conservation of historical values and urban design. In: Crişan R, Franco G, Kealy L, Musso SF (eds) European association for architectural education transactions on architectural education, vol 58, pp 231–250. Eaae Bucharest

Ciolfi L (2015) Embodiment and place experience in heritage technology design. In: Macdonald S, Leahy HR, Henning M (eds) The international handbook of museum studies, pp 419–446. Wiley-Blackwell, Hoboken, NJ

Council of Europe–CoE (2005) Convention on the value of cultural heritage for society (Faro convention). https://www.coe.int/en/web/culture-and-heritage/faro-convention. Last Accessed 16 Apr 2021

Demetrescu E (2018) Virtual reconstruction as a scientific tool: the extended matrix and source-based modelling approach. In: Digital research and education in architectural heritage. UHDL DECH 2017. Springer, Cham

Diemer J, Alpers GW, Peperkorn HM, Shiban Y, Mühlberger A (2015) The impact of perception and presence on emotional reactions: a review of research in virtual reality. Front Psychol 6:26

Domingo P (2019) Plácido Domingo sends open letter to two leaders of Cyprus calling for their urgent action to protect the endangered heritage in the buffer zone of Nicosia. Europa Nostra. https://www.europanostra.org/placido-domingo-sends-open-letter-to-two-leaders-of-cyprus-calling-for-their-urgent-action-to-protect-the-endangered-heritage-in-the-buffer-zone-of-nicosia/. Last Accessed 20 Mar 2019

Europa Nostra (2018) Bulgaria: European experts put forward action plan to preserve the Buzludzha monument. Europa Nostra. https://www.europanostra.org/bulgaria-european-experts-put-forward-action-plan-to-preserve-the-buzludzha-monument/. Last Accessed 16 Apr 2022

Frampton K (1992) Modern architecture: a critical history. Thames and Hudson, London

Future Earth (2017) Participation in the Seoul international biennale of architecture and urbanism. https://futureearth.org/2017/08/28/updated-participation-in-the-seoul-international-biennale-of-architecture-and-urbanism/. Last Accessed 12 May 2022

Georgiou A, Iacovou P, Mesaritis G, Sioulas M, Siandou E (2023) The value of the wholesale market of Nicosia. In: Kathinerini, Art & Literature, Architecture.

Goffman E (1974) Frame analysis: an essay on the organization of experience. Harper & Row, New York

Hamilton D, Mckechnie J, Edgerton E, Wilson C (2021) Immersive virtual reality as a pedagogical tool in education: a systematic literature review of quantitative learning outcomes and experimental design. J Comput Educ 8:1–32. https://doi.org/10.1007/s40692-020-00169-2

Hassapopoulou M (2018) Playing with history: collective memory, national trauma and dark tourism in virtual reality docugames. New Rev Film Telev Stud 16(4):365–392

Hruby F (2019) The sound of being there: audiovisual cartography with immersive virtual environments. KN J Cartogr Geogr Inf 69:19–28

Iacovou P, Artopoulos G (2024) The architecture exhibition as a stage of mediated narratives. Digit Creat. https://doi.org/10.1080/14626268.2024.2304811

Iacovou P, Artopoulos G, Sioulas M, Christodoulidou M (2021) Past-forward: Stavros Economou unarchived, at the state gallery of contemporary art–SPEL.

International Council of Museums (ICOM) Extraordinary General Assembly at the 26th General Conference (2022) ICOM Prague 2022. https://prague2022.icom.museum/. Last Accessed 10 Sept 2022

Kenderdine S (2016) Embodiment, entanglement, and immersion in digital cultural heritage. In: Schreibman S, Unsworth J, Siemens R (eds) A new companion to digital humanities, pp 22–41. John Wiley & Sons, Ltd. https://doi.org/10.1002/9781118680605.Ch2

Konstantakis M. Caridakis G (2020) Adding culture to UX: UX research methodologies and applications in cultural heritage. ACM J Comput Cult Herit 13(1)

Laparelli PI (2018) OMA. Palermo atlas. Italy: Humboldt Books Manifesta 12:340–43

Latour B (2003) The promises of constructivism. In: Ihde D, Selinger E (eds) Chasing technoscience: matrix for materiality, pp 27–46. Indiana University Press

Mccurry J (2023) Legacy of Japan's Nakagin capsule tower lives on in restored pods. The Guardian. https://www.theguardian.com/world/2023/jan/06/legacy-japan-nagakin-capsule-tower-lives-on-restored-pods. Last Accessed 9 Apr 2023

Michael MS (2020) Famagusta dialogues project. Report, Cyprus Academic Dialogue, Funded by Australian Department of Foreign Affairs and Trade, and Friedrich Ebert Stiftung Foundation

Ministry of Foreign Affairs, Republic of Cyprus (2022) Varosha: declaration by the high representative on behalf of the European Union. https://mfa.gov.cy/press-releases/2021/07/27/eu-declaration-on-illegal-actions-of-turkey-in-varosha/#:~:text=the%20european%20union%20strongly%20condemns,fenced%2doff%20town%20of%20varosha. Last Accessed 22 Aug 2022

Münster S (2013) Workflows and the role of images for a virtual 3D reconstruction of no longer extant historic objects. In: ISPRS annals of the photogrammetry, remote sensing and spatial information sciences, XXIV international CIPA symposium, 2–6. 9. 2013, pp 197–202. Strasbourg

Nonument (2023) The Nonument group. https://nonument.org/. last Accessed 10 June 2022

Penz F, Lu A (2011) Urban cinematics. Understanding urban phenomena through the moving image. Intellect, UK

Perry S, Roussou M, Economou M, Young H, Pujol L (2017) Moving beyond the virtual museum: engaging visitors emotionally. In: 23rd International conference on virtual system & multimedia (VSMM), pp 1–8. IEEE, Dublin. https://doi.org/10.1109/vsmm.2017.8346276

Petrelli D (2019) Making virtual reconstructions part of the visit: an exploratory study. Digit Appl Archaeol Cult Herit 15

Pinheiro J, Ivanova D (2018) Bulgaria: European experts put forward action plan to preserve the Buzludzha monument. Europa Nostra. https://www.europanostra.org/bulgaria-european-experts-put-forward-action-plan-to-preserve-the-buzludzha-monument/. Last Accessed 10 Jan 2019

Poole S (2018) Ghosts in the garden: locative gameplay and historical interpretation from below. Int J Herit Stud 24:300–314. https://doi.org/10.1080/13527258.2017.1347887

Ram R (2023) Curating contemporary art and design: archives and collections intensive. https://www.rca.ac.uk/study/programme-finder/curating-contemporary-art-and-design-archives-and-collections-intensive/. Last Accessed 20 Mar 2023

Slater M (1999) Measuring presence: a response to the Witmer and singer presence questionnaire. Presence 8(5):560–565

Smaczynski M, Horbinski T (2021) Creating a 3D model of the existing historical topographic object based on low-level aerial imagery. KN J Cartogr Geogr Inf 72:33–43

Smith L, Campbell G (2015) The elephant in the room: heritage, affect and emotion. In: Logan W, Craith MN, Kockel U (eds) A companion to heritage studies. Wiley-Blackwell, Oxford, pp 443–460

Soto-Martin O, Fuentes-Porto A, Martin-Gutierrez J (2020) A digital reconstruction of a historical building and virtual reintegration of mural paintings to create an interactive and immersive experience in virtual reality. Appl Sci 10:597

Victoria and Albert Museum (2023) Robin hood gardens. Victoria and albert museum, London. https://www.vam.ac.uk/articles/robin-hood-gardens. Last Accessed 20 May 2023

Chapter 8
From Physical to Digital and Back: Novel Modalities for Interaction with Cultural Heritage Through 3D Digital Fabrication

Myrsini Samaroudi and Karina Rodriguez Echavarria

Abstract The development of 3D digital technologies to facilitate a range of cultural heritage management processes within Galleries, Libraries, Archives and Museums and Higher Education Institutions now exceeds two decades of impactful presence. Over the last decade, digital fabrication and particularly low-cost and accessible 3D printing has emerged as a popular means to enable novel modalities for interaction with collections through multisensorial experiences which involve physical access to replicas. Such experiences have the potential to transform our relationship with cultural heritage, while touch gradually regains its place amongst heritage engagement strategies. This chapter reviews the state-of-the-art in 3D digital fabrication for heritage communication by looking at different examples where this technology has been deployed. A further focus is also directed towards communities' participatory approaches, alongside the employment of such technologies for decolonisation efforts. Lastly, we look at the adoption of 3D technologies with emphasis on digital fabrication during the COVID era while discussing the means to unleash the potential of such technologies in future.

8.1 Introduction

Efforts to develop efficient 3D digital technologies to facilitate cultural heritage (CH) documentation, study, conservation, exhibition design, interpretation and more, now exceed two decades of impactful presence in Galleries, Libraries, Archives and Museums (GLAMs) and Higher Education Institutions (HEIs). Over the last decade, as part of this technological fruition and experimentation, digital fabrication and particularly low-cost and accessible 3D printing has emerged as a popular means to enable research and practice around CH interpretation. Within this frame,

M. Samaroudi (✉) · K. Rodriguez Echavarria
School of Architecture, Technology and Engineering, University of Brighton, Brighton, UK
e-mail: m.samaroudi3@brighton.ac.uk

K. Rodriguez Echavarria
e-mail: k.rodriguez@brighton.ac.uk

F. Liarokapis et al. (eds.), *Interactive Media for Cultural Heritage*, Springer Series on Cultural Computing, https://doi.org/10.1007/978-3-031-61018-9_8

novel modalities for interaction with collections target audience engagement through multisensorial experiences with the involvement of physical access to replicas. Such interactive encounters with 3D replicas include educational programmes for young audiences, artistic explorations of collections and digital remixes to create new 3D objects, smart replicas working as tangible interfaces, 3D replicas to enable access to CH assets for the visually impaired and more. All these experiences have the potential to transform people's relationship with CH, while touch gradually regains its place amongst heritage engagement strategies.

Of course, accessing a copy of an artefact or museum object is not new. Different civilisations and artists throughout the centuries have been copying and replicating objects to fulfil needs which range from mastering artistic skills to satisfying spiritual needs or demonstrating certain social status. The potential of digitally fabricated objects as novel modalities for interaction with our heritage lie within their predecessor, i.e. the digital file that can be easily stored, exchanged and manipulated to satisfy curatorial and/or users' needs. Such features constitute some of the main advantages of digital imaging and thereafter fabrication, as file processing, customisation for specific uses, sharing of data and unlimited physical replication (either in-house or by outsourcing manufacturing) provide a feasible and flexible environment to enable digital fabrication.

This chapter reviews the state-of-the-art in digital fabrication for CH communication by looking at different examples where this particular technology—ultimately a negotiation between the digital and physical world—has been deployed for interpretation. In Sect. 8.2, we examine 3D replicas' background and production processes, as well as issues around authenticity. In Sect. 8.3, we investigate through a 'functional lens' how 3D replicas have been used in CH to enhance audiences' experiences. Section 8.4 focuses on current trends in the deployment of 3D replicas in CH, including participatory approaches and decolonisation efforts. Lastly, in Sect. 8.5 we look at the adoption of 3D technologies with emphasis on digital fabrication during the COVID era while discussing the means to unleash the potential of such technologies in future. Section 8.6 presents the conclusions of this chapter.

8.2 Digitally Fabricated Artefacts or 3D Replicas

8.2.1 Background: Digital Fabrication

Fabricating an object, through a process that takes raw material and transforms it into an object is the closest connection that exists between graphics software and the physical manifestation of such product. The story of fabrication, though, is not new. The roots of subtractive manufacturing date back in the 1940s and the first experimental numerically controlled milling machine. In the 1950s, the MIT created the first computer numerical controlled machine (CNC). A decade later, CAD/CAM software was connected to CNC and the technology became cheaper with the arrival of minicomputers and lower cost machines. In the 1970s, the technology had already become attractive and was more widely used. On the other hand, rapid prototyping or 3D printing, i.e. the additive technique to build an object gradually, appeared in the 1980s. In 1981, a layer-by-layer approach to create models by using polymers that reacted to light and solidified was introduced. In 1984, stereolithography (SLA) was invented and in 1986 the first selective laser sintering (SLS) machine working with powder polymers appeared. In 1991, the first operational fusion deposition modelling machine (FDM) was created. In almost ten years, the three major technologies behind the idea of rapid prototyping (SLA, SLS and FDM) had been introduced. It took another 20 years to explore materials, develop software, add colour to prints and experiment with applications, from the medical domain to industry, food production and space research (Bensoussan 2016; Lipson and Kurman 2013).

Digital fabrication became popular and gained visibility when several initiatives, involving the public in accessible and open manufacturing processes, were launched. All these 'making' movements were driven by the unique idea of democratisation, which brings people closer to manufacturing processes, tools, technology, software and knowledge to produce objects for a variety of purposes, from artistic expression, to personal and commercial use. Some of the significant actions and innovations which have changed the scenery of digital manufacturing in the last decades are (Mota 2011): *Online providers of fabrication services*: companies (e.g. Shapeways, Sculpteo, i.materialise) offering online fabrication services; *Manufacturing networks*: places or networks, like 100kGarages, where people could have their design produced by a local shop and tool owner; *Local production places*: community places, such as FabLabs and Hackerspaces, to bring amateurs, designers and technology enthusiasts together to collaborate and realise their ideas; *Personal printers*: open-source projects like RepRap, aiming at creating an affordable printer that could replicate itself. Thereafter, companies like Makerbot, Stratasys and 3DSystems started selling low-cost desktop printers; *Public databases of blueprints*: Thingiverse is one of the public repositories where people upload their 3D models for others to download and print. SketchFab, is one of the most popular platforms where 3D models are published and shared. Today, there are more than 1470 CH/education organisations publishing their content on SketchFab and more than 195000 CH models can be found on it

8.2.2 Producing and Defining 3D Replicas

The production pipeline of a 3D replica can be structured in two phases:

1. Acquisition and processing of 3D data: This process involves acquisition methods, such as 3D scanning, computed tomography (CT) scanning or photogrammetry to 'capture' information about the artefact's shape and appearance. Also, a 3D digital object can be created by using 3D modelling software.

This process will result in a 3D model or mesh which can be visualised and digitally edited to manipulate its shape and other physical behaviours. Nowadays, there is also the option to download or purchase a 3D model file through online databases.

2. Digital fabrication: This is the manufacturing phase that can be realised in different ways. It includes the process of taking a 3D model, producing code for the fabrication machine and physically fabricating it. Then, post-processing steps need to take place, including joining parts, removing any supportive material around the object, cleaning it, sanding it and painting it if necessary.

The production pipeline varies in every project and will involve choices in each step of the workflow. Different technologies can be deployed for fabricating an object which can be divided into subtractive and additive techniques. The former work by removing volume from a block of material by using CNC for a cutting machine which is usually a mill, lathe or router. Conversely, additive techniques are gaining popularity, as they become more accessible in terms of cost, ease of use and sustainability (they waste less material than CNC processes). The additive approach is mostly described as *3D printing* or *rapid prototyping* and it builds an object layer-by-layer. New 3D printing and hybrid techniques constantly emerge.

The product of the above workflow is described in literature with terms, such as *3D print, replica, 3D replica, reproduction.* Selecting the most appropriate can become and extensive discussion. Yet, in the era of fast technological advancement, when the distinction between the original and the other item becomes vague, most of these terms could become outdated. For this reason, the use of the term *digitally fabricated artefact* might appear as appropriate. Firstly, the word *artefact* refers to the products of work involving a degree of intentionality and agency (Hilpinen 2011) while also constituting a low-value term which is related to practical aspects (i.e. artifice) and hence is applied to material with humble, ordinary character (Pearce 2012). Secondly, *digitally fabricated* indicates activities which use computer-controlled tools for manufacturing and is broad enough to include products made from digitally synthesised materials. While taking this into consideration, it must be pointed out that the terms *replica* or *3D replica* dominate literature. Therefore, in this chapter, the terms *replica* and *3D replica* appear alongside the term *digitally fabricated artefact* as common terms corresponding to the related body of knowledge.

8.2.3 A Note on Authenticity

The discourse on the authenticity of artefacts has long been a vivid topic in heritage studies. In 1935, the German philosopher Walter Benjamin in his famous art critique *The Work of Art in the age of Mechanical Reproduction* argues that reproducing art has always been a fact. The introduction of mechanical methods to reproduce art, is something different, mainly because mechanical means can capture an aspect of the object, which might not be obvious on the original piece (this happens with 3D imaging); and replication can 'transfer' the object to places where the original could never be (this physically happens with fabrication). Nonetheless, replicas miss some important elements: the unique spatiotemporal existence (aura) of the original artefact; the 'essence' and the 'history' the object has experienced; its ritual function, i.e. original usage value; and the wholeness of the original. The enjoyment when experiencing a replica, as Benjamin concludes, hides behind politics and the production of sensorial imagery to satisfy the masses (Benjamin 1935).

Almost a century later, different approaches are challenging such ideas. Manually made replicas have long been introduced in the CH sector. What distinguishes the digitally fabricated replicas from the 'traditional' ones is the technological mediation that brings several advantages with it. Replicas—regardless of their provenance and context—can still provoke aesthetic appreciation and contribute to holistic experiences for audiences. Research further addresses the relation between experiences, authenticity and ethics. Some authors even characterise as fetishists those who insist on it (Sandis 2016). The key decision with respect to authenticity, whether it refers to the original context where an artefact was made, its creator, its original function and all the parameters defining the 'aura' of the authentic object, is to be honest about the exhibition context of the replica and its purpose (Sandis 2016).

Findings from Hede and Thyne (2010) show how people negotiate with 'inauthentic', supporting the idea about truth and honesty. Most visitors in this research did not mind dealing with replicas when they knew what they were. They also appreciated the narrative of replicas, engaged with exhibits, touched objects and enjoyed the imaginative process of projecting their own thoughts and feelings on them. As Di Giuseppantonio Di Franco et al. (2015) corroborate, their findings demonstrated that participants were more concerned with experiencing a 3D-printed object through the senses rather than having the original in front of them.

Being honest highlights that by no means a given replica intends to substitute the original object or deceive audiences. In fact, a physical and/or a digital replica can work as complementary interpretative materials within a CH experience. Perceiving replicas in this way might seem difficult. For instance, some CH professionals are still reluctant to use 3D digital and physical tools either because they might 'take away' some of their authoritative power by 'allowing' new interpretations to emerge (King et al. 2016), or because they cannot understand such potential due to lack of digital literacy (Parry et al. 2018). However, providing honest access to replicas agrees with the movement towards the democratisation of CH institutions, which focus on the provision of services to the public while becoming less 'authoritative' holders of objects and knowledge.

8.3 3D Replicas as Novel Modalities for Interaction

Our focus in this section builds on presenting the state-of-the-art in using 3D replicas for CH communication. Application examples can be grouped by different criteria, depending on the fabrication technology; the type of object the replica represents;

the targeted audience group and more. Our classification employs criteria related to *purpose*, i.e. what is the purpose and goal when using a replica, and *function*, i.e. the task assigned to a replica, under the 'umbrella' of CH communication (education, learning, enjoyment, appreciation, emotions, etc.). In case examples might fall under more than one category, the application is presented under the most obvious one, without eliminating alternative categorisations. While an effort has been made to include as many representative examples as possible, the review is not exhaustive as more applications of 3D replicas to support interpretation exist. The following subsections present examples of usage of replicas within such context.

8.3.1 3D Replicas to Enjoy Multisensorial Experiences

Replicas can be part of CH exhibitions to 'facilitate' more holistic experiences of artefacts that are usually out of reach, placed behind glass displays or not physically accessible. In this way, replicas become interpretative materials which can be included in an exhibition (with or without the original), along with other informative content to support CH interpretation, appreciation and enjoyment.

In one of the early examples, Guidazzoli et al. (2014) mention that, for the exhibition of the *Etruscan heritage* at the Museum of the History of Bologna, a detailed full-size 3D print of the Sarcophagus of the Spouses would be presented. Hence, people would have the chance to access by sight and touch an iconic artefact of the Etruscan world which is located in Rome. The authors argue that having the 3D replica along with a variety of digital applications could lead to better results, satisfying both CH institutions and the public. Similarly, a 3D replica of a marble statue representing a human-lion creature belonging to the Museo Civico of Viterbo was 3D scanned in Italy and 3D printed in the USA to form part of an exhibition about Egypt at the Yale Peabody Museum of Natural History (Urcia et al. 2018). 3D-printed reliefs representing illustrations of Santiago Ramon y Cajal, the father of modern neuroscience, have also been included in an exhibition of the National Institutes of Health in the USA along with Cajal's original illustrations to support the exhibition experience in more tangible ways (National Institutes of Health 2015). Other deployments of the technology come from the Archaeology Gallery (launched in 2019) of the Brighton Museum and Art Gallery, where replicas have been used to support the creation of facial reconstructions, as well as the interpretation of archaeological artefacts (Fig. 8.1).

The Visual Computing Lab of ISTI-CNR, in collaboration with the Opificio delle Pietre Dure and the Peggy Guggenheim Collection, have digitised in 3D Jackson Pollock's *Alchemy* and then produced a physical reproduction of the painting that was exhibited in Venice (Visual Computing Laboratory ISTI-CNR 2015). Another famous example is the replica of the prehistoric cave in Lascaux, France. As the original cave has been closed to the public for decades (because of the deterioration of the wall paintings), several efforts have been made to make the paintings accessible to the public. The latest one is the *Lascaux IV International Centre for Cave Art*,

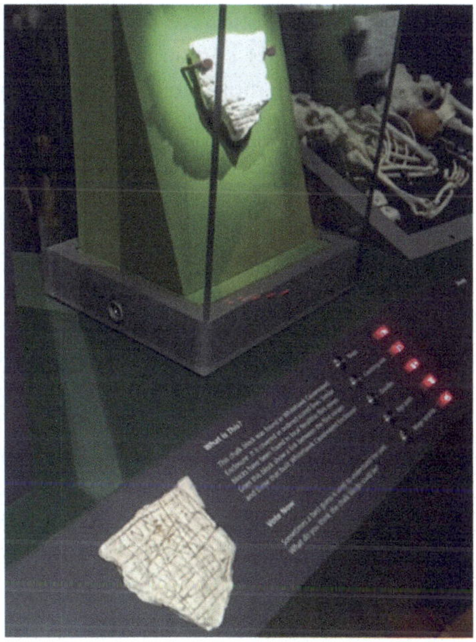

Fig. 8.1 3D-printed replica of the incised chalk block from Whitehawk in front of the museum display with the original item

where 3D-printed replicas of the paintings are exhibited along with a 1:1 replica of the original cave. Inside the cave replica, the light is low and the atmosphere is dark, while sounds are muffled to imitate the environment of the cave (Lascaux IV International Centre for Cave Art n.d.). Another example comes from the Madrid-based Factum Arte Company and Factum Foundation, who have produced several replicas of artworks. One of their most well-known projects is a replica of Tutankhamun's tomb in the Valley of the Kings in Egypt, which is accessible to the public (Factum Foundation 2014).

Some of the latest efforts in the context of multisensorial experiences come from the Google Arts and Culture institute, CyArk and Stratasys, who announced an extended collaboration on the *Open Heritage* project. By printing small-scale versions of CH sites, the project aims to bring to life monuments and artefacts around the world (Jackson 2019). More recently, Google teamed up with the CH project *Scan the world* to enrich its open-source 3D printable art data (Everett 2021).

8.3.2 3D Replicas to Artistically Remix

An interesting idea to enhance appreciation and connection with CH involves 3D imaging, 3D remixing and 3D printing of hybrid collection objects (i.e. mixing museum objects together or with other imaginary additions). The new hybrid objects reflect the expression and creativity of the audiences/artists and can be considered as physical manifestations of their ideas. Such activities constitute innovative applications of 3D in CH communication, as people are not limited to just accessing information but are motivated to 'play' with it. Showcasing remixed examples goes one step further into the idea of democratisation, as organisations gradually detach from their authoritative profile and give space to other voices.

A tomb figurine from the Eastern Han dynasty and an architectural brick with ogre mask from the Tang dynasty at the Art Institute of Chicago were mixed by Tom Burtonwood, who created the *Ogre puppy* (Neely and Langer 2013). The same institution (Neely and Rozner 2015) ran the programme *Object: Remixed, Reconfigured* for tweens. The participants chose artefacts and remixed them to create their own version of artworks. The Metropolitan Museum of Art (Met) in New York invited digital artists to capture and print their 3D models during a Hackathon. Artists created remixed objects from the museum's collections and uploaded them online. One of the most interesting results was a 3D mashup of statues named *Leda and the Marsyas*, designed by Jonathan Monaghan who stated that the experience 'illustrates the mutability of 3D models and the ease with which users can create new content out of what already exists' (Undeen 2013).

Finally, an activity that involved physically remixing 3D-printed parts of Rodin's sculptures took place at the Portland Art Museum during the exhibition *Rodin: The human experience*. 3D-printed parts from Rodin's sculptures with magnets on were made available to visitors to assemble their own versions of Rodin's work. Apart from the creative aspect of the process, the museum officers discuss the educational benefits from the involvement of the audience in such activities (Noto 2017).

8.3.3 3D Replicas to Enhance Learning and Education

In accordance with the constructivist approach, suggesting that children engage and learn when interacting with objects, CH organisations were amongst the first to deploy replicas in educational activities for children, families and schools. Many examples of such deployments exist, so only few of them are mentioned here.

A megalithic stone from Anglesey (Wales) was segmented into pieces to create a puzzle, that children could assemble using a central pillar, for the outreach activities of the *Heritage Together* project (UK). The activity has proved to be engaging for older children but not very successful for the younger ones (Miles et al. 2015). The reason could be that people did not know what features to incorporate into replicas and then how to successfully introduce them in CH activities for the targeted audience. In 2013, the American Museum of Natural History launched an educational programme for high school children, who were asked to digitise, process and 3D print dinosaur bones and then assemble the skeleton to identify the dinosaur species. The activity engaged children with palaeontology, introduced them to comparative anatomy and worked as a critical thinking and practical skill acquisition framework, fundamentally beneficial for learning (AMNH 2013). Another interesting project comes from the collaboration of the University of Brighton with the Brighton Museum and Art Gallery. Researchers

Fig. 8.2 3D-printed replicas of tools and pottery for the Stone Age educational activity at the Brighton Museum and Art Gallery

3D scanned and 3D-printed replicas of objects from the archaeological collection for primary school children participating in the Stone Age educational sessions (Fig. 8.2). The children were invited to associate the fabricated artefacts to fictional characters and engage in an exchange of goods game to imitate neolithic trading activities. The hands-on activities and especially the trading activity were engaging for the children and generated interesting discussions. Another 3D-printed puzzle activity of an Iron Age funerary urn was also produced for the Archaeology Gallery of the museum to engage young visitors within the exhibition (Rodriguez Echavarria et al. 2020).

8.3.4 3D Replicas to Experience the Physical and the Digital World

In the frame of digital fabrication for heritage interpretation, many parties have been exploring ideas which combine replicas with alternative digital content presentations, embedding hardware into physical objects that behave in intelligent ways. Such objects, known as *smart replicas*, are essentially 3D replicas that work as tangible interfaces, enabling novel modes of interaction by triggering some response in the form of a reaction or behaviour (e.g. projection of an animation, audio response) (Marshall et al. 2016). Integrating smart replicas in the CH environment attempts to unite the physical and the digital (sometimes described as *phygital*) into one experiential framework. The EU funded project MeSch (2017), employed replicas and other copies of objects to provide further layers of interpretative information and physical engagement with artefacts in exhibitions (Marshall et al. 2016). Another relevant example is the Virtex system. For this project, touch sensors were placed inside two replicas (statue of Augustus of Prima Porta and the Ara Pacis monument in Rome) for the exhibition *Keys to Rome* in Amsterdam. When visitors touched the tiny buttons that were integrated into the replicas, relevant storytelling content was projected on a screen, complementing the tactile experience (Capurro et al. 2015).

Replicas can also trigger interaction without having any kind of hardware (sensors, NFC tags or other) embedded into them. Thus, they can be used as input devices, such as a computer mouse or joystick, to activate some content on an output or input/output device. Such a hybrid solution was deployed for the outreach activities of the *Heritage together* project in the UK. 3D-printed miniatures of megalithic monuments (created through crowdsourced photogrammetry) were placed on a multitouch table. The replicas acted as fingers touching different points on the screen and triggered relevant interpretative information. The application received positive feedback and it was successful especially with children. Nonetheless, the use of the replicas was not always clear, as people did not know whether this was a game activity and in some cases adults were not confident when using the touch table (Miles et al. 2015).

Replicas have also been used in AR/VR applications. Some interesting examples come from Maaike Roozenburg's studio. The designer collaborated with academics and curators for the exhibition *I cook therefore I am* at the Wereldmuseum of Rotterdam. Video mapping was used on the surface of three scaled-up replicas of cuneiform tablets to present information about the cooking recipes described on them, witnessing some of the oldest culinary data in the world (Studio Maaike Roozenburg 2017). An application from the same studio ulitises physical ceramic replicas 'enriched' with content from an AR mobile application. The user can download the app and point a mobile phone to an open foldable cardboard that works as a marker. Then, a timeline appears providing textual, visual and sound information about the replica which is placed at the centre of the box (Studio Maaike Roozenburg and Like-Friends Creative Agency 2016). Another relevant example deployed an HTC VIVE headset and the integration of a VIVE tracker within a 3D-printed replica to navigate a VR environment and interact with artefacts, providing further interpretations for the lifecycle of an Iron Age pot (Gaugne et al. 2018).

8.3.5 3D Replicas to Assist Visually Impaired People to Experience Artefacts

Numerous projects focus on multisensorial experiences for the visually impaired (VI), as this is one of the audiences that can benefit the most by such provision. Here, we mention some of these projects to showcase how such efforts gradually move from simple tactile explorations to more sophisticated responsive systems which enable independent user interactions.

One of the early examples was a 3D-printed figurine of the artist Rita Furrer covered with cloth, made at the Vienna University of Technology in 2010. The figurine was used by blind visitors during a museum 'touch tour' (Neumüller et al. 2014). Also, four paintings from the Kunsthistorisches Museum in Vienna were produced and 3D printed in the form of 'layered-diagrams' and 'textured reliefs' by the VRVis research centre. These reliefs were tested with VI users with the support of trained guides. Users reported that they had a clearer understanding of the composition of paintings and depth details (Reichinger et al. 2011). A series of guided tours took place at the Art Institute of Chicago in 2014 to enhance the visiting experience for people with low vision. Four artefacts from each gallery were fabricated and given to people to touch, while listening to descriptions by the museum staff, along with other sensorial input, such as music and sounds produced by the objects (bell, whistle). The evaluation demonstrated that VI people developed a deeply emotional relationship with the objects which had an 'awakening' power (Neely and Rozner 2015). Further efforts come from the National Museum in Bloemfontein, South Africa, where micro Computed Tomography (micro-CT) was used to capture the shape of natural specimens, which were then processed, fabricated and placed in the museum for VI visitors to explore (du Plessis et al. 2020).

Other projects make use of 3D replicas and multimedia content to support non-guided interpretation for VI users. For instance, the Orasis project deployed Arduino boards, touch sensors and a mobile app to enhance access to museums for blind users (Anagnostakis et al. 2016). Participants valued the application and would like to deploy it in museum environments, yet controlling the audio through gestures on a phone while exploring the replica proved easier for totally blind users than for the partially sighted. A similar project in Italy utilised 3D replicas, NFC technology and QR codes along with a mobile app to enable visitors to enjoy audio descriptions about the artefacts (3D ArcheoLab). The users reported that they discovered more about local history by using touch. Another project deployed touch sensors on a 'digital touch replica' of an Egyptian cat sarcophagus to trigger audio descriptions. People expressed positive comments about the wood composite material of the replica, resembling the original artefact. However, they found difficult to explore the object freely, as the audio would always trigger when touching the cat (Reichinger et al. 2016b).

Work investigating functional and non-functional requirements of the VI community for 3D-printed haptic objects for CH exploration comes from the Aptos project 'smart exhibit' prototypes. For this project, three different interactive systems were developed integrating technologies in the spectrum of the Internet of Things, such as WiFi, single board computers, microcontrollers, RFID tagging, on-demand triggering and proximity sensors to support the interpretation of monuments in Greece. The evaluation demonstrated that such systems are welcomed by the VI community, yet user retention is ultimately related to people's interests, while high fidelity prints along with narrations might overwhelm some users due to information and haptic input overload (Pistofidis et al. 2023).

Reliefs have also been introduced to communicate 'flat' information, such as architectural facades and paintings. Artworks in the form of 3D-printed reliefs were produced for the Bendigo Art Gallery in Australia as a 'value-sensitive' methodology providing access to artefacts to VI users (Butler et al. 2019). The Tooteko app (D'Agnano et al. 2015) deployed NFC technology to provide audio descriptions of a 15th century church facade in Italy. The USA-based company Tactile Images produced coloured tactile prints of paintings and photos with embedded touch sensors to trigger audio descriptions for the *Sight Unseen* exhibition at the Canadian Museum for Human Rights. As Tactile Images stated, providing such assets is a step towards independent, unaided exploration, which is a basic human right (Tactile Images

2016). In addition, the *Touch the Prado* exhibition featured coloured replicas of famous paintings along with audio descriptions (Hewitt 2015).

The *Out Loud* exhibition at the Andy Warhol Museum (USA) showcased tactile representations of Warhol's artwork and supported the tactile experience with audio descriptions using location-aware technology and a mobile app. VI people collaborated as consultants during the development of the audio application (Blakemore 2016). A similar system was developed at the Booth Museum of Natural History (UK) to enable the VI to explore the otherwise inaccessible Victorian environmental dioramas of the museum through touch and audio via a 3D-printed relief and a context-aware mobile application (Samaroudi et al. 2017). A system using a camera and gesture recognition to provide audio descriptions for Klimt's Kiss tactile painting has been created by the VRVis research centre in Vienna. Users gave positive feedback about the system, nonetheless some problems with the audio occurred because of wrong hand/gesture positioning and limitations in hand/gesture recognition by the camera (Reichinger et al. 2016a). Similar applications have also been deployed within the ARCHES project (Arches 2019), to make CH environments more inclusive for people with difficulties associated with perception, memory, cognition and communication. Another relevant system (Buonamici et al. 2016) used a Microsoft Kinect depth-sensing scanner to detect users' finger position on a bas-relief and provide audio information. Yet, the application presented some problems with the hand tracking system and identification of touch.

8.3.6 3D Replicas to Enhance Socialisation, Remembrance and Comfort

3D replicas have been utilised in programmes designed for older audiences having an impairment; for people facing age-related difficulties, such as dementia; for trauma survivors; or audiences receiving treatment in health settings. Such activities present common elements of social interaction, collaboration, memory retrieval, which have a 'healing' potential and present benefits for people facing various conditions (Chatterjee et al. 2009).

For the *Please Touch* project (Knowlson 2016), curators and researchers presented replicas of objects from the Social History Collection of Museums Sheffield to older VI people. The tactile exploration of the objects and related audio, motivated participants to narrate stories from their childhood and difficult periods such as the Second World War. A series of reminiscence workshops worked as an 'engagement vehicle' for people and prompted them to explore and share personal and community narratives. Another project at the Brighton Museum and Art Gallery (Collectingbulldogs.com 2017) explored the creative use of a replica of a ceramic bulldog exhibit, significant to a member of a group experiencing trauma or mental health issues. The group was involved in a series of art workshops and also attended a session about 3D printing, where miniatures of the selected object were printed live. A 1:1 replica of the

Fig. 8.3 3D-printed replica of a Bulldog (right) as painted by the museum group on display next to the original item (left)

selected artefact was provided to the group and was painted by them in their chosen colours (with David Bowie's eyes) (Fig. 8.3). The museum mentors received positive comments about the experience, emphasising how the group creatively engaged with the activity.

An interesting project that intersects creativity, remixing and comfort was a collaboration between the Victoria and Albert Museum (V&A), the GOSH Arts programme at Great Ormond Street and other hospitals. Officers from the museum visited young patients in hospital wards and asked them to remix 3D models of museum artefacts to create their desired models. Then the designs were 3D printed and presented to the patients. The activities generated various discussions around the objects and patients' ideas in an environment where they often experience isolation and distancing from creative processes (Flowers 2018). A follow up of this project by the V&A and GOSH was also launched in 2021 called *Museum in your Room*. Selected animal models from the museum's collections were 3D printed and then provided to the hospital's school to support teachers and students with flexible educational activities, as well as further sensory and artistic activities (Tucker 2021).

8.3.7 3D Replicas to Explore Through Workshops and Creative Sessions

GLAMs have also launched workshops, usually addressed to families, teenagers, young adults and professionals, to engage them in creative activities via 3D technologies. During sessions, people become involved in 3D scanning, designing, editing and 3D printing models of museum artefacts and their own artwork inspired by museum objects. At the Art Institute of Chicago teenagers explored 3D printing during the *Teen Lab* workshops. The same institute organised workshops for teachers to introduce them to 3D printing, by employing museum objects as inspiration for artwork. Another event, invited families to sit on a turn-platform, posing as sculpture from the museum galleries. A facilitator digitised them, while other people observed 3D printers working. All workshops have proved valuable opportunities to trigger people's interest around technology and art, perception and reproduction of artwork (Neely and Rozner 2015). Further examples include a Scanathon by the British Museum, and a 3D-printed jewellery workshop at the V&A (Bryce 2015; Flowers 2015). The Design Museum in London offered 3D design and 3D printing events to families (Design Museum 2017); and the Met in collaboration with Ultimaker (2019) offered the *Met Set* lessons to bring the museum artefacts and 3D printing into the classroom.

8.3.8 3D Replicas to Enjoy Focusing on Smell and Taste

Enjoying replicas through multisensorial experiences often neglects smell and especially taste, because they are perceived as 'irrelevant' senses. Nonetheless, smell is one of the strongest mechanisms for memory retrieval and engagement. Similarly, taste can provoke thinking or inspiration and constitutes an alternative method to connect with objects' narratives. Researchers at the Met in New York created edible replicas of museum artefacts to allow visitors to enjoy multisensorial experiences of CH, while emphasising on smell and taste (due to the edible materials used). They also produced a kit for visitors to make their own edible artefacts (Tang and Zhao 2015). These approaches might appear unusual, but they demonstrate innovative ways to engage audiences with collections through important yet forgotten senses.

8.3.9 3D Replicas to Offer and to Take Home

3D replicas have also made their appearance in museum shops for visitors to purchase. The Van Gogh Museum in Amsterdam was one of the pioneers when selling replicas in 2013 (Alberge 2013). The British Museum also started selling replicas of objects from its collections after collaborating with the company ThinkSee3D (Young 2017). In Italy, researchers have collaborated with the National Etruscan Museum of Villa Giulia, to create 3D-printed miniature versions of Ati (a fictional character) and the famous Sarcophagus of the Spouses, to sell at the museum store (Guidazzoli et al. 2014). By purchasing a replica, people can take artefacts home and keep them close to them. They can also offer them as gifts. In these ways, people establish connections with artefacts, which might have a significance further than that of a mere souvenir purchased from a museum shop.

8.4 Topical Discussion Around 3D Replicas

8.4.1 3D Replicas Within Participatory Community Approaches

Leveraging the possibilities of 3D technologies and especially 3D printing can serve as valuable mechanisms to bring communities closer to CH organisations or initiatives. Such opportunities engage people in activities which enhance community dialogue, ‘allow’ different voices to be heard, embrace alternative interpretations, while challenging the authoritative character of institutions. Some activities with a co-design, co-production aspects have been presented in the previous Sect. (8.3). Yet, here we focus on examples where community groups have been actively involved in making decisions, deploying tools and curating the outputs of creative processes through digital fabrication.

As part of the ACCORD project (UK), community groups engaged in deciding on appropriate 3D imaging technologies to capture and in some cases to produce 3D replicas of CH sites. The community was also encouraged to integrate community-generated material into the output resources relating to CH sites, such as photos, oral histories and more. Participants, appreciated the opportunities to explore CH in novel ways and also made new ‘connections’ through a process of further valorising local heritage (Maxwell 2017). Another project in Hove, East Sussex (UK) involved artists, civic groups, CH organisations and technical experts to produce the *Constellation* public sculpture celebrating and sharing Hove’s heritage. Through a series of workshops, the local community group selected objects/ideas that hold significance for the city and further elaborated on their integration in the ‘urban grain”. Museums, citizens and the artist of the sculpture contributed with artefacts which were 3D scanned and then physically produced through digital fabrication. The replicas were processed with appropriate surface materials and then placed on the *Constellation* statue (Rodriguez Echavarria et al. 2018).

Lastly, a project to engage the public with the collection of Asante goldweights held at the Brighton Museum and Art Gallery, involved curators, academics and community groups, including people from the communities of origin of the artefacts, to research and provide interpretations of the collection. The community groups, not only engaged in the selection of the objects and research of their narratives, but also became involved in photogrammetry activities and had the chance to see 3D printing in action. Such step, moves further in terms of enabling access to tools and processes. Yet, there is still potential to explore how such initiatives could overcome knowledge, cost, hardware and software barriers and actively co-produce with communities even through the more ‘technical’ aspects of the replica workflow.

8.4.2 3D Replicas in Decolonisation and Repatriation Efforts

Producing replicas for repatriation and decolonisation is a topical and open matter of discussion. When deploying 3D for such purposes, collaboration of the interested parties is essential to overcome difficulties related to copyright, cost, ethics and the crucial question of who keeps the original.

The Smithsonian's National Museum of Natural History has worked with the Tlingit native community of Alaska to return objects which were sacred, of special importance or related to funerary practices of the community. Some of the objects that were returned to the Tlingit were digitised in 3D and a significant Killer Whale clan crest hat was digitally fabricated and accurately replicated to be kept at the possession of the museum (Hollinger et al. 2013). Another case of repatriation comes from Finland. Seventy artefacts were repatriated from the Hämeenlinna City Museum and the Museum Centre Vapriikkiin in Tampere to the Sámi Museum Siida in Inari. In this project, photogrammetry was used to digitally capture several repatriated artefacts and then offer their 3D models to the local artisans' community to facilitate copying designs and education. The community was further involved in discussions around data ownership and data access (Magnani et al. 2018). Lastly, a controversial example of repatriation was the project that artists Nora Al-Badri and Jan Nikolai Nelles undertook secretly at the Neues Museum. The artists claimed that they scanned the bust of Nefertiti using a Microsoft Xbox 360 Kinect. Then, they released the 3D data online. A 3D replica of Nefertiti's bust was created and exhibited at the *Something Else Off Biennale* in Cairo and another one was printed by the American University of Cairo. The artists claimed that their intention was to return Nefertiti to her homeland and criticised Western museums' colonialist practices (Voone 2016). However, there was controversy around the fact that such a detailed model could never be the result of the acquisition done by the artists. Instead, it seems that the data was released to them through other means. Following this, the artist and 3D scanning expert, Cosmo Wenman, was able to acquire the scanning data from the Neues Museum after a three-year freedom of information effort and then released them online (Wenman 2019).

By looking at the above examples, it becomes clear that the employment of advanced technological methods to digitally capture and replicate—physically and virtually—CH assets is a powerful tool to promote the discourse on decolonisation and repatriation. Such efforts are currently shaped through collaborative practices and projects around the world. Yet, it is crucial to understand that such efforts should involve CH institutions, initiative groups and most importantly the communities of origin of these artefacts in order to decide the most appropriate way/s to move forward. For instance, mutually agreed decisions should be made on the choice of technology, data ownership, data access, the possibility to physically replicate, as well ownership of the physical object/s. Therefore, a case-by-case examination should be adopted and communities' positions should not be prejudged. This is important, as there are examples of community groups who mostly care about the sacred knowledge of the process of making an object and not so much about the final product itself, while others assign special meaning to artefacts through spiritual ceremonies without looking that much at their 'originality' (Isaac 2011; Csoba DeHass and Taitt 2018).

8.5 3D Replicas During/Post the COVID Era and Future Perspectives

Given the multiple examples of digital fabrication and especially 3D printing for CH interpretation, using replicas during the COVID lockdowns would have been a sensible solution to enable access to CH. Recent research (Samaroudi et al. 2020) demonstrates that the pandemic forced CH organisations to find new means to engage standard audiences and support other emerging ones through a variety of offerings usually relating to the museums' collections. Nonetheless, 3D models, which could be further 'materialised' into digitally fabricated artefacts, constituted just a small percentage of these offerings. Some of the limited known examples of deploying fabrication during the pandemic come from the UCL Museums, which had to adapt to the 'new normal'. Thus, a set of gorilla bones was scanned through Computer Tomography and then 3D printed to become part of a skeleton assembly loan kit for secondary schools. Similarly, four objects were 3D printed to support pupils at a London primary school to learn about Ancient Sudan and the Petrie Museum (Abankwah 2021).

The pandemic demonstrated the need to rapidly adapt to unexpected circumstances, while contributing to a 'shift' in rethinking about digital data infrastructure, practices and strategies. In the context of CH, being 'data ready' and adopting open access practices is crucial to enable HEIs and GLAMs to fulfil their role as accessible and inclusive institutions for the benefit of the community. Within this frame, leveraging the potential of digital fabrication to enable physical access to CH assets can work as an engagement vehicle, while prompting interesting discussions, supporting creative explorations and ultimately democratising culture and knowledge. Yet, several challenges still hinder the fruition of digital fabrication for CH communication. These are summarised below.

Data acquisition: Even though digitisation methods, such as photogrammetry, are more accessible in terms of cost, accessing a structured light scanner, a LiDAR system or CT is still out of reach for many GLAMs or HEIs. Lowering costs of equipment or enabling access to it would facilitate capturing 3D data.

Data processing: Many free software packages exist to process 3D data, yet these might not always produce good quality 3D models and often come with limitations regarding the amount of data which can be processed without paying a fee. Using 3D graphics software also requires a certain level of knowledge and skills to produce the desirable 3D model ready for fabrication. The lack of standardisation or guidance in terms of workflows to perform necessary processes (e.g. hole filling, segmenting, adding fixtures, slicing) further hinders the production of 3D replicas.

Data preservation, sharing and reuse: Storing, curating and sharing 3D data for a variety of purposes requires certain knowledge and skills to apply FAIR (Findable, Accessible, Interoperable, Reusable) data management principles to facilitate open access to data, while enabling data customisation and reuse. Accessible data infrastructure is also needed to support all the above processes and enable data-driven approaches, including digital fabrication.

Digital fabrication: The cost of digital fabrication devices, apart from some FDM printers, is still high and hence difficult to access. Outsourcing, when requiring another fabrication method (possibly to achieve better quality or accurate colours), is often very expensive. Time is another constraint, as to fabricate an object which is not small, many hours or even days are needed to complete fabrication.

Post-processing: Post-processing depends on the type of object that is digitally fabricated in terms of shape, size and details. It comprises processes such as removing the supportive material, sanding, joining, polishing and painting. These require manual labour and skills with regards to materials, tools and execution. Post-processing can be time-consuming and costly, yet it is necessary in many cases, e.g. when a 3D replica is printed in parts or needs to be painted to resemble a museum artefact.

8.6 Conclusion

This chapter detailed the development of digital fabrication, the production and the definition of 3D replicas while also addressing issues around authenticity in the context of CH interpretation. Through numerous applications, we presented the state-of-the-art in deploying digitally fabricated artefacts for CH communication, focusing on the purpose and function of replicas as novel modalities for interaction within different experiential frameworks. The contribution of replicas in participatory approaches and decolonisation efforts was also discussed.

Although there is great benefit in including 3D replicas as standard interpretative, interactive 'devices' in heritage communication, several challenges still need to be addressed to unlock the potential of digital fabrication for effective CH communication. From the technology point of view, while considerable efforts are happening towards this direction, 3D imaging software, hardware as well as fabrication technologies need to become more accessible in terms of cost, workflows and possibly standardisation to overcome knowledge barriers. From the infrastructure point of view, 3D data need to become widely available via systems facilitating data storage, access, use and reuse for CH communication and beyond. From the practice perspective, digital literacy with regards to the potential that 3D technologies have to offer needs to be supported through cross-sectorial efforts, including the development of appropriate strategies to promote digital fabrication.

References

3D ArcheoLab (2016) Museo tattile di Marzabotto. https://www.3d-archeolab.it/portfolio-items/museo-tattile-marzabotto/. Last Accessed 03 Apr 2024

Abankwah J (2021) Gorillas and frogs: the use of 3D printed replica objects for handling in schools during the pandemic. https://blogs.ucl.ac.uk/public-engagement/2021/08/11/gorillas-and-frogs-3d/. Last Accessed 03 Apr 2024

Alberge D (2013) Van Gogh in 3D? A replica could be yours for £22,000. https://www.theguardian.com/artanddesign/2013/aug/24/3d-replicas-van-gogh. Last Accessed 03 Apr 2024

AMNH (2013) Students use 3D printing to reconstruct dinosaurs. https://www.amnh.org/explore/news-blogs/education-posts/students-use-3d-printing-to-reconstruct-dinosaurs. Last Accessed 03 Apr 2024

Anagnostakis G, Antoniou M, Kardamitsi E, Sachinidis T, Koutsabasis P, Stavrakis M, Vosinakis S, Zissis D (2016) Accessible museum collections for the visually impaired: combining tactile exploration, audio descriptions and mobile gestures. In: Proceedings of the 18th international conference on human-computer interaction with mobile devices and services adjunct. MobileHCI'16. https://doi.org/10.1145/2957265.2963118

Arches (2019) Arches project–accessible resources for cultural heritage EcoSystems. https://www.arches-project.eu. Last Accessed 03 Apr 2024

Benjamin W (1935) The work of art in the age of mechanical reproduction. Tech Rep. https://www.marxists.org/reference/subject/philosophy/works/ge/benjamin.htm. Last Accessed 03 Apr 2024

Bensoussan H (2016) The history of 3D printing: from the 80s to today. https://www.sculpteo.com/en/3d-learning-hub/basics-of-3d-printing/the-history-of-3d-printing/. Last Accessed 03 Apr 2024

Blakemore E (2016) Visually impaired people can now explore Andy Warhol's work with their ears and fingers—smart news—Smithsonian. https://www.smithsonianmag.com/smart-news/visually-impaired-people-can-now-explore-andy-warhols-work-their-ears-180960935/?no-ist. Last Accessed 03 Apr 2024

Bryce E (2015) The British Museum uses 3D scanning to bring artefacts to life. In: Wired. https://www.wired.com/story/reprinting-history/. Last Accessed 03 Apr 2024

Buonamici F, Carfagni M, Furferi R, Governi L, Volpe Y (2016) Are we ready to build a system for assisting blind people in tactile exploration of bas-reliefs? Sens (Switz) 16(9). https://doi.org/10.3390/s16091361

Butler M, Holloway L, Marriott K (2019) A closer look: multi-sensory accessible art translations. In: ASSETS 2019-21st international ACM SIGACCESS conference on computers and accessibility. https://doi.org/10.1145/3308561.3354617.

Capurro C, Nollet D, Pletinckx D (2015) Tangible interfaces for digital museum applications. In: Digital heritage

Chatterjee H, Vreeland S, Noble G (2009) Museopathy: exploring the healing potential of handling museum objects. Mus Soc 7(3)

Collectingbulldogs.com (2017) 3D Printed bulldog figurine donated to the Collectibulldogs. https://www.collectibulldogs.com/little-3d-printed-puppy/. Last Accessed 03 Apr 2024

Csoba De Hass MK, Taitt A (2018) 3D Technology in collaborative heritage preservation. Mus Anthropol Rev 12(2). https://doi.org/10.14434/mar.v12i2.22428

D'Agnano F, Balletti C, Guerra F, Vernier P (2015) Tooteko: a case study of augmented reality for an accessible cultural heritage. Digitization, 3d printing and sensors for an audio-tactile experience. In: The international archives of the photogrammetry, remote sensing and spatial information sciences XL-5/W4. https://doi.org/10.5194/isprsarchives-XL-5-W4-207-2015

Design Museum (2017) Innovative product design. https://designmuseum.org/whats-on/families-and-young-people/get-into-design-past/innovative-product-design. Last Accessed 03 Apr 2024

Di Giuseppantonio Di Franco P, Camporesi C, Galeazzi F, Kallmann M (2015) 3D Printing and immersive visualization for improved perception of ancient artifacts. Presence: Teleoperators Virtual Environ 24(3). https://doi.org/10.1162/PRES_a_00229

du Plessis A, Els J, Le Roux S, Tshibalanganda M, Pretorius T (2020) Data for 3D printing enlarged museum specimens for the visually impaired. Gigabyte. https://doi.org/10.46471/gigabyte.3

Everett H (2021) Scan the world partners with Google Arts & Culture for open-source 3D printable artefacts. https://3dprintingindustry.com/news/scan-the-world-partners-with-google-arts-culture-for-open-source-3d-printable-artefacts-188977/. Last Accessed 03 Apr 2024

Flowers A (2015) Samsung digital classroom: 3D printed jewellery. https://www.vam.ac.uk/blog/museum-life/samsung-digital-classroom-3d-printed-jewellery. Last Accessed 03 Apr 2024

Flowers A (2018) Taking sculptures for a walk: 3D Printing and museum outreach. https://www.vam.ac.uk/blog/digital/taking-sculptures-for-a-walk-3d-printing-and-museum-outreach. Last Accessed 03 Apr 2024

Factum Foundation (2014) Factum foundation-exhibitions. https://factumfoundation.org/our-projects/exhibitions-and-conferences/the-theban-necropolis-preservation-initiative/the-burial-chamber-of-tutankhamun/the-authorized-facsimile-of-the-tomb-of-tutankhamun. Last Accessed 03 Apr 2024

Gaugne R, Samaroudi M, Nicolas T, Barreau J-B, Garnier L, Rodriguez Echavarria K, Gouranton V (2018) Virtual Reality (VR) interactions with multiple interpretations of archaeological artefacts. In: GCH 2018-Eurographics workshop on graphics and cultural heritage. https://doi.org/10.2312/gch.20181339

Guidazzoli A, Baglivo A, De Luca D, Imboden S, Liguori MC, Rivalta A (2014) Crossmedia integration of 3D contents for cultural communication. In: 2014 3DTV-conference: the true vision-capture, transmission and display of 3D video (3DTV-CON). https://doi.org/10.1109/3DTV.2014.6874732

Hede A-M, Thyne A (2010) A journey to the authentic: museum visitors and their negotiation of the inauthentic. J Mark Manag 26(7–8). https://doi.org/10.1080/02672571003780106.

Hewitt D (2015) Please touch the art: 3D Printing helps visually impaired appreciate paintings. https://www.smithsonianmag.com/innovation/please-touch-art-3-d-printing-helps-visually-impaired-appreciate-paintings-180954420/?no-ist. Last Accessed 03 Apr 2024

Hilpinen R (2011) Artifact. In: Zalta EN (ed). https://plato.stanford.edu/entries/artifact/. Last Accessed 03 Apr 2024

Hollinger RE, John E Jr, Jacobs H, Moran-Collins L, Thome C, Zastrow J, Metallo A, Waibel G, Rossi V (2013) Tlingit-Smithsonian collaborations with 3D digitization of cultural objects. Mus Anthropol Rev 7(1–2). https://scholarworks.iu.edu/journals/index.php/mar/article/view/2173/4567

Isaac G (2011) Whose idea was this? Museums, replicas, and the reproduction of knowledge. Curr Anthropol 52(2). https://doi.org/10.1086/659141

Jackson B (2019) Google and Stratasys collaborate to preserve cultural heritage with 3D printing. https://3dprintingindustry.com/news/google-and-stratasys-collaborate-to-preserve-cultural-heritage-with-3d-printing-148118/. Last Accessed 03 Apr 2024

King L, Stark JF, Cooke P (2016) Experiencing the digital world: the cultural value of digital engagement with heritage. Herit Soc 9(1). https://doi.org/10.1080/2159032X.2016.1246156

Knowlson A (2016) The please touch project. https://pleasetouchproject.wordpress.com. Last Accessed 03 Apr 2024

Lascaux IV International Centre for Cave Art (n.d.) LASCAUX IV. https://lascaux.fr/en/. Last Accessed 03 Apr 2024

Lipson H, Kurman M (2013) Fabricated: the new world of 3D printing, 1st edn.

Magnani M, Guttorm A, Magnani N (2018) Three-dimensional, community-based heritage management of indigenous museum collections: archaeological ethnography, revitalization and repatriation at the Sámi Museum Siida. J Cult Herit 31. https://api.semanticscholar.org/CorpusID:139732155

Marshall MT, Dulake N, Ciolfi L, Duranti D, Kockelkorn H, Petrelli D (2016) Using tangible smart replicas as controls for an interactive museum exhibition. In: TEI'2016. https://doi.org/10.1145/2839462.2839493

Maxwell M (2017) Power is in the process: the ACCORD project. Internet Archaeol 44. https://doi.org/10.11141/ia.44.10.
MeSch (2017) MeSch-material encounters with digital cultural heritage. https://www.mesch-project.eu. Last Accessed 03 Apr 2024
Miles HC et al (2015) Alternative representations of 3D reconstructed heritage data. J Comput Cult Herit 9(1). https://doi.org/10.1145/2795233
Mota C (2011) The rise of personal fabrication. In: Proceedings of the 8th ACM conference on Creativity and cognition-C&C'11. https://doi.org/10.1145/2069618.2069665
National Institutes of Health (2015) NIH exhibits original Cajal neuroscience drawings. https://www.youtube.com/watch?v=QIDUKHXqtg4&feature=youtu.be. Last Accessed 03 Apr 2024
Neely L, Langer M (2013) Please feel the museum: the emergence of 3D printing and scanning. In: Museums and the web 2013. https://mw2013.museumsandtheweb.com/paper/please-feel-the-museum-the-emergence-of-3d-printing-and-scanning/. Last Accessed 03 Apr 2024
Neely L, Rozner E (2015) Museum3D: experiments in engaging audiences using 3D. In: Museums and the web 2015. https://mw2015.museumsandtheweb.com/paper/museum3d-experiments-in-engaging-audiences-using-3d/. Last Accessed 03 Apr 2024
Neumüller M, Reichinger A, Rist F, Kern C (2014) 3D Printing for cultural heritage: preservation, accessibility, research and education. In: Ioannides M, Quak E (eds) 3D Research challenges in cultural heritage: a roadmap in digital heritage preservation. https://doi.org/10.1007/978-3-662-44630-0_9
Noto J (2017) Rodin remix: 3D Printing and museum engagement. https://artmuseumteaching.com/2017/06/08/rodin-remix/. Last Accessed 03 Apr 2024
Parry R, Eikhof DR, Barnes S-A, Kispeter E (2018) Development, supply, deployment, demand: balancing the museum digital skills ecosystem. First findings of the 'One by One' national digital literacy project. In: Museums and the web 2018. https://mw18.mwconf.org/paper/development-supply-deployment-demand-balancing-the-museum-digital-skills-ecosystem-first-findings-of-the-one-by-one-national-digital-literacy-project/. Last Accessed 03 Apr 2024
Pearce SM (2012) Museum objects, 1st edn. In: Dudley S (ed) Museum objects: experiencing the properties of things
Pistofidis P et al (2023) Design and evaluation of smart-exhibit systems that enrich cultural heritage experiences for the visually impaired. J Cult Herit 60. https://doi.org/10.1016/j.culher.2023.01.004
Reichinger A, Maierhofer S, Purgathofer W (2011) High quality tactile paintings. J Comput Cult Herit (JOCCH) 4(2). https://doi.org/10.1145/2037820.2037822
Reichinger A, Fuhrmann A, Maierhofer S, Purgathofer W (2016a) Gesture-based interactive audio guide on tactile reliefs. In: Proceedings of the 18th international ACM SIGACCESS conference on computers and accessibility-ASSETS'16. https://doi.org/10.1145/2982142.2982176
Reichinger A, Schröder S, Löw C, Sportun S, Reichl P, Purgathofer W (2016b). Spaghetti, sink and sarcophagus: design explorations of tactile artworks for visually impaired people. In: Proceedings of the 9th Nordic conference on human-computer interaction-NordiCHI'16, pp 1–6. ISBN: 9781450347631. https://doi.org/10.1145/2971485.2996471
Rodriguez Echavarria K, Janzon K, Wright J (2018) Participatory co-creation of a public sculpture incorporating 3D digital technologies. In: GCH 2018-Eurographics workshop on graphics and cultural heritage, pp 211–214. https://doi.org/10.2312/gch.20181364
Rodriguez Echavarria K, Samaroudi M, Weyrich T (2020) Fracturing artefacts into 3D printable puzzles to enhance audience engagement with heritage collections. J Comput Cult Herit 13(1). https://doi.org/10.1145/3351343
Samaroudi M, Rodriguez Echavarria K, Song R, Evans R (2017) The fabricated diorama: tactile relief and context-aware technology for visually impaired audiences. In: Schreck T, Weyrich T, Sablatnig R, Stular B (eds) Eurographics workshop on graphics and cultural heritage. The Eurographics Association. https://doi.org/10.2312/gch.20171315

Samaroudi M, Rodriguez Echavarria K, Perry L (2020) Heritage in lock-down: digital provision of memory institutions in the UK and US of America during the COVID-19 pandemic. Mus Manag Curatorship. https://doi.org/10.1080/09647775.2020.1810483

Sandis C (2016) An honest display of fakery: replicas and the role of museums. R Inst Philos Suppl 79:241–259. https://doi.org/10.1017/S1358246116000163

Studio Maaike Roozenburg and LikeFriends Creative Agency (2016) Smart replicas. http://smartreplicas.blogspot.com. Last Accessed 03 Apr 2024

Studio Maaike Roozenburg (2017) The oldest recipes of the world. https://cargocollective.com/maaikeroozenburg/The-oldest-recipes-of-the-world. Last Accessed 03 Apr 2024

Tactile Images (2016) Canadian museum for human rights. https://www.tactileimages.com/custom-projects. Last Accessed 03 Apr 2024

Tang J, Zhao Y (2015) Edible met: eating art to understand. https://www.metmuseum.org/blogs/digital-underground/2015/edible-met. Last Accessed 03 Apr 2024

Tucker F (2021) Bringing the V&A to hospital schools. https://www.vam.ac.uk/blog/museum-life/bringing-the-va-to-hospital-schools. Last Accessed 03 Apr 2024

Ultimaker (2019) Bringing 3D printing to the metropolitan museum of art. https://ultimaker.com/learn/bringing-3d-printing-to-the-metropolitan-museum-of-art. Last Accessed 03 Apr 2024

Undeen D (2013) Creative technologist interview: Jonathan Monaghan's Leda and the Marsyas. https://www.metmuseum.org/blogs/digital-underground/posts/2013/jonathan-monaghan-interview. Last Accessed 03 Apr 2024

Urcia A, Zambruno S, Vazzana A, Anderson M, Darnell CM (2018) Prototyping an egyptian revival. Laser scanning, 3D prints and sculpture to support the Echoes of Egypt exhibition. Archeologia e Calcolatori 29(1). https://doi.org/10.19282/ac.29.2018.24

Visual Computing Laboratory ISTI-CNR (2015) Jackson Pollock Alchemy in 3D. https://vcg.isti.cnr.it/alchemy/. Last Accessed 03 Apr 2024

Voone C (2016) Artists covertly scan bust of Nefertiti and release the data for free online. https://hyperallergic.com/274635/artists-covertly-scan-bust-of-nefertiti-and-release-the-data-for-free-online/. Last Accessed 03 Apr 2024

Wenman C (2019) A German museum tried to hide this stunning 3D scan of an iconic Egyptian artifact. Today you can see it for the first time. https://reason.com/2019/11/13/a-german-museum-tried-to-hide-this-stunning-3d-scan-of-an-iconic-egyptian-artifact-today-you-can-see-it-for-the-first-time/. Last Accessed 03 Apr 2024

Young J (2017) British museum now offers 3D printed replicas of parts of its collection. https://3dprint.com/182710/british-museum-3d-printing/. Last Accessed 03 Apr 2024

Chapter 9
Photogrammetric Computer Vision—Good Practices and Pitfalls

Andreas Georgopoulos and Sevasti Tapinaki

Abstract During the past decade or so, standard photogrammetric practice has experienced an impressive influence by computer vision algorithms, which have led to its automation and democratization. Although this radical change has obvious advantages, it is also escorted by some severe disadvantages. Potential users are faced with numerous parameter choices about which they have no expert knowledge and consequently, the results are not always ideal, to say the least. In this chapter, we try to pinpoint the lurking dangers and help non-expert users to take knowledgeable decisions and be able to evaluate their results. The few—unavoidable—theoretical aspects are escorted by rich illustrated examples, thus leading to practical guidelines for achieving optimum results.

Keywords 3D reconstruction · SfM–MVS software · Photogrammetry · Computer vision · Good practices · Cultural heritage

9.1 Introduction—Democratization of Photogrammetry: A Tool for Everyone?

The Geoinformatics profession has experienced a dramatic, but positive, influence by the Computer Vision Community in the past decades. This "democratization" of complex and difficult to understand photogrammetric procedures until a decade or so ago, undoubtedly helped to spread the use and, consequently, the demand for photogrammetric products such as orthophotography and 3D models. However, and unfortunately, it also led to the use and application of these automated software by many so-called "experts", engineers, and non-engineers (!!), who do not have

A. Georgopoulos (✉) · S. Tapinaki
Laboratory of Photogrammetry, School of Rural, Surveying and Geoinformatics Engineering, National Technical University of Athens, Zografou, Greece
e-mail: drag@central.ntua.gr

S. Tapinaki
e-mail: sevi@survey.ntua.gr

F. Liarokapis et al. (eds.), *Interactive Media for Cultural Heritage*, Springer Series on Cultural Computing, https://doi.org/10.1007/978-3-031-61018-9_9

the necessary theoretical background for photogrammetry, nor the necessary practical experience of photogrammetric applications for the detailed and strict control and evaluation of the results. This phenomenon of the "*sorcerer's apprentices*" has inevitably caused multiple negative effects, such as the devaluation of the method on the one hand and on the other the production of very often incorrect outcomes, which, when the time comes for their use, will prove to be wrong or even dangerous.

In this chapter, we are trying to present the lurking traps and pitfalls for applying Photogrammetry using the automated software without prior knowledge of the basics of the Science, which requires several courses to be mastered in those university departments that educate Geoinformatics experts. In addition, we present good practices by illustrating practical examples from our long-term practical experience. Firstly, in Sect. 9.2, we present the evolution of science from its digital era to that of almost complete automation. We examine the raw material, i.e., the digital images, which nowadays are so easy to acquire, yet too diverse in their properties, which directly affect the quality and accuracy of the final products. Then, in Sect. 9.3, we present the working principles of the automated software available today for the reader to understand their operation and grasp the numerous sources of errors. This is concluded by a short reference to the available software, either commercial or freeware. Section 9.4 deals with the object properties and how they might affect the results. Photogrammetric procedures deal with objects which may be very large, e.g., the surface of the earth, or very small, e.g., an ancient coin, with very simple to very complicated shapes. In general, object diversity is very often dictating the actions needed for proper raw data acquisition, which will lead to successful results. In addition, we present two illustrated examples from our vast experience, to stress our main argument, which is that application of Photogrammetric Computer Vision must always be performed with expert knowledge for accurate metric results. The chapter finishes with the most important conclusions and take-away remarks in Sect. 9.5.

9.2 From Digital Photogrammetry to Photogrammetric Computer Vision

9.2.1 Brief Historic Review—How We Arrived to SfM–MVS

SfM–MVS stands for Structure-from-Motion and Multiple View Stereo, implying that many overlapping images, hence multi-view, from different viewpoints, hence motion, of the camera, contribute to 3D reconstructing of the desired scene and the shape, hence structure, of the object of interest. The development of SfM–MVS software can be traced back to the early days of computer vision research, when researchers began exploring techniques for estimating the 3D structure of a scene from multiple 2D images for the sake of enabling flawless robot movements.

One of the earliest methods for this task was photogrammetric stereo vision, which uses two images of the same scene captured from slightly different perspectives to compute depth information. Stereo vision was dominant in photogrammetric applications since the early days of Photogrammetry in the nineteenth century. It is still required for mapping applications from aerial or satellite images. However, stereo vision has limitations, such as the need for precisely calibrated cameras and the difficulty of handling complex scenes with many occlusions. To address these limitations, researchers began exploring SfM and MVS techniques in the 1990s.

SfM algorithms use point correspondences between multiple images to estimate the camera position parameters and consequently the 3D structure of the scene. These algorithms became popular in the 2000s with not only the emergence of digital cameras and the availability of large datasets of images but also with the development of the necessary computer power to process them simultaneously. MVS algorithms use multiple images to generate a dense point cloud from multiple ray intersections and then use surface reconstruction algorithms to generate a mesh, a surface, and, finally, a 3D model. Hence, SfM–MVS software combines both SfM and MVS techniques to estimate both the camera parameters and the 3D structure of the scene from multiple images and, consequently, generate high-quality 3D textured models. The development of SfM–MVS software has been driven by advances in computer vision, image processing, and hardware technology, as well as the increasing demand for 3D modeling and scanning by various industries.

9.2.2 Cameras, Sensors, and Platforms

Nowadays, people assume that any camera is suitable for 3D reconstruction despite the efforts of many experts to explain the contrary. In fact, people even think that smartphone cameras can compete with DSLR and mirrorless digital cameras, which is a big misconception as far as 3D reconstruction is concerned. Digital cameras are in abundance, but also, they vary significantly in terms of sensor size, megapixels, and lenses. As the camera is the only source of the raw data for the 3D reconstruction, it is imperative that users know exactly the capabilities of their camera, but most of all its limitations. Sensor size, pixel pitch, and number of pixels, but also the quality of the optical system which concentrates and focuses the rays on the sensor are of utmost importance. The worse the system components, the lower the quality of the results both in resolution and accuracy. Moreover, users must master the basics of photography to exploit their camera system to the fullest for correctly exposed images. Hence, careful planning of the acquisition process must be conducted to ensure the desired outcome.

The means of positioning the camera to the correct and desired position is also a critical action and users should be fully aware of the available platforms to do that. These platforms may include tripods, scaffoldings, cranes, kites, balloons, unmanned aerial vehicles (UAV), helicopters, airplanes, and satellites, to name but a few.

9.2.3 The Digital Image

An image is generally defined as "*the representation of a 3D scene on a planar surface.*" This presupposes (i) a light-sensitive means for capturing the light rays emitted or reflected by the objects in the 3D scene and (ii) a light source to illuminate the objects for the light reflectance. Since the turn of the century, film has been gradually replaced by light sensitive digital sensors either of CCD or CMOS technology. This technology produces planar rectangular arrays of pixels, for each of which the color information is known and stored in the digital image file.

Digital image files can be of various formats, depending on the way the image information is stored. Tagged Image File Format (TIFF) and Joint Photographic Experts Group (JPEG) are quite popular formats, illustrating the non-compression and the compression of the data, respectively, thus resulting to large or smaller file sizes. RAW format, which contains the maximum possible information the camera can record, is also used but is proprietary for different manufacturers and needs special treatment. In many cases, it would be advisable to shoot in RAW and JPG if necessary. Several image processing software can read the RAW format of most camera manufacturers, and thus they are able to exploit their content to the fullest.

Some particularly important parameters to consider before the image acquisition are the calibration of the camera, the image resolution, and the ground sampling distance. *Camera Calibration* is the description of the internal camera geometry, which determines the accuracy of all photogrammetric measurements. It is the model of central projection, which describes the geometric behavior of the camera. The parameters which determine the internal camera geometry are the *principal distance* (c), i.e., the physical distance of the lens projection center from the plane of the sensor, the *principal point* (x_o, y_o), i.e., the projection of the projection center on the sensor plane, and the values of the *radial distortion* of the lens. In addition, *decentering distortion* values, *skewness, and scale variation in x and y* could also be considered. These parameters may be determined either with pre-calibration of the camera(s) or, alternatively, with inclusion of autocalibration algorithms in the photogrammetric adjustment. Autocalibration requires many conjugate points for reliability, which, fortunately, is often the case when automated software is employed for the photogrammetric adjustments.

Image resolution relates to the information content of the digital image and is related to the color depth and to the number of pixels forming the image but also to their physical size, also referred to as pixel pitch. The pixel pitch depends on the physical size of the sensor and the number of pixels along and across the sides of the sensor. If more pixels are to be included in a given sensor size, their size must be obviously smaller. Pixels of physical size less than 3 μm result to lower image quality, as they are unable to record small number of light photons and hence their digital number is inevitably the result of interpolation. Hence, the number of megapixels of a digital camera should always be evaluated in relation to the pixel pitch.

The *focal length* of the camera lens is also a very significant parameter in the data acquisition process. The focal length characterizes the lens as wide-angle, normal,

Table 9.1 Indicative relations of sensor sizes, MP, and pixel pitch

Sensor	Physical size (mm)	MP	X	Y	Pixel pitch (μm)
1/3″	4.8 × 3.4	16	4920	3264	1
1/2″	6.4 × 4.8	16	4920	3264	1.4
1″	12.8 × 9.6	24	6000	4000	2.2
4/3″	18 × 13.5	24	6000	4000	3.2
APS-C (1.8″)	23.7 × 15.7	24	6000	4000	4.0
Full frame	36 × 24	36 42	7360 7952	4912 5304	4.9 4.5

or telephoto. It also changes the field of view angle and has an impact on the magnification on the image. One may easily understand that the angle of the field of view depends not only on the focal length but also on the size of the sensor. Hence, whether a lens is wide-angle, or telephoto depends on the ratio f/d of its focal length (f) and the diagonal (d) of the sensor. If the ratio is smaller than 1 the lens is a wide-angle lens, if it approximately equals to 1, the lens is characterized as normal and if the ratio is greater than 1 it is a telephoto. To avoid confusing calculations due to different sensor sizes and focal lengths, the manufacturers calculate the equivalent focal length of all lenses for a standard sensor size. This standard is the 35mm film of the analogue era, which is today called full-frame sensor and has dimensions 36 × 24 mm^2. This, of course, does not reveal the actual focal length of the lens, which may be easily back calculated using the ratio of the actual size of the sensor and the equivalent 35 mm standard.

In Table 9.1, the pixel pitch of various combinations of popular digital sensor sizes and megapixels is shown.

The ground sampling distance (GSD) is the area of the object's surface imaged in one pixel of the digital image. It represents the notion of image scale in the digital era and is a decisive factor of the resolution and accuracy of the final photogrammetric product. Obviously, it is not constant for the whole image, as it depends on the scale variations. A rule of thumb states that the final photogrammetric product cannot have smaller GSD than the original images, as this would imply generating information that has not been initially recorded and, consequently, does not exist in the first place. Hence, it is particularly important to consider the GSD before the image acquisition.

9.3 Automated Software (SfM–MVS)—Advantages and Disadvantages

Digital automation has undoubtedly broadened the implementation of photogrammetric methods to a much wider spectrum of applications. This has been performed by a much wider range of scientists not only Geomatics Engineers. This is a great advantage on one hand, which must be escorted with extreme caution on the other. As already mentioned, the automated photogrammetric and computer vision algorithms have just over a decade or so of life and have contributed to the speedy production of 3D models and orthophotographs.

9.3.1 SfM–MVS Algorithms Simply Explained

Structure-from-Motion (SfM) software is used to reconstruct 3D models of objects or scenes from 2D images taken from different viewpoints, i.e., exploiting the motion of the camera. Multi-View Stereo (MVS) software, on the other hand, is used to create detailed 3D models of objects or scenes from multiple images, by estimating the depth of each point in the scene with the intention to form a dense colored point cloud. When combined, SfM–MVS software takes a carefully acquired set of 2D images and produces a 3D model by first estimating the camera positions and orientations from the images using SfM algorithms. It then computes the depth information for each point in the scene using MVS algorithms, which are based on intersecting by triangulation corresponding points in multiple images. The SfM–MVS software then generates a dense point cloud, which is a set of 3D points representing the surface of the object or scene. The point cloud can be further processed to create a 3D mesh or textured 3D model (Fig. 9.1). The degree of the detail content of the 3D model, alias its resolution, is dependent on the properties of the digital images and the camera system, i.e., the lens and the sensor.

SfM–MVS software operates by using computer vision algorithms to estimate the camera parameters and the 3D geometry of a scene from a set of 2D images. The term *camera parameters* imply the intrinsic and extrinsic parameters, meaning the geometry of the camera and its pose estimation in a specific reference system. In SfM, the software first estimates the camera positions and orientations by finding point correspondences between the images and solving for the camera parameters using techniques such as bundle adjustment methods. Once the camera parameters

(a) (b)

Fig. 9.1 A surface (**a**) and a 3D textured model (**b**) of the Cannon Gate in Rhodes (© Authors) have been estimated, MVS algorithms are used to compute the 3D geometry of the scene. These algorithms typically use a patch-based approach to estimate the depth of each point in the scene. For each point, the MVS algorithm selects a set of patches in the images that correspond to that point and computes the depth by minimizing the photometric error between the patches using techniques such as graph cuts or variational methods (Stathopoulou 2022).

9.3.2 3D Reconstruction Software—Commercial and Freeware

There is a great number of 3D SfM–MVS automated reconstruction software available in the market which use similar algorithms and techniques to generate 3D models from 2D images. One may choose from mainly two groups: Commercial and freeware software. Freeware software may be equally functional and powerful; however, they present the usual shortcomings of non-commercial software, which are (i) the lack of documentation and manuals, (ii) the lack of support, and (iii) the unstable installations, which greatly depend on the updates of the operational system (Windows, iOS, etc.) and the particulars of the hardware. Analytical reviews of the 3D reconstruction software available may be found in the web.[1]

Overall, 3D reconstruction software can improve the efficiency and accuracy of 3D modeling and scanning. However, it is important to carefully evaluate different software options and choose one that best fits the specific needs and requirements of each project.

9.3.3 Advantages—Disadvantages and Pitfalls

Automated software for 3D reconstruction has become increasingly popular exactly due to its ability to generate 3D models from 2D images quickly and efficiently. The undeniable advantages of the spread of this technology are, of course, speed and automation, which imply avoidance of human errors since they enforce impartiality and objectivity by minimizing human intervention. This is true in theory, as practice has proven the opposite, as will be shown in the next paragraphs.

Among additional advantages, one could mention (i) the independence from costly and complicated in use digital photogrammetric workstations (DPW) with

[1] https://www.3dnatives.com/en/photogrammetry-software-190920194/#!.
https://manufactur3dmag.com/top-8-best-photogrammetry-software-free-paid/?utm_content=cmp-true.
https://www.3dbeginners.com/list-of-free-photogrammetry-software/.
https://www.makeuseof.com/best-photogrammetry-software-free-paid/.
https://all3dp.com/1/best-photogrammetry-software/.
https://formlabs.com/eu/blog/photogrammetry-guide-and-software-comparison/.

Fig. 9.2 Example of low-quality images (© Authors)

steep learning curves and demand for stereoscopic acuity, (ii) the alleged freedom in taking images randomly, which might, unfortunately, lead to problems, and (iii) the easy implementation of the automated SfM–MVS software, which again is a source of problematic outcomes if it is not escorted by deep knowledge of geometry and photogrammetric procedures.

Hence, there are several pitfalls associated with this technology that can affect the quality and accuracy of the reconstructed models. Some of these pitfalls include:

1. Image Quality: The photographic quality of the input images can greatly affect the accuracy of the reconstructed 3D models. Images that are blurry, have low contrast, or are poorly lit (Fig. 9.2) can lead to inaccurate reconstructions. Hence, great care should be given to the correct exposure and focusing of the initial images.
2. Occlusions: Automated 3D reconstruction software relies heavily on feature correspondences between images to estimate camera parameters and 3D geometry. If parts of the object or scene are occluded in some of the images, it can be difficult for the software to accurately estimate the camera parameters and produce an accurate and reliable 3D model. In addition, in these cases the software may produce wrong description of the object's surface which will lead to erroneous results (Fig. 9.3).
3. Symmetry: Objects with symmetrical features or repeating patterns (e.g., a checkerboard) can cause problems for automated 3D reconstruction software, as it will have difficulty distinguishing between the left and right sides of the object or identifying conjugate points to establish geometry.
4. Lack of texture: Objects without texture (e.g., white walls), or with problematic textures, i.e., black surfaces which absorb light, shiny surfaces, which diverge light, etc., completely "confuse" the automated algorithms and lead to extremely problematic results (Fig. 9.4). Such cases must be foreseen and prevented, if possible, at the time of image acquisition (Evgenikou and Georgopoulos 2015; Stathopoulou 2022).
5. Post-processing: Automated 3D reconstruction software often requires post-processing to refine the resulting 3D models. This can be a time-consuming

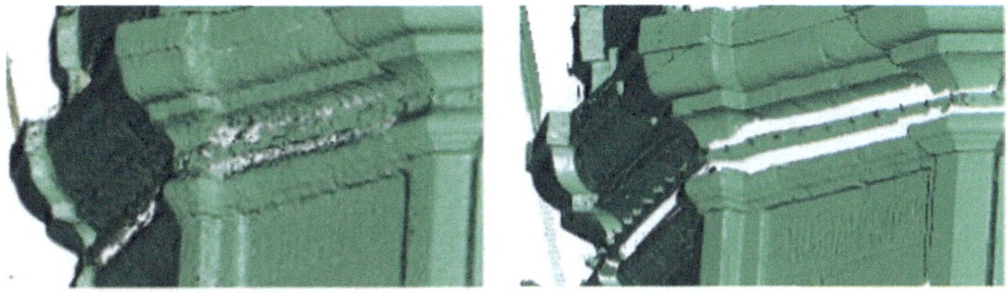

(a) (b)

Fig. 9.3 In the point cloud from the Image Based Modeling (IBM) software in **(a)** wrong points have been included due to occlusions by objects in the foreground. In **(b)** the point cloud after "cleaning", i.e. after removing the noise.

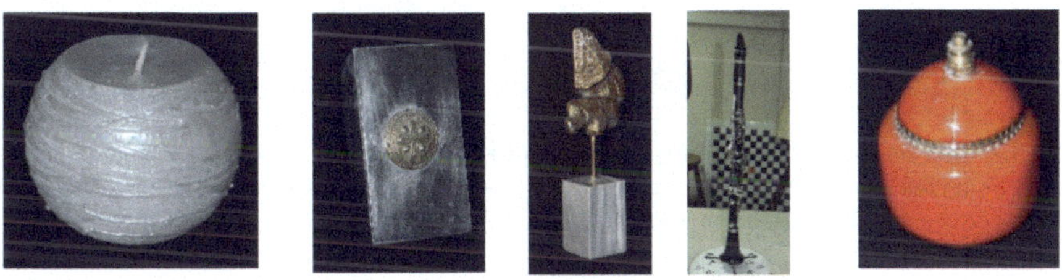

Fig. 9.4 Examples of problematic objects, with shiny or transparent surfaces and black color (Evgenikou and Georgopoulos 2015)

process and can require a high level of expertise to achieve the desired level of accuracy and quality. Experience has shown that at least ten times the time necessary for data acquisition is required for post-processing.

6. Large Scenes: For larger scenes, the amount of data generated by the reconstruction software can become overwhelming, leading to slower processing times and potential inaccuracies in the resulting 3D models. Moreover, in the case of lengthy objects (Fig. 9.5), special care should be taken at the time of image acquisition, for ensuring robust photogrammetric network and reliable bundle adjustment. This is achieved, e.g., by adding images with convergent camera axes and adequate number of control points.

In conclusion, while automated 3D reconstruction software has many benefits, it is important to be aware of the pitfalls associated with this technology to ensure accurate and high-quality results. This requires deep and thorough knowledge of the basic photogrammetric and computer vision algorithms implemented by the automates SfM–MVS software and perfect grasp of the network geometry.

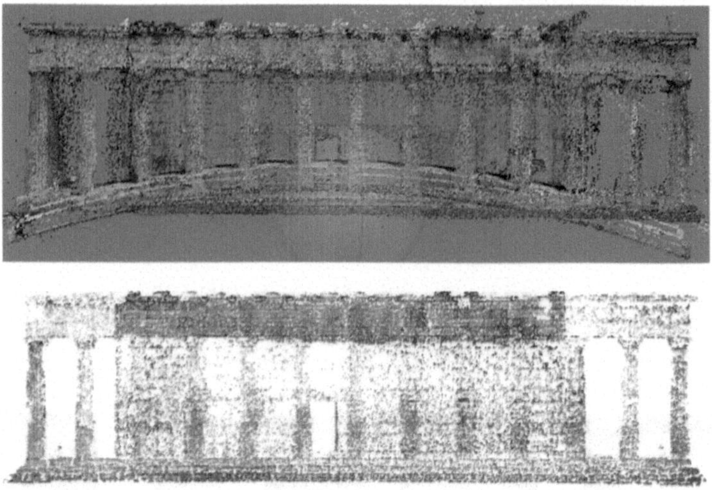

Fig. 9.5 Deformation of lengthy object (Temple of Hephaestus) due to wrong orientation (alignment) of the images, because of geometrically unstable photogrammetric network (top). The same object corrected with additional images (bottom) (© Authors)

9.4 From Images to 3D Models and Orthophotos

9.4.1 Object Diversity and Complexity

The complexity of objects has been the subject of studies since ancient times and continues to be of research interest today (European Union 2022). Complexity is a quality inherent in cultural heritage artifacts, monuments, and sites, and a critical consideration when planning a geometric documentation project (European Union 2022).

Cultural heritage objects can be of different sizes, for example, an ancient coin or a statue or a building or even a collection such as an entire archeological site. At the same time, objects can be simple or complex in shape.

A comprehensive understanding of object complexity is crucial since it has a direct and high impact on various aspects of 3D reconstruction while it presents severe difficulties for raw data acquisition for that purpose. Complexity requires different strategies to be implemented and directly reflects on the required results or achievable quality. It may limit the intended purpose of use and impact on the time and budget of a 3D reconstruction survey.

In the case of complex objects that include multiple surfaces, fine details and possibly hidden segments, great care must be taken to capture images for all segments so that no "holes" occur. Therefore, where required, multiple oblique, i.e., from various angles and at different scales, images should be taken to ensure adequate and flawless 3D reconstruction. Depending on the needs and properties of the object, the method and means of capturing the images should be adapted. Different cameras, different lenses, and different mounting platforms should be used for each different case. Although it is preferable to use normal or wide-angle lenses for the SfM–MVS procedures, in some special cases, very close shooting distances with ultra-wide-angle and sometimes spherical lenses can be used.

In case the images are taken outdoors, cloudy or overcast weather is preferable; otherwise, the images should be taken during the hours of the day when there are fewer or uniform shadows. Images of different segments of the object can be captured at different times of the day so that each segment is photographed under the same conditions. In case the images are taken indoors, suitable artificial lighting should be used to optimize the quality and the uniformity of brightness, contrast, and colors.

There are cases where the objects are submerged, for example, a shipwreck or a submerged building, where the images are taken with the same rationale, but additional pre-processing of the images is required depending on whether the photography is fully or partially underwater (Agrafiotis et al. 2018b; Georgopoulos and Agrafiotis 2012; Skamantzari et al. 2020).

In any case, the appropriate study of the object and its peculiarities is necessary, to choose and implement the proper methods and execute the right planning of data collection and processing tasks. This practice, which is developed with experience, ensures the correct production of the required outcomes, either 2D or 3D.

9.4.2 Illustrated Examples

In this section, we will present two illustrated examples from our own projects, which have contributed to our experience and showcase the dangers of the automation. Not only the cases included here but also many others performed by our Laboratory[2] have led us to formulate the guidelines included in this chapter for avoiding the main errors and pitfalls.

9.4.3 The Medieval Castle of Chios[3]

The Medieval Castle of Chios Island, located at the north side of the city's port, was constructed in the tenth century AD. The structures that survive to this day date back to the time when the Genoese ruled the island from the fourteenth to the sixteenth century AD. We conducted a 3D Geometric Documentation of a specific part of the Medieval Castle of Chios with the goal to produce the accurate 3D detailed textured model of a bastion, a watch tower, and a significant part of the walls as well as a set of colored orthophotos and 2D vector drawings at 1:25 and 1:40 scales (Tapinaki

[2] http://photogrammetry.survey.ntua.gr/ (last accessed April 2025).

[3] This section is largely based on Tapinaki et al. (2019).

et al. 2019). The main challenge of this case study was that dense scaffolding had been placed, in direct contact with the object to be documented, making both the data acquisition process and the data processing afterward extremely challenging and time-consuming, since the scaffolding should not appear in the final products of course (Fig. 9.6).

Close-range automated photogrammetry and image-based modeling, as well as topographic surveys were implemented, using standard equipment, i.e., a total station (Topcon GPT3003LN), two DSLR cameras (Canon EOS 6D and Canon 80D with 8–15 mm, 24 mm and 18–55 mm lenses), and a UAV (DJI Phantom 4 Pro). Because of the scaffolding, images were acquired from very close distances (approx. 1.0–1.5 m) with the super wide-angle lens (15 mm), to get "clear" parts of the surface (Fig. 9.7).

General images with normal (50 mm) and wide-angle lenses (35 and 24 mm) were also acquired from various distances, to support the orientation of all images together. The GSD of all datasets ranged from 0.6 to 2.4 mm. Also, pre-marked points were placed and measured to ensure correct orientation of images from different cameras

Fig. 9.6 The part of the Medieval Fortress of Chios with the scaffolding in almost direct contact (© Authors)

Fig. 9.7 Example of a very close-up image with super wide-angle lens (15 mm) (© Authors)

(a) (b)

Fig. 9.8 Result of automated determination of masks Evgenikou and Georgopoulos (2015). Original image (**a**) and the automatically determined masks (**b**)

and lenses, since it was possible to identify and measure the points on all images, even on the oblique ones.

For data processing, an Image-Based Modeling (IBM) software (Agisoft Photoscan—now Metashape®) was employed for the orientation of the images and the production of the dense point cloud. Masks were applied on all images where the scaffolding appeared. Masks are used to mark areas in images that should not be used in processing, because they may lead to incorrect image orientation or incorrect reconstruction results. The masks were applied using the tools provided by the IBM software, which was used, investing a lot of manual work and time. We consider it extremely important that the software provides such masking tools, but also the possibility to add masks at any time of the SfM–MVS processing. This time-consuming process led to further research (Kogeorgos 2020) for automating the detection and extraction of entities from images, using classification and segmentation algorithms (Fig. 9.8). Automated masking methods are still being investigated.

The data was georeferenced via the coordinates of all pre-marked points determined in a common geodetic network, which was initially established. Further processing of point clouds for the correct and accurate representation of the object's surface was carried out in a dedicated software (Geomagic Wrap®), which offers special point cloud editing tools, like construction and editing of Triangulated Irregular Network (TIN), clever decimation of triangles according to the surface's complexity, possibility to "repair" triangles and fill eventual holes (Fig. 9.9). This surface editing is necessary for its accurate description, which will lead to correct orthophotos and proper texturing of the 3D model. Surface reconstruction from point clouds is extensively analyzed and described in Remondino (2023) and Berger et al. (2014).

The orthophoto production with a ground pixel size of 2 mm, was performed in the IBM software with the corrected mesh by carefully selecting the clear parts from the appropriate images. The final deliverables were prepared after applying appropriate and controlled radiometric corrections. The architectural details and the typology of the monument played a fundamental role in the determination of the projection

Fig. 9.9 The oriented images (top), the dense point cloud (middle), and the surface (bottom) (© Authors)

planes for each orthophoto and drawing, to avoid any geometric distortions since each architectural structure presented different orientations in 3D space.

9.4.4 The Cannon Gate in Rhodes[4]

The Cannon Gate is located at the southeast corner of the Medieval Palace and provides access to battle positions on the ramparts of the walls surrounding and fortifying the Medieval City of Rhodes (Fig. 9.10). It was constructed during Jean de Lactic's Magistery (1437–1454). The Gate was protected by two cylindrical towers (Fig. 9.11), symmetrically situated one on each side, a fact indicating the presence of a drawbridge connecting the Gate with the ramparts over the moat. The bastions were equipped with cannons, hence the name of the Gate (http://www.medievaltown.gr/item/gate-of-the-canons/).

The geometric documentation of such complex fortified constructions presents challenges and difficulties, especially when it comes to the need for development of curved, cylindrical, conical, spherical, parabolic, or ellipsoidal surfaces. Nowadays, modern technological advances have enabled digital automated methods to be applied for accurate and detailed 3D documentation of archaeological sites and monuments (Georgopoulos and Ioannidis 2004; Tapinaki et al. 2021).

[4] This section is largely based on Georgopoulos et al. (2020).

Fig. 9.10 A view of the Medieval City of Rhodes with the position of the Cannon Gate (© Google Earth)

Fig. 9.11 The Cannon Gate in Rhodes (© Authors)

For the 3D geometric documentation of the Cannon Gate in Rhodes, apart from the bird's eye view, the four façades, all with orthophotos, and the detailed 3D textured model, the development of the western façade was also required. The 1:50 scale of the products dictates a final accuracy of 12.5 mm.

The standard SfM–MVS methodology and workflow was followed for the data acquisition, including close range automated photogrammetry, image-based modeling, terrestrial laser scanning, and topographic surveys. The equipment used included a standard total station (Topcon GPT3003N), a time-of-flight phase shift 3D Terrestrial Laser Scanner (FARO Focus 110), two DSLR cameras (Canon EOS 6D and Canon 80D with 24 mm and 18–55 mm lenses, respectively) and an unmanned aerial vehicle (DJI Phantom 4 Pro).

Suitable digital images, both aerial and terrestrial, were taken, in such a way to fulfill the Structure-from-Motion (SfM) requirements, from key positions and directions according to the part of the fortified structure that should be documented, and the difficulties presented in terms of shape, obstacles, illumination, etc. The

Fig. 9.12 The point cloud with the footprints of all images indicating their position after orientation (© Authors)

UAV was used to document the upper parts of the fortification and the parts that were difficult or unattainable to get digital images with the handheld DSLR camera. While multiple scans were needed to overcome any eventual lack of information about the correct shape of the complicated surface that could arise and record all the necessary details of the object.

The digital images were processed with the Image-Based Modeling (IBM) software Agisoft Photoscan v.1.4.2., (now renamed to Metashape®) to produce the detailed 3D textured model (Fig. 9.12) as well as the orthophotos and the required developments.

In this way, three complementary point clouds were produced, each covering in detail different parts of the structure (Fig. 9.13). They were cleaned and filtered using the Geomagic Wrap® 2017, a powerful point cloud and mesh processing software and combined into one complete point cloud from which the final object surface was produced. This step is necessary in most cases, as the IBM software is generally unable to determine some fine details of complicated surfaces, depending, of course, on the image acquisition and should be executed meticulously, as the surface determination affects all subsequent steps.

Nowadays, there is a variety of software (e.g., 3DReshaper, Cloud Compare, Gomagic Wrap) that can produce surface developments. It was necessary to decide which method should be used for the process, providing a complete, accurate, detailed, and useful result with orthophoto. The development of the Cannon Gate towers was very challenging, because of the different and complicated shapes composing them. The western façade consists of three parts, the main gate in the center and two towers on either side. Thorough geometric analysis and examination of the whole object led to the conclusion that the towers are not symmetrical. Each part is composed of the wall at its lower part, the protruding battlements on top and the corbels supporting them (Fig. 9.14).

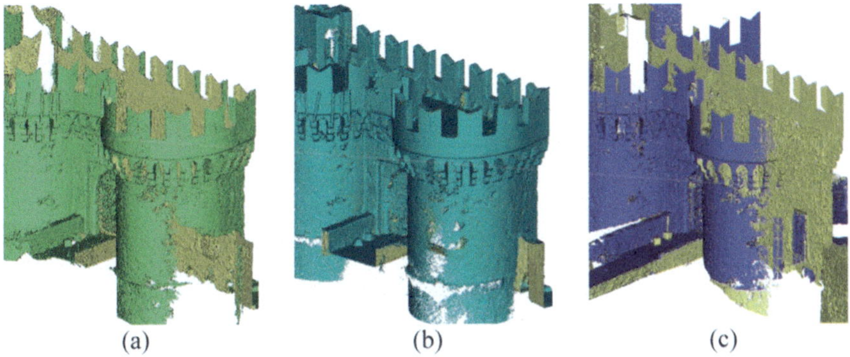

Fig. 9.13 IBM point cloud from DSLR images (a), IBM point cloud from UAV images (b) and Scanner point cloud (c) (© Authors)

Fig. 9.14 The complicated details of the Cannon Gate (© Authors)

In Fig. 9.15, the horizontal section is shown, and the bold numbers indicate where the surface changes from planar to cylindrical. Standard orthophotos were produced for the planar parts, while the cylindrical parts were developed using the specific methodology mentioned above. The details for the development of the Cannon Gate may be found in Georgopoulos et al. (2020). The development of the whole object is shown in Fig. 9.16, where the three parts are positioned at a distance, so that the drawing becomes more legible and useful. Furthermore, the wall between the corbels has no raster for the same above explained reasons. The numbers correspond to the ones of Fig. 9.15.

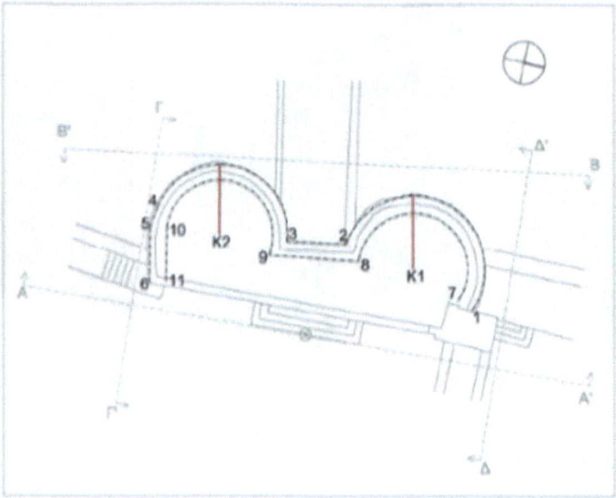

Fig. 9.15 Horizontal section and vertical section footprints of Cannon Gate in Rhodes (© Authors)

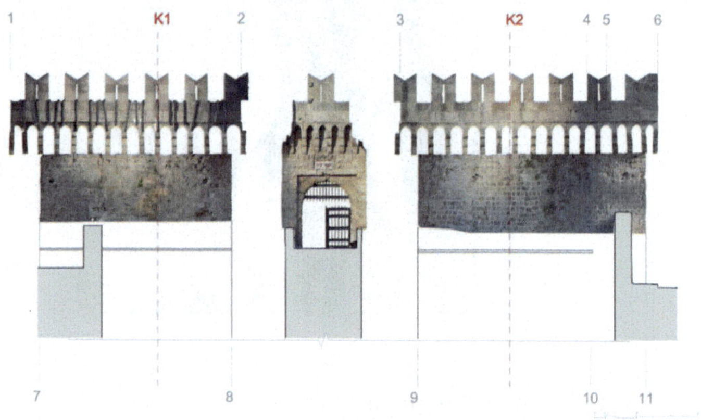

Fig. 9.16 The development of the Cannon Gate in Rhodes (© Authors)

9.5 Lessons Learnt—Recommendations and Guidelines

In this section, we will try to summarize all the experience gained while executing all the projects that we have undertaken in the Laboratory of Photogrammetry at NTUA.[5] Automated photogrammetric and computer vision techniques follow certain stages in their implementation. All these stages should be performed with extreme caution and deep knowledge for optimal results. These steps are image acquisition, orientation of the acquired images, surface determination, and production of the final 2D and 3D documentation products.

[5] http://photogrammetry.survey.ntua.gr/ (last accesses April 2025).

9.5.1 Image Acquisition

Photogrammetric computer vision has completely changed the way image acquisition is performed. Since human stereovision is no longer a prerequisite, the image axes can be of any orientation in 3D space. This, however, does not mean that careful planning is no longer necessary. On the contrary, image acquisition must follow a different approach always keeping in mind that (i) all details of the object must be imaged on at least three images, (ii) considerable overlap between images is favorable, (iii) more images at the time of acquisition make no harm, as they may be deleted later, (iv) occlusions should be taken into account by taking additional images, (v) maintaining constant image scale is not a prerequisite, (vi) GSD must never be larger than the desired one in the final product, and (vii) all photographic rules for sharp, evenly illuminated and as noiseless as possible images are naturally still valid. Not all cameras and not all shooting sequences are able to produce the desired results. Hence, great care must be taken for choosing the suitable instrumentation and the most advantageous course of taking the pictures, always bearing in mind that a great number of decisions might affect the method to achieve the desired result, in terms of accuracy, reliability, resolution, and completeness.

For cases of *terrestrial imaging* to document buildings or small artifacts, special care should be taken for the correct exposure, focusing and the depth of field, especially in difficult cases such as museum artifacts under difficult illumination conditions. Special techniques of computational photography, like HDR imaging and focus stacking, should always be an option. It has been shown that they do not affect the SfM–MVS techniques in a negative way (Ntregka et al. 2013; Kontogianni and Georgopoulos 2014; Kontogianni et al. 2017a, 2017b).

For cases of *UAV imaging*, additional care must be taken for geometrically correct images. Usually, image acquisition with slightly oblique camera axis and large forward and side overlaps ensures favorable coverage of the object. Sometimes additional images from special viewing angles may be needed for the complete coverage of objects with complicated surface, like an ancient Greek temple. A very serious source of geometric deformation, which very often is ignored, is the *Rolling Shutter*. The rolling shutter effect is a phenomenon that occurs in digital cameras or video recorders that use a rolling shutter mechanism to capture images. Unlike a global shutter, which captures the entire frame simultaneously, a rolling shutter captures the image by scanning the frame from top to bottom (or vice versa) or from left to right (or vice versa). When the rolling shutter captures a moving object, the exposure time for different parts of the frame is not the same. As a result, the moving object appears distorted or skewed in the captured image. This distortion is caused by the time gap between the start and end of the exposure for different parts of the frame. The magnitude of this adverse effect depends on the camera used, on the relative speed of the camera to the object and the scale of the images. Correcting the rolling shutter effect in post-processing can be challenging since the distortion is a result of the way the image was captured. However, there are a few techniques that can help minimize or reduce the impact of the rolling shutter effect (Bruno and Forlani 2023).

9.5.2 Orientations

The orientation of the images must obviously be done with great care, especially the relative orientation, which determines the shape of the object. Calculations made during the bundle adjustment are very likely to be incorrect when performed without user supervision and control escorted by complete awareness of the mathematical processes. When the data is wrong and the bundle adjustment is allowed to uncontrollably determine all the parameters, then the errors will most likely be distributed, hence hidden, and the user will end up with small errors but with wrong parameters. The correct relative orientation of the images, and consequently the correct shape of the object, must be ensured before control point coordinates are introduced into the adjustment for scaling and georeferencing the model. It is then that the interior orientation parameters can be added to the adjustment for the global and final solving for the exterior orientation parameters.

This, of course, is not new to photogrammetrists, who are trained to pay great attention to the correct performance of relative orientation. The same rules apply in automated computer vision photogrammetry. Even distribution of enough number of tie points on the images and on the 3D object, optimal image network geometry with favorable ray intersections, preferably multiple ones, are of utmost importance.

Special care should be taken at the time of image acquisition for objects with relatively huge depth differences and cases of submerged objects, where the refraction negatively affects the adjustment if special procedures are not undertaken. In such cases, processing should consider the characteristics of the special underwater case for the camera, and the ratio of two media, i.e., air and water, that are between the camera and the object (Agrafiotis and Georgopoulos 2015; Menna et al. 2018). Especially for UAV imaging, there are a lot of studies that compensate for the bending of the light rays due to refraction (Agrafiotis et al. 2017, 2018a, 2018b, 2020). This compensation is crucial for the subsequent geometric adjustments, especially the relative orientation of the images, to correctly determine the shape of the object imaged.

9.5.3 Surface Reconstruction

In cases of complex objects, especially when great precision is required, it is recommended to use a separate special 3D data processing software to produce a correct as possible surface from the point cloud. During surface reconstruction, automations such as noise removal, repairing, filling holes, decimation, and smoothness of the surface must be implemented gradually and very cautiously.

Point clouds produced from IBM software, like those from 3D scanners, usually include a lot of noise and outliers, i.e., undesirable, or misplaced points in 3D space, that must be removed. Large sections containing such noise, and which can be recognized and selected may be manually deleted. Automatic noise reduction can be performed using certain IBM software which provide such tools or, better, using 3D data processing software. In any case, these tools must be applied gradually and controlled to avoid distortions and deformation.

The point cloud is a step toward the 3D surface description required for either the orthophoto production or the formation of a 3D model. The point cloud is firstly used to develop a polygon mesh and then this is used to produce the object's surface. Many refinements can be performed on a polygon mesh which cannot be applied on a point cloud. For the representation of the continuous surface, usually, the triangulated irregular network (TIN) is recommended, because it is an effective and simple way to reliably describe the surface based on a set of irregularly spaced points such as the point cloud. In smooth parts of the surface, the points may not be as dense as in areas with more complicated relief, where the density of the points is increased. In this way the number of points and hence the number of triangles required for modeling complex surfaces and, consequently, the size of the file is reduced. TINs, on the other hand, may be stored in various file formats and thus can be used in a variety of software for further 3D processing, analysis, and production of different products, such as cross-sections, contours, raster DSMs, textures, and orthophotomosaics.

Very often cases are encountered, where IBM processing fails to provide a complete point cloud, which later leads to incorrect surface description. This is usually caused by incurring occlusions which were not taken into consideration at the time of image acquisition. This could be corrected by taking additional images, but this may not be feasible or may cause illumination variations in the different image sets which will introduce additional problems. Our recommendation is that this problem be remedied by supplementing the IBM point cloud with information derived from terrestrial laser scanning. The lack of reliable color can be compensated using the high-resolution images already available.

9.5.4 *Orthophoto Production*

Perhaps the most important imagery product for cultural heritage documentation is the orthophoto. It is the projection of the object's geometry and texture onto a plane, thus producing an invaluable documentation product containing geometric and qualitative information. Although most of the photogrammetric computer vision (IBM) software available offer the automated production of orthophotos, very often the results are incorrect for various reasons. These reasons include the erroneous description of the object's surface, the wrong definition of the projection planes, the careless selection of the texture from the images, and the lack of necessary details imaged. Consequently, to produce a correct orthophoto, it is necessary to ensure that all previous steps, i.e., image acquisition (see Sect. 9.5.1), image orientation (see Sect. 9.5.2), surface reconstruction (see Sect. 9.5.3), determination of the projection planes, and selection of the images to apply texture onto the orthophoto are very carefully and knowledgably performed. Usually, the final orthophoto is a mosaic of individual orthophotos separately produced, which, of course, must be geometrically correct.

The projection planes for the orthophotos should be carefully determined so that the orthophoto has minimum deformations, hence they should be as "parallel" as possible to the main planes of the projected objects. In cases where the object consists of multiple non-parallel planes or curved surfaces, the solution is to produce developments instead of orthogonal projections (see Sect. 9.4.2).

As for texturing, theoretically the pixels closest to image centers should be used, but very often this is not possible, when, e.g., the acquired images were inclined, or occlusions were present. In these cases, a careful and controlled selection of the images to be used in the composition of the final orthophoto must be made, provided of course the software allows it. Alternatively, or in combination, masks should be applied to remove specific parts from the initial images. As an example, the orthophoto of the archeological site of Ancient Messini (Fig. 9.17) was produced with a GSD of 5 cm. Although the initial data were of better specifications than required, the method failed to produce the correct surface for the columns and hence they were projected incorrectly in the orthophoto (Fig. 9.17). The solution was given firstly by densifying the images above the columns, i.e., taking additional images directly above the columns, from the same height, and secondly by carefully selecting the individual orthophotos which imaged the column correctly, i.e., as a true ortho.

The colors in the final orthophoto must be as realistic as possible. This, of course depends on the correct exposure of the initial images and the color and illumination balancing in the final orthophotos. Very often the natural illumination may not be favorable, causing strong shadows or intense color differences. If that cannot be avoided at the time of image acquisition, digital image processing should be employed either *before* the photogrammetric processing or *after* the orthophoto production on the final mosaic.

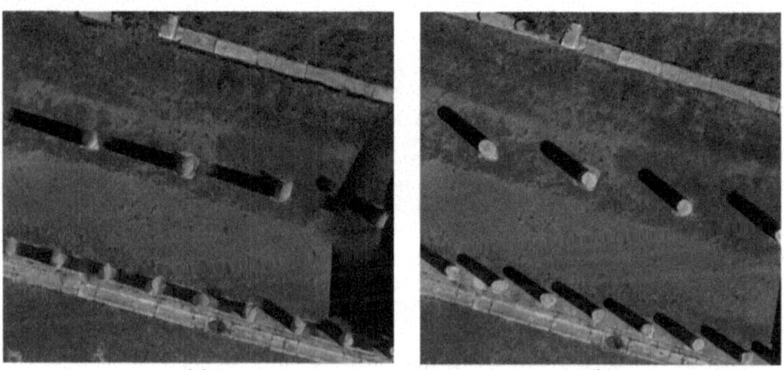

(a) (b)

Fig. 9.17 The initial orthophoto of a colonnade in Messini (**a**) and the corrected orthophoto (**b**)

9.5.5 *Quality Control of the Results*

It is imperative not to forget that the results of the automated procedures be thoroughly examined for errors. The criteria used for the quality control of the products, i.e., the 3D model, the orthophotos, and, eventually, the developments, are those of conformity, completeness, and accuracy. The concept of conformity is the degree of faithful depiction of the object, while the concept of completeness, the degree of coverage of the object documented and all its details that should appear in the final product. The completeness and conformity checks are usually performed by visual observation which entails a high degree of subjectivity. The spatial accuracy of the 3D models is assessed by examining the reprojection errors of the Ground Control Points (GCPs), or even better of Check Points. With the illustrated examples presented, it has been clearly demonstrated that special care must be taken during all stages of the procedure, i.e., from data acquisition to the final outcomes. Only in this way will photogrammetric computer vision to be as helpful as possible for cultural heritage documentation.

References

Agrafiotis P, Georgopoulos A (2015) Camera constant in the case of two media photogrammetry. ISPRS Arch XL-5/W5:1–6. In: Menna F, Nocerino E, Del Pizzo S, Bruno F, Remondino F (eds) Underwater 3D Recording and Modeling, 16–17 April 2015, TC V, CIPA, Piano di Sorrento, Italy. http://www.int-arch-photogramm-remote-sens-spatial-inf-sci.net/XL-5-W5/1/2015/isprsarchives-XL-5-W5-1-2015.pdf

Agrafiotis P, Drakonakis GI, Skarlatos D, Georgopoulos A, (2017) The effect of underwater imagery radiometry on 3d reconstruction and orthoimagery. Int Arch Photogramm Remote Sens Spat Inf Sci XLII-2/W3:25–31. https://doi.org/10.5194/isprs-archives-XLII-2-W3-25-2017

Agrafiotis P, Drakonakis GI, Skarlatos D, Georgopoulos A (2018a) Underwater image enhancement before three-dimensional (3D) reconstruction and orthoimage production steps: is it worth?. In: Remondino F, Georgopoulos A, González-Aguilera D, Agrafiotis P (eds) Latest developments in reality-based 3D surveying and modelling (1st Chapter: Underwater 3D surveying and modelling). MDPI editions, Basel, Switzerland. https://doi.org/10.3390/books978-3-03842-612-7/12

Agrafiotis P, Skarlatos D, Forbes T, Poullis C, Skamantzari M, Georgopoulos A (2018b) Underwater photogrammetry in very shallow waters: main challenges and caustics effect removal. Int Arch Photogramm Remote Sens Spat Inf Sci XLII 2:15–22. https://doi.org/10.5194/isprs-archives-XLII-2-15-2018

Agrafiotis P, Karantzalos K, Georgopoulos A, Skarlatos D (2020) Correcting image refraction: towards accurate aerial image-based bathymetry mapping in shallow waters. Remote Sens. 12(2):322. https://doi.org/10.3390/rs12020322

Berger M, Tagliasacchi A, Seversky LM, Alliez P, Levine JA, Sharf A, Silva CT (2014) State of the art in surface reconstruction from point clouds. Eurographics. https://doi.org/10.2312/egst.20141040

Bruno N, Forlani G (2023) Experimental tests and simulations on correction models for the rolling shutter effect in UAV photogrammetry. Remote Sens 2023(15):2391. https://doi.org/10.3390/rs15092391

Evgenikou V, Georgopoulos A (2015) Investigating 3d reconstruction methods for small artifacts. ISPRS Arch XL-5/W4:101–108. In: Gonzalez-Aguilera D, Remondino F, Boehm J, Kersten T, Fuse T (eds) WG V/4, CIPA—3D-Arch 2015—3D virtual reconstruction and visualization of complex architectures 25–27 February 2015, Avila, Spain. http://www.int-arch-photogramm-remote-sens-spatial-inf-sci.net/XL-5-W4/101/2015/isprsarchives-XL-5-W4-101-2015.pdf

European Union (2022). Study on quality in 3D digitisation of tangible cultural heritage. https://digital-strategy.ec.europa.eu/en/library/study-quality-3d-digitisation-tangible-cultural-heritage

Georgopoulos A, Ioannidis Ch (2004) Photogrammetric and surveying methods for the geometric recording of archaeological monuments FIG international week, Athens. https://www.fig.net/pub/athens/papers/wsa1/WSA1_1_Georgopoulos_Ioannidis.pdf

Georgopoulos A, Agrafiotis P (2012) Documentation of a submerged monument using improved two media techniques. In: 2012 18th international conference on virtual systems and multimedia (VSMM), pp 173–180, 2–5 Sept 2012, Milan, Italy. https://doi.org/10.1109/VSMM.2012.6365922. http://ieeexplore.ieee.org/stamp/stamp.jsp?tp=&arnumber=6365922&isnumber=6365890

Georgopoulos A, Skamantzari M, Tapinaki S (2020) Digitally developing medieval fortifications. In: Navarro Palazón J, García-Pulido LJ (eds) FORTMED2020—defensive architecture of the mediterranean, vol X, pp 317–324. Universitat Politecnica de València. https://ocs.editorial.upv.es/index.php/FORTMED/FORTMED2020/paper/viewFile/11468/5305

Kogeorgos Ch-M (2020) Detection and extraction of entities from images using classification and segmentation algorithms. MSc thesis, Lab of Photogrammetry, NTUA (in Greek)

Kontogianni G, Georgopoulos A (2014) Investigating the effect of HDR images for the 3D documentation of Cultural heritage. In: Ioannides M et al. (eds) Proceedings of the EUROMED 2014 international conference, Short Papers. Multi-Science Publishing Co. Ltd., pp 27–36. ISBN 978-1-907132-47-6

Kontogianni G, Chliverou R, Koutsoudis A, Pavlidis G, Georgopoulos A (2017a) Investigating the effect of focus stacking on SFM-MVS algorithms. Int Arch Photogramm Remote Sens Spatial Inf Sci XLII-2/W3:385–389. https://doi.org/10.5194/isprs-archives-XLII-2-W3-385-2017

Kontogianni G, Chliverou R, Koutsoudis A, Pavlidis G, Georgopoulos A (2017b) Enhancing close-up image based 3D digitisation with focus stacking. Int Arch Photogramm Remote Sens Spatial Inf Sci XLII-2/W5:421–425. https://doi.org/10.5194/isprs-archives-XLII-2-W5-421-2017

Menna F, Agrafiotis P, Georgopoulos A (2018) State of the art and applications in archaeological underwater 3D recording and mapping. J Cult Heritage 33:231–248. https://doi.org/10.1016/j.culher.2018.02.017

Ntregka A, Georgopoulos A, Santana-Quintero M (2013) Photogrammetric exploitation of HDR images for cultural heritage documentation. In: ISPRS annals—volume II-5/W1, 2013 TC V XXIV international CIPA symposium, 2–6 September 2013, Strasbourg, France, pp 209–214. https://doi.org/10.5194/isprsannals-II-5-W1-209-2013. http://cipaheritagedocumentation.org/fileadmin/template/doc/STRASBOURG/ANNALS/isprsannals-II-5-W1-209-2013.pdf

Remondino F (2003) From point cloud to surface: the modeling and visualization problem. Int Arch Photogramm Remote Sens Spat Inf Sci XXXIV-5/W10

Skamantzari M, Georgopoulos A, Palyvou C (2020) Sunken Roman villa of ancient Epidaurus: documentation and enhancement using virtual reality. ISPRS Ann Photogramm Remote Sens Spat Inf Sci V-2-2020:981–988. https://doi.org/10.5194/isprs-annals-V-2-2020-981-2020

Stathopoulou E-K (2022) Integrating scene priors in Multi-View Stereo (MVS). PhD dissertation, Lab of Photogrammetry, NTUA. https://dspace.lib.ntua.gr/xmlui/handle/123456789/56640. https://doi.org/10.26240/heal.ntua.24338

Tapinaki S, Skamantzari M, Chliverou R, Evgenikou V, Konidi A-M, Ioannatou E, Mylonas A, Georgopoulos A (2019) 3D image based geometric documentation of a medieval fortress. Int Arch Photogramm Remote Sens Spat Inf Sci XLII-2/W9:699–705. https://doi.org/10.5194/isprs-archives-XLII-2-W9-699-2019

Tapinaki S, Skamantzari M, Anastasiou A, Koutros S, Syrokou E, Georgopoulos A (2021) 3D holistic documentation of heritage monuments in Rhodes. Int Arch Photogramm Remote Sens Spat Inf Sci XLVI-M-1-2021:739–744. https://doi.org/10.5194/isprs-archives-XLVI-M-1-2021-739-2021

Chapter 10
Digital Cultural Heritage Twins: New Tools for a Complete Fruition of the Cultural Heritage Entities

Gian Piero Zarri

Abstract This chapter concerns the possibility of creating a *generalized access*, in digital form, to all the physical and symbolic/conceptual features of any kind of Cultural Heritage (CH) entities. With the term *physical*, we denote all those measurable/easily quantifiable/descriptive features that are currently used to characterize a Cultural Heritage item, e.g., dimensions, support, style, and name of the artist. The term *symbolic/conceptual* refers to the, often disregarded, immaterial properties of these items, like the full descriptions of their inner meaning and of the emotional messages transmitted to the users. Accordingly, we conceive an in-depth digital representation of a CH item under the form of a *twofold entity* according to a sort of Digital Cultural Heritage Twin approach. The first component of this entity consists of the usual description of the physical characteristics of the original cultural item; the second concerns its associated Digital Cultural Heritage Twin reproducing its symbolic/conceptual properties. To validate this methodology, we have taken into account, in a first step, those very important Cultural Heritage entities like paintings, drawings, frescoes, mosaics, sculptures, and murals that represent the support of the iconographic (or pictorial) narratives, i.e., illustrated stories told to the user/observer using only visual/illustrative modalities. The Chapter will then describe how—making use of NKRL, the Narrative Knowledge Representation Language—it will be possible to create complete and expressive Digital Cultural Heritage Twins for complex iconographic narratives, like Da Vinci's "hidden painting" that lies beneath the very famous Mona Lisa's portrait or the Surrender of Breda by Velasquez.

Keywords Digital twins · Digitalization procedures · Iconographic narratives · NKRL

G. P. Zarri (✉)
STIH Laboratory, Sorbonne University, 75005 Paris, France
e-mail: zarri@noos.fr; gianpzarri@gmail.com

F. Liarokapis et al. (eds.), *Interactive Media for Cultural Heritage*, Springer Series on Cultural Computing, https://doi.org/10.1007/978-3-031-61018-9_10

10.1 Introduction

This chapter concerns the use of advanced Artificial Intelligence and Knowledge Representation technologies to allow a full digital access to all the important features, both *physical* and *symbolic/conceptual*, of any possible kind of Cultural Heritage (CH) entities, and to make then possible their real *global fruition*.

We include under the label *physical features* all those measurable/easily quantifiable properties that are currently utilized to describe in digital format a Cultural Heritage item, i.e., dimensions, support, execution technique, style, name of the artist, information about the owner, places, and collections to which the item belongs. The term *symbolic/conceptual* refers, on the contrary, to those *immaterial features* that, still in digital format, should be used to characterize these entities from an *inner meaning* point of view. These features include then, all those stylistic, historical, aesthetic, emotive, communicative, temporal-related, and behavior-related properties that the cultural heritage specialists denote as *particularly important for the full characterization, understanding and interpretation* of the cultural entities considered. That is to say that those *immaterial features* we have collected under the *symbolic/conceptual label* must be considered as *absolutely needed* for defining *the specific inner content/meaning conveyed by the corresponding cultural entities.* Note that these features are, quite often, forgotten or expressly neglected in those "digitalization" activities of the cultural domain that are currently so fashionable.

This means that we consider the CH items from two strictly related but independent perspectives, i.e., as usual, like physical tangible artifacts, but also as a bundle of symbolic intangible features defining, in practice, their *inner content/meaning.* To insert this vision within a well-defined methodological framework, we will refer to this advanced conception of the digitization practices by saying that an exhaustive representation in digital format of all the possible CH items should consist of a *twofold entity* on the model of what suggested by the, now popular, *Digital Twins paradigm.* The first component of this entity will then involve the usual description of the physical (as explained above) characteristics of the original cultural entity. The second component will be its associated Digital CH Twin, encoding, in computer-usable form, the symbolic/intangible/conceptual properties of the original entity as evoked above.

Digital Twin is a relative recent notion (Barricelli et al. 2019; Grieves 2016; Fuller et al. 2019; Semeraro et al. 2021) that is now spreading very quickly in an (applied) research context, from engineering to architecture to aerospace to AI-inspired domains like IoT and robotics, and which is concretely used at present, among others, in manufacturing, healthcare and software engineering settings. At the origin, a digital twin was represented by *a high-fidelity, virtual image of a real-world entity*, constantly synchronized with its physical counterpart. It was then utilized to evaluate, optimize and predict the behavior, life, and performance of the physical entity in a timely fashion in order to, e.g., predicting failures of this entity and/or mitigating related unexpected events. Conforming to the recent developments of a new generation of information technologies where *the integration/interaction between the physical and virtual spaces is becoming increasingly important*, the notion of Digital Twin tends now to generalize in order to include the description in digital form of the *immaterial/symbolic/semantic aspects of any possible real-world entity*. The introduction in the CH domain of a new "*Digital Cultural Heritage Twin*" notion seems to be, then, quite justified.

To concretely test the feasibility, from a Computer Science point of view, of the dual approach described above and, in particular, to verify the possibility of implementing really expressive Digital CH Twins entities, a few successful experiments have been recently carried out, see Amelio and Zarri (2020), Zarri (2019c), for example—some of these results will be described and commented later this paper. In this context, an important problem to be solved has concerned the choice of the specific category of Cultural Heritage objects to be used for experimentation. We have then decided to utilize some instances of that *quantitatively and qualitatively particular important class of CH entities* represented by the supports (paintings, drawings, frescoes, sculptures, bas-/high-reliefs, tapestries, mosaics, etc., but also, more in general, photographs, films, posters, comics, cartoons, billboards…) of what are conventionally denoted as *iconographic (or pictorial) narratives*. These narratives typically relate, making use of *visual/illustrative modalities*, particular episodes of larger dynamic stories that we can assume as well known to an educated public, see, for example, the iconographic narratives dealing with events like The Raft of the Medusa (Gericault), the Surrender of Breda (Velasquez), or Napoleon at the Marengo's battle (Louis David). For the sake of generality however, and in agreement with some recent theoretical results (Speidel 2019) showing that the general public is ready to discover deep narrative aspects even in face of pictures, etc., describing *static situations*—see a panoramic view like The Garden at Sainte-Adresse (Monet), a still life as The Vase with Fifteen Sunflowers (Van Gogh) or even a portrait like Da Vinci's Mona Lisa—we have associated to the category of the iconographic/pictorial narratives all those CH entities (paintings, drawings, frescoes, etc.) denoting some sort of *illustrative/narrative aim*. The rationale behind this decision can be found—see again (Speidel 2019)—in the remark that the user/observer will always be in a position to *create some sort of personal story/narrative* about the visible content of the observed CH entity, even when this was, e.g., a Mondrian's work. In this case, the resulting description (the story/narrative) will probably consist of a *mix of feelings, memories, evocations of aesthetic experiences*, leading eventually (as a kind of paradox) to produce some sort of "*tangible*" representation of what, normally, *is deemed not to be explicitly representable*.

The setup of really operational Digital CH Twins can then represent—with respect, e.g., to the metadata-based approaches still largely in use—an important step forward an in-depth description of the inner meanings and the symbolic features of the CH entities. It is evident, however, that the realization of this step requires the use of *high-level knowledge representation tools*; this requirement is even more stringent in the context of our current approach where *iconographic narratives*—characterized then by the presence of *particularly complex inner contents/meanings*—will be used in an experimental framework. This problem can represent an important blocking point with respect to the correct implementation of our Digital CH Twins, given also the well-known *lack of expressiveness* of the Computer Science (CS) tools—OWL, RDF(S), SPARQL, SWRL, etc.—used in a Semantic Web (SW) context and improperly considered as *de facto standards* in a Knowledge Representation context, see also next Section.

For our experiments, we have then made use a *high-level of expressiveness tool* as NKRL, the *Narrative Knowledge Representation Language* (Zarri 2009), both a powerful knowledge representation language and a fully implemented CS environment. Expressly created, thanks mainly to several European projects, to formalize and manage as accurately as possible *those real-world, dynamically characterized and highly ubiquitous entities denoted as "narratives,"*[1] NKRL is particularly well tailored to our aims where, as explained above, *the word narrative can take a quite extensive meaning*. See Zarri (2010, 2011, 2014), e.g., for references to some additional examples of narrative domains where NKRL has been successfully used.

In the following, Sect. 10.2 introduces a short "state of the art," dealing with topics like the digitalization of CH entities, the formal representation of iconographic narratives and the use of the Digital Twin notion in the CH domain. Section 10.3 presents some general notions about NKRL, limited to those strictly necessary to understand the examples of formal representations presented in Sect. 10.4—detailed information about this language can be found in Zarri (2009). Section 10.4 uses the description of a few particularly advanced features of NKRL to introduce some fragments of those Digital CH Twins that have been implemented in the past experiments; these fragments would have been very difficult to realize in a simple and concise way making use of the traditional knowledge representation tools. Section 10.6 is a short Conclusion of the paper.

10.2 A Short State of the Art

Over the past thirty/forty years, the so-called *digitization procedures* in the Cultural Heritage domain—i.e., the production of some forms of *digital images*, directly usable on a computer, of the original CH entities—have progressed considerably both in quantity and in quality.

At the beginning, they were based simply on the use of *standard annotations techniques* created making use, e.g., of keywords (*metadata*) extracted from thesauri like the Art and Architecture Thesaurus, AAT, the Thesaurus of Geographic Names, TGN, the Union List of Artist Names, ULAN, and ICONCLASS, a specialized library

[1] In an operational NKRL context, and in agreement with the Narratology's principles (Bal 2017; Jahn 2021), a *narrative* is seen as a *coherent set* (i.e., its components are logically and chronologically related), possibly of cardinality = 1, *of spatio-temporally constrained elementary events* describing the activities, states, experiences, behaviors, etc., of the (human and non-human) entities involved in the global narrative.

classification designed for art and iconography.[2] Another way of creating basic annotations was to make use of some (relatively simple) *data models*. The Dublin Core, for example—issued originally in 1995 (Weibel 1995)—included, in its basic version, 15 elements like "Title", "Subject", "Description", "Source", "Creator", "Date", "Format", and "Language". A more sophisticated model, the VRA Core 4 XML Schema,[3] was created by the Visual Resources Association—its first version, VRA Core 1.0, dates back to 1996. This model brought in new *structured annotating elements* in the style of CULTURAL CONTEXT, STYLE, PERIOD, TECHNIQUE, etc. The introduction and utilization of the CIDOC CRM Conceptual Reference Model (Bekiari et al. 2021) has, in a sense, marked the peak of this early digitization era, characterized by a strong *documentary/information retrieval attitude*. CIDOC CRM is a well-known and widely used object-oriented *domain ontology* that aims at providing definitions for describing the main implicit and explicit *classes and relationships* used in a Cultural Heritage documentation context. Since December, 2006, it has been recognized as an official ISO international standard (ISO 21127:2023) for the controlled exchange of cultural heritage information from museums, libraries and archives. The (continuously evolving) current model includes now more than 110 classes and 160 properties; the top-class of the hierarchy is denoted as CRM Entity that directly subsumes important classes like Temporal Entity (*Perdurants*, according to the SW terminology) Persistent Item (*Endurants* in SW), Time Span, Place, Dimension. FRBR ("Functional Requirements for Bibliographic Records") was, originally, an entity relationship-oriented ontology created, independently from CIDOC CRM, for the management of bibliographic information. The two ontologies have been successively integrated following an object-oriented model and giving rise, then, to the $FRBR_{OO}$ ontology, see Bekiari et al. (2016).

The introduction in the CH domain, at the turn of the new century, of Semantic Web techniques combined with the use of ontologies and of RDF(s)-based models, has had, undoubtedly, *beneficial effects* on the CH digitization procedures *from an interoperability and standardization point of view*—as also proved, inter alia, by the conversion of several of the models previously mentioned into RDF-compatible tools like the DCMI, the Dublin Core Metadata Initiative Abstract Model (Nilsson et al. 2008) or the RDF(S) versions of the CIDOC CRM tool (CIDOC CRM Team 2022).

In spite of these progresses, the limits of what we have called the *documentary/information retrieval approach* (symbolized by the CIDOC CRM/SW tools association) to the digitization procedures are well evident—in particular with regards to the possibility of taking into account the most abstract/immaterial/symbolic/semantic aspects of the Digital Heritage entities, i.e., those primarily concerned by the introduction of the Digital CH Twins.

With respect to CIDOC CRM, let us consider, for example, a recent successful paper by Carboni and De Luca (2019), describing an extension of CIDOC CRM

---

[2] https://vocab.getty.edu/aat; https://www.getty.edu/research/tools/vocabularies/tgn/; https://www.getty.edu/research/tools/vocabularies/ulan; https://iconclass.org/, accessed Dec 10, 2023.

[3] https://www.loc.gov/standards/vracore/schemas.html; Accessed Dec 10, 2023.

through the implementation of an ontological tool called VIR (Visual Representation)—see also.[4] In particular, VIR expands the key entities and properties of CIDOC CRM by introducing *seven new classes* (e.g., "Iconographical Atom") and *20 new relationships* (e.g., "portray/is portrayed") corresponding, according to the Authors, to the needs of the visual and art historical community. This paper is undoubtedly noteworthy, and has also an interest from an iconographic narratives point of view given that it takes as example the formal representation of a well-known *iconographical character*, Saint George, by following the evolutions in time of the *set of attributes that illustrates this character*. However, the contribution of the paper to the representation of the *inner content/meaning* of the iconographic items examined is practically *non-existent*. According to the Authors, in fact, these attributes can be simply reduced to *horse* and *spear* in the iconographic narrative frescos of the Panagia Phorbiotissa church in Cyprus, to which can then be added *Castle, Princess, Lake and Dragon* when the "Saint George killing the dragon" painting by Vittore Carpaccio is taken into account. Limiting now ourselves to the Carpaccio's painting, its formal modeling—fully coherent, furthermore, with the standard CIDOC CRM approach—is reduced here to a simple *binary form of representation* where an individual, Saint George, is denoted by a set of static CIDOC CRM-like properties as horse, spear, castle, etc. These, being interrelated, can give rise together, as explained in the paper, to a sort of *map of information* that can be of some significance in general, but that tells us nothing about *the highly complex, dramatic and dynamic illustration* of the fight of the Saint with the dragon, which is totally ignored.

With respect now to the specific Semantic Web aspects of the CIDOC CRM/SW association, we have already alluded to the *lack of expressiveness* characteristics of the SW tools, a problem that is well known within the Semantic Web community itself. We can note, in this context, the questioning of certain fundamental theoretical principles of the SW carried out by outstanding figures of this movement (Bernstein et al. 2016) and, from a more technical/operational point of view, the analysis carried out by Trame et al. (2013) about the *systematic failure* of all the attempts—RDF reification, named graphs, RDF blank nodes plus rdf:value properties, quad-tuples, *n*-ary design patterns, F-events, etc.—developed to try to improve the *inherently binary nature* of the SW tools. In the so-called binary model in fact (now also used by CIDOC CRM and the similar/associated tools), the properties/attributes coupled to a given concept can only link an individual to another individual or a value i.e., individual1-property-individual2/value. The limitations of this approach become quickly apparent as soon as we must represent *everyday situations* implying (as, among others, in the iconographic narrative domain) the presence of *several different, human and non-human entities, linked by multiple relationships characterized by strong spatio-temporal constraints.*

Returning then to the digitization operations evoked at the beginning of this Section, a canonical example of the difficulties linked to the adoption of a SW-like purely binary approach is represented by the *SW/RDF-based description* of Claude Monet's "Garden at Sainte-Addressee" painting included in the Image Annotation on

[4] https://ncarboni.github.io/vir/. Accessed Dec 10, 2023.

the Semantic Web W3C Incubator Group Report (Troncy et al. 2007). This description supplies, in fact, an impressive number of details about the *physical (dimensions, etc.) characteristics* of the painting. However, with respect to the proper inner content/meaning of this picture, the representation in digital form is reduced to *three xml-like statements* relating the presence on the picture of three persons (three Claude Monet's relatives). No information is given about *the important immaterial properties that characterize the painting*, e.g., the mode of sitting of the personages facing of the sea, their mutual relationships, their attitude about the peaceful, and bright landscape. The Incubator Group Report goes back to 2007, but, apparently, few real progresses with respect to a (at least partial) description of the symbolic/conceptual properties of the CH items have been made in recent years. We can see in this context, e.g., the *flat statements* in the style of "the subject of the painting is a woman" included in the formalization of the Mona Lisa painting carried out in 2013 in an Europeana context (Isaac 2013). Another example is the formal description of a Giambologna's sculpture (Lodi et al. 2017) denoting the kidnapping of a Sabin woman by a Roman warrior, on display at the Capodimonte museum in Naples. This description is restricted to purely documentary-oriented statements telling us that the sculpture is part of the Collezione Farnese, *without any attempt to model the frightened woman, the kidnapper, the man who tries to stop the kidnapping*, etc.

To conclude this fast "state of the art" analysis, we can mention here that the idea of using the Digital Twin approach to improve the digitalization techniques is far from being our exclusivity. See in this context, e.g., all the references to the necessity of implementing Digital Twins and Digital Twins Repositories included in the authoritative European Commission Report about the creation of an "European Collaborative Cloud for Cultural Heritage."[5] From an implementation perspective of these Twins, however, important divergences still subsist.

In recent papers like (Niccolucci et al. 2022, 2023), e.g., the Authors describe a work that, at first, seems to share at least part of the Digital CH Twin vision expounded in this paper. They affirm in fact, see Niccolucci et al. (2022), that, "Due to the complexity of the cultural heritage data and of their intrinsic inter-relationships, it is necessary to introduce a novel ontology … based on the Digital Twin concept, i.e., the digital counterpart of cultural heritage assets incorporating all the digital information

[5] https://data.europa.eu/doi/10.2777/64014, Accessed 10 Dec 2023. As an example of the several references, in this Report, to the need of creating Digital Twins in the context of the collaborative Cloud for Cultural Heritage, we can mention a very explicit passage about this topic in sub-section 1.3.3 of the Report that concerns the design of the Cloud. In this it is affirmed, in fact, that the creation of digital twins of heritage objects represents *an essential component of the vision underlying this design*, given that it will allow us *to move from fragmented and episodic digitization operations to the establishment of permanent digital counterparts of these objects*, which can then be continuously enriched and enhanced. To temper however the enthusiasm we can note that, even in a European Commission context, *"digital twin" is often understood as a simple synonymous of "digital replica."* Digital replica normally refers to the three-dimensional acquisition and reconstruction methods that make use of photogrammetry and laser scanning techniques to capture *the structural characteristics of physical cultural heritage objects*, in an architectural context, for example. They have nothing to do, then, with the *digital representation of the inner content/meaning of the CH entities*.

pertaining to them"; they suggest then *to collect in a Digital Twin all the semantic/conceptual aspects of a given Cultural Heritage entity.* Concretely, however, their proposal comes down to representing this Twin *under the form of a standard, CIDOC CRM-like, ontology of classes and properties.* How this ontology is concretely structured is far from being evident, even if examples are supplied in the two papers. The core of the ontology seems to consist in an extension (another one…) of CIDOC CRM with additions derived from the Europeana Data Model, EDM and other standard ontological proposals. This ontology is, then, *a purely static one*, formed of classes/concepts defined a priori according to what we have called a *documentary/information retrieval approach*, directly derived, then, from a (dated) terminology-oriented way of thinking. This approach can face strong difficulties when it must be used *to denote complex, interlinked dynamic situations* and preclude then, among other things, the possibility of ensuring a correct and in-depth handling of any sort of iconographic narratives. Another reason of perplexity about this approach concerns the fact that, according to the original definition of any possible kind of Digital Twins, these must correspond to *specific, full-fledged, autonomous digital entities* expressly created to represent the most important semantic/conceptual, aspects of the original ones. They are obviously related to the original "physical" entities, but are, e.g., independently stored on specific platforms, and independently used. Simply identifying the Digital CH Twins *with the nodes of standard, undifferentiated, CIDOC CRM derived, cultural heritage ontologies*, seems then to be in sharp contradiction to the very concept of "digital twin."

10.3 Basic Notions About NKRL

From an ontological point of view, the most important characteristic of NKRL concerns the use of *two different but coordinated ontologies*, a *relatively traditional* ontology of concepts, and an *innovative one* ontology of elementary events.

The ontology of concepts is called *HClass* (hierarchy of classes) in NKRL terms; it consists of a simple *tree data structure* and includes presently (December 2023) more than 5000 *standard concepts. Standard* means here that the properties used to define a given HClass concept are, on purpose, expressed in a quite simple way according to the usual *binary relationships of the property/value type* already discussed in the previous Section. From a strictly formal point of view the HClass ontology—see Zarri (2009: 43–55)—is not fundamentally different from many SW ontologies and, in particular, from those that can be built up by using the original frame version of Protégé (Fridman Noy et al. 2000). Even if rather traditional from a strictly formal point of view, this hierarchy presents, however, some interesting aspects from an ontological perspective, with respect, e.g., to the solutions adopted for representing *particularly difficult notions like color and substance* (Zarri 2009: 123–137).

As already said, a simple binary-based approach undergoes, however, *major difficulties* when the entities to be represented are no more simple, independent notions/concepts that can be defined ahead and inserted then in a usual graph-shaped static ontology, but they denote *complex and dynamically created situations/actions/episodes/experiences,* etc., describing the real-time interactions among a number ≥ 1 of entities like the above HClass items. Stories/narratives (and then iconographic narratives) concern clearly this second category of entities. To allow their formal, computational management, and in agreement with the operational definition of narrative given in Note 1 above, a set (possibly of cardinality $= 1$) of *logically, spatio-temporally and semantically coordinated information units, each corresponding to an elementary event,* must be identified in the context of any of the above stories/narratives. Following a typical Davidsonian/neo-Davidsonian approach (Davidson 1967; Parson 1990), every single elementary event of the set can be recognized thanks the detection, within the natural language (NL) formulation of the whole story/narrative, etc., of a specific *generalized predicate.*[6]

The formal representation of the above basic elementary events is provided in NKRL under the form of *instances* of high-level conceptual structures called *templates.* Each template—i.e., each node of the second NKRL ontology, called HTemp, the hierarchy of templates—*corresponds to a semantically coherent category of elementary events.* Templates are built up according to a specific *augmented n-ary approach,* neatly more expressive than the simple binary one utilized for HClass More precisely:

- Using an *n-ary approach* means, in general, to make use of a sort of formal representation where a *given predicate can be associated with multiple arguments*—using a simple example, representing the *n*-ary "purchase" relation implies associating with the specific "purchase" predicate several arguments as a seller, a buyer, a good, a price, a timestamp, etc.
- *Augmented* means that—following a suggestion that goes back to the seminal "What's in a Link" paper by Woods (1975)—in the context of *n*-ary representations, the logico-semantics links between the predicate and its arguments are *explicitly represented* making use of the notion of *role*—more precisely, of *functional role* (Zarri 2019a) in an NKRL context.

The formal description of a template corresponds then to the structure of Eq. 10.1:

$$(L_l(P_j(R_1, a_1)(R_2, a_2) \ldots (R_n, a_n))) \tag{10.1}$$

In Eq. 10.1, L_l is the *symbolic label* identifying the particular conceptual structure corresponding to a given template. P_j is a *conceptual predicate* defining the general conceptual category of the template and derived from an NL *generalized predicate,* see Note 6. R_k is a *functional role* used to identify the specific logico-semantic function (subject/agent, object, beneficiary, modality, etc.) performed by its filler a_k, an HClass term or a combination of these terms, with respect to the predicate P_j.

[6] An NL generalized predicates can correspond to the usual *tensed/untensed verbs* but also to *adjectives* ("… *worth* several dollars…", "…a *dormant* volcano…"), *nouns* ("…Jane's *amble* along the park…", "…a possible attack…), etc., when they have an evident *predicative function.*

Table 10.1 Deriving a predicative occurrence from a template

```
name: Move:TransferMaterialThingsToSomeone
father: Move:TransferToSomeone
position: 4.21
natural language description: "Transfer a Material Thing (e.g., a product, an object, a letter...)
to Someone".

MOVE:
   SUBJ: var1: [var2]
   OBJ: var3
   [SOURCE: var4: [var5]]
   BENF: var6: [var7]
   [MODAL: var8]
   [TOPIC: var9]
   [CONTEXT: var10]
   { [modulators], ≠abs }

var1: human_being_or_social_body
var3: artefact_
var4: human_being_or_social_body
var6: human_being_or_social_body
var8: process_, sector_specific_activity, service_
var9 : sortal_concept
var10 : situation_, symbolic_label
var2, var5, var7: location_

ex.c1:  MOVE:
          SUBJ: PETER_
          OBJ: ART_BOOK_1
          BENF: MARY_
          MODAL: as_a_gift
          date-1: 2022-07-08
          date-2:
```

As an example, the HTemp template Move:TransferMaterialThingsToSomeone is instantiated to provide the representation of a simple elementary event like "Peter has given an art book to Mary as a gift," see Table 10.1—the resulting formal representation, a "*predicative occurrence*" (according to the NKRL's terminology), denoted as ex.c1 in Table 10.1, *could be interpreted as a component of the Digital CH Twin associated, for example, with a photo describing this event.*

In ex.c1, the predicate MOVE, corresponding to the surface NL verb "give", introduces its four arguments a_k—PETER_, MARY_, ART_BOOK_1 (individuals, i.e., instances of HClass concepts) and as_a_gift (a specific HClass concept)—via, respectively, the four relationships (R_k roles) SUBJ(ect), BEN(e)F(iciary), OBJ(ect) and MODAL(ity), see Table 10.1.[7] Note that, to avoid the ambiguities of natural language and any possible combinatorial explosion problem, see Zarri (2009: 56–61), both the predicates P_j of Eq. 10.1 and the associated functional roles are *primitives.* Predicates P_j belong to the set {BEHAVE, EXIST, EXPERIENCE, MOVE, OWN, PRODUCE, RECEIVE}, and roles R_k to the set {SUBJ(ect), OBJ(ect), SOURCE,

[7] In the *external* NKRL format, *individuals* are denoted in uppercase and *concepts* in lowercase.

BEN(e)F(iciary), MODAL(ity), TOPIC, CONTEXT}.[8] HTemp is then arranged into *seven branches*, where each of them includes only the templates created using *one* of the seven predicate P_j above. Move:TransferMaterialThingsToSomeone, the template used to create occurrence ex.c1 of Table 10.1, is included in the Move:TransferToSomeone sub-tree of the Move: branch of the HTemp hierarchy.

In a template, the arguments of the predicate (the a_k terms in Eq. 10.1) are actually represented by variables (var_i) with *associated constraints*. These are expressed as concepts or combinations of concepts, i.e., *using HClass terms*. When creating a predicative occurrence as instance of a template, the constraints linked to the variables are used to specify *the legal sets of HClass terms*, concepts or individuals, *that can be substituted for these variables within the occurrence*. In Table 10.1 we must verify, e.g., that PETER_ and MARY_ are instances of individual_person, a specific term of human_being_or_social_body, see the constraints on the SUBJ and BENF roles of the Table 10.1 template. The individual ART_BOOK_1 is an instance of art_book, a specific term, through intermediate elements, of artefact_, see the constraint associated with OBJ in Table 10.1, etc.

10.4 Examples of Digital CH Twins Fragments Implemented Using Advanced NKRL Features

We will describe in this Section some examples of how it could be possible to create advanced Digital CH Twins making use of *specific high-level NKRL's features*, very difficult to replicate by means of the usual SW tools. To this aim, we will make use of two of the recent results about the utilization of NKRL in a Digital CH Twin context, concerning the first the digital representation of the central episode included in the "The Surrender of Breda" by Velazquez) (Zarri 2019c) and the second a detailed formal analysis of the identification problems posed by so-called "hidden painting" associated with the universally known "La Gioconda/Mona Lisa" portrait by Da Vinci (Amelio and Zarri 2022).

Several good reproductions of the "Surrender of Breda" can be found, e.g., on Wikipedia at Velazquez-The Surrender of Breda.jpg. With respect to the "hidden painting," the reference paper is (Feldman Schwartz 1988). In this, Lillian Feldmann Schwartz presents a detailed analysis of both the well-known "surface" Mona Lisa's

[8] We can note that the *seven NKRL functional roles* coincide basically with the *seven semantic roles* used in the—well known and widely used in a Computational Linguistics (CL) framework—EAGLES (Expert Advisory Group on Language Engineering Standards) system (The EAGLES Lexicon Interest Group 1999). Both the NKRL and EAGLES roles originate from the *roles/cases* introduced by Charles Fillmore in its ground-breaking paper on the *Case Grammars Theory* (Fillmore 1968). With respect to some CL initiatives aimed at getting free from any discussion about the specific names to associate with these roles and consisting, for supposed generality's reasons, in *simply numbering them beginning with zero*—i.e., Arg0 for Agent/Subject, Arg1 for Patient/Theme, Arg2, etc., see (Palmer et al. 2005) for example—they do not look like as very useful and add, possibly, only further confusion.

portrait and of a second *"hidden" portrait*, revealed only thanks to an x-ray analysis, which lies beneath the surface painting on the same wooden panel. While it was initially thought that the two images represented the same person, i.e., Mona Lisa, Feldmann Schwartz's analysis has shown, as we will see in the next sub-sections, that the "surface" and the "hidden" woman do not denote the same person, and that the "hidden woman" is probably Isabella, Duchess of Aragon, the wife of the Duke of Milan Ludovico il Moro, one of the Leonardo's employers. Feldmann Schwartz's paper includes several illustrations; in particular, Fig. 4 represents a (not particularly well-defined) x-ray photograph of the "hidden painting."

10.4.1 Structured Arguments (Expansions)

Structured arguments (or expansions) represent a very powerful, flexible and, at the same time, *strictly defined* knowledge representation feature that gives us the possibility of building up the predicate arguments a_k of Eq. 10.1 under the form of *sets of recursive lists*. These lists are introduced using the four *AECS operators*: the *disjunctive operator* ALTERN(ative) = A, the *distributive operator* ENUM(eration) = E, the *collective operator* COORD(ination) = C and the *attributive operator* SPECIF(ication) = S. As a simple introductive example to the representation possibilities offered by the AECS mechanism, we can mention here how it could be possible to enhance the description of the ex.c1 event of Table 10.1 by introducing, e.g., (COORD_ PETER_ JOHN_) as filler of the SUBJ(ect) functional role—i.e., Peter and John have, *together*, made a present to Mary—and (SPECIF ART_ BOOK_1 expensive_) as filler of the OBJ(ect) role. In the last case, the operator SPECIF(ication) is used *to define in a more precise way the characteristics of the book* by introducing the information that the book is costly: expensive_ is an HClass term belonging to the intensity_attribute branch of the qualifier_ sub-tree of HClass. From a formal point of view, we can note that, e.g.,:

$$(\text{SPECIF}\,\text{e}_i\,a\,b) = (\text{SPECIF}\,\text{e}_i\,b\,a); \tag{10.2}$$

$$(\text{ENUM}\,\text{e}_1\,\text{e}_2) = (\text{e}_1 \wedge \text{e}_2 \wedge \neg\,(\text{COORD}\,\text{e}_1\,\text{e}_2)),\ \text{etc.} \tag{10.3}$$

As a more complex example we can make reference to the *hidden painting problem*, see above. The predicative occurrence gio2.c4 (an instance of the Own:CompoundProperty template) in Table 10.2 provides *a relatively simple, initial description* of the hidden painting and of its main properties. In NKRL, the instances of the Own:Property and Own:CompoundProperty templates are used to introduce the properties of *inanimate entities*; the templates of the type Behave:HumanProperty introduce, on the contrary, the properties of *human (animate) entities*. The difference between the Own:Property and Own:CompoundProperty's instances concerns the way of denoting the specific property, which is represented by the filler of

Table 10.2 A complex example of structured argument (expansion)

```
gio2.c4: OWN:
        SUBJ: PAINTING_2
        OBJ: property_
        TOPIC: (COORD (SPECIF painted_on POPLAR_PLANK_1 (SPECIF under_ PAINTING_1))
                (SPECIF labelled_as HIDDEN_PAINTING))
        { obs }
        date-1: today_
        date-2:
Own:CompoundProperty (5.42)
```

PAINTING_2 *has been painted under* PAINTING_1 *on the same plank, and is known as the* HIDDEN_PAINTING.

the TOPIC role. This filler is simply a *HClass term*, concept or individual, in the Own:Property instances, while it is a *structured argument (expansion)* in the instances of Own:CompoundProperty.

In the gio2.c4 occurrence, PAINTING_2 denotes *the hidden painting*. Its properties, represented by the filler of the TOPIC functional role, are formalized under the form of a COORD(ination) list including *two arguments* represented by SPECIF(ication) lists:

- The first argument states (i) that the property painted_on of PAINTING_2 refers to the same POPLAR_PLANK_1 that represents the support of PAINTING_1, i.e., of the Mona Lisa's "*surface*" portrait, and (ii), using an additional SPECIF list, that PAINTING_2 is *located under* PAINTING_1.
- The second argument tells us that PAINTING_2 is known as "the HIDDEN_PAINTING."

Given that an unruly utilization of the AECS operators *could give rise to inconsistent conceptual structures*, impossible to interpret and disentangle, they are used according to a so-called priority rule, *mnemonically visualized* according to this expression: (ALTERN (ENUM (COORD (SPECIF)))). This means that it is forbidden to use within the scope of a list introduced by an operator B_i a list labeled in terms of one of the AECS operators appearing *on the left of* B_i in the priority expression above. It is impossible, e.g., to use a list COORD within the scope of a list SPECIF—the inverse is perfectly legal, see the example of Table 10.2.

10.4.2 Determiners and Attributes

The semantic predicate P_j, the seven functional roles R_k and the (simple or structured) arguments a_k of the predicate, see Eq. 10.1, are *the three basic building blocks* strictly needed to give rise, together, to a meaningful representation of templates or predicative occurrences—and then to valid Digital CH Twins. When the addition of further information-carrying elements is required to better specify the meaning expressed by this basic core, *these additional elements (basically locations, modalities and temporal information) are dealt with simply as "determiners/attributes"* (Zarri 2009: 70–86).

In Table 10.1, e.g., the variables *var2, var5,* and *var7* included in the template denote *determiners/attributes of the location type* that are represented, in the corresponding predicative occurrences, *by specific terms of the HClass concept location_ or by individuals derived from these terms*. In the case of Table 10.1, let us suppose that both the donor (Peter) and the recipient (Mary) are in Paris. The fillers of the SUBJ and BENF roles of ex.c1 will be then SUBJ: PETER: (PARIS_) and BENF: MARY_: (PARIS_). PARIS_ is an individual, instance of the concept french_city and then, through some intermediary steps, of the high-level concept location_ that, in the template Move:TransferMaterialThingsToSomeone of Table 10.1, expresses the constraints on the filler of the *var2, var5* and *var7* variables.

Modulators (modalities) represent an important category of determiners/attributes which, unlike "locations" that can only be linked to specific fillers of functional roles, see above, *necessarily apply to complete and well-formed templates or predicative occurrences* to particularize their *full meaning*. They are classed into three categories, *temporal* (begin, end, obs(erve)), *deontic* (oblig(ation), fac(ulty), interd(iction), perm(ission)) and *modal* (abs(olute), against, for, main, ment(al), wish, etc.) modulators, see Zarri (2009: 71–75). "begin" and "end" are used to denote that the date associated with the operator date-1 (see below) corresponds, respectively, to *the beginning or the end* of the event/state/situation/action, etc., represented by the predicative occurrence where they appear. An example of use of the temporal modulator obs(erve) is given in Table 10.2: we can see, *as of today*, that PAINTING_2 is…; note that today_ is a legal HClass concept.

Another important category of attribute/determiners concerns the two operators date-1 and date-2. They can only be associated *with full predicative occurrences* (see, e.g., the two occurrences in Tables 10.1 and 10.2). They are used, in general, to materialize in NKRL terms the temporal interval (or a specific date) associated with the elementary event that was at the origin of the corresponding predicative occurrence; they take on special meanings in association with the temporal modulators, see the previous paragraph. A recent paper about the representation of temporal information in NKRL is (Zarri 2019b).

To emphasize the importance of the attribute/determiner tools in NKRL, we reproduce in Table 10.3 another fragment of the formalization of the *hidden painting narrative*. In this, occurrence gio2.c6 represents a typical example of NKRL modeling of the *notion of negation*, a very debated and controversial topic in Knowledge Representation and Computational Linguistics. The solution adopted in NKRL for dealing with negation *consists in adding to a predicative occurrence a specific modal modulator*, negv (negated event) to denote that the corresponding elementary event *did not take place*.[9]

[9] We prefer to speak about *negated event* rather than *negative event* as, e.g., in the Stanford Encyclopaedia (Casati and Varzi 2020)—even if, in the two cases, the meaning is not so different, "things that do not actually happen, including 'negative actions' of various sort", according to the

Table 10.3 An example of "negated event"

```
gio2.c6: BEHAVE:
          SUBJ: (SPECIF WOMAN_53 (SPECIF identified_with WOMAN_52))
          { obs, negv }
          date-1: today_
          date-2:

Behave:HumanProperty (1.1)
```

We can remark today that the elementary event represented by gio2.c6 *is a* negated event *(modulator* negv*), i.e.,* WOMAN_53 *is not* WOMAN_52.

In this example, WOMAN_53, the woman of the hidden painting, has not been recognized as WOMAN_52, i.e., as Mona Lisa—as already stated above, WOMAN_53 is probably Isabella d'Aragona, the wife of the Duke of Milan Ludovico il Moro, see Feldman Schwartz (1988). The association of the temporal modulator obs with today_ has the usual "as of today" meaning.

10.4.3 Linking Elementary Events

What described until now illustrates the NKRL solutions to the problem of representing *single elementary events*. In the context of larger dynamic situations like complex events, narratives, scripts, scenarios, etc., several predicative occurrences must be associated using specific tools that formalize the meaning/behavior of *surface—i.e., linguistic—connectivity constructions* like causality, goal or indirect speech. In NKRL, these connectivity constructions are represented using *Higher Order Logic (HOL) structures* obtained via the *reification* of "generic" (i.e., not only predicative, see below) occurrences. As already stated, these reification operations rely on the utilization of the L_i symbolic labels of Eq. 10.1; they concern in particular, as usual in Computer Science, the possibility of creating new objects out of existing entities and to say something about them without making explicit reference to the original entities.

10.4.3.1 Completive Construction

A first example of HOL structure in NKRL is represented by the *completive construction*. This consists in using as filler of a functional role in a *predicative occurrence pci* the symbolic label *Lj* of another occurrence *cj*, where this second occurrence,

Encyclopaedia. The version *negated events* is, in fact, more coherent with the general philosophy of NKRL, based on the existence of *neutral* building blocks represented by elementary events that are then specified, manipulated, negated, aggregated, etc., and with the *particular operational modalities proper to the modulators*, which are *added* to pre-existing pieces of code.

(indirectly) used as fillers, can correspond not only to a *predicative occurrence* but also to those *binding occurrences bci* introduced below. The (single) label *Lj* used as a filler is prefixed, in the external NKRL format, by a sharp, "#", code; the format of a completive construction filler corresponds then to #symbolic_label.

As an example, we supply in Table 10.4 the NKRL's formulation—simplified here, see a more complete version in (Zarri 2019c)—of the *key moment* of the narrative expressed by Velazquez' masterpiece "The Surrender of Breda." In this Ambrosio Spinola, Commander in Chief of the Spanish Army during the Eighty Years' War, receives, on June 5, 1625, the keys to the city of Breda by its Dutch governor, Justinus van Nassau, after the surrender of the city. The main interest of this scene—see, e.g., the reproductions that, as already mentioned, can be found on Wikipedia at Velazquez-The Surrender of Breda.jpg—resides in the *benevolent attitude of the winner*, Spinola, toward the loser, van Nassau, a not so common behavior at that time. In the picture, we see in fact Spinola preventing, by a hand gesture, the Justinus' attempt to genuflect in front of him; the corresponding NKRL encoding is represented in Table 10.4. We can note here the NKRL's capabilities with respect to the *computerized representation of abstract entities* like feelings, behaviors, attitudes, etc.—see also (Zarri 2014) in this context—very important, as already noticed in Sects. 10.1 and 10.2, from a Digital CH Twins point of view.

In Table 10.4, breda.c5 and breda.c6 *represent together (completive construction) a sort of unique, coherent entity*—in linguistic terms, a connectivity structure similar to a sort of *indirect speech*. This entity formalizes the *most important narrative element of the picture*: while he receives the keys to the city (breda.c6), Ambrosio Spinola *prevents*, (PRODUCE activity_blockage), a Justinus' attempt to

Table 10.4 Formal representation of the "key moment" in the "Surrendcer of Breda"

```
breda.c5: PRODUCE:
            SUBJ: AMBROSIO_SPINOLA: (BREDA_)
            OBJ: activity_blockage
            MODAL: hand_gesture
            TOPIC: (SPECIF GENUFLECTING_1 JUSTINUS_VAN_NASSAU)
            CONTEXT: #breda.c6
            date-1: 05/06/1625
            date-2:

Produce:CreateCondition/Result (6.4)
```

(Within the breda.c6 *framework), Spinola stops van Nassau who is starting to genuflect.*

```
breda.c6: RECEIVE:
            SUBJ AMBROSIO_SPINOLA: (BREDA_)
            OBJ (SPECIF key_to_the_city BREDA_)
            SOURCE JUSTINUS_VAN_NASSAU
            CONTEXT CELEBRATION_1
            date-1: 05/06/1625
            date-2:

Receive:TangibleThing (7.1)
```

Spinola receives the keys to the city from van Nassau in the context of particular celebrations

Table 10.5 Examples of NKRL's concept reification technique

```
breda.c7: OWN:
          SUBJ: (SPECIF GENUFLECTING_1 JUSTINUS_VAN_NASSAU)
          OBJ: property_
          TOPIC: (COORD sketched_ (SPECIF in_front_of AMBROSIO_SPINOLA))
          date-1: 05/06/1625
          date-2:

Own:CompoundProperty (5.42)
```

Van Nassau's genuflecting in front of Spinola is only sketched.

```
breda.c8: OWN:
          SUBJ: CELEBRATION_1: (BREDA_)
          OBJ: property_
          TOPIC: (SPECIF surrender_ BREDA_)
          date-1: 05/06/1625
          date-2:

Own:CompoundProperty (5.42)
```

The celebrations are about the surrender of Breda.

genuflect in front of him (breda.c5). activity_blockage is a specific term of activity_in HClass; genuflecting_ is a specific term of negative_relationship and then of relationship_. Note that the genuflecting_ concept has been *reified* through its transformation into an *individual*, GENUFLECTING_1, to allow us to *quote unambiguously this term within several occurrences*. It appears, in fact, in another predicative occurrence (breda.c7) which is part of the full coding of the episode, see Zarri (2019c), and in the first predicative occurrence of Table 10.5, where it is stated that the genuflecting is both sketched_ (specific term of qualifier_ via general_characterising_property) and in_front_of (specific term of binary_relational_property) Ambrosio Spinola.

This *concept reification technique*, largely utilized in a NKRL context, is interesting in itself given that it represents an easy and very effective solution to (at least) some aspects of the so-called *entity linking* (or *entity resolution*) problem that bothers the Computational Linguistics community, see Rao et al. (2013) for a paper on this topic. Another example of application of this technique is represented by breda.c8 (see the second occurrence of Table 10.5) that corresponds, in a sense, to a *definition* of the HClass term CELEBRATION_1 introduced in occurrence breda.c6 of Table 10.4. With respect to breda.c8, we have already noticed in Sect. 4.1 above that making use of the instances of the Own:Property and Own:CompoundProperty templates represents the standard NKRL techniques for introducing the properties of *inanimate entities*.

10.4.3.2 Binding Occurrences

A second kind of HOL structures is used to associate together, through several kinds of formalized *connectivity operators*, the NKRL representations—*fully independent*, at the difference of what happens in a completive construction context—of elementary or *complex events* (complex events are formed of *coherent set of elementary events*). This mechanism is called *binding occurrences*, see Zarri (2009: 91–98), and it is implemented under the form of lists composed of a *binding operator* Bn_i and its *Li arguments*, see Eq. 10.4:

$$(Lb_k(Bn_i\, L_1, L_2 \ldots L_n)), \tag{10.4}$$

where Lb_k is the symbolic label identifying the global binding structure. The Bn_i operators are: ALTERN(ative), COORD(ination), ENUM(eration), CAUSE, REFER(ence), the *weak causality* operator, GOAL, MOTIV(ation), the *weak intentionality* operator, COND(ition), see again (Zarri 2009: 91–98) for more details.

The binding structures are particularly important in an NKRL context, given that the top-level occurrence introducing the full representation of any kind of NKRL-encoded narrative structure—and then of full Digital CH Twins—*has necessarily the form of a binding occurrence*, see the example of Table 10.6. In this, it is explained that the CAUSE of what declared in occurrence gio2.c6 of Table 10.3—i.e., that WOMAN_52, Mona Lisa, *is not* WOMAN_53, the hidden painting woman—is related to the publication (see gio2.c7, an instance of the Move:StructuredInformation template) of a paper of Feldman Schwartz (1988). In this, she had listed all the *incoherencies*—like the strong dissimilarities existing among the mouths, eyes, noses, chins, hairlines, etc., of the two women—that prevent any possible identification. In the corresponding NKRL encoding, all these incoherencies are denoted under the form of a set of *predicative occurrences* grouped within a *binding occurrence* of the COORD(ination) type labeled as gio2.c8 in Table 10.6—because of their *repetitive nature*, only one of these predicative occurrences, gio2.c9, is presented in Table 10.6. We can note that the binding occurrence gio2.c8 is introduced in gio2.c7 under the form of a *completive construction.* This particular form of completive construction, created using the template Move:StructuredInformation, is very important in an NKRL context because it represents the *standard way* to denote any sort of *transmission of messages* (Zarri 2009: 165–167).

10.5 Some Remarks About the Inference Procedures

Setting up *particularly expressive Digital CH Twins* without having the possibility of demonstrating the interest of making use of their high-level representation features in the context of attractive inference procedures can be considered *quite a nonsense.* Unfortunately, implementing this possibility would require the existence of a *sufficiently large Knowledge Base (KB) of Digital CH Twins* to be utilized for carrying on the inferences, knowledge base that is clearly missing in this preliminary phase of our work. Using, however, information represented in Tables 10.4 and 10.5, we can try to provide an at least general idea about the way these inference procedures could be used in a concrete context.

Table 10.6 Examples of binding occurrences

```
gio2.c5: (CAUSE gio2.c6 gio2.c7 #gio2.c8)
```
The elementary event modelized by gio2.c6 *has been caused by what is collectively described in the completive construction involving occurrences* gio2.c7 *and* gio2.c8.

```
gio2.c6: BEHAVE.
        SUBJ: (SPECIF WOMAN_53 … { obs, negv } (see Table 10.3)
```
The elementary event represented by gio2.c7 *is a "negated event" …*

```
gio2.c7: MOVE:
        SUBJ: LILLIAN_FELDMANN_SCHWARTZ
        OBJ: #gio2.c8
        MODAL: (SPECIF SCIENTIFIC_PAPER_2 (SPECIF published_on
                                    THE_VISUAL_COMPUTER_JOURNAL))
        date-1: 1/1/1988, 31/1/1988
        date-2:
Move:StructuredInformation (4.42)
```
Mrs. Schwartz has circulated what denoted in gio2.c8 *by means of a paper in "The Visual Computer" journal.*

```
gio2.c8: (COORD1 gio2.c9 …)
```
The binding occurrence gio2.c8 *includes a list of predicative occurrences denoting a difference between* WOMAN_52 *and* WOMAN_53.

```
gio2.c9: OWN
        SUBJ: (SPECIF eye_ (SPECIF cardinality_ 2) WOMAN_53))
        OBJ: property_
        TOPIC: (SPECIF different_from (SPECIF eye_ (SPECIF cardinality_ 2) WOMAN_52))
        MODAL: x_ray_analysis
        { obs }
        date-1: today
        date-2:
Own:CompoundProperty (5.42)
```
Only the dissimilarity between the eyes of WOMAN_52 *and* WOMAN_53 *has been taken into account in this Table. In reality, also the mouth, nose, chin and hairline of the two women are incompatible.*

We will show, then, how it could be possible to automatically infer some confirmation about the positive attitude of Ambrosio Spinola versus his opponent. As a first move, we will make use of the simple *search pattern* p_i of Table 10.7, derived from the template Behave:ConcreteVersusHumanAttitude. In NKRL, search patterns are *partially instantiated templates that represent,* in the first place, *formal queries posed by the user to a knowledge base of NKRL statements,* but that can also be *generated automatically during the execution of high-level inference procedures*, see Zarri (2009: 183–202).

Table 10.7 A search pattern about data included in Tables 10.4 and 10.5

```
BEHAVE:
    SUBJ: AMBROSIO_SPINOLA
    OBJ: JUSTINUS_VAN_NASSAU
    MODAL: positive_attitude
    date1:
    date2:
```

Given the extremely reduced quantity of data at our disposal, this search pattern in itself will be *unable to find direct unifications* with the data of Tables 10.4 and 10.5. We can however imagine to find, within the *rule repository* associated with a hypothetical complete Digital CH Twins system, a (sufficiently general) "*transformation rule*" stating that, "should a given person stop a submissiveness expression towards herself/himself from another person, this implies a positive attitude of the first person against the second." *Transformation rules* represent an important class of *high-level NKRL inference rules*, see Zarri (2009: 212–216), used *to try to adapt* (from a semantic point of view) a search pattern p_i that *failed*—i.e., that was unable to find a unification with the information in the knowledge base—to the *actual contents of this base* using a sort of *analogical reasoning*. This means, concretely, that transformations try to *automatically convert pattern* p_i *into one or more different patterns* $p_1, p_2 \ldots p_n$ *that, overall, are not strictly "equivalent" but only "semantically close" to the original one*. A formal expression of the above rule in NKRL terms is given in Table 10.8.

To activate this rule we must verify, as a first step, if the rule is *likely, at least in principle, to transform the particular* p_j *pattern*. This verification will be carried out by checking whether the pattern to transform is really able to *unify* the left-hand component of the rule (the *antecedent*). Looking at Tables 10.7 and 10.8, this is of course possible—the antecedent of Table 10.8 is, in fact, a *generalization* of

Table 10.8 A transformation rule example

t41: *"recovering from a submissive condition" transformation*

antecedent:

BEHAVE:
    SUBJ: *var1*
    OBJ: *var2*
    MODAL: positive_attitude

var1: individual_person
var2: individual_person
var1 ≠ *var2*

first consequent schema (*conseq1*):

PRODUCE:
    SUBJ: *var1*
    OBJ: activity_achievement
    TOPIC: (SPECIF *var3 var2*)

var3: negative_relationship

second consequent schema (*conseq2*):

OWN:
    SUBJ: *var3*
    OBJ: property_
    TOPIC: (SPECIF *var4 var1*)

var4: binary_relational_property

If a given person stops a manifestation of submission concerning herself/himself which is expressed by another person, this could imply a positive attitude of the first person towards the second.

the pattern of Table 10.7; moreover, this unification will allow us to associate some values with variables *var1* and *var2* i.e., *var1* = AMBROSIO_SPINOLA and *var2* = JUSTINUS_VAN_NASSAU. These values will be then transferred to the first consequent schema (*conseq1*) in the right side of the rule. This consequent schema, *transformed then into a new search pattern* p_j *characterized by the presence of a new variable*, *var3* (see Table 10.8) will try in turn to find successful unifications with information included in Tables 10.4 and 10.5 that correspond to our (extremely reduced) KB producing, among other things, *new values* for the new variable. All these values will be transmitted to the second consequent schema (*conseq2*) and so on; the transformation will be validated *iff all the consequents can find at least a valid unification within the KB*. In our example, the search pattern derived from *conseq1* will unify breda.c5 of Table 10.4; the value GENUFLECTING_1 will be linked to *var3* and transferred to the pattern derived from *conseq2*. This last will unify breda.c7 (Table 10.5). The two occurrences, breda.c5 and breda.c7, will be supplied then to the user as a sort of an *indirect answer* to the original question.

Additional details about the characteristics of the NKRL's *inference engines*—which run according to *backward chaining procedures* making use of *backtracking operations* in case of deadlocks can be found, e.g., in Zarri (2009: 201–234, 2013).[10]

Making use of a normal size KB, it could be possible to employ a second class of NKRL inference rules, the *hypothesis rules* (Zarri 2009: 205–212), to evaluate some of the *possible reasons* already introduced to explain the behavior of Spinola versus his adversary and for proposing, in case, new ones. Among those already suggested—see, e.g., the Encyclopaedia Britannica entry about "The Surrender of Breda" by Velazquez—we can mention (i) an astute propaganda operation to the benefit of the Spanish royal household, (ii) the fact that the Spanish Army had really admired the bravery of the Dutch soldiers, (iii) Velazquez's wish to promote a sort of Christian way of conducting warfare, (iv) Velazquez's friendship for Spinola, etc. Other investigations paths could concern exploring the *possible influences* on Velazquez exerted by well-known masterpieces dealing with similar topics, e.g., Rubens' "Meeting of King Ferdinand of Hungary and the Cardinal-Infante Ferdinand of Spain at Nördlingen" or "The reconciliation between Jacob and Esau."

[10] We can also note, from a general *automatic reasoning point of view*, that the possibility of profiting from the high-level of expressiveness of NKRL is particularly important to create inference rules whose *atoms*, see Table 10.8, for example, *can represent directly complex situations and events, actions, scenarios, narratives, etc*. We are no more constrained, then, to express these atoms, as usual, in terms of *simple binary clauses* that make use of just monadic (unary) and dyadic (binary) predicates. Modeling all the rule atoms according to a uniform binary format implies, among other things, the impossibility of stating even relatively simple implications of the "if-then" type *making use of a reduced number of clauses*. This leads in practice to the necessity of a decomposition of the original formulation of the rules into (possibly very large) amounts of binary clauses implying, eventually, *serious problems both from a logical and an operational point of view*.

10.6 Conclusion

In this paper, we have proposed the use of advanced digital representation techniques to allow a generalized access to all the important features, both physical and symbolic/conceptual, of any kind of Cultural Heritage (CH) entities, and to make possible their *global fruition*. According then to the so-called *Digital Cultural Heritage Twin approach*, we suggest to conceive the digitalized image of any CH entity as the *association of two components*, the first describing the *physical* (in the largest meaning of this word) properties of this entity, and the second supplying the formal description of at least the most important *immaterial/symbolic aspects* of the same entity. NKRL, the Narrative Knowledge Representation Language, has been chosen for the implementation of the second component of this approach, because of its well-known capacity for *dealing with important immaterial/symbolic aspects* of many different realities.

To demonstrate the viability of this methodology and the validity of the NKRL's choice, we have illustrated in some depth the use of NKRL to *digitally represent complex expressive cultural heritage entities*, with particular reference to those *iconographic narrative entities* corresponding to stories told in visual form that are conveyed by works of art like paintings, drawings, frescoes, mosaics, sculptures, and murals. They represent a particularly important component—both numerically and culturally—of the whole Cultural Heritage domain. In particular, we have utilized NKRL *to represent in digital form some interesting aspects of two Renaissance works of art*, the *hidden painting* that lies beneath Mona Lisa on the same poplar panel and the *Surrender of Breda painting* by Velasquez; these formal representations can *correspond to possible components of the Digital CH Twins proper to the two works of art*. As a result of this study, the well-known generality and efficiency properties of NKRL with respect to the representation and management of any possible form of narrative (both in written and pictorial form) have been confirmed, both from a specific knowledge representation and an inferential point of view. The potential of NKRL overcomes, in fact, *some important imitations* linked with the use of simple descriptions under metadata form and/or with the choice of knowledge representation tools unsuitable for representing complex situations/events, and allows us to explore the *immaterial components* (including some emotional factors) associated to any possible Cultural Heritage entities in a *very expressive, complete and meaningful form*.

As stated at length in this paper, the work presented here represents only *a very preliminary experiment* whose initial results should be confirmed in the framework of *larger and more stable initiatives*. In any case, we are particularly pleased to have led to a good end a challenge whose *positive result*—taking into account all the difficulties liked with our commitment to represent *in the more expressive way and with a minimum loss of information* the conceptual complexities of the Cultural Heritage domain—*was far from being evident at the outset*.

References

Amelio A, Zarri GP (2020) Conceptual encoding and advanced management of Leonardo da Vinci's Mona Lisa: preliminary results. Information 10(10):321, 1–20, MDPI—Special issue on Visual pattern extraction and recognition for cultural heritage understanding. https://doi.org/10.3390/info10100321. Accessed 10 Dec 2023

Amelio A, Zarri, GP (2022) A knowledge representation framework for managing Leonardo Da Vinci's Mona Lisa: case study of the hidden painting. In: Proceedings of the 1st international virtual conference on visual pattern extraction and recognition for cultural heritage understanding (CEUR Publications vol 3266). CEUR, Aachen. http://ceur-ws.org/Vol-3266/. Accessed 10 Dec 2023

Bal M (2017) Narratology: introduction to the theory of narrative, 4th edn. University Press, Toronto

Barricelli BR, Casiraghi E, Fogli D (2019) A survey on digital twin: definitions, characteristics, applications, and design implications. IEEE Access 7:167653–167671. https://doi.org/10.1109/ACCESS.2019.2953499. Accessed 10 Dec 2023

Bekiari C, Doerr M, Le Bœuf P, Riva P (eds) (2016) Definition of $FRBR_{OO}$, A conceptual model for bibliographic information in object-oriented formalism. International Federation of Library Associations and Institutions, Den Haag

Bekiari C, Bruseker G, Doerr M, Ore CE, Stead S, Velios T (eds) (2021) Definition of the CIDOC conceptual reference model (version 7.1.1). ICOM/CIDOC Documentation Standard Group, Heraklion

Bernstein A, Hendler J, Noy N (2016) A new look at the semantic web. Commun ACM 59(9):35–37

Carboni N, Luca L (2019) An ontological approach to the description of visual and iconographical representations. Heritage 2(2):1191–1210

Casati R, Varzi A (2020) Events. In: The Stanford encyclopaedia of philosophy (Summer 2020 Edition), Metaphysics Research Laboratory of the Stanford University. Stanford, CA (2020). https://plato.stanford.edu/archives/sum2020/entries/events. Accessed 10 Dec 2023

CIDOC CRM Team (2022) RDFs implementation of CIDOC-CRM (version 7.1.2). ICOM/CIDOC Documentation Standard Group, Heraklion

Davidson D (1967) The logical form of action sentences. In: Rescher N (ed) The logic of decision and action. University Press, Pittsburg, PA, pp 81–95

Feldman Schwartz L (1988) The Mona Lisa identification: evidence from a computer analysis. Vis Comput 4(1):40–48

Fillmore CJ (1968) The case for case. In: Bach E, Harms RT (eds) Universals in linguistic theory. Holt, Rinehart and Winston, New York, pp 1–25

Fridman Noy N, Fergerson RW, Musen MA (2000) The knowledge model of Protégé-2000: combining interoperability and flexibility. In: Knowledge engineering and knowledge management. methods, models, and tools—Proceedings of EKAW 2000 (LNCS, vol 1937). Springer, Berlin, pp 17–32

Fuller A, Fan Z, Day C (2019) Digital twin: enabling technology, challenges and open research. https://arxiv.org/abs/1911.01276v1. Accessed 10 Dec 2023

Grieves M (2016) Origins of the digital twin concept—working paper. Florida Institute of Technology, Melbourne, FL. https://www.researchgate.net/publication/307509727. Accessed 10 Dec 2023

Isaac A (ed) (2013) Europeana data model primer (14/07/2013). Europeana. http://travesia.mcu.es/portalnb/jspui/bitstream/10421/5981/1/EDM_primer.pdf. Accessed 10 Dec 2023

Jahn M (2021) Narratology 2.3: a guide to the theory of narrative. English Department of the University, Cologne. https://www.researchgate.net/publication/344239602. Accessed 10 Dec 2023

Lodi G, Asprino L, Nuzzolese AG, Presutti V, Gangemi A, Reforgiato Recupero D, Veninata C, Orsini A (2017) Semantic web for cultural heritage valorisation. In: Hai-Jew S (ed) Data analytics in digital humanities. Springer, Cham, pp 3–37

Niccolucci F, Felicetti A, Hermon S (2022) Populating the data space for cultural heritage with heritage digital twins. MDPI Data 7(8):105. https://doi.org/10.3390/data7080105. Accessed 10 Dec 2023

Niccolucci F, Markhoff B, Theodoridou M, Felicetti A, Hermon S (2023) The heritage digital twin: a bicycle made for two. The integration of digital methodologies into cultural heritage research. arXiv:2302.07138. Accessed 10 Dec 2023

Nilsson M, Powell A, Johnston P, Naeve A (2008) Expressing Dublin core metadata using the resource description framework, RDF (DCMI Recommendation 2008-01-04). Dublin Core Metadata Initiative, Silver Spring, MD

Palmer M, Kingsbury P, Gildea D (2005) The proposition bank: an annotated corpus of semantic roles. Comput Linguist 31(1):71–106

Parson T (1990) Events in the semantics of English. The MIT Press, Cambridge, MA

Rao D, McNamee P, Drezde M (2013) Entity linking: finding extracted entities in a knowledge base. In: Poibeau T, Saggion H, Piskorski J, Yangarber R (eds) Multi-source, multilingual information extraction and summarization. Springer, Berlin, pp 93–115

Semeraro C, Lezoche M, Panetto H, Dassisti M (2021) Digital twin paradigm: a systematic literature review. Comput Ind 130:103469

Speidel K (2019) What narrative is—reconsidering definitions based on experiments with pictorial narrative. An essay in descriptive narratology. Front Narrative Stud 4(s1):s76–s104

The EAGLES Lexicon Interest Group (1999) EAGLES LE3-4244 preliminary recommendations on lexical semantic encoding—final report. ILC-CNR, Pisa. http://www.ilc.cnr.it/EAGLES96/EAGLESLE.PDF. Accessed 10 Dec 2023

Trame J, Kessler C, Kuhn W (2013) Linked data and time—modeling researcher life lines by events. In: Proceedings of the 11th international conference on spatial information theory, COSIT 2013 (LNCS, vol 8116). Springer, Berlin, pp 205–223

Troncy R, van Ossenbruggen J, Pan JZ, Stamou G (eds) (2007) Image annotation on the semantic web, W3C Incubator Group Report 14 August 2007. https://www.w3.org/2005/Incubator/mmsem/XGR-image-annotation/. Accessed 10 Dec 2023

Weibel S (1995) Metadata: the foundations of resource description. D-Lib Magazine 1(1) July 1995

Woods WA (1975) What's in a link: foundations for semantic networks. In: Bobrow DG, Collins AM (eds) Representation and understanding: studies in cognitive science. Academic Press, New York, pp 35–82

Zarri GP (2009) Representation and management of narrative information—theoretical principles and implementation. Springer, London

Zarri GP (2010) A conceptual methodology for dealing with terrorism 'narratives. Int J Digit Crime Forensics 2(2):47–63 (2010)

Zarri GP (2011) Knowledge representation and inference techniques to improve the management of gas and oil facilities. Knowl-Based Syst 24(7):989–1003

Zarri GP (2013) Advanced computational reasoning based on the NKRL conceptual model. Expert Syst Appl (ESWA) 40(8):2872–2888

Zarri GP (2014) Sentiments analysis at conceptual level making use of the narrative knowledge representation language. Neural Netw 58(1):82–97

Zarri GP (2019a) Functional and semantic roles in a high-level knowledge representation language. Artif Intell Rev 51(4):537–575

Zarri GP (2019b) Modelling and exploiting the temporal information associated with complex 'narrative' documents. Int J Knowl Eng Data Min 6(2):135–167

Zarri GP (2019c) Use of a knowledge patterns-based tool for dealing with the 'narrative meaning' of complex iconographic cultural heritage items. In: Proceedings of the 2019 international VIPERC workshop on visual pattern extraction and recognition for cultural heritage understanding (CEUR Publications vol 2320). CEUR, Aachen, pp 25–38. https://ceur-ws.org/Vol-2320/. Accessed 10 Dec 2023

Chapter 11
Motion Labeling and Recognition: A Case Study on the Zeibekiko Dance

Maria Skublewska-Paszkowska, Pawel Powroznik, Marilena Lemonari, and Andreas Aristidou

Abstract Performing arts is part of our Intangible Cultural Heritage (ICH), a mainspring of humanity's cultural diversity. Folk dance is one of the most important aspects of ICH that is still alive and continues to influence arts in modern days. Digitizing, documenting, and understanding folk dance and other structured movement systems, is important in the larger scheme of cultural forms. Nowadays, modern and sophisticated equipment, such as optical motion capture systems, allow for accurate dance acquisition, advancing our ability to digitally store, curate, study, present, portray, and re-use intangible dance creations. However, motion captured data do not contain labels, annotations, or semantics to assist organization and indexing. In addition, the large diversity of dance motions and their complexity makes automatic motion segmentation and movement recognition challenging, especially for such highly dynamic, heterogeneous, and stylized motions. In this work, we utilize the Spatial Temporal Graph Convolutional Networks (ST-GCN) to recognize particular dance moves, enabling motion segmentation and annotation. ST-GCN takes advantage of the human topology in temporal order, achieving great success in human motion recognition. We use Zeibekiko as our case study; Zeibekiko is a Greek dance, which is included in the Greece's National Inventory of Intangible Cultural Heritage. It is a unique, soulful dance that requires an inner tension, as it is based on the improvisation of the dancer, mainly expressing the performer's emotions (e.g., pride, happiness, sadness), by making their own unique and characteristic steps. The used classification measures indicate that this is an appropriate tool to classify these kinds of dance patterns. Our method can be useful in several applications in the

M. Skublewska-Paszkowska · P. Powroznik
Department of Computer Science, Lublin University of Technology, Lublin, Poland
e-mail: maria.paszkowska@pollub.pl

P. Powroznik
e-mail: p.powroznik@pollub.pl

M. Lemonari · A. Aristidou (✉)
Department of Computer Science, University of Cyprus, Nicosia, Cyprus
e-mail: a.aristidou@ieee.org

M. Lemonari
e-mail: lemonari.marilena@ucy.ac.cy

F. Liarokapis et al. (eds.), *Interactive Media for Cultural Heritage*, Springer Series on Cultural Computing, https://doi.org/10.1007/978-3-031-61018-9_11

cultural heritage domain, for example in dance motion analysis and indexing to find potential contextual similarities between dances from different countries, as well as e-learning applications, providing detailed step-by-step education on how to imitate specific dance moves (pirouettes), etc.

Keywords Motion labeling · Motion recognition · Zeibekiko · Dance analysis · Intangible cultural heritage · Spatial temporal graph

11.1 Introduction

Intangible Cultural Heritage (ICH) encompasses the practices, expressions, knowledge, and skills that communities, groups, and individuals recognize as part of their cultural legacy. It comprises a diverse array of non-physical elements, including performing arts, oral traditions, rituals, social practices, traditional craftsmanship, and knowledge systems. Unlike tangible cultural heritage, such as monuments or artifacts (Barszcz et al. 2021; Montusiewicz et al. 2022), ICH is rooted in living traditions and passed down from one generation to another. It plays a vital role in shaping identities, fostering social cohesion, and promoting cultural diversity, reflecting the cultural, social, and historical values of communities, and contributing to their sense of belonging and continuity (Aristidou et al. 2022). Often intertwined with local environments, natural resources, and traditional knowledge systems, dance holds particular significance as an essential aspect of ICH (Doulamis et al. 2017; Rallis et al. 2020; Shay and Sellers-Young 2016).

Dance is a form of artistic expression through body movements, conveying emotions to the public. It is a complex art that encompasses a wide variety of movements with various characteristics (Faridee et al. 2019), and can be categorized into folk, standard, and competitive dances (Ni and Yao 2021). As elements of culture, each of these dance forms should be documented and preserved to ensure their protection and accessibility to the public. However, folk dances deserve special attention as their preservation becomes more challenging in modern societies. Digitizing such cultural phenomena becomes crucial for preserving their essence over time.

Recent technological advancements allow us to capture precise dance data, store, identify, and analyze them to gain a deeper understanding of human behavior (Mindoro et al. 2021; Skublewska-Paszkowska et al. 2022). Motion capture systems enable the recording of accurate data that can be further stored and processed. The application of motion capture for ICH purposes spans various domains, including technical, academic, choreographic, commercial, and educational (Skublewska-Paszkowska et al. 2022). Among the most accurate motion capture systems are those using infra-red cameras (optical) or active markers. These systems acquire three-dimensional coordinates of markers attached to body parts, which are crucial for capturing the nuances of the dance of interest.

The primary objective of this study is to capture and recognize the traditional Greek dance, Zeibekiko, an important element of ICH that is included in the

Greece's National Inventory of Intangible Cultural Heritage (Howitt-Marshall 2022). To achieve this, we utilized data acquired through a state-of-the-art PhaseSpace motion capture system, stored in the widely used .C3D format. This format stores time-series data representing the three-dimensional coordinate positions and movements of markers attached to the dancers' bodies during motion capture sessions. To recognize specific dance moves in the captured data, we employed Spatial Temporal Graph Convolutional Networks (ST-GCNs). This approach enables motion segmentation and annotation by leveraging the human topology in temporal order, resulting in remarkable success in human motion recognition. Our experiments demonstrated the efficiency of this method across various examples, achieving high accuracy in labeling and segmenting dance movements.

11.2 Related Work

One of the key elements of ICH is the performance of art, often presented in the form of dances and music. The recent advent of capturing technology has opened new possibilities for storing and preserving these valuable aspects of culture for future generations. In recent years, various fields of study, such as image analysis, machine intelligence, computer vision, and pattern recognition, have found specific applications in this domain (Reshma et al. 2023). These techniques have significantly impacted dance capturing, dance processing, understanding the meaning of different dance styles, and pose recognition for dance movements.

11.2.1 Dance Capturing

Several techniques have been employed for capturing dance movements, including marker-based and marker-less approaches, as well as the use of wearable devices like Inertial Measurement Units (IMUs). Each approach has its own advantages and limitations.

Marker-based systems use infrared cameras and retro-reflective/active markers attached to the dancer's body or costumes, allowing for precise tracking of individual elements in the silhouette. This technology provides accurate three-dimensional marker positions, enabling detailed movement analysis. However, it requires marker placement and maintenance, which can be time-consuming and may limit the natural flow of the performance. Marker-based systems can also be sensitive to occlusion or marker misplacement, potentially affecting data accuracy. On the other hand, marker-less systems rely on cameras and structured light to capture the entire body using real-time depth maps. They offer a more convenient solution as they eliminate the need for markers. Marker-less systems, like those using Microsoft Kinect sensors, are widely available and relatively affordable. They provide greater freedom of movement for the dancer and are less intrusive. However, they may be less accurate in capturing subtle details and can be affected by changes in lighting conditions or occlusion. Wearable devices like IMUs offer portability and flexibility in capturing dance movements. They can capture joint rotations, velocities, and linear accelerations, providing valuable data for analysis. IMUs are less restrictive than marker-based systems and can be used in various environments. However, they may have limitations in capturing precise details and movements requiring fine-grained tracking. In summary, marker-based systems excel in capturing detailed movements but can be cumbersome, while marker-less systems offer convenience but may sacrifice some accuracy. IMUs provide portability but may have limitations in capturing fine-grained movement details. The choice of technology depends on the specific requirements of the dance analysis, trading off accuracy, convenience, and the desired level of detail.

In the context of digitizing folk dances, notable works include those of (Stavrakis et al. 2012), who utilized the Phasespace Impulse X2 motion capture system with active LEDs to create a dance database for Cypriot folk dances. Similarly, (Łukasik et al. 2022; Skublewska-Paszkowska et al. 2021), employed a Vicon motion capture system, introducing a unique marker model to capture hand gesticulation in Uzbekistan's Lazgi dance. (Xie et al. 2021) presented a symbolic recording system for preserving folk dances and performing arts, utilizing an OptiTrack motion capture system. Other systems, such as Microsoft Kinect sensors, have been used for marker-less motion capture in capturing folk dance sequences (Li and Zheng 2021) and human skeleton tracking in dance performances (Alexiadis et al. 2011). Furthermore, (Mindoro et al. 2021) recorded the Aeta folk dance from the Philippines using the SmartSuit Pro system, which incorporates inertial sensors, representing data in the form of joint movements and rotations. IMUs were also employed by researchers to capture movements in various dance styles, including waacking (Samprita et al. 2020).

Additionally, in the field of dance ethnography, (Aristidou et al. 2019) explored the cultural significance and contextual understanding of specific folk dances. This ethnographic approach provides valuable insights into the social, historical, and cultural aspects of the dances, enriching the digitization and preservation efforts. In the realm of preserving dance heritage, a noteworthy development is the creation of virtual dance museums, as seen in (Aristidou et al. 2021). These digital platforms enable the preservation, documentation, and interactive exploration of dance forms, making them widely accessible to audiences across geographical boundaries. Collectively, these diverse techniques contribute to the comprehensive study, preservation, and analysis of cultural dances. They shed light on their cultural significance and ensure accessibility for future generations.

In addition to employing motion capture systems, numerous studies explore alternative and simpler methods such as image or video-based approaches. Among many others, a framework for Balinese dance registration, involving the extraction of features from individual frame images, was proposed in (Kesiman et al. 2020). This framework progresses from initial feature extraction, which includes fundamental Histogram of Gradient features, to the ultimate formation of features in the Bag of Visual Movement. Moreover, an autostereoscopic display system that integrates image capturing, displaying, and playback functionality for street dance is presented in (Chen et al. 2024). This system incorporates a framework featuring depth map generation, a Multiview point generation and optimization module, and encoding and displaying of 3D content. Similarly, in the context of Flamenco dance, video capturing was employed for recording performances, as detailed in (Baena-Chicón et al. 2023). The communication codes of Flamenco dance, including signals like "llamada" to start singing, "remate" to conclude a section, "subida" to accelerate the rhythm, and "desplante" as a static position ending the performance, were described and analyzed. The integration of 3D graphics and sensor technology is showcased in (Song et al. 2015) for stage performances. The Illimitable Space System, applied with real-time animation and interaction, combines Kinect, cameras, and microphones for capturing participants' actions. This approach enables the creation of both virtual and real-time performances. For an extensive exploration of motion capture technologies and motion analysis techniques in dancing, consult the research conducted by Aristidou et al. (2019), and Ami-Williams et al. (2014).

11.2.2 Dance Recognition and Analysis

Folk dances hold significant importance in ICH, and their recognition and analysis pose unique challenges. Numerous studies have explored various approaches to dance performance and recognition, leading to the development of different methods. A comprehensive survey is presented in (Reshma et al. 2023), where a range of dance analysis techniques is described, emphasizing the importance of choreography in ICH studies. Various methods, such as Dynamic Time Warping with Fuzzy Inference System, Principal Component Analysis (PCA), Support Vector Machine (SVM), and Convolutional Neural Networks (CNNs), were used to analyze a dataset created with EMG, accelerometer, and Kinect motion capture tools.

In particular, in (Li and Zheng 2021), characteristic dancers' postures from Kinect images were recognized using a proposed Target Detection algorithm based on a Gaussian Mixture Model. This approach outperformed other methods with a higher precision of up to 93%. Later, (Mindoro et al. 2021), used CNN networks including InceptionV3, MobileNetV2, and VGG19 to classify the Aeta dance. They successfully recognized dances of the bird and dragonfly, with all classifiers achieving accuracy above 92%. Yao and Chen (2022) used Labanotation to recognize the upper and lower limb movements on BVH motion capture data, resulting in an accuracy level of 95%. Other challenges in video-based activity recognition for traditional Greek dances were addressed in (Kapsouras et al. 2013), with a proposed approach involving feature extraction, K means clustering, and SVM classification for recognizing sequences of five traditional Greek dances. Similarly, methods that use the Laban Movements Analysis (LMA) principles have been used to compare and analyze motion qualities and emotions in dancing (Aristidou et al. 2015a, b). Moreover, in (Ni and Yao 2021), step recognition of sport dances was proposed using SVM, achieving an average recognition rate of 92%. The study also proposed a system for training dancers, which automatically detects falls to prevent injuries.

In (Samprita et al. 2020), a heuristic approach was introduced to analyze the movements of hip-hop dance, with data collected using a 3-axis IMU and LSTM networks employed for classifying movement phases with distinct motion sequences. (Yuan and Pan 2022) utilized an LSTM-based method for dance recognition, achieving an accuracy of up to 94.33% on dance movements comprising 270,000 frames. Lastly, in (Xie et al. 2021), a double-stream fusion method of directed graph neural networks was proposed for dance classification, with an average classification accuracy of 87.79%.

Another motion analysis framework derived from the LMA entities was introduced by (Aristidou et al. 2017) for emotion recognition and stylization in dancing. This framework addresses potential issues with transitions and ensures the synthesis of dance motions that are consistent with the desired style. In a later work, the same group analyzed dance movements to form the first digital dance ethnography (Aristidou et al. 2019). This method breaks down dance motion sequences into temporal overlapping feature descriptors and clusters them to define motifs, capturing contextual correlations, while being capable of distinguishing fine-grained differences.

Considering the latest scientific advancements in the preservation of folk dances for ICH, further research is warranted, particularly in studying traditional dances like Zeibekiko, through novel motion labeling and recognition systems. These advancements can facilitate in-depth analysis of these ICH elements.

11.3 Zeibekiko Dance: History and Description

Zeibekiko is a traditional Greek dance of cultural and historical significance (Howitt-Marshall 2022). Known for its passionate and improvisational nature, it is often performed to slow or moderate Greek folk music. Zeibekiko's origins date back to the late 18th and early nineteenth century, during the Greek Revolution. This dance is inspired by the Zeybek tribe, a group of mountain warriors known for their bravery and resistance to the Ottoman Empire. The Zeybek family fought for independence and their dance moves were influenced by their warrior spirit. Zeibekiko is a highly improvisational dance form that allows individuals to express their emotions, conflicts, and joys through movement. It is often performed by one dancer who interprets the music through spontaneous gestures, footwork, and body movements. The dance is characterized by an intense, free-spirited style, with dancers often immersing themselves in the performance, as if they were lost in their own world.

Zeibekiko's importance lies in its connection to Greek culture and history (Holst-Warhaft 2012; Topalidis 2022). It embodies the Greek spirit, resilience, and longing for freedom. The dance has become a symbol of Greek identity and is often performed at social gatherings, festivals, and celebrations. Additionally, Zeibekiko serves as personal expression and catharsis. This allows dancers to express their emotions, frustrations and triumphs through movement and gestures, providing an opportunity to break free from the music and their inner self and create a connection. Therefore,

Zeibekiko is not just a dance, it is also a cultural treasure that preserves Greek traditions and serves as a powerful vehicle for self-expression that connects individuals with history, emotion and community, hence documenting and archiving this dance is immensely important and much needed.

11.4 Systems and Methodology

11.4.1 Data Acquisition

In this study, we utilized data from the Dance Motion Capture Database (DMCD) (Stavrakis, et al. 2012), with a specific focus on the culturally significant Zeibekiko dance. To capture and preserve these invaluable intangible cultural creations, (Aristidou et al. 2019) employed the PhaseSpace Impulse X2E motion capture system, which utilizes active optical motion capture through modulated LEDs. This system provides high frequency optical tracking, allowing to document and record the dance movements with great accuracy. It supports a high-frequency capability of up to 960 Hz, ensuring precise three-dimensional motion data capture while maintaining natural human proportions and movement.

The DMCD comprises performances by experienced dancers from various cultural organizations and dance schools, forming a rich dataset that includes over 250 dance performances, featuring more than 30 folk dances. Notably, selected folk dance recordings have been included in EUROPEANA, the European Digital Library of Cultural Heritage. (Aristidou et al. 2021) later recognized the importance of capturing longer choreographies involving multiple dancers, each showcasing their unique styles. This approach was essential in truly capturing the essence of each performance, as individual idiosyncrasies influenced by factors such as performers' experiences, backgrounds, body types, age, and emotions play a crucial role in the representation of the dance. Consequently, no standardization or normalization of dances was applied during the capture process.

It is important to note that, the dedicated efforts of both the (Aristidou et al. 2019; Stavrakis et al. 2012) works were aimed at creating a comprehensive and scalable dance database that allows for long-term maintenance and the addition of new data over time. Their work combined motion capture techniques, as well as the development of dance ethnography, and virtual dance museum (Aristidou et al. 2021), thus contributing to the preservation, analysis, and accessibility of cultural dances for research, education, and future generations.

In this study, we carefully selected dance data of skilled male and female performers who possess extensive dance experience and actively participate in cultural organizations and dance schools. Specifically, we included five variations of the Zeibekiko dance performed by four different dancers, as well as 14 other Greek and Cypriot folk dances, such as Antikristos, Hasapiko, Haniotikos, Tsamikos, Tatsia, Pentozali, and more, performed by five different dancers. This diverse dataset allowed

Table 11.1 Zeibekiko sequences

No. sequence	Sequence name
1	Left single turn
2	Right foot strike
3	Seat on the right
4	Seat on the left
5	Leg kick with counterclockwise turn
6	Step right
7	Hand clap shot floor
8	Double hand clap
9	Double pretense right
10	Back heel strike

us to capture a broad range of dance styles and expressions. To ensure efficient storage and computational processing, we stored the motion capture data in both C3D and BVH formats, initially sampled at varying rates between 120 and 480 frames per second. However, to enhance efficiency without sacrificing crucial temporal information, we downsampled the data to 24 frames per second. This downsampling allowed us to retain the essential characteristics of the dance movements while reducing data size and computational requirements.

11.4.2 Data Preparation

The data underwent segmentation and labeling, a process carried out by a professional dancer affiliated with the Nicosia Folk Association. It is crucial to emphasize that we utilized the raw C3D data without any post-processing or cleaning. Fortunately, the data was generally free from artifacts and occlusions, ensuring its reliability and suitability for analysis. Using the C3D Python library and based on specified frame numbers, we extracted the following sequences from the obtained C3D files. The professional dancers specified ten sequences from one registered Zeibekiko dance, as detailed in Table 11.1.

11.4.3 Spatial Temporal Graph Convolutional Networks (ST-GCNs)

Human motion recognition is a fundamental task in computer vision, finding applications in areas like video surveillance and human–computer interaction. Over the years, numerous approaches have been explored to address this challenging problem. One promising technique that has garnered considerable attention is the use of

Spatial–Temporal Graph Convolutional Networks (ST-GCNs) (Yan et al. 2018). This study delves into the application of ST-GCNs in human motion recognition, showcasing its effectiveness and potential for advancing the field.

ST-GCNs combine two fundamental concepts in deep learning: Graph Convolutional Networks (GCNs) and temporal modeling (Yan et al. 2018). GCNs extend Convolutional Neural Networks (CNNs) to irregular graph-structured data, facilitating efficient processing and capturing spatial dependencies. Temporal modeling techniques enable the network to analyze the temporal evolution of data, making them well-suited for time-series analysis.

ST-GCNs are designed to capture spatial and temporal information from human motion data using a graph-based representation. Nodes represent body joints, edges encode pairwise relationships, and store spatial features and temporal dependencies between consecutive frames. The architecture includes multiple temporal stages with graph convolutional layers, non-linear activation functions, and temporal pooling. These stages enable the network to learn hierarchical representations at different temporal scales, incorporating both local and global motion information.

In the context of motion capture data, dance sequences are recorded in successive time frames, rendering the data inherently time-dependent. The movement is discerned based on markers that are strategically positioned on the dancer's body, reflecting the complete silhouette and essential elements for dance analysis. These markers form a graph with nodes corresponding to markers and edges connecting them. Consequently, the adoption of the ST-GCN network emerges as a logical and fitting choice. An inherent strength of the ST-GCN network lies in its capacity to process data presented in a graph format. Unlike images, where convolution operates on a fixed number of neighbors, graphs allow for a variable number, enhancing the efficiency of feature map generation. However, a fundamental limitation of the employed ST-GCN is its constrained inner structure, specifically tailored to a predetermined number of nodes aligned with the motion capture model. This lack of flexibility in modifying the node count necessitates a complete network rebuild, thereby requiring a repetition of the entire study.

The initial step involves constructing a graph representing the human skeleton, with joints as nodes and edges encoding pairwise relationships. The graph is typically defined as an adjacency matrix, capturing both spatial and temporal dependencies between body joints, forming the basis for further processing in the network.

In ST-GCNs, spatial convolution aims to capture local spatial relationships between body joints within each frame. Operating independently on each frame, it extracts features from individual joints, enabling the network to learn local patterns and joint-specific information like positions and orientations. On the other hand, temporal convolution models the temporal dependencies between consecutive frames. It operates on the graph structure, considering features from individual joints and their connecting edges, capturing evolving patterns of human motion and learning sequential information and motion dynamics. The core of the ST-GCN architecture lies in its graph convolutional layers. These layers perform spatial–temporal convolutions by combining spatial and temporal convolutional operations. Taking features from individual joints as input, they propagate them through the graph structure, considering both local and temporal dependencies. This allows the network to learn joint interactions and hierarchical relationships between joints at different temporal scales.

To introduce non-linearities, non-linear activation functions like ReLU and Leaky ReLU are applied to the outputs of the graph convolutional layers. These transformations enable the network to capture complex patterns and enhance the model's discriminative power. Temporal pooling aggregates features across consecutive frames, reducing the temporal dimensionality of the data. By focusing on capturing the most discriminative motion information while reducing complexity, pooling strategies like max pooling or average pooling are utilized, selecting the maximum or average values, respectively, from the features across consecutive frames.

Following graph convolutional layers and temporal pooling, fully connected layers are often incorporated to perform high-level feature aggregation and classification. Combining spatial and temporal features learned by earlier layers, these fully connected layers make predictions about specific motion classes or actions. The number and sizes of these layers can vary based on the task's complexity and the network's depth. It is important to note that the architecture of ST-GCNs can be extended with additional components, such as attention mechanisms to focus on informative joints or frames, or regularization techniques to prevent overfitting. These extensions further enhance the model's performance and generalization capabilities.

Skeleton Graph Construction. A skeleton is represented as a series of vectors in 3D coordinates, where each node is related to human joints and edge to connection between them. The ST-GCNs process the undirected graph $G = (V, E)$, $V = \{v_{ji} | j = 1, ..., J, i = 1, ..., N\}$; N denotes the number of joints. The graph includes two sets of edges. The first set, called spatial edges, represents natural connections between joints within a frame, denoted as $V_S = \{v_{ji} v_{jk} | i, k \in H\}$, where H is the set of naturally connected human joints. The second set, temporal edges, connects corresponding joints between adjacent frames, denoted as $V_T = \{v_{ij} v_{i(j+1)}\}$. The edges in V_T capture the dynamics of a specific joint i across T frames.

Graph Convolution. Through graph convolution, inputs undergo a series of GCN layers to generate high-level features. As stated in Yan et al. (2018), the graph convolution operation for vertex v_i is defined as follows:

$$\varphi_{out}(v_i) = \sum_{v_i \in \beta_i} \frac{1}{z_{ij}} \varphi_{in}(v_j) \star \omega(\tau_i(v_j)) \tag{11.1}$$

In Eq. (11.1), φ represents feature maps, with φ_{in} and φ_{out} correspond to the input and output feature maps, respectively. The variable v denotes the graph vertex, and is the weighting function, similar to the original convolution operation. β_i represents the neighboring vertices (v_j) at a unit distance from the corresponding vertex v_i, participating in the convolution operation with v_i. . In ST-GCN (Yan et al. 2018), τ_i was introduced to group the variable number of neighboring vertices in β_i into three clusters (C_{ik}): the vertex itself, neighboring vertices closer to the center of gravity, and vertices farther away from the center of gravity. The variable Z_{ij} is used to balance the contribution of each cluster, representing the count of C_{ik} in v_j.

GCN Implementation. To implement the GCN, it is necessary to convert Eq. (11.1) into tensor form. The shape of the skeleton features for the model is $C \times F \times N$, where C represents the number of channels, F is the number of frames, and N denotes the number of vertices. The transformation of Eq. (11.1) is as follows (inspired from Ghosh et al. (2022)):

$$\varphi_{out} = \sum\nolimits_{k}^{K_v} \Gamma_k(\varphi_{in} A_k) \cdot M_k \tag{11.2}$$

where K_v represents the spatial kernel size, set as 5, A_k denotes an adjacency matrix, while M_k is $N \times N$ attention map that represents the significance of each vertex.

Spatio-temporal Graph Convolutional Block. The Spatio-temporal graph convolutional block consists of spatial (SCL) and temporal (TCL) convolution layers. The SCL is responsible for extracting spatial features using Eq. (11.2), while the TCL follows the methodology of ST-GCN (Yuan and Pan 2022) to obtain temporal features. The SCL operates on spatial edges, and the TCL performs graph convolutions on temporal edges, extracting spatial and temporal features, respectively. For input data of shape $C \times F \times N$, the TCL incorporates a 2D convolution layer with a $kf \times 1$ kernel size. Fig. 11.1 illustrates the structure of a single block of our ST-GCN, comprising an SCL and a TCL. Both spatial and temporal convolution layers include Batch Normalization (BN) and Rectified Linear Unit (ReLU) layers. This approach enables simultaneous and independent extraction of spatial and temporal features using our redefined spatio-temporal graph convolutional block. Additionally, we employ a 1×1 convolutional layer to reduce the output channel size, as done in (Aristidou et al. 2015a, b).

Spatio-Temporal Graph Convolutional Layers. Figure 11.2 illustrates the configuration of the ST-GCN network, composed of a series of interconnected blocks.

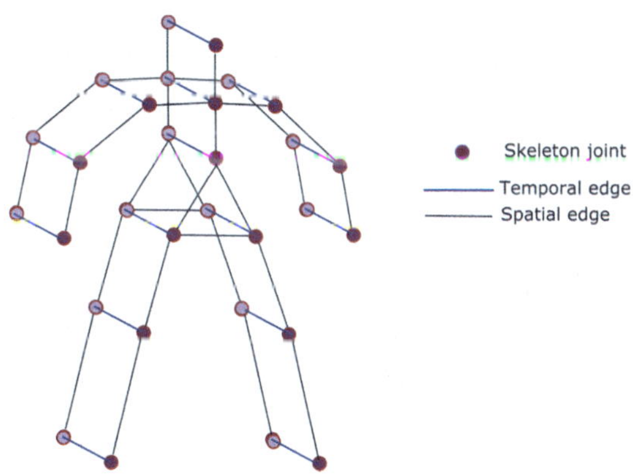

Fig. 11.1 Spatio-temporal graph

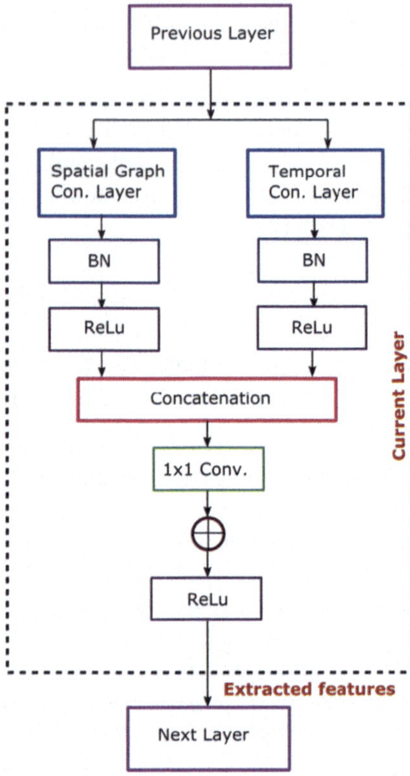

Fig. 11.2 Convolution block (Ghosh et al. 2022)

The network comprises a total of ten blocks, each serving a specific function. The initial four blocks produce 64 output channels, followed by blocks five to seven, which generate 128 output channels. The remaining blocks yield 256 output channels. To ensure input normalization, a Batch Normalization (BN) layer is introduced at the network's inception. Finally, to consolidate and condense the extracted features for the ultimate prediction, a fully connected (FC) layer equipped with a Softmax function is employed.

11.5 Experiment and Results

The limited amount of recorded data required duplicating the collected sequences through data augmentation. This involved separating elements corresponding to 46 frames from individual dance moves and modifying marker locations within $\pm 10\%$. The chosen length was based on the duration of the shortest dance moves, resulting in 1419 sequences used for training (60%), validation (20%), and testing (20%).

The Zeibekiko classification results are presented in Tables 11.2, 11.3, 11.4 and 11.5. The ST-GCN network was validated for ten various sequences through 20 test iterations (see Table 11.2). The mean accuracy for each sequence exceeded 80.9%, with the highest classification accuracy achieved for the "right foot strike" sequence, and the lowest for the "leg kick with counterclockwise turn."

Precision results, see Table 11.3, indicate that the mean precision for all analyzed sequences was higher than 79%, with the "leg kick with counterclockwise turn" sequence yielding the best precision result, and the "Double pretense right" sequence showing the weakest. Table 11.4 lists the recall results indicating that the average values ranged from 54% for the "leg kick with counterclockwise turn" sequence to 96.32% for the "Double pretense right" sequence. Similarly, the F1-score (harmonic means of precision and recall) in Table 11.5 ranged from 77.80 to 87.30%, with the "Right foot strike" sequence achieving the highest F1-score and "Seat on the right" sequence obtaining the lowest. The low standard deviation values confirm the suitability of the applied model for this experiment. The results demonstrate that the ST-GCN classifier is an appropriate choice for Zeibekiko movement recognition.

Table 11.2 Obtained accuracy results (%)

	1	2	3	4	5	6	7	8	9	10
Mean	83.06	86.63	82.69	83.33	80.92	82.32	82.60	81.92	81.51	82.15
Max	87.99	87.73	87.92	87.92	87.79	87.48	87.88	86.28	86.34	87.63
Min	79.19	77.19	77.28	77.28	77.48	77.16	77.77	77.79	77.07	77.65
±SD	2.92	2.98	3.57	3.58	2.63	2.59	3.44	2.93	3.04	2.76

Table 11.3 Obtained precision results (%)

	1	2	3	4	5	6	7	8	9	10
Mean	79.71	86.28	87.97	86.43	90.25	87.21	87.86	86.62	78.83	81.37
Max	88.28	90.79	94.33	92.22	94.25	92.53	93.44	92.11	87.63	88.88
Min	73.41	83.33	83.33	83.00	88.17	82.66	83.82	83.33	72.22	75.55
±SD	4.97	3.99	6.42	3.15	2.19	3.45	3.88	3.89	5.06	4.34

Table 11.4 Obtained recall results (%)

	1	2	3	4	5	6	7	8	9	10
Mean	94.49	88.55	69.81	77.49	54.00	71.51	76.23	88.03	96.32	88.99
Max	96.47	93.87	81.96	84.69	65.60	80.51	86.36	95.89	97.33	94.48
Min	92.82	85.71	62.50	72.80	43.32	64.58	68.67	84.33	95.36	85.25
±SD	3.58	2.41	8.72	3.28	6.51	5.44	5.85	3.75	2.68	3.23

Table 11.5 Obtained F1-score results (%)

	1	2	3	4	5	6	7	8	9	10
Mean	86.40	87.39	77.80	81.71	67.42	78.57	81.61	87.32	86.63	85.00
Max	91.98	92.30	87.71	88.30	77.36	86.11	89.76	93.95	92.16	91.60
Min	82.22	84.66	71.14	77.57	60.74	72.94	75.49	83.83	82.22	80.08
±SD	8.98	5.16	8.76	3.44	5.55	4.15	4.99	3.33	7.35	8.26

11.6 Conclusions and Future Work

In conclusion, this study successfully achieved its primary objective of analyzing the traditional Greek dance, Zeibekiko, an essential element of Intangible Cultural Heritage that has been inscribed on the Greece's National Inventory of Intangible Cultural Heritage. The significance of technological advancements in preserving and promoting cultural heritage was highlighted, emphasizing the importance of safeguarding and comprehending traditional dances for future generations.

The application of Spatial Temporal Graph Convolutional Networks (ST-GCN) demonstrated exceptional performance in recognizing specific dance moves from the captured data. ST-GCN's efficiency in motion segmentation and annotation by leveraging the human topology in temporal order resulted in remarkable success in human motion recognition. Our comprehensive experiments consistently achieved high accuracy in labeling and segmenting dance movements, showcasing the method's potential to advance research in this field. The classification of specific dance elements holds significant importance in teaching the fundamentals steps, enabling trainees to grasp the basics of folk dance and familiarize themselves with the unique dance style. Leveraging motion capture technology facilitates a realistic three-dimensional representation of dance, simplifying the preservation of key elements in folk dance. By identifying and classifying relevant dance sequences, this technology streamlines the comparison of various dance elements. Such comparisons prove valuable in discerning disparities between a novice learner and a professional, as well as in tracking the evolutionary trajectory of the dance over time. This study holds particular relevance in educational settings, offering a detailed examination of the Zeibekiko dance. Future research can explore distinguishing Zeibekiko dance from other Greek folk performances, further enriching the understanding and preservation of this unique cultural heritage. By embracing innovative methodologies, we can secure the rich tapestry of cultural traditions, fostering cultural diversity, and strengthening the bonds of identity and belonging within communities worldwide.

Acknowledgements This project has received funding by the University of Cyprus under the project titled "Demonstration." The authors extend their gratitude to the dancers who performed in our studio.

References

Alexiadis DS, Kelly P, Daras P, O'Connor NE, Boubekeur T, Moussa MB (2011) Evaluating a dancer's performance using kinect-based skeleton tracking. In: Proceedings of the 19th ACM international conference on Multimedia, pp 659–662

Ami-Williams T, Serghides C-G, Aristidou A (2014) Digitizing traditional dances under extreme clothing: the case study of Eyo. J Cult Herit 67:145–157

Aristidou A, Charalambous P, Chrysanthou Y (2015) Emotion analysis and classification: understanding the performers' emotions using LMA entities. Comput. Graph Forum 34(6):262–276

Aristidou A, Stavrakis E, Charalambous P, Chrysanthou Y, Himona SL (2015) Folk dance evaluation using Laban movement analysis. J Comput Cult Heritage (JOCCH) 8:1–19

Aristidou A, Zeng Q, Stavrakis E, Yin K, Cohen-Or D, Chrysanthou Y, Chen B (2017) Emotion control of unstructured dance movements. In: Proceedings of the ACM SIGGRAPH/ Eurographics symposium on computer animation, pp 1--10

Aristidou A, Shamir A, Chrysanthou Y (2019) Digital dance ethnography: Organizing large dance collections. J Comput Cult Heritage (JOCCH) 12:1–27

Aristidou A, Andreou N, Charalambous L, Yiannakidis A, Chrysanthou Y (2021) Virtual dance museum: the case of greek/cypriot folk dancing. In: Hulusic V, Chalmers A (eds) Proceedings of the eurographics workshop on graphics and cultural heritage (GCH). EG, Bournmouth, UK

Aristidou A, Chalmers A, Chrysanthou Y, Loscos C, Multon F, Parkins JE, Sarupuri B, Stavrakis E (2022) Safeguarding our dance cultural heritage. In: Proceeding of the 43rd annual conference of the European association for computer graphics—tutorials (Eurographics 2022). Reims, France

Baena-Chicón I, Gómez-Lozano S, Fernández-Falero MR, García de Vicuña OA, Vargas-Macías A (2023) Hidden communication codes in flamenco dance choreography. Res Dance Educ 1–17

Barszcz M, Montusiewicz J, Paśnikowska-Łukaszuk M, Anna S (2021) Comparative analysis of digital models of objects of cultural heritage obtained by the "3D SLS" and "SfM" methods. Appl Sci 11:5321

Chen W, Zhang D, Ma J, Wu G (2024) A comprehensive system for 3D display: from image capture to autostereoscopic playback. Displays 81:102572

Doulamis N, Doulamis A, Ioannidis C, Klein M, Ioannides M (2017) Modelling of static and moving objects: digitizing tangible and intangible cultural heritage. In: Mixed reality and gamification for cultural heritage, pp 567–589

Faridee AZ, Ramamurthy SR, Roy N (2019) Happyfeet: challenges in building an automated dance recognition and assessment tool. GetMobile Mob Comput Commun 22:10–16

Ghosh DK, Chakrabarty A, Moon H, Jalil Piran M (2022) A spatio-temporal graph convolutional network model for internet of medical things (IoMT). Sensors 22:8438

Holst-Warhaft G (2012) National steps: can you be Greek if you can't dance a Zebekiko?. Mod Greek Stud (Australia and New Zealand) 14

Howitt-Marshall D (2022) Zeibekiko and Bouzouki added to Greece's intangible cultural heritage list. March. Accessed January 13, 2024. https://www.greece-is.com/news/zeibekiko-and-bouzouki-added-to-greeces-intangible-cultural-heritage-list/

Kapsouras I, Karanikolos S, Nikolaidis N, Tefas A (2013) Feature comparison and feature fusion for traditional dances recognition. In: Engineering applications of neural networks: 14th international conference, EANN 2013, Halkidiki, Greece, September 13–16, 2013 proceedings, Part I 14, pp 172–181. Springer, Halkidiki

Kesiman MWA, Made Dendi Maysanjaya I, Made Ardwi Pradnyana I, Made Gede Sunarya I, Suputra PH (2020) Profiling balinese dances with silhouette sequence pattern analysis. In: 2020 international conference on computer engineering, network, and intelligent multimedia (CENIM), pp 423–428. IEEE

Li X, Zheng H (2021) Target detection algorithm for dance moving images based on sensor and motion capture data. Microprocess Microsyst 81:103743

Łukasik E, Skublewska-Paszkowska M, Powroźnik P, Smołka J, Miłosz M, Mukhamedova D, Miłosz E (2022) Analysis of selected Lazgi dance sequences using three-dimensional motion capture data. In: Computer technologies in sharing the cultural heritage and education of the Silk Road from Uzbekistans, pp 107–118

Mindoro JN, Festijo ED, de Guzman MTG (2021) A comparative study of deep transfer learning techniques for cultural (aeta) dance classification utilizing skeleton-based choreographic motion capture data. In: 2021 international conference on computational intelligence and knowledge economy (ICCIKE), pp 74–79. IEEE

Montusiewicz J, Barszcz M, Korga S (2022) Preparation of 3D models of cultural heritage objects to be recognised by touch by the blind—case studies. Appl Sci 12:11910

Ni S, Yao D (2021) Sports dance action recognition system oriented to human motion monitoring and sensing. Wirel Commun Mob Comput 2021:1–10

Rallis I, Voulodimos A, Bakalos N, Protopapadakis E, Doulamis N, Doulamis A (2020) Machine learning for intangible cultural heritage: a review of techniques on dance analysis. Vis Comput Cult Heritage 103–119

Reshma MR, Kannan B, Jagathy Raj VP, Shailesh S (2023) Cultural heritage preservation through dance digitization: a review. Digit Appl Archaeol Cult Heritage e00257

Samprita S, Koshy AS, Megharjun VN, Talasila V (2020) LSTM-based analysis of a hip-hop movement. In: 2020 6th international conference on control, automation and robotics (ICCAR), pp 519–524. IEEE

Shay A, Sellers-Young B (2016) The Oxford handbook of dance and ethnicity. Oxford University Press

Skublewska-Paszkowska M, Milosz M, Powroznik P, Lukasik E (2022) 3D technologies for intangible cultural heritage preservation—literature review for selected databases. Heritage Sci 10:1–24

Skublewska-Paszkowska M, Powroznik P, Smolka J, Milosz M, Lukasik E, Mukhamedova D, Milosz E (2021) Methodology of 3D scanning of intangible cultural heritage—the example of Lazgi dance. Appl Sci 11:11568

Song M, Mokhov SA, Grogono P, Mudur SP (2015) HCI in performance arts and the case of Illimitable Space System's multimodal interaction and visualization. In: SIGGRAPH ASIA 2015 art papers, pp 1–11

Stavrakis E, Aristidou A, Savva M, Himona SL, Chrysanthou Y (2012) Digitization of cypriot folk dances. In: Progress in cultural heritage preservation, pp 404–413. Springer Berlin Heidelberg, Berlin, Heidelberg

Topalidis S (2022) An introduction to traditional greek dance: Part 3. Accessed January 13, 2024. https://pontosworld.com/index.php/pontus/news/805-an-introduction-to-traditional-greek-dance-part-3

Xie N, Miao Z, Zhang X-P, Wanru X, Li M, Wang J (2021) Sequential gesture learning for continuous labanotation generation based on the fusion of graph neural networks. IEEE Trans Circuits Syst Video Technol 32:3722–3734

Yan S, Xiong Y, Lin D (2018) Spatial temporal graph convolutional networks for skeleton-based action recognition. In: Proceedings of the AAAI conference on artificial intelligence

Yao J, Chen Y (2022) A motion capture data-driven automatic labanotation generation model using the convolutional neural network algorithm. Wirel Commun Mob Comput (2022)

Yuan X, Pan P (2022) Research on the evaluation model of dance movement recognition and automatic generation based on long short-term memory. Math Prob Eng (2022)

Chapter 12
Virtual Restoration of Archaeological Artifacts

Ilan Shimshoni and Ayellet Tal

Abstract The task of restoring the look of an artifact as it used to be thousands of years ago, is a fascinating task, for a variety of reasons. The first reason is the very nature of the task of generating information that is not in the input. Second, the condition the artifacts are found—eroded, broken and noisy—differ from those of natural images in two dimensions or smooth geometries in three dimensions. Finally, datasets from which algorithms may learn, are rarely available; and even when available they are small. These aspects make state-of-the-art general algorithms prohibitive in the archaeological domain and special methods need to be developed. This chapter focuses on four sub-problems of restoration: reassembly, reconstruction of artifacts from drawings, re-colorization, and ancient document enhancement. It reviews our recent advances in terms of methods and results.

12.1 Introduction

Archaeology provides a unique window into the past and offers valuable insights into the history and culture of humanity. It enables us to delve into and acquire knowledge about societies that have ceased to exist, their cultures, and their accomplishments. Additionally, it has the potential to contribute to scientific advancements by offering insights into various areas like climate change, technology, the development of human societies, and even the downfall of ancient civilizations.

It is an exhilarating era in terms of technology, with transformative changes taking place across the world. However, certain fields have been left lagging behind, and archaeology is one of them. This is regrettable, considering the immense potential technology holds to incorporate archaeology into the ongoing technological

I. Shimshoni (✉)
The University of Haifa, Haifa, Israel
e-mail: ishimshoni@is.haifa.ac.il

A. Tal
Technion, Haifa, Israel
e-mail: ayellet@ee.technion.ac.il

F. Liarokapis et al. (eds.), *Interactive Media for Cultural Heritage*, Springer Series on Cultural Computing, https://doi.org/10.1007/978-3-031-61018-9_12

revolution and enhance the scientific investigation of the past with improved efficiency. Specifically, advancements in computer vision and computer graphics can be leveraged to automate certain aspects of the study of archaeological artifacts.

From the perspective of computer vision and graphics, the tasks performed by archaeologists studying sites with a focus on small artifacts can be categorized into four main areas:

1. Excavation: This involves the physical act of digging and uncovering the artifacts.
2. Documentation: It entails the creation of textual and visual records of the findings, which are typically documented in books and site reports.
3. Localization: This involves determining the temporal and spatial context of the findings through various means such as visual comparisons, chemical tests etc.
4. Restoration: This refers to the process of restoring the artifacts to their original state before any damage occurred.

It is worth noting that the latter three tasks are fundamental challenges in computer vision & graphics. In particular, the visual aspect of documentation can be interpreted as edge detection, non-photo realistic rendering or even domain transfer (Gilboa et al. 2013; Hayon et al. 2024; Kolomenkin et al. 2013, 2009; Lawonn et al. 2016; Luo et al. 2011; Wilczek et al. 2018); The visual component of location may be viewed as classification and retrieval (Anwar et al. 2021; Barucci et al. 2021; Canul-Ku et al. 2018; Chetouani et al. 2020; Hayon et al. 2024; Lerner and Shimshoni 2022; Ma and Arandjelović 2020; Phillips et al. 2016; Romanengo et al. 2020; Sipiran et al. 2021; Tal 2014); Restoration, which is the focus of this chapter, will be discussed in detail below.

Nonetheless, the application of cutting-edge computer vision techniques to the field of archaeology is prone to significant challenges and may not yield satisfactory results. This can be attributed to two primary factors. First, archaeological artifacts typically lack clean and well-behaved geometries. Rather, they are often broken, noisy, and extremely eroded. Second, the availability of massive datasets, which is crucial for training deep learning algorithms, is limited in the domain of archaeology. This is due to two problems: the number of existing artifacts and that these artifacts usually have to processed or labelled by experts, such as conservators or archaeologists who specialize in the specific domain. Without an ample supply of labeled data, deep learning approaches that heavily rely on large datasets may not be effectively utilized.

The primary focus of this chapter revolves around the fourth task, namely restoration, which aims to revive the original appearance of damaged artifacts. Within the scope of restoration, this chapter provides an overview of our research efforts in four distinct sub-tasks: re-assembly, reconstruction of artifacts from drawings, recolorization, and document enhancement. In the subsequent sections, we delve into each of these sub-tasks.

Reassembly. The objective is to reconstruct a broken artifact by accurately assembling its fragmented pieces, similar to solving a puzzle (Derech et al. 2021; Dimov 2020; Saalfeld et al. 2021; da Silva Teixeira et al. 2021). Currently, the prevailing practice in archaeology involves manual reassembly, which is a painstaking and time-consuming process, where pieces are meticulously glued together one by one. Instead, our aim is to automate this intricate puzzle-solving task. Unfortunately, even the "easy" variants of puzzle solving, such as rectangular pieces of equal size, are NP hard. Our case is more difficult, as the fragments come in all sizes and shapes, their boundaries are eroded and do not align perfectly, and there may be missing pieces. Within this general problem, reassembly might be attempted on different input domains, such as frescoes, papyri, ceramic objects, and even statues. In each case a different type of matching transformation between the pieces is required. In Sect. 12.2 we will discuss the recent advancements in this field, on the first two types of objects, discussing the progress made towards automated reassembly techniques.

Reconstruction of artifacts from drawings. Oftentimes, artifacts are securely stored within museum and storage rooms, with access limited to their drawings found in site reports and books. These drawings, created by archaeological artists during the documentation process, serve as the sole means of visualizing these artifacts. The challenge lies in the reverse engineering process, where the goal is to generate three-dimensional virtual objects based on these drawings (Kolomenkin et al. 2011; Zeng et al. 2014; Zhang et al. 2021). Section 12.3 elaborates on this task.

Re-colorization. A prevailing belief regarding the great statues of ancient Greece and Rome is that they were originally crafted from pure, unpainted stone. However, researchers have been arguing that these statues used to be quite alive, vibrant, and full of color. Unfortunately, due to centuries of deterioration and subsequent cleaning processes, any remnants of pigments that may have existed on the statues have been lost. This poses the question: can we restore the original appearance of these scanned statues? In Sect. 12.4 we present methods for doing so (Leifman and Tal 2012, 2013).

Document enhancement. Ancient transcript might be damaged due to stains, ink spills or natural degradation that occur over time. Our objective is to automatically extract the text from these transcripts (Kligler et al. 2018; Souibgui and Kessentini 2020; Tensmeyer and Martinez 2020; Xiong et al. 2021). Specifically, our aim is to *binarize* the image pixels, distinguishing between background and foreground (text) pixels. Section 12.5 presents some results.

It is worth noting that Some of the methods presented in the following sections may differ in terms of the input representation. Some approaches assume that the input consists of images of artifacts, while others assume that the objects are three-dimensional and captured through scanning processes. The choice between these representations depends on the available data.

12.2 Reassembly

Reassembling fragmented artifacts is a fundamental and essential challenge in archaeology. Frequently, artifacts discovered during archaeological excavations are found in a broken state, with both structural and visual degradation. Additionally, there may be missing fragments, further complicating the reassembly process. Consequently, considerable effort and time are dedicated by expert conservators to manually reconstruct these artifacts with utmost precision and completeness.

In computer vision, reassembly can be seen as a specialized form of puzzle solving. The task becomes particularly challenging due to the complexity of the inputs described earlier. When tackling the reassembly problem, it can be divided into two main stages. The first stage involves matching, where the goal is to find the relative geometric transformation between two adjacent fragments and assign a confidence score to each potential match. This matching process serves as a fundamental step within the broader placement algorithm, which aims to reassemble the artifact from its fragments. When considering reassembly problems, they can be characterized in different ways. Firstly, the matching process can be based on the shape and/or appearance of the fragments. However, in cases where the fragments have undergone geometric degradation, shape matching may not be straightforward. The second criterion for reassembly characterization is the type of local matching transformation employed. It can be discrete or continuous. In the continuous case, the transformation can be a 2D translation or a general 2D rigid transformation, typically applied to 2D artifacts. For 3D objects, a general 3D rigid transformation is utilized. In certain special cases, such as surfaces of revolution (e.g., jars, jugs, or vases), more limited 3D transformations are applicable.

In this section, we will review two of our works on the subject. The first work focuses on the reassembly of colored 2D fragments, specifically addressing the reconstruction of artifacts like frescoes (Derech et al. 2021). The second work deals with matching papyrus fragments (Abitbol et al. 2021).

12.2.1 Reassembly of Colored 2D Fragments

Given N images, each capturing a single fragment of an artifact, our goal is to reassemble the artifact. In particular, each fragment should be assigned a 2D rigid transformation that indicates how to place it within the re-assembly. Our proposed algorithm consists of four steps, as illustrated in Fig. 12.1. We briefly discuss each of the steps below.

Fragment Extrapolation. In the first step, each fragment is extrapolated. This serves two goals. First, it shows how the fragment used to look before it was damaged and eroded. Second, it reduces the problem of continuity from one fragment to another into the problem of matching pieces within the extrapolated region. Formally, given a fragment, the goal is to produce a k-pixel wide band around it. The algorithm extrapolates the image using patches from the original image, utilizing patch-based optimization. This optimization takes into account not only colors and image gradients, but also geometric and photometric transformations, which is vital for our case.

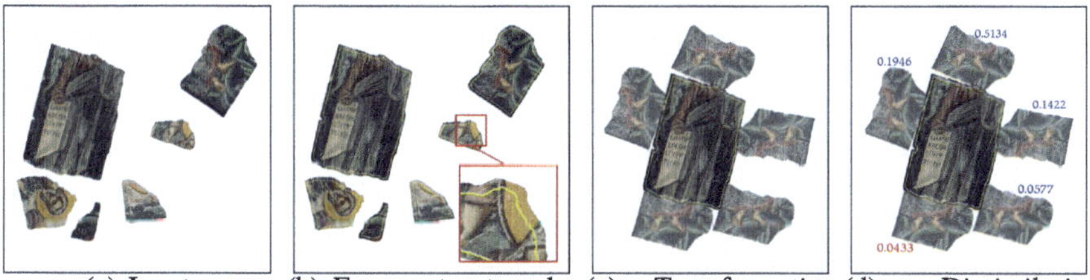

(a) Input (b) Fragment extrapolation (c) Transformation sampling (d) Dissimilarity scores

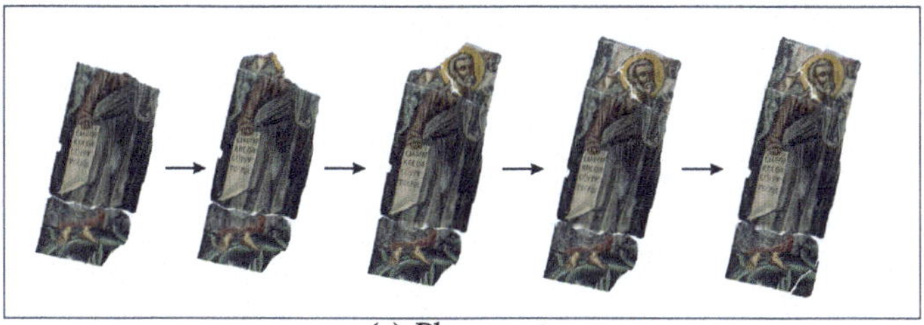

(e) Placement

Fig. 12.1 Reassembly algorithm outline

Sampling a set of valid transformations. The objective of this stage is to sample the space of transformations between a given pair of fragments. When sampling these transformations, three conditions need to be satisfied. First, the transformations must be valid. In our context, a valid transformation is one that brings the fragments closer to each other, increasing the likelihood of adjacency, without causing overlap. Thus, we require that the original pixels of the fragments do not overlap, but the extrapolated pixels of the fragments do overlap. Second, it is important to ensure that the number of sampled transformations is feasible. To address this, we demonstrate how the set of valid transformations can be represented as a configuration space problem, similar to those used in robotics. This allows for easier sampling within this space. Finally, due to the sampling process, some of the initially promising transformations may be imprecise. To refine these transformations, a fine-tuning approach is necessary. In our algorithm, we this fine-tuning is performed during the placement stage.

Finding good matches. Computing a dissimilarity score for a given transformation between a pair of fragments lies at the core of re-assembly. Thanks to Step 1, the continuity problem was reduced to matching the extrapolated region of one fragment and the other original fragment, on the overlapping region. The strongest cues for matching are the colors and the color edges, which should continue from one fragment to its adjacent piece. Matching becomes challenging in our domain due to three additional difficulties: (1) faded colors (2) imprecise transformations (due to sampling) that cause misalignment of the edges and (3) degradation that may yield spurious edges that should be ignored.

Our algorithm handles these problems. However, even when the dissimilarities are computed, our problem is not yet solved. This is so since a low dissimilarity value does not necessarily imply confidence in a match, as other matches with the same fragment may be almost as likely. We propose to compute a confidence score, which predicts the likelihood of the pair of fragments to be neighbors. The confidence in the match takes into account, in addition to the dissimilarity score, also the scores of competing matches in the same region of the fragment.

Placement. In line with previous works, our placement strategy follows a greedy approach, where fragments are added iteratively, one at a time. However, our algorithm incorporates new considerations to address additional complexities arising from the continuity of the transformation space and the shape of the fragments. To handle the challenge of imprecise transformations, the selected transformation is refined within a small neighborhood around it. For a visual demonstration of our placement algorithm, we refer the reader to its visualization available on YouTube (Derech et al. 2019).

Several results of running the algorithm on frescoes are shown in Fig. 12.2.

Limitations. If the gaps between fragments are substantial, the algorithm may encounter difficulty in accurately reconstructing the fresco. This is due to the potential mismatch of neighbors on either side of the gap.

12.2.2 Matching Papyrus Fragments

In this work we proposed a method for matching and assembling pairs of ancient papyrus fragments containing mostly unknown scriptures. Papyrus paper is manufactured from papyrus plants and therefore portrays typical thread patterns resulting from the plant's stems. The proposed algorithm is founded on the hypothesis that

(a) a fresco from the Ferapontov monastery, Russia (17 pieces)

(b) a fresco from the Sistine Chapel, Vatican City, 1512, (32 pieces).

(c) A fresco from the church of Christ Antiphonitis in Cyprus, (6 pieces).

Fig. 12.2 Fragments are re-assembled by our algorithm. The borders of the fragments are marked in cyan. The fragments are faded, stained, scratched, and the boundaries do not accurately match these thread patterns contain unique local attributes, such that nearby fragments show similar patterns reflecting the continuations of the threads. We posit that these patterns can be exploited using image processing and machine learning techniques to identify matching fragments. The algorithm and system support the quick and automated classification of matching pairs of papyrus fragments as well as the geometric alignment of the pairs against each other.

Since we have no ground truth of previously matched fragments, we synthetically generate a suitable training set with label. For this purpose, we utilize three relatively large scroll pieces from a nearly complete papyrus scroll as the basis for a training and validation set. We start by digitally tearing the three pieces into three distinct sets of small fragments. We train the algorithm on two of the sets and attempt to match the third set's fragments. We perform the tearing in several randomized iterations while altering the number of fragments and their shape in each iteration.

The algorithm consists of a series of steps and is based on deep-learning and machine-learning methods. The first step deconstructs the problem of matching fragments into a smaller problem of finding thread continuation matches in local edge areas (squares) between pairs of fragments. Due to the local nature of the thread pattern similarity, we focus on seeking matches only within squares that are cropped from the edges of the fragments. In order to produce the squares we slide a "crop window" of 250×250 pixels along the edges of each fragment and crop corresponding square images at regular intervals. Figure 12.3 shows an example of the traversal of the "crop window" and the resulting squares.

Each pair of squares is given as input to a convolutional neural network, yielding local matching scores. During training we take into account that matching pairs might not be accurately aligned and due to the tearing between the fragments might be at a certain distance from each other. The result of this stage yields very high recall but low precision.

To deal with this problem we combine the results of the first step by verifying them geometrically. For each match a suggested relative translation between the fragments

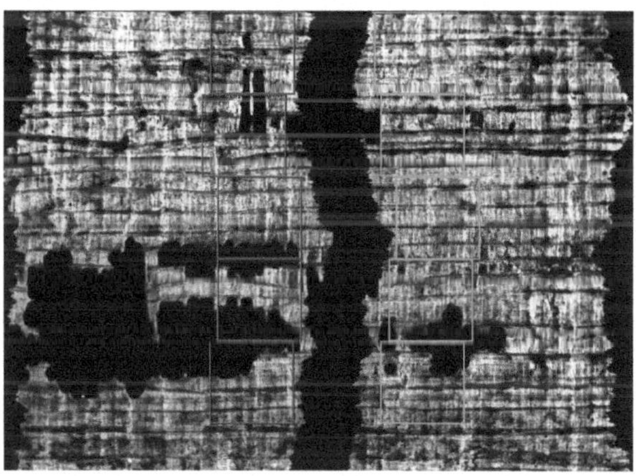

Fig. 12.3 An example of two adjacent artificially torn fragments (from plate 303) with a set of candidate squares to be used in the matching phase

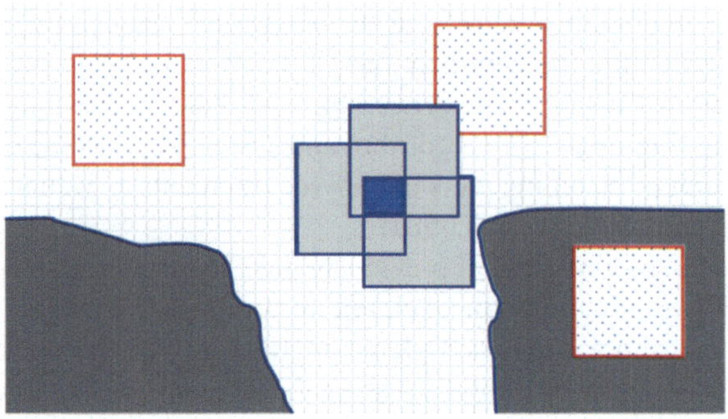

Fig. 12.4 An illustration showing edges of two potentially matched fragments and squares representing the fragments' proposed relative position alignment as voted by their matching square pairs. Three of the squares in this illustration overlap each other, thereby creating a strongly supported alignment area, while the three others are not supported by other votes and are are therefore not considered in the alignment process nor as part of the spatial features used for classification

is produced. Since it is not accurate, it votes for a rectangle in the translation space, as can be seen in Fig. 12.4. Correct matches will generate a region in the translation space with a large number of overlapping rectangles.

We enhance this voting with geometric alignment techniques from which we extract additional spatial information. Eventually, we feed all the data collected from these steps into a Random Forest classifier in order to produce a higher order classifier capable of predicting whether a pair of fragments is a match.

Our algorithm was trained on a batch of fragments which was excavated from the Dead Sea caves and is dated circa the 1st century BCE. The algorithm shows excellent results on a validation set, which is of a similar origin and conditions. An example of these results can be seen in Fig. 12.5. However, on a test batch, which is considered extremely challenging due to its poor condition and the small size of its fragments, the performance is sub optimal, returning a relatively large ratio of false positives. Nevertheless, the algorithm was quite useful by eliminating 98% of the possible matches, thus reducing the amount of work needed for manual inspection. Indeed, experts that reviewed the results have identified some positive matches as potentially true and referred them for further investigation.

Limitations. The geometric matching component depends on the size of the fragments and for relatively small fragments the algorithm struggles to find the correct matches. In addition, multi-spectral images (which exist) could be used as the input to the algorithm, which might improve its results.

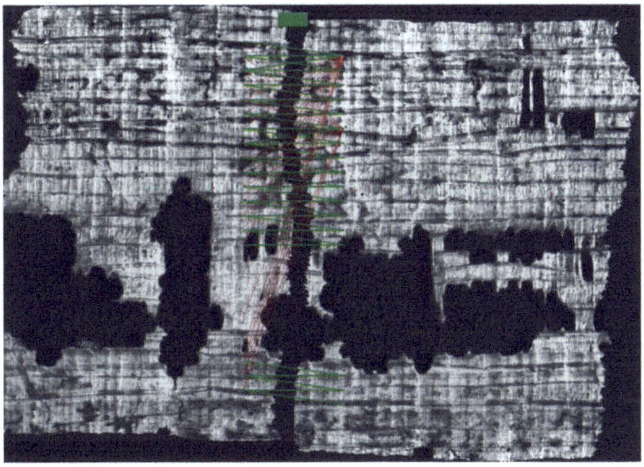

Fig. 12.5 An example of a pair of matched fragments (from plate 303) from the validation set showing the concatenation based on the relative positioning as well as lines connecting between the centers of the supporting matching squares on each fragment. Green lines indicate well supported squares while red lines are not supported. The green square at the top reflects the highly voted area for the relative alignment point

12.3 Reconstruction of Artifacts from Drawings

Line drawings have been the standard method of archaeological artifact documentation for many years. While many findings might have been lost or destroyed, their illustrations remain. Therefore, the only existing inputs for reconstruction are the line drawings appearing in an archaeological report (Fig. 12.6a, c). Usually, production of such drawings is derived from the analysis of an expert archaeologist. The archaeologist translates into a drawing his interpretation of the object. So our goal is not to recreate a digital replica of the object itself, but to recreate a missing object as it was perceived by the scientist who drew the archaeological report (Fig. 12.6b, d). These inputs are usually highly complex. State-of-the-art algorithms for automatic reconstruction were not designed with such drawings in mind. In our

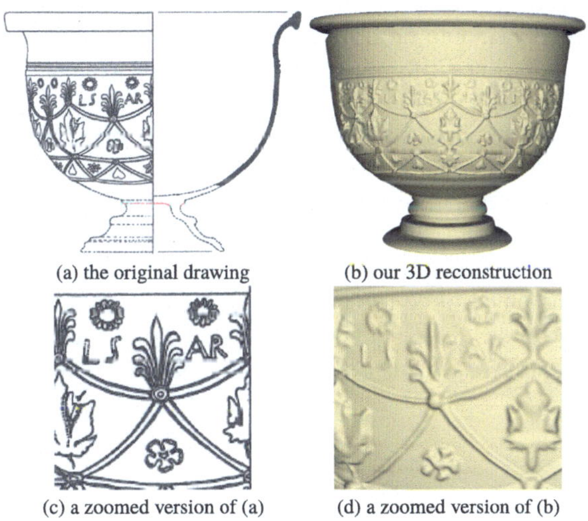

(a) the original drawing (b) our 3D reconstruction

(c) a zoomed version of (a) (d) a zoomed version of (b)

Fig. 12.6 Reconstruction of a Roman vase from a manual drawing consisting of 571 curves

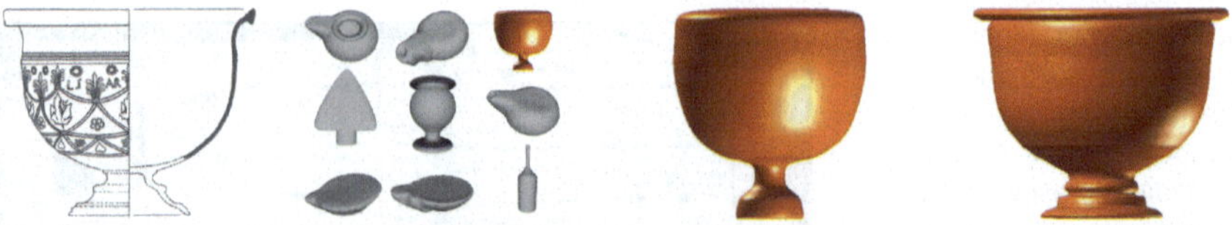

(a) The input drawing (b) The database (partial) (c) The most similar model (d) The deformed model

Fig. 12.7 Base estimation algorithm. Given a line drawing (**a**) and a database (**b**), our algorithm first retrieves the most similar model from the database (**c**) and then deforms it to better suit the line drawing (**d**). In this example, we used a database of 1830 models

work (Kolomenkin et al. 2011, 2013), we focus on artifacts containing reliefs. They are important sources of information, since they are fingerprints of periods and cultures. We applied our algorithm to real examples from archaeological reports of two types: Hellenistic and Roman relief pottery (Brusić 1999) and Cosa lamps (Fitch et al. 1994). Our approach solves two subproblems: reconstruction of the base and reconstruction of the details (the relief) on top of the base.

Base Estimation. Given the drawing of the artifact (Fig. 12.7a), its silhouette is first extracted. In some cases more than one view exists and they are also used. The silhouettes are then compared to a large number of 3D objects from a database, as seen in Fig. 12.7b. The object with the smallest $L2$ distance is chosen. It is seldom the case that the database contains a base model that perfectly fits the drawing, as can be seen in Fig. 12.7c. Therefore, we deform the retrieved model to better match the drawing. The key idea of our algorithm is to move the points on the orthographic projections to their matched points on the drawing and move the other points of the model so as to preserve its shape. The final result can be seen in Fig. 12.7d.

Relief Reconstruction. For most relief objects, the details can be described as a height function defined on a surface, termed the base. The lines of drawings of relief objects typically indicate changes of the height function. This height function is usually smooth far from the lines and constant along them. Its gradient is strongest near the lines in the direction perpendicular to the lines. Hence, the value of the height function in the line's neighborhood depends only on the distance from the line. A drawing consists of drawing curves, junctions, and margins (Fig. 12.8). We define the drawing curves, or simply the curves, as the lines of the given drawing. They indicate visually-meaningful locations on the relief. The curves may be connected by junctions, but cannot cross them. Margins are the borders of a curve's neighborhood. A drawing defines the relief (the height function). Outside the margins, the relief is assumed to be smooth. Inside the margins the relief is approximated by a step edge of height h and width w. Height h can be positive or negative, representing the direction of the edge. The shape of the relief defined by step edge $s(x)$ is $p(u)$:

$$p(u) = h \cdot s(u/w), \tag{12.1}$$

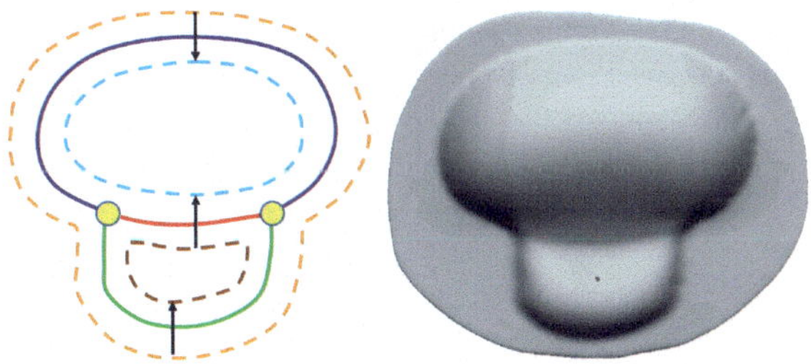

(a) Drawing data types (b) The corresponding relief

Fig. 12.8 Notations. Curves are solid lines, junctions are yellow circles, margins are dashed lines, and step edge directions are arrows. Each curve and margin is drawn in a different color

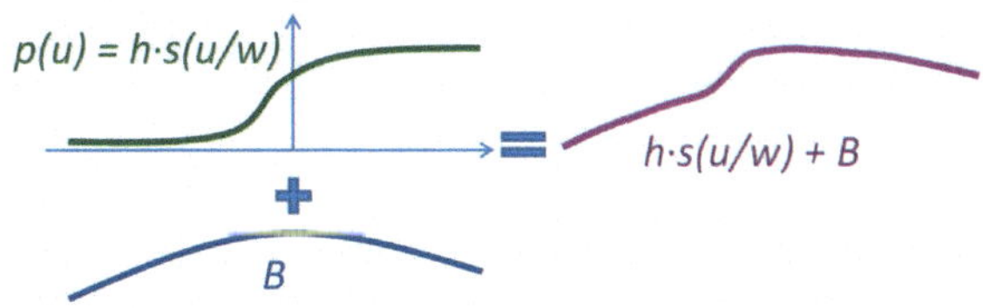

Fig. 12.9 The relief in a curve's neighborhood is a combination of the step edge $p(u)$ & the base B

where $u \in [-w, w]$ is the width parameter of the step edge. The sought-after surface is a combination of the base B and the relief. See Fig. 12.9 for an illustration.

Interpreting the line drawing requires setting the height of the step edge of each curve. Doing this manually for a complex drawing composed of dozens, or even hundreds of curves is a cumbersome process. Moreover, the set of assigned heights has to be consistent. Consistency refers to the requirement that two different paths between points should result in the same height difference. Interestingly, the key idea of our method for computing the heights of the step edges is to reduce this problem to the problem of a constrained topological ordering of a graph.

Reconstruction Given a base, a set of curves, and the heights of their step edges that were computed above, the goal is to reconstruct the relief surface. The output of the algorithm is a height function defined for every point on the base, yielding the resulting surface. The main problem the algorithm addresses is the sparsity of the input curves. This is approached by producing a smooth interpolation in regions in which curves do not exist. The interaction challenge requires that the reconstructed surface will not contain undesired artifacts due to interactions between close curves.

To achieve this goal, we require that the reconstructed height function satisfy two constraints. Locally, the relief in the curve's neighborhood is defined up to a constant using only the step edges of the margins. Globally, the relief should be the smoothest function that coincides with the relief obtained locally for every curve. During the reconstruction, the algorithm should compute for each curve its constant. This is done using the Laplacian operator. Let us denote by Δ the Laplacian operator on a scalar function. We are seeking the Laplacian L of the required surface R, which is a scalar function defined on the base surface. L should be equal to the Laplacian of relief in the neighborhoods of the curves and its Laplacian $\Delta(L)$ should be zero elsewhere. Solving this linear set of equations yields the resulting surface. Figure 12.10 illustrates a couple of results of our algorithm.

Fig. 12.10 Reconstruction of two artifacts. **a** Hellenistic relief large light-brown krater (Found in V. Mrdakovica-Croatia, (Brusić 1999) catalog number 1.) The drawing consists of 1300 tightly interconnected lines. **b** Roman triangular nozzle lamp of Eros, A.D. 50-ca 100. (Fitch et al. 1994) catalog number 504

Limitations An underlying assumption of the algorithm is that the surface can be accurately portrayed by a step edge in the line's neighborhood. When this assumption is violated, the relief cannot be reconstructed automatically, and some user interaction is needed.

12.4 Re-Colorization

Researchers have been arguing that classic statues and buildings of ancient Greece and Rome were not pure unpainted stone or green tarnished bronze, but rather quite alive, vibrant, and full of color (Bonn-Muller 2008). The colors were created using mineral and other organic materials. Unfortunately, after centuries of deterioration only little traces of pigments remained, yet chemical analysis can often estimate the original color.

Since the number of colors and hues used by the artists was limited, re-colorization algorithms may be able to restore the look of the scanned statues. Recolorization is defined as a computer-assisted process for adding color to monochrome visual data. It was originally defined for black & white images (Levin et al. 2004; Qu et al. 2006). However, in order to handle scanned ancient statues, the problem was extended to three-dimensional objects (Leifman and Tal 2012), as described hereafter.

The interactive colorization process begins with an artifact represented by a polygonal mesh. The user initiates the process by applying a few color strokes on the mesh surface. Based on these initial scribbles, the system proceeds to colorize the entire mesh accordingly. The user has the option to further refine the colorization by adding more scribbles, and the system updates the colorization in response to these additional inputs. Notably, the scribbles do not require high precision and can be loosely placed. An example session, as depicted in Fig. 12.11, showcases a typical process that can be completed within a few minutes. The algorithm that realizes this process proceeds in three steps:

(a) scribbling 2 colors (b) adding red, 2 grays and lip pink (c) adding 2 scribbles to column

Fig. 12.11 A typical colorization session. a The user starts by scribbling two colors. **b** Then, the user adds red to the head band, light gray to the column, dark gray to the base and pink to the lips (middle). **c** Finally, the user fine-tunes the results by adding color scribbles close to the column boundaries, to prevent color bleeding

1. Initialization: For each face the scribble passes through, the closest vertex is colorized with the color of the scribble.
2. Vertex similarity. A similarity measure between neighboring vertices is computed. This is done by seeking a descriptor that robustly characterizes the local geometry of the vertex. In (Leifman and Tal 2012) we propose to use a variation of *spin images* (Johnson and Hebert 1999) as vertex descriptor. Then, a similarity measure between vertex descriptors, which must be robust to small changes in the mesh, is computed. We use the *diffusion distance* as a similarity measure (Ling and Okada 2006).
3. Propagation: Given these similarities, the algorithm propagates the colors to the remaining vertices of the mesh. The basic assumption is that adjacent vertices that have similar descriptors should get similar colors. This stage is naturally the key of the algorithm. It is done through optimization, in which we impose the constraint that two neighboring vertices should have similar colors if their geometry is similar.
   In particular, for all the vertices of mesh M, we minimize the difference between the color at vertex v_i and the weighted average of the colors at neighboring vertices $v_j > \in N(v_i)$. This is done for each color channel C in the YUV color space, by minimizing the following loss:

$$\Omega(C) = \sum_{v_i \in M} \left(C(v_i) - \sum_{v_j \in N(v_i)} k_{ij} C(v_j) \right)^2. \tag{12.2}$$

   In this equation, k_{ij} is a weight function, which is large when the descriptor of v_i is similar to that of v_j and small otherwise, and for which $\sum_{v_j \in N(v_i)} k_{ij} = 1$. It is defined as

$$k_{ij} \propto e^{s_{ij}^2/2\sigma_i^2}, \tag{12.3}$$

Fig. 12.12 Only a few scribbles are needed to colorize the cloth, despite its folded structure. Note how the fingers are correctly separated from the folded cloth or the hand-held objects

where s_{ij} is the similarity of v_i and v_j, as computed in the second stage and σ_i is the standard deviation of the similarity values between each of the vertices in $N(v_i)$ and v_i.

The output is a mesh in which every vertex has a designated color. We note that to prevent color bleeding we define a new vector field on meshes, which is in accordance with the valleys of the object. Figure 12.12 demonstrates some of the results.

A drawback of the above algorithm is that it does not handle repetitive patterns. As a result, to colorize an objects with patterns, color strokes on each pattern instance are needed, which might be very time consuming. In (Leifman and Tal 2013), a method for colorization, which performs also pattern classification, is presented.

The key idea is that the few strokes, which are provided for colorization, can be extremely helpful also for pattern classification. Thus, once the patterns are classified, even highly complex surfaces can be automatically colorized using the user's strokes around and within a single instance of each pattern. The interactive session is similar to the one described above. However, the user needs scribble only on and around one instance of the pattern. The approach consists of three steps, which are performed for each pattern in turn.

1. *Pattern-aware filtering*. The surface is filtered in a pattern-preserving manner. In the filtered surface, the pattern boundaries are kept intact, whereas the details in the pattern region are filtered out. This is done by first segmenting the sub-surface into its foreground (a single pattern instance) and its background, by the colorization technique of (Leifman and Tal 2012), using the user's scribbles. Then, a uniform Laplace smoothing is applied. The result of this stage facilities subsequent steps, where sharp pattern boundaries are important for achieving the desirable colorization.

2. *Pattern-driven region descriptors*. Each vertex is associated with a descriptor that characterizes its neighborhood, in accordance with the pattern to be colorized. In particular, for each vertex its surrounding region is first extracted, which is segmented into foreground (pattern) and background. Then, two types of descriptors of the foreground region are considered: region-based and boundary-based. The region-based descriptor captures the geometry of the region, whereas the boundary descriptor relies only on the shape of the region's boundary. Utilizing two different descriptors not only characterizes the region better, but is also essential for the co-training described next.
3. *Pattern classification*. The aim is to determine which vertices of the surface belong to the pattern and which do not. The key idea is to classify a subset of the classified vertices to automatically produce additional colorization strokes in accordance with the pattern. These strokes are the input to (Leifman and Tal 2012). More specifically, for each face the scribble passes through, the closest vertex gets the color of the scribble. The result is a very small number of training examples. To handle shortage in training examples, the set of positive examples is enriched by using the foreground vertices found in Step 1. We face a two-class classification problem, for which there is a large number of positive examples and a small number of negative examples. Fortunately, classification of all the vertices can be avoided, as the goal is to classify only a representative subset of vertices with very high confidence (as additional strokes), which will suffice for colorization. In the proposed method semi-supervised learning is utilized.

Figure 12.13 shows a couple of challenging examples, jointly with their scribbles.

In the time since the publication of these works, progress has been made in the development of 3D re-colorization algorithms, primarily focusing on applications in interior design for scenes and furniture, as well as CAD models. It is anticipated that generative models, previously employed in the aforementioned domains (Hou et al. 2019; Yang et al. 2018), will be expanded to tackle the complex archaeological domain. Additionally, an alternative approach involves considering the problem as interactive segmentation and employing advanced segmentation algorithms tailored to our specific domain.

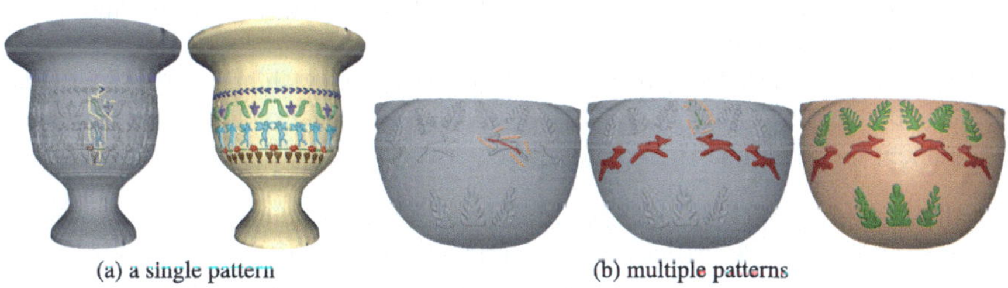

Fig. 12.13 Pattern-driven colorization. Given a 3D surface, the user scribbles a handful of strokes within and around a single pattern instance. The algorithm colorizes the whole surface accordingly

Limitations. The algorithms necessitate a reasonably dense input mesh. If the input mesh exhibits high irregularity or sparsity, or if the vertices of two valleys are one vertex apart, remeshing may be necessary. Additionally, in the presence of patterns, our assumption is that instances of the pattern are distinguished by a background area that separates them.

12.5 Ancient Document Enhancement

Binarization is the process of converting a multi-tone image into a binary image. When the image is a document, binarization classifies every pixel as text (foreground) or non-text (background). Binarization facilitates other document processing tasks, such as layout analysis and character recognition. Historical document images might be more difficult to binarize than modern scanned documents, due to their degraded state, as well as to the digitization process. There exist several excellent reviews of the problem and the methods that attempt to address it (Ismail et al. 2018; Lins et al. 2019; More and Dighe 2016; Mustafa et al. 2018; Sezgin and Sankur 2004; Tensmeyer and Martinez 2020). These are categorized into the following types (Tensmeyer and Martinez 2020):

- *Thresholding*. Setting a threshold that distinguishes between foreground and background, based on either local or global statistics (or both).
- *Edge detection*. These approaches perform edge detection in an attempt to find the boundary between foreground and background.
- *Image transforms*. These approached extract local features based on image transforms such as Gabor filter banks or Fourier Transform.
- *Mixture of Gaussians*. This is a parametric probability distribution whose function is a weighted sum of Gaussian distributions, which can be fit to any set of unlabeled data points (features). Then, each data point is assigned to its most probable cluster, each of which is either a foreground or a background class.
- *Conditional Random Fields*. A CRF is associated with an energy (cost) function that scores the binarization. Thus, it may incorporate spatial dependencies among pixels into the binarization process. Usually, the energy function is hand-crafted and does not learn parameters.
- *Machine Learning*. Like in many other fields, recently machine learning methods, especially deep learning models, have become the state of the art in historical document binarization. The goal of these networks is to directly classify pixels.

Rather than proposing a new algorithm, we introduce a novel general approach (Kligler et al. 2018), which improved the results of any state-of-the-art algorithm, by providing it with new information (input). Interestingly, this information is based on a solution to a seemingly unrelated problem of visibility detection in $\mathbb{R}^3$. The key idea is that if we choose a suitable representation of pixels as points in $\mathbb{R}^3$ and then detect the subset of the points that are visible from a viewpoint (and/or

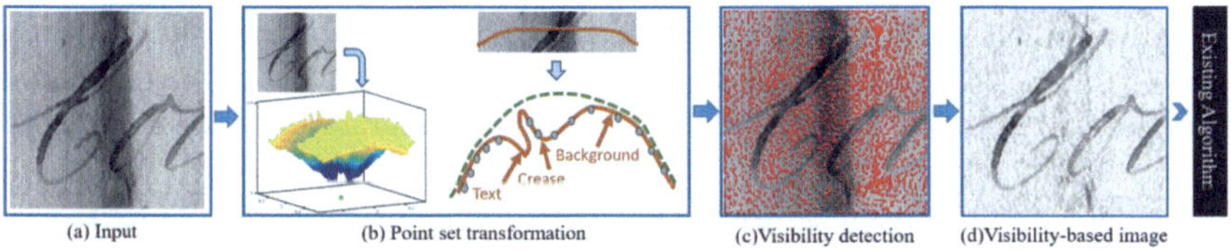

Fig. 12.14 Algorithm outline: The intensity image **a** is transformed to a 3D point set on a "globe", where the distance of a point from the globe's center (in green) is determined according to the intensity (**b**). Visibility detection operators detect which pixels have been transformed to visible/occluding points from/to the viewpoint (the globe's center). Visible/occluding pixels are marked red in (**c**). Notice that the letters hardly have any red points, whereas the background and the stain have many. This implies a strong visibility–foreground correlation. Using the information of (**c**), a visibility-based image is created (**d**). It maintains the text of (**a**), while making stains disappear. This image is used to alter existing algorithms

occluding it), hidden information about the image is revealed. This information is used to create a new image, which when given as input to an existing algorithm, will improve its own results, while leaving the algorithm's general structure as usual.

Visibility has been defined in various dimensions and for different types of objects, however our focus is on a specific variant of it: Given a point set in $\mathbb{R}^3$ and a viewpoint, the goal is to determine the subset of points visible from the viewpoint. Since points cannot occlude each other (unless they accidentally fall on the same ray from the viewpoint), the more precise problem definition is to determine the subset of points that would be visible, if the surface from which the points were sampled, was known.

Why does visibility information assist us? The representation we propose will assign text pixels, which are dark on white background, to points in deep valleys. Background, which is constant and of high intensity, will turn to elevated plateaus. Stains on text, which have no distinct intensity characteristics, will be represented as structure-less, resembling "volcanic" terrains. Stains on background, which normally cause darker local regions, will outcome in craters or shallow valleys upon the elevated plateaus. It turns out that visibility detection operators manage to distinguish between deep valleys and "volcanic" terrains (text) to elevated plateaus, craters and shallow valleys (background).

Our approach proceeds as follows: Given an image of a document (Fig. 12.14a), which might be stained, shadowed or otherwise distorted, our goal is to produce another image (Fig. 12.14d), which better distinguishes the foreground from the background. This image will benefit any algorithm that processes the document. Our approach is encapsulated into four stages:

Stage 1: Transform each pixel to a 3D point. Intuitively, one could imagine the image as if it was pasted onto a portion of the world globe, such that (1) valleys and craters on the surface are created from pixels of low intensity relatively to their vicinity; (2) ridges and mountains are created from high intensity pixels relatively to their vicinity; (3) plateaus are created from areas of pixels with low varying intensity.

To realize it, let p_i be a pixel within the image at location (x_i, y_i) and intensity level $\mathrm{I_i} \in [0, 1]$. The transformation first spreads the image onto a portion of the unit sphere's surface and then brings the pixels closer or further away according to their intensity, as demonstrated in Fig. 12.14b. This figure shows both the full point cloud representing the whole image, as well as the transformation of a single (orange) curve through the image.

In spreading, p_i is first translated to a scaled coordinate system relatively to the image coordinate system, having its origin located in the center of the image s.t.:

$$x_i' = \frac{x_i - \frac{width}{2}}{M}, \quad y_i' = \frac{y_i - \frac{height}{2}}{M}, \tag{12.4}$$

where M is the maximum image dimension. This guarantees that $\left(x_i', y_i'\right) \in ([-0.5, 0.5] \times [-0.5, 0.5])$.

To set the height of a point on the globe, an initial height is defined for all pixels and p_i is then represented in polar coordinates (r_i, θ_i, ϕ_i). Then, each pixel is transformed to the unit sphere at $(1, \theta_i, \phi_i)$. Finally, r_i is set relatively to p_i's intensity using a linear transformation to $\mathrm{I_i}$ s.t.:

$$r_i = a_1 \cdot \mathrm{I_i} + a_0. \tag{12.5}$$

Stage 2: Detect the visible/occluding points from (/to) the center of the globe. As illustrated in Fig. 12.14c, red (occluding) dots exist on the background, including the stain, but not on the foreground letters. This is the key to the success of our approach. This stage is performed by applying the visibility detection algorithm described in (Katz and Tal 2015; Katz et al. 2007).

Stage 3: Create a visibility-based image by using the information of Stage 2 above, as shown in Fig. 12.14d. In particular, a smoothed image is created using only the intensity values of the pixels that generated the occluding points. For the rest of the pixels, we apply the *natural-neighbor interpolation* (Sibson et al. 1981), using only the occluding pixels. Hence, their values are approximated by their neighboring occluding (background) pixels. Next, the smoothed image is subtracted pixel-wise from the input image and subsequently normalized to the range of [0, 1], resulting in a visibility-based image. Since the value of a background pixel in the original image and in the smoothed image are equal, its value in the visibility-based image will be 1, as desired. Even if it is not detected occluding, the fact that it resides on a plateau or a ridge, means that its vicinity contains points that originated from pixels with similar intensity values. Consequently, the pixel will end up with a value approaching 1. On the other hand, if the pixel is a text pixel, then its 3D point will end up within a valley. This point, as well as points around it, are unlikely to be marked occluding. Thus, its interpolated value in the smoothed image will be much greater than its true intensity. Upon creation of the visibility-based image, its value will be close to 0.

Stage 4: Apply any existing binarization algorithm, using the visibility-based image rather than the input image.

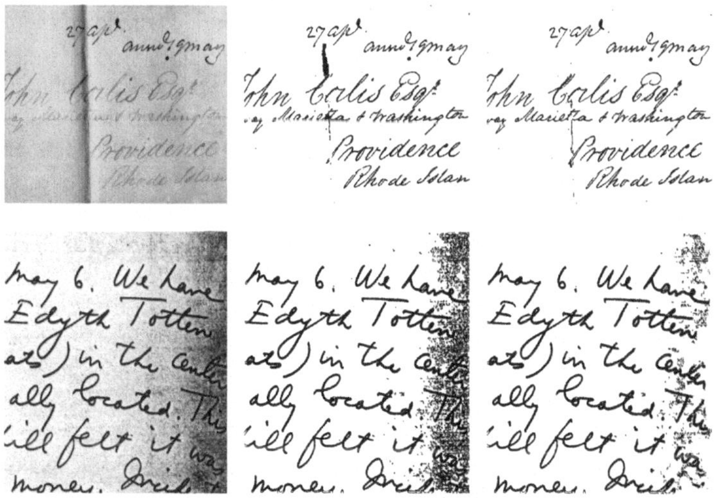

(a) Input (b) Original output (c) Our output

Fig. 12.15 **Binarization results**: **a**: Images out of (Pratikakis et al. 2011). An algorithm's output in **b** is improved by using our approach in (**c**). Top: (Howe 2013) Alg. 3 is improved from 92.06% to 93.61%. Our algorithm manages to detect the vertical crease as background. Bottom: (Su et al. 2013) is improved from 76.18% to 90.18%. Our algorithm enables better treatment of the noisy region in the right side of the image. Scores are in PF-measure

The main dataset used in the literature for this application comes from the DIBCO series of competitions, e.g., (Gatos et al. 2009; Pratikakis et al. 2011, 2013, 2019). Every year, since 2009 (except 2015), a new dataset of 10-20 images of representative degradations, are released. The data and the evaluation software can be downloaded. Figure 12.15 shows a couple of examples out of (Pratikakis et al. 2011), where the results of the original algorithms are improved. Note how the vertical crease (top) is detected as background and how the noisy region on the right-hand side of the bottom image is better treated.

Limitation. The algorithm might produce suboptimal outcomes in cases where the fonts are small, and there is minimal color variance.

12.6 Conclusion

In this chapter we reviewed our work on cultural heritage restoration problems. We covered very diverse types of artifacts, from papyrus fragments, to ancient documents, archaeological drawings, and Hellenistic and Roman statues. These represent artifacts, which are 2D by nature and 3D artifacts. The algorithms presented in this chapter are very diverse by nature, showing how challenging are the problems in the field of computational archaeology.

Future work may benefit from the integration of image processing techniques with deep learning models. Furthermore, as is the case with all applications of archaeology, large datasets are a necessity, in particular when deep learning models are used. This is a major challenge since large datasets are very hard to come by in the field of archaeology and therefore the big challenge will be to develop deep learning algorithms, which can work on relatively small datasets. Moreover, another challenge is to get the data labeled. This is also difficult since it usually can be done only by experts. Thus, exploiting unlabeled examples with a small set of labeled examples is also of great importance.

As mentioned earlier, there are numerous unresolved challenges in the field of restoration. One such intriguing aspect that was discussed in this chapter pertains to the reassembly of 2D objects. However, an equally fascinating area of study involves the reassembly of 3D objects. This encompasses a broad range of objects, including general 3D shapes (Niu et al. 2022; Zhang et al. 2018) as well as specific categories like surfaces of revolution (Hong et al. 2021) (e.g., pots, vases, etc.). While there has been considerable research dedicated to this problem, it is important to note that it is still an ongoing endeavor and not yet considered solved.

Additionally, we explored research related to document enhancement. This could be enhanced using deep learning techniques (Souibgui and Kessentini 2020; Lin et al. 2020). Such algorithms can serve as components of a comprehensive end-to-end pipeline aimed at extracting the text content from documents. Deep learning techniques, specifically OCR (Optical Character Recognition) methods, in conjunction with large language models, can be leveraged to accomplish this task. These models have the capability to not only recover the text from documents but also correct errors that arise during the process.

References

Abitbol R, Shimshoni I, Ben-Dov J (2021) Machine learning based assembly of fragments of ancient papyrus. J Comput Cult Herit (JOCCH) 14(3):1–21

Anwar H, Anwar S, Zambanini S, Porikli F (2021) Deep ancient roman republican coin classification via feature fusion and attention. Pattern Recogn 114:107871

Barucci A, Cucci C, Franci M, Loschiavo M, Argenti F (2021) A deep learning approach to ancient Egyptian hieroglyphs classification. IEEE Access 9:123438–123447

Bonn-Muller E (2008) Carved in living color. Archaeology 61(1):14–15

Brusić Z (1999) Hellenistic and roman relief pottery in liburnia: North-East Adriatic, Croatia. BAR Int Ser 817

Canul-Ku M, Hasimoto-Beltran R, Jiménez-Badillo D, Ruiz-Correa S, Román-Rangel E (2018) Classification of 3d archaeological objects using multi-view curvature structure signatures. IEEE Access 7:3298–3313

Chetouani A, Treuillet S, Exbrayat M, Jesset S (2020) Classification of engraved pottery sherds mixing deep-learning features by compact bilinear pooling. Patt Recog Let 131:1–7

Derech N, Tal A, Shimshoni I (2019) Placement visualization. https://www.youtube.com/watch?v=2-pjbiiJ1GQ&feature=youtu.be
Derech N, Tal A, Shimshoni I (2021) Solving archaeological puzzles. Pattern Recogn 119:108065
Dimov DT (2020) Rotation-invariant NCC for 2d color matching of arbitrary shaped fragments of a fresco. Pattern Recogn Lett 138:431–438
Fitch CR, Goldman NW, Goldman N (1994) Cosa, the lamps, vol 39. University of Michigan Press
Gatos B, Ntirogiannis K, Pratikakis I (2009) ICDAR 2009 document image binarization contest (dibco 2009). In: 2009 10th international conference on document analysis and recognition. IEEE, pp 1375–1382
Gilboa A, Tal A, Shimshoni I, Kolomenkin M (2013) Computer-based, automatic recording and illustration of complex archaeological artifacts. J Archaeol Sci 40(2):1329–1339
Hayon O, Münger S, Shimshoni I, Tal A (2024) ArcAid: analysis of archaeological artifacts using drawings. In: Proceedings of the IEEE/CVF winter conference on applications of computer vision (WACV), pp 7264–7274
Hong JH, Yoo SJ, Zeeshan MA, Kim YM, Kim J (2021) Structure-from-sherds: incremental 3d reassembly of axially symmetric pots from unordered and mixed fragment collections. In: Proceedings of the IEEE international conference on computer vision, pp 5443–5451
Hou JU, Zhao B, Ansari N, Lin W (2019) Range image based point cloud colorization using conditional generative model. In: 2019 IEEE international conference on image processing (ICIP). IEEE, pp 524–528
Howe NR (2013) Document binarization with automatic parameter tuning. Int J Doc Anal Recognit 16(3):247–258
Ismail SM, Abdullah S, Fauzi F (2018) Statistical binarization techniques for document image analysis. J Comput Sci 14(1):23–36
Johnson AE, Hebert M (1999) Using spin images for efficient object recognition in cluttered 3d scenes. IEEE Trans Pattern Anal Mach Intell 21(5):433–449
Katz S, Tal A (2015) On the visibility of point clouds. In: Proceedings of the IEEE international conference on computer vision, pp 1350–1358
Katz S, Tal A, Basri R (2007) Direct visibility of point sets. In: ACM SIGGRAPH 2007 papers, ACM, pp 24–es
Kligler N, Katz S, Tal A (2018) Document enhancement using visibility detection. In: Proceedings of the IEEE conference on computer vision and pattern recognition, pp 2374–2382
Kolomenkin M, Shimshoni I, Tal A (2009) On edge detection on surfaces. In: 2009 IEEE conference on computer vision and pattern recognition. IEEE, pp 2767–2774
Kolomenkin M, Leifman G, Shimshoni I, Tal A (2011) Reconstruction of relief objects from line drawings. In: CVPR 2011. IEEE, pp 993–1000
Kolomenkin M, Leifman G, Shimshoni I, Tal A (2013) Reconstruction of relief objects from archeological line drawings. J Comput Cult Herit (JOCCH) 6(1):1–19
Lawonn K, Trostmann E, Preim B, Hildebrandt K (2016) Visualization and extraction of carvings for heritage conservation. IEEE Trans Vis Comput Graph 23(1):801–810
Leifman G, Tal A (2012) Mesh colorization. Comput Graph Forum 31(2):421–430
Leifman G, Tal A (2013) Pattern-driven colorization of 3d surfaces. In: Proceedings of the IEEE conference on computer vision and pattern recognition, pp 241–248
Lerner J, Shimshoni I (2022) Thin section analysis for ceramic petrography using motion analysis and segmentation techniques. Mach Vis Appl 33(5):70
Levin A, Lischinski D, Weiss Y (2004) Colorization using optimization. In: ACM SIGGRAPH 2004 papers. ACM, pp 689–694
Lin YH, Chen WC, Chuang YY (2020) Bedsr-net: a deep shadow removal network from a single document image. In: Proceedings of the IEEE/CVF conference on computer vision and pattern recognition, pp 12905–12914
Ling H, Okada K (2006) Diffusion distance for histogram comparison. In: 2006 IEEE computer society conference on computer vision and pattern recognition (CVPR'06), vol 1. IEEE, pp 246–253

Lins RD, Bernardino R, Jesus DM (2019) A quality and time assessment of binarization algorithms. In: 2019 international conference on document analysis and recognition (ICDAR). IEEE, pp 1444–1450
Luo T, Li R, Zha H (2011) 3d line drawing for archaeological illustration. Int J Comput Vis 94:23–35
Ma Y, Arandjelović O (2020) Classification of ancient roman coins by denomination using colour, a forgotten feature in automatic ancient coin analysis. Sci 2(2):37
More PK, Dighe D (2016) A review on document image binarization technique for degraded document images. Int Res J Eng Technol 3(3):1132–1138
Mustafa WA, Aziz H, Khairunizam W, Ibrahim Z, Shahriman A, Razlan ZM (2018) Review of different binarization approaches on degraded document images. In: 2018 international conference on computational approach in smart systems design and applications (ICASSDA). IEEE, pp 1–8
Niu X, Wang Q, Liu B, Zhang J (2022) An automatic chinaware fragments reassembly method framework based on linear feature of fracture surface contour. ACM J Comput Cult Herit 16(1):1–22
Phillips SC, Walland PW, Modafferi S, Dorst L, Spagnuolo M, Catalano CE, Oldman D, Tal A, Shimshoni I, Hermon S (2016) GRAVITATE: geometric and semantic matching for cultural heritage artefacts. In: Catalano CE, Luca LD (ed), Eurographics workshop on graphics and cultural heritage. The Eurographics Association
Pratikakis I, Gatos B, Ntirogiannis K (2011) DIBCO 2011: document Image Binarization Contest. In: International conference on document analysis and recognition (ICDAR)
Pratikakis I, Gatos B, Ntirogiannis K (2013) DIBCO 2013: document image binarization contest. In: International conference on document analysis and recognition (ICDAR)
Pratikakis I, Zagoris K, Karagiannis X, Tsochatzidis L, Mondal T, Marthot-Santaniello I (2019) Competition on document image binarization (dibco 2019). In: International conference on document analysis and recognition (ICDAR), pp 1547–1556
Qu Y, Wong TT, Heng PA (2006) Manga colorization. ACM Trans Graph (ToG) 25(3):1214–1220
Romanengo C, Biasotti S, Falcidieno B (2020) Recognising decorations in archaeological finds through the analysis of characteristic curves on 3d models. Pattern Recogn Lett 131:405–412
Saalfeld P, Böttcher C, Klink F, Preim B (2021) Vr system for the restoration of broken cultural artifacts on the example of a funerary monument. In: 2021 IEEE virtual reality and 3D user interfaces (VR). IEEE, pp 739–748
Sezgin M, Bl S (2004) Survey over image thresholding techniques and quantitative performance evaluation. J Electron Imaging 13(1):146–168
Sibson R et al (1981) A brief description of natural neighbour interpolation. Interpret Multivar Data 21:21–36
da Silva TT, de Andrade M, Da Luz MR (2021) Reconstruction of frescoes by sequential layers of feature extraction. Pattern Recogn Lett 147:172–178
Sipiran I, Lazo P, Lopez C, Jimenez M, Bagewadi N, Bustos B, Dao H, Gangisetty S, Hanik M, Ho-Thi NP et al (2021) Shrec 2021: retrieval of cultural heritage objects. Comput Graph 100:1–20
Souibgui MA, Kessentini Y (2020) DE-GAN: a conditional generative adversarial network for document enhancement. IEEE Trans Patt Ana Mach Intel 44(3):1180–1191
Su B, Lu S, Tan CL (2013) Robust document image binarization technique for degraded document images. IEEE Trans Image Proc 22(4):1408–1417
Tal A (2014) 3d shape analysis for archaeology. 3D research challenges in cultural heritage: a roadmap in digital heritage preservation, pp 50–63
Tensmeyer C, Martinez T (2020) Historical document image binarization: a review. SN Comput Sci 1(3):173
Wilczek J, Monna F, Jébrane A, Chazal CL, Navarro N, Couette S, Smith CC (2018) Computer-assisted orientation and drawing of archaeological pottery. J Comput Cult Herit (JOCCH) 11(4):1–17
Xiong W, Zhou L, Yue L, Li L, Wang S (2021) An enhanced binarization framework for degraded historical document images. EURASIP J Image Video Process 1:13

Yang Z, Liu L, Huang Q (2018) Learning generative neural networks for 3d colorization. Proc AAAI Conf Artif Intell 32:2580–2587

Zeng Q, Martin RR, Wang L, Quinn JA, Sun Y, Tu C (2014) Region-based bas-relief generation from a single image. Graph Models 76(3)

Zhang Y, Li K, Chen X, Zhang S, Geng G (2018) A multi feature fusion method for reassembly of 3d cultural heritage artifacts. J Cult Herit 33:191–200

Zhang YW, Wang J, Wang W, Chen Y, Liu H, Ji Z, Zhang C (2021) Neural modelling of flower bas-relief from 2d line drawing. Comput Graph Forum 40(6):288–303

Chapter 13
Low-Barrier-to-Entry Multispectral Imaging: Enhancing Understanding of and Furthering Access to Cultural Heritage Artifacts

Juilee Decker, David W. Messinger, and Roger L. Easton Jr.

Abstract Through the creation of a low-cost, low barrier-to-entry Multispectral Imaging (MSI) system called MISHA (Multispectral Imaging System for Historical Artifacts) and the development of software and user manuals to support the processing and visualization of images captured by the system, we have demonstrated that scholars in a variety of humanities fields, library, archive, and museum professionals, conservators, and other researchers and practitioners can use such a system to capture and process images in an easy-access manner. The image capture and processing facilitate ways to better represent, interpret, characterize, uncover and, ultimately, gain access to collections across a wide range of artifacts and constituent materials. For the purposes of this chapter, interactive media applies to two facets: *both* the material collections *and* the digital surrogates rendered through the MISHA capture, processing, and visualization. We examine image processing and visualization techniques as exemplars to frame methods for enhancing our understanding and furthering access to collections. We demonstrate the utility of such a system through four examples of artifacts we have examined, imaged, processed, and evaluated.

Keywords Digitization · Cultural heritage imaging · Multispectral imaging · Advanced imaging and analysis

13.1 Introduction

Humanities scholars, library, archive, and museum professionals, conservators, and other researchers and practitioners who privilege object-based inquiry are driven to understand artifacts, their histories, practices surrounding their use, and their mere coming into existence. In the absence of fully-narrativized paper ledgers or blockchain provenance, gaps in an artifact's history leave us to wonder about its past.

J. Decker (✉) · D. W. Messinger · R. L. Easton Jr.
Rochester Institute of Technology, Rochester, NY, USA
e-mail: jdgsh@rit.edu

F. Liarokapis et al. (eds.), *Interactive Media for Cultural Heritage*, Springer Series on Cultural Computing, https://doi.org/10.1007/978-3-031-61018-9_13

How has an item come to be in the state it is? What do differences in the materials in the artifact tell us about its history? Answers may emerge from beneath the surface and could be revealed by "seeing" what lies beyond our visibility. Non-invasive methodologies developed in the field of cultural heritage imaging have the capacity to yield new knowledge about artifacts by revealing features that are otherwise imperceptible without the employ of such imaging and processing techniques.

13.1.1 Cultural Heritage Imaging

The history of multispectral imaging (MSI) of historical manuscripts arguably dates from 1844 to 1846, when William Henry Fox Talbot published "The Pencil of Nature" in London (Talbot). There, Talbot wrote about imaging with "invisible rays" and the use of a camera as tool for imaging, that is, for seeing beyond what was possible for the eye to see. An application of imaging was applied to historical manuscripts in the 1890s by Ernst Pringsheim and Otto Gradenwitz. Their work enabled an understanding of palimpsests, the phenomenon whereby an earlier text is erased, worn off, or otherwise rendered invisible: however, through illumination, the visible traces of the earlier text or embellishment become apparent (Gradenwitz 1900). Multispectral imaging with ultraviolet sources was demonstrated by Father Raphael Kögel of the Order of Saint Benedict who employed ultraviolet to increase the contrast between the background and the text. His work led to the publication of the full edition of the palimpsested text *Codex Sangallensis 193* in 1913 (Jerome 1913; Kögel 1920). This was intended to be the first in a series of published palimpsests that was immediately interrupted by the First World War and never restarted. Other efforts included Fr. Alban Dold's fluorescent imaging of palimpsests documented in two papers (1917 and 1928) and Charles Samaran's use of ultraviolet light to read manuscripts (1925).

The development of digital technologies roughly beginning in the 1970s enabled the application of scientific methods for digital image processing to humanities disciplines. John Frederick Benton, paleographer and professor of Medieval history at California Institute of Technology, applied image processing techniques developed for space exploration for digitally "uncovering" erased, faded, or damaged texts (Benton 1978). The studies of the Archimedes Palimpsest from 2000 to 2011 further demonstrated the value of MSI in studies of cultural heritage (Easton and Noel 2010) and the technology has since been applied to a wide variety of objects, including the palimpsests at St. Catherine's Monastery in Sinai, the Biblioteca Ambrosiana in Milan, and the Biblioteca Capitolare in Verona. Fischer and Kakoulli (2006) review the use of multispectral and hyperspectral imaging in the field of conservation, providing an overview of the technology uses and applications including the study of palimpsests and other works on paper and parchment. Giacometti et al. (2017) consider various methods of processing multispectral imagery with a focus on historical texts. Here, they deliberately degrade samples cut from a historical text (deemed to "hold no historical or scholarly value") and then image them, developing both quantitative and qualitative assessments of image capture and processing. They use a multispectral setup similar to that described below and conclude that processing algorithms such as Principal Components Analysis (also described below) provide an accurate method of degraded text recovery. McGillivray and Duffy (2017) used the MegaVision Cultural Heritage EV Imaging Systems, a commercially available multispectral imaging system (described below) to study illuminations in a medieval manuscript, particularly focusing on potential underdrawings, abrasion or fading of the illuminations, and pigment analysis. These contributions provide evidence of the utility of multispectral imaging for Cultural Heritage studies, however existing commercially available systems, while providing outstanding imagery, are expensive, complex, and difficult to use. Additionally, processing software is typically expensive and designed for other purposes such as remote sensing, and therefore inaccessible to most potential users. The result is that the number of systems available is relatively small and therefore, the number of artifacts that can benefit from multispectral imaging is also small.

Building upon this long and rich history of imaging as a significant and accessible tool promoting access and discoverability, the authors define cultural heritage imaging as any in a continuum of practices that involves the digitization of tangible or intangible heritage. From document camera and related scanning methods to multispectral and hyperspectral imaging, digitization seeks to produce a surrogate of the source item. The key difference in the technologies is in the digital representations they produce. Traditional digitization aims to produce a digital product that represents what the artifact "looks like" to a human observer. Hyperspectral imaging is typically used to quantitatively understand the chemical nature of the materials in the artifact, thus producing a more detailed description of what the artifact is "made of," without necessarily producing a visually representative image. Multispectral imaging is "in between," leveraging the material differences to produce visualizations that enhance otherwise sub-visual content. The goal is to enhance our knowledge of the artifact, both the material features as well as the content.

The focus in this article is multispectral imaging, a camera-based technique that involves taking tens of images (in our case, 16) of an object at different wavelengths from the ultraviolet (365, 385, and 395 nm) to the visible (420 nm through 660 nm) and infrared (730 nm through 940 nm) (see Table 13.1). Each image is collected independently of the others and after completion, combined into a single, large, "spectral cube" that includes all of the spatial and spectral information. The spectral information is compounded as it is composed layer-by-layer with one image stacked on top of another. In contrast, and beyond the scope of this article, is hyperspectral imaging (HSI) which captures many more (up to thousands) of images across a wider range of wavelengths, resulting in higher spectral resolution (but typically worse spatial resolution). Hyperspectral imaging uses a dispersive element (such as a prism or diffraction grating) in the optical instrument, while multispectral imaging uses either wavelength selective illumination or transmission filters. Both MSI and HSI, however, are non-invasive methods to reveal and enhance non-visible features such as erasures or earlier markings on papyrus, vellum, parchment, paper, and a

Table 13.1 MISHA is a camera-based multispectral imaging technique that involves taking 16 images at different wavelengths from the ultraviolet to the visible and infrared

Band	Length (nm)
UV	365
UV	385
UV	395
Violet blue	420
Royal blue	450
Long blue	470
Cyan	505
Green	530
Lime	560
Narrow amber	590
Red–orange	615
Red	630
Deep red	660
IR	730
IR	850
IR	940

variety of other materials (Arnold et al 2022; Davies 2020; Easton and Noel 2010; Easton et al. 2010, 2019; Falotico et al. 2023; Zawacki et al. 2023).

13.1.2 Multispectral Imaging

Multispectral imaging (MSI) has its origins in remote sensing and has been used in environmental monitoring, medical imaging, and astronomy. As a result, it has been out of the reach of many heritage professionals, scholars, and researchers. Nevertheless, a brief literature review involving results from electronic searches of federated portals such as Google Scholar yielded the following results when searching for multispectral, cultural heritage, and artifact: 3880 results with 183 results from 2023; 401 results for 2022; and 372 results from 2021. These results show the range of scholarship around case studies of a particular artifact or development of a workflow related to digitization. More interestingly, a growing body of scholarship addresses MSI's application to humanities-based inquiry of analyzing collections materials exists (Davies 2020; Frühmann et al. 2018; Lanigan and Hirshberg 2001). In addition, and representing a new addition to the field, a recent article published by researchers at University College London, British Library, and University of Edinburgh employed Action Research methodology to characterize MSI workflows and to make recommendations for project management, documentation, and the practice of MSI (Jones et al. 2020).

Contributing to this growing body of work and seeking to assist researchers, scholars, and practitioners, the authors have been funded by the United States' National Endowment for the Humanities Preservation and Access Division and since 2021 have led an interdisciplinary team comprising students and faculty in imaging science and museum studies in the creation of a low-cost, low barrier-to-entry MSI system called MISHA (Multispectral Imaging System for Historical Artifacts) that is supported by open-source software and user manuals to support the processing and visualization of images captured by the system. A primary goal of the research project is the democratization of the technology, providing access to multispectral imagery for small to medium sized institutions to enhance their collections. Through this grant-funded effort thus far, the authors have demonstrated that library, archive, and museum professionals, conservators, and scholars in a variety of humanities fields can use such a system to capture and process images without the need for specialist training in imaging science or technical photography.

13.1.3 Interactive Media

Extracting meaningful information from MSI occurs in two phases: capture and processing. If capture yields sixteen digital surrogates, then processing unleashes numerous opportunities for discovery by bringing together these spectral images created as a result of illumination by a particular wavelength and the resultant creation of an image cube. The cube contains spectral data which can be calibrated and processed. The calibrated and processed image cubes can then be transformed into images with the goal of enhancing the visibility of features that may be otherwise imperceptible. These images combine spectral bands from the image cube and processing results with the goal of improving the visibility and legibility of features such as erased or faded text (Easton et al. 2016, 2018). In these images (called "pseudocolor" and defined fully below), areas of similar material properties will appear in a similar rendered color, although this color is not related to the visual color of the material. This visualization technique has long been used to leverage the human visual system's ability to differentiate differences in color to enhance subtle material differences such as erased text on parchment.

Thus, as a method, MSI provides two opportunities for engagement with interactive media for cultural heritage. First, by handling material collections directly as part of the staging for image capture, the media (artifact) is itself interactive. For it is through our direct, unmediated engagement with material collections that researchers, practitioners, and the public can come to know more about artifacts, and as a result, understand them more fully. Once transformed into a digital surrogate (or several surrogates), the artifact's digital surrogates become the basis for interactive media through image processing which facilitates ways to better represent, interpret, characterize, uncover and, ultimately, gain access to collections. Both phases of MSI serve as opportunities for media interactivity: the creation of digital surrogates and their transformation through processing techniques made available through MISHA.

Whereas the first form of interactivity is not the focus of this chapter—because it is driven by the lived experience and direct encounters with tangible cultural heritage—the second form of interactivity through image processing and visualization is emphasized here. The following section outlines processing methods and is followed by four case studies that offer examples to examine how image processing and visualization techniques can enhance our understanding and provide further access to collections. Figures 13.1 and 13.2 show the layout diagrams of the RIT MIHSA Image Capture Software and the RIT Spectral Analysis App. The two phases, capture and processing, will be introduced below with more emphasis placed on the image processing and visualization stages.

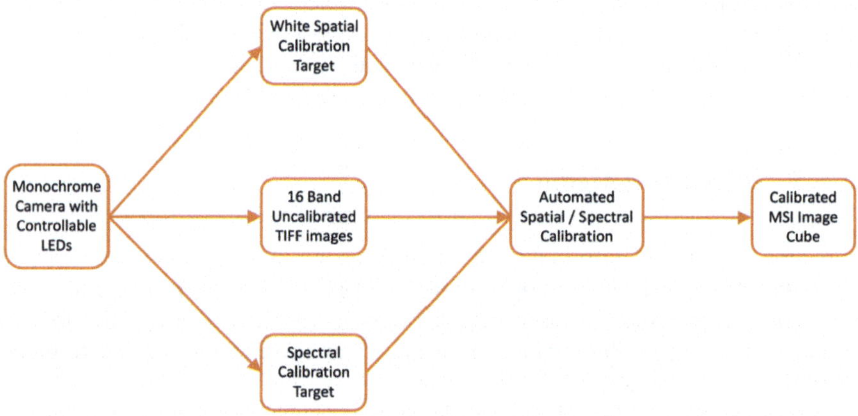

Fig. 13.1 Image capture workflow with MISHA. Camera and LED hardware collect images of the artifact, a uniform white calibration target, and a spectral calibration target to automatically produce spatially flattened, spectrally calibrated images saved in a binary image cube format

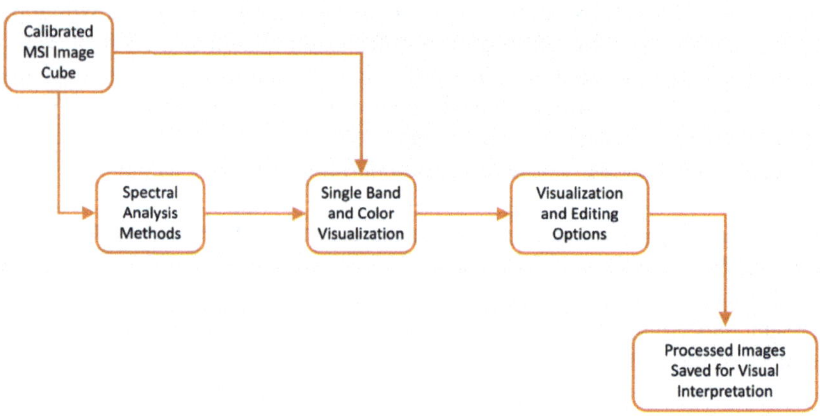

Fig. 13.2 RIT spectral analysis software allows for both visualization of data and the results from various processing algorithms

13.2 Multispectral Image Capture

The MISHA hardware and capture software are intended to provide a simple, step by step guide through image collection, calibration, and creation of the image cube. We achieve multispectral imaging through use of a monochrome camera and colored illumination in a dark environment. The camera is sensitive across the visible spectrum and into the near infrared, from about 400 to 1000 nm. In the absence of external illumination, we use selectively colored LEDs to illuminate in narrow spectral bands. We collect images that represent both the reflection of the light by the artifact, as well as fluorescence stimulated by that artifact when illuminated by light in the ultraviolet (UV). By imaging during illumination by only one LED, we record an image of the signal that is either reflected from the surface at that wavelength, or a fluorescence signal stimulated by the ultraviolet LEDs. By sequentially illuminating with the 16 LEDs, and capturing 16 distinct images during the process, we acquire 16 individual TIFF files. In addition to these, we collect "flat field" images to remove non-uniformities in the illumination field. If required, we also collect "dark images" to remove sensor noise. Additionally, we place a small calibration target in each scene to remove the effects of varying illumination levels and convert the final images to estimated reflectance, as a function of wavelength, of the object.

The 16 individual images are flat fielded, calibrated, and then combined into a single binary file called a "data cube". This data structure contains all of the spectral and spatial information and is convenient for spectral image processing. However, one must note that the final image can be quite large. The process of collecting, calibrating, and building the final image cube are shown in Figs. 13.1 and 13.2.

13.3 Image Processing (RIT Spectral Analysis App)

After image capture, the image cube can be run through various image analysis techniques such as Principal Component Analysis (PCA), Minimum Noise Fraction (MNF), and Spectral Angle Mapping (SAM). While there are many commercially available software products for MSI processing, for the MISHA project, we created a spectral analysis software program to process the images. As noted elsewhere, the RIT Spectral Analysis App may be used with multispectral imagery collected with our system or others. For instance, our application can process imagery collected with the MEGAVISION EV multispectral imaging system (Megavision 2022). The aforementioned software is free and open-source, and users can incorporate their own desired tools and processing techniques as the code base is Python, PyQT5 with a GUI toolkit, NumPy, and a Python library. However, again, the target audience is non-scientist users and those who may have little-to-no coding experience.

13.3.1 Spectral Image Processing

The primary method suggested for image processing is Principal Component Analysis (PCA). PCA is commonly used in data science to reduce variables in large, high dimensional data sets, to a reduced dimensionality while maintaining the wealth of information in the large set. PCA is a statistical processing technique that seeks a new representation of the data where it is maximally uncorrelated. In spectral image processing, PCA is used to identify materials of similar properties that reflect light in similar ways and groups them together in order to create contrast from the other materials in the image. Minimum Noise Fraction (MNF) is a similar approach that seeks to maximize the signal to noise ratio in the data. While text can be recovered through the aforementioned statistical processing, if the text is damaged beyond recognition the standard processes such as PCA and MNF may not be sufficient enough to visualize the undertext. In such cases, multiple rounds of image processing may need to occur. Both PCA and MNF produce a new image with the same number of channels as the original spectral image. These new bands can be visualized as described below.

Spectral Angle Mapping is a spectral similarity approach to identify materials of similar properties. Given a portion of the image that contains a known material of interest, e.g., a low-contrast but visible section of erased text, the spectral signature (i.e., its brightness as a function of wavelength) can be used as a "target" signature. Every other pixel can then be compared to that target producing a measure of similarity between each pixel and the target. This similarity measure is called the spectral angle. By representing the pixels in a mathematical space where each axis represents the brightness of a given pixel in that color, each pixel can be thought of as a point in that high-dimensional space. Treating each point as a vector from the origin to the pixel value, similar pixels will have small angles between these vectors. Thus, spectral angle mapping produces a grayscale image where in each pixel, the value represents how similar that pixel is to the chosen target.

Visualization of both the spectral bands in the original cube, as well as the processed results, is a highly interactive process with the aim of enhancing the contrast of features of interest. Images can be created that are either grayscale or color. Color images can be representations of the "true color" of the object, or pseudocolor (sometimes called "false color") images. In the former, the digital representation is meant to "look like" the visual artifact. In the latter, we render other bands, either in the original or processed images, into the red, green, and blue display channels to produce visualizations enhancing features not visible to the naked eye. For example, we can create a pseudocolor visualization of the first, second, and third PCA bands, the fifth, first, and second PCA bands, or any other combination.

This is particularly useful for inks, for which it is known that several different types of ink that are visually similar have strong reflectance differences in the infrared. For example, iron gall and carbon black inks have differences across the spectral range we consider here. It is sometimes possible to differentiate between them by creating a visualization that includes the infrared bands in a pseudocolor rendering.

In addition to pseudocolor visualizations, we provide options in the software to change the display characteristics of the rendered images. Users can "stretch" the image to change the relative brightness of pixels on the screen, modify the color palate used in the rendering, set a brightness threshold to produce a binary output, or invert a grayscale image, turning dark content to white, and vice versa.

With the goal of ease-of-use on the part of the end user, the processing software, in particular, strives to enable greater exploration and opportunities for interactivity and resulting media that lay as the basis for further access and discoverability. For example, the captured images rendered into a PCA cube are processed through a series of actions deliberately taken by the user and evaluated by the user to determine where to look for areas of interest. The bands can be selected and "shuffled" to identify meaningful visualizations.

13.4 MISHA Use Cases

The authors have partnered with a number of institutions and individuals since 2021 to deliver a set of use cases that validate MISHA's use on a variety of substrates and artifact forms (see Tables 13.2 and 13.3). Inexpensive and small, the system has imaged more than 300 items of varying media types—from parchment, vellum, and other format manuscripts to autograph letters, thermal fax papers, and other sheet, leaf, folio, and book materials—deposited in archival collections in the US and Europe. The system enables enhancement of sub-visual text to enable clarity of content, such as reading erased or palimpsested texts; enhancing text or imagery on damaged materials; fostering codicological studies through pigment differentiation; and providing insight into the creation and potential modification process of artifacts.

In addition, our software has processed data imaged by the system, as well as other multispectral data created by other systems, thereby bringing the image count to approximately 500 image samples either collected, processed, or both.

By democratizing the technology and its processing software, the authors are providing opportunities for scholars and practitioners to enhance understanding of material collections and to provide further access to cultural heritage artifacts that can, in turn, foster opportunities for discoverability, expanded access, and preventive collections care. This chapter now turns to several examples of MISHA's image processing and visualization techniques as means of enhancing our understanding of the artifacts themselves. To demonstrate these capabilities and access, the authors have imaged and processed a variety of materials from their own institution (Rochester Institute of Technology, hereafter RIT) and universities in the United States. They have taken the system or lent it to collaborators at institutions in the United States to test the ease of use and to demonstrate the capacities of MSI for cultural heritage documentation, interpretation, and contextualization. See Table 13.2 for a complete list of collections and Table 13.3 for the list of example materials imaged. Both Tables are frequently updated, as we continue to deploy the system and build additional systems to share among the academic and professional communities.

Table 13.2 Cultural heritage artifacts from the following collections have been imaged with MISHA, as of February 2024

university-held collections:
Arizona State University from NASA/Psyche Mission
Cary Graphic Art Collection at RIT
Case Western Reserve University, OH
Cleveland Institute of Art, OH
Colorado College
Dyer Arts Center at RIT
Harry Ransom Center, UT-Austin, TX
Haverford College, PA
Image Permanence Institute (IPI) at RIT
National Technical Institute for the Deaf, RIT
Oberlin College, OH
Ohio State University, OH
Ohio University, OH
Princeton University, NJ
SUNY, Binghamton, NY
Syracuse University, Syracuse, NY
University of Cincinnati, OH
University of Colorado, Colorado Springs, CO
University of Rochester, Rochester, NY
Vignelli Center for Design Studies (VCDS) at RIT
Washington University in St. Louis
Private collections (multiple)
other archives, libraries, and museum-held collections:
Archivio Capitolare, Vercelli, Italy
Cleveland Public Library, OH
Corning Museum of Glass, Corning, NY
Genesee Country Village & Museum, Mumford, NY
George Eastman Museum
History Colorado
Public Library of Cincinnati and Hamilton County, OH
Rochester & Monroe County Public Library
Rochester Museum and Science Center
St. John's Episcopal Church, Fort Washington, MD
State Archive of Croatia, Dubrovnik, Croatia
Strong, the National Museum of Play, Rochester, NY

Elsewhere, the authors have provided an overview of the image capture and processing software that offer a basis for demonstrating the possibilities for low-cost, low barrier-to-entry software on cultural heritage imaging, research, preservation, and dissemination (Falotico et al. 2023) As noted, the software and system can increase the accessibility of multispectral imaging systems and software so that researchers, scholars, and staff of small-to-medium-sized institutions can have access

Table 13.3 MISHA has imaged a range of sheet, leaf, autograph letter, and folio collection items in these mediums, as well as some 3-D items, Summer 2021 through present

Ink on papyrus: Book of the Dead

Ink on parchment: c. 800-1400 French parchment; 12th-century binder's waster; Ege, c. 1400 ink on parchment with gold leaf through 16th-century as well as palimpsests/reused parchment:

Ink on vellum:

12th-century vellum with Latin text

13th-century Vercelli Mappamundi

Ink on paper:

16th-century print of Wittenberg, Germany;

17th-century autograph document;

18th-century scroll Book of Esther;

c. 18th-century illustrated book (of 10th century Shahnameh);

18th-century printed book;

19th-century diary from Ellis Island

19th-century hand-color lithographic print of Rochester, NY;

19th-century autograph diaries and maps;

pastedowns on plat maps (early 20th century);

20th-century Vogue magazine graphic blandishment (multiple media, including ink, pencil, paint)

Pencil on paper: including 19th-century autograph letters; 20th-century Hayden Furniture Co. drawings with watercolor/paint treatment

3-D Objects: meteorite; Greek and Roman coins; 19th-century medicine bottle; small, 35mm film canisters c. 1895; 20th-century fine art glass damaged in flood; mid-20th-century baseball

Digital source on paper: thermal fax paper; IPI digital print substrates

Other material: c. 17th century palm leaf; 19th-century oil painting; 19th-20th-century photographic prints

to the tools they need to uncover distinct features in cultural heritage objects to better know, understand, contextualize, and share their collections. As noted in Tables 13.2 and 13.3, these use cases have validated that MISHA can be used on a variety of substrates, from medieval manuscripts, Renaissance artwork, and autograph letters from the nineteenth century to thermal papers of the 1980s and contemporary glass. Below, four case studies demonstrate these capacities.

As noted above, the use cases below serve only as examples of both the types of materials/artifacts for which imaging with MISHA has provided important discoveries, as well as demonstrating the ease of use of the system across a variety of objects and users. Results from these imaging sessions are continually being studied by scholars with the relevant interest and expertise. The multispectral imaging system described here serves as a tool to enable these, and other, historical investigations.

13.4.1 20th-Century Thermal Fax Paper

During the summer 2022, the authors imaged several items from the Washington University in St. Louis libraries (WUSTL). Objects ranged from manuscripts with faded/damaged text, books with paste-downs, and intriguingly, thermal fax paper that had virtually completely faded. This form of communication is known to fade after a relatively short period of time, and WUSTL has an extensive collection which is largely un-readable. Example sheets were imaged with MISHA and with minimal imaging processing, significant text was recovered.

Upon learning of this potential with thermal fax paper, the authors sought out samples from collections on the RIT campus. The authors visited the Vignelli Center for Design Studies, a modern design collection at RIT comprising 750,000 items. To build upon our learnings from the imaging and processing of the aforementioned fax sheets, we sought several comparable artifacts of around the same time period. Five sheets of thermal paper dating from 1987 to 1996 were imaged and processed. The results were startling, such that with minimal processing, the previously visible text and notations were clear. For this collection, in particular, the recovery is immensely helpful because much of the notation is not text, but rather hand drawings by Lella and Massimo Vignelli, as demonstrated in Fig. 13.3, *Floor Plan Sketches Windber Coal Heritage Center* (c. 1995). Learning of the capabilities of the system with minimal processing required opened up the potential for MISHA to recover lost text *and* drawings, thereby recovering incremental evidence of artistic practice.

At the same time, a second MISHA system was on loan to the Harry Ransom Center (HRC) at the University of Texas, Austin. During the authors' after-briefing with staff from the HRC, we learned that they too had independently discovered this unintended application of the MISHA system. They had successfully retrieved text from faded thermal fax paper in their collection as well. These independent discoveries of this capability have opened extensive doors for use of the MISHA system, or systems like it. This low cost, easy to use technology can now be deployed extensively to recover previously lost information contained in this, at the time, common method of communication.

13.4.2 *15th-Century Parchment,* Horae Beatae Mariae Virginis*: Fragment*

This manuscript leaf is one of several in the Cary Collection at RIT that illustrates the art of the manuscript during the period of its greatest development and influence. These items reflect the work of European scriptoria by Benedictine, Franciscan, Carthusian, Dominican, and other orders of monks.

Although created in the fifteenth century, this leaf took on a new context in the twentieth century when it was bound into a volume of manuscript leaves by Otto F. Ege (1888–1951), Dean of the Cleveland Institute of Art and Lecturer on the

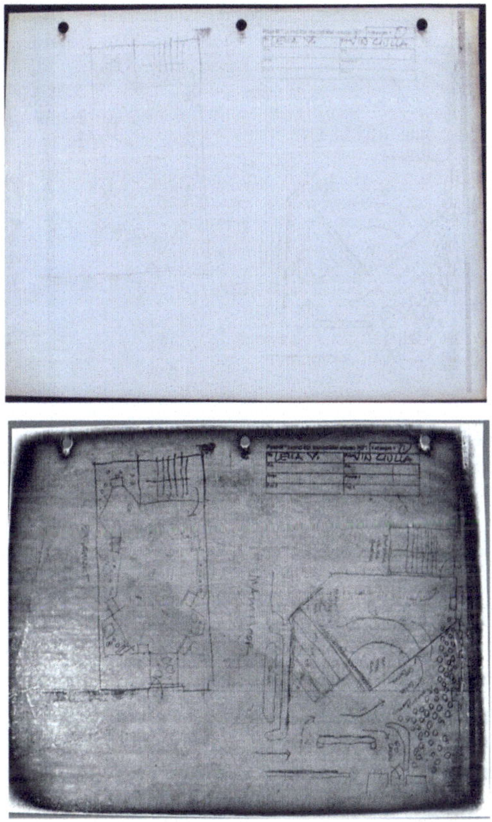

Fig. 13.3 Windber Coal Heritage Center exhibition layout sketch facsimile page from Vincent Ciulla to Lella Vignelli, Massimo and Lella Vignelli papers, Courtesy Vignelli Center for Design Studies, RIT

History of the Book at the School of Library Science, Western Reserve University (now Case Western Reserve University). His assemblages of gathered leaves were distributed under the title *Fifty original leaves from medieval manuscripts, Western Europe, XII-XVI century, collected by Otto F. Ege.* Each volume represents a series of unique groupings of illuminated manuscript leaves derived from more than 50 source volumes. The dismembering of entire volumes and their "mixing up" into new collections arranged by Ege brought medieval art into the hands of patrons of libraries and students and faculty of public libraries and universities in the United States, which had scare access to such materials at the time. Ege's practices, which are considered butchery today, offered many the opportunity to study and have tangible experiences with authentic medieval manuscripts. Modestly funded and smaller institutions were able to acquire and provide access to manuscripts in ways that they could not otherwise.

This particular item was held in RIT's Cary Collection for multiple decades before it was imaged in 2020 when it was found to be palimpsested. By imaging this object, knowledge about the leaf was enhanced, beyond what was in the catalog and "known." (Kleynhans et al. 2021; LaLena 2021).

Fig. 13.4 *Horae Beatae Mariae Virginis*: fragment, "Ege 30" Courtesy RIT Libraries, Cary Graphic Arts Collection Portfolio Box 2–30. Left is RGB; Right is UV, grayscale

Such an artifact offers an opportunity to demonstrate the type of materials where multispectral imaging is highly successful and widely available as a use case. On the left in Fig. 13.4 is an RGB true color image, on the right is UV fluorescence image collected with MISHA and visualized to heighten and contrast the image's appearance. The image on the right shows text that is revealed when images are manipulated to disclose text beneath the illuminations applied around 1450. As palimpsested images are encountered, it is possible to begin to illuminate the history of each leaf in ways that have not been possible, without the new knowledge that can be revealed through MSI. Such new information has the capacity to change the interpretation of items. Conceptually, technical methods such as MSI and appropriate research and further understanding of these materials can serve as a starting point for conversations around agency and authority by de-centering Ege and his role as connoisseur and curator in order to draw attention to the manuscripts and their rich, unique histories.

13.4.3 14th-Century Parchment, Statuta Antiqua et Nova Ordinis Cartusiensis

A late fourteenth century manuscript that has had the cover removed *Statuta antiqua et nova ordinis Cartusiensis* (RIT Cary Collection) requires more processing due to the higher degree of loss perceived. In particular, the back page is heavily damaged with significant portions of the text worn off. Additionally, annotations are visible in the side and bottom margins of many of the leaves with varying levels of contrast. On the right of Fig. 13.5 is the result of processing the multispectral image collected with MISHA through the Spectral Analysis App using Principal Component Analysis and producing a false color representation of the result. In this case, the statistics of only a damaged portion of the manuscript were collected to develop the PCA

Fig. 13.5 Back cover of the *Statuta antiqua et nova ordinis Cartusiensis*, imaged with MISHA and processed with the RIT Spectral Analysis App. Note the improved contrast of the text in the upper left and lower right corners, as well as in the bottom margin. Courtesy RIT Cary Collection

transformation, which was then applied to the entire image. This method has been shown to be of great utility in cases where a significant portion of the image is undamaged which will dominate any statistical measures. Of particular interest is the dramatically increased contrast of worn away text in the upper left, lower left, and lower right corners. Additionally, the annotations in the bottom margin have been greatly enhanced after processing, yielding opportunities to read the Latin text. In this case, an observer has the chance to digitally go back and forth between the damaged leaf and the recovered text, piecing together the text and learning about both the contents and context of the manuscript page.

13.4.4 18th-Century Scroll, Book of Esther

A different type of artifact that shows the utility of the MISHA system is the Esther Scroll, also contained in the Cary Collection at RIT. When the item entered the collection, the documentation was sparse. The provenance is unknown, beyond being transferred to the Cary from the New York Times Museum of the Recorded Word. As such, the catalogue record inherited the information that accompanied the donation, indicating that it was an 8th-century scroll depicting the story of Esther, the 5th-century BCE Jewish heroine, Queen Esther, and her cousin Mordecai, who devised a plan to rescue the Jewish people from Persia. The scroll celebrates the days of feasting and joy that are commemorated as part of the festival of Purim.

In appearance, the spindle upon which the scroll is housed seemed fairly un-aged though the leading approximately 6 inches of the scroll are heavily damaged through extensive use. Even though the text itself came from a textual source that is otherwise known, this artifact still provided an excellent use case for MSI and was imaged to see if any of the worn decoration could be discerned. The first results were encouraging enough that the artifact was re-imaged and analyzed in greater detail in the early summer 2022. Original results from this re-processing are presented in Arnold et al. (2022) which detail how MSI was able to extract key details on the damaged portion of the scroll, in particular an illustration in the first panel.

As part of an ongoing project, the processed images were provided to Hebrew text scholars for analysis in the summer and fall of 2022. After extensive discussion and investigation it was determined that the scroll was actually an eighteenth-century artifact, meant to look more than a thousand years older than it was. This information was then conveyed to the collection curator and collections staff to include this contextual information as part of the catalogue record, and also to correct the item's date of creation. We note that the date of the scroll was incorrectly identified in Arnold et al. (2022), though that date was based on our knowledge of the artifact at the time of that publication.

While not a false reproduction, per se, the scroll was meant to visually represent another time. In this case, the MSI was able to reveal features on the artifact not otherwise visible. These images and features allowed scholars to better understand the object and changed our understanding of the artifact itself. This new interpretation was provided to curatorial staff of the collection. While the catalogue record has already been updated to reflect a new date of around 1750 (rather than the eighth century), ongoing research may lead to further insight about this object and can better inform future scholars studying this particular artifact.

13.5 Conclusion and Further Implications

Multispectral imaging offers opportunities for curators, collections professionals, scholars and researchers to understand their collections more fully as a result of capturing and processing images of collections as a means of visualizing both the raw data as well as the results of image processing. These results enable these users opportunities to understand their collections better, produce novel visualizations of the digital imagery, and enhance the digital representations of their collections.

Here, we have presented a unique multispectral imaging system for use in cultural heritage studies that is low-cost, easy to use, and highly portable. This will allow for further democratization of the technology, providing access the multispectral imaging for scholars, practitioners, and institutions who otherwise would not have it. However, there are trade offs in designing and building such as system. In particular,

MISHA does not have the high spatial resolution or large field of view of state-of-the-art commercially available systems. Nor does it provide options for transmissive imaging or a larger number of spectral bands. Given the wide application and use of MISHA, these trade-offs are in general acceptable to a significant number of practitioners.

Our interest lies, also, in communicating these findings with the public in engaging, interactive methods. For this, we have taken cues from a GIS (geographic information systems) and online storytelling platform: ArcGIS. ArcGIS is a storytelling platform that offers digital content in an engaging, interactive manner. The images in the online exhibition clearly communicate the relationship between artifacts as they appear to the naked eye and how they can be transformed after imaging, processing, and visualization (https://arcg.is/1fy5Df; https://arcg.is/1P9n5S). In particular, the slider tool in ESRI's "StoryMaps" is used to compare and contrast two visualizations. The slider tool can enable the viewer to toggle back and forth between an RGB image and the pseudocolor image which shows hidden text that is not visible in the RGB image.

As described above, multispectral imaging in the context of cultural heritage facilitates interactivity in multiple ways. During the image capture phase, users of the system, and scholars interested in the artifact, interact with the object, camera system, and environment to ensure imagery is collected in a manner that will enable future processing of the data. Secondly, during the processing phase, users of our Spectral Analysis App interact directly with the captured images, working with data that reveals features not able to be seen by the naked eye. Image processing further enhances this experience, modifying, transforming, and enhancing the data to further extract information about the artifact content and context. Finally, visualization of the data, both as collected and after processing, allows users to leverage the human visualization system to produce images for human consumption, both in color and grayscale, at the original resolution or zoomed in, and in both true color and pseudocolor. These final visualization products aim to improve our understanding of the artifacts being studied. This end-to-end system is designed to be low cost, easy to use, and portable, bringing Multispectral Imaging technology to as many practitioners as possible.

Future work in this area largely lies in the dissemination of the plans for creation of the MISHA system, as well as the distribution of the open source image capture and image processing software. To facilitate this, our focus will be on training and educational materials to bring multispectral imaging to as many practitioners as possible, further broadening the impact multispectral imaging can have on an ever-growing number of artifacts and collections.

Acknowledgements Authors Messinger and Decker received a grant from the National Endowment for the Humanities (PR-268783-20) to fund the development of a low-cost, portable imaging system with processing software known as MISHA (Multispectral Imaging System for Historical Artifacts) which is described here: https://securegrants.neh.gov/publicquery/main.aspx?f=1&gn=PR-268783-20. A second grant focusing on education and training was awarded in 2024, https://apps.neh.gov/publicquery/AwardDetail.aspx?gn=PE-303737-25. Access to the open-access parts list, software for capture and processing, and educational tools is available on our website: https://www.rit.edu/chipr/misha. All authors would like to acknowledge Tania Kleynhans, who wrote the initial capture software in MatLab, the 2022–23 software engineering team: Cecelia Ahrens, Mallory Bridge, Eric Gao, Troy Potter, Rob Maron, and Larry Kiser; and the 2023–24 graduate computer science co-op Keshav Sasanapuri. They would also like to acknowledge curators; library, archive, and museum professionals; conservators; scholars in a variety of humanities fields and others who given us access to their collections materials. Among these are Steven Galbraith, Curator of the Cary Graphic Arts Collection, RIT; Jennifer Whitlock, Archivist, Vignelli Center for Design Studies, RIT; and Donna Fae Dadson, great-granddaughter to Theron Loomis and custodian of the Loomis letters.

References

Arnold E, Moyer A Bourgeois P, Decker MJ, Easton R Jr, Messinger D (2022) "Multispectral imaging for historical artifacts: a case study using an 8th-century Biblical scroll." *GCH 2022—Eurographics workshop on graphics and cultural heritage*, proceedings 2022. https://diglib.eg.org/handle/10.2312/gch20221231

Benton JF (1978) "Nouvelles Recherches sur le Déchiffrement des Textes Effacés, Grattés ou Lavés, communication du 2 Juin 1978". *Comptes rendus des séances de l'Académie des Inscriptions et Belles-Lettres*, 122e année, N. 3, 1978:580–595

Davies H (2020) "Multispectral imaging of the vercelli mappamundi: a progress report." *Imago Mundi* 72(2):181–191. https://doi.org/10.1080/03085694.2020.1748378

Dold A (1917) Prophetentexte in Vulgata: Übersetzung nach der ältesten Handschriften-Überlieferung der St. Galler Palimpsete no. 193 and no. 567. Beuron: Kunstschule der Erzabtei

Dold A (1928) Lateinische Fragmente der Sapientialbücher aus dem Münchener palimpsest CLM 19105. Beuron: Verlag der Kunstschule der Erzabtei

Easton RL, Noel W (2010) "Infinite possibilities, ten years of study of the Archimedes palimpsest." *Proc Am Philos Soc* 54:50–76

Easton, Jr RL, Knox KT, Christens-Barry WA, Boydston K, et al (2010) "Standardized system for multispectral imaging of palimpsests." https://doi.org/10.1117/12.839116. Accessed 5 May 2023

Easton Jr RL, Knox KT, Christens-Barry WA, Boydston K (2019) "Spectral imaging methods applied to the Syriac Galen palimpsest." *Manuscript Stud* 3(1):7–20, Article 4. https://repository.upenn.edu/mss_sims/vol3/iss1/4

Falotico J, Schultz K, Arnold E, Moyer I, Amiri MM, Decker J, Messinger D, Easton Jr R (2023) "Build, select, reshuffle: uncovering distinct features of cultural heritage objects with multispectral imaging." *IS&T archiving conference proceedings*, June 2023, Oslo. https://doi.org/10.2352/issn.2168-3204.2023.20.1.38

Fischer C, Kakoulli I (2006) "Multispectral and hyperspectral imaging technologies in conservation: current research and potential applications." *Stud Conserv* 51(sup1):3–16. https://doi.org/10.1179/sic.2006.51.Supplement-1.3

Frühmann B, Cappa F, Vetter W, Schreiner M, Petrus F (2018) "Multianalytical approach for the analysis of the codices Millenarius Maior and Millenarius Minor in Kremsmuenster Abbey, Upper Austria." *Heritage Sci* 6(1):1. https://doi.org/10.1186/s40494-018-0176-3

Giocametti A, Campagnolo A, MacDonald L, Mahony S, Robson S, Weyrich T, Terras M, Gibson A (2017) "The value of critical destruction: evaluating multispectral image processing methods for the analysis of primary historical texts." *Digital Scholarship in the Humanities*, vol 32, no. 1, 2017

Gradenwitz O (1900) Einführung in die Papyruskunde. S. Hirzel, Leipzig. https://archive.org/details/einfhrungindiep00gradgoog/

Jerome S, Manser A (1913) Codex sangallensis 193: Continens Fragmenta Plurium Prophetarum Secundum. Beuronae: Lipsiae Prostat Apvd O. Harrassowitz. https://archive.org/details/codexsangallensi0000unse/

Jones C, Duffy C, Gibson A, Terras M (2020) "Understanding multispectral imaging of cultural heritage: determining best practice in MSI analysis of historical artefacts." *J Cult Herit* 45:339–350. https://doi.org/10.1016/j.culher.2020.03.004

Kleynhans T, Carr ML, Messinger DW (2021) "Low-cost, user friendly multispectral imaging system for the recovery of damaged, faded or palimpsested historical documents." *Proceedings of SPIE 11727 algorithms, technologies, and applications for multispectral and hyperspectral imaging XXVII,* 117270F. https://doi.org/10.1117/12.2585629

Kögel PR (1920) Enzyklopädie der Photographie, Heft 96, Die Palimpsestphotographie (Photographie der radierten Schriften)

LaLena Z (2021) "Imaging Palimpsests in the Otto F. Ege Collection" Presented at international congress on medieval studies

Lanigan D, Hirshberg C (2001) "The hidden hand of Philodemus." *Popular Sci* 259(6):22

McGillivray M, Duffy C (2017) "New light on the *Sir Gawain and the Green Knight* manuscript: multispectral imaging and the Cotton Nero A.x. illustrations." *Speculum* 92/S1. https://doi.org/10.1086/693361

Megavision (2022) https://mega-vision.com/products/#

National Endowment for the Humanities (2020) https://securegrants.neh.gov/publicquery/main.aspx?f=1&gn=PR-268783-20

Samaran C (1925) "Application des rayons ultra-violet au déchiffrement des passages grattés ou effacés dans les manuscrits" Comptes rendus des séances de l'Académie des Inscriptions et Belles-Lettres, 69e année, N. 5:348–355. https://www.persee.fr/doc/crai_0065-0536_1925_num_69_5_75203

Talbot WHF (1844-1846) The pencil of nature. https://www.metmuseum.org/art/collection/search/267022

Zawacki AJ et al (2023) Fragments under the lens: a case study of multispectral versus hyperspectral imaging for manuscript recovery. *Digit Philo J Medieval Cult* 12(1):123–143. https://muse.jhu.edu/issue/49139

Part III
Interactive and Immersive Experiences for Storytelling in Cultural Heritage

Chapter 14
Gameplay Elements in Digital Cultural Heritage Applications

Selma Rizvic, Bojan Mijatovic, Ivona Ivkovic-Kihic, and Dusanka Boskovic

Abstract Interactive media offer outstanding possibilities for the presentation and preservation of tangible and intangible cultural heritage. The users are transferred to the past where they can experience historical events, see original appearances of cultural monuments, and learn about customs, skills, and traditions of people long gone and forgotten. Digital cultural heritage applications aim to introduce them to historical topics in an educational and entertaining way and create a so-called "edutainment" factor. This is easiest achieved through gameplay elements. In this chapter, we will show how to obtain a high level of immersion and edutainment through the combination of interactive digital storytelling and gameplays in selected VR applications for cultural heritage. We will explain how this methodology helps in overcoming the narrative paradox problem. We consider gamification a great tool to improve learning and user experience in any topic, not just cultural heritage, and recommend the application of the presented methods to other education fields.

S. Rizvic (✉) · I. Ivkovic-Kihic · D. Boskovic
Faculty of Electrical Engineering, University of Sarajevo, Sarajevo, Bosnia and Herzegovina
e-mail: srizvic@etf.unsa.ba

I. Ivkovic-Kihic
e-mail: iivkovic2@etf.unsa.ba

D. Boskovic
e-mail: dboskovic@etf.unsa.ba

B. Mijatovic
Sarajevo School of Science and Technology, Sarajevo, Bosnia and Herzegovina
e-mail: bojan.mijatovic@ssst.edu.ba

I. Ivkovic-Kihic
Graz University of Technology, Graz, Austria

F. Liarokapis et al. (eds.), *Interactive Media for Cultural Heritage*, Springer Series on Cultural Computing, https://doi.org/10.1007/978-3-031-61018-9_14

14.1 Introduction

The shift in media from newspapers, radio, and television, to the Internet opened the possibility of interacting with media content. Due to this transformation, digital technologies found their place in the presentation and preservation of cultural heritage. Not only that cultural monuments and sites, as well as museums, benefited from digital content that shows the original appearances of historical buildings and artifacts, but now the viewers can experience life in the past using Virtual and Augmented Reality.

The way of communicating information has also been changed. Storytelling became digital, trying to catch the attention of Internet users, bombarded every day with so much content, that their attention span became very short. They are expecting content available on demand and presented in the form of short audiovisual snippets. Interactive Digital Storytelling (IDS) (Miller 2019) offers a new way of approaching users, enabling them to control the flow of the story.

However, moving the information into an interactive form created another problem called "the narrative paradox". It is the conflict between the interactor's freedom of choice (or agency) and the author's control over the story world (Smed et al. 2019). In digital heritage applications, historical information is presented in the form of short stories. As those stories are implemented to be watched on demand, some of them may never be selected. In our storytelling methodology called hyper-storytelling, we introduced a motivation factor for users to watch all stories (Rizvic et al. 2017a, b). It could be a quiz containing information presented in storytelling and, if users reply correctly, they would be offered additional attractive activities (sailing the ancient boat, exploring historical monuments, interacting with museum exhibits).

Another way of conveying information in the digital storytelling world is "gamification", defined as "using game design elements in non-gaming contexts" (Deterding et al. 2011). Gamification has shown to be very successful in all kinds of learning (Stieglitz et al. 2017) and we applied it in learning about cultural heritage. In this chapter, we will describe how IDS can be combined with gameplays to create immersive and educational cultural heritage experiences. More information about the methodology can be found in (Rizvic et al. 2023a, b, September) and (Rizvic et al. 2023a, b, October).

In the Related Work Section, we discuss the state-of-the-art and similar projects with their advantages and drawbacks. Through the Case studies Section, we will show various combinations of IDS and gameplays in Virtual Reality (VR) applications. In the Battle on Neretva VR, users become participants in a famous WWII battle in Jablanica, Bosnia and Herzegovina. They are tasked to destroy a bridge, fight against enemy airplanes, and save wounded comrades. Trebinje Fortresses VR takes the users on virtual travel through Austro-Hungarian fortresses, where they become carrier pigeons and explorers of underground spaces. In Battle on Kozara VR, they follow stories told by trees in Kozara mountain, which witnessed a famous WWII battle, and learn how partisans succeeded in surviving the siege of numerous enemies and broke out while saving civilians.

The success of the presented methodologies has been confirmed through the User experience evaluation studies we present in the User Satisfaction Section. Finally, we offer our conclusions and lessons learned to be potentially applied to future similar applications.

14.2 Related Work

War has played a significant role throughout human history, shaping civilizations, cultures, and societies in profound ways. Unfortunately, the passage of time, natural decay, and the impact of war itself often lead to the loss or damage of crucial artifacts and documents that make up our war heritage. Recently, digitization has emerged as a vital tool in protecting and preserving this war heritage, but also cultural heritage (CH) in general, allowing us to document, protect, and disseminate these invaluable resources for present and future generations.

As an increasingly critical aspect of cultural heritage, digitization serves not only as a tool for preservation but also as a means to disseminate knowledge. As the author (Bekele et al. 2018) assert, "Digitization enables the spread of knowledge, and the use of innovative immersive reality tools could further facilitate the access to CH in a more appealing and innovative way."

This holds across all facets of cultural heritage, and as pointed out by (Ch'ng et al. 2005), " Efforts by the community of virtual heritage researchers to reconstruct sites considered worthy of preservation span through the whole history. These digital reconstructions have, to date, contributed significant awareness and interest among the general public, providing educational benefits to concerned parties and new research opportunities to archaeologists and conservationists."

The digitization of war heritage itself, on the other hand, comes with its own set of challenges and ethical considerations. The digitization process calls for careful handling of delicate artifacts, and appropriate standards and protocols must be adhered to for accurate representation and preservation. Digitization workflows need to be established, and many authors are focusing on these subjects (Bogdanova et al. 2013; Heuberger et al. 2015). These sites endure not just the passage of time but also vandalism, as one author highlights: "There is no doubt that the built cultural heritage, as a shared history and culture, remains in danger because of the natural and human risks to which it is exposed on a daily basis. The problems of management and strategies for its conservation, in particular, are still critical. Cultural heritage is, therefore, not without challenges" (Mechiche and Zeghlache 2020). Examples of this can be found globally (Fadli and AlSaeed 2019; López-Menchero Bendicho et al. 2020).

This delicate process is being approached by many researchers, and among them, the war heritage is the most sensitive. The scars left by wars are increasingly becoming important cultural heritage, as a group of authors suggests: "In the last twenty years, restoration/recovery/enhancement projects focused more on the permanent fortifications, leaving in the background the interest in the "care" of minor vestiges such as trenches, walkways, defensive posts, craters due to bombings, underground shelters." (Aldrighettoni and D'Urso 2022). Additionally, many disputed territories lack laws regulating cultural heritage (Hisari and Fouseki 2020), and the reconstruction of cultural heritage post-war can be a challenging task (Legnér 2018), underscoring the potential of digitization. Yet, it is not just the preservation of cultural heritage that is significant, but also its tourism potential.

Waagen et al. (2023) emphasize that Virtual and Augmented reality technologies are considered to be memory-stimulating environments and therefore suitable for presenting complicated and contrasting views on conflicted heritage. In Hornoiu et al. (2023) it is stated that Virtual Reality technology has the potential to revolutionize the way people experience and understand the destinations affected by war. In this study, it was concluded that ease of use is one of the important aspects to consider when creating such applications. Authors in Mulders (2023) explored the effects of mediators in the process of learning in Virtual Reality applications for war heritage and concluded that guided/mediated experience leads to a better understanding of the materials. This is an important aspect to consider when creating immersive experiences.

Digital models of fortresses can give tourists a virtual tour of these historical sites, promoting tourism and enhancing visitor engagement. This explains the proliferation of projects centered on fortresses, such as the Lost Bastion of Cáceres Wall (Franco et al. 2020), the Russian Fortress Koporye (Borisov and Smolin 2013), the Famosa fortress in Malaysia (Izani et al. 2010), and Catalhoyuk (Forte 2014). As (Franch et al. 2017) posit: "Tourism based on the valorization of places in which historical heritage is the main attraction is one of the fastest growing segments of cultural tourism." Thus, cultural heritage sites draw many tourists and adventurers. Research in Northern Finland indicates that "The activities of hobbyists using metal detectors can be regarded in some cases as an asset to archaeological research." (Thomas et al. 2016).

Yet, what may be even more appealing to people is the ability to visit sites that no longer exist or that are inaccessible due to dangerous conditions. This is where Virtual Reality technology comes into play. Projects such as (Okanovic et al. 2022) demonstrate immense potential in using extended reality for these purposes. Our projects about Sarajevo survival tools (Rizvic et al. 2012) and Sarajevo War tunnel (Prazina et al. 2020; Rizvic et al. 2019a, b) have shown promising results in user experience evaluation. Users enjoyed listening to the stories and having the opportunity to experience the passage through the war tunnel in a virtual environment. We believe that this innovative approach to reliving historical events through gamification is a critical step in preservation. Numerous other projects also underscore the advantages of digitization in cultural heritage, ranging from digitizing cities (Psomadaki et al. 2019) and leveraging digital technology for reconstruction (Chalmers and Debattista 2005) to developing serious educational games for museums (Djaouti et al. 2009; Germak et al. 2021).

How to approach the creation of projects like this can also be gleaned from (Allal-Chérif 2022; Edler et al. 2019; Walmsley and Kersten 2020). Each of these projects presents both advantages and drawbacks that warrant further examination.

Many of these advantages and drawbacks are shared across different virtual reality applications (Hamad and Jia 2022).

The most important advantages are:

Immersive experience and interactive learning—VR applications offer immersive experiences that can be more engaging than other forms of presentations and offer a better way of learning through interaction.

Preservation and reconstruction of cultural sites—VR technology can be used to reconstruct and visualize cultural heritage that has been lost or damaged over time or help preserve existing ones by creating digital replicas.

Enhanced accessibility—VR allows for more accessibility to people with disabilities by providing virtual access to sites that might be physically challenging to visit.

On the other side, the biggest drawbacks are:

Technology limitations—The quality of the VR experience can be limited by the technology available to users depending on different factors such as geographic, economic, and social factors.

High costs—The development and maintenance of VR applications can be expensive, requiring significant investment in technology, software, and expertise.

Physical discomfort—Some users may experience physical discomfort, such as motion sickness (cybersickness) or eye strain, from using VR headsets, which can limit the duration of their engagement with the content.

Delicate workflow—As mentioned earlier, when it comes to war heritage, special care must be taken to ensure the objective and ethical creation of content. This content can also require parental guidance which must be noted.

In the following section, we aim to demonstrate how our Interactive Digital Storytelling (IDS) method can enhance immersion and educational entertainment in digital heritage applications with gameplays.

14.3 Case Studies

The combination of IDS and gameplays will be showcased through three VR applications. Battle on Neretva VR and Battle on Kozara VR commemorate two very important WWII battles from Bosnia and Herzegovina. Trebinje Fortresses VR shows how Austrian-Hungarian fortresses around the city of Trebinje, Bosnia and Herzegovina, barely accessible in reality and almost completely destroyed, can be virtually visited in an amusing and educational way.

14.3.1 Battle on Neretva VR

Battle on Neretva Virtual Reality application (Rizvic et al. 2022) presents one of the most significant battles in World World II that happened in Yugoslavia. In this battle,

German-Italian forces along with their allies were defeated by Tito's Partisans. The Partisans, despite being outnumbered and outgunned, managed to successfully resist the enemy forces and inflict significant casualties upon them.

One of the key elements of the battle was the destruction of the Neretva River Bridge, which was crucial for the German-Italian supply lines. The Partisans managed to demolish the bridge, impeding the advance of the enemy forces.

In the Battle of Neretva VR application (Rizvic et al. 2022), users are brought into action by giving them the task of destroying the bridge and rescuing their wounded allies. Through storytelling and gameplay, users are taught about this historical event in an interesting and immersive way. The application is created as an extension of a physical exhibition in the Jablanica Museum (Fig. 14.1).

To create informative, but also interesting applications, elements of storytelling and gameplay are intertwined in realistic and interactive virtual environments (Fig. 14.2). The ultimate goal of the application is to transfer knowledge to the user in an easy-to-understand and memorable way.

The users initially find themselves in the virtual recreation of a Museum area, where the VR equipment is physically situated, and are introduced to the essential details of the Battle by an actor portraying a curator. In the following scene, the user is taken back in time to World War II, witnessing the meeting of Partisans. The Commander of Partisans explains the mission to his comrades and delegates the task of destroying the Neretva Bridge to the user. To make sure that the users understood the assignment, they have to correctly answer one simple question related to the

Fig. 14.1 Physical exhibition at Museum of Battle on Neretva, Jablanica, Bosnia and Herzegovina

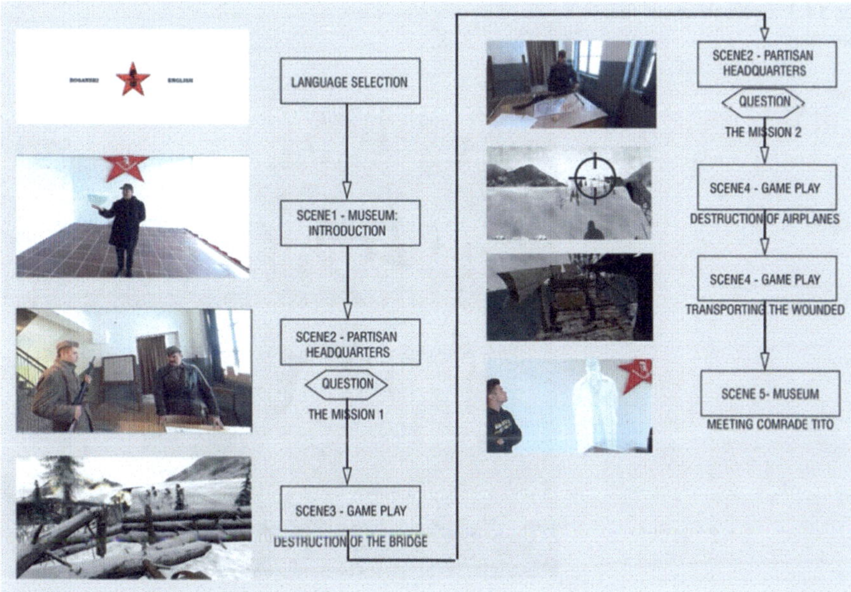

Fig. 14.2 Structure of Battle of Neretva VR application

previously given task. After that, they are placed in the middle of the battlefield and they have to set the explosives on the bridge.

After the successful completion of the first task, users are taken back to the Partisan's headquarters, where they are assigned the next task. After confirming that they understood the assignment, they are back on the battlefield trying to destroy enemy airplanes to protect Partisans who are building the improvised bridge. The mission is considered accomplished if the user manages to destroy three airplanes. Then the user has a chance to rescue a wounded comrade by taking him/her over the improvised bridge. After the successful completion of all tasks, users are back in the museum virtual environment, where comrade Tito congratulates them on helping the Partisans win the battle.

Stories told by the curator and commander are set in the prerecorded 360° environment. The historical information is provided by the museum curators and authenticity is thus confirmed. They were recorded in the museum and a special set-up room which imitated how the Partisan headquarters looked like. Special costumes were created and props were used to create realistic recordings. The user is placed among the actors to make him/her feel included and immersed in the action. Gameplay parts were created in Unity 3D, using a 3D virtual environment, 3D objects, and weather simulations such as fog and rain. Special audio effects were used throughout the whole application. Each of these elements had its role in creating a very realistic and immersive environment (Fig. 14.3).

Fig. 14.3 Screenshots of the gameplay

14.3.2 Trebinje Fortresses VR

Another project in which we incorporated gaming elements to serve educational purposes is Trebinje Fortresses VR (Rizvic et al. 2023a, b, October). Trebinje is a city in Bosnia and Herzegovina that was once home to a strategic military fortification network consisting of 36 different structures, including close to 100 military-purpose facilities distributed in two defense circles—one within the city center, and the other surrounding the city in the hills.

The fortifications were built beginning in 1883, during the Austro-Hungarian administration, when they encountered unexpected difficulties such as resistance to occupation and an 1881–82 rebellion against the introduction of military service. Despite the garrison, which typically housed around 4500 soldiers and officers, most of these fortifications were in a state of disrepair by the time the Austro-Hungarian army took control of Bosnia and Herzegovina in 1878 due to the 1875 rebellion and the subsequent battles in 1878.

Today, the garrison building is home to the Museum of Herzegovina, but the fortresses remain in ruins, abandoned and difficult to access. This is the reason why such locations show great potential for Virtual Reality presentations. Venturing to the location of these fortresses can be quite hazardous and even there, one can learn very little about these monumental structures. On the other hand, reading about them off-location can decrease the connection between the reader and the actual location.

The Virtual Reality (VR) application for this purpose was created in collaboration with the Museum of Herzegovina. The idea of the application is to start the story in the virtual replica of the very room the VR headset is in, where holographic Baron Leigther introduces the VR tour (Fig. 14.4).

The VR tour employs two historical figures: Engineer Baron Leightner and General Ferdinand Zahradnik, both portrayed by the same actor. It is important to add that this is a real-life actor recorded on the green screen, with full costume and makeup, later added to these 3D-modeled locations to guide users through the application, providing short narratives about the fortresses and life within them. The narrations are organized as tasks or "missions" for the users to undertake.

Fortresses Klicanj, Golo Brdo, and Petrinja each have a single corresponding narrative, while Strac contains five separate narratives in various locations. The reason behind that decision is the fact that Strac is a very interesting fortress that was built inside a cliff featuring a complex system of underground tunnels, which are completely inaccessible today. To emphasize the importance of those tunnels a more

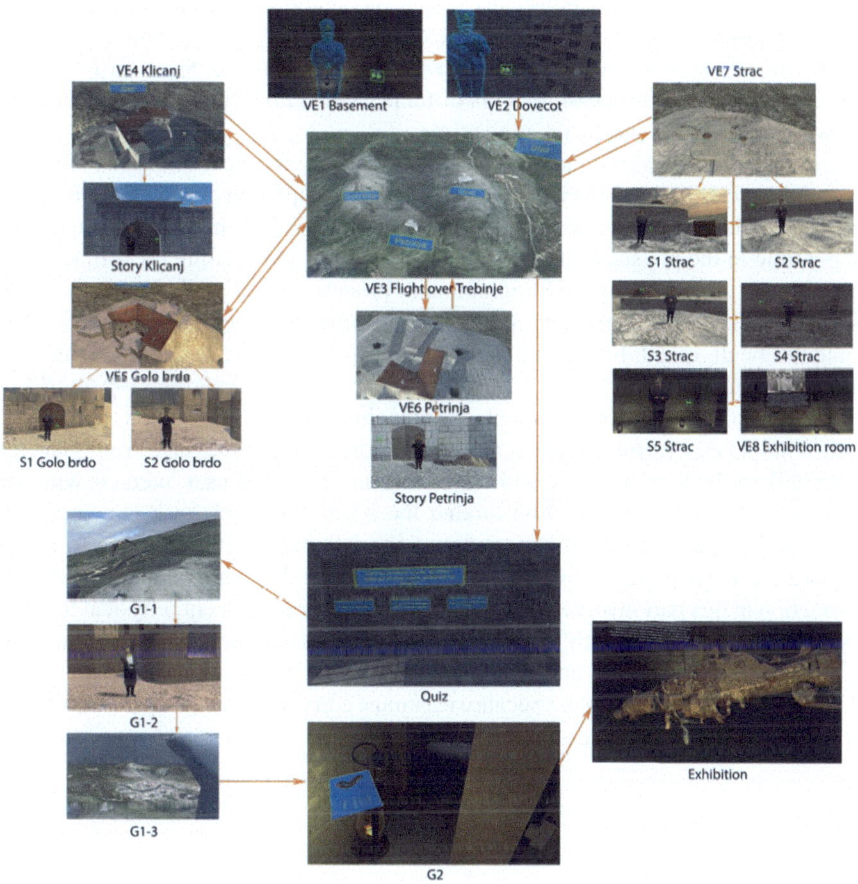

Fig. 14.4 Trebinje Fortresses VR Application structure

complex story was designed around Strac. Users can navigate the virtual environment with a controller joystick and are encouraged to pay attention to the narratives by answering questions based on the stories. The historical information is collected and authenticated by museum curators.

A Virtual Reality (VR) headset is installed in the basement of the Museum of Herzegovina. As stated before, the exhibition room is transferred into the VR environment so the user can have a smooth transition to the VR tour where they are greeted by Baron Leigther. After his introduction, visitors transform into carrier pigeons flying over the Strac, Golo Brdo, Petrina, and Klicanj fortresses. During these virtual visits, Baron Leightner continues to narrate the history of each fortress. After visiting all fortresses, users return to their initial location, where they are quizzed and tasked with delivering a message to the Strac fortress.

This is the place where the application transitions into gameplay. The user is now turned into a carrier pigeon trying to deliver the message while avoiding attacks from an eagle. Users must physically dodge incoming attacks making the experience more immersive than just using the controllers. If they accomplish this task, another mission awaits them in the underground tunnels of the Strac fortress. This part emphasizes the inaccessible parts of tunnels and allows the user to experience the way tunnels were used back in the time.

Once all missions are completed, users can virtually visit the Exhibition room. It is a special underground room created as a reward for completing the application. Here, they can explore and interact with digitized museum exhibits in ways that would not be possible in the physical museum, such as handling and rotating the artifacts. 3D models were created using a photogrammetry process so they could look as realistic as possible. The virtual exhibition also includes images of significant artifacts that could not be digitized. Informational texts are available for each exhibit, providing basic information about them.

As mentioned before, two gameplays are included in this application. In the first, users role-play as carrier pigeons, tasked with delivering a message from General Zahradnik to the Strac fortress, while avoiding an eagle. The user interacts with the application by physically moving around the room. Once this task is completed, they find themselves in the underground of Strac Fortress with a mission to find a key to a secret room and activate a mechanism to reveal machine guns for defense. Interaction in this part involves using VR controllers for movement. Physical moving here would require too much room while teleporting would decrease the immersion of movement through stiff underground corridors. In addition, darkness is another obstacle that the user faces, and because of it must carry the torch using the controller all the time while moving around.

14.3.3 Battle of Kozara VR

The following project was another one from WWII. The Battle of Kozara holds great importance in Ex-Yugoslavia history books, and it deserves a VR experience of its own.

In the spring of 1942, Yugoslav Partisans in Central and Western Bosnia liberated Bosanski Petrovac, Drvar, Glamoc, and Prijedor. On 20th May the 1st Krajina Assault Brigade was founded, and the next day it obtained tanks and a modest air force. The free territory stretched from the river Sava south across the mountains Kozara and Grmec. During the winter, Partisans inflicted heavy casualties on the Germans. In the summer of 1942, the West Bosnia fascist combat group surrounded Kozara with three rings of soldiers. The famous Battle of Kozara lasted from mid-June to mid-July 1942, when partisan forces tried to break through the enemy's encirclement and save the population of Kozara on several occasions. The biggest breakthrough took place in the night between July 3rd and 4th. It would be difficult to mark all the places and preserve the memory of all those who were part of it but in 1972, a memorial complex on Mrakovica was built, consisting of the Revolution Monument, the Memorial Wall, and the Memorial Museum. The Virtual Reality application allows visitors of the Memorial Museum in Mrakovica to become participants in this famous battle and to solve the tasks that are set before them in trying to free themselves from the encirclement of fascist forces.

Battle on Kozara VR application (Rizvic et al. 2023a, b, October) consists of 360 videos of locations where the Battle took place inhabited by actors playing selected historical characters, a virtual environment of Kozara forest with trees-storytellers, a quiz with questions from stories, and a virtual environment with a 3D model of Kozara monument. Five gameplays are implemented in the application, each in a different 3D scene.

The application starts with the 360 video cinematic of the forest in Kozara where the commander of partisan forces Dr. Mladen Stojanovic and Mika Mandic introduce you to the story. After that, the users find themselves in the virtual forest where they should move from one storytelling tree to another. Next to each talking tree, a portal opens and the user starts a gameplay part of the experience.

In the first gameplay, the task is to find shelter from the enemy. The second gameplay enables the user to experience the fear of bombs. The third gameplay is happening in a meadow, where the grass needs to be mowed using the traditional mowing tool. In the fourth gameplay, a bag with food should be prepared and taken to the partisans. The user is inside a village house looking for various food items and placing them inside the bag. Finally, in the fifth gameplay, a stretcher needs to be assembled from elements that could be found inside the shelter. The interaction was again implemented through the usage of VR controllers and movement was achieved using locomotion. Teleport proved to be impractical in this case as well, since we emphasize strategic movement through some of the gameplays to avoid shelling and obstacles around the terrain. This did introduce a certain level of nausea

Fig. 14.5 Storytelling tree and a portal for entering gameplay

for some users leaving more room for further research on the movement methods in VR applications (Fig. 14.5).

After the successful completion of all gameplays, the user is again in VR cinematic, getting familiar with the tragic destiny of Mira Cikota, who was killed by enemies leaving her little daughter an orphan. Lastly, the users are presented with questions from stories they heard. This is again the quiz part of the application that ensures the users have followed the story. It is a part of the hyper-storytelling concept we envisioned before (Rizvic et al. 2017a, b, November). The initial material for the scenarios was prepared by the museum curators, so there is no doubt about the authenticity of the data.

The use of 360 videos in VR applications for cultural heritage contributes to the immersion of users, as they see the real appearance of the historical sites around them. Based on that video, 3D models of cultural monuments' virtual reconstructions can be added using compositing. In our applications, we add actors-storytellers recorded on a green screen to emphasize the connection to the characters in the story. In the Battle on Kozara VR application, we recorded 360 videos of the monument area and several places in the forest around to provide backgrounds for the storytelling parts of the application. We also used 360 videos as a reference for adjusting the 3D model of the monument. 360 videos were recorded using Garmin VIRB 360 camera. It has two lenses and can record up to 5.7 K video quality.

Recording in 360 degrees poses many challenges. Everything is now inside the camera frame, and there is no framing technique involved. Each user becomes the director of their own story so it is important to make them feel as if they belong to the environment. The crew needs to hide as well as any additional equipment which might be used. Filming exteriors is easier due to the natural illumination of the scene, while interiors need to be illuminated with practical lights, which are part of the shot itself. For this particular filming, the main challenge was the bright sunlight creating sharp shadows in the forest, so some parts of the shot tended to be overexposed. We performed some color corrections in postproduction to overcome this problem (Fig. 14.6).

For our application, we created 3D models of talking trees, a village house, and the Kozara monument. Talking trees were modeled in 3ds max and animated upon

Fig. 14.6 Mika Mandic shows the player the way through the forest

the voiceover of the actor recorded before, using professional sound recording equipment. Trees models were created based on 360 videos and photographs of the forest around the monument and museum. Kozara monument was created using drone photogrammetry. Some modeling has been added to the final mesh obtained from the photogrammetry software. The number of polygons was reduced as well as the size of textures. The village house was created based on photographs from the Ethnological Museum in Prijedor. We recreated the original textures and materials, as well as the small objects from the interior. Some of these objects were made interactive in the Unity scene, so the users could explore them and move them around. The rest of the assets, such as the forest environment, gameplay environments, headquarters house, shelter for wounded, herbs models, and smaller objects used in gameplays were either modeled or purchased online.

Battle on Kozara VR application features four storyteller characters to help users learn about Kozara. Dr. Mladen Stojanovic, the leader of the Partisans in the Bosanska Krajina region where mountain Kozara is situated, is an educated and distinguished individual. His popularity and respect in the region, coupled with his participation in the resistance, inspired many others to join as well. In our narrative, he invites the user to Kozara. Mika Mandic, an elderly woman from a village in Kozara, was known for her defiance against the Croat Fascist forces ("ustase"). She was later captured and brutally murdered. In our narrative, Mika guides the user through the forest. Mira Cikota was part of the covert resistance against fascist forces. After being driven out of Prijedor, she was captured by enemies, separated from her young daughter, tortured, and eventually hanged. Her final letter to her parents was recovered and is kept in the Memorial Museum as a testament to the bravery and rebellion of the Kozara people. In our narrative, she shares her emotional story. At the end of the application, she invites users to build the monument based on their quiz responses as a tribute to Kozara. The fourth character is an anonymous partisan who narrates the story of Mira Cikota and her tragic fate. Lastly, we introduced narrating trees that tell brief stories, thus recreating the timeline of the Battle.

Our storytelling primarily focuses on the suffering of the Kozara people, who were forced to seek shelter from enemies in the forest and caves, without access to food or medicine. Selecting from the abundance of critical historical facts presented by Museum curators was a challenging task. We aimed to maintain a balance between storytelling and gameplay while keeping users engaged until the end of the application.

Melding storytelling with gameplay elements has emerged as an effective strategy for enhancing the educational entertainment value of digital cultural heritage applications. Gameplay elements motivate users to explore the entirety of the digital content, thus solving the narrative paradox problem. They infuse elements of gamification into cultural heritage presentations and present users with challenges.

In the first gameplay of the Battle on Kozara VR application, users are immersed in the terrifying experiences of the Kozara people who were relentlessly pursued by enemies, and forced to hide in forests, caves, and shelters. The user must navigate through the terrain towards a destination marked by a red arrow as the clock ticks away, sometimes needing to crawl under branches or jump over obstacles.

The second gameplay reenacts the frequent bombings that occurred during WWII in Kozara. Enemy aircraft fly overhead dropping their lethal payloads while the user must take cover in terrain dips, crouching to avoid the blasts and flying shrapnel. The objective is to reach the house that serves as the partisan headquarters, with the user given three lives to complete this challenge.

The third gameplay tasks the user with traditionally mowing the grass using an old-fashioned cutter tool, thereby providing an insight into pre-modern mowing techniques. This skill now forms part of the intangible cultural heritage. After mowing, the user must collect three types of herbs that were used as medicinal remedies for injured partisans during the battle.

The fourth gameplay takes place inside a traditional Kozara village house. The user is tasked with locating food items suitable for packing into a peasant bag and delivering to comrades on the battlefield. The mission is deemed accomplished once all items have been found and stowed in the bag.

The fifth gameplay requires the user to construct a stretcher for carrying wounded soldiers from materials found within the shelter. The user must determine which items in their surroundings are suitable and arrange them to assemble the stretcher. All gameplay elements represent activities the people of Kozara undertook and the events they lived through. This experiential learning allows museum visitors to fully comprehend the challenging times of the Battle, supplementing the knowledge gained through storytelling and physical exhibits.

Recognizing that museum visitors encompass a wide range of ages, computer literacy levels, and intellectual backgrounds, the gameplay was designed to be challenging enough for younger users and not too complex for older or less tech-savvy visitors. The Unity 3D game engine was again our choice for the development of this application.

14.4 User Satisfaction

The user experience created by involving the user in Virtual Reality is specific concerning all other experiences of interaction with other technologies because it enables a unique feeling of immersion in another world and exclusion from the real world. Approaches to the evaluation of user experience (UX) differ according to the objective: whether it is (1) finding flaws in the implementation and helping developers to improve the interaction or (2) obtaining standardized metrics data for general conclusions based on the research hypothesis test.

A quantitative approach to UX evaluation is important when assessing the level of application development or comparing different solutions, and we primarily focus on measuring success in achieving features such as immersion and edutainment. The edutainment as a feature is of specific importance for cultural heritage applications.

We primarily use the results of the UX evaluation to identify flaws in the user interface and the overall presentation of the narrative, since our goal is to improve the solution and rarely to generalize the results. In our quantitative studies, we follow an established framework to enable comparison of studies and identify patterns in user preferences.

The evaluation of the overall UX for the selected case studies is designed according to our benchmarking framework (Boskovic et al. 2017, October). This approach is based on systematized questionnaires employing the Likert scale items measuring levels of users' performance and users' effort. The consistent nature of the questionnaires also provides for comparison of different VR applications and helps to identify users' preferences. User performance is measured using Immersion and Edutainment, and user effort is measured by perceived Ease of Use.

UX evaluations for the case studies presented in the Chapter are described in more detail in Rizvic et al. (2022, 2023a, 2023b). The common experiment protocol includes participants' recruitment at museum sites and by invitation for experiments in the university lab. The participants are informed about the experiment objectives and procedures, and provided with the Informed Consent Statement. The questionnaires contain parts with relevant demographic data. The demographic data are important to assess if participants are a representative sample of the targeted population, and also to enable comparison of user satisfaction across different user types.

Although our approach to UX evaluation is quantitative, users' engagement with the VR applications demands the evaluator's presence to monitor the participant's well-being and offer assistance and explanations when needed. Consequentially, evaluators observe the users during the engagement with the VR application and collect relevant information about user behavior, and movements, evaluating their independence in interaction, and noting when and why assistance was needed. The typical duration of the evaluation session for one participant is 30–40 min. A user engaged with the Battle on Kozara VR application during the experiment at the University of Sarajevo Graphics Lab is presented in Fig. 14.7.

Fig. 14.7 User during engagement with Battle on Kozara VR application

Participants answered the questionnaire immediately after completing the experiment. The questionnaire comprises the following sections defined by our UX framework:

- Demographics data as their age, their professional sector, gender, VR technology expertise, and previous knowledge of the VR application topic.
- UX evaluation by Likert items organized in 3 sub-scales measuring previously identified features: Immersion, Edutainment, and Ease of Use, and
- Open-type questions for user feedback and recommendations.

Respective summary statistics for selected case studies: Battle on Neretva, Trebinje Fortresses, and Battle on Kozara; are shown in Table 14.1. Results are presented for each case study for the previously identified UX features: Immersion, Edutainment, and Ease of Use, and per specific statistics: Range, Mean, and Standard Deviation (SD).

Table 14.1 Summary statistics

Item	Range of means	Mean	SD
Battle on Neretva			
Immersion	3.82–4.76	4.47	0.81
Edutainment	4.53–4.71	4.66	0.61
Easy of use	3.24–4.59	3.93	1.09
Trebinje Fortresses			
Immersion	3.89–4.41	4.20	0.91
Edutainment	4.15–4.63	4.36	0.75
Easy of use	2.70–4.30	3.78	1.08
Battle on Kozara			
Immersion	4.00–4.59	4.41	0.65
Edutainment	4.27–4.59	4.48	0.60
Easy of use	2.32–4.32	3.47	1.39

The results confirm the affirmative grading for performance measures (Immersion and Edutainment) even in the presence of the lower grading for the measure of effort (Ease of Use). This confirms our previous findings that users are driven by engagement in VR stories, overcoming difficulties in using a new non-familiar technology. Detailed analysis of users' behavior and open answers indicates the positive effects of introducing the Gameplays to promote Edutainment and retain Immersion even in the presence of decreased satisfaction regarding the Ease of Use.

The challenging topic of the Battle on Kozara VR application motivated us to focus our UX research on the balance of Gameplays and Narrative to obtain informative and specific feedback for designers and developers of War Heritage VR applications. Our standard UX questionnaire was extended with user satisfaction related to gameplays and narrative and subjective assessment of the balance between these components of the VR application.

The results for this specific evaluation are illustrated in Fig. 14.8 presenting the frequencies of answers per each Likert item linked to the specific preference: Narrative (N1–N3), Gameplays (G1–G5), and Balance (B1–B2). The summary statistics strongly indicate users' preference for Gameplays, and grading for Balance items is comparable to grading for the Gameplays. The more precise comparison would demand two versions of the VR application—with and without Gameplays, comparing not only user satisfaction but also retention of the historical information presented.

Limitations of our evaluation study are linked to standard challenges as the number of participants, with specific relation to time and equipment constraints. To overcome these limitations, in addition to experiments at the museum sites, experiments were organized also at the University of Sarajevo lab. Cultural context presents a limitation not yet addressed in the case studies described in the Chapter, but this limitation was explored in our previous research with the international partners conducting the same experiment in their environment (Selmanović et al. 2020).

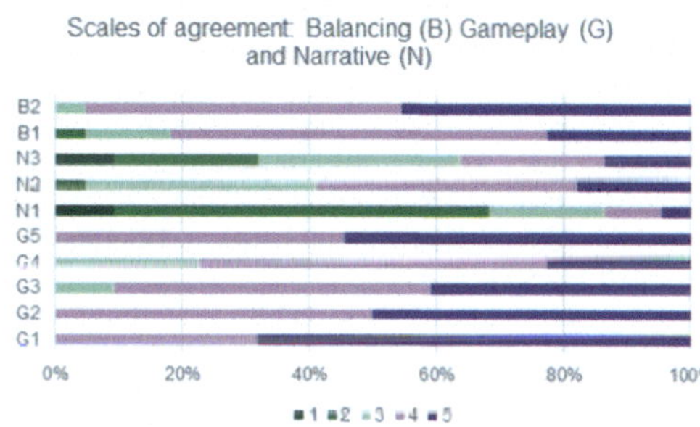

Fig. 14.8 Graph visualizing frequencies of answers linked to the preference of Narrative and Gameplays

14.5 Conclusion

The presented VR applications and their User Evaluation studies show that gamification indeed improves learning and attractiveness of cultural heritage monuments and sites. Gameplays combined with Interactive Digital Storytelling enable the users to experience historical events and visit the cultural monuments in their original shape. All museums where our applications have been installed greatly appreciated this addition to their exhibitions. They trained dedicated curators to work with the users of VR headsets and facilitate their experiences.

We noticed that all generations of museum visitors and users of our VR applications found them equally challenging and engaging. Even the people without any VR or IT knowledge did not hesitate to try on the headsets and move into different realities. All users appreciated the involvement in historical topics provided by gameplays and information about historical objects and sites provided by the storytellers. They particularly empathized with characters from VR applications due to the fact that they are humans (Rizvic et al. 2019a, b).

Occasional negative impressions were mostly related to motion sickness, as a small number of users felt uncomfortable during the movement implemented through the VR controller's joystick. We plan to solve this problem by implementing teleport movement as an alternative. User evaluation suggests that gameplays are the most appreciated part of our applications. Therefore we will continue in this direction, balancing the amount of storytelling with challenges and missions for our users to obtain the highest level of edutainment.

References

Aldrighettoni J, D'Urso MG (2022) An interdisciplinary approach for unveiling and enhancing the first world war heritage in the landscape. ISPRS Ann Photogramm Remote Sens Spat Inf Sci 5:17–24. https://doi.org/10.5194/isprs-annals-V-5-2022-17-2022

Allal-Chérif O (2022) Intelligent cathedrals: using augmented reality, virtual reality, and artificial intelligence to provide an intense cultural, historical, and religious visitor experience. Technol Forecast Soc Change 178:121604. https://doi.org/10.1016/j.techfore.2022.121604

Bekele MK, Pierdicca R, Frontoni E, Malinverni ES, Gain J (2018) A survey of augmented, virtual, and mixed reality for cultural heritage. J Comput Cult Herit (JOCCH) 11(2):1–36. https://doi.org/10.1145/3145534

Bogdanova G, Todorov T, Noev N (2013) Digitization and 3D scanning of historical artifacts. Digit Presentation Preserv Cult Sci Herit 3:133–138

Borisov N, Smolin A (2013) Virtual reconstruction of the ancient Russian fortress koporye. In: Proceedings of third international conference for digital presentation and preservation of cultural and scientific heritage, pp 18–20, Veliko Tarnovo. https://doi.org/10.55630/dipp.2013.3.16

Boskovic D, Rizvic S, Okanovic V, Sljivo S, Sinanovic N (2017) Measuring immersion and edutainment in multimedia cultural heritage applications. In: 2017 XXVI international conference on information, communication and automation technologies (ICAT), pp 1–6. IEEE

Chalmers A, Debattista K (2005) Investigating the structural validity of virtual reconstructions of prehistoric Maltese temples. In: Proceedings of the 6th international conference on virtual reality,

archaeology and intelligent cultural heritage, pp 107–112. https://doi.org/10.2312/VAST/VAST05/107-112
Ch'ng E, Stone RJ, Arvanitis TN (2005) A virtual reality archaeological framework for the investigation and interpretation of ancient landscapes. In: EuroIMSA, pp 527–532
Deterding S, Sicart M, Nacke L, O'Hara K, Dixon D (2011) Gamification. using game-design elements in non-gaming contexts. In: CHI' 11 extended abstracts on human factors in computing systems, pp 2425–2428. https://doi.org/10.1145/1979742.1979575
Djaouti D, Alvarez J, Rampnoux O, Charvillat V, Jessel JP (2009) Serious games & cultural heritage: a case study of prehistoric caves. In: 2009 15th international conference on virtual systems and multimedia, pp 221–226. IEEE. https://doi.org/10.1109/VSMM.2009.40
Edler D, Keil J, Wiedenlübbert T, Sossna M, Kühne O, Dickmann F (2019) Immersive VR experience of redeveloped post-industrial sites: the example of "Zeche Holland" in Bochum-Wattenscheid. KN-J Cartogr Geogr Inf 69(4):267–284. https://doi.org/10.1007/s42489-019-00030-2
Fadli F, AlSaeed M (2019) Digitizing vanishing architectural heritage; the design and development of Qatar historic buildings information modeling [Q-HBIM] platform. Sustainability 11(9):2501. https://doi.org/10.3390/su11092501
Forte M (2014) 3D archaeology: new perspectives and challenges—the example of Çatalhöyük. J East Mediterr Archaeol Herit Stud 2(1):1–29. https://doi.org/10.13140/2.1.3285.0568
Franch M, Irimiás A, Buffa F (2017) Place identity and war heritage: managerial challenges in tourism development in Trentino and Alto Adige/Südtirol. Place Brand Public Dipl 13:119–135. https://doi.org/10.1057/s41254-016-0019-5
Franco PAC, Márquez R, de la Plata A, Cruz Franco J (2020) From the point cloud to BIM methodology for the ideal reconstruction of a lost bastion of the cáceres wall. Appl Sci 10(18):6609. https://doi.org/10.3390/app10186609
Germak C, Di Salvo A, Abbate L (2021) Augmented reality experience for inaccessible areas in museums. In: Proceedings of EVA London 2021, pp 39–45. BCS Learning & Development. https://doi.org/10.14236/ewic/eva2021.7
Hamad A, Jia B (2022) How virtual reality technology has changed our lives: an overview of the current and potential applications and limitations. Int J Environ Res Public Health 19(18):11278. https://doi.org/10.3390/ijerph191811278
Heuberger R, Leone LE, Evers R (2015) The challenges of reconstructing cultural heritage: an international digital collaboration. IFLA J 41(3):223–229. https://doi.org/10.1177/0340035215597235
Hisari L, Fouseki K (2020) Post-war cultural heritage preservation in Kosovo: Rethinking the implementation of ahtisaari plan annex v. Heritage 3(1):98–115. https://doi.org/10.3390/heritage3010006
Hornoiu RI, Popescu D, Militaru IA (2023). Exploring war tourism through the use of virtual reality in the context of conflict situations
https://doi.org/10.1145/1877922.1877927
https://doi.org/10.4995/FORTMED2020.2020.11415
Izani M, Bridges A, Razak A, Calder B, Grant M (2010) Digital preservation of a famosa fortress in Malaysia. In: Proceedings of the second workshop on eHeritage and digital art preservation, pp 7–12
Legnér M (2018) Post-conflict reconstruction and the heritage process. J Archit Conserv 24(2):78–90. https://doi.org/10.1080/13556207.2018.1463663
López-Menchero Bendicho VM, Maschner HD, McLeod JB, du Vernay JP, Hervás Herrera MÀ (2020) The work of Global Digital Heritage for the massive digitization of fortifications in Spain
Mechiche R, Zeghlache H (2020) The digitization of shared cultural built heritage highlighted in "Heritage at Risk in Algeria". In: IOP conference series: materials science and engineering, vol 949, no 1, p 012021. IOP Publishing. https://doi.org/10.1088/1757-899X/949/1/012021
Miller CH (2019) Digital storytelling 4e: a creator's guide to interactive entertainment, 4th edn. CRC Press. https://doi.org/10.1201/9780429440045

Mulders M (2023) Learning about victims of holocaust in virtual reality: the main, mediating and moderating effects of technology, instructional method, flow, presence, and prior knowledge. Multimodal Technol Interact 7(3):28. https://doi.org/10.3390/mti7030028

Okanovic V, Ivkovic-Kihic I, Boskovic D, Mijatovic B, Prazina I, Skaljo E, Rizvic S (2022) Interaction in extended reality applications for cultural heritage. Appl Sci 12(3):1241. https://doi.org/10.3390/app12031241

Prazina I, Ivkovic-Kihic I, Chahin TA, Jajcanin A, Rizvic S, Okanovic V (2020) Sarajevo war tunnel-mobile virtual cultural heritage application. In: 2020 43rd international convention on information, communication and electronic technology (MIPRO), pp 224–227. IEEE

Psomadaki OI, Dimoulas CA, Kalliris GM, Paschalidis G (2019) Digital storytelling and audience engagement in cultural heritage management: a collaborative model based on the Digital City of Thessaloniki. J Cult Herit 36:12–22. https://doi.org/10.1016/j.culher.2018.07.016

Rizvic S, Sadzak A, Hulusic V, Karahasanovic A (2012) Interactive digital storytelling in the Sarajevo survival tools virtual environment. In: Proceedings of the 28th spring conference on computer graphics, pp 109–116

Rizvic S, Boskovic D, Okanovic V, Sljivo S (2017) Kyrenia-hyper storytelling pilot application. In: Eurographics workshop on graphics and cultural heritage. https://doi.org/10.2312/gch.20171311

Rizvic S, Djapo N, Alispahic F, Hadzihalilovic B, Cengic FF, Imamovic A, Boskovic D, et al (2017a) Guidelines for interactive digital storytelling presentations of cultural heritage. In 2017 9th international conference on virtual worlds and games for serious applications (VS-Games), pp 253–259. IEEE. https://doi.org/10.1109/VS-GAMES.2017.8056610

Rizvic S, Boskovic D, Bruno F, Petriaggi BD, Sljivo S, Cozza M (2019b) Actors in VR storytelling. In: 2019 11th international conference on virtual worlds and games for serious applications (VS-Games), pp 1–8. IEEE. https://doi.org/10.1109/VS-Games.2019.8864520

Rizvic S, Boskovic D, Okanovic V, Ivkovic-Kihic I, Sljivo S (2019) Virtual reality experience of Sarajevo war heritage. In: GCH, pp 1–6. https://doi.org/10.2312/gch.20191340

Rizvic S, Mijatovic B, Boskovic D, Ivkovic-Kihic I (2022) Workflow of extended reality applications for museum exhibitions. In: 2022 international Balkan conference on communications and networking (BalkanCom), pp 189–194. IEEE

Rizvic S, Boskovic D, Mijatovic B (2023a) Advanced interactive digital storytelling in virtual reality presentation of Austrian-Hungarian fortresses around Trebinje.https://doi.org/10.2312/gch.20231173

Rizvic S, Boskovic D, Mijatovic B (2023b) Balancing gameplay elements and interactive digital storytelling in virtual reality applications of war heritage.https://doi.org/10.2312/imet.20231257

Selmanović E, Rizvic S, Harvey C, Boskovic D, Hulusic V, Chahin M, Sljivo S (2020) Improving accessibility to intangible cultural heritage preservation using virtual reality. J Comput Cult Herit (JOCCH) 13(2):1–19

Smed J, Suovuo T, Trygg N, Skult P, Hakonen H (2019) The digital campfire: an ontology of interactive digital storytelling. In: Thakur J (ed) Modern perspectives on virtual communications and social networking, pp 174–195. IGI Global. https://doi.org/10.4018/978-1-5225-5715-9.ch007

Stieglitz S, Lattemann C, Robra-Bissantz S, Zarnekow R, Brockmann T (2017) Gamification. Springer, Berlin, pp 1–164

Thomas S, Seitsonen O, Herva VP (2016) Nazi memorabilia, dark heritage and treasure hunting as "alternative" tourism: understanding the fascination with the material remains of World War II in Northern Finland. J Field Archaeol 41(3):331–343. https://doi.org/10.1080/00934690.2016.1168769

Waagen J, Lanjouw T, de Kleijn M (2023) A virtual place of memory: virtual reality as a method for communicating conflicted heritage at Camp Westerbork. Herit Mem Confl 3(1):87–93. https://doi.org/10.3897/ijhmc.3.71198

Walmsley AP, Kersten TP (2020) The imperial cathedral in Königslutter (Germany) as an immersive experience in virtual reality with integrated 360 panoramic photography. Appl Sci 10(4):1517. https://doi.org/10.3390/app10041517

Chapter 15
Virtual Agents and Interactive Digital Narrative in XR Experiences for Cultural Heritage. Designing for Engagement

Akrivi Katifori, Angeliki Chysanthi, Androniki Agelada, Maria Vayanou, and Vlasios Kasapakis

Abstract Traditionally, the communication of cultural heritage has relied on oral and written narratives. In the digital realm, informative and interpretive narratives for cultural heritage are delivered in various ways, with applications serving as virtual guides (VGs). These range from neutral, impersonal system narratives to engaging, role-playing VGs. The latter are widely utilized in commercial contexts for the communication and promotion of cultural heritage. While Non-Immersive Virtual Reality (N-IVR) applications predominantly employ VGs, their use in Immersive Virtual Reality (IVR) and Immersive Augmented Reality (IAR) applications is significantly less. Considering the interpretative significance of narration for a digital heritage experience, this study focuses on the use of VGs in immersive XR experiences from the perspective of narrative design. It critically reviews selected existing approaches to VGs in XR for heritage, aiming to deepen our understanding of the current state of interactive narrative design in this context.

Keywords Immersive XR · Cultural heritage · Interactive narrative design · Virtual guides

---

A. Katifori (✉) · M. Vayanou
Department of Informatics and Telecommunications, National and Kapodistrian University of Athens, Athens, Greece
e-mail: vivi@di.uoa.gr

M. Vayanou
e-mail: vayanou@di.uoa.gr

A. Chysanthi · A. Agelada · V. Kasapakis
Department of Cultural Technology and Communication, University of the Aegean, Lesvos, Greece
e-mail: a.chrysanthi@aegean.gr

A. Agelada
e-mail: androniki.agelada@aegean.gr

V. Kasapakis
e-mail: v.kasapakis@aegean.gr

F. Liarokapis et al. (eds.), *Interactive Media for Cultural Heritage*, Springer Series on Cultural Computing, https://doi.org/10.1007/978-3-031-61018-9_15

15.1 Introduction

The communication of cultural heritage has traditionally relied on oral and written narratives. Information about heritage artefacts and monuments has been made available to the public through informative texts in the form of labels or leaflets as well as the narration of tour guides or museum hosts. In 1957, Freeman Tilden introduced the concept of "interpretation" as "an educational activity which aims to reveal meanings and relationships" (Tilden 2009), at the same time defining principles that should guide the creation of such narratives. According to Tilden, the provision of factual information does not equal interpretation, but is rather one of its constituents. Interpretative narratives, akin to an art form, aim not merely to instruct, but to provoke and establish a connection between the display and the visitor's personal life and personality. In this context, the design of museum labels has been the subject of a long debate leading to a multitude of guidelines, such as "effective museum labels anticipate and answer visitors' unspoken questions about the artwork or object they accompany." (Faherty 2022).

As digital technology becomes increasingly pervasive in our everyday lives, its integration into heritage practice strengthens. Digital experience design, long present in museums and heritage institutions, has established digital storytelling as an effective method for communicating and interpreting the past (Bedford 2001; Birchall and Faherty 2016; Coerver 2016; Lombardo and Damiano 2012; Pau 2017; Poole 2018; Roussou and Katifori 2018). At the same time, significant progress in hardware supporting XR applications has stabilized and enhanced user experiences, making them suitable for a wider audience, including home users. This hardware maturity, coupled with an increasing number of digitized sites, enables both reconstructions and faithful 3D representations of sites in their current state.

In this wider spectrum of digital applications for cultural heritage, informative and interpretive narratives are offered in a multitude of ways as the application assumes the role of a VG. These ways range from a neutral and impersonal narrative offered by the system, such as audio/text guides (Tsepapadakis and Gavalas 2023), to virtual characters represented using digital humanoid 3D/2D models (Butz et al. 2021), scanned 3D models (Papaefthymiou et al. 2018), or volumetric/holographic videos of real individuals (Martí-Testón et al. 2021), which may assume different roles, aiming in each case to convey a specific atmosphere while immersing and engaging the user.

VGs are widely utilized in commercial contexts for the communication and promotion of cultural heritage, and they have also been extensively examined as a subject of scientific inquiry in this context. However, it is worth noting that non-Immersive Virtual Reality (N-IVR) applications predominantly employ VGs, while Immersive Virtual Reality (IVR) and Immersive Augmented Reality (IAR) applications with VGs represent a relatively minor percentage within the broader spectrum of the field. Considering the interpretative significance of narration for a digital heritage experience, this study focused on the use of VGs in immersive XR experiences from the perspective of narrative design. We examine the use of virtual agents in XR for heritage through a critical review of selected existing approaches, seeking a deeper understanding of interactive narrative design in this context.

The following Section presents the methodology employed for this review, while Sect. 15.3 offers an overview of the broader field of narrative design and the role of VGs in both physical and digital experiences. Section 15.4 presents the examined systems, focusing mainly on the VGs' role, appearance, and narrative design. Finally, Sect. 15.5 discusses the outcomes while Sect. 15.6 concludes the chapter.

15.2 Methodology

As previously emphasized, the focal point of this review concerns the narrative aspects of immersive XR heritage experiences facilitated by VGs. In pursuit of this objective, we conducted a comprehensive literature review to identify pertinent research publications and applications. We searched freely in Google Scholar as well as in several journals and conference proceedings, including Virtual Reality (Springer)[1] and ACM International Conference on Intelligent Virtual Agents,[2] on topics related to VR, AR, XR used in the domain of Digital Cultural Heritage. Apart from works focusing on individual systems, we also sought existing surveys and reviews on the specific topic of VGs in XR.

The identified research studies, concerning the use of VGs in immersive VR and/or AR environments that meet the criteria of this survey's topic, were published within the last five years and number nine. These studies are chronologically presented in Table 15.1, alongside their respective application type and the VG high-fidelity representation methods. The discussion of these studies, along with their technical descriptions and categorizations, focuses on five main themes. These themes have emerged from the analysis of the research items and related work in the field of interactive narrative in CH as follows:

- VG Characteristics
  - VG Role/character (guide, historical character, co-visitor etc.)
  - VG appearance/quality of graphics
  - VG body motion, facial expressions etc.
- Narrative Design
  - Linear
  - Non-linear
- Narrative Content Type
  - Information provision by an expert or generic guide
  - Information-based narrative by a historical character, real or fictional

[1] https://www.springer.com/journal/10055.

[2] https://dl.acm.org/conference/iva.

Table 15.1 Types of experiences and technical characteristics of VGs identified in existing research

	XR type		VG generation			VG animation	
	VR	AR	Video-recorded	3D-modelled	3D-captured	Motion capture	Manual
Papaeftthymiou et al. (2018)	✓	×	×	×	✓	×	✓
Microsoft (2018)	×	✓	✓	×	×	×	×
Rzayev et al. (2019)	✓	×	×	✓	✓	✓	×
Sylaiou et al. (2020)	✓	×	×	✓		✓	×
Muñoz and Martí Testón (2020)	×	✓	✓	×	×	×	×
Bönsch et al. (2021)	✓	×	×	✓	×	✓	×
Butz et al. (2021)	✓	×	×	✓	×	×	✓
Karuzaki et al. (2021)	✓	✓	×	✓	×	✓	×
O'Dwyer et al. (2021)	×	✓	✓	×	×	×	×

  - Personal narrations by a historical character, real or fictional

- Interaction with the user
  - User-initiated (free-exploration) or guided by the VG (linear)
  - Possibility to converse with the agent.
- Social experience
  - Possibility for social interaction or absence
  - Possibility for dialogue between users.

Important observations with regards to the current state, the identified limitations of implementations and future directions are then synthesized and discussed in the final sections of this chapter.

15.3 Related Work

To our knowledge, only three recent studies provide in-depth analyses of Virtual Guides (VGs) in the context of cultural heritage (Machidon et al. 2018). These studies comprehensively review literature and applications of VGs, addressing various aspects such as technology setup, user representation, and interaction design. However, they do not focus on the narrative design aspect of VGs, and particularly on their role in conveying interpretation through narratives, which is the central theme of our review. Our work contributes to the existing knowledge on narrative design trends and recommendations for VGs in the cultural heritage domain by examining several related research efforts and commercial applications, specifically through the lens of this previously overlooked element.

In conducting the review of VGs' role in these experiences, we reference the extensive literature on narrative as a means of communicating heritage, drawing from various heritage experience contexts, including purely physical guided tours as well as digitally enhanced tours.

15.3.1 The Role of the Guide in Physical Tours

As early as 1985, Cohen (1985) discusses the role of the human tourist guide in cultural heritage environments as one beyond information provision and identifies activities such as guiding the group in the exhibition, maintaining cohesion between the group members, applying tension management and conflict resolution techniques, while promoting the social integration of the group and animating them when required (Cohen 1985). According to Ap and Wong (2001), tour guides, through their knowledge and interpretation of a heritage site, their communication skills and ability to adjust to their audience needs, can transform the visit from a tour into an experience (Ap and Wong 2001).

As Antoniou et al. (2021) discuss, the traditional role of guides is increasingly challenged by a variety of engaging digital experiences and evolving attitudes of contemporary audiences. The conventional one-sided and linear delivery of information by experts is gradually becoming less effective in capturing visitors' attention. Nowadays visitors, whether as individuals or in groups, are increasingly seeking more interactive and engaging content delivery methods. In this context, the role of guides shifts from being mere information providers to acting as heritage interpreters. These individuals engage with participants to provoke interest, foster engagement, and encourage reflection, thus enhancing the experience of exploring natural, historical, or cultural themes (Hanani et al. 2013). This development is evident in the emergence of new types of physical guided tours. Such tours prioritize dialogue facilitation, joint exploration, active participation, and communication among group members, rather than focusing solely on the tour guide as the primary source of information. This type of tour, pioneered in practice by the International Coalition of Sites of Conscience (ICSC),[3] has been recognized as an effective practice in physical settings (Abram 2007) to help visitors make connections between the past and present.

[3] https://www.sitesofconscience.org/.

15.3.2 *Digital Narrative Design for Cultural Heritage: The System as a Storyteller*

The role of the human tour guide is constantly transforming, in an attempt to adapt to the digital age, finding inspiration also in the ways technology has been applied to heritage communication and interpretation. Moving beyond traditional audio guides, which substitute the expert human guide with recorded exhibit-centric narrations, there has been a great variety of digital experiences inspired by the art of storytelling.

Storytelling can be characterized as the first, most essential form of human learning, an imaginative form of discourse, which guides the listener to a process of meaning-making in the openness of an "imaginative state" (Bruner 1990). As a predominantly oral tradition in its initial, non-digital form, storytelling is an interactive performance. Here, the storyteller adapts the content and presentation of the narration to better align with the audience's needs (Bull and Kajder 2005) and to create a specific atmosphere (Bailey 1999). Pujol et al. (2012) discuss the effectiveness of storytelling to provoke curiosity, foster engagement and promote learning. Coerver (2016) emphasizes the importance of transitioning from mere facts to relatable stories in cultural heritage, arguing that these narratives should evoke emotions and curiosity. He asserts, "What most visitors really need is a story—a memorable, emotionally resonant way to connect with a fundamentally foreign object."

Storytelling can be characterized as "interactive" when there is at least a basic amount of user agency in relation to how the narrative unfolds. The term "interactive storytelling" in cultural heritage has been used to characterize a wide spectrum of narrative types (Chrysanthi et al. 2021). Existing digital storytelling approaches range from pre-defined and mostly linear narratives that attempt to balance between fiction and facts (Pau 2017; Poole 2018) to more dynamic and interactive experiences (Katifori et al. 2019; Lombardo and Damiano 2012; Vrettakis et al. 2021). The digital medium allows the use of multimedia combined with the narration, often resulting in experiences that combine sound, images, video, and animation.

In the related field of history education, the use of storytelling and interpretation as critical practice has also been recognized (Gallagher 2011). During a storytelling experience we enter another's standpoint through the story, as well as the circumstances that give rise to it. This indicates that participating simply as a listener of stories is still an important act of negotiation and diplomacy (Mello 2001). Robin (2008) identifies three main types of digital storytelling for education (Robin and Robin 2017): personal narratives, stories that inform or instruct, and stories that examine historical events. The Center for Digital Storytelling (Robin 2006) is known for developing and disseminating a guide that describes the seven main elements of digital storytelling. These include, among others, dramatic questions that provoke curiosity, emotional content, which connects the story to the audience, and the use of multimedia, sound and music to support the story line and convey emotion. According to (Katifori et al. 2020a, b), narrative elements such as "humor, links to everyday contemporary life, an informal tone, the perhaps surprising use of unconventional characters" have been identified as important in supporting the learning objectives of informal education institutions (Roussou and Katifori 2018). In this wider, theoretical context, incentives by associations such as Europeana[4] have also recognized the "exciting—and sometimes overwhelming—array of possible storytelling methods available online" as well as the fact that "the best examples all engage people on a personal and emotional level", also moving on to propose guidelines for context creation. Digital narratives on the web or mobile-based media are conveyed by the system in the form of either neutral narrators, assuming a nonspecific identity, or through the identity of a real or fictional character, this being a virtual tour guide or heritage expert or even a personality of the past (Katifori et al. 2020a, b; Sylaiou and Fidas 2022).

15.3.3 The VGS Role in Non-immersive Experiences: From Storytelling to Dialogue Facilitation

Moving beyond the use of the digital medium as a storyteller with the objective to convey narratives, interactive or linear, there have been several digital experiences proposing different roles for the device, beyond that of a storyteller. Chatbots (Bouras et al. 2023) and question-answering systems (Mishra and Jain 2016), in general, have already been established in other fields as an interactive way for the user to access information. Several cultural heritage chatbot initiatives operate within a site's physical space, most often serving as exhibition guides (Gerber 2018; Kopp et al. 2005; Vassos et al. 2016). Their primary aim is to offer information to the visitor. Bots such as ChatÇat (Roussou et al. 2019), Bo the Chatbot (McKinney et al. 2020) and Hermias the Bot (Petousi et al. 2021) were designed to engage with the user or users in conversation that moves beyond user-initiated information provision. These bots attempt to promote reflection and meaning making by posing questions to the users, as they are designed to provoke with their views, offering a new perspective about the past, and its comparison with the present. Bo and Hermias for instance are designed to act as dialogue facilitators to small groups of users, guiding the group to engage in dialogue and joint meaning making, with the cultivation of historical empathy (Endacott and Brooks 2013) as their ultimate objective. Chatbots are one way to implement such experiences in a digital design. There are other variations, where the digital experience assumes the role of a neutral agent that combines dialogue facilitation for perspective sharing with storytelling (Gargett 2018; Katifori et al. 2020a) or even gaming (Vayanou et al. 2021).

4 https://pro.europeana.eu/post/seven-tips-for-digital-storytelling-with-cultural-heritage.

15.3.4 The VG's Role to Promote Social Interaction

The value of social interactions has been stressed out in the cultural heritage field (Falk and Dierking 2018), manifesting the cultural visit as a social, rather than individual experience. Non-immersive digital designs that support group visits range from leveraging a single mobile device that is at all times shared between the members of small groups (Lanir et al. 2016), to posing reflective, open-ended questions (Shaer et al. 2011), or even providing multiple VGs that explicitly prompt the group members to interact at specific points of the experience (Katifori et al. 2020a). For instance, in (Katifori et al. 2020a), two different VGs are leveraged to provide a joint experience for visitor pairs: one group member is guided by *Abla*, a resident of the Neolithic site of Catalhoyuk, and the other is guided by *Archie*, an archaeologist working at the excavation site. The two VGs progressively cover the same set of topics, yet from different perspectives and offering complementary information, which the visitors are explicitly prompted to explore by (physically or/and verbally) conversing with their companion, at several parts of the visit.

The use of Augmented Reality technology has also been considerably explored to that end, since, instead of directing each visitor's attention to their personal mobile screens, it allows the creation of shared interaction areas (Ch'ng et al. 2023; Franz et al. 2019). Tackling larger groups, such as in the case of school visits (Schaper et al. 2018), several works move away from the "Window-on-the-World" (WoW) technique (Olaz et al. 2022), and adopt the "World-as-support" interaction paradigm (Malinverni et al. 2017), directing the visitors' attention over the museum's space and using handheld projection devices to meaningfully overlay digital elements over the physical world, thus shaping viewing areas that are shared by all the group members (Malinverni et al. 2017; Schaper et al. 2018). In the same direction, a recent work that presents the outcomes of a multi-disciplinary design workshop, describes a VG that is projected on the wall of a cultural environment and provides a device-less experience to the visitors: The wall simulates a mine (using 3D mapping projection) and the VG's avatar represents a miner who narrates stories about the cultural objects displayed in the room -as the visitors interact with these objects. In this way, the entire room provides a shared interaction space for the group members, hence enabling social interaction and collaboration (although not explicitly guiding it, through the VG) (Olaz et al. 2022).

15.4 Virtual Agents as Guides in Immersive XR Experiences

In this section we report on the selected research studies by discussing and analyzing the experiences taking place in immersive XR environments, focusing on the role of VGs to convey a narrative as described in the Methodology section. The analysis will commence from the VR implementations followed by examples in AR environments and conclude with a case that has implemented experiments in both environments. A summary of the identified narrative characteristics of the research studies are reported in Table 15.2 and further discussed in the following section.

Table 15.2 Narrative characteristics identified in the research studies

Experience	VG role	Narration design	Narration content	VG interaction with user
Papaefthymiou et al. (2018)	Priest	Linear	Information provision by an expert	No direct interaction with VG. The user selects buttons to play animations and segments of narrative
Microsoft (2018)	Monk	Linear	Information provision by an expert	No direct interaction with the VG. The user follows some gestural prompts performed by the VG to trigger animations
Rzayev et al. (2019)	Researcher	Linear	Information provision by an expert	The user is a passive observer
Sylaiou et al. (2020)	Curator/ Co-visitor/ Museum guard	Linear	Information provision by an expert	The user is a passive observer
Muñoz and Martí Testón (2020)	Clelia, a fictional historical character	Non-linear	Information-based narrative by a fictional historical character	The user is prompted by the VG to look at specific objects. Her gaze towards virtual objects activates the narrative
Bönsch et al. (2021)	Tour guide	Linear/ Non-linear	Information provision by an expert	Direct interaction with VG in two conditions: (a) the user is prompted to follow the VG (linear narrative) and (b) the VG follows the user (non-linear narrative)
Butz et al. (2021)	Generic model	Linear	Information provision by an expert/instruction	The user receives instructions to perform an activity
Karuzaki et al. (2021)	Mastic workers	Non-linear	Personal narrations and information provision by fictional historical characters	The user is prompted to select a story each time from a menu
O'Dwyer et al. (2021)	Jonathan Swift, Dean of Trinity College	Linear	Humorous personal narrations by a real historical character	The user is a passive observer

In their study, Rzayev et al. (2019) investigated the influence of VGs in both real and virtual exhibition settings. The study involved a female researcher delivering a predetermined linear presentation about four music composers to visitors of a physical exhibition. Subsequently, a 3D representation of the exhibition was generated, and the researcher's live performance was recorded using audio recording and motion capture technology, specifically an Optitrack Motion Capture system.[5] This recorded performance was then applied to three VG variations: (a) a VG reconstructed to replicate the researcher's actual appearance through the utilization of facial and body reconstruction software (FaceGen Pro 1[6] and Daz3D[7]); (b) a VG embodied by a humanoid robot model; and (c) an auditory guide without any visual representation. The overall application development took place inside Unity engine.[8] Real participants were given the opportunity to observe the VGs delivering the presentations through an HTC Vive[9] Head-Mounted Display (HMD) from a fixed distance of 2 m, with no interaction capabilities provided. The findings of this study indicate that the influence of VG's appearance on visitors' acquisition of knowledge is comparatively limited. Moreover, the accurately reconstructed VG exhibited lower levels of co-presence, humanness, and attractiveness when compared to the presence of a real human guide. Conversely, the audio-only VG variant enabled visitors to concentrate on the content but resulted in reduced overall connection with the guide (Rzayev et al. 2019).

Sylaiou et al. (2020) studied the influence of different embodiments of VGs on the persuasive quality of their narratives and the emotions experienced by visitors in a virtual museum. The research focuses on several key aspects, including (a) the diversity of participant characteristics based on gender and prior experience, (b) the variability of emotions elicited by each VG, and (c) the correlation between the emotions of VGs and those of the visitors. The authors devised three distinct linear narratives recounting the story of the Arria and Paetus sculpture, showcased at the renowned Louvre Museum. These narratives were specifically designed for presentation by a female exhibition curator, a male museum security guard, and a female visitor of the exhibition (see Fig. 15.1a).

To bring these narratives to life, actors recorded performances utilizing audio recording and Vicon Blade[10] motion capture technology. These performances were applied to VGs generated through Adobe Fuse 3D Character Creator,[11] while facial expressions and lip syncing was simulated using Salsa Lip-Synch.[12] Using Unity[8], the authors constructed a minimalistic virtual environment reminiscent of a museum,

---

[5] https://optitrack.com/.

[6] https://facegen.com/.

[7] https://www.daz3d.com/.

[8] https://unity.com/.

[9] https://www.vive.com.

[10] https://www.vicon.com/.

[11] https://www.adobe.com/ie/products/fuse.html.

[12] https://crazyminnowstudio.com/unity-3d/lip-sync-salsa/.

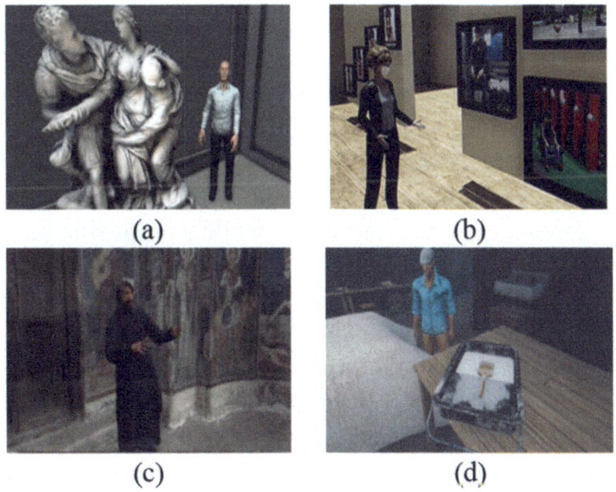

Fig. 15.1 **a** VG conveying information about a famous sculpture; **b** VG following visitors inside a virtual memes museum; **c** VG showcasing a church to visitors; **d** VG instructing visitors on how to repair a cultural heritage artefact

where both a digital twin of the Arria and Paetus sculpture, created using photogrammetry, and the VGs were placed. Visitors could experience the narrations using an Oculus Rift HMD.[13] This study findings suggest that avatars lacking explicit professional identities can not only fulfil their intended functions effectively but can potentially offer an optimal solution due to their propensity for fostering emotional empathy and providing a natural and approachable VG. Particularly noteworthy is the possibility that users may unconsciously regard a VG personifying an astute and well-informed visitor as an aspirational ideal when assuming the role of a (virtual) museum visitor themselves (Sylaiou et al. 2020).

Bönsch et al. (2021) investigated user preferences regarding independence within a virtual museum setting presenting the history of internet memes. To achieve this, two distinct behaviors were devised for a VG, portraying a female museum staff member (see Fig. 15.1b). The first case study involved her leading the user along a predetermined path within the museum. She would position herself near the exhibits and await the visitor's approach before offering information about them. She would discipline visitors in the case they moved away from an exhibit by interrupting her presentation and verbally asking for them to come back, or even approach them and ask them to follow her back to the exhibit. The second case was designed for the VG to emulate a virtual companion, thereby enabling the user to freely explore the museum. Whenever the user displayed interest in a particular exhibit by approaching it, she would follow and provide relevant information about it. Once more, if visitors lost interest in a particular exhibit, the VG made efforts to re-engage their attention, employing a more nuanced approach while she would subtly interrupt her presentation and accompany them to the subsequent exhibit should they decide to proceed. In both cases she would convey personality traits such as expressing her likeness for certain exhibits.

[13] https://www.oculus.com/.

Overly, the VG was depicted as a generic female 3D model, her body motion was generated using MCO Mocap Basics[14] library of Unreal Engine,[15] and her verbal communication was produced through the utilization of the IBM Watson[16] text-to-speech engine, specifically employing the Allison V3 voice. As for the visitors, they utilised an HTV Vice[9] HMD to access the virtual world and an HTV Vive Controller[17] to navigate through it. The results of a within-subjects pilot study yielded no clear preferences to either use cases, while a promising idea for combining both roles can be derived (Bönsch et al. 2021).

Papaefthymiou et al. (2018) compared usability and appropriateness of using photogrammetry, via Agisoft Photoscan,[18] or 3D scanning, using Fast Avatar Capture[19] or Occipital Structure Sensor,[20] for creating a VG based on a real individual (priest), delivering a predefined presentation on history of the Asinou church located at Nikitari village (Nicosia, Cyprus) to users observing its digital twin using an Oculus Rift[8] HMD (see Fig. 15.1c), a HoloLens[21] device, or a mobile device. According to the findings of their study, Occipital Structure Sensor offered the highest level of reconstruction detail and the most practical pipeline for VG creation allowing for detailed body and facial animations (Papaefthymiou et al. 2018).

Butz et al. (2021) investigated the impact of VG appearance on perceived presence, attractiveness, and sense of agency in immersive virtual environments aimed to exhibit and promote cultural heritage. Initially, the writers created a virtual reality application called Enter the Hindenburg, which allows visitors to see and explore the historic airship and intangible cultural treasure Hindenburg. Visitors could tour the airship using an HTC Vive HMD[9] and Vive Controllers[17] and get articulated information about its historical backdrop. Aside from this passive option, the application allowed visitors to follow verbal commands from a VG on how to repair and paint the airship. The VG was shown as either (a) audio-only with no embodiment; (b) an object; (c) an anthropomorphic object; or (d) a human 3D model created using Reallusion Character Creator[22] software (see Fig. 15.1d). The findings of this study reveal that the agent's presence and agency are unaffected by the style of VG visualization. It is also concluded that with current virtual human representation capabilities, the VG can be swapped with an anthropomorphic object without loss of attraction (Butz et al. 2021).

Contrary to immersive VR experiences, which strive to use virtual agents for introducing visitors to recreated virtual CH spaces and scenarios, AR storytelling

---

[14] https://www.unrealengine.com/marketplace/enUS/product/28fc3cc4332541e3b0037d67a65e5d6d.

[15] https://www.unrealengine.com/.

[16] https://www.ibm.com/products/text-to-speech.

[17] https://www.vive.com/eu/accessory/controller/.

[18] https://www.agisoft.com/.

[19] http://ict.usc.edu/prototypes/fast-avatar-capture/.

[20] https://structure.io/.

[21] https://www.microsoft.com/en-us/hololens.

[22] https://www.reallusion.com/character-creator/.

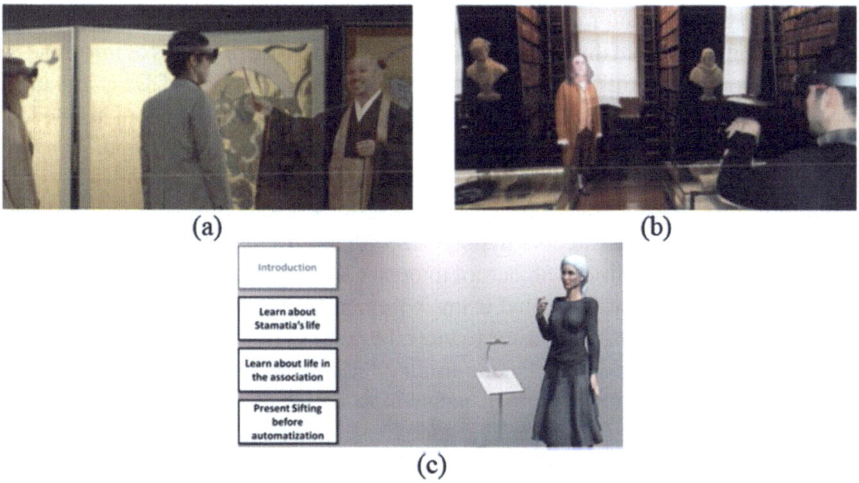

Fig. 15.2 VGs in AR applications. **a** VG presenting a real heritage object to visitors; **b** VG presenting the history of a library in situ; **c** VG presenting the process of mastic production and living in this context

applications focus on the seamless integration of real and virtual elements of CH at the same perceptual level. While AR storytelling deployments have used so far various display components and solutions, this survey narrows its focus on studies and implementations that employ immersive glasses and head-mounted displays (HMDs) to maintain consistency with the reported VR immersive experiences.

In a relatively early work by Microsoft (2008), the use of a digital agent, specifically a virtual monk, is showcased in an MR museum experience at the MR Museum in Kyoto.[23] This digital agent who serves as a guide is a real Kennin-ji monk providing detailed knowledge about the Folding Screen of Fujin and Raijin, a National Treasure. The monk was filmed at Microsoft's Mixed Reality Capture Studios, explaining the intentions of Tawaraya Sotatsu, the artist who painted the Folding Screen. This digital guide immerses viewers, using a Hololens HMD[21], in a dynamic narrative that combines the artwork with 3D graphics, creating a unique and engaging museum experience. The digital agent, in the form of a holographic monk, enhances the viewer's understanding and appreciation of the artwork, demonstrating the potential of digital agents in enhancing cultural and educational experiences (Fig. 15.2a). However, to the best of our knowledge, this application has not reported any systematic evaluation results that validate the positive indications suggested by the use of the digital agent.

In a recent study by O'Dwyer et al. (2021), an AR application was developed with the goal of presenting objects of historical, scientific, artistic, and cultural interest to

[23] https://news.microsoft.com/apac/features/mixed-reality-museum-kyoto-unique-insight-centuries-old-japanese-artwork/.

the public. The application employs a playful and humorous mode of communication, breaking away from the traditional informative and formal modes of information delivery in museum exhibitions. The VG, a live-action portrayal of Dean Jonathan Swift, humorously recounts an embarrassing biographical anecdote from his student days at Trinity (Fig. 15.2b). This decision to adopt a playful narrative approach was informed by observations from library staff, who noted that many visitors exhibit symptoms of information overload and often overlook details of aesthetic and historical significance. The researchers hypothesized that a friendly AR tour guide could help draw visitors' attention to objects of interest within the museum space (O'Dwyer et al. 2021). The guide was created using Volumetric Video (VV), a 3D live-action recording technique that allows users to view the content from any chosen viewpoint. The prototype scene consisted of a one-minute linear monologue narrative featuring a simulation of Jonathan Swift imparting a whimsical, idiosyncratic anecdote linked to the Long Room and its context. The same experience was evaluated in a comparative study that used both a tablet and a HoloLens HMD[21]. Based on the qualitative data analysis, it became evident that a majority of users exhibited a preference for the HMD owing to its ability to provide a heightened sense of immersion and conversational presence. However, the users noted that the HMD headset offered a solitary experience when viewing VV content, and it was no longer a shared, communal experience as with the use of the tablet. Furthermore, VV is captured in a way that does not afford any interactivity with objects or the cultural space itself. The visitor merely assumes the role of an active observer of the narrative (Chrysanthi et al. 2021). The motion of the character was fixed, much like traditional video, whereas 3D computer-generated imagery (CGI) could be programmed to react to visitor interactions.

In a different study, Muñoz and Martí Testón (2020) conducted experiments, using HoloLens HMD[21], in various applications and contexts to determine the most effective techniques for utilizing AR storytelling in museum settings. The archaeological museum of the Almoina in Valencia, Spain, served as the testbed for their study, with the VG Clelia playing a central role in the designed experience. Clelia, a fictional video character, assumed the role of a personal historical guide. The decision to employ a video character, as opposed to a 3D animated recreation, prevailed after previously testing with 3D animated characters and deciding that the expressions of a real person would enhance engagement, vitality, and empathy. In the AR application, the visitor's interaction was designed to be intuitive, resembling natural communication with real individuals, without the need for button presses or text input. Clelia consistently appeared as a flat video layer positioned approximately two or three meters away from the viewer, with her gaze continually directed towards the visitor. At the outset of the experience, Clelia prompted the visitor to approach her before commencing the narrative about the site. Once the visitor assumed the correct position, Clelia's initial task was to introduce herself and instruct the visitor on how to interact with the content. Clelia taught the audience that by directing their gaze toward specific 3D plates within the room, they could activate particular segments of the story. The system was programmed to assess whether the visitor had acquired the necessary head movements for interaction. If not, Clelia would repeat the instructions until the visitor demonstrated the "correct body response." Each plate or coin triggered synchronized sequences of animated video, 3D reconstructions, and music, offering narrative segments that elucidated the history of Valencia during the Roman Republic era. In one particular scene, titled "Sanctuary," Clelia appeared wearing various costumes to illustrate the potential use of the water from the lost pool for healing purposes with the assistance of the god Asclepios. She invited the visitor to explore the area and discover four items placed around the ruins of the pool. Each item contained a two-minute story regarding sacrifices, the city's demise during a civil war, or an explanation of the water's connection to the gods (Martí-Testón et al. 2021).

The study concluded that AR holds significant pedagogical value, primarily in revealing how lost archaeological artefacts were once situated in real space and how they functioned and were used in the past. Additionally, it found that depicting characters in videos, rather than using 3D avatars or cartoons, was more effective in engaging visitors. The decision to present Clelia through video, as opposed to alternative approaches such as 3D avatars or cartoons, proved successful as none of the test participants expressed dissatisfaction with the absence of three-dimensionality. On the contrary, visitors found it intriguing that Clelia seemed to maintain direct eye contact throughout and even waited for their specific actions when required. However, the authors noted that AR technology is still quite expensive and immature to be fully integrated as part of museums' main offerings. The study also acknowledges that this format is less flexible to changes during production because all the necessary lines in the story must be recorded in advance, including any reaction or bifurcation in the plot that may be necessary as a response to specific interactions with visitors.

In the research study titled "Realistic Virtual Humans for Cultural Heritage Applications," the authors present a cost-effective methodology for creating realistic Virtual Humans (VHs) to enhance user experiences in cultural heritage applications (Karuzaki et al. 2021). The study focuses on the Chios Mastic Museum, where eight VHs, mirroring the gender distribution at the Chios Gum Mastic Growers' Association, serve as VGs. The latter narrate personal and work-life stories and explain the functionality of machines in the mastic factory. The VH models were created using Reallusion Character Creation software[22], and their animations were recorded using the Rokoko suit and gloves,[24] which utilize inertial sensors. These models, animations, and recorded audio clips were then imported into the Unity game engine, and the Salsa Lip-Sync[12] software was used to produce realistic lip-synch animations and facial expressions. Visitors interact with the VGs through a camera-controlled user interface. Upon approaching a VG, the latter begins to speak, introducing themselves and presenting available stories in the form of selectable buttons. The narrative content is categorized into sections, including family background, early and adult years of life, work-life in the Chios Gum Mastic Growers Association, and explanations of the processes. The study concludes that the proposed methodology is

[24] https://www.rokoko.com/products/.

cost-effective and results in the production of realistic avatars. The combination of motion and voice recordings has proven beneficial for both realism and development time, providing valuable guidelines for future research in this area (Fig. 15.2c).

15.5 Discussion

Concerning the technology perspective of the examined systems, we identify a clear pattern regarding the utilization of widely adopted design and development engines, such as Unity and Unreal Engine, in conjunction with commercially accessible HMDs such as HTC Vive and Oculus Rift (Bönsch et al. 2021; Butz et al. 2021; Papaefthymiou et al. 2018; Rzayev et al. 2019; Sylaiou et al. 2020). This tendency indicates a preference among researchers investigating VGs within immersive settings for readily available solutions that facilitate convenient access to high quality virtual environments. Another noteworthy observation pertains to the use of advanced technologies for VG animation. Specifically, most of the studies rely on automated motion capture solutions, which in many cases are rather expensive to use to animate VGs. They, however, result in a more precise portrayal of the human body and the capture of body language and nonverbal cues, that further enhances communication with visitors (Bönsch et al. 2021; Rzayev et al. 2019; Sylaiou et al. 2020). Consequently, this practice contributes to an elevated standard of service and augments the overall quality of VG experiences.

In terms of VGs representation, several studies employ dedicated software for the purpose of creating virtual characters (Bönsch et al. 2021; Butz et al. 2021; Karuzaki et al. 2021; Papaefthymiou et al. 2018; Sylaiou et al. 2020). This highlights the significance of achieving a superior quality representation for VGs within immersive virtual reality and augmented reality environments. 3D scanning and photogrammetric software as well as software for adjusting various VG characteristics, are employed to ensure the precise transfer of the visual appearance of real individuals to VGs operating in the virtual world (Karuzaki et al. 2021; Papaefthymiou et al. 2018; Rzayev et al. 2019). These techniques serve to enhance realism, with the objective of supporting social presence.

However, despite the researchers' focus on quality graphics and photorealism, VGs portrayed as high-fidelity virtual humans continue in many cases to exhibit suboptimal or similar performance when compared to audio-only guides or VGs depicted as simpler 3D objects. Researchers who attempt to interpret this discrepancy focus primarily on the fact that audio-only guides or VGs represented as simpler objects enable visitors to concentrate on the presented narrative content rather than the VG itself (Butz et al. 2021). Another possible factor could be that of the visitors' prior familiarity with audio-only guides and more "traditional" 2D technologies (Rzayev et al. 2019). When it comes to the generation of high fidelity VGs, a comparative study showed that video recorded characters are preferred to 3D modelled and animated VGs as they exhibit more realistic human expressions, gestures and emotions, while interactivity limitations of this option are also acknowledged (Martí-Testón et al.

2021). An interesting hybrid workflow is proposed by Karuzaki et al. (2021) which utilizes ultra-high-resolution VGs to achieve a more realistic appearance, mo-cap technologies to ensure that animations look natural, and software that can use voice recordings, lip-synching and facial expressions (Karuzaki et al. 2021). Nonetheless, aiming to create a virtually identical, human-like representation entails potential pitfalls. Users may confront the unsettling phenomena known as the uncanny valley (Mori et al. 2012) while engaging with such avatars. Overall, avatars characterized by high fidelity are found to be more appealing, less unsettling, and more human-like, as well as more cheerful compared to lower fidelity VGs.

In the same vein, recent studies have also indicated that a human voice is still preferable over state-of-the-art Text-to-Speech (TTS) synthesizers, both in terms of exhibited listener facial expressions indicating emotions during storytelling, as well as in terms of non-verbal gestures involving the head and arms. The narrator's voice should sound clear and natural, with slight fluctuations in the narrator's tone, speed, and volume to draw users' attention to what's important. Overall, as discussed in the systematic review on social presence presented in Oh et al. (2018), visual and behavioral realism of the virtual human are considered in most studies as strong predictors for enhanced social presence.

The examination of the selected systems in this review shows a strong prioritization for technological solutions towards realistic virtual humans in terms of both appearance, facial expressions and bodily motion. However, less emphasis seems to be given on the design of the narrative content offered to the user by the avatar. As it can be remarked from Table 15.2, two out of the nine systems follow the narrative approach of information provision by a VG in the role of an expert (Butz et al. 2021; Papaefthymiou et al. 2018; Rzayev et al. 2019; Sylaiou et al. 2020). This deliberate approach ensures stability of experimental variables when comparing the visual appearance or performance of VGs. Nonetheless, the incorporation of interactive narrative design in such instances may yield divergent outcomes pertaining to the acceptance of VGs by visitors of virtual cultural heritage sites.

Even in the case of Muñoz and Martí Testón (2020), where the VG is a fictional historical character, the narrative itself is purely informational. The VG, thus, in this case, is an expert guide in disguise (Martí-Testón et al. 2021). Karuzaki et al. (2021) and O'Dwyer et al. (2021) assign to the VGs narratives that are more fitting to their role. In both cases, the VGs, in a more informal note, adopt a more personal storytelling approach and narrate episodes of their (real or fictional) everyday life (Karuzaki et al. 2021; O'Dwyer et al. 2021).

In terms of interactivity in the narrative design, again in most cases we note a predominantly linear approach. The visitor, in most cases, is a passive observer that is expected to consume the content provided by the VG without any control or choice. Karuzaki et al. (2021), Muñoz and Martí Testón (2020) and Bönsch et al. (2021) allow interactivity at the level of object or story selections (Bönsch et al. 2021; Karuzaki et al. 2021; Martí-Testón et al. 2021) and Butz et al. (2021) adopt a more participatory approach including in the narrative scenario instructions for activities (Butz et al. 2021). Direct interaction with the VG, two-way communication and dialogue is again not included in the XR experience design. The VGs narrate or instruct, while the user listens.

15.6 Conclusions and Future Work

The road travelled towards the provision of "human-like" VGs in the highly immersive XR has been long and important. In this work, we attempt to take a step back, and reflect over the road ahead: Which research directions seem to be most promising? Which aspects are currently under-investigated, or entirely missing, to create VGs that can fulfil their exciting potential for the communication and interpretation of heritage? The outcome of this review shows that existing approaches focus on realism and immersion through the application of the state of the art in motion capture and 3D agent design, gradually working towards the objective of a realistic, life-like appearance and body motion for the VGs. What is also evident however is that comparatively much less importance and focus is placed upon the design of the narrative itself, resulting in VGs that lack key features of an engaging tour guide.

Going back to the early work of Cohen (Cohen 1985) about the role of the human tourist guide in cultural heritage environments, different roles are assigned to the guide. As their human guide counterparts, VGs, are expected to be "instrumental", supporting navigation and time management of the group visit, "interactionary", acting as a mediators between the group and the site, "social", with the responsibility for maintaining cohesion between the group members, including tension management and conflict resolution, social integration of all participants and morale booster, and, lastly, "communicative", capturing the guide's role as a "culture broker", pointing out objects of interest and mediating precise information.

The research reported in this chapter focuses almost entirely on the last category, that of communicating information. But what about the other ones? And what about new approaches to guided tours, including those transforming the role of the guide to that of a dialogue facilitator? How should they be (re)shaped in immersive XR digital heritage experiences? Here we posit that the "Social role of VGs" remains an important issue to explore further. Earlier in this work, we reported several recent narrative design approaches that implement VGs over mobile devices and attempt to promote not only historical reflection on an individual level, but also social interactions, perspective sharing and joint meaning making between the group members. This is accomplished in different ways, including interactive storytelling, direct interaction with the VG through question answering as well as by assigning dialogue facilitation responsibilities to the VGs. How can such approaches be combined with the "immersive" condition? This review revealed the mismatch between the strong visualization capabilities for VGs in XR and the lack of advanced, elaborate and effective designs for their narrative and communicative aspects.

The visualization capabilities of VGs raise questions about their effectiveness as well. Many studies discussed above utilize state-of-the-art solutions, such as 3D scanning, motion capture, non-verbal communication, and high-polygon humanoid visualization, to accurately depict and animate VGs. Nevertheless, comparisons between abstract VGs, such as audio-only ones, and state-of-the-art VGs visualization techniques reveal that the latter are not always as effective, even when expected to be. What aspects of strongly visualized VGs contribute to this result? Is it their appearance, their clothes, their body language, or perhaps the absence of a virtual body for the users themselves, preventing them from sympathizing with VGs?

These questions lead to another important aspect of VGs which is not considered by the studies presented above: the impact of the technological infrastructure used to interact with VGs on the overall user experience, as most of the studies utilize conventional commercial solutions. Does the type of technological equipment used to interact with VGs affect the user experience? Are the affordances provided to users sufficient, or could new ones, such as fully controllable virtual bodies, voice commands, and gesture interaction, enhance VGs' acceptance and effectiveness? Comparative studies among VGs visualization/user interaction techniques, considering popular theories such as the uncanny valley and the social identity model, should shed light on this crucial factor in VGs design for XR experiences.

XR has indeed specific characteristics that need to be taken into account for an effective design combining realistic virtual humans as VGs and a narrative design that promotes a deeper understanding of heritage. However, in this wider context of designing XR experiences for the communication of heritage, there are similar challenges for effective interpretative narratives, with their physical and more conventional digital counterparts. Identified principles for storytelling, narration or dialogue facilitation in these other contexts could be transferred in VR and AR. The different affordances and characteristics of these mediums, along with the newly added affordance of Artificial Intelligence and Chatbots, which may be used to further increase the lifelikeness of VGs, imply that these principles require further experimentation with immersive designs before being turned into concrete design guidelines towards maximizing the potential of XR for heritage.

Acknowledgements Angeliki Chrysanthi, Androniki Agelada and Vlasios Kasapakis research for this chapter was funded by the Research e-Infrastructure "Interregional Digital Transformation for Culture and Tourism in Aegean Archipelagos" Code Number MIS 5047046 which is implemented within the framework of the "Regional Excellence" Action of the Operational Program "Competitiveness, Entrepreneurship and Innovation". The action was co-funded by the European Regional Development Fund (ERDF) and the Greek State Partnership Agreement 2014–2020.

References

Abram RJ (2007) Kitchen conversations: democracy in action at the Lower East Side Tenement Museum. Public Hist 29(1):59–76

Antoniou A, Vayanou M, Katifori A, Chrysanthi A, Cheilitsi F, Ioan-nidis Y (2021) Real change comes from within!: towards a symbiosis of human and digital guides in the museum. ACM J Comput Cult Herit (JOCCH) 15(1):1–19. https://doi.org/10.1145/3465557

Ap J, Wong KK (2001) Case study on tour guiding: professionalism, issues and problems. Tour Manage 22(5):551–563

Bailey P (1999) Searching for storiness: story-generation from a reader's perspective. In: Working-notes of the narrative intelligence symposium, pp 157–164

Bedford L (2001) Storytelling: the real work of museums. Curator Museum J 44(1):27–34. https://doi.org/10.1111/j.2151-6952.2001.tb00027.x

Birchall D, Faherty A (2016) Big and slow: adventures in digital storytelling. Museums and the Web

Bönsch A, Hashem D, Ehret J, Kuhlen TW (2021) Being guided or having exploratory freedom: user preferences of a virtual agent's behavior in a museum. In: Proceedings of the 21st ACM international conference on intelligent virtual agents, pp 33–40. https://doi.org/10.1145/3472306.3478339

Bouras V, Spiliotopoulos D, Margaris D, Vassilakis C, Kotis K, Antoniou A, Lepouras G, Wallace M, Poulopoulos V (2023) Chatbots for cultural venues: a topic-based approach. Algorithms 16(7):339. https://doi.org/10.3390/a16070339

Bruner JS (1990) Acts of meaning: four lectures on mind and culture, vol 3. Harvard University Press

Bull G, Kajder S (2005) Digital storytelling in the language arts classroom. Learn Lead Technol 32(4):46–49

Butz M, Hepperle D, Wölfel M (2021) Influence of visual appearance of agents on presence, attractiveness, and agency in virtual reality. In: Proceedings of the international conference on ArtsIT, interactivity and game creation, pp 44–60. https://doi.org/10.1007/978-3-030-95531-1_4

Ch'ng E, Cai S, Feng P, Cheng D (2023) Social augmented reality: communicating via cultural heritage. ACM J Comput Cult Herit 16(2):1–26. https://doi.org/10.1145/3582266

Chrysanthi A, Katifori A, Vayanou M, Antoniou A (2021) Place-based digital storytelling. The interplay between narrative forms and the cultural heritage space. In: Proceedings of the international conference on emerging technologies and the digital transformation of museums and heritage sites, pp 127–138. https://doi.org/10.1007/978-3-030-83647-4_9

Coerver C (2016) On digital content strategy. Retrieved Oct 17, 2019

Cohen E (1985) The tourist guide: the origins, structure and dynamics of a role. Ann Tour Res 12(1):5–29. https://doi.org/10.1016/0160-7383(85)90037-4

Endacott J, Brooks S (2013) An updated theoretical and practical model for promoting historical empathy. Soc Stud Res Pract 8(1):41–58. https://doi.org/10.1108/ssrp-01-2013-b0003

Faherty A (2022) What makes a great museum label? Retrieved from https://www.museumnext.com/article/what-makes-a-great-museum-label/

Falk JH, Dierking LD (2018) Learning from museums. Rowman & Littlefield

Franz J, Alnusayri M, Malloch J, Reilly D (2019) A comparative evaluation of techniques for sharing AR experiences in museums. Proc ACM Hum Comput Interact 3(CSCW):1–20. https://doi.org/10.1145/3359226

Gallagher KM (2011) In search of a theoretical basis for storytelling in education research: story as method. Int J Res Method Educ 34(1):49–61

Gargett K (2018) Re-thinking the guided tour: co-creation, dialogue and practices of facilitation at York Minster. Unpublished MA dissertation, University of York. https://doi.org/10.1017/eaa.2019.24

Gerber K (2018) Tour Akron art museum with dot the Chatbot. Retrieved from https://www.theformgroup.com/articles/2018/10/17/tour-akron-art-museum-with-dot-the-chatbot

Hanani N, Mohamed R, Noor SM, Lim KY (2013) The effectiveness of tour guide's interpretation in creating mindful tourists: a study on the Penang World Heritage Sites. In: Paper presented at the proceedings of international conference on tourism development

https://doi.org/10.1016/S0261-5177(01)00013-9

Karuzaki E, Partarakis N, Patsiouras N, Zidianakis E, Katzourakis A, Pat-takos A, Kaplanidi D, Baka E, Cadi N, Magnenat-Thalmann N, Ringas C (2021) Realistic virtual humans for cultural heritage applications. Heritage 4(4):4148–4171. https://doi.org/10.3390/heritage4040228

Katifori A, Roussou M, Kaklopoulou I, Servi K (2019) Mobile interactive storytelling in the Athens Ancient Agora: exploring the right balance between the Site and the App. XVII. Cult Comput Sci 47–60. https://doi.org/10.5281/zenodo.3545761

Katifori A, Perry S, Vayanou M, Antoniou A, Ioannidis IP, McKinney S, Chrysanthi A, Ioannidis Y (2020a) "Let them talk!" exploring guided group interaction in digital storytelling experiences. J Comput Cult Herit (JOCCH) 13(3):1–30. https://doi.org/10.1145/3382773

Katifori A, Tsitou F, Pichou M, Kourtis V, Papoulias E, Ioannidis Y, Roussou M (2020b) Exploring the potential of visually-rich animated digital story-telling for cultural heritage: the mobile experience of the Athens university history museum. Vis Comput Cult Herit 325–345. https://doi.org/10.1007/978-3-030-37191-3_17

Kopp S, Gesellensetter L, Krämer NC, Wachsmuth I (2005) A conversational agent as museum guide–design and evaluation of a real-world application. In: Proceedings of the 5th international working conference on intelligent virtual agents, pp 329–343. https://doi.org/10.1007/11550617_28

Lanir J, Wecker AJ, Kuflik T, Felberbaum Y (2016) Shared mobile displays: an exploratory study of their use in a museum setting. Pers Ubiquit Comput 20:635–651. https://doi.org/10.1007/s00779-016-0931-y

Lombardo V, Damiano R (2012) Storytelling on mobile devices for cultural heritage. New Rev Hypermedia Multimed 18(1–2):11–35. https://doi.org/10.1080/13614568.2012.617846

Machidon OM, Duguleana M, Carrozzino M (2018) Virtual humans in cultural heritage ICT applications: a review. J Cult Herit 33:249–260. https://doi.org/10.1016/j.culher.2018.01.007

Malinverni L, Maya J, Schaper M-M, Pares N (2017) The world-as-support: embodied exploration, understanding and meaning-making of the augmented world. In: Proceedings of the CHI conference on human factors in computing systems, pp 5132–5144. https://doi.org/10.1145/3025453.3025955

Martí-Testón A, Muñoz A, Solanes JE, Gracia L, Tornero J (2021) A methodology to produce augmented-reality guided tours in museums for mixed-reality headsets. Electronics 10(23):2956. https://doi.org/10.3390/electronics10232956

McKinney S, Perry S, Katifori A, Kourtis V (2020) Developing digital archaeology for young people: a model for fostering empathy and dialogue in formal and informal learning environments. Communicating the past 12:179

Microsoft (2018) Mixed reality in a Kyoto museum offers a unique insight into centuries-old Japanese artwork. https://news.microsoft.com/apac/features/mixed-reality-museumkyoto-unique-insight-centuries-old-japanese-artwork/

Mello R (2001) The power of storytelling: how oral narrative influences children's relationships in classrooms

Mishra A, Jain SK (2016) A survey on question answering systems with classification. J King Saud Univ Comput Inf Sci 28(3):345–361. https://doi.org/10.1016/j.jksuci.2014.10.007

Mori M, MacDorman KF, Kageki N (2012) The uncanny valley [from the field]. IEEE Robot Autom Mag 19(2):98–100. https://doi.org/10.1109/MRA.2012.2192811

Muñoz A, Testón AM (2020) New storytelling for archaeological museums based on augmented reality glasses. Bulletin of the Council of Heads of National Antiquities Departments 41. https://doi.org/10.5334/bch.g

O'dwyer N, Zerman E, Young GW, Smolic A, Dunne S, Shenton H (2021) Volumetric video in augmented reality applications for museological narratives: a user study for the long room in the library of Trinity college Dublin. J Comput Cult Herit (JOCCH) 14(2):1–20.https://doi.org/10.1145/3425400

Oh CS, Bailenson JN, Welch GF (2018) A systematic review of social presence: definition, antecedents, and implications. Front Robot AI 5:409295. https://doi.org/10.3389/frobt.2018.00114

Olaz X, Garcia R, Ortiz A, Marichal S, Villadangos J, Ardaiz O, Marzo A (2022) An interdisciplinary design of an interactive cultural heritage visit for in-situ, mixed reality and affective experiences. Multimod Technol Interact 6(7):59. https://doi.org/10.3390/mti6070059

Papaefthymiou M, Kanakis ME, Geronikolakis E, Nochos A, Zikas P, Papagiannakis G (2018) Rapid reconstruction and simulation of real characters in mixed reality environments. In: Proceedings of the final conference of the Marie Skłodowska-Curie initial training network for digital cultural heritage, pp 267–276

Pau S (2017) Audio that moves you: experiments with location-aware story-telling in the SFMOMA app. Museums Web.https://doi.org/10.1007/978-3-319-75826-8_22

Petousi D, Katifori A, McKinney S, Perry S, Roussou M, Ioannidis Y (2021) Social bots of conviction as dialogue facilitators for history education: promoting historical empathy in teens through dialogue. Interact Des Child 326–337.https://doi.org/10.1145/3459990.3460710

Poole S (2018) Ghosts in the garden: locative gameplay and historical interpretation from below. Int J Herit Stud 24(3):300–314. https://doi.org/10.1080/13527258.2017.1347887

Pujol L, Roussou M, Poulou S, Balet O, Vayanou M, Ioannidis Y (2012) Personalizing interactive digital storytelling in archaeological museums: the CHESS project. In: Proceedings of the 40th annual conference of computer applications and quantitative methods in archaeology, pp 93–100

Robin B (2006) The educational uses of digital storytelling. In: Proceedings of the international conference on society for information technology & teacher education, pp 709–716

Robin BR (2017) Digital storytelling: a powerful technology tool for the 21st century classroom. Theory Pract 47(3):220–228. https://doi.org/10.1080/00405840802153916

Roussou M, Katifori A (2018) Flow, staging, wayfinding, personalization: evaluating user experience with mobile museum narratives. Multimod Technol Interact 2(2):32. https://doi.org/10.3390/mti2020032

Roussou M, Perry S, Katifori A, Vassos S, Tzouganatou A, McKinney S (2019) Transformation through provocation? In: Proceedings of the CHI conference on human factors in computing systems, pp 1–13. https://doi.org/10.1145/3290605.3300857

Rzayev R, Karaman G, Wolf K, Henze N, Schwind V (2019) The effect of presence and appearance of guides in virtual reality exhibitions. In: Proceedings of mensch und computer, pp 11–20.https://doi.org/10.1145/3340764.3340802

Schaper M-M, Santos M, Malinverni L, Berro JZ, Pares N (2018) Learning about the past through situatedness, embodied exploration and digital augmentation of cultural heritage sites. Int J Hum Comput Stud 114:36–50. https://doi.org/10.1016/j.ijhcs.2018.01.003

Shaer O, Olson J, MaCheire E, Valdes C (2011) Art App-reciation: fostering engagement and reflection in museums through a social-mobile application. In: Museums and the web 2011. Archives & Museum Informatics

Sylaiou S, Fidas C (2022) Virtual humans in museums and cultural heritage SITES. Appl Sci 12(19):9913. https://doi.org/10.3390/app12199913

Sylaiou S, Kasapakis V, Gavalas D, Dzardanova E (2020) Avatars as storytellers: affective narratives in virtual museums. Pers Ubiquit Comput 24(6):829–841. https://doi.org/10.1007/s00779-019-01358-2

Tilden F (2009) Interpreting our heritage. University of North Carolina Press
Tsepapadakis M, Gavalas D (2023) Are you talking to me? An audio augmented reality conversational guide for cultural heritage. Pervasive Mob Comput 92:101797. https://doi.org/10.1016/j.pmcj.2023.101797
Valdes C. Art apprcciation: fostering engagement and reflection in museums through a social-mobile application
Vassos S, Malliaraki E, Falco FD, Di Maggio J, Massimetti M, Nocentini MG, Testa A (2016) Art-bots: toward chat-based conversational experiences in museums. In: Proceedings of the 9th international conference on interactive digital storytelling, pp 15–18. https://doi.org/10.1007/978-3-319-48279-8_43
Vayanou M, Katifori A, Ioannidis Y (2021) Perspective sharing in culture group games: passing around the social mediator role. Proc ACM Hum Comput Interact 1–24. https://doi.org/10.1145/3474676
Vrettakis E, Katifori A, Ioannidis Y (2021) Digital storytelling and social interaction in cultural heritage-an approach for sites with reduced connectivity. In: Proceedings of the 14th international conference on interactive digital storytelling, pp 157–171. https://doi.org/10.1007/978-3-030-92300-6_14

Chapter 16
Delving into Fairy Tales: Designing for Digital Interactions in a Children's Museum

Maria Shehade, Theopisti Stylianou-Lambert, Panagiotis Kyriakou, Fotos Frangoudes, Maria Pavlou, Stefanos Papadas, and Kleanthis Neokleous

Abstract With the rapid advancement of technology, children's museums have integrated interactive installations to engage young visitors in immersive and educational experiences. The advantages of interactive installations lie in their ability to cater to different learning styles and enhance children's engagement with educational content. However, it is important to acknowledge the limitations and challenges that such interactive technologies can have in these settings. This chapter explores the design of two interactive installations in a children's museum, examining the advantages that can be achieved and also the challenges and limitations that can be addressed through a well-thought-out design process. By focusing on fairy tale museums, and through a real case example, the chapter explores how interactive technologies can foster fantasy, imagination and allow children to be transported

M. Shehade (✉) · T. Stylianou-Lambert · P. Kyriakou · F. Frangoudes · M. Pavlou · S. Papadas · K. Neokleous
CYENS Centre of Excellence, Nicosia, Cyprus
e-mail: m.shehade@cyens.org.cy

T. Stylianou-Lambert
e-mail: t.stylianou@cyens.org.cy

P. Kyriakou
e-mail: p.kyriakou@cyens.org.cy

F. Frangoudes
e-mail: f.frangoudes@cyens.org.cy

M. Pavlou
e-mail: m.pavlou@cyens.org.cy

S. Papadas
e-mail: s.papadas@cyens.org.cy

K. Neokleous
e-mail: k.neokleous@cyens.org.cy

M. Shehade · T. Stylianou-Lambert
Cyprus University of Technology, Limassol, Cyprus

F. Liarokapis et al. (eds.), *Interactive Media for Cultural Heritage*, Springer Series on Cultural Computing, https://doi.org/10.1007/978-3-031-61018-9_16

in magic worlds. The chapter explores and analyses specific design considerations and principles that can be applied in order to harness the advantages of interactive installations while addressing their limitations and explains how these were applied in a fairy tale museum in Cyprus.

Keywords Children's museums · Interactive installations · Design principles · Fairy tale museum · Fantasy and imagination

16.1 Introduction

Children are natural-born explorers, armed with boundless curiosity and an insatiable appetite for discovery. To foster their intellectual and creative growth, children's museums have long been recognized as spaces that captivate young minds, ignite their imaginations and foster exploration, discovery, and hands-on learning for young visitors. Over the years, these institutions have evolved, adapting to the rapid advancements in technology, and are now considered as dynamic and interactive environments that actively engage young visitors.

The integration of technology within children's museums has facilitated the way we engage and educate our future generations. Interactive installations, ranging from touchscreen displays and immersive Virtual Reality (VR) experiences to Augmented Reality (AR) applications, can provide unique, engaging and immersive experiences designed to captivate and educate children. These innovative technological tools offer many advantages, allowing children to actively participate, learn through play, and personalize their museum visit.

In today's digital age, interactive installations have emerged as powerful tools in engaging young minds. These installations seamlessly blend the physical and digital worlds, creating multisensory environments that encourage active participation and experimentation. Through the use of interactive technologies, children can explore various subjects in ways that traditional museum exhibits often cannot provide. The interactive nature of these installations can promote curiosity, critical thinking, and problem-solving skills, enabling children to become active learners rather than passive observers.

However, it is crucial to recognize that interactive installations also come with certain limitations and challenges that need to be carefully addressed during the design process. For example, one of the primary concerns is the potential for overstimulation and information overload. While technology offers exciting possibilities, an excessive reliance on sensory stimulation can overwhelm children, hindering their ability to process and retain information effectively. Therefore, to ensure that these technologies truly benefit all children, designers and curators must set particular design principles, accommodate diverse needs and provide equal opportunities for engagement.

The aim of this chapter is to delve into the design of interactive installations within children's museums, through a real case example, and to highlight design considerations and principles that should be applied for both augmenting the advantages of these technologies but also for better addressing their inherent limitations. In particular, the chapter presents two interactive installations created for a fairy tale museum in Cyprus and discusses the design and development process in an attempt to explore how interactive technologies in a children's museum can promote fantasy, imagination and wonder. Although many attempts have been made to incorporate such technologies in children's museums, very few projects focused on fairy tale and story museums, that place an emphasis on magic worlds and fantasy. Thus, this chapter places a special emphasis on these characteristics to address this gap.

The chapter begins with an overview of children's and fairy tale museums, discussing their development and special characteristics. It then examines the uses of technology in these museums, summarizing the advantages and limitations that these technologies may have in these settings. Finally, the next sections present our case study, the concept of the exhibition, a detailed description of the installations and their technical characteristics and offer an analysis of the design considerations and principles followed.

16.2 The Development of Children's Museums and Fairy Tale Museums

Children's museums play a vital role in providing educational and interactive experiences tailored specifically to the needs and interests of young visitors. The aim of these museums is usually to engage children in hands-on learning, foster creativity, and inspire a love for knowledge and exploration. According to the Association of Children's Museums, these museums constitute "places where children learn through play and exploration in environments designed just for them".[1]

Children's museums have a rich history that can be traced back to the late nineteenth century, when the importance of hands-on learning experiences for children was recognised for education and child development.[2] One of the earliest examples of a children's museum is the Brooklyn Children's Museum, founded in 1899 in Brooklyn, New York (Mayfield 2005). It was established by the Brooklyn Institute of Arts and Science, and it was the first museum in the United States dedicated to children, aiming to provide a space where children could explore and engage with objects from different cultures, natural history specimens, and interactive exhibits. This groundbreaking initiative served as a catalyst for the establishment of similar museums around the world. This particular museum pioneered "the philosophy that now governs all children's museums: that the museum was for somebody rather than about something" (Cleaver quoted in Mayfield 2005, 180).

[1] Available at https://findachildrensmuseum.org/about/ [Last access July 1, 2023].

[2] For an overview on the history of Children's museums refer to Mayfield (2005); Fouad and Elsaid (2021); Schofield-Bodt (1987).

In the early twentieth century, the concept of children's museums gained momentum, and several other museums dedicated to children's education were established across the United States, such as the Boston's Children Museum in 1913 and the Children's Museum of Indianapolis in 1925 (Fouad and Elsaid 2021). Children's Museums in the twentieth century were driven by advancements in child psychology, educational philosophies of the time (such as those by Maria Montessori for the importance of hands-on learning and play in children's development), and by an increased focus on early childhood education. These ideas influenced the design and programming of children's museums, which aimed to provide interactive and experiential learning opportunities. Apart from the expansion of children museums, this was a time when museums began to embrace child-centred approaches, focusing on open-ended exploration, sensory experiences, and fostering creativity.

During the late 20th and the twenty-first century, children's museums evolved to encompass a broader range of educational objectives, and expanded their offerings to include exhibits and programs that explore science, technology, art, culture, and the environment. To facilitate their educational offerings, children's museums were the first to work with interactive machines to demonstrate science concepts, relating to the principles of physics, the space, the environment etc. In recent decades, the global expansion of children's museums has been notable, with more than 300 such museums existing globally (Fouad and Elsaid 2021) in diverse forms, ranging from large institutions in urban centres to smaller community-based museums. Although museums dedicated to children's learning and play have been established in many countries, most of them are located in the USA (ibid).

In today's children's museums, the emphasis shifted towards creating dynamic and immersive environments that can stimulate children's curiosity, creativity, and critical thinking. The incorporation of interactive exhibits, role-playing areas, and sensory experiences became integral to the design of children's museums in the twenty-first century. The technological advancements of the twenty-first century, allowed children's museums to integrate emerging technologies, interactive digital displays, and virtual experiences, in order to offer even more interactive and immersive learning opportunities, further expanding the possibilities for engagement and education. As will be explained in the following sections, these advancements have both created an array of advantages and new potentials for these museums, but also created some challenges in their daily operations.

One particular type of children's museum that captures the imagination of young visitors is the fairy tale museum. Over the last two decades, fairy tale and story museums have emerged, reflecting the approaches of the 'participatory museum' (Simon 2010), moving towards more interactive curatorial practices (Hamer 2019). Some of these museums may be dedicated to fairy tales in general, such as for example the Story Museum in Oxford, UK[3] or the Museum of Fairy tales (Mesemúzeum) in Budapest.[4] Other such museums may be devoted to particular well-known authors of fairy tales, such as for example the Hans Christian Andersen House and Museum

---

[3] See https://www.storymuseum.org.uk/ [Last accessed: 4th July 2023].

[4] See https://mesemuzeum.hu/en [Last accessed: 4th July 2023].

in Denmark,[5] or the Grimm Welt Kassel in Germany, dedicated to the work of the Grimm Brothers.[6]

Fairy tale museums have a unique and specialized focus on the world of folklore, mythology, and traditional tales. These museums aim to preserve and celebrate the rich cultural heritage of fairy tales while providing an engaging and educational experience for children. Their aim is to serve as gateways to imagination, allowing children to explore the realms of fantasy and develop a deeper appreciation for storytelling. Thus, the role of fairy tale museums extends beyond mere entertainment, since they also serve as educational platforms, promoting literacy, critical thinking, and cultural understanding (Hamer 2019). By immersing children in the world of fairy tales, these museums aim to spark their imagination and ignite their creativity. Through these museums, children can develop important skills such as problem-solving, empathy, and moral reasoning as they navigate the moral dilemmas and ethical complexities often present in fairy tales. Fairy tale museums also provide opportunities for children to explore different cultures, as fairy tales are a universal form of storytelling found in diverse traditions and countries.

16.3 Technology in Children's Museums

In recent years, many children's museums are attempting to embrace the opportunities presented by the digital age, by incorporating new technologies to enhance the visitor experience and expand learning possibilities. The integration of digital elements, such as interactive displays, AR, VR, and mobile applications, has changed the way children interact with exhibits and engage with educational content. Through the adoption of hybrid approaches, blending traditional hands-on experiences with digital elements, many children's museums around the world aim to create dynamic and multisensory learning environments that cater to the evolving interests and digital fluency of young visitors.[7]

Especially in the context of fairy tale museums, mediated experiences with the use of technologies are increasingly created, in an attempt to create more interactive and immersive exhibits for engaging with children's literature texts, the act of story-telling and other related material (Hamer 2018). The use of technologically mediated engagement of children with fairy tales, creates an experience which combines traditional children literature with the so-called 'new literacies', that is "practices that draw upon technical affordances of new media technologies but also cultivate a new ethos that is often defined as participatory, collaborative and distributed" (Hamer 2018, 438).

---

[5] For a detailed overview of the museum refer to Hamer (2018, 2019).

[6] See https://www.grimmwelt.de/en/ [Last accessed: 4th July 2023].

[7] See for example the Indianapolis Children's Museum in the US and the Egyptian Child Museum in Cairo, discussed in Fouad and Elsaid (2021).

Undoubtedly, there is an array of advantages that can be gained from the use of technologies in children's museums, which have also been recognised in recent literature (for an overview refer to Shehade and Stylianou-Lambert 2020). Interactive and emerging technologies can offer enhanced interactivity and immersion, providing unique experiences that traditional exhibits cannot replicate. As noted by Moorhouse et al., "interactivity is increasingly seen as essential to children's museum learning experiences and is a key feature of AR learning applications because it can assist with making connections between museum artefacts and images and visitors lives and memories" (2019, 5). AR and VR technologies, for example, enable children to explore virtual worlds, reconstruct historical environments and provide the feeling of actually being there (Economou 2016), or present scientific concepts in a hands-on and immersive manner.

This can in turn enrich learning experiences by providing dynamic and personalized content tailored to the individual needs and interests of children (Fouad and Elsaid 2021; see also Debailleux et al. 2018; Hsu and Liang 2017). Interactive displays and digital exhibits can present information in engaging ways, utilizing gamification elements to promote experiential learning, problem-solving, and critical thinking skills (Sung et al. 2010; Lai et al. 2007). Moreover, interactive touchscreens, and AR and VR simulations can bring abstract concepts to life, enabling children to explore and experiment in ways that traditional exhibits may not permit. Relevant studies have also found that the level of immersion and presence of such learning experiences can also affect how easily children can recall what they learned (Araiza-Alba et al. 2020). It was also found that the incorporation of a technological exhibit in a museum setting may evoke children's curiosity, critical thinking and exploration (Andre et al. 2017). The technology itself, especially if tried out by children for the first time, can also evoke curiosity and excitement, as indicated in the study of Cianciarulo (2015), examining children's interactions in museums.

Interactive technologies can also address accessibility concerns in children's museums, by promoting inclusivity and accessibility and ensuring that all visitors, including those with physical or cognitive disabilities, can fully engage with the exhibits. Assistive technologies, such as audio descriptions, adaptive interfaces or tactile interactions, can create inclusive and barrier-free environments, allowing visually impaired and other children with special needs to equally access the museum offerings (see for example Vistisen and Jensen 2012).

Especially in the context of fairy tale museums, interactive and emerging technologies can allow children to advance their imagination and get immersed into the world of fairy tales and fantasy (Cassell and Ryokai 2001). As noted by Hamer, "within the context of an immersive exhibit, the visual and verbal elements of print texts are not only adapted across multiple media platforms, but the design of each affiliated text has the opportunity to meaningfully extend, inform, or potentially subvert the central discourses of the fairy tale or children's literature narrative" (2018, 439).

Nevertheless, despite the advantages of technologies identified in children's museums, there are also several concerns and limitations identified, that should also be considered. As Mayfield notes, "the place of technology in children's museums is an area of debate both inside and outside the museum community" (2005, 185), with many curators expressing concerns over the role of technology in children museums (see for example Brister 2017).

While emerging technologies can enhance engagement, technology applications may also become distractions rather than facilitators of learning, overshadowing the exhibition's educational objectives. Relevant concerns were raised in literature and by curators noting that children may become absorbed in the novelty of the technology itself, rather than focusing on the educational content or engaging with other visitors (Brister 2017; Mayfield 2005). Others also argue that in many cases such applications aim to create a 'wow factor' in children, in an attempt to compete theme parks and other family recreational activities, without providing meaningful interactions (Lord 2003). The absorption to the screens and the distraction of the visitor from the objects and concepts of the museum is a concern that has also been discussed in relation to adults in museums (see Shehade and Stylianou-Lambert 2020).

The isolation of visitors (and in this case children) from the surrounding environment, has also been noted as an important limitation of technologies such as VR. This can also impede social interaction, which is of paramount importance in museum settings. Especially in the case of children's museums, that are mostly visited by school groups and families with children, technologies such as VR, that are designed to be used by a single user can create problems in the social interactions between these particular visiting groups. The same problem may also appear with other types of technology, such as touch screen-based interactive kiosks. For example, in a study by Vishkaie et al. (2021) it was noted that most families that visited the touch screen-based interactive kiosks, did not complete the tasks included in the kiosk, since the screen size did not allow the entire family to participate.

The incorporation of interactive and emerging technologies in children's museums also requires a substantial investment for the purchase and maintenance of the necessary equipment as well as an investment in the necessary training of the museum personnel on how to use and troubleshoot the equipment. Additionally, keeping up with rapidly evolving technology trends may require continuous investment and staff training (for an analysis of the challenges associated with financial investment in technology and training needs of museums refer to Shehade and Stylianou-Lambert 2020). Particular types of technologies also have the limitations of age restrictions. For example, it is not advised to use VR in children younger than 12 years old, and this can create problems especially in children museums, if such applications are only available for particular ages (ibid).

Some studies also indicted that when a technological application is complicated and difficult to use, this can negatively affect children's experiences in museums (Wolf and Wood 2012). This is especially so in cases where the adults accompanying the children find it difficult to use the technology and cannot guide their children, which may produce negative impacts on children's learning (compared to children effectively guided by adults) in their interaction with technology (ibid).

Despite the growing attempts of children's museums to incorporate technology in their exhibits, and the discussion of the advantages and challenges that this technology may pose, relevant literature on the topic is still rather limited. Moreover, it seems that there is a lack of a 'critical children's museology', since as Hamer notes, "while a number of critical curatorial movements are in effect in academic museum studies [...], very few of these projects involve young people in their critical practices across media or feature children's museum exhibits in their scholarly studies" (2019, 391).

Existing research on children's museums mostly focuses on museum education, with a special emphasis usually on science museums and interactive learning opportunities (Andre et al. 2017; Moorhouse et al. 2019; Anderson et al. 2002; Piscitelli and Anderson 2001). Relevant studies also focus on art education in museums and galleries, especially through hands-on education (Terreni 2015; Kortbek and Grønbæk 2008). When it comes to technological applications for children's museums, relevant literature mostly focuses on the role of different types of media in museum education and specific experimentation with different types of technologies (Hall and Bannon 2005, 2006; Pallud 2016; Radeta et al. 2017; Rodrigo et al. 2019; Vishkaie et al. 2021) or on projects of digital storytelling in which children act as co-creators (Cassell and Ryokai 2001; Jones et al. 2003). Especially in the case of interactive media for fairy tale museums or related exhibitions, relevant literature is even more limited, with only very few studies presenting relevant projects designed for children (Taylor et al. 2015).

Therefore, this chapter aims to present a project especially designed for a fairy tale museum and to discuss the design considerations that should be taken into account in such cases. The sections that follow provide an overview of the museum and its exhibition, the interactive installation designed and the technology used, with a special attention to the design considerations followed during the development process.

16.4 The Fairy Tale Museum in Cyprus and the Designed Exhibition Concept

The Fairy Tale Museum in Cyprus was founded in 2017 as a non-profit organisation and is housed in a renovated Grade II listed building. The aim of the museum is to safeguard fairy tales, legends, myths and traditions from Cyprus and Greece, as well as from many different parts of the world, together with internationally renowned fairy tales.

According to the objectives set out by the museum, through its exhibitions, the museum aims to preserve an important element of intangible heritage linked to fairy tales, legends and traditions, but also highlight the universality of fairy tales and allow children to become familiar with other cultures through their fairy tales, to help children develop a love of reading and to strengthen children's mental resilience through fairy tales. The museum is addressed to families with children and also to groups of school children that regularly visit the museum as part of the curriculum.

The museum includes a series of interactive exhibits relating to fairy tales and their main characteristics, such as the concept of time, climax fluctuations, and their universality. It also organises book reading sessions, thematic exhibitions, tributes to

Fig. 16.1 The "magic library" that includes a book installation stretching towards the ceiling, located at the entrance of the museum. *Photo* Maria Shehade

authors and illustrators and educational programs aimed at children, families, school groups and those who love the world of fairy tales and storytelling.

The museum also includes rooms that highlight particular fairy tales and objects related to them such as Alice in Wonderland, Aladdin and Cinderella. The exhibits are designed to allow for interaction, through a series of hidden doors, drawers that can be opened, gears that can be turned, and magic objects that can be handled. One of the main attractions of the museum is the "magic library" that includes a book installation stretching towards the ceiling, which is dedicated to fairy tale writers and folk researchers (Fig. 16.1).

Although most of the museum's exhibits promote interactivity, none of the exhibits used technology to facilitate new ways of interaction and immersion. Thus, in 2019, the museum partnered with the CYENS Centre of Excellence[8] to enhance some of its exhibits with technology. The collaboration of the museum with CYENS was the result of an Open Competition for Museums and Heritage Sites,[9] announced by the Museum Lab of CYENS, in which the Fairy Tale Museum was the winner. The competition was addressed to museums and cultural sites interested in incorporating interactive media and emerging technologies in their premises, to help them meet the needs of the current digital era and become more visible and attractive. CYENS Centre of Excellence, in close consultation and collaboration with the winning museum, designed, developed and funded a technological solution for the needs of the museum.

[8] See https://www.cyens.org.cy/en-gb/.

[9] For more information on the aims of the competition see https://museumlab.cyens.org.cy/project/let-technology-rise-you-up/.

16.4.1 Overview and Concept of Developed Exhibition

For the purposes of the collaboration between the two organisations, a room of the museum was selected to be enhanced with technology. The selected room was the 'magic objects' room, situated on the ground floor of the museum. The particular room is the first room visited during the guided tours offered by the museum, after an introduction that is made to the visitors in the museum's foyer.

The room is dedicated to well-known magic objects found in internationally known fairy tales and to the concept of the 'magic helpers'. The room includes a cabinet which hosts a series of replicas of magic objects such as the flying carpet, the magic mirror from Snow White, the hat that makes its bearer invisible, the hen with the golden eggs, the mill that makes wishes come true, the magic wand, and Aladdin's lamp amongst others (Fig. 16.2).

The magic objects room aims to immerse children in the world of fairy tales and explore the uses of such magic objects in fairy tales, for fulfilling the desires of the heroes, from the most basic and material ones to their deepest desires, such as overcoming human abilities. The conceptual design of the room also aims to explain the role of magic helpers in fairy tales, i.e., supernatural or other creatures that help heroes overcome the hardships they face or battles against monsters, wicked witches, or dangerous creatures, by providing them with the magic objects mentioned above.

Throughout a typical guided tour of the museum, the guide usually asks children to imagine how these objects were used and by whom, remember fairy tales they

Fig. 16.2 The cabinet with the magic objects. *Photo* Maria Shehade

know that include these objects, and even use them in a re-enactment of scenes from fairy tales.

The team involved in the project, in collaboration with the museum, decided to create a technological installation that would 'bring these objects to life', help children get immersed in the world of these objects and related fairy tales and get a chance to truly experience the effects of these objects.

For this reason, six objects from the room were selected:

1. The magic flying carpet that transports anyone who seats on it to faraway places
2. The lamp of Aladdin, which produces a genie that makes wishes come true
3. The mill, that when turned produces anything that its owner asks for
4. The magic mirror from Snow White
5. The magic flute, that mesmerises people with its music
6. The hen with the golden eggs.

The particular objects were selected in close consultation with the founder and director of the museum, since they constitute well-known objects from important fairy tales, and they are usually the objects drawing more attention from the children.

Since the aim of the installation would be to bring fairy tales and objects to life and immerse the visitor in the world of fairy tales, it was considered as a great start to the museum visit, since the installation would allow the visitor to be detached from the ordinary, leave behind everyday life, and get immersed into a fantasy world. Getting immersed in a fantasy world, would also help visitors follow the rest of the exhibits; it was also one of the reasons why the particular room was selected (as the first stop to a typical visit or tour). Apart from this, the theme of the room, focusing on the abilities of magic objects, was considered very appropriate for attempting to re-create an immersive experience with these objects.

16.4.2 Design Considerations and Principles

Before developing any digital interactive for a children's museum, one must ensure that particular considerations and principles are in place for designing the installation as effectively as possible. Throughout this process, the team involved was in close consultation with the museum personnel to understand the needs of the museum, and tailor the installation according to these needs, but to also understand the challenges faced by the museum and take them into consideration through the design process. The narratives of the museum were also considered to tailor the technology to fit the needs and context of these narratives. This was extremely important given that past studies indicate that the people that use the museum spaces, such as museum educators, teachers, and pupils, who can share their experiences and insights on the space are very rarely consulted before developing interactive exhibits in museums, which in many cases impedes the successful design of these interactives (Rogers and Edwards 2002; see also Hall and Bannon 2005).

The cabinet, including the magic objects, already had a distinctive purple light in each segment, creating a 'magical' and 'mysterious' atmosphere in the room, which intrigued the children to explore what was hidden behind the cabinet doors, when these were closed. Building on this element, it was decided that the aim would be to create an 'enriched' space that would combine this light with sound, interactive storytelling elements, and animations to further augment the children's curiosity and fantasy and make the environment of the room appear as truly 'magical'.

An important consideration during the design phase, was with regard to the role of technology in the overall narrative of the museum, and the need to seamlessly integrate the digital interactives as facilitators in the storytelling, and not as exhibits on their own merit. As emphasised by Wyman et al., "the question is how to leverage new forms of technology while ensuring that they don't detract from the power and significance of stories and content" (2011, 464). Thus, one of the guiding principles of the design process was the blending of the interactive exhibits with the physical space (and its limitations), so that the physical space, its atmosphere and objects, remain the centre of attention. This was also based on Falk and Dierking's vision for interactive technologies in museum settings:

> virtuality will never replace reality [...] although people might be thrilled to [...] view objects through the electronic medium, our guess, [...], is that if given the opportunity, most people will readily choose the real experience every time. The future [of technology in museums] lies in the blending, not the separation, of the virtual and the real world. (Falk and Dieking 2000, p. 231).

Thus, the technology used should be unobtrusive and it should also respect the authentic design of the room, the furniture and the artefacts.

Multi-modality was also considered during the design process and it was decided that the designed interactives would allow the inclusion of tactile, auditory and visual elements to facilitate multi-modal interactions with the fairy tale narratives. This was also based on previous studies, in which it was found that children remembered more strongly exhibits that were associated with tactile experiences (Andreson et al. 2002). Since tactile interaction plays an important role in children's learning and meaning- making, we also aimed to include in the digital interactive the actual objects included in the magic room, so that we can combine the material aspect with a digital augmentation, and provide the chance to children to handle and touch the objects of the exhibit.

The overall design was guided by a human-centred and participatory perspective, in an attempt to create an engaging experience that would both promote storytelling and also incorporate some kind of activity so that children are not passive receivers but active creators of their own stories, promoting fantasy play and creativity. We also aimed to include aspects of discovery learning in the associated activities, through hidden content in the designed interactives that the children can discover.

Since one of the most important limitations of technological applications in museums (and children's museums) is the visitor isolation and lack of social interaction, the group dynamics of the museum experience were one of the guiding designing principles of the project. As a matter of fact, most visitors at the Fairy Tale Museum are school groups or family groups so it was important to design an application with a group audience in mind. Thus, we aimed to promote the social dimension of the museum visit, by designing an experience that would allow children to learn through social interactions with other children and schoolmates and also allow all family members to take part in the exploration of the exhibit.

Some functionality and other practical considerations were also taken into account during the design process. Based on the experience of the Director of the museum, any digital interactive incorporated into the room should be easy to use and should not require sophisticated or difficult to use equipment, so that it is easily accessible to all, even to very young children. Given that the museum is also visited by very young audiences (3–4 years of age), it was also important to include equipment that does not break easily and technologies that are appropriate for all ages and don't have age restrictions. Moreover, based on the needs of the museum, it was important to design a technology that is easy to maintain due to the budget restrictions that the museum has, and that does not malfunction often, to reduce repair costs. As discussed in Sect. 16.3, budgetary restrictions are a serious impediment for many museums that wish to incorporate technology in their spaces, and we aimed to design an interactive installation that would respect these restrictions.

16.5 The Development of the Interactive Installation

Based on the design considerations and principles presented in the previous section, we created five interactive experiences, following the same logic, for the magic carpet, the lamp of Aladdin, the mill, the flute and the hen and another experience for the magic mirror, with different technical parameters. The developed exhibition was fully funded and developed by the CYENS Centre of Excellence, as a collaboration between two of its research groups: the Museum Lab[10] and the ITICA group.[11] The Museum Lab is dedicated to the exploration of emerging technologies inside and outside museums and other heritage sites, while the ITICA group aims to bring together elements from fine arts with computational intelligence and emerging technologies. The team involved followed an interdisciplinary approach, which is of extreme importance in such projects and consisted of museologists, computer scientists, 3D modelers and sound designers. This multidisciplinarity allowed for designing the most suitable interactives, taking into account both museological and museum education perspectives as well as technical considerations, based on the design principles set out at the beginning of the project.

For all the experiences created, the aim was to keep the original 'magic' objects at the centre of attention, also taking into account the narrative of the museum for the particular room, and the way these objects were used during the educational programs of the museum. Based on the original program of the museum, the museum educator

[10] https://museumlab.cyens.org.cy/.

[11] https://itica.cyens.org.cy/.

guiding the experience in the room has a dual role, aiming to both provide the contextual information relating to the role of these objects and of the 'magic helpers' in fairy tales, but also to mediate the experience to allow for the scaffolding of social interactions between the children and families in the room and the encouragement of role play for some objects. In this context, the museum educator would ask children to imagine what these objects can do or how they work and also imagine how they would use them if they were in the shoes of the heroes of the fairy tale. Children are also asked to role play and imagine that they can use these objects. Therefore, we aimed to create an experience that can augment this narrative and facilitate these social interactions and role play. We also selected technologies that are as 'invisible' as possible, to also enhance this sense of wonder and magic so that the physical objects remained the centre of attention.

16.5.1 Magic Objects Installation

For the first five objects—the magic carpet, the lamp of Aladdin, the mill, the flute and the hen—the experience was designed around the handling of these objects to which radio frequency identification (RFID) tags were attached. Each individual object was assigned a passive RFID tag. When a reader scans a passive RFID tag, it transmits energy to power the tag's chip and antenna, allowing it to relay information back to the reader. This information is then sent to an RFID computer program for interpretation. To maintain a discreet appearance, each RFID tag was attached to its corresponding object or hidden within the object, when possible.

To incorporate the physical environment of the room, we used an antique wooden chest that was available in the room, under which we 'concealed' the technical equipment (the computer and sound speakers) (Fig. 16.3a). The RFID reader, used for recognizing each object, was placed underneath a wooden board inside the chest (Fig. 16.3b). Based on the designed experience, after children are prompted to imagine what each object does, they are asked to place the object on the wooden chest. This activates a set of animations that are projected both on the wall in front of the children and on the floor underneath their feet, to allow for a semi-immersive experience (Figs. 16.4a and b). These animations were projected using two separate short-throw projectors.

For each of the five objects, different animations were created depicting the object 'coming to life', with a set of two different animations for each object, aiming to transport the users into a magical world linked to the particular object. For example, for the magic carpet the floor animation depicts a moving carpet (on which children are asked to sit to be transported to a faraway city) while the wall animation shows the journey while flying between the buildings of an ancient city (Fig. 16.4). For the magic hen, the wall animation shows the hen moving around in roller blades, while the floor fills with eggs that are then transformed into golden eggs. Thus, the installation offers young visitors a unique opportunity to not only physically engage with objects from fairy tales but also become fully immersed in the enchanting worlds

Fig. 16.3 **a** (on the left) Shows the wooden chest used for technical equipment. **b** Shows the wooden board used for concealing the RFID reader. The circle indicates the exact position that the objects should be placed to be recognized by the reader. *Photo* Maria Shehade

Fig. 16.4 Overview of the projections of the animations on the floor and the walls. *Photo* Nicolas Karatzas (Used with permission)

associated with these objects. The installation was developed using the game engine Unity3D (Unity3d.com).

All animations were designed based on the actual objects, using the same forms and colours so as to give the impression that the particular object comes to life. (Figs. 16.5a and b) Moreover, in some animations other objects from the room were also incorporated; for example, the animation for the lamp of Aladdin shows the genie coming out, standing next to a wooden chest, which resembles the chest in the room.

Fig. 16.5 **a** (on the left) shows the original object for the hen with the magic eggs. **b** Shows the corresponding animation created for the particular object. *Photo 16.5a* Maria Shehade. *Photo 16.5b* Maria Pavlou

Apart from the animations, each object is accompanied by its own music theme and voice over. All music themes were enriched with sound effects matching the animations. The narrations of the voice overs were written by the museum staff to better reflect the narratives used in the guided tours and educational programs. Based on previous studies with technology in children's museums it was found that pre-scribed narratives were usually found long and tiresome (Hall and Bannon 2005) and thus all voice overs were kept short.

All animations were designed with the aim to engage the children and allow them to build their own narratives, so that they do not act as passive receivers of information. For example, the genie coming out of the lamp asks children to make a wish and write it down on a piece of paper that is then placed in the wooden chest; the magic flute prompts all children to dance together to its music. Therefore, the designed interactive inspires creative storytelling, allowing the children both to discover the 'hidden' content behind each object and to also create their own stories around them. The content is also non-restrictive, to help the museum educator encourage children's imagination and the scaffolding of personal experiences. For example, the flying carpet takes children on a journey to a far away, ancient city, without pre-scribing which city this is. During the experience children are asked to imagine which city they would like to see and why and they also have the chance to hear what their peers are saying. Therefore, through these group interactions children have the chance to collaborate and hear multiple perspectives and diverse opinions with the use of technology.

16.5.2 Magic Mirror Installation

The second installation, created for the 'magic mirror', had a different concept and used different technical parameters. The magic mirror is also included in the cabinet together with the rest of the objects, hidden behind a closed door. During the regular museum visits, the museum educator usually asks children to imagine that this is the magic mirror from the Snow White fairy tale. The mirror is used together with a replica of the bitten apple in a performative way, to reenact parts of the fairy tale 'Snow White and the Seven Dwarfs', with some children acting as the 'Evil Queen', others as 'Snow White' and others as the 'Magic Mirror's' voice.

The aim of our designed interactive for the mirror was to literally bring the mirror to life and provide the experience of talking to the mirror and interacting with it. Based on the concept of the designed interactive, as soon as the door is opened and a child stands in front of it, the mirror 'becomes alive' and a face appears in the mirror and talks to the child (Fig. 16.6). This effect was achieved by utilizing a special type of glass that functioned as a mirror when no light was present behind it, while still allowing light to pass through from the rear. Behind the glass, we positioned a vertical monitor of similar size to the mirror. Upon activation, the monitor displayed an animation of a face against a black background. The surrounding areas appeared reflective, but the region where the face was rendered appeared as if it was emerging from the mirror. To trigger the animation, we employed a concealed web camera, also positioned behind the faux mirror, which was programmed to recognize faces using specific algorithms from the OpenCV computer vision library (https://opencv.org/). This installation was also developed using the game engine Unity3D. The mirror animation is also accompanied by its own music theme with sound effects to enrich the mirror's 'magical' aura.

Based on the new script developed by the museum, although the mirror in the fairy tale points out Snow White as the most beautiful of them all, the mirror at the Fairy Tale Museum states to the children that everybody is beautiful in their own way and asks them to think of three things they like about themselves, prompting them to reply and interact with it.

The interaction with the magic mirror can work both with an individual user and with a group of children, who may either take turns in interacting with the mirror or 'discover' the mirror together. As with the previous interactive, this also allowed for active participation and engagement, since children are not passive receivers of what the mirror says but they are prompted to think about their preferred characteristics. The experience also respects group dynamics and interactions since the children also have the opportunity to hear the characteristics chosen by the rest of the children and discuss them with the museum educator.

The mirror is usually shown after the other five objects and the different concept usually surprises children, who become excited when they realise that the mirror can interact with them. The haptic aspect is also incorporated in this experience, with children being asked to open the door to reveal the mirror.

Fig. 16.6 The magic mirror with its animation. *Photo* Maria Shehade

Therefore, both experiences designed for the magic objects room, enrich the space, while respecting the authentic aura of the room and of the objects, allow for muti-modal interactions, active participation of the children in the experience, and for the development of social interactions.

16.5.3 Addressing Technical Limitations

The experiences created attempted to address some of the limitations usually noted during the use of technology in children's museums (see Sect. 16.3). In both experiences the physical objects remained at the centre of attention and the technology was built around these objects so as not to distract the children or take their attention away from the narratives associated with each object.

The technology was designed to augment the physical experience of the children in the magic objects room and to allow for their meaningful and active engagement. The design considered the museum's needs and narratives, and the technology was designed in such a way so as to have a meaningful impact on the visit rather than just create a wow factor or impress the visitors.

We also used simple and screen-less technologies that offered many advantages and allowed us to address many limitations noted in relevant literature. First, the designed experiences allowed children to 'disentangle' from screens and spend creative time away from smartphones and tablets. They also allowed social experiences that provided for group/family interaction, which is the reason why we moved away from technologies such as VR, that could be considered as more isolating and less social in the context of a children's museum. This also helped to avoid age restrictions in the designed experiences, since the nature of the technology we used also allowed very young children (from 3 to 4 years old) to participate in the experience (which would not be possible with technologies such as VR).

Finally, the designed technology was very easy to use both by children and by the museum staff, which also provided many advantages. First, this allowed us to address the limitations described in Sect. 16.3 for the use of complex technologies in children's museums and to also address the concerns of the museum staff regarding the vulnerability of the equipment, especially when used by very young children. Second, due to the ease of use of the technology, no extensive training of the museum staff was needed (which is also a concern for most museums), apart from some initial guidance on basic troubleshooting. Finally, although the cost of the project was covered entirely by CYENS, the maintenance of the technology is cost efficient for the museum, compared to other more complex technologies that also require high maintenance costs.

Regarding the limitations identified during the use of the interactive experiences, we identified two issues that relate mostly to functionality and use. First, the camera of the magic mirror was placed at a specific height so that it can easily recognize the faces of young children (which are the largest audience of the museum). However, when taller (or older) children or adults participate in the experience, the camera may not be able to easily detect their faces at a different height (and they may have to bend their knees a bit to reach the camera level). Second, in some cases when very young children handled the objects, some RFID tags fell off or were lost and had to be replaced. Thus, some extra attention was needed by museum staff when very young children participated in the experiences.

16.6 Conclusion

The integration of technology in children's museums presents immense opportunities to create dynamic, engaging, and educational experiences for young visitors. However, it is crucial to consider the characteristics that technology should possess in this unique setting, through a well-thought-out design process. The project presented in this chapter is an illustrative example of the design considerations and principles that can be applied when creating digital interactives for a children's museum, with a special focus on fantasy and fairy tales.

Although the incorporation of interactive technologies in these museums can offer many advantages, there are also many challenges that should be taken into consideration. For example, technology in children's museums should strike a balance between screen time and hands-on experiences. While digital technologies offer exciting possibilities, it is important to ensure that they are integrated alongside other tactile and physical play elements, so as to create a holistic environment that promotes active exploration, creativity, and social interaction. By carefully curating the digital content and providing opportunities for children to manipulate physical objects, children's museums can foster a well-rounded and enriching visitor experience. Therefore, as this chapter emphasised, technology in children's museums should be interactive, immersive, and it should encourage active participation and critical thinking.

As emphasised by the presented example, the design and implementation of technology in children's museums should be guided by thoughtful curatorial planning. The incorporation of a multidisciplinary team in such projects is of crucial importance to address many different perspectives, so that both museological, educational and technical considerations are taken into account. Consultation with the museum staff is also critical before, during and after the design of digital interactives to address the needs of the museum and its visitors. This also facilitates the selection of age-appropriate content to align with the educational and other objectives of the museum and to incorporate technology in a seamless way.

Especially in the context of fairy tale museums, which place an emphasis on fantasy and imagination, interactive technology should be 'concealed' to provide a sense of wonder and magic. This will also allow to keep the children's attention on the actual narratives and objects of the museum, rather than distracting them. Multi-modality is also an important element in these experiences, since the combination of auditory and visual elements with tactile ones, can create more memorable experiences for children.

By incorporating technology with these characteristics, children's museums can provide meaningful and enriching experiences that foster lifelong learning, creativity, and a sense of wonder in the minds of young learners. Interactive technologies in these museums should strive to create a harmonious blend of digital innovation with the magic of traditional, hands-on exploration, facilitating engaging and transformative educational journeys for children in the modern era, and the aim of this chapter was to present an example of how these design considerations can be applied in the case of a fairy tale museum.

The application of emerging technologies in children's museums offers exciting opportunities to enhance interactivity, enrich learning experiences, and facilitate engagement. However, challenges related to the social aspects of the visit, maintaining engagement, and avoiding prolonged screen time and isolation must be carefully navigated. By following specific design considerations and principles, children's museums can successfully integrate interactive technologies to create immersive and educational environments that cater to the diverse needs and interests of young visitors. Regular evaluation and feedback from visitors and the museum staff can provide insights into the effectiveness and impact of technology applications, allowing for continuous improvement and refinement. Collaboration between educators, museum professionals, and technology experts is essential to ensure that technology in children's museums remains purposeful, engaging, and aligned with educational goals. By embracing the potential of technology while upholding the core principles of children's museums, we can create transformative and inspiring learning environments that ignite curiosity, creativity, and a lifelong love of exploration in the minds of young learners.

Acknowledgements This project has received funding from the European Union's Horizon 2020 Research and Innovation Programme under Grant Agreement No 739578 and from the Government of the Republic of Cyprus through the Deputy Ministry of Research, Innovation and Digital Policy.

References

Anderson D, Piscitelli B, Weier K, Everett M, Tayler C (2002) Children's museum experiences: identifying powerful mediators of learning. Curator Museum J 45(3):213–231

Andre L, Durksen T, Volman ML (2017) Museums as avenues of learning for children: a decade of research. Learn Environ Res 20:47–76

Araiza-Alba P, Keane T, Chen W, Kaufman J (2020) Children's memory of a story experienced with virtual reality versus traditional. J Virtual Reality 20(2):55–69

Brister S (2017) Does digital technologies belong in children's museums?. https://childrensmuseums.blog/2017/07/27/digital-technology-in-childrens-museums/. Retrieved July 1, 2023

Cassell J, Ryokai K (2001) Making space for voice: technologies to support children's fantasy and storytelling. Pers Ubiquit Comput 5:169–190

Cianciarulo D (2015) From local traditions to "augmented reality". The MUVIG museum of Viggiano (Italy). Proc Soc Behav Sci 188:138–143

Debailleux L, Hismans G, Duroisin N (2018) Exploring cultural heritage using virtual reality. In: Ioannides M (ed) Digital cultural heritage. Lecture notes in computer science. Springer International Publishing

Economou M (2016) Heritage in the digital age. In: Logan W, Craith M, Kockel U (eds) A companion to heritage studies. Wiley and Sons, Sussex, UK, pp 215–228

Falk JH, Dierking LD (2000) Learning in museums. Whalesback Books, Washington, DC

Fouad RAE-D, Elsaid H (2021) Promoting children tourism through applying virtual reality to the Egyptian child museum. Int J Herit Tour Hosp 15(2):1–19

Hall T, Bannon L (2005) Co-operative design of children's interaction in museums: a case study in the hunt museum. CoDesign 1(3):187–218

Hall T, Bannon L (2006) Designing ubiquitous computing to enhance children's learning in museums. J Comput Assist Learn 22(4):231–243

Hamer N (2018) 'Children's museums'. In: Greenhill P, Rudy JT, Hamer N, Bosc L (eds) The Routledge companion to media and fairy-tale cultures, pp 435–442. Routledge, New York

Hamer N (2019) The hybrid exhibits of the story museum: the child as creative artist and the limits to hands-on participation. Museum Soc 17(3):390–403

Hsu TY, Liang HY (2017) A cyclical learning model to promote children's online and on-site museum learning. Electr Libr 35(2):333–347

Jones C, McIver L, Gibson L, Gregor P (2003) Experiences obtained from designing with children. In: Proceedings of the 2003 conference on interaction design and children, pp 69–74

Kortbek KJ, Grønbæk K (2008) Communicating art through interactive technology: new approaches for interaction design in art museums. In: Proceedings of the 5th Nordic conference on human-computer interaction: building bridges, pp 229–238

Lai CH, Yang JC, Chen CF, Ho CW, Chan WT (2007) Affordances of mobile technologies for experiential learning: the interplay of technology and pedagogical practices. J Comput Assist Learn 23:326–337

Lord GD (2003) The power of cultural tourism. http://www.lord.ca/publications/articles/powerculturaltourism.html. Accessed July 1, 2023

Mayfield MI (2005) Children's museums: purposes, practices and play? Early Child Dev Care 175(2):179–192

Moorhouse N, Claudia Tom Dieck M, Jung T (2019) An experiential view to children learning in museums with augmented reality. Museum Manage Curatorsh 34(4):402–418

Pallud J (2016) Impact of interactive technologies on stimulating learning experiences in a museum. Inf Manage 54(4):465–478
Piscitelli B, Anderson D (2001) Young children's perspectives of museum settings and experiences. Museum Manage Curatorsh 19(3):269–282
Radeta M, Cesario V, Matos S, Nisi V (2017) Gaming versus storytelling: understanding children's interactive experiences in a museum setting. In: Interactive storytelling: 10th international conference on interactive digital storytelling, ICIDS 2017 Funchal, Madeira, Portugal, November 14–17, 2017, proceedings 10, pp 163–178. Springer International Publishing
Rodrigo MMT, Vidal ECE, Herras IYD, Agapito JL, Diy WD, Ortega VA, Bugayong NA, Ong A, Santos JM, Lim LRT (2019) Tuklas: design, development and testing of an augmented reality experience for a children's museum. In: 2019 IEEE international conference on engineering, technology and education (TALE), pp 1–6. IEEE
Rogers R, Edwards S (2002) The Big Sink: a report on the key factors for designing building, equipping, using and managing creative spaces in galleries, museums and schools. In: Group for education in museums (GEM) news, no 86, pp 8–9
Schofield-Bodt C (1987) A history of children's museums in the United States. Child Environ Q 4(1):4–6
Simon N (2010) The participatory museum. Museum 2.0, Santa Cruz, CA
Shehade M, Stylianou-Lambert T (2020) Virtual reality in museums: exploring the experiences of museum professionals. Appl Sci 10(11):11–13
Sung Y, Hou H, Liu C, Chang KE (2010) Mobile guide system using problem-solving strategy for museum learning: a sequential learning behavioural pattern analysis. J Comput Assist Learn 26(2):106–115
Taylor R, Bowers J, Nissen B, Wood G, Chaudhry Q, Wright P, Bruce L, Glynn S, Mallinson H, Bearpark R (2015) Making magic: designing for open interactions in museum settings. In: Proceedings of the 2015 ACM SIGCHI conference on creativity and cognition, pp 313–322
Terreni L (2015) Young children's learning in art museums: a review of New Zealand and international literature. Eur Early Child Educ Res J 23(5):720–742
Vishkaie R, Seyed T, Emmons CT, vom Lehn D (2021) Take me to Greece: exploring intergenerational interactivity in a mixed reality children's museum exhibition. J Museum Educ 46(1):93–112
Vistisen P, Jensen T (2012) Transforming learning and visitor participation as a basis for developing new business opportunities in an outlying municipality: case study of Hjørring Municipality and Børglum Monastery, Denmark. In: Kristiansen E (ed) The transformative museum: proceedings, pp 164–175. DREAM—Danish Research Center on Education and Advanced Media Materials Institute for Literature, Culture and Media Studies University of Southern Denmark
Wolf B, Wood E (2012) Integrating scaffolding experiences for the youngest visitors in museums. J Museum Educ 37(1):29–38
Wyman B, Smith S, Meyers D, Godfrey M (2011) Digital storytelling in museums: observations and best practices. Curator Museum J 54(4):461–468

Chapter 17
Reinheriting Cultural Heritage Spaces: Performance Design and Practice

Andreas Papapetrou, Fotos Frangoudes, Alexis Polydorou, Stefanos Papadas, Maria Shehade, Niki Kyriakou, and Kleanthis Neokleous

Abstract Two interdisciplinary immersive performances were organised within the framework of ReInHerit, funded by Horizon 2020 (https://www.reinherit.eu), which is an international project focused on promoting a digital ecosystem connecting cultural heritage collections and sites, in order to present Europe's tangible and intangible heritage to citizens and tourists in its wider historical and geographical contexts. The immersive performances will provide a template for collaborations for developing similar projects, which are shaped by cultural heritage sites and will in turn help to attract wider audiences to them. These were planned, developed and realised in parallel to the setup of a digital platform, in which all key stakeholders (museums, cultural heritage sites, policy makers, professionals and communities) have an open and collaborative space to experiment, share, co-create and innovate. A diverse group of professionals joined forces to create this project, resulting in two interdisciplinary performances that invited audiences to take initiative in shaping their experience of them.

A. Papapetrou (✉) · F. Frangoudes · A. Polydorou · S. Papadas · M. Shehade · N. Kyriakou · K. Neokleous
CYENS Centre of Excellence, 23 Lellou Demetriadi Square, 1016 Nicosia, Cyprus
e-mail: andreaspapapetrou@gmail.com

F. Frangoudes
e-mail: f.frangoudes@cyens.org.cy

A. Polydorou
e-mail: a.polydorou@cyens.org.cy

S. Papadas
e-mail: s.papadas@cyens.org.cy

M. Shehade
e-mail: m.shehade@cyens.org.cy

N. Kyriakou
e-mail: n.kyriakou@cyens.org.cy

K. Neokleous
e-mail: k.neokleous@cyens.org.cy

F. Liarokapis et al. (eds.), *Interactive Media for Cultural Heritage*, Springer Series on Cultural Computing, https://doi.org/10.1007/978-3-031-61018-9_17

Keywords Interdisciplinarity · Immersion · Interactivity · Performance · Cultural heritage · Improvisation · Aleatoric music · Sound installation · Augmented reality

17.1 Introduction

This chapter aims to provide an in-depth presentation and analysis of the two immersive performances created as case studies within the framework of the ReInHerit H2020 project, with a focus on interactive media used for the project's design and development, discussing objectives, challenges and solutions sought, as well as points for consideration in planning and realising similar future endeavours. Furthermore the chapter offers a detailed discussion of the objectives, museological perspectives, technical characteristics, artistic aspects for both immersive performances, followed by an evaluation of audience engagement strategies and ending with an examination of challenges and limitations faced within the project.

17.2 The ReInHerit Project: Redefining the Future of Cultural Heritage

Finding an alternative way of experiencing cultural heritage sites is a crucial part of ReInHerit. *Redefining the future of cultural heritage through a disruptive model of sustainability*, or ReInHerit,[1] is a Horizon2020 project that aspires to disrupt the current status quo of communication, collaboration and innovation exchange between museums and cultural heritage sites, connecting them in order to present Europe's tangible and intangible heritage to local communities and tourists in its wider historical and geographical contexts. In short, the ReInHerit project proposes an innovative model of sustainable cultural heritage management, through which a dynamic network of collaboration is created, comprising of cultural heritage professionals, innovation and cultural heritage solution tech experts, researchers, national museums, regional and local museums, and representative managers of Heritage Label sites. The proposed model is based on a digital ecosystem in which all the stakeholders, such as museums, cultural heritage sites, policy makers, professionals and communities, are provided with the tools and resources to communicate, experiment, innovate and disseminate European cultural heritage in real time.[2]

[1] See https://www.reinherit.eu.

[2] Tools, such as apps and educational toolkits, and a collection of resources (on training, tourism, conservation, preservation, knowledge creation, content use/reuse, illicit trafficking of goods), which are necessary for sustainable management are already being shared through the digital platform hosting the ecosystem. This ecosystem also aims to be an experiential open-ended space that will support and generate entrepreneurial initiatives, knowledge produced through co-creation, curation of digital content and visitor experiences. This will be achieved through the creation of an innovative Digital Hub (see https://reinherit-hub.eu/).

CYENS Centre of Excellence,[3] and specifically the Multidisciplinary Research Group ITICA (Immersive Technologies for Intelligent and Creative Applications)[4] and the Multidisciplinary Research Group Museum Lab,[5] is a partner institution and a member of the consortium for ReInHerit H2020. The centre's role within the project is to address the ReInHerit Digital Hub's requirements mentioned earlier on content generation and its dissemination, resulting from the curation of visitor experiences in cultural heritage sites.

CYENS CoE was responsible for the creation of two immersive performances in cultural heritage sites, which would be thoroughly documented in order to function as case studies for the ReInHerit Digital Hub, setting standards for collaboration and co-creation between partner institutions. The two immersive performances were planned, developed and realised in parallel to the setup of the Digital Hub, which now hosts a thorough description and documentation of both, including hardware and software requirements, a smartphone app, anonymous user data collected during the events, as well as music scores and instructions for re-creating similar performances in other venues.

The proposed objectives of the immersive performances in focus included inducing audience participation in museums and cultural heritage sites, by hosting interactive activities (i.e. the performances) and making the visitors' experiences intuitive within them. An important extension of this was to measure the extent to which technology incorporated in performance may help audience members think creatively and even improvise musically, regardless of whether they have formal musical education or not. Furthermore, the objectives included increasing awareness on and visibility of the ReInHerit project, aiming to promote the sharing of ideas, and the re-use of content and resources related to the project in disruptive ways, and to create opportunities for audience engagement, cultivating active citizenship and encouraging EU cohesion.

Some of these objectives were achieved during the performances, while others through the dissemination of the performances' documentation in the ReInHerit Digital Hub. The creative team faced challenges during the development stage for both case studies and had to adapt the proposed performance plans several times before reaching the final outcome of the two immersive performances, which are outlined in the next sections.

---

[3] See https://www.cyens.org.cy.

[4] ITICA MRG is an interdisciplinary team with a research focus that combines elements from fine arts with computational intelligence and emerging technologies, such as Virtual Reality (VR) and Augmented Reality (AR), to develop evidence-based applications. (See https://itica.cyens.org.cy/).

[5] Museum Lab MRG is dedicated to the exploration of emerging technologies inside and outside museums and other heritage sites, with a special emphasis on visitors' experiences and their interactions with technology. (See https://museumlab.cyens.org.cy/).

17.3 A Review of Audience Immersion in Cultural Heritage

It can be argued that audience immersion has a long history. Depending on technological means and the nature and intensity of such experiences, the history of audience immersion is intertwined with the development of theatre and opera set design and special effects. As early as in ancient Greece, theatrical performances often took place in amphitheatres, where the audience was seated around the stage. The circular shape of these theatre spaces, allowed maximum eye contact and intervisibility among the audience, fostering a shared experience. Greek tragedies and comedies sometimes involved direct interaction between performers and audience in choruses (Grzega 2013).

Specifically for its use in cultural heritage, the focus lies in exploring the 'experience (physical vs. virtual), the narratives (content vs. context) and the meaning (interpretation vs. action)' (Dogan 2020). The concept of immersion in cultural heritage was adopted after projects of media art such as multimedia art installations and performance arts gained recognition and popularity by creating environments or experiences that deeply immersed viewers and encouraged their active engagement (Wiener 2022). Whereas museums have traditionally privileged the use of visual or textual resources, the inclusion of other cues to promote types of visitor immersion, such as embodied and spatial interaction, allows the flow of information between a site, a participant and technology to be multidirectional, providing unique experiences for participants (McAvoy 2019).

Recent efforts to digitise cultural heritage, such as the CHROMATA platform, focus on 'facilitating the creation of novel immersive experiences to sustain intangible cultural heritage' (Pistola et al. 2021), providing heritage professionals with tools to enhance visitor experiences in educational contexts, while it is widely recognised that gamification can 'positively impact the educational process, as it integrates game mechanisms and elements into teaching and learning activities' (Kleftodimos et al. 2023). This idea has a wide following and within archaeology, heritage and video game circles, the playful yet scholarly engagement with the past through video games is now known as 'archaeogaming' (Politopoulos et al. 2023).

Digital games are considered an effective tool for public engagement with heritage, attracting an increasing amount of academic attention (Varinlioglu and Halici 2019). To achieve visitor immersion in a museum setting, augmented reality is often preferred to using virtual reality headsets, as they are currently impractical in a museological context as they can be antisocial and difficult to operate (Choi 2023). However, a hybrid combination of live immersive performance and digitally enhanced experience, using augmented reality can render visitors into active participants in their cultural heritage experience, fusing the virtual with the real (Dima and Maples 2021). ReInHerit combines elements from the aforementioned ideas in its case studies, the two immersive performances discussed in the following sections.

17.4 Case Study 1: ReInHerit in Performance: The Hadjigeorgakis Kornesios Mansion

17.4.1 Overview

"ReInHerit In Performance: The Hadjigeorgakis Kornesios Mansion" was organised on the evening of October 29th 2022. A diverse group of professionals, namely artists, museologists and computer scientists, joined forces to create this project, resulting in an interdisciplinary performance, consisting of a combination of live music, sound art, video art, lighting design, programming, 3D printing and temporary exhibition curation, that invited its audience to take initiative in shaping their experience of it.

The performance was hosted at the Ethnological Museum of Cyprus in Nicosia. The venue is mostly known as the mansion of the Dragoman Hadjigeorgakis Kornesios, a high-ranking official in Ottoman Cyprus and the palace of the House of Podocataro, dating back to the fifteenth century. The venue was chosen because of its significance as a unique monument of cultural heritage that combines several layers of Nicosia's rich history. It is also a space that attracts only a small number of daily visitors, coming mostly from school field trips and privately guided tours.

The project's objective was to create a performance that would offer visitors an alternative mode of experiencing exhibits and spaces within this cultural heritage site, inviting them to interact and engage with the spaces or exhibits in a holistic way, i.e. a specially designed multimedia experience, which is site-specific, exhibit-specific, time-limited, unique and deeply personal for each visitor that comes to the space during the performance. It is a case study in developing a performance that is informed by a cultural heritage site, that grows within, respects and helps enhance pre-existing exhibitions and museum spaces. The performance was open to different types of interpretation and did not require the use of complicated verbal instructions, prior accustomisation with specialised equipment or familiarity with the cultural heritage site in question.

Upon entering the cultural heritage site on the day of the performance, visitors witnessed a small group of musicians standing silently in the mansion's courtyard (Fig. 17.1) with large video projection on the wall behind them, and were given a small brown envelope, containing a set of text-based treasure hunt prompts on postcard-sized paper. Visitors were provided with simple guidelines on how to navigate the performance space and interact with the immersive environment it contained, and the musicians started producing sounds and moving in both outdoor and indoor spaces of the mansion. The performers' sounds mixed with the sounds of the interactive audio installation, which was triggered by the audience's proximity to its sensors. Visitors were encouraged to wander in the mansion's spaces freely and explore the exhibits, while interacting with the audio installation. The performance ended when all musicians gathered on a terrace at the edge of the courtyard, cueing all sound and video projection to fade out.

Fig. 17.1 Visitors and performers in the courtyard of the Mansion of Hadjigeorgakis Kornesios at the beginning of the performance. Photo credit: Andreas Papapetrou

17.4.2 Treasure Hunt and Museological Perspectives

One of the main ideas behind the immersive performance was that the Hadjigeorgakis Kornesios mansion would not constitute just a performance site hosting the event, but that the performance would merge with the place and constitute an enhancement of the visitor experience. The aim was to provide the visitors a way of experiencing a heritage site that goes beyond the typical museum visit, which is usually centred around textual ways of interpretation, and to provide a combination of visual, haptic, textual and auditory cues, allowing visitors to create meanings based on their personal interests.

To allow this, the experience (both from a museological and from a performative aspect) was not designed to be linear, following a particular script, but visitors could walk freely within the mansion, deciding where to spend more time as they wished and according to their interests. To achieve non-linearity, a treasure hunt was designed around 15 particular objects of interest that are found in different areas of the mansion, located both inside the rooms and in the courtyard, including, a fountain, a traditional dress, a grandfather clock, a decorated chest, a tea set, pottery and jewellery amongst others.

Short texts were prepared for each of the selected objects, written in simple language and avoiding academic jargon, so that they were easily read by younger audiences as well. These provided basic information regarding each object and its use in the daily life of the mansion. The texts were designed in such a way to briefly provide a general historical context, since many of the selected objects originated from different historical periods and emphasised the use of these objects or stories of the mansion's inhabitants related to these objects. The aim of the texts, apart from providing a basic way of interpretation, was to help visitors relate to the people that inhabited the mansion and imagine their daily life in the specific environment.

The texts deliberately omitted information on where in the mansion each object was located, as the treasure hunt-type of activity asked the visitors to spot them. Each object included in the treasure hunt was linked to a sonic activity, so once visitors approached an object, they would start to receive extra auditory cues.

It should be noted that another important aspect addressed in this performance was its suitability and availability to groups with disabilities. To achieve this, a temporary multisensory exhibition was set up in the mansion, specifically created for people with visual impairments. This exhibition included replicas prepared by CYENS Thinker Maker Space[6] specifically for the performance evening: replicas of the traditional dress exhibited in the space, 3D-printed scans of small parts for the exhibits (namely a wooden carved ceiling decoration), a small-scale haptic sound installation, consisting of a line-art black-and-white reduction of the Podocataro coat of arms bas-relief that produced corresponding sounds when touched in certain coordinates, plus a booklet of the exhibition's texts in braille.

17.4.3 Interactive Sound Installation

Sound and music were an essential component of this performance, created using an interactive audio installation and a group of nine moving performers. As audience and performers navigated the performance space, they triggered sonic events, depending on locations of sound installation receivers. The sound installation was set up in both outdoor and indoor spaces of the mansion and it was designed to interact with audience members moving in the performance space, based on their number and proximity to receivers placed in various locations.

Even though the sound installation's stations were spread across the mansion, enveloping the performance space, all sound coming from the installation was localised, meaning that each station functioned independently from the rest. The sounds used for each sound station (i.e. a receiver-smartphone and a Bluetooth speaker) corresponded to specific exhibits in the mansion (for instance, grandfather clock chimes or sewing machine sounds—Fig. 17.2) adjacent to them or to the surrounding space's original use within the venue (for instance, the guest reception room had different sounds to those played back in the kitchen space).

To create the sound stations, two applications which both run on smart mobile phones were developed using Android Studio. The first application (*the "station"*) was responsible for the detection of users in an area while streaming the appropriate sounds to a speaker. The second application, (*the "Remote"*) had remote control and

[6] See https://makerspace.cyens.org.cy.

Fig. 17.2 Musician performing in front of a grandfather clock, interacting with corresponding audio coming from an adjacent sound station. Photo credit: Andreas Papapetrou

connecting functionalities of the various stations that were spread across the museum. The applications developed are now available in the ReInHerit Digital Hub.

The *Station* application was able to track users' behaviour within its Field of View (FOV), using the integrated back-facing camera of the mobile devices., The integrated algorithms were responsible for the scanning of the space for changes in its FOV (such as number of people or their movement), and triggered accordingly different sonic evens associated with the corresponding changes. Several sonic events were designed based on specific thresholds that were calibrated with associated changes on the number of people and level of their movement in each station. Specifically, each station was designed to play up to five different sounds, while at the same time, a constant background sound (drone) was played regardless of the users' behaviour.

Tracking the number and movement of users was done indirectly by analysing changes of pixel value within the captured frames due to limitations in lighting conditions or placement of smartphone cameras. Initially, a base image of the observed area was captured and used for calibration and for comparison purposes with the continuously new frames that were captured. Since this procedure produced a high CPU load, each frame was converted to a grayscale image and rescaled to a lower resolution, allowing a stable framerate for the application. Moreover, this process also computed pixel differences between consecutive frames to track motion in real time. These two values were then combined using a weighted average, with an adjusted threshold weight defined for the specific conditions of each location. Finally, a sonic event was triggered depending on the level of threshold that was passed.

The Remote application was connected through Bluetooth with the Sound Stations and was used by the technical team of the project for controlling specific parameters of each station. Thus, the team members were able to walk around the performance space and control the Sound Stations remotely for real time calibration when changes in lighting or object placement took place. The main functionalities of the Remote application include the adjustment of the volume of the stations and the control of their audio playback. The application can also adjust the weights and thresholds used for the recognition algorithm so it can be optimised in real-time. These settings and the operation of the stations can also be monitored by retrieving the status of each station. Finally, the number of musicians present within each room can be optionally tracked, and this information was logged for analysis.

17.4.4 Visual Elements: Lighting and Video Art

To establish coherence between performance space and the sonic elements added within the performance, dramatic coloured lighting and video projections were included. The lighting did not change throughout the performance as its function was to enhance specific spots within the performance space and to set the general mood during the event. While the colour and intensity of the lights used were fixed throughout the performance, a natural change in lighting occurred during the first of the three performance slots organised, as this slot started at dusk. This was deliberately set at this time to allow easier access to audience members with visual impairments.

On the other hand, video art was used to provide visual rhythms for the performance. This was used in the performance space in two locations: a large-scale projection on an adjacent building's façade that visually dominated the courtyard during the event, and a smaller indoor projection that created an intimate, meditative atmosphere in a hidden room of the mansion that is usually not accessible by the museum's visitors. In terms of concept, the video artist's focus was to breathe new life into the museum by representing the mansion's breath in a symbolic way. The video projections used intricate details of textures and patterns found in the venue, combined in a highly abstract collage that was slowly morphing and constantly moving for 40 min to set the pace of the performance (Fig. 17.3). Thus, subtle changes on screen were also used to cue the musicians to move to different spots in the performance space and change the sounds they produced.

17.4.5 Performative Aspects: Spatial Music and Guided Improvisation

A group of nine musicians (violinists and violists) provided by the Cyprus Symphony Orchestra performed within the sound installation, to add a necessary element of live performance to the event. The musicians moved throughout the duration of the performance. They had fixed starting and ending points, with loosely set routes

Fig. 17.3 The courtyard of the Mansion of Hadjigeorgakis Kornesios during performance, with video art projection visible in the background. Photo credit: Andreas Papapetrou

through the performance space. The sounds they created were produced following a set of verbal and notated instructions for guided improvisation. The instructions were easy to memorise as the performers could not use a score during performance space because of lighting restrictions and constant movement.

The instructions for performers included a short description of the general concept of the performance, directions for the locations in the venue, in which the musicians would be performing and indications on when to go to them and how fast to move. The score used a floor plan of the venue to facilitate instruction. Furthermore, a series of tones (pitches) or extended playing techniques for each section of the piece was included, along with instructions on how to approach these as material for guided improvisation. In addition, the instructions indicated timings for sound, such as when to make gradual or abrupt changes in the style of improvised playing, or sectional changes that required synchronisation to other performers. Section changes (timings) were also cued by the large-scale video art piece projected in the courtyard.

The sounds produced by the performers blended with the audio coming from the sound installation, parts of which were at times triggered by the musicians as they moved in the space, and created a fluctuating cloud of drones,[7] short melodic motifs and noise loops that set the mood for each part of the performance. The performers did not interact with audience members, but instead set their courses through the space and gently prompted the audience to move around and explore the venue during the performance.

[7] In the context of music, a drone is a tone sustained for a long time.

17.5 Case Study 2: ReInHerit a Museum: Immersive Performance at the BoCCF

17.5.1 Overview

"ReInHerit a Museum: Immersive Performance at the BoCCF" was the second case study for the project, realised on 19 May 2023, as part of the International Museum Day and European Museum Night events organised at the Bank of Cyprus Cultural Foundation. As with the previous case study, a diverse group of professionals joined forces to create this project, resulting in an interdisciplinary performance that invited its audience to take initiative in shaping their experience of the event, this time while exploring *digital and physical exhibits* and the space hosting them.

The performance was organised at the premises of the Bank of Cyprus Cultural Foundation (BoCCF)[8] in Nicosia. The goal for this project was to create an immersive environment that would use both indoor and outdoor spaces of the venue in a way that would allow audiences to still attend it as a museum and visit its exhibitions, but that would also enhance their experience of these (Fig. 17.4). Thus, the environment designed had to coexist with the permanent and temporary exhibitions and envelop all spaces and items in the building with layers of sound, augmented reality exhibits, coloured light and video art (used in the courtyard).

This immersive performance was created within and around the museum space, consisting of a temporary large-scale audiovisual installation, combining live electronic sound with a group of 20 live music performers, theatrical lighting, generative video art, a digital exhibition and an augmented reality smartphone app that allowed visitors to interact with the installation during the event. In the event, the audience and performers navigated the performance space. Performers interacted with the sounds coming from the audio installation that was spread across various locations in the museum, by adjusting the dynamics (volume) and textural density in their playing, according to changes in audio levels and layers. In addition, the audience interacted with the audio installation by discovering the locations of a selection of augmented reality exhibits and engaging with them on their devices, using the smartphone app. Thus, each audience member received an individualised experience of the museum, shaped by their personal choices on where to go, what to focus on, who or what to interact with and for how long, within the venue, during the performance.

As with the previous performance, the main objective was to create a performance that would offer visitors an enhanced, alternative mode of experiencing exhibits and spaces within a museum, inviting them to interact and engage with the spaces or exhibits in a holistic way, receiving a personalised multimedia experience of them.

[8] The BoCCF was established in 1984 and is housed in the old administrative building of the Bank of Cyprus. It was built in 1936 and is situated in the historical center of Nicosia, near Phaneromeni Church. The Foundation maintains five Cyprological collections and curates two museums: the Museum of the History of Cypriot Coinage and the Archaeological Museum of George and Nefeli Giabra Pierides. The building includes small halls for periodical exhibitions and an amphitheatre, used as an outdoor performing arts venue. (See https://www.boccf.org).

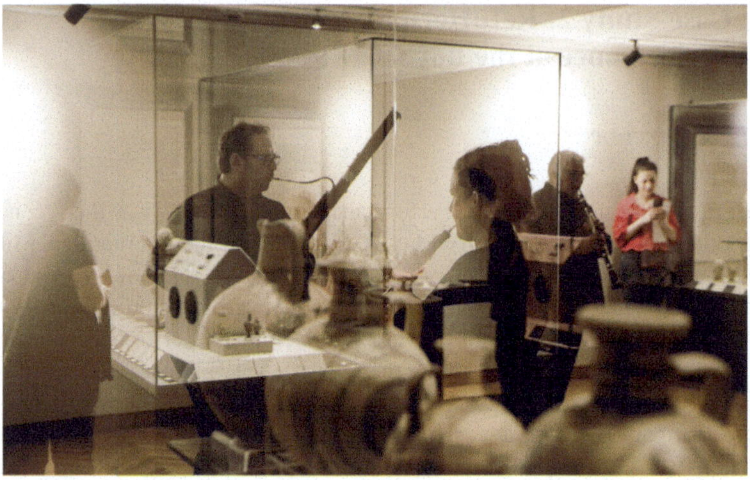

Fig. 17.4 Musicians performing amidst the exhibits of the archeological collection of the BoCCF, with audience members using the ReInHerit app on their phones. Photo credit: Kyriakos Xristodoulides

17.5.2 Museological Perspectives

The BoCCF has a large and very rich ethnographic collection, which is not accessible to the public. Therefore, it was decided that an AR application would be designed for the performance, which could be used to bring these objects to the public and create a virtual exhibition, presented alongside the Museum of George and Nefeli Giabra Pierides Collection and the temporary exhibitions of the BoCCF.

Artefacts from the ethnographic collection of the BoCCF were selected and 3D scanned, and were available through the AR application, such as a traditional vase, a brazier, a throne, a wooden chest, a gilded buckle and a talisman, amongst others. The exhibits of this virtual exhibition were scattered around the premises of the building and became visible in the app based on the audiences' interactions. The virtual exhibition consisted of 12 objects of folk art from the Pierides ethnographic collection, mainly from the nineteenth century, such as examples of silversmithing, woodcarving, ceramics and metalwork. Through this virtual exhibition, the digital exhibits coexisted with the artefacts currently on display from the archaeological collection and the other temporary exhibitions.

Through the smartphone application, visitors could see these objects and interact with them, by rotating them and zooming in to observe details. For each object, an accompanying text was available through the application, which provided thoroughly researched context and described its use in the daily life of the people in the nineteenth century. As with the previous performance's treasure-hunt activity, these texts were written in a simple, easily comprehensible language. The interpretation material created was standalone for each object, so that visitors could have a full experience even if they did not see all objects and irrespective of the order in which they saw the objects and texts. Thus, the experience was not designed to be linear, but visitors could explore the space freely, deciding where to spend more time as they wished and according to their interests.

It is worth noting that the venue's main function as a museum space had an interesting effect on visitors: museum visitor etiquette dictates that people are either silent or limit the level of their conversations to a minimum while exploring the space. With this performance, this expectation was turned on its head and produced a situation which made the museum into a concert hall of sorts, and its exhibition spaces into sounding boards of a large, traversable instrument that spanned the entire building. The environment of this immersive performance enveloped the museum's exhibits and added new layers of information—namely sound and interaction with performers, something that is uncommon in a museum setting—to its visitors' experience.

17.5.3 Interactive Sound Installation

As with the first performance, sound and music were also an essential part of this second performance, which combined pre-recorded tracks and live electronics (as part of a sound installation) with live performers improvising, following instructions for melodic loops and movement in the performance space. As in the previous performance, the sound installation used 14 sound stations, each consisting of a smartphone receiver and a Bluetooth speaker, placed in pre-determined spots within the performance space. Twelve of these stations were placed inside the museum, the exhibition spaces and the staircase, while two were placed outdoors,[9] close to where the video projection was happening.

In contrast to the previous performance, the sounds produced by the sound installation were of an abstract nature (i.e. tones or rhythms) and did not hint towards specific exhibits. The audio used for each station consisted of a long drone sound, of a duration of roughly 33 min (set to C—i.e. 65.41 Hz—for spaces with strings, percussion and brass groups and to D—i.e. 73.42 Hz—for spaces with woodwinds) and six additional layers of sounds (different pitches, with pulse, looping) that could be combined to create harmonies and polyrhythms in combination with the original drone sound and with each other, depending on when they would be triggered for playback.

The sounds were triggered by a smartphone app designed specifically for this performance. The app allowed audience members to search for a group of 12 augmented reality exhibits, which were scattered in various locations in the BoCCF interior. Each time an audience member found one of these objects and interacted with it (by tapping on it), an audio track was triggered in the nearest sound station to

[9] The two sound stations placed outdoors were not interactive and played a drone that developed in density and dynamics for 50 min.

the object, which lasted for about a minute and a half before stopping.[10] Each audience member could interact with an exhibit and its assigned sound station only once. Every interaction produced a layer of sound, of a limited duration, that would be overlayed on the drone sound produced by the sound station throughout the performance. Depending on the number of audience members interacting with a digital exhibit at any given time, the sound installation could produce anything from simple combinations of two audio files up to complex polyrhythmic harmonic textures of sound, created by 7 layers of audio files. Thus, the sound installation provided the conditions for the audience to *co-create* an aleatoric[11] piece, which the performers in the space would react to in real time.

17.5.4 Smartphone Application

The "ReInHerit a Museum" smartphone application was designed to allow the audience of the performance to experience a virtual exhibition of artefacts of the BoCCF, using AR technology. In this app, visitors could find out more information about the exhibits and interact with them, triggering various sounds which enhanced the performance and created a dynamic composition, combined with the sounds of live musicians. The application was available to the audience in both Greek and English through the Google Play Store for Android devices and the Apple App Store for iOS devices.

The application allowed users to find 12 virtual exhibits in the museum. By clicking on the app's camera button, the user is presented with the locations within the venue where the virtual exhibits can be activated from. S. When the user selected a location, the smartphones' camera was turned on, activating the AR function of the application. Over the camera feed, an outline of what the user should be facing was displayed, prompting the user to match this outline with the physical representation. Once the latter was achieved, the virtual exhibits were then virtually placed within the space at pre-defined locations, with the objective to promote further exploration of the venue.

When the user was within a specified range, the exhibits, was displayed rotating around their axis, and could be zoomed in and out freely, allowing the user to view more details of their texture and geometry. When tapped on, their texture (colour) changed to negative as an alternative to their default and this interaction triggered a nearby Bluetooth speaker, which played various sounds simultaneously based on the number of single tapping interactions. The interactions and views of each exhibit were stored remotely in a database for monitoring purposes and for guiding other visual elements of the performance (see Sect. 17.5.5). The user was prompted to find all 12 exhibits in the museum, while and when the user successfully found all the artefacts in that area, a success message was displayed.

[10] Each digital object and its location had a pre-assigned physical sound station.

[11] Aleatory or chance music (from Latin *alea*, "dice").

The "ReInHerit a Museum" application was developed using the Unity gaming engine while for the AR part, Lightship Augmented Reality Developer Kit (ARDK) from Niantic[12] was used which can detect areas and place objects accurately in place. To use the ARDK, the areas of the museum that were selected for the virtual exhibits needed to be scanned, and this was done using another application from Niantic, the Wayfarer.[13] The corresponding scans were then downloaded and used within Unity, to control the placement of the AR objects in their corresponding locations.

During the performance, the application also recorded anonymised data from users, such as number of visitor views and interactions per AR exhibit. All the data were stored at real time in a remote NoSQL database implemented using Cloud Firestore within the Google Firebase[14] service for synchronising data across the application through real time listeners. The real time listener was attached to the interaction events, sending a signal for each of them to a separate smartphone-based application, which in turn, was connected with each of the designated Bluetooth speakers at the venue (i.e. the audio installation's sound stations), controlling the playback of the sounds.

17.5.5 Visuals: Real-Time Generated Video and Projection Mapping

The visual part of this performance is a hybrid artwork that connects elements of the BoCCF using Generative Art and Video Art. Historical artefacts and algorithms were combined to create a distinctive audiovisual landscape, in which the visual artist's approach aims to enhance the sense of audience immersion during this performance, using moving images to evoke emotions, mental states and a journey through time. Its moving images are based on a combination of exhibits from the BoCCF and AI-generated images of dancers, modified in real-time either through audience choices or a MIDI controller, utilising algorithmic graphics.

The software used for the visual elements of the project included Adobe Photoshop, Adobe Lightroom, Adobe Premiere, TouchDesigner,[15] Syphon,[16] Mad Mapper[17] and internal software (data collection and transmission of metrics related to audience interactions) implemented using Unity3D. To develop the visuals, 12 three-dimensional scans of exhibits from the museum's ethnographical collection were created using photogrammetry. These were imported in TouchDesigner, a node-based software, maintaining only their wire frames and using a variety of techniques to generate the moving image. Additionally, AI-generated images of dancers were

[12] See https://lightship.dev/products/ardk/.

[13] See https://wayfarer.nianticlabs.com.

[14] See https://firebase.google.com.

[15] See https://derivative.ca.

[16] See https://syphon.github.io.

[17] See https://madmapper.com.

Fig. 17.5 Musicians performing on the seating rows of the BoCCF amphitheatre while video art is projected directly onto them. Photo credit: Kyriakos Xristodoulides

created through e-Dally[18] and placed in a timeline, utilising the morphing technique to generate intermediate states or images occurring during the transition from one image to another. All of these elements were integrated into a system created in TouchDesigner. The final artwork was shaped by variable values occurring from the audience's interactions with the performance's smartphone app and a MIDI controller input. Finally, projection mapping was applied on the exterior wall of the BoCCF building and on the seating rows of the the courtyard's amphitheatre (Fig. 17.5). The two diametrically opposed points in the courtyard were selected to effectively immerse the audience in both visuals and music. For the projection mapping, three programs were simultaneously used in real time. TouchDesigner generated the graphics, Syphon transported them to Mad Mapper and Mad Mapper facilitated the mapping of the graphics onto the building's surface.

17.5.6 Performative Elements: Spatial Music and Guided Improvisation

The music composed for this performance followed the requirements set by the space and the objectives for this project, which were interactivity, interdisciplinarity, immersion, and a focus on cultural heritage. The composition was created for 20 musicians—a combination of string, woodwind, brass and percussion players—who were provided by the Cyprus Symphony Orchestra and the Cyprus Youth Symphony Orchestra. The instructions to create it consisted of a short description of the general

[18] See https://openai.com/dall-e-2.

concept of the performance, directions on locations in the venue in which the musicians would be performing with indications on when to go to them and how fast to move, and a series of tones (pitches) for each section of the piece with guidelines on how to approach them as material for guided improvisation.[19]

The performers did not have to interact with audience members. They were instructed to set their courses through the space and gently prompt the audience to move around and explore the venue during the performance alongside them. The musicians were also required to adjust their playing (the loudness and density of their improvisation) to correspond to the textures of sound produced by the audio installation and occasionally to each other's playing, building up in intensity over the course of the performance.

The performers were split into three groups and started their performance in different parts of the building, including the permanent and temporary exhibition spaces. The decision on where each group of performers would be placed was not based on the groups' type of instruments but instead on the groups' sizes. By the middle of the performance all groups were mixed, and performers were moving in and out of other groups' spaces freely. This was done to prompt the audience to move around in the space more and explore every aspect of it during performance.

17.6 Audience Engagement

17.6.1 Target Audience

Attracting an audience for both performances was important for the success of the project. Hoping to create a new generation of museum and cultural heritage site visitors and increase their numbers in the long run, the goal was to bring in audiences coming from a younger demographic of teenagers and young adults, who would not typically be attracted to cultural heritage sites and museums. Consideration was given to the fact that many of our guests might be visiting cultural heritage sites or museums for the first time after the pandemic and that, given their young age, this might be the first museum they visited in person, as teenagers or young adults. Thus, the aim was to encourage visitors to actively engage with the cultural heritage space, using interactive technology and gamification techniques. In the immersive performances, this was a combination of an interactive audio installation blended with a group of live performers, captivating visuals, social media and blog posts to increase pre-show and post-show engagement with the project, and finally a treasure hunt-type mission set up as prompts on a collection of cards or a bespoke smartphone application,

[19] These guidelines included instructions on timings, such as when to make gradual or abrupt changes in the style and content of the improvised playing, or sectional changes that required synchronisation to other performers, instructions on how and when to interact with other musicians and with the sound installation's harmonies and rhythms, and lastly instructions on how to interpret the video art projection as a moving, developing graphic score for improvisation.

allowing audience members to spot specific points of interest in the space where sonic activity would take place.

Given the wealth of multisensory stimuli available during the performances, it was possible for people with different backgrounds and varied interests to find parts of it to focus on, whether these would be completing the treasure hunt or augmented reality activity, following performers moving around in the exhibition rooms, watching the live video art projection, listening to the sound fluctuations of the audio installation or simply observing the museum's exhibits, which were visitable just like any other day, but this time with additional layers of information (i.e. sound, augmented reality objects, moving crowds, etc.). In terms of performance theory, the visitors' experience of the ReInHerit case studies fluctuates between being a *simple* and a *diffused audience*, (Abercrombie and Longhurst 1998), as there are constant shifts of attention, the physical distance between performers and audience is often eliminated, and while interacting with the audio installation audience members also become performers as they can interfere with the sound world of the performance.

It is worth noting that, in both events, having performers provided a sense of live performance and a necessary human dimension—in other words, people to watch and interact with, instead of physical or virtual exhibits, an abstract video or sound—which filled the gap between the world of the video and sound installations, and that of their audience. Even though they did not necessarily engage with the audience, the performers acted as a sort of choros,[20] i.e. intermediaries between visitors and the cultural heritage space, keeping the audience engaged and helping the performance run its course (Fig. 17.6).

17.6.2 Pre-show and Post-show Audience Interaction

The pre-show strategy set to generate interest in the first case study, ReInHerit in Performance, consisted of a series of daily social media posts, using a collection of pictures and texts about the mansion's history and exhibits, curated by a museologist with a focus on easily comprehensible expressions to address younger audiences. Some of these posts, which were not published in time for the event, were used instead to create a treasure hunt activity during the performance. For the second performance, ReInHerit a Museum, the BoCCF planned an advertisement campaign in social media platforms and an article in a local newspaper (online version). The focus of these posts was sharing the event's concept and showing the main collaborating organisations. One of the final posts published contained the link to download the latest version of the app, with which audience members could interact with the performance. This was released prior to the performance so that audience members could familiarise

[20] The Choros in ancient Greek drama was a group of performers, occupying a special part of the stage, commenting the actions of the protagonists (much like the audience would) and narrating parts of the play (Bacon 1994).

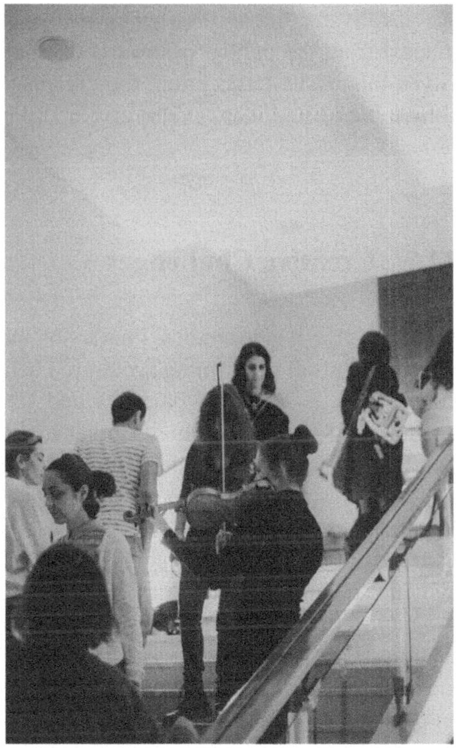

Fig. 17.6 Performer navigating the performance space, moving alongside the audience. Photo credit: Kyriakos Xristodoulides

themselves with the concepts of the performance and learn about the AR objects they would be looking for during the performance.

Following the performances, a selection of photos from the event was published online as a post-show interaction with the audience. QR codes with links to a feedback-and-comments form were displayed in the performance space. In addition, anonymous user data was collected during and after the performances, through the sound stations or the smartphone app, or by using online questionnaires to examine the performances' impact on the audience's interactions and experience of the cultural heritage spaces. Furthermore, a performance highlights video and a full-length edit of the video documentation is now available on the ReInHerit YouTube channel and on social media platforms.[21] The documentation and promotional material is also published in the ReInHerit Digital Hub, to openly communicate the lessons learned as well as detailed instructions for stakeholders interested in recreating the proposed immersive performance.

On both occasions, the hosting organisation, BoCCF, shared insights about the outcomes of the project, consisting of largely positive feedback received for the performances and the audience's experience of the cultural heritage spaces in question during the event. According to feedback received from the hosting organisation

[21] See https://www.youtube.com/watch?v=tZ9VoZDAsro.

specifically for the second performance, the inclusion of AR elements generated interest from the public, offering a distinctive and immersive museum experience. Given this positive reception, the organisation expressed a willingness to organise similar interdisciplinary events and incorporate the use of technology into upcoming projects.

17.7 Creative Challenges

In the ReInHerit case studies, immersion meant that audiences would have to escape modern habits of performing accultured behaviours from television watching, (Heim 2016), such as sedentary passivity and selective inattention, or from rock concert attendance, such as cheering or other highly physicalised expressions of participation, and instead explore the cultural heritage site in question with an inquisitive mindset, like playing a game. Since audience immersion was part of the objectives for the project, this entailed certain specifications in terms of performance development and realisation: Immersion in the context of a performance means that the audience (or immersant) experiences the world of the aforementioned performance in a multisensory way and is able to navigate the environment created within it, using their body as if it were an avatar in the world of this performance.[22] This meant that the audience had to be prompted to explore the museum spaces during performance and that they had to experience these spaces (and exhibits) with more than their sense of sight.

However, creating a performance within a cultural heritage space brought about several challenges that needed to be addressed. In both case studies, these were mainly the lack of sound amplification and lighting equipment, the absence of a delineated stage or audience seating space, and the fact that all performance activity had to be coordinated in a highly compartmented space (i.e. the numerous rooms of the museum, split into ground level and first floor, plus a courtyard, etc.) that is quite different to a stage or concert hall and enforces severe limitations on the communication between musicians (and even audience members) during performance.

The compartmentalisation of performance space was a challenge for performers, as it did not allow them to maintain eye contact or hear each other clearly unless they were located close to each other. This meant that it would be difficult, if not impossible to coordinate a performance using a conductor or even to require extended passages with absolute synchronisation between performers, as they would all be scattered and walking around in the space at a later point. To mitigate this, stopwatches were used as part of the installation and by the performers, so that they could adhere to the same timestamp throughout the performance, in addition to having timed actions

[22] The performance's "world" is experienced as part of physical reality but not quite of it; it only lasts for as long as a performance takes place. There are parallels of immersivity with gamification in performance experiences to consider.

(changes in sound or location) that would be cued by a single performer leading the group. The fact that the visible timestamps on the installation's sound stations had to be manually cued led to minor inconsistencies in the synchronisation between performers.

In both immersive performances, the composition required musicians to walk around for extended periods and frequently change locations in the performance space, often in situations in which lighting was not ideal for viewing scores or maintaining eye contact with each other. At the beginning of both performances, the musicians were dispersed in the performance space, playing simultaneously throughout the performance. They were divided into groups to spread the sound evenly throughout the performance space and seamlessly blend with the sounds coming from the audio installation. This requirement dictated that the compositions had to consist of largely text-based instructions for guided improvisation and movement that allowed a great amount of flexibility for the performers.

Another challenge was the limitation on the amount of people experiencing the performance at the same time: The first case study had a cap of up to 100 attendees per performance slot, because of the structural attributes of the ancient mansion it was set it. The second case study had attracted an unexpectedly large crowd at the BoCCF, meaning that the function of the smartphone app was often compromised and that some visitors did not have the chance to find all the AR objects. Specifically, the technological applications employed in the two immersive performances had functional limitations due to large crowds and varying light settings impacting their stability and reliability in both performances.

For the first performance, difficulties in calibration were experienced due to variations in lighting conditions across three different performance slots (afternoon with sunlight, evening from twilight to dusk and nighttime). Accordingly, these lighting inconsistencies affected the accuracy of the computer vision algorithms, leading to challenges in real-time data processing and the subsequent sound events triggering. One way to go around this challenge for future implementations could be by taking into account diverse lighting conditions during the testing phase, as well as incorporating adaptive calibration mechanisms. In addition, the presence of a large number of people in each sound-station location led to algorithm saturation, triggering the highest threshold constantly. Therefore, the sonic events associated with the highest threshold dominated the performance, limiting the variety of triggered sound events. A solution to this would be the refinement of algorithms to handle high traffic scenarios more effectively and a consideration of alternative triggering mechanisms to enhance the diversity of sonic experiences.

Crowd dynamics played a significant part in shaping the experience of the second performance. Specifically, the movement of visitors in the AR display space of the second performance caused interference, hindering the stability of triggered virtual objects. This resulted in difficulty for visitors to maintain interaction with virtual objects, as the movement of individuals behind them disrupted the AR experience. A possible adjustment could be to strategically position the projected digital objects in areas inaccessible to visitors, such as spaces higher than 3 m or within restricted sections of the museum, where entry is prohibited. The fact that only a fraction of visitors interacted with the virtual objects, indicates that the specific feature's design was problematic and not well understood by the audience. Future versions of the application could be adjusted to provide better instructions on how to interact with the artefacts. These are possible solutions that may be tested in future iterations of these ideas.

The most interesting limitation, however, was the requirement to produce a performance that enters in a creative discourse with the hosting space. In our case, the performance didn't just happen at a cultural heritage site and it wasn't a performance of heritage, as all the music in it was new. According to Haldrup and Bærenholdt's categorisation, the type of event created was a performance with heritage, which draws on pre-existing scripts on heritage provided by the media and wider society (McKerrell and Pfeiffer 2020). Thus, besides the venues' architectural characteristics, the pre-existing information about them shaped the performance design: A performance in these museum spaces had to envelop the collection of exhibits and enhance the visitors' experience of them. Accordingly, this type of event was difficult to define, categorise and advertise beyond the fact that it was an immersive performance within a cultural heritage site. In our case it was a non-representational and non-mimetic activity (Kirby 2005), that required the time-limited co-presence of performers and spectators (Fischer-Lichte 2008), involving several modes of communication (sound, texts, etc.) and engaging multiple senses as the audience members were 'immersed' in the same world as the performance taking place (Machon 2013), In other words, performers and audience members navigated the same spaces, listened to the same sounds, watched the same video projections, observed the same exhibits, for a set amount of time.

17.8 Conclusions

The type of events created as case studies for ReInHerit H2020 is difficult to define, categorise and advertise beyond the fact that they were interdisciplinary immersive performances within cultural heritage sites. Following the described development process, the performances were open to different types of interpretation depending on the cultural, educational, social backgrounds of the audience. Audience members experiencing each event, interacting with performers and equipment, and navigating the performance space during the immersive performance would not need to receive complicated instructions or to be guided in the space. Any prompts on where to go and what to do in the space would occur subtly, within a smartphone application or a treasure hunt card, or by following a musician around the performance space. In other words, the audience would not need to have prior training in music or any other performing art, to be accustomed to using specialised equipment other than their smartphones or to demonstrate familiarity with the cultural heritage site in question. They could simply explore the space depending on their interests and previous experiences.

It is recommended that the following considerations should be taken into account for future iterations of the project's performances:

- Using a smartphone application makes the performance and cultural heritage site more appealing to digital natives, but including meaningful tactile experiences (for instance, exhibit replicas for the visually impaired, etc.) provides an important layer of information during a performance. Consider using both.
- Using a larger number of performers increases difficulties in group coordination and synchronisation. The number of performers should be cautiously decided based on venue size and the musicians' experience with similar projects.
- Differences in sound coming from the audio installation may not be easily perceivable, as was the case in our second performance. As such, it is suggested that creators limit the sounds they use to three per sound station.
- Setting up multiple performance slots rather than a single one, allows the event's organisers to limit audience numbers in each performance, providing them with a more comfortable and meaningful experience, and avoiding health and safety hazards.
- Video art speed could be adjusted to suit the performance's pace and maintain audience engagement at a high level during the performances.
- Lighter graphics in the smartphone app, or even less AR objects to discover, would reduce loading times for users.
- Improvisation and written instructions are important in creating the sound environments without the need for notation. However, if the style of the performance allows it, composers could opt for recognisable motivic repetitions to create a sense of performance identity or brand.

Summing up, a long and ambitious development process resulted in two performances that combined elements from different disciplines and invited audiences to take initiative in shaping their experience of it. Both immersive experiences, "ReInHerit in Performance: The Hadjigeorgakis Kornesios Mansion" and "ReInHerit a Museum: Immersive Performance at the BoCCF" are case studies in developing performances that are informed by a cultural heritage site, that grow within, respect and help enhance pre-existing exhibitions and museum spaces, making them places that not only preserve culture but also help people create it today.

Acknowledgements and Credits The work presented in this chapter has received funding from the European Union's Horizon 2020 Research and Innovation Programme under the ReInHerit project with Grant Agreement no. 101004545. ReInHerit funding was secured in the framework of the Horizon 2020 CSA Programme, on the theme Culture beyond borders—Facilitating innovation and research cooperation between European museums and heritage.

Performance direction and music composition: Andreas Papapetrou
Programming and mobile app design: Fotos Frangoudes, Alexios Polydorou
Programming: Giorgos Hadjiantonis
Video Art: Stefanos Papadas
Lighting Design: Demetris Shammas
Graphic Design: Maria Loizou, Avgi Papapetrou
2D animation design: Alexis Baldwin
3D scanning and model reconstruction: Andreas Lernis

Technical Support: Marios Charalambous
Mobile application UI: Tereza Kourra
Museologist: Maria Shehade
Communication Officer: Chrystalla Charalambous-Papadopoulou
Project Manager: Niki Kyriakou
Project Coordinator: Kleanthis Neokleous
Performers from the Cyprus Youth Symphony Orchestra:
Christian Bishara, Panos Milios, Anfisa Antonova, Sofia Kleopa, Ladyslava Korolenko, Lydia Mattheou, Leto Syrimi, Michalis Vassiliades
Performers from the Cyprus Symphony Orchestra:
Kelly Alijani, Konstantinos Anastasiades, Angelos Angelides, Virginie Bove, Giovanni Galetti, George Georgiou, Gareth Griffiths, Catherine Heaver, Ayse Karaoglan, Giovanni Magni, Varvara Merzlova, Marios Nicolaou, Kumiko Okutomi, Laura Rodgers, Hasmik Sargsyan, Simeon Spasov, Andreas Yiannakouras, Tefkros Xydas, Dusko Žarković

References

Abercrombie N, Longhurst B (1998) Audiences: a sociological theory of performance and imagination. Sage, London, Thousand Oaks and New Delhi, pp 68–76

Bacon HH (1994) The chorus in greek life and drama. Arion J Humanit Class 3(1):6–24. http://www.jstor.org/stable/20163562

Choi C (2023) Immersive art exhibitions: spellbinding, or forgettable? The New York Times, May 5, 2023, sec. Arts. https://www.nytimes.com/2023/05/05/arts/design/immersive-art-exhibits.html

Dima M, Maples H (2021) Affectual dramaturgy for augmented reality immersive heritage performance. Body Space Technol 20(1):25–36. https://doi.org/10.16995/bst.368

Dogan E (2020) Bringing heritage sites to life for visitors: towards a conceptual framework for immersive experience. Adv Hosp Tour Res (AHTR) 8(1):76–99. https://doi.org/10.30519/ahtr.630783

Fischer-Lichte E (2008) The transformative power of performance: a new aesthetics, p 32 (trans: Jain SI). Routledge, London

Grzega J (2013) Methodological challenges of semantic and pragmatic studies in eurolinguistics. J EuroLinguistiX Jelix 10:4–14

Heim C (2016) Audience as performer: the changing role of theatre audiences in the twenty-first century. Routledge, London and New York, p 172

Kirby M (2005) The new theatre. In: Sandford MR (ed) Happenings and other acts, p 27. Routledge, London and New York

Kleftodimos A, Moustaka M, Evagelou A (2023) Location-based augmented reality for cultural heritage education: creating educational, gamified location-based AR applications for the prehistoric lake settlement of Dispilio. Digital 3(1):18–45. https://doi.org/10.3390/digital3010002

Machon J, Theatres I (2013) Intimacy and immediacy in contemporary performance. Palgrave Macmillan, Houndmills, p xvi

McAvoy EN (2019) Immersive experiences in museums, galleries and heritage sites: a review of research findings and issues. Creative Industries Policy and Evidence Centre

McKerrell S, Pfeiffer K (2020) On the relationship between performance in intangible cultural heritage. In: Kockel U, Clopot C, Tjarve B, Craith MN (eds) Heritage and festivals in Europe, p 42. Routledge, London and New York

Pistola T, Diplaris S, Stentoumis C, Stathopoulos E, Loupas G, Mandilaras T, Kalantzis G, Kalisperakis I, Tellios A, Zavraka D, Koulali P, Kriezi V, Vraka V, Venieri F, Bacalis S, Vrochidis S,

Kompatsiaris I (2021) Creating immersive experiences based on intangible cultural heritage, pp 17–24. https://doi.org/10.1109/ICIR51845.2021.00012
Politopoulos A, Angus AAM, Lammes S (2023) Finding the fun: towards a playful archaeology. Archaeol Dialog 30(1):1–15. https://doi.org/10.1017/S1380203823000053
Varinlioglu G, Halıcı S (2019) Gamification of heritage through augmented reality, pp 513–518. https://doi.org/10.5151/proceedings-ecaadesigradi2019_168
Weiner A (2022) The rise of 'immersive' art. The New Yorker, February 10, 2022. https://www.newyorker.com/news/letter-from-silicon-valley/the-rise-and-rise-of-immersive-art

Chapter 18
Human Animatronics in Museum Experience: *Casa Parlante—The Living Museum*, Corfu, Greece

Sofia Paschou and Georgios Papaioannou

Abstract This paper discusses the results of a survey on visitors' experience in a museum exhibition with human-resembling animatronics (robotic puppets). It is based on the assumption that animatronics comprise novel and interesting exhibits for visitors, trigger their imagination and enrich their museum experience. The museum under study is the *Casa Parlante—A Living Museum* in Corfu, Greece, established in March 2014. The research addressed visitors' feelings, the role of animatronics in the exhibition's narrative, the perceived gained knowledge and the quality of the visit in general. The survey consisted of a two-page questionnaire that was filled in by visitors at the exit of the exhibition. We collected 65 questionnaires filled-in by adults. Findings showed that incorporating human-like animatronics models as part of a museum exhibition enhance learning and entertainment, and that human-resembling animatronics have a significant impact in terms of cognitive and introspective museum experience.

Keywords Museum · Museum experience · Visitors' emotion · Animatronics · Casa Parlante

18.1 Introduction

Museums have gone through many phases: from object-oriented to visitor-centred and more recently to technology-driven (Virto and Lopez 2019). They cope with the needs of researching, exhibiting, educating and entertaining (Sheng and Chan 2012), while striving to stay visitor focused (Desvallées and Mairesse 2010; Parry 2019) and advance the visitors' museum experience (Csikszentmihalyi and Robinson 1990Derbaix and Gombault 2016; Dierking 1989; Falk and Dierking 1992, 1995,

S. Paschou · G. Papaioannou (✉)
Museology Research Laboratory, Ionian University, 49100 Corfu, Greece
e-mail: gpapaioa@ionio.gr

S. Paschou
e-mail: spaschou@ionio.gr

F. Liarokapis et al. (eds.), *Interactive Media for Cultural Heritage*, Springer Series on Cultural Computing, https://doi.org/10.1007/978-3-031-61018-9_18

2016; Joy and Sherry 2003; Kesner 2006; Neumann 1988). The museum experience has been approached as a pleasant experience (Roppola 2013; Volo 2009) depending on various factors (Packer 2008) and criteria. It has been classified into four categories: 1. The object experience that focuses on the features of exhibits, 2. The cognitive experience that aims at enriching knowledge, 3. The introspective experience that relates to reactions and (personal) emotions triggered by an object and 4. The social experience that comes about the interaction with other visitors (Doering 1999; Pekarik et al. 1999). In addition, the ongoing evolution of technological innovations has added innovative and creative ways to engage visitors by offering new tools (Budge and Burness 2017). Advanced technological tools and media have given museums the opportunity for more immersive and interactive experiences to satisfy a wider range of visitors (Hede et al. 2014; Wilson-Barnao 2017). The norm has been that visitors enjoy using hi-tech devices, apps and tools because of the unique and entertaining visit tour they experience. Robots have also been incorporated and used mainly as museum guides, telepresence and installation (Germak et al., 2015), but also as museum exhibits in the form of animal or human resembling animatronics.

This paper presents the results of a questionnaire-based visitors' study on the impact of animatronics in visitors' museum experience. The research questions were *how animatronics affect visitors' experience* and *how visitors perceive animatronics in relation to the other exhibits*. Further research questions were *what visitors notice and feel while viewing animatronics as part of an exhibition, how animatronics (specifically human-resembling ones) capture visitor and add to the museum experience, and to what extent animatronics enhance visitors' experience and understanding of the exhibition's narrative*. The research methodological approach is via a survey with a two-page filled-in questionnaire. Visitors filled in the questionnaire after visiting the museum and at the exit of the exhibition. The research was conducted just before the pandemic. The sample consisted of 65 adult visitors, each measured once as the scope was to look at causality (Sukamolson 2007). The questionnaire consisted of question sets of closed and open-ended questions.

The museum under study was the *Casa Parlante—A Living Museum* in Corfu, Greece, established in March 2014. *Casa Parlante* is housed in a nineteenth-century Corfiot cosmopolitan aristocratic residence and attempts to revive everyday life of the island's nineteenth-century upper class by employing human-resembling animatronics and accurate reproductions of the décor and domestic furnishing. It is the first (and so far the only) visitors' study conducted on this museum.

The paper starts with the introduction, followed by a literature review/related work on animatronics and museum visitors. Section 18.3 presents the *Casa Parlante Museum*, its exhibition and the museum's human-resembling animatronics. In Sects. 18.4, 18.5 and 18.6 our research design, processes and findings are analysed and discussed. Section 18.7 offers concluding remarks and future work.

18.2 On Animatronics and Related Work

In the following pages we explore the notions of animatronics in museum exhibitions, focusing on related work and specific examples. As modern museums have shifted their focus on visitors' expectations and participation (Black 2006), museums have adopted innovative technologies to advance their operation and services, and to encourage and increase visitors' participation and involvement. Modern technologies attract visitors and offer beneficial and holistic experiences (Bounia 2012) via the interaction evolving from the triangular relationship among visitor, place and digital technologies (McCarthy and Ciolfi 2008). Robotics and the use of robots, the so-called animatronics, comprise part of this effort. Animatronics are well known and form very popular parts of periodical exhibitions, especially on dinosaurs. A good example is that of the "Dinosaurs Extreme" exhibition at The Museum of Natural History of Crete, in Herakleion, Crete (November 2015–November 2017) (Dinosaurs Extreme 2015).

Animatronics (also known as animation electronics) are life-like robots that resemble to people or animals (Tunnicliffe 1999). The term is also attributed to the whole process of creating and handling robotic models (Critchlow 1985). Animatronics usually have motion (Tunicliffe 1999). Advanced versions are equipped with extra features beyond movement, such as voices and smells. Animatronics are mostly used in films (Maheswari 2015) and in entertainment and/or educational environments, such as museums (Chandrashekhar 2016). Their early appearance goes back at '90s (Tunnicliffe 1995) with the emergence of robots that have entered museum spaces and exhibitions. The use of autonomous robots in public spaces poses several challenges, particularly if they are to interact socially with humans. Minerva is an example of tour-guide robots at museums. The robot was featured at the Smithsonian's National Museum of American History in the summer of 1998. During a two-week installation period, the robot was successfully used to educate many visitors (Thrun et al. 1999). In 2000, a group of three different robots have been launched at the Museum for Communication in Berlin, providing instruction, incitation and entertainment (Schraft et al. 2001). London's Science Museum opened a temporary exhibition on robotics in 2017, showcasing a collection of over 100 objects focusing on humanoid robots from the sixteenth century to the present (Dittmann and Lange 2018). Another example is Lindsey, an autonomous robot at Collection Museum in Lincoln, UK. Lindsey has been operating as an autonomous tour guide for visitors since October 2018. Lindsey can provide information about specific exhibitions in the Gallery, direct visitors to where to view an exhibition or give guided tours. Lindsey performs the same function every day during the museum's opening hours (Del Duchetto et al. 2019).

Science museums choose to use animatronics as effective means to exhibit scientific methods and principles, such as rules of physics or the function of the human body. Natural history museums use animatronics to liven animals, with dinosaurs being the most frequent choice (Tunnicliffe 2000). Dinosaurs of different types, including water birds in the Los Angeles Museum of Natural History are the most popular category of animals represented as animatronics (Tunnicliffe 1999). Dinosaur models are spectacular and high-profile public attractions especially when they are designed to move their limbs, head and jaws.

Creating animatronics, especially human-like ones, is a demanding and challenging task involving complex mechanical assemblies. Due to the potential for wear, tear and mechanical damage, proper care and attention is required when displayed in a museum environment (Mayet et al. 2019). For this reason, the presence of animatronics in museums can be a strain on staff, especially if there are insufficient resources for maintenance.

Research on animatronics, despite their establishment as a popular form of presentation in museums, is limited and focuses mainly on their technical development, addressing and highlighting technical and technological manners, issues and points of view (Chandrashekhar 2016; Maheswari 2015; Peel 2008; Poor and Jacob 2011). In terms of visitors' experiences, research so far concentrates on children and animal-like animatronics, mainly dinosaurs. Tunnicliffe's work published in 1999 and 2000 is still the best example of this trend. He focused on school groups visiting a dinosaur-animatronics exhibition and on relevant questions and conversations that have arisen. Tunnicliff (1999) chose the method of a comparative study between animatronics displayed in the zoo as a temporary exhibit and in a natural history museum as part of the permanent exhibits: "The study indicated that the moving animal models -the animatronics—in themselves are insufficient to induce many visitors to talk about them in other, than a superficial, cursory manner" (Tunicliffe 1999: 23). His follow-up research (2000) illustrated comments on animatronics' features and concepts in museum environments. Families and primary school groups were studied as self-guided groups visiting an exhibition about dinosaurs. The research was conducted in terms of the content of their conservations and responses regarding two different robotics dinosaur exhibits in the Natural History Museum, London. Findings have indicated that animatronics could be a valuable and supportive tool in students' learning. Animatronics have a simple story line, which could be easily read by both families and school groups and hence increases and supports the understanding of the topic of exhibit.

The first robots in museums have been museum guides. Asimo has been one of the most famous and advanced humanoid robot museum guide at the National Museum of Emerging Science and Innovation in Japan (Sakagami et al. 2002). Recently, robot Maven, a virtual human character (avatar) on a mobile robotic platform and Edgar, a humanoid avatar that produces speech in English and Mandarin have been developed for the Chinese Heritage Centre to study the use of robotic technologies within heritage museum settings. The aim was to offer innovative ways to provide information, especially to young children, for learning heritage languages and cultures (Pang et al. 2018).

More recent research focused on robotic museum guides. In the case of Robovie robot, for example, researchers examined its ability to hold visitors' attention at a science museum and guide them around (Shiomi et al. 2006). Another robots-related research endeavour in museum settings focused on modalities such as robot's gaze. The study revealed that visitors' ability to remember a story was affected by the robot's gaze. Specifically, visitors were better able to remember the story when the robot looked at them, compared to when the robot was looking at random (Multlu et al. 2006).

An interesting major online survey just before the pandemic helped towards learning more about people's attitude towards robots. This research by Webster and Ivanov (2022) was conducted from March 2018 to October 2019. It explored how the public views the suitability of using robots in museums and galleries. The data obtained from an international survey of 1589 participants indicated that the perceived appropriateness of robot implementation in museums and galleries is primarily influenced by perceptions of the usefulness and emotional skills of robotic technologies, as well as their perceived advantages over human employees.

This research deviated from the norm of studying children-visitors in dinosaur-resembling animatronics by studying human-resembling animatronics on adult visitors' experience in the *Casa Parlante—A living Museum* in Corfu, Greece.

18.3 The *Casa Parlante Museum* in Brief

The Museum under study is the *Casa Parlante—A living Museum* in Corfu Greece, established in March 2014. The museum won the Greek Entrepreneurship Award 2013 and it is at the top of the TripAdvisor list for Corfu, Greece, since its opening. The museum's website is http://casaparlante.gr. "Casa Parlante" in Italian means the "speaking house". The choice of this specific name indicates the house has voice and talks about the habits, the manners and the everyday life of a typical noble nineteenth-century Corfiot family.

The *Casa Parlante Museum* presents a typical Corfiot aristocratic mansion of the period 1814–1864. Corfu's aristocratic residences exhibited the past of the noble owners and their family through valuable objects, paintings, relics and furniture. They confirmed the family's social status, they outlined the owners' style and displayed the noble aristocracy's past and habits. The museum exhibition unfolds inside the building where the everyday life of a typical noble 19th-century Corfiot family is represented with the help of nine (9) animated human figures (animatronics), as well as reproductions of smells and sounds of that era. The museum aims to guide visitors in the past by offering a unique experience, involving human senses other than sight, such as hearing, smell and taste. A tour-guide accompanies visitors, presents the exhibition, offers traditional drinks and sweets, and answers visitors' questions.

There are eight rooms in this aristocratic Corfiot mansion house: the living room (the largest and brightest room of the house), the study room (serving reading and business needs), the bathroom, the main/master bedroom, the children's bedroom with the piano, the servants' room, the kitchen and the cellar.

There is at least one human-resembling animatronic in the *Casa Parlante Museum* in every room. Each of the nine animatronic represents either a family member or a member of the household staff. Therefore, guests have the opportunity to meet the aristocratic family via their animatronics: conte-Spyros (the grandfather of the

Fig. 18.1 Conte-Spyros, animatronic in the *Casa Parlante Museum* (photo by the authors)

family who belongs to the old aristocracy, Fig. 18.1), conte-Ioannis (the son of conte-Spyros), contessa-Eleonora (wife of the conte-Ioannis), contessa-Theodora (wife of the grandfather conte-Spyros), and the children Spyros and Theodora (Fig. 18.2), traditionally named after their grandfather and grandmother. Visitors also meet staff members, i.e. the children's music teacher (Fig. 18.2), Mrs Maria (the maid taking care of children), and Miss Katina, the cook, preparing the meal or dinner (Fig. 18.3). Visitors meet the children during their music lesson with their teacher of music, i.e. the animatronic of a woman music teacher whose name is not known. All animatronics are animated and there is an effort to add sound to them. Visitors see them moving parts of their bodies but maintaining their positions in the space. Animatronics are dressed in original clothes of the nineteenth century.

The *Casa Parlante Museum* is a sui generis museum. Its exhibition addresses human senses other than vision, such as hearing, smell and taste, offering an innovative, interactive and sense-involving experience, in which visitors are invited and challenged to be part of a Corfiot aristocrat narrative in a nineteenth century replica house of the Corfiot aristocracy.

18.4 Research Questions, Design and Limitations

This research aims to measure the impact of animatronics in the museum experience perceived as an introspective and cognitive condition. More specifically, we study the impact of human-resembling animatronics on visitor's experience in terms

Fig. 18.2 The music teacher and the children Theodora and Spyros, animatronics in the *Casa Parlante Museum* (photo by the authors)

Fig. 18.3 Miss Katina, the cook, animatronic in the *Casa Parlante Museum* (photo by the authors)

of emotions, gained knowledge and overall satisfaction. We also study the animatronics as part of an alternative curatorial approach and the way that is perceived and experienced by visitors.

This is a survey research based on a questionnaire of 19 question sets, all related to the research questions mentioned above and repeated here:

- how animatronics affect visitors' experience?
- how visitors perceive animatronics in relation to the other exhibits?

Further research questions were What do visitors notice and feel while viewing animatronics as part of an exhibition, how animatronics (specifically human-resembling ones) capture visitor and add to the museum experience, and to what extent animatronics enhance visitors' experience and understanding of the exhibition's narrative.

To build up the questions on the questionnaire, we had a pilot phase followed by discussion with researchers of the Museology Research Laboratory of the Ionian University, Corfu, Greece, and their friends. This research received ethical clearance from the Ionian University, questionnaires were filled-in anonymously with all participants' full consent. We employed no control group in this study as this would be very difficult have for practical reasons. In terms of sample size, we decided to randomly reach the number of 70, as this is the number of visitors of the museum on an average summer day. The final questionnaire was in paper, two pages, and would need about 7 min to be filled-in by a visitor. Visitors filled in the questionnaire after visiting the museum at the exit of the exhibition. For the compilation of the questionnaire, we used Casaleiro (1999) and Tunnicliffe (2000) with a focus on mining information regarding visitors' opinion and feelings. We, therefore, used nouns such as "indifference", "deception" "enthusiasm", "satisfaction" at a specific question (Q14), which referred to emotions evoked by the animatronics' presence. By doing so, we wanted to give visitors the option to tick as many options as they wished.

The quantitative research design was descriptive, since the subjects (visitors) have been measured once and the scope was to look at causality (Sukamolson 2007). As mentioned above, the sample consisted of adult visitors. Questionnaires consisted of closed and open-ended questions. Data was collected and subjected to statistical analysis, whilst data of the open-ended questions were elaborated via content analysis.

The final questionnaire consisted of 19 questions in two parts:

Part A: Questions on demographic information, including gender, age, nationality, education, whether visitors have visited museum(s) with animatronics before and, if yes, what kind of animatronics. (Q 1–6).

Part B: Question sets (closed and open-ended) on the exhibition with emphasis on animatronics' impact. (Q 7–15 and Q 16–19 respectively).

We addressed 70 visitors, and we collected 65 questionnaires by adults, 47 of which were women and 18 were men. Five visitors (mainly visitors as part of a couple) refused to fill in the questionnaire.

The majority of participants were high educated (university and post graduate degree) and 20 of them had already visited an exhibition with animatronics in the past. Most of them were under 35 years old; 20 participants were between 18 and 24 years old; 17 were between 25 and 34; 15 visitors were between 35 and 44; 11 visitors at the age of 45–54; only 2 at the age of 55–64.

In terms of limitations and challenges, this survey was conducted solely with adults (i.e. it did not include children), and it will be challenging to use it in comparative approaches with research on animatronics and children (e.g. the early work of Tunicliffe). Also, the sample of 65 adults consisted of more women than men, and therefore it may refer more to how women, rather than men, experience the animatronics' presence at the museum. Also, the survey took place just before the pandemic during summer months, meaning that it covers both local and tourist populations. Moreover, most visitors were under the age of 35 and very few visitors declared an age of more than 54 years, which means that (a) the results may not be valid for elder visitors, and (b) elder people tend not to visit the *Casa Parlante Museum*.

18.5 Research Results

Having presented the demographic information collected in part A of the questionnaire (questions 1–7), in this chapter we present the answers we received from the question sets (closed and open-ended) of Part B, on the exhibition with emphasis on animatronics' impact. More specifically:

In the question set no 7 "What of the following has/have impressed you or have provided you with more knowledge?", participants indicated that they were impressed or got more knowledge about the everyday life of the nineteenth century in Corfu (81%), the social status of the society at the time (58%), the furniture (46%) and the objects (40%).

In the question set no 8 "How much have the following satisfied you?" (five-scale, from "very much" to "not at all") participants were very satisfied with the museum topic (76%) and the exhibition settings (97% the "very much" or "much"). They were also satisfied (76%) with the time they had to explore the exhibition on their own, highlighting the importance of the unguided tour option at the museum.

In question no 9 "Have the moving robotic puppets (animatronics) made any difference regarding the exhibition's quality/experience?", 82% of the participants stated that the animatronics made a big or very big difference regarding the exhibition's quality/experience. The latter confirms the animatronics' choice as an alternative and differentiated interpretation approach.

This was also confirmed by the answers in the next three question sets (no 10–12). In these questions most participants noted that, in comparison with an exhibition without animatronics, the Casa Parlante exhibition was more alive (84%), took them back to the past (55%), did not seem fake or phony (97%) and made them feel part of the exhibition (37%). They also stated that they experienced going back to the time that the museum aims to revive (92%), they gained historical information (92%), they discovered new knowledge (92%) and felt that the exhibition's message was better delivered via the animatronics (82%).

In question no 13 "To what extent did you feel that the moving robotic puppets (animatronics) have overtaken the rest of the artefacts?", almost a third of participants claimed that animatronics did overtake the rest of artefacts, another third claimed they did not, and the rest did not take a side.

In question no 14 "What was the feeling you have experienced by the presence of the moving robotic puppets (animatronics)?", 30 visitors experienced satisfaction by their presence and 34 experienced enthusiasm, whilst only 2 visitors felt that their presence was indifferent or deceiving, getting scores 46%, 52% and 3% respectively.

In question 15 "Have you been satisfied by the museum visit experience in total?", aiming at information mining regarding the overall experience, almost all participants answered "very much" (76%) or "much" (18%).

The last part of the questionnaire had four open-ended questions (q. 16–19) on the reasons for visiting the Casa Parlante (q. 16), on what visitors liked in the museum (no 17), on what they disliked in the museum (q. 18), and if they had suggestions for improvement (q. 19). Reasons for the visit included "curiosity", "learn about noble life in nineteenth century", "animatronics", "reviews on the internet", with animatronics and curiosity being most frequently stated. In terms of what visitors liked in the museum, indicative answers are: "presence of animatronics attributes a more realistic character to museum", "staff, setting and atmosphere", "it feels like I was part of the nineteenth century for 30 min", "moving puppets gave a realistic sense to the exhibition", "guidance tour was exceptional, giving us the opportunity to dialogue", "accurate era illustration", "stylish decoration, moving puppets, furniture and the whole story that resemble to fairytale", "good behaviour, nice setting, great atmosphere", "informative and interesting tour". Dislikes included: "hot", "not taking photo", "not so much move to animatronics", "more interaction with place. To be able to open the closet for example". Suggestions for improvement were: "photos allowed", "permission for more rooms", "voice to animatronics", "more advertising, as not many people seem to know about it".

18.6 Discussion

Having presented the demographic information collected in part A of the questionnaire (questions 1–7), in this chapter we present the answers we received from the question sets (closed).

According to our findings, the animatronics' impact on the Casa Parlante Museum exhibition was noteworthy. The use of animatronics has been positive and favourable for visitors. Findings pointed out that, regardless of sex, age, nationality and educational background, visitors gained new knowledge and were entertained, illuminating the restorative element of museum experience as claimed by Packer (2008). We have focused on visitors' experience regarding human-resembling animatronics in terms of learning, feelings, expectations and overall impact, what is described as cognitive and introspective experience as argued by Pekarik et al (1999). These answers evinced the effect of animatronics on the adults' overall museum experience, expanding the audience categories that react positively and get excited by their presence beyond children. The specific findings signify the need for adopting unconventional options, such as animatronics, when it comes to museum interpretation and narratives. Given their wide acceptance, animatronics have turned out to be a form that could serve the purpose of museum inclusivity in an efficient way.

Regarding our first research question (i.e. how animatronics affect visitors' experience), visitors' answers indicated that the inclusion of animatronics as part of exhibition offered them the chance to augment their imagination. The latter contributes to the embodiment element for aesthetic museum experience as argued by Joy and Sherry (2003). In addition, their answers stressed that they experienced the visit in a participatory and vivid way. Animatronics contributed to the excitement and to the feeling of being involved, as well as to absorbing information on the history, the habits, the status and the ways of living of a noble Corfiot family of the nineteenth century.

Moreover, the adoption and the incorporation of animatronics, together with the experience of smells and sounds of that era, satisfied visitors' expectations and resulted to a feeling of travelling to the past. Visitors' museum experience included act and activation, feel and sense, knowledge and entertainment. They felt that they were not passive observers, but active participators, since they took and played imaginary roles, they interacted with the characters represented through the animatronics humanoid puppets, and lived an imaginary museum-driven narrative. Even though there were no real actors performing roles as in a living history museum, participants featured the choice of animatronics as an alternative, dynamic, costumed interpretation medium that has created an immersive learning environment. In our case, it was not the costumed actors or costumed museum staff that formulated social and cultural connections with the past through their performance, but it was the presence of the humanoid animatronics that did that. Their presence and moves captured visitors' imagination and offered them a back to the past journey, upgrading their experience.

This feeling of participation has given Casa Parlante a high ranking in visitors' preferences and agendas, since almost all stated that they would visit it again. The latter is noteworthy, since it indicates that their presence as part of the exhibit continues to affect visitors during the after-visit period, constituting a considerable reason for revisiting. Based on the given answers, the results showed that animatronics do affect the museum experience in its cognitive and introspective dimension.

Referring to our second research question (how visitors perceive animatronics in relation to the rest of the exhibits), participants' answers showed that animatronics seem to noticeably contribute to learning. They offer a unique and amusing educative path, as they blend favourably with the rest exhibits and the narrative of exhibition. As indicated via participants' answers, animatronics were perceived as a medium for understanding the exhibition's message in depth and upgrading the overall experience.

Furthermore, it is argued that people pay more attention to things that interest them and learn best if something captures their attention or intrigues their feelings. Animatronics can offer to cultural and heritage tourism, since they are tourist-attractive and fulfil the main criterion, i.e. striking attraction, for the choice of a destination (Nowacki 2005). According to Augustyn and Samuel "the environment quality, the opportunity to learn something new, the complexity and authenticity of an experience will make the tourist choose a destination" (1998: 71). Furthermore, Kozak and Rimmington claim that "it is the tourists' satisfaction with destination attractions (e.g. museums) that makes them visit a place again" (2000). Satisfaction is a significant factor for returning to a place such as museums. Based on these claims, museum experience could extend beyond learning outcomes, without of course slighting this role, by invigorating emotional benefits.

In the case of the Casa Parlante Museum discussed in this paper, animatronics in the form of human-resembling robots have totally capsized a classical subject-oriented exhibition. Along with historically documented information, they have significantly contributed to a romantic, imaginary story in a way that offers mental, sensory and imaginative excitement. As pointed out by this research here, animatronics serve this need in a satisfactory way. They managed to capture visitors' attention and interest, and offer different content referring to museum experience. This was mainly achieved by the complementary way they harmonized with the rest of the exhibits.

Consequently, the need for visitor studies has emerged and continues to increase, and visitors' experience and attitudes are constantly under study. As resulted here, animatronics provide novelty museum exhibits and unprecedented experiences. In this context, they can contribute and enrich both to exhibition and exhibits sets.

18.7 Conclusions and Future Research

This study addressed the relationship and interaction among museum visitors and human-resembling animatronics as exhibits. It delivered findings regarding how animatronics affect visitor's museum experience and how visitors perceive animatronics' presence in relation to other exhibits. It outlined the contribution of animatronics to cognitive and introspective museum experience, while it shed more light on the aspect of aesthetic experience with the concept of embodiment. Findings showed that incorporating human-like animatronics models as part of a museum exhibition offers an immersive and unique museum experience. Animatronics' presence in museum exhibition spaces enhance learning and entertainment expectations, and they contribute in a vivid way to a 'back in time' visitor experience. The latter is a key element in terms of introspective museum experience.

We concluded that human-resembling animatronics comprise a valuable tool in twenty-first century museum exhibitions, since they attract attention and provoke a 'wow' feeling to visitors. Visitors were impressed and stated their enthusiasm. Visitors felt they learnt via animatronics and experienced nineteenth century Corfu in a unique way. Not only did they gain knowledge and provide themselves with historical information, but they also felt that they travelled back in time in an emotional way. Thus, they admitted via their given answers that they had a good, creative and restorative time. As visitors suggested, more advanced animatronics with extra movements, voice and smells would add to their experience and fulfil their expectations.

In terms of future research and good practices, it is important to maintain a balance between the presence of animatronics and the exhibits. Visitors' attention should not be distracted from the exhibits, as this would diminish their value and the experience they provide. Also, as this research involved adult museum visitors, it is important to expand it to children, as they tend to be more enthusiastic and enjoy interactive exhibits in a museum environment. Therefore, exploring children's experiences in museums and their interactions with animatronics is our next research step.

Acknowledgements The authors would especially like to thank the owners of the *Casa Parlante Museum*, Mrs. Rantou and Mr. Mitsopoulos, who were very helpful and hospitable. We also thank the rest of personnel of the Casa Parlante Museum, who have always been willing to guide us, comment on our views and answer our questions.

References

Augustyn M, Samuel K (1998) Service quality and tourism. J Travel Res 3(1):71–76

Black G (2006) The engaging museum. Developing museums for visitors involvement. Routledge, London

Bounia A (2012) Στα παρασκήνια του μουσείου. Η διαχείριση των μουσειακών συλλογών. Patakis, Athens (in Greek, 3rd edn)

Budge K, Burness A (2017) Museum objects and Instagram: agency and communication in digital engagement. Continuum 32(1):137–150

Casaleiro P (1999) Evaluating the moving dinosaurs: surveys of the blockbuster exhibition in four European capital cities. Visitor Stud Assoc 9(11):157–170

Chandrashekhar K (2016) Review on animatronics. Imp J Interdiscip Res 2(9):1168–1170

Del Duchetto F, Baxter P, Hanheide M (2019) Lindsey the tour guide robot-usage patterns in a museum long-term deployment. In: 2019 28th IEEE international conference on robot and human interactive communication (RO-MAN), New Delhi, India, pp 1–8

Derbaix M, Gombault A (2016) Selling the invisible to create an authentic experience: imagination at work at Cézanne's studio. J Mark Manag 32(15/16):1458–1477

Desvallées A, Mairesse F (eds) (2010) Key concepts of museology. Armand Colin, Paris

Dierking LD (1989) The family museum experience: implications from research. J Museum Educ 14(2):9–11

Dinosaurs Extreme (2015) Περιοδική έκθεση στο ΜΦΙΚ με ακραίες μορφές δεινοσαύρων. http://www.nhmc.uoc.gr/cl/news/28641. Accessed 10 March 2024 (in Greek)

Dittmann F, Lange N (2018) Robots: the 500-year quest to make machines human. Technol Cult 59(1):159–167. https://doi.org/10.1353/tech.2018.0010

Doering ZD (1999) Strangers, guests, or clients? Visitor experiences in museums. Curator Museum J 42(2):74–87

Falk JH, Dierking LD (1992) The museum experience. Whalesback Books, Washington DC

Falk JH, Dierking LD (1995) Recalling the museum experience. J Museum Educ 20(2):10–13

Falk JH, Dierking LD (2016) The museum experience revisited. Routledge, London

Germak C, Lupetti ML, Giuliano L, Ng MEK (2015) Robots and cultural heritage: new museum experiences. J Sci Technol Arts 7(2):47–57

Joy A, Sherry JF (2003) Speaking of art as embodied imagination: a multisensory approach to understanding aesthetic experience. J Consum Res 30(2):259–282

Kesner L (2006) The role of cognitive competence in the art museum experience. Museum Manage Curatorsh 21(1):4–19

Kozak M, Rimington M (2000) Tourist satisfaction with Mallorca, Spain, as an off-season holiday destination. J Travel Res 38(3):260–270
Maheswari BU (2015) Animatronics and multi-disciplinary technologies. Int J Adv Res Comput Sci Softw Eng 5(3):1260–1262
Mayet R, Diprose J, Pandey AK (2019) Towards automatic visual fault detection in highly expressive human-like animatronic faces with soft skin. In: 2019 28th IEEE international conference on robot and human interactive communication (RO-MAN), New Delhi, India, pp 1–6
McCarthy J, Ciolfi L (2008) Place as dialogue: understanding and supporting the museum experience. Int J Herit Stud 14(3):247–267
Mutlu B, Forlizzi J, Hodgins J (2006) A storytelling robot: modeling and evaluation of human-like gaze behavior. In: 2006 6th IEEE-RAS international conference on humanoid robots, Genova, Italy, pp 518–523
Neumann M (1988) Wondering through the museum: experience and identity in a spectator culture. Border/Lines 12(summer 1988):21–27
Nowacki M (2005) Evaluating a museum as a tourist product using the SERVQUAL method. Museum Manage Curatorsh 20(3):235–250
Pang WC, Wong CY, Seet G (2018) Exploring the use of robots for museum settings and for learning heritage languages and cultures at the Chinese heritage centre. Presence Teleoper Virtual Environ 26(4):420–435
Packer J (2008) Beyond learning: exploring visitors' perceptions of the value and benefits of museum experiences. Curator Museum J 51(1):33–54
Parry R (2019) How museums made (and re-made) their digital user. In: Giannini T, Bowen J (eds) Museums and digital culture. Springer series on cultural computing, pp 275–293. Springer, Switzerland, Cham
Peel CT (2008) An investigation into the construction of an animatronic model. Dissertation, University of Bradford
Pekarik AJ, Doering ZD, Karns DA (1999) Exploring satisfying experiences in museums. Curator Museum J 42(2):152–173
Poor GM, Jacob RJK (2011) Introducing animatronics to HCI: extending reality-based interaction. In Jacko JA (ed) Human-computer interaction, Part II, HCII 2011, LNCS 6762, pp 593–602. Springer, Berlin Heidelberg
Roppola T (2013) Designing for the museum visitor experience. Routledge, New York
Sheng CW, Chan MC (2012) A study of experience expectations of museum visitors. Tour Manage 33(1):53–60
Shiomi M, Kanda T, Ishiguro H, Hagita N (2006) Interactive humanoid robots for a science museum. In: Proceedings of the 1st ACM SIGCHI/SIGART conference on Human-robot interaction, Salt Lake City, Utah, USA, pp 305–312
Schraft RD, Graf B, Traub A, John D (2001) A mobile robot platform for assistance and entertainment. Int J Ind Robot 28(1):29–35
Sakagami Y, Watanabe R, Aoyama C, Matsunaga S, Higaki N, Fujimura K (2002) The intelligent ASIMO: system overview and integration. In: IEEE/RSJ international conference on intelligent robots and systems, Lausanne, Switzerland, vol 3, pp 2478–2483
Sukamolson S (2007) Fundamentals of quantitative research. Language Institute Chulalongkorn University 1(3):1–20
Thrun S, Bennewitz M, Burgard W, Cremers AB, Dellaert F, Fox D, Hahnel D, Rosenberg C, Roy N, Schulte J, Schulz, D (1999) MINERVA: a second-generation museum tour-guide robot. In: Proceedings 1999 IEEE international conference on robotics and automation, Detroit, MI, USA, vol 3. https://doi.org/10.1109/ROBOT.1999.770401
Tunnicliffe SD (1995) Talking about animals: studies of young children in zoos, a museum and a farm. Dissertation, King's College London
Tunnicliffe SD (1999) It's the way you tell it! What conversations of elementary school groups tell us about the effectiveness of animatronic animals exhibits. J Elem Sci Educ 11(1):23–26

Tunnicliffe SD (2000) Conversations of family and primary school groups at robotic dinosaur exhibits in a museum: what do they talk about? Int J Sci Educ 22(7):739–754

Virto N Lopez M (2019) Robots, artificial intelligence, and service automation to the core: remastering experiences at museums. In: Ivanov S, Webster C (eds) Robots, artificial intelligence, and service automation in travel, tourism and hospitality, pp 239–253. Emerald Publishing Limited, UK. https://doi.org/10.1108/978-1-78756-687-320191018

Volo S (2009) Conceptualizing experience: a tourist based approach. J Hosp Market Manag 18(2–3):111–126

Webster C, Ivanov S (2022) Public perceptions of the appropriateness of robots in museums and galleries. J Smart Tourism 2(1):33–39

Part IV
Innovative Approaches to Interactive Cultural Heritage Visualization

Chapter 19
Multimodal Presentations of the Tangible and Intangible Dimensions of Traditional Crafts

Nikolaos Partarakis, Paraskevi Doulgeraki, Efrosyni Karouzaki, Emmanouil Zidianakis, and Xenophon Zabulis

Abstract In this chapter, we discuss the possibilities for multimodal presentation of the tangible and intangible dimensions of traditional crafts rooted in their semantically rich representation and complemented with digital assets and semantic annotations, in a way that captures their socio-historic context and preserves both their tangible and intangible Cultural Heritage dimensions. These meaningful and experiential multimodal presentations are delivered to the target audience through multimodal narratives rendered by a range of presentation modalities, including personalized storytelling, interactive Augmented Reality (AR), augmented physical artefacts, Mixed Reality (MR) exhibitions, and the Web. In this chapter, we argue that this novel form of presentation can support impactful cultural experiences on interest growth and tourism and thus support Traditional Craft communities and Cultural Heritage institutions.

Keywords Craft preservation · Cultural heritage · Digitization · Documentation · Digital curation

N. Partarakis (✉) · P. Doulgeraki · E. Karouzaki · E. Zidianakis · X. Zabulis
Foundation for Research and Technology Hellas, Institute of Computer Science, Vassilika Vouton, N. Plastira 100, 70013 Heraklion, Crete, Greece
e-mail: partarakis@ics.forth.gr

P. Doulgeraki
e-mail: vdoulger@ics.forth.gr

E. Karouzaki
e-mail: karuzaki@ics.forth.gr

E. Zidianakis
e-mail: zidi-an@ics.forth.gr

X. Zabulis
e-mail: zabulis@ics.forth.gr

F. Liarokapis et al. (eds.), *Interactive Media for Cultural Heritage*, Springer Series on Cultural Computing, https://doi.org/10.1007/978-3-031-61018-9_19

19.1 Introduction

Crafts, such as handicrafts, traditional arts, or "heritage crafts" (Jennings 2012), hold significant cultural value (Lenzerini 2011; UNESCO 2003a). Unfortunately, many of these crafts face endangerment due to a decline in the number of practitioners and apprentices (UNESCO 2003b). Unlike other intangible cultural heritage forms, traditional crafts encompass both tangible and intangible aspects, serving as the most tangible expression of intangible cultural heritage.[1] The ICCROM has classified craft dimensions as tangible (materials, tools, workspaces, and artefacts) and intangible (knowledge, skills, social, technological, and historical context) (Donkin 2001). The objective of this chapter is to provide accurate representations, documentation, instructions, and training resources to digitally and actively preserve craft knowledge and practice so as to enable multimodal presentation for information, education and leisure. The main challenge addressed in this chapter is representing the practice itself (Schatzki et al. 2001), rather than focusing solely on structures and movements. Craft actions involve material transformation and incorporate invisible elements such as knowledge and dexterous motion. This knowledge often reflects social aspects of human activity, including collective values and memories depicted in traditional motifs. Crafts encompass various dimensions, requiring multiple types of representations. The appearance, and geometric structure of products, tools, materials, and actions are digitized using signal representations, including audiovisual and 3D/4D formats. Knowledge is encoded using semantic representations, encompassing craft production methods, required materials and skills, as well as their cultural, economic, and historical significance.

This chapter proposes a protocol to (a) identify, organize, and collect the necessary information, digital assets, and knowledge, (b) organize them into a digital representation, and (c) utilize this representation to digitally preserve craft knowledge and physically re-enact digitized craft processes. Given the relevance of multiple information types, the proposed protocol provides a structured framework for achieving a comprehensive craft representation. The work described in this paper is situated within the multidisciplinary Mingei Innovation Action of the European Commission.[2] Several digital tools have been developed as a foundation for implementing the proposed protocol. The core infrastructure is the Mingei Online Platform (MOP), a collaborative web-based authoring platform for craft representations (Partarakis et al. 2021). Accompanying this platform are various supporting editors that facilitate the digital curation of relevant digital assets. The platform builds upon previous work on representing crafting processes (Zabulis et al. 2022) and contextualization narratives. A set of tools has been developed to make the represented knowledge more accessible to the general public and researchers, leveraging the achieved representation.

The rest of this chapter is organised as follows. Section 19.2 presents existing and related work on the discussed research subjects. Section 19.3 presents our approach towards crafts representation and Sect. 19.4 the multimodal presentation empowered

[1] Traditional craftsmanship: https://ich.unesco.org/en/traditional-craftsmanship-00057.

[2] Mingei Horizon 2020 project: https://www.mingei-project.eu/.

by the rich representation. Section 19.5 provides a discussion of the lessons learned while Sect. 19.6 gives an overview of the next research steps.

19.2 Related Work

19.2.1 Craft Documentation

UNESCO's recognition of traditional crafts as Intangible Cultural Heritage (ICH, UNESCO 2003b) has raised awareness and promoted adherence to scientific and ethical guidelines for craft descriptions fostering approaches to their representation, presentation and safeguarding (Partarakis and Zabulis 2023a, b). Descriptions following these guidelines can be found in UNESCO's Representative List of the ICH of Humanity (UNESCO 2003c), as well as national inventories (Barra 2012; French Republic Ministry of Culture 2008; Government of India Ministry of Textiles and Ministry of Textiles 2021). These craft descriptions emphasize cultural content, social aspects, ownership, intellectual property rights (IPR), and authenticity certification. However, they often lack sufficient technical descriptions to support understanding and reenactment of the crafts. In 1990, UNESCO published a data collection guide for traditional crafts (Jocelyne 1990), which, although technologically outdated, identifies the essential elements to be recorded, including artefacts, materials, tools, and the crafting process. Photographic documentation is considered necessary to capture the practical aspects of the craft-making process, which are often better conveyed visually than through verbal descriptions, such as the manipulation of tools and their proper usage.

Ethnography (Mauss 1967) is a method that identifies and describes the activities of social groups as "textual reconstructions of reality" (Atkinson 1990). In recent years, ethnography has been applied in workshops focusing on various crafts, such as carpentry (Vannini and Vannini 2020), glasswork (Atkinson 2013), and textile manufacturing (Konstantinou and Anagnostopoulos 2019). UNESCO's Living Human Treasures program has specifically focused on talented tradition bearers and practitioners, utilizing ethnographic documentation to facilitate the transmission of their knowledge and skills to younger generations.[3]

Cinematography and digital technologies have played a crucial role in recording easily understandable visual examples of craft processes. Video dictionaries capturing crafting gestures have been proposed (Wang et al. 2011). The concept of a worn camera has been suggested to capture the practitioner's viewpoint (Bellu and Blanc 2012). Additionally, 3D recording techniques have been employed to enable viewing from any perspective (Dimitropoulos et al. 2014). Digital ethnographic tools have also been proposed (Wood 2009). These advancements have provided valuable resources for documenting and studying traditional crafts (Zabulis et al. 2023).

[3] UNESCO's Living Human Treasures program: https://ich.unesco.org/en/living-human-treasures.

19.2.2 Prior Work on Craft Representations

The Crafts Ontology (CrO), that we employ in this chapter, is based on the CIDOC Conceptual Reference Model (CIDOC-CRM, Doerr 2003) and allows for the formal representation of crafts. It incorporates the Narrative Ontology (Bartalesi et al. 2016; Meghini et al. 2021) for representing narratives, the FRBRoo ontology for bibliographic records, and the OWL Time ontology recommended by W3C for time representation (Cox and Little 2017).

The CrO is utilized to formally represent crafting processes, as demonstrated in (Zabulis et al. 2022). In CrO, Process schemas model a recipe decomposed into process schema steps and each step into sub-steps until the desired level of detail is achieved. Within the schema, crafting events are connected by transition nodes (Simple, Fork, Merge, Join, and Branch). The execution of a process schema is encoded in the form of a Process that encodes events that occurred during the actual execution of a crafting process. A process represents one of the potential flows within a process schema, meaning that different sets of events can still conform to the same schema.

The digital narratology approach described in (Partarakis et al. 2021) is adopted to represent narratives that provide context to artefacts, collections, and techniques. A key concept in this approach is the term "Fabula," referring to the series of events that constitute a narrative in chronological order. Events within the Fabula are connected through mereological, causal, and temporal relationships and are used to individually model a narrative. A Narrative may be told in multiple ways called Narrations. To organize the stimuli presented during a Narration on a specific medium, a class called "Presentations" is introduced. Each presentation depicts a different way to present a narration facilitating one of the discussed presentation modalities.

The MOP integrates the aforementioned craft process and narrative models. It offers a graphical user interface (GUI) for creating instances of craft representations. The GUI simplifies the process and encourages user collaboration by providing different access roles. MOP is built on ResearchSpace[4] (Oldman and Tanase 2018), a research platform that incorporates CIDOC-CRM modules and integrates a repository of digital assets with assigned Internationalized Resource Identifiers (IRIs). Connective links are established in the MOP knowledge base to resources that have other identifiers in Wikidata or other knowledge bases. Each digital asset is enriched with metadata, including semantic annotations from controlled vocabularies for objects, activities, and locations.

[4] Researchspace: https://www.researchspace.org/.

19.2.3 Digital Technologies for the Presentation of Cultural Heritage

The integration of digital technologies has influenced the preservation and presentation of cultural heritage (Zhou et al. 2012) with a direct effect on traditional crafts (e.g., Chatterjee and Alvelos 2021; Kolay 2016; Vilbrandt et al. 2010). Capturing both the tangible and intangible dimensions of crafts is essential for providing new perspectives on understanding and appreciating (Mezzino 2017). As such this section provides an overview of these advances.

19.2.3.1 Digitization of Tangible Craft Artifacts

Digital technologies have contributed to the digitization of tangible craft artefacts (Adamopoulos et al. 2020; Pavlidis and Koutsoudis 2022). High-resolution imaging has contributed to conservation (Filippidis et al. 2015; Huang et al. 2016) while 3D scanning and advanced documentation techniques have allowed for the creation of virtual replicas that capture the details of craft objects but also enhanced the capacity of the craft sector to deliver products that are based on digital innovation (Mongeon 2015). This not only facilitates preservation efforts by mitigating physical deterioration but also enables broader accessibility to these artefacts including in times where access restrictions have been applied (Palit 2022). Virtual museums and online repositories have emerged as platforms for the public to explore and study these digital renditions, transcending geographical and cultural boundaries (Kiriyama et al. 2002).

19.2.3.2 Virtual and Augmented Reality (VR/AR) and Digital Storytelling

The integration of virtual and augmented reality has revolutionized the presentation of crafts by providing immersive and interactive experiences (e.g., Chakraborty 2022; Fuchigami and Ishida 2023; Ishida et al. 2019; Iyobe et al. 2016). Through VR, users can engage with lifelike simulations of craft workshops, gaining insights into the artisanal processes (Lee 2023; Yiyi and Lingxuan 2022). AR applications enhance physical exhibits by overlaying digital information, creating enriched narratives around craft objects (Chakraborty 2022). Crafts embody not only physical artefacts but also intangible aspects such as techniques, stories, and cultural practices. Digital story telling on Cultural Heritage (Lu et al. 2011, Vrettakis et al. 2019) and the relevant digital platforms have the potential to present narratives surrounding crafts. Crafts often come with stories that are passed down through generations, contributing to the narrative tapestry of a community (Gibson 2021). Digital storytelling techniques, including podcasts, video documentaries, and interactive multimedia presentations, provide a platform to share these stories. Craftsmen, communities, and historians can collaborate to create compelling narratives that contextualize the craft within its cultural, historical, and social context (Zabulis et al. 2020).

19.2.3.3 Web-Based Platforms

The advent of crowdsourced digital platforms has democratized the documentation and interpretation of craft heritage. Online communities and collaborative initiatives allow enthusiasts, researchers, and practitioners to contribute their perspectives, knowledge, and personal experiences (Sabiescu et al. 2015, 2017). This collective approach not only enriches the understanding of crafts but also creates a dynamic, evolving representation of cultural heritage that reflects diverse viewpoints. At the same time, online platforms dedicated to oral histories allow community members to share personal narratives, anecdotes, and folklore associated with crafts (Mathioudakis et al. 2022). This digital archive of oral histories not only preserves the authenticity of cultural expressions but also offers insights into the socio-cultural significance of crafts within specific communities (Mason 2005).

19.2.3.4 Digital Documentation

The digital documentation of craft techniques through high-definition videos, interactive tutorials, and virtual workshops allows artisans to demonstrate their skills in a digital format (Hasoğlu 2015). These resources serve as valuable educational tools, preserving the intricate processes involved (Lehmann 2012) in crafting and ensuring the transmission of knowledge to future generations (Partarakis and Zabulis 2023a, b). Digital platforms also facilitate the exchange of skills among artisans across different regions, fostering a global community of practitioners (Gu 2018). Festive events and traditions associated with crafts are part of the intangible heritage and may include ceremonies, festivals, and community gatherings. Through digital documentation and presentation, these can be transformed into new experiences (Chan and Cai 2023).

19.2.4 Contribution

Based on the aforementioned analysis the contributions of this chapter can be considered under multiple perspectives. A major contribution is a representation that captures both tangible and intangible dimensions of crafts as cultural heritage introducing semantically enhanced representation that can assist towards sustainable and multidisciplinary preservation efforts. In addition, by preserving the socio-historic of craft practice the proposed approach aims to ensure that the cultural heritage associated with these crafts is accurately conveyed to the audience and links to the living history, social practices and traditions of the communities that practice them. By introducing the concept of meaningful and experiential multimodal narratives this chapter aims to enhance the ways that traditional crafts are presented through various presentation modalities, including personalized storytelling, interactive Augmented Reality (AR), augmented physical artefacts, Mixed Reality (MR) exhibitions, and the Web.

The proposed novel form of presentation has the potential to significantly impact cultural experiences, interest growth, and tourism. By leveraging immersive technologies like AR and MR, the goal is to enhance the audience's engagement with traditional crafts, leading to a broader appreciation of cultural heritage. This has the potential to have a profound impact towards supporting craft communities and cultural heritage institutions. The suggested multimodal presentation approach is positioned as a means to not only showcase the richness of traditional crafts but also to contribute to the sustainability and economic well-being of the communities involved.

19.3 Representation

19.3.1 Understanding and Recording

In the process of documenting crafts and their social and historical context, a mapping of related topics and knowledge items is established. The goal is to identify the entities necessary for understanding the craft practice and its community context. Prior knowledge of the topic serves as a starting point for discussions with practitioners and communities. Secondary sources provide information on basic concepts and their names. Visual recordings of objects and events complement the documentation by capturing craft tools, workshops, machines, and products.

Understanding the craft practice and context involves interactions with practitioners and cultural heritage (CH) professionals. This includes collaborative creation workshops where communities are involved in defining craft roles, traditions, and contextual elements. Ethnography is employed as a methodology to comprehensively document the crafting processes. Practitioners demonstrate and explain the making of artefacts, identify required skills, and suggest teaching or demonstration processes. Communities and CH professionals contribute historical and social context, sharing information about community history, traditions, and the broader significance of the craft. Stakeholder mapping is conducted to identify relevant stakeholders and determine the information to be collected from each group.

To understand craft practice, various types of concepts and their names are identified. Physical items encompass materials, artefacts, tools, machinery, protective clothing, and workspaces. Actions refer to the transformation of materials into intermediate or final craft products. Narratives and stories that are directly relevant to craft representation are selected, considering historical events, technological advances, and artistic movements that have influenced the craft's history and economy. In

(Zabulis et al. 2019), potential methods for identifying relevant topics are proposed. The outcome of this task is preliminary documentation in the form of a vocabulary for the crafting process, including physical items and crafting actions, and a collection of narratives related to the craft's genre, technological evolution, and social/historical context. A catalogue of recording or digitization targets is prepared, which may include objects of historic or symbolic significance. References to the sources of each piece of information are included.

Recording involves capturing objects (endurants) and events (perdurants). Endurant recordings involve photographic documentation and 3D digitization, while event recordings utilize audio, video, and 4D reconstruction (reconstruction over time). Contextualization items, literature, and other information-carrying media such as documents, technical drawings, images, and audio recordings are also digitized. Technical metadata is associated with digital assets to interpret them appropriately as computer files. The concept of digital assets allows for the management of multiple types of files, linked to the knowledge base regardless of their file type or storage location.

When documenting endurant items (e.g., tools, machines, products) photography and 3D reconstruction are commonly used. Comprehensive guides on the photographic recording of cultural heritage artefacts and sites are recommended (Brosseau et al. 2006, CARLI 2022). For 3D documentation, 3D-ICONS provides a comprehensive exploration of the data processing pipeline and recommendations for conventional digitization methods.[5] The digital assets in this case consist of images and 3D models that capture the structure and appearance of the items, typically encoded as 3D textured meshes.

The digitization of endurants encompasses structures of varying spatial scales. The choice of 3D scanning modality depends on the size of the subject, the material it's made of, and the type of environment. For large spaces such as rooms and outdoor areas, a combination of laser scanning and aerial photogrammetry is used to ensure comprehensive coverage. Smaller artefacts can be reconstructed using photogrammetry and active illumination sensors, which have become more accessible. Rourk (2019) proposes an approach to 3D data curation that covers the collection, processing, archiving, and distribution of data from multiple scanning modalities.

The digitization of perdurants primarily focuses on craft practice and archival data related to extinct techniques or historical events. The collection of archival recordings follows conventional practices of linked audiovisual data in the semantic web. For craft practice recordings, the events of interest are the postures and gestures of practitioners. The digital assets in this case are audio, video, and 4D motion recordings, referred to as "nimations." The choice of motion capture (MoCap) or video modalities depends on the environment. In cluttered workshop spaces, inertial MoCap is more suitable due to reduced installation requirements and independence from occlusions. Markerless visual methods are employed for video-based motion digitization

[5] 3D-ICONS exploration of the data processing pipeline and recommendations for conventional digitization methods: http://3dicons-project.eu/guidelines-and-case-studies/guidelines.

(Colyer et al. 2018), although they are less accurate than MoCap recordings. Such methods only require a camera and are essential for treating archive video.

Both objects and animations have parts of individual importance. Objects may have spatial regions associated with meaning or affordances, such as symbols or handles. Human motion is interpreted in terms of actions, gestures, or postures per body member. Segmenting animation recordings into body postures and gestures is facilitated by an editing tool developed for this purpose (Partarakis et al. 2020a, b).

For the technical implementation of storing digital assets, we facilitate the MOP (Mingei Online Platform), where the collected digital assets are linked to the knowledge base as "media objects." When new digital assets are added to the MOP repository, they are uploaded, assigned new URIs, and associated with the MOP Web server, which serves them via the HTTP protocol. Existing online resources require no additional operations.

19.3.2 Formulation of Knowledge Elements

Basic knowledge elements are categorized into Events, Materials, Objects, Places, and Persons. The instantiation of these knowledge elements involves creating a record for each element by asserting semantic metadata, establishing relations, and linking relevant digital assets. All classes presented in this section follow the naming conventions of CIDOC-CRM.

Events in the ontology (Doerr 2003), are defined as changes of state in cultural, social, or physical systems that are influenced by phenomena or other events. In the ontology, events are instances of the class E5 Event. Events can be associated with multiple places, objects, and locations. Participants, including individuals and social groups, are linked to events as relevant participants or actors. Places are related to events based on their occurrence or relevance to the event. Objects and materials may be used or produced as part of the event, capturing their involvement in the crafting process. Two types of events are of interest in representing craft practice and its context: contextual events and crafting events. Contextual events represent changes in social, technological, and economic systems, providing the building blocks for contextualization narratives. Crafting events, on the other hand, represent changes in materials that are transformed into craft products serving as the building blocks for crafting processes.

Materials are represented by facilitating the class E57 Material which is extended to include an optional attribute called Place. This extension allows for the representation of the origin of a material, which can be significant in terms of the quality, reputation, authenticity, and cost of the craft article produced from that material.

Objects include craft products, tools, machines, and historically significant artefacts, and are represented using the E22 Man-Made Object class in ontology. These objects are crucial for contextualizing craft practices. They are associated with relevant digital assets, such as photographs and 3D documentation, which provide visual representations and additional information about the objects. Objects include optional links to the materials that are used in τηειρ composition, as well as a Place attribute to indicate their location. Craft products can be associated with the specific process involved in their creation, the place where the process occurs, and the practitioner(s) responsible for crafting them.

Places in the craft ontology are represented as instances of the E53 Place class. They can be associated with one or multiple links to geographical locations. In the context of crafting processes, both the geographical location and the type of place hold significance. The geographical location is particularly relevant when considering the origin of materials or the specific site where craft products are manufactured. The classification of places is crucial for accurately representing the types of locations where crafting processes take place. For example, it can distinguish between a workshop where crafts are created or a harvesting site where raw materials are collected. This classification helps provide a comprehensive understanding of the specific environments and settings involved in craft practices.

In the case of contextualization narratives, geographical locations play a crucial role in documenting historical events. They allow for the identification and documentation of specific places where significant events occurred, enriching the narrative with spatial information.

Person entities in the craft ontology are instances of the E21 Person class and are used to represent individuals. On the other hand, social groups are represented as instances of the E74 Group class and refer to organizations or collectives of individuals. In process representations, persons and groups play a crucial role in depicting individual practitioners and workgroups involved in crafting processes. Additionally, persons are semantically classified based on their roles within the crafting process, further enriching the representation.

In narrative representations, person and social group entities are used to represent historical figures and social collectives such as companies, parties, guilds, or art movements. These entities help contextualize craft practices within a broader historical and social framework.

To enhance semantic annotation, the craft ontology leverages established thesauri such as the Getty Arts and Architecture Thesaurus[6] and the UNESCO Thesaurus.[7] Additionally, the option to incorporate additional thesauri from National Documentation Centers is available. Geographical references and location names are integrated into the craft ontology through a dedicated geographical reference.[8]

19.3.3 Semantic Representation

The representation of craft context is based on the collection of narratives established during Understanding and Recording, utilizing the computational approach

[6] Getty Arts and Architecture Thesaurus: https://www.getty.edu/research/tools/vocabularies/aat/.

[7] UNESCO Thesaurus: https://vocabularies.unesco.org/.

[8] Geonames: http://www.geonames.org/.

to narratology presented in (Meghini et al. 2021). A key concept in this approach is the term "Fabula," which refers to the series of events that constitute a narrative in chronological order. The Fabula can include parallel and simultaneous events but has a single version.

Each narrative is individually modelled using the events that form its Fabula. Events within the Fabula are connected through mereological, causal, and temporal relationships (Allen and Hayes 1989). Mereological relationships are employed to analyze complex events into simpler ones, while causal relationships encode the curator's interpretation of events. The instantiation of the Fabula for each narrative is carried out using the MOP.

Crafting process schemas capture the actions involved in executing a particular crafting process. A distinctive characteristic of crafting process schemas is the presence of branching points in their workflow, where the choice of action depends on the practitioner's judgment and can be influenced by various factors. To ensure a visual, unambiguous, and formal encoding of schemas, UML activity diagrams[9] are adopted. The visual nature of activity diagrams facilitates collaboration between technical and heritage partners.

Process schemas are decomposed into process schema steps. The analysis continues until the desired level of detail is achieved, typically reaching simple actions identifiable by practitioners. This recursive decomposition results in a hierarchy of schemas, starting from a broad description and gradually delving into the analysis of elemental actions. The finest sub-steps encompass individual postures and elemental gestures, such as "grasping a hammer" or "striking a nail with a hammer."

Within the schema and activity diagram, crafting events are connected by transition nodes (Simple, Fork, Merge, Join, and Branch), which are sufficient for defining crafting workflows (OMG UML 2022). Fork, Merge, and Join nodes enable the representation of simultaneous and synchronized actions performed by multiple individuals or body parts. Branching nodes depict conditional actions taken by practitioners, leading to different actions within the execution of the same process schema. Transition nodes establish temporal and causal relationships between process steps, while sub-step decomposition organizes them hierarchically.

The MOP is utilized to convert the process schema into a semantic representation. Both the creation of process schemas and fabulae are facilitated by the MOP.

19.3.4 Narratives

Narratives involve the authoring and semantic representation of fabulae. They serve as a means to present or narrate fabulae. Contextual events, which are past occurrences, are incorporated into narratives. The representation of narratives follows the guidelines provided in (Bartalesi et al. 2016, Meghinin et al. 2021), with the MOP being utilized for implementation, as described in (Partarakis et al. 2021).

[9] UML activity diagrams: https://www.omg.org/spec/UML/.

A narrative serves as a presentation or narration of a fabula and can have multiple narrations. Each narration refers to events from the Fabula, presented in a specific order that may not necessarily be chronological. Different narrations may exist to cater to diverse audiences and presentation modalities, allowing for multiple ways of presenting subsets of the Fabula. Each narrative references a fabula and utilizes a reference function to determine the order in which the Fabula's events are narrated. This enables access to knowledge elements and digital assets associated with the events. Narrations can be adapted based on factors such as language, age, or special needs. Furthermore, narrations may differ depending on the format of the presentation medium, whether it is audio, visual, textual, or multimodal.

To organize the stimuli presented during a narration on a specific medium, a class called "Presentations" is introduced. For each event referenced in the narration, a presentation segment is authored, containing links to the digital assets to be presented or their spatiotemporal arrangement. The MOP assists in authoring these presentation segments by retrieving relevant knowledge entities and digital assets.

Processes consist of events that occur during the crafting process. If these events adhere to a process schema, they are considered as executing that schema. A process represents one of the potential flows within a process schema, meaning that different sets of events can still conform to the same schema. A process includes a reference function that identifies and chronologically orders the events that took place during its execution. The knowledge entities and digital assets linked to these events are also available for presenting the process. The digital assets can be recordings of the events and digitized versions of the involved objects.

Various media can be utilized for delivering process and narrative presentations, ranging from verbal and visual formats to immersive and interactive narrations. The MOP facilitates the authoring of presentation segments that align with narrative events and crafting process steps by retrieving relevant knowledge elements and digital assets for each event.

19.4 Presentation

Craft presentations are constructed based on events and event schemas referenced in the narrative. These events are associated with knowledge elements and digital assets, which can be retrieved to illustrate the narration. Narrations are linked to events and, consequently, to knowledge elements and media objects. Alternative presentations of these narrations are enriched by incorporating 3D objects and actions within a virtual environment. Within this environment, human actions are re-enacted through motion recordings and animations performed by virtual humans. This allows for a multi-perspective view of human motions and interactions with tools and machines, enhancing comprehension.

The MOP serves as the underlying infrastructure for providing content to the presentation tools across all modalities. As a result, the content can be directly imported and reused in these applications. In addition to conventional digital assets, the knowledge base contains semantic representations of narratives and motion-driven narratives, which can be queried and systematically accessed by software clients.

19.4.1 Basic Presentation Modalities

19.4.1.1 Place-Oriented Presentation Modalities

Spatial presentation modalities play a crucial role in facilitating the visualization of environments. In Step 4, the geographical organization of narratives can directly benefit from presentation modalities designed for conveying spatial and geographical information. Spatial representations are enhanced by incorporating points of interest, which are associated with knowledge elements in the CrO and are predefined locations on the map. These locations, along with their associated digital assets, can be retrieved from the knowledge base or other repositories. This enables spatial presentations to be enriched with various types of digital assets available in the knowledge base, such as 3D reconstructions, historical information, video data, and more. For large-scale representations, map-oriented presentation modalities are proposed, specifically utilizing 3D geophysical maps that are relevant to the local environment and its resources (Partarakis et al. 2022).

To explore and navigate 3D environments, the utilization of an immersive visualization system like a wide-projection setup or a VR headset can be employed. Specifically, software capable of generating video output for a predetermined walk-through of the virtual camera within the 3D environment is required (see Fig. 19.1). The resulting video can then be further enhanced with narration, subtitles, music, and other elements.

Fig. 19.1 (left) 3D reconstructions of large-scale sites. (right) Integration of reconstructions in a geophysical 3D map to present immersive place-based narrations

Fig. 19.2 Screenshots from the Chios exploration game

19.4.1.2 Virtual Exploration

To create more intricate presentations, a virtual exploration of the natural environment can be employed, providing a terrestrial viewpoint enriched with 3D reconstructions of heritage sites and landscapes. This concept is exemplified through the implementation of a 3D game (Partarakis et al. 2020a, b). The terrain of the game is generated by importing the geophysical map into Unity3D, a popular game development platform. Additionally, flora and fauna elements are incorporated, along with 3D reconstructions of villages. The objective of the game is to explore the island in different eras and gain knowledge about the cultivation and trade of mastic through mission-oriented tasks. The inclusion of digitized rural environments contributes to the realism of the application. Furthermore, the game benefits from reusing digital representations of garments, machinery, and original tree structures obtained from the Mastic Museum at Chios (refer to Fig. 19.2).

19.4.1.3 Virtual Exhibits in Real Places

Virtual museum modalities offer the opportunity to showcase collections of digital assets within a physical space. These modalities address two key considerations: (a) the existence of museums with extensive artefact collections that cannot be fully displayed due to spatial limitations, and (b) the ability to virtually revisit past exhibitions even after they have concluded. The implementation of virtual museum applications exemplifies this concept (refer to Fig. 19.3).

19.4.1.4 Virtual Storytellers

Virtual storytellers play a crucial role in enriching the museum visit by providing narrations about the lives and experiences of individuals from the craft community. This concept is exemplified by the incorporation of virtual humans within the factory space of the Mastic Museum of Chios. These virtual humans, representing workers from the factory, share their personal stories and anecdotes (Ringas et al. 2022) (refer to Fig. 19.4). By utilizing virtual storytellers, visitors can engage with the narratives and gain a deeper understanding of the human aspect behind the craft and its community.

Fig. 19.3 (left) Web-based virtual museum collection, (right) Web-based 3D virtual museum collection

Fig. 19.4 (left) Computer vision-based avatar localization, (middle) Avatar storyteller in the museum, (right) Avatar storyteller in a Virtual environment

19.4.2 Narratives

19.4.2.1 Web-Based Narratives

The primary presentation method in the MOP involves a form of documentation that comprehensively outlines the contents of a craft representation, offering an overview of the craft itself and its broader context. This documentation is presented digitally and accessible online, providing an introductory narrative that serves as an initial orientation to the craft instance. The overview narrative offers a holistic perspective of the craft while allowing users to explore various aspects through multiple views.

These views include temporal (timeline-based), geographical (map-based), event based (calendar-based), object-based (galleries showcasing artefacts and tools), person-based (galleries highlighting key individuals), and more. The MOP offers predefined "templates" that facilitate the authoring and presentation of web based narratives, enabling users to create engaging and interactive presentations. An example of such a presentation is depicted in Fig. 19.5.

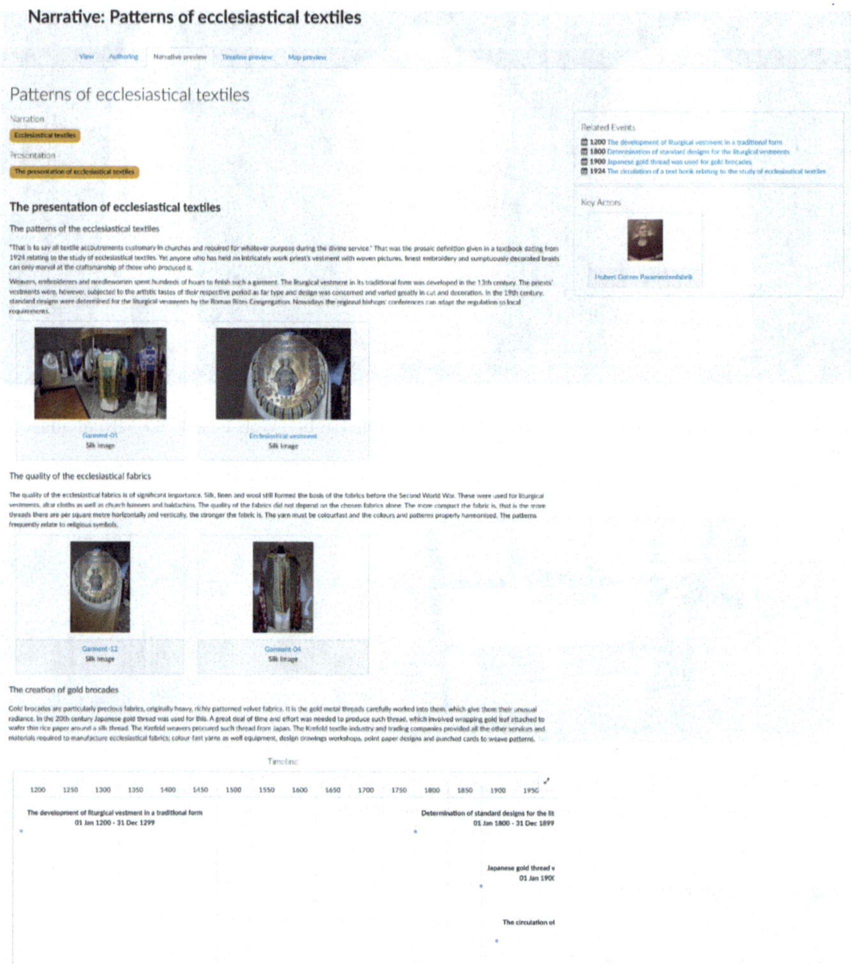

Fig. 19.5 Web-based narrative presentation

19.4.2.2 Augmented Physical Artifacts

Object-oriented presentation modalities can be achieved by augmenting contemporary objects with digital stories that connect them to history, society, traditions, and values. These stories serve to enhance the meaning, value, and uniqueness of the objects, thereby generating new interest in them. An example of this is illustrated through a handbag that serves as both a woman's accessory and a contemporary craft creation (refer to Fig. 19.6). To unveil its unique history and identity, the handbag is enhanced with an augmented reality (AR) application that utilizes three layers of pattern recognition. The first layer focuses on the bag itself, revealing its individual story and creative process. The second layer incorporates multiple patterns

Fig. 19.6 A handbag acting as a storyteller

that expose the story of textile weaving in Krefeld, providing further contextual background. Lastly, the third layer highlights that the patterns themselves possess their own stories, adding another layer of depth and narrative to the overall experience. Through the AR application, users can engage with the handbag and explore its multi-layered narratives, ultimately fostering a deeper appreciation for the object and its cultural significance.

19.4.3 Processes

19.4.3.1 2D Presentation of Actions

Two-dimensional visualization of actions plays a valuable role in conveying motion and instructions, especially in printed materials (Rigaki et al. 2020) and physical surfaces, opening up a range of applications in mixed reality involving physical objects and surfaces. Our approach draws inspiration from the world of art to create meaningful visualizations of human motion on 2D media. By leveraging concepts employed by artists, we aim to utilize their insights in motion visualization to efficiently depict and communicate human motion (McCloud 1993).

Artists, including painters, illustrators, and directors, have extensively studied the perceptual appeal of motion visualization methods through centuries of experimentation. Techniques such as motion lines, contrast, and the superimposition and juxtaposition of visual frames have been employed to aid the mental recreation of depicted motion by observers. Abstractions, like motion lines, offer valuable insights into understanding motion dynamics.

To simplify the authoring process for visualizing human motion, the MotiVo computer-aided authoring system was developed (Rigaki et al. 2020). An example of the visualization of glassblowing techniques, specifically the carafe glassmaking process, presented as a graphical story enriched with verbal content and visual annotations (Carre et al. 2022) is presented in Fig. 19.7.

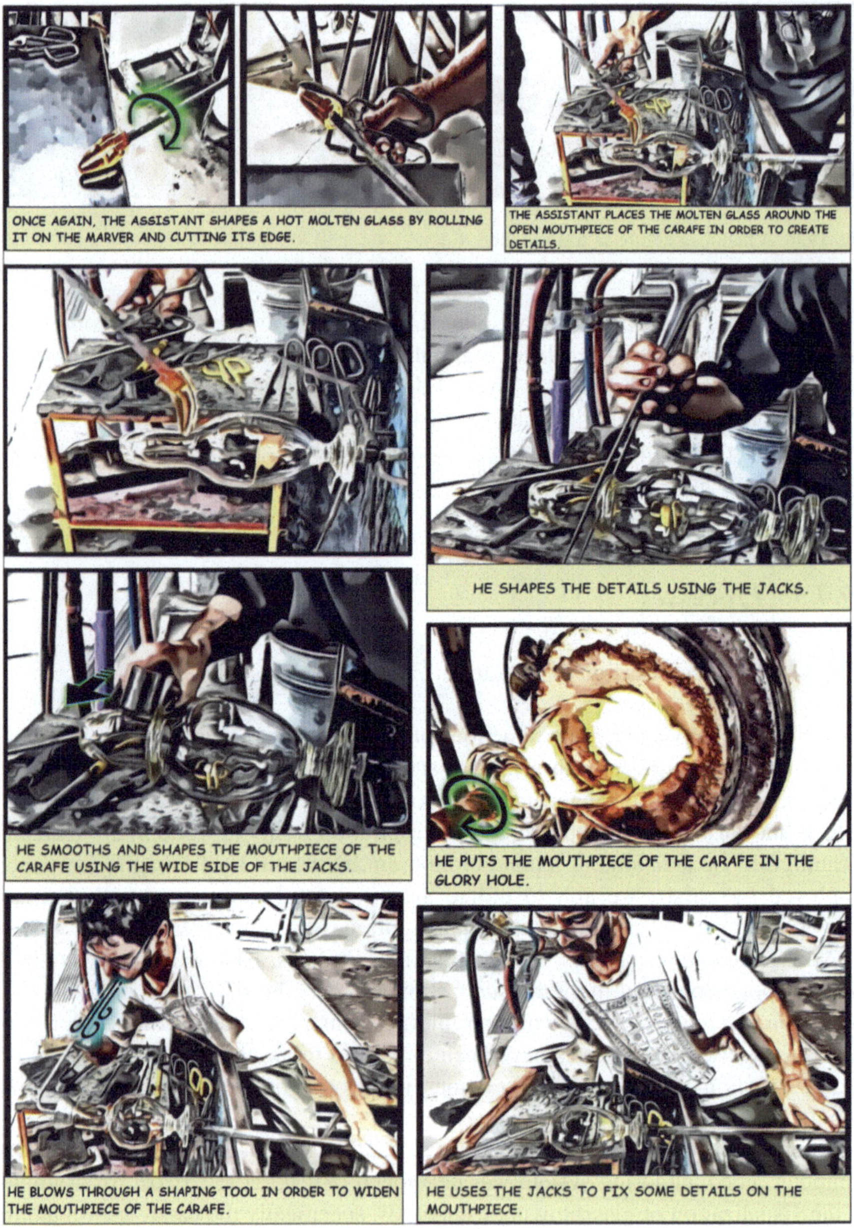

Fig. 19.7 Illustrated demonstration of glassblowing

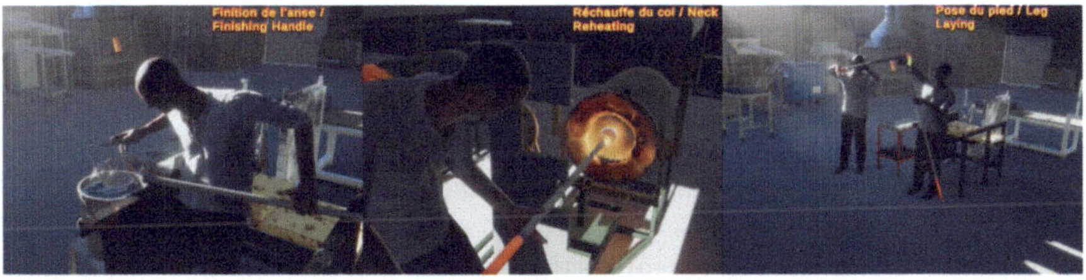

Fig. 19.8 Intuitive visualizations of practitioner actions and techniques of glassblowing

19.4.3.2 3D Presentation of Actions

Virtual humans can be employed as effective tools to present craft processes and demonstrate the usage of tools and machines. A key component in representing specific motion segments is the utilization of motion vocabulary items. These items serve as instances of distinct motion segments, which can be combined and interleaved to depict complete procedures. They act as fundamental building blocks within a motion vocabulary. By leveraging the motion vocabulary, it becomes possible to create "sentences" that encode various actions and procedures. This allows for the representation of complex craft processes in a structured and organized manner. Visualizations of practitioner actions and abstractions of tool usage configurations are used to demonstrate the motion vocabulary (refer to Fig. 19.8).

Through the use of virtual humans, these visualizations can effectively showcase the step-by-step execution of craft processes, highlighting the precise movements and interactions involved. The motion vocabulary provides a standardized framework for representing and communicating actions and procedures, enabling a clear understanding of the craft processes and facilitating their learning and replication.

19.5 Lessons Learned

In this section, we summarise the challenges faced in the process of representing and presenting HCs. Indeed, the need for interdisciplinary collaboration posed a significant challenge in applying the representation methodology. The involvement of multiple scientific disciplines with diverse approaches, tools, and research methods required a cohesive and unified framework to ensure effective collaboration. The MOP, serving as a single point of representation for research data, played a crucial role in enhancing collaboration within the team by providing a common platform for researchers to collaborate and share their findings in a structured and coherent manner, despite differences in terminology and disciplinary perspectives.

The iterative refinement of the representation was another important aspect that emerged during the application of the methodology. While the linear execution of the representation steps initially assumed the acquisition of all digital assets beforehand, it became apparent that new knowledge and non-digitized items could surface during later stages of the process. As a result, the need for additional digitization and refinement arose. This highlighted the importance of flexibility and adaptability within the methodology. The methodology proved to be highly adaptive to such iterations, allowing for adjustments and modifications to incorporate new needs and acquired assets.

The main lesson learned regarding the presentation was that due to the solid representation, we were able to enhance the delivery of information to visitors mainly due to the presence of a knowledge base and a comprehensive representation. This allowed us to employ several heterogeneous presentation modalities all strongly bound to the representation and thus being able to target different communication goals to support information, education, and entertainment. Thus, the separation of the representation from its usage enabled the use of a diverse range of technical tools, harnessing the creative abilities of UX designers and developers.

19.6 Conclusions and Future Work

In the context of crafts, a significant aspect of knowledge is the "felt," "tacit," or "embodied" knowledge, which relies on practitioners' sensory perception and their understanding of tool and material affordances. This type of knowledge includes the tactile sensations of materials (e.g., feeling the dampness of plaster as a potter or the roughness of a textile), the sensory experiences of heat and smell (e.g., in glass-making), or the perception of colour, which skilled practitioners utilize in their craft. It is crucial to recognize that understanding a craft cannot be solely accomplished through theoretical means. While narrations, documentaries, and VR demonstrations can provide valuable insights, they cannot fully recreate the "felt experiences" of craft. Therefore, in addition to conventional digital tools, the acquired representations include knowledge for craft re-enactment by meticulously capturing and representing craft processes and techniques.

This chapter proposes an initial step in digitizing intangible dimensions, such as purpose and causal dependencies, present in various vocational domains. The utilization of contextualization narratives can address more complex challenges, including the representation of technological history, social and historical events, and their impact on social groups and their practices. By incorporating these dimensions, the representation of crafts can pave the way for capturing and preserving the broader knowledge associated with different domains of human activity.

Regarding our future endeavours, our research efforts will focus on the generality of understanding of the making process, as the purposeful interaction of the mind with the world through senses and actions. Formal representation of knowledge is essential for reenactable preservation, but also computational under-standing of human creative tasks, enabling us to provide more specific tools for its aid. Generative, realistic reenaction (simulation) and simulated imagery allow us to assess the correctness of the representation of elusive concepts such as tacit knowledge. Craft-specific simulations are a powerful tool for learning but also optimizing workflow efficiency. Short-term predictive imagery of intended actions can be seen as a "pre-cautious undo" for mistakes in work of risk. The aforementioned objectives will serve towards expanding the phenomenological representation of TC we have achieved in this research work to a deeper understanding of the making process thus enhancing the capacity of comprehending and re-enacting TC processes for education and training.

Acknowledgements The work presented in this chapter has been implemented under the European-funded projects Mingei and Craeft, which received funding from the European Union's Horizon 2020 and Horizon Europe research and innovation programs under grant agreements No 822336 and No 101094349.

References

Adamopoulos E, Rinaudo F, Ardissono L (2020) A critical comparison of 3D digitization techniques for heritage objects. ISPRS Int J Geo Inf 10(1):10

Allen JF, Hayes PJ (1989) Moments and points in an interval-based temporal logic. Comput Intell 5:225–238

Atkinson P (1990) The ethnographic imagination: textual constructions of reality. Routledge, London, UK. https://doi.org/10.4324/9781315852065

Atkinson P (2013) Blowing hot: the ethnography of craft and the craft of ethnography. Qual Inq 19:397–404. https://doi.org/10.1177/1077800413479567

Barra G (2012) Chinese craft project. Master's Thesis, Politecnico Di Milano, Milano, Italy

Bartalesi V, Meghini C, Metilli D (2016) Steps towards a formal ontology of narratives based on narratology. In: 7th workshop on computational models of narrative (CMN 2016). Schloss Dagstuhl-Leibniz-Zentrum fuer Informatik, Dagstuhl Publishing, Germany

Le Bellu S, Le Blanc B (2012) How to characterize professional gestures to operate tacit know-how transfer. Electron J. Knowl Manag 2:142–153. https://hal.archives-ouvertes.fr/hal-00984750. Accessed 29 March 2022

Brosseau K, Choquette M, Renaud L (2006) Digitization standards for the Canadian museum of civilization corporation; Version 1.1. Canadian Museum of History, Gatineau, Quebec, Canada. ISBN 0-662-49507-1

CARLI Digital Collections Users' Group (2022) Guidelines for the creation of digital collections. Consortium of Academic and Research Libraries at the University of Illinois. CARLI Digital Collections, Illinois, U.S.A. https://mid-coast.com/Downloads/CARLI.pdf. Accessed 23 February 2022

Carre AL, Dubois A, Partarakis N, Zabulis X, Patsiouras N, Mantinaki E, Manitsaris S (2022) Mixed-reality demonstration and training of glassblowing. Heritage 5:103–128

Chan SC, Cai S (2023) Preserving and exhibiting intangible cultural heritage via virtual museum: a case study of the hungry ghosts festival in Hong Kong. Int Arch Photogramm Remote Sens Spat Inf Sci 48:405–411

Chatterjee A, Alvelos H (2021) Hands versus fingers: leveraging digital technology towards sustaining traditional crafts and industrial practices. In: Perspectives on design and digital communication: research, innovations and best practices, pp 197–209

Colyer SL, Evans M, Cosker DP, Salo AIT (2018) A review of the evolution of vision-based motion analysis and the integration of advanced computer vision methods towards developing a markerless system. Sports Med Open 4:1–15. https://doi.org/10.1186/s40798-018-0139-y

Cox S, Little C (2017) Time ontology in OWL, W3C recommendation. https://www.w3.org/TR/owl-time/. Accessed 19 October 2017

Dimitropoulos K, Manitsaris S, Tsalakanidou F, Nikolopoulos S, Denby B, Al K, Crevier-Buchman L, Pillot-Loiseau C, Adda-Decker M, Dupont S, et al (2014) Capturing the intangible: an introduction to the i-treasures project. In: International conference on computer vision theory and applications, Lisbon, Portugal, pp 773–781. Institute of Electrical and Electronics Engineers, Lisbon, Portugal

Doerr M (2003) The CIDOC conceptual reference model: an ontological approach to semantic interoperability of metadata. AI Mag 24:75–92

Donkin L (2001) Crafts and conservation. In: Synthesis report for ICCROM. https://www.iccrom.org/publication/crafts-and-conservation-synthesis-report-iccrom. Accessed 29 March 2022

Filippidis G, Tserevelakis GJ, Selimis A, Fotakis C (2015) Nonlinear imaging techniques as non-destructive, high-resolution diagnostic tools for cultural heritage studies. Appl Phys A 118:417–423

French Republic Ministry of Culture (2008) The national inventory of intangible cultural heritage. https://www.culture.gouv.fr/Sites-thematiques/Patrimoine-culturel-immateriel/La-politique-du-Patrimoine-culturel-immateriel/L-inventaire-national-du-Patrimoine-culturel-immateriel. Accessed 29 March 2022

Fuchigami R, Ishida T (2023) Virtual traditional craft simulation system in mixed reality environment. Int J Grid Util Comput 14(6):553–561

Gibson MA (2021) Making meaning: informal craft communities as sites of learning and identity development, Doctoral dissertation, University of Otago

Government of India Ministry of Textiles and Ministry of Textiles (2021) Development commissioner (Handicrafts). http://www.handicrafts.nic.in/. Accessed 29 March 2022

Gu X (2018) Crafts community. Craft Econ 17

Hasoğlu R (2015) Building a community platform for artisans and designers: artisans in Istanbul, Doctoral dissertation

Huang X, Uffelman E, Cossairt O, Walton M, Katsaggelos AK (2016) Computational imaging for cultural heritage: recent developments in spectral imaging, 3-D sur-face measurement, image relighting, and X-ray mapping. IEEE Signal Process Mag 33(5):130–138

Ishida T, Iyobe M, Miyakawa A, Sugita K, Shibata Y (2019) Implementation of an AR traditional Japanese craft presentation system: presentation of traditional crafts using the Kansei retrieval method. Artif Life Robot 24:430–437

Iyobe M, Ishida T, Miyakawa A, Uchida N, Sugita K, Shibata Y (2016) Development of a mobile virtual traditional crafting presentation system using augmented reality technology. Int J Space-Based Situated Comput 6(4):239–251

Jennings H (2012) Towards a definition of heritage craft. Report prepared for creative and cultural skills of the national skills academy, pp 1–30. http://creative-blueprint.co.uk/library/item/towards-a-definition-of-heritage-craft1. Accessed 29 March 2022

Jocelyne E (1990) Methodological guide to the collection of data on crafts. Technical Report. UNESCO, Paris, France

Kiriyama T, Otake M, Tanaka H, Tokuda J, Tanji H, Matsushita T, Shibasaki R, et al (2002) Exploring exhibit space in a personal perspective: an interactive photo collage of a folk crafts museum. In: Proceedings of the 4th conference on designing inter-active systems: processes, practices, methods, and techniques, pp 393–398

Kolay S (2016) Cultural heritage preservation of traditional Indian art through virtual new-media. Proc Soc Behav Sci 225:309–320

Konstantinou K, Anagnostopoulos A (2019) Interweaving contemporary art and traditional crafts in ethnographic research. Art/Res Int A Transdiscipl J 4:58–82. https://doi.org/10.18432/ari29420

Lee IJ (2023) Applying virtual reality for learning woodworking in the vocational training of batch wood furniture production. Interact Learn Environ 31(3):1448–1466

Lehmann AS (2012) Showing making: on visual documentation and creative practice. J Modern Craft 5(1):9–23

Lenzerini F (2011) Intangible cultural heritage: the living culture of peoples. Eur J Int Law 22:101–120

Lu F, Tian F, Jiang Y, Cao X, Luo W, Li G, Wang H, et al (2011) ShadowStory: creative and collaborative digital storytelling inspired by cultural heritage. In: Proceedings of the SIGCHI conference on human factors in computing systems, pp 1919–1928

Mason R (2005) The meaning and value of home-based craft. Int J Art des Educ 24(3):261–268

Mathioudakis G, Klironomos I, Partarakis N, Papadaki E, Volakakis K, Anifantis N, Stephanidis C et al (2022) InCulture: a collaborative platform for intangible cultural heritage narratives. Heritage 5(4):2881–2903

Mauss M (1967) Manuel d'Ethnographie; Payot & Rivages: Paris, France

McCloud S (1993) Understanding comics. Harper Collins Publishers Inc., New York, USA. ISBN 0-87816-244-5

Meghini C, Bartalesi V, Metilli D (2021) Representing narratives in digital libraries: the narrative ontology. Semantic Web 12:241–264. https://doi.org/10.3233/sw-200421

Mezzino D (2017) Cultural built heritage's tangible and intangible dimensions and digital-ization challenges, Doctoral dissertation, Carleton University

Mongeon B (2015) 3D technology in fine art and craft: exploring 3D printing, scanning, sculpting and milling. CRC Press

Object Management Group (2007) OMG unified modelling language (OMG UML), Superstructure version 2.1.1. Specification formal/2007-02-05. W3C. https://www.omg.org/spec/UML/. Accessed 23 February 2022

Oldman D, Tanase D (2018) Reshaping the knowledge graph by connecting researchers, data and practices in ResearchSpace. In: International semantic web conference, Monterey, CA, USA, pp 325–340. Springer, Cham, Switerland

Palit, S. (2022). Digital museums and hybrid models of craft studies during COVID-19. NIFT J Fashion 200

Partarakis N, Zabulis X (2023a) Applying cognitive load theory to elearning of crafts. Multimod Technol Interact 8(1):2

Partarakis N, Zabulis X (2023b) Safeguarding traditional crafts in Europe. Encyclopedia 3(4):1244–1261

Partarakis N, Patsiouras N, Evdemon T, Doulgeraki P, Karuzaki E, Stefanidi E, Zabulis X (2020a) Enhancing the educational value of tangible and intangible dimensions of traditional crafts through role play gaming. In: International conference on arts11, interactivity and game creation, pp 243–254. Springer, Cham, Switzerland

Partarakis N, Zabulis X, Chatziantoniou A, Patsiouras N, Adami I (2020b) An approach to the creation and presentation of reference gesture datasets, for the preservation of traditional crafts. Appl Sci 10:7325. https://doi.org/10.3390/app10207325

Partarakis N, Doulgeraki P, Karuzaki E, Adami I, Ntoa S, Metilli D, Bartalesi V, Meghini C, Marketakis Y, Theodoridou M, et al (2021) Representation of socio-historical context to support the authoring and presentation of multimodal narratives: the Mingei online platform. J Comput Cult Herit 16(1). https://doi.org/10.1145/3465556

Partarakis N, Zabulis X, Patsiouras N, Chatjiantoniou A, Zidianakis E, Mantinaki E, Kaplanidi D, Ringas C, Tasiopoulou E, Dubois A et al (2022) Multi-scale presentation of spatial context for cultural heritage applications. Electronics 11:195. https://doi.org/10.3390/electronics11020195

Pavlidis G, Koutsoudis A (2022) 3D digitization of tangible heritage. Handbook of cultural heritage analysis. Springer International Publishing, Cham, pp 1363–1404

Rigaki A, Partarakis N, Zabulis X, Stephanidis C (2020) An approach towards artistic visualizations of human motion in static media inspired by the visual arts. In: Proceedings of the international conference on advances in computer-human interactions (ACHI), Valencia, Spain. https://doi.org/10.5281/zenodo.4409664

Ringas C, Tasiopoulou E, Kaplanidi D, Partarakis N, Zabulis X, Zidianakis E, Patakos A, Patsiouras N, Karuzaki E, Foukarakis M et al (2022) Traditional craft training and demonstration in museums. Heritage 5:431–459. https://doi.org/10.3390/heritage5010025

Rourk W (2019) 3D cultural heritage informatics: applications to 3D data curation. In: 3D/VR in the academic library: emerging practices and trends. Grayburn 3:24–38. ISBN 978-1-932326-60-4. Council on Library and Information Resources, Arlington, VA, USA. https://doi.org/10.13140/RG.2.2.19944.93449

Roy Chakraborty K (2022) Craft stories: an augmented reality animated interactive documentary on craft artists from South Asia, Doctoral dissertation, OCAD University

Sabiescu A, Woolley M, Cummings C, Prins J (2015) Online maker communities: craft and engagement with cultural heritage. In: Conference communities and technologies, Limerick

Sabiescu AG, Woolley M, Cummings C, Prins J, Forbes N (2017) Online maker communities: craft and new spaces of engagement with cultural heritage. In: Cultural heritage communities, pp 38–59. Routledge

Schatzki TR, Knorr-Cetina K, Savigny E (2001) The practice turn in contemporary theory. Routledge, London, UK

UNESCO (2003a) Intangible cultural heritage domains in the 2003 convention. https://ich.unesco.org/en/intangible-heritage-domains-00052. Accessed 29 March 2022

UNESCO (2003b). Text of the convention for the safeguarding of the intangible cultural heritage. https://ich.unesco.org/en/convention. Accessed 29 March 2022

UNESCO (2003c) Representative list of the intangible cultural heritage of humanity. https://ich.unesco.org/en/lists. Accessed 29 March 2022

UNESCO (2014) Mali launches an inventory of intangible cultural heritage. https://ich.unesco.org/en/news/mali-launches-an-inventory-of-intangible-cultural-heritage-00084. Accessed 29 March 2022

Vannini P, Vannini A (2020) Artisanal ethnography: notes on the making of ethnographic craft. Qual Inq 26:865–874. https://doi.org/10.1177/1077800419863456

Vilbrandt T, Pasko G, Vilbrandt C, Pasko A (2010) Digital preservation of traditional crafts and three-dimensional modeling technologies. Int J Arts Sci 3(9):1–10

Vrettakis E, Kourtis V, Katifori A, Karvounis M, Lougiakis C, Ioannidis Y (2019) Narralive–creating and experiencing mobile digital storytelling in cultural heritage. Digit Appl Archaeol Cult Herit 15:e00114

Wang K, Liao Y, Chu W, Chiang J, Chen Y, Chan P (2011) Digitization and value-add application of bamboo weaving artifacts. In: International conference on Asian digital libraries, pp 16–25. Springer, Beijing, China

Wood (2009) Transmitting craft knowledge: designing interactive media to support tacit skills learning. ProQuest Number: 10701209. PhD thesis. Sheffield Hallam University, South Yorkshire, UK

Yiyi X, Lingxuan W (2022) Feasibility study of VR and AR technologies on the revitalization of intangible cultural heritage: taking Putian wood carving techniques as an example. In 2022 International conference on computation, big-data and engineering (ICCBE), pp 127–130. IEEE

Zabulis X, Meghini C, Partarakis N, Kaplanidi D, Doulgeraki P, Karuzaki E, Beiss-wenger C (2019) What is needed to digitise knowledge on heritage crafts? Memoramedia Rev 4:1–25

Zabulis X, Meghini C, Partarakis N, Beisswenger C, Dubois A, Fasoula M, Galanakis G et al (2020) Representation and preservation of heritage crafts. Sustainability 12(4):1461

Zabulis X, Partarakis N, Demeridou I, Doulgeraki P, Zidianakis E, Argyros A, Krivokapic J et al (2023) A roadmap for craft understanding, education, training, and preservation. Heritage 6(7):5305–5328

Zabulis X, Meghini C, Dubois A, Doulgeraki P, Partarakis N, Adami I, Karuzaki E, Carre A, Patsiouras N, Kaplanidi D, et al (2022) Digitisation of traditional craft processes. J Comput Cult Herit. https://doi.org/10.1145/3494675

Zhou M, Geng G, Wu Z (2012) Digital preservation technology for cultural heritage. Higher Education Press, Beijing

Chapter 20
Re-mediating Interaction with Online Art Collections: How Creative Curating Can Enhance Discovery Through Recommendations Towards a New Model of Cultural Participation

Stéphanie Bertrand, George Papagiannakis, George Margetis, Stavroula Ntoa, Nikolaos Partarakis, Xenophon Zabulis, and Constantine Stephanidis

Abstract For over 25 years, art museums have digitized their collections and made them available online for broad public access and reuse, tapping citizens to become curators and content creators. Yet, public engagement remains scarce, owing in large part to the lack of necessary social and technical skills among non-expert users to take part in existing digital cultural participation models. While facilitating reuse continues to be seen as an effective engagement strategy, the chapter instead argues that fostering broad public participation towards collective cultural production depends on developing an alternative approach to algorithmic curation to facilitate user-driven exploration and aesthetic choice by means of a novel, interactive recommender system for online collections. To support this claim, the chapter critically examines the parallels between curation and personalization, highlighting both the importance of pre-filtering for user-driven choice, and the drawbacks of current

S. Bertrand (✉) · G. Papagiannakis · G. Margetis · S. Ntoa · N. Partarakis · X. Zabulis · C. Stephanidis
Foundation for Research and Technology Hellas, Heraklion, Greece
e-mail: bertrandstephanie@gmail.com

G. Papagiannakis
e-mail: papagian@ics.forth.gr

G. Margetis
e-mail: margetis@ics.forth.gr

S. Ntoa
e-mail: ntoa@ics.forth.gr

N. Partarakis
e-mail: partarak@ics.forth.gr

X. Zabulis
e-mail: zabulis@ics.forth.gr

F. Liarokapis et al. (eds.), *Interactive Media for Cultural Heritage*, Springer Series on Cultural Computing, https://doi.org/10.1007/978-3-031-61018-9_20

recommender systems when it comes to automating art curation, including their limited ability to sustain discovery and reduce external influences on aesthetic judgment as well as their interference with personal taste. To address these different issues, the chapter turns to a rare physical exhibition making approach, which it coins "creative curating", as an alternative model for algorithmic curation. Drawing on associative theory, it describes how creative curating diverges from current recommendation methods, which rely on principles of similarity and serendipity, in that it exploits a third associative approach known as mediation to establish complex semantic relationships between different artworks. The chapter concludes by speculating how a novel, interactive recommender system for online art collections powered by this curatorial model could be used to nudge users into making personally indicative choices as they intuitively explore collection contents, thus providing art institutions with actionable data on users' unique perspective towards power sharing on a mass scale. In doing so, the chapter ultimately advances a new digital cultural participation model based on an unprecedented method to reverse-engineer aesthetic judgment.

20.1 Introduction

For over 25 years, museums have digitized their collections and made them available online for broad public access and reuse, tapping citizens to become curators and content creators in a bid to recruit multiple and diverse perspectives on their holdings so as to expand, enrich and diversify their institutional narratives (the canon), viz. foster polyvocality, while drumming up public interest. Yet, despite these concerted efforts, public engagement remains scarce (Roued-Cunliffe 2021) owing in part to the lack of necessary social and technical skills among non-expert users to take part in prevailing digital cultural participation models (e.g., folksonomies, citizen curation and online endorsements) (Sacco 2021). While facilitating reuse continues to be seen as an effective strategy to sustain digital cultural participation, this chapter instead sets out to show that a small change in how users interact with online, digitized art collections typically found on museum websites and art aggregators: that is, how users navigate and discover the art digitizations[1] contained in these vast databases, can have a profound impact on cultural participation. It has the potential to not only increase non-expert engagement with online collections, but also generate actionable data to facilitate power sharing on a much larger and more inclusive scale than today's time- and resource-intensive participatory projects.

Contrary to prevailing participatory models, this chapter's core argument is that such a change in user behavior or response does not depend on the development of a new suite of interactive tools enabling users to further manipulate, arrange, annotate and/or modify (e.g., crop, remix) cultural content in novel ways. Instead, it hinges on a shift in mediation, viz. content curation: that is, how art digitizations

[1] Digital reproductions or surrogates of artworks originally created for the physical space of the gallery (definition adapted from Cameron (2019: 55)).

are selected, filtered and contextualized. As this chapter aims to show, changing how online collection content is curated can facilitate and incentivize non-expert participation, and at the same time nudge users towards making aesthetic choices that are indicative of their evolving concerns and worldview—as opposed to gravitating towards museum highlights and crowd favorites—thus providing cultural institutions with uniquely valuable data. Given that cultural institutions' main societal role is to underwrite and secure collective meaning and value (Boltanski 2011; Gielen et al. 2015; Pasnak 2013), real-time user data accurately capturing what makes sense and holds importance to their diverse audiences is vital to these organizations' continued relevance, which effectively depends on their transition to a more democratic and participatory model of culture.

Far from having to reinvent the wheel, viz. come up with a brand-new curatorial strategy tailored to art digitizations online, the claim is that prompting users to make telling (personally meaningful, and therefore revealing) choices can be achieved by converting certain existing, in-gallery curatorial practices into an interactive[2] recommender system for online art collections. This claim is based on a simple hypothesis: if art perception, interpretation and appreciation are derived from each individual's unique memories, experiences, cultural background and knowledge—as has been amply theorized (De Duve 1996; Weil 2002) and empirically demonstrated (Darda and Chatterjee 2023; Falk 2016; Vessel et al. 2023)—then it follows that when presented with different suggestions that specify conflicting interpretations, users are bound to be drawn to the option that makes the most sense to them in light of their personal worldview. Of course, the key to this model lies in applying the right kind of mediation. It hinges on implementing a computational curation approach capable of specifying particular interpretations simply by juxtaposing different artworks, which current algorithms can only superficially achieve. Accordingly, the following chapter will examine a distinct, associative approach to group exhibition making dubbed "creative curating", and discuss why this approach is uniquely tailored to the development of such an interactive recommender system and how it differs from existing methods.

In this respect, it is worth clarifying, from the get go, that the ideas advanced in this chapter run counter to the popular view that recommender systems offer a viable solution to automate curation. Contrary to this view, the argument is that creative curating can instead help solve one of recommender systems' main issues when it comes to the discovery of online art collections: namely, the accuracy-originality trade-off of these systems' content suggestions.

[2] In accordance with He et al. (2016), the word interaction here refers to "user involvement through dialogue with the system" (9).

20.2 Fostering Digital Cultural Participation by Resolving Curating's Narrative Paradox

To appreciate the radical impact of the proposed strategy, it is incumbent to first grasp what cultural participation might mean in the context of online digitized art collections, where content mainly consists of digital images of visual artworks along with their related metadata (e.g., title, artist, material, date). Broadly speaking, cultural participation is defined as "the activities of audiences and participants in consuming cultural products and taking part in cultural activities and experiences (book reading, dancing, participating in carnivals, listening to radio, visiting galleries)" (UNESCO Institute for Statistics 2009: 20). What this definition initially suggests is that cultural participation in the context of digitized visual art collections mainly involves searching, browsing, viewing images and reading descriptions (label copy), not unlike visiting an art gallery, or, more analogously, a museum storage space, such as the recently opened Depot Boijmans Van Beuningen. Without further clarification, it follows that this standing definition can be somewhat misleading. Even while it accurately describes how audiences continue to engage with cultural content today, it glosses over the fact that the meaning of the expressions "to consume" and "to take part" has substantially changed over the past two decades in society and in multiple industries (e.g., retail, music, publishing, journalism), evolving from passive consumerism and spectatorship to prosumerism and responsive (two-way), even collaborative involvement.

This recent reconceptualization of the roles of citizen and consumer has equally extended to the notion of audience engagement in the cultural sphere. Whereas the primary mission of traditional cultural institutions was once to care for collections and transmit expert knowledge about these collections to the public in order to educate and enlighten (Bennett 1996), contemporary museum studies and practice have increasingly adopted a more audience-centered approach, placing visitors' needs on equal footing with collection care (Samis and Michaelson 2017; Villeneuve and Love 2017). At its most radical, this audience-centered paradigm shift has given rise in the LAM sector to a multitude of cooperative models, loosely gathered under the banner of what has been coined "the participatory turn" (Bonet and Negrier 2018; Huvila et al. 2022). Broadly driven by values such as equality, empowerment, democracy, and inclusion, these participatory models range from crowdsourcing to co-design and co-creation (Huvila et al. 2022). Even while the intensity and extent of participation varies from one model to the next from "short-lived casual involvement to radical and profound redistribution of responsibilities and power" (ibid.: 160), these models are all driven by the common aim to sustain power sharing: that is, reduced gatekeeping and the partial delegation of institutional authority to the public.

As with other sectors, networked technologies (the internet, social media) have played a major role in the emergence of these new participatory models and facilitated their integration in cultural institutions (Margetis et al. 2021). The Open Access movement, which supports the public reuse of LAM collection materials, for instance, was originally modeled after the new political economy of open source of the mid-2000s, whereby tech companies strategically opened their development environment to broad communities to enhance the value of their products and services through broad iterative use (Verwayen et al. 2011). Likewise desirous to enhance the value of their assets and their brand while promoting culture to a broader public, a number of prominent museums (e.g., The Rijksmuseum, The Metropolitan Museum of Art) and cultural aggregators (e.g., Europeana) have not only opted to make their digitized collections available online for public viewing; they also actively encourage users to annotate, appraise, recontextualize and reuse this content through various digital strategies, including folksonomies, endorsement features (e.g., "like" buttons), citizen curation (e.g., tools enabling users to curate their own digital galleries) and cultural hackathons.

Yet, despite LAM organizations' efforts to sustain more audience participation, the public's response to these projects has been mostly limited to contributions by experts (e.g., curators, researchers) and amateur groups with niche interests. As digital humanist Henriette Roued-Cunliffe (2021) bluntly puts it, there is a desperate lack of users for digital tools and online collections. This scarcity in usership has been attributed to several factors, chief among which: insufficient digital literacy (viz. the necessary technical and social skills to feel at ease expressing opinions online) among non-expert users (Sacco 2021) and the inadequate curation of online collections (Roued-Cunliffe 2020: 58). Indeed, when it comes to participatory projects involving digitized visual art collections, insufficient digital and artistic literacy among general public users has meant that organizing institutions have had to invest considerable staff time and resources to recruit and ensure the sustained and constructive involvement—via intense mediation—of relatively small numbers of participants. The Irish Museum of Modern Art's (IMMA) Deep Viewpoints is a paradigmatic case. This web application was designed to enable different underrepresented groups, including migrant women, Black and Irish and Black Queer advocacy groups and asylum seekers, to interpret and curate the museum's collection based on their unique concerns and perspective. However, the app was not intended to be used on its own. It was integrated as part of an extensive workshop, which first included an exhibition tour and process of Slow Looking with an IMMA mediator prior to the digital engagement (Stoneman et al. 2021). While the project was certainly successful in terms of generating new readings of the museum's collection, public participation was greatly constrained.

On the whole, participatory projects, such as Deep Viewpoints, have undoubtedly proven their worth in terms of diversifying institutional perspectives by recruiting different users' unique insight. At the same time, they have also revealed the challenges of scaling up this type of cultural participation model to effectively sustain more equality, democracy, and inclusion within cultural institutions—and this, despite networked technologies' ubiquitous access, automation capabilities and computational processing, which originally seemed to hold the promise of mass cultural participation. Far from the "Field of Dreams" scenario once envisioned, however, it has become increasingly plain that crowdsourcing platforms are no guarantee of public participation, regardless of the source material's interest and value. In fact, Ridge et al. (2021) emphasise the need for outreach, community building and management to ensure the success of crowdsourcing projects in cultural heritage, noting that even "if you build it, people rarely just show up" (n.p.).

If digital participation models that require explicit feedback (e.g., folksonomies, citizen curation) may feel or be out of reach for non-expert publics owing to a self-perceived lack of artistic and technological knowledge or skill, it follows that capturing user preferences through consensual data tracking might offer a more viable avenue for power sharing on a mass scale—provided, of course, that art institutions are willing to leverage this data to shape their programs and mission. This being said, the success of such a power sharing model depends on at least two conditions. It is contingent on: (1) effectively recruiting a critical mass of diverse non-expert users, and (2) accurately capturing user preferences—i.e., ensuring that the data is not overly distorted by design features (interaction modalities) and/or external spheres of influence: e.g., expert taste, the media, social feedback (Bertrand 2023). Our claim is that both of these conditions can be met by overcoming the second aforementioned barrier to non-expert engagement with online art collections: that is, inadequate content curation (Bertrand 2022b).

As museum technologist Keir Winesmith remarks, without adequate context, the open and transparent practice of uploading digitizations and collection metadata online is the equivalent of a data dump that excludes non-specialist audiences who do not know where and how to look (Winesmith et al. 2019: 49). When engaging with online collections, knowing where and how to look is key because, generally speaking, content can only be accessed through a search box (which requires having a clear sense of what one is looking for) or generous interface (which entails browsing through hundreds, if not thousands of artworks). These two main access modalities inadvertently create an important handicap for non-expert users who usually consult online collections without knowing what they are looking for (making the standard collection search box virtually useless), and without the necessary knowledge to make sense of and properly appraise unfamiliar artworks. Indeed, even basic background knowledge: e.g., semantic contextual information such as artist and technique, has been proven to enhance the aesthetic appreciation of unfamiliar artworks, and crucially reduce prejudices against artworks and artists originating from an outgroup (Darda and Chatterjee 2023). While basic contextual information can usually be found in the metadata on individual artwork pages, it is unreasonable to expect the average user to look up this information, let alone pay attention to it, every time they come across an unfamiliar artwork whilst scanning vast online collections. As follows, without adequate content curation, power sharing models based on consensual data tracking are liable to exclude non-expert publics, and moreover exploit biased data privileging familiar museum highlights over underrepresented practices, thus defying the goal of recruiting outside perspectives to sustain more inclusion, equality and diversity in art institutions.

Within physical galleries, the question of where and how to look does not arise owing to exhibition curation. Contemporary curating sets up subtle cues directing visitors' attention and guiding their interpretation of the artworks on view without excessive text, simply by means of a careful selection, juxtaposition and display, which still affords visitors a fair amount of interpretive freedom and control (Falk

2016). Nevertheless, directly transferring physical exhibition making practices to an interactive online context by creating static virtual exhibitions—as is currently the norm—runs counter to the primary demand of today's audience-centered paradigm, which calls for more dynamic cultural participation models capable not only of sustaining, but also harnessing user-centered perspectives.

For art institutions, this audience-centered demand poses a particular challenge. Indeed, art galleries and museums have been far more reluctant than other cultural organizations (e.g., science and history museums) to relinquish authorial control and let visitors define the message (Samis and Michaelson 2017), doubtless owing to their societal function to secure a hierarchy of collective meanings and values, viz. serve as society's "moral compass". It follows that developing an adequate content curation strategy for online digitized art collections hinges on resolving this fundamental "narrative paradox"[3] pitting institutional authority against user agency in a way that enables users to take a more active but adequately mediated role in collective cultural production. This basically entails facilitating access to collection content without overdetermining the choice of artworks or their interpretation by providing tools and contextual indications supporting personal exploration, discovery, meaning-making and appraisal. The most obvious and prevailing solution to this challenge is to personalize user experience by means of a recommender system.

20.3 Recommender Systems and Virtual Museums

First pioneered in the 1990s, recommender systems (or recommendation engines) are both the result and the cause of the global expansion of the internet (Schrage 2020), which has simultaneously emerged as an unprecedented source of feedback on users' likes and dislikes, and an overwhelming and chaotic informational environment demanding increasingly sophisticated and personalized access tools (Aggarwal 2016). Recommendation engines are information filtering systems that are programmed to identify and return the most personally relevant items from an overabundance of possibilities by making predictions based on individual users' preferences and constraints (Ricci et al. 2011). Simply put, they are tools designed to help individuals navigate choice on a mass scale (Schrage 2020). To do so, these systems establish and continuously update data-driven relationships between users and items based on the relevant characteristics and attributes of each group, and infer missing values by relying on three methods: 1. content filtering, which is based on "the assumption that items with similar properties and features will be rated similarly" (Schrage 2020: 124); 2. collaborative filtering, which is based on "the assumption that people with similar tastes will rate things similarly" (ibid.); and 3. hybrid models, which are a combination of the two. Depending on the specific aims of each platform, these methods are fine-tuned to target different recommendation

[3] Term borrowed from Riggs (2019), where it is used to designate the conflict between classic (static) storytelling and user agency (capacity to affect the narrative) within immersive experiences.

goals: namely, relevance (by proposing items most likely to trigger the user's engagement, viz. items that are highly similar to past choices), novelty (by proposing new, viz. never-before encountered, items) and serendipity (by proposing surprising and unexpected items to facilitate "chance" discoveries) (Aggarwal 2016: 3–4).

Owing to recommender systems' capacity to select and present personally and contextually relevant items, numerous parallels have been drawn between personalization and curation (Bhaskar 2017; Shrage 2020: 61), with some going so far as to describe recommendation engines as a natural fit to automate curation (Noehrer et al. 2021). In this sense, writer and publisher Michael Bhaskar (2017) recently proposed a new definition of curation to capture today's expanded notion as using "acts of selection and arrangement to add value", whereby value is generated by "cutting down complexity" and overcoming overload (7–8), which is precisely what recommender systems are programmed to do. As an example, Bhaskar describes what he terms the "Curator Model" of business retail as "the correct product pre-selected from an infinite catalogue" (100), viz. an always-accurate, personalized selection from a profusion of items designed to prevent jam (the inability to make decisions) arising from the "tyranny of choice". Unsurprisingly, given their role as curatorial pioneers, art museums first begin to experiment with recommender systems as early as 1999 to aid end-users—especially non-expert users—locate and discover relevant artworks in their collection. Much like conventional in-gallery curating, the benefits of recommender systems for cultural institutions are described as: facilitating access to desired resources in unfamiliar domains (Benouaret and Lenne 2015: 743) by filtering information overload (Iaquinta et al. 2010), and streamlining the discovery process (Kontiza et al. 2018: 6–7) by suggesting "contents that the visitor would not have been likely to discover without being recommended" (Keller and Viennet 2015: 67).

This being said, it is worth highlighting that not all recommender systems developed for the cultural domain have been designed to automate curation online. In fact, many, if not most, of these systems have been otherwise created as mobile tour managers to help onsite museum visitors maximize their in-gallery experience by pinpointing artworks of particular personal relevance across the museum's multiple spaces, often through context-awareness. Such recommender systems have included Hippie (Oppermann and Specht 1999), Sotto Voce (Aoki et al. 2002), PEACH (Rocchi et al. 2004), SMARTMUSEUM (Ruotsalo et al. 2013), AMMICO (Keller and Viennet 2015), MyMuseum (Benouaret and Lenne 2015), meSch (Hashemi and Kamps 2017), M5SAR (Cardoso et al. 2017), CrossCult (Kontiza et al. 2018) and CHARS (Colace et al. 2019).[4] This contextual distinction is vital when thinking about the purpose and impact of recommender systems in the cultural domain because the intentions and expectations of onsite museum visitors often diverge from those of online users owing to the time, cost and fatigue associated with physical museum visits, not to mention the phenomenological differences between physical and digital displays favoring certain artworks over others (Sanchez 2013), inevitably impacting users' interactions with the system and resulting preference profile. For

[4] A more detailed summary of most of these projects can be found in Pavlidis (2019).

instance, many punctual onsite visitors, notably international tourists—which these mobile tour managers frequently target (e.g., Konstantakis et al. 2020)—are motivated by a "been there, done that" identity-related goal, which tends to orient their time-constrained visit towards hitting the museum's main attractions (Falk 2016).

By comparison, online collections' free and unlimited access[5] is more conducive to the pursuit of discovery-driven goals. Accordingly, a number of leading museums and cultural aggregators have begun to introduce recommendation features as part of their online collection interface to satisfy this purpose: that is, to recirculate users and promote discovery (Andrews 2023). Noteworthy examples include Tate's "You Might Like", the Metropolitan Museum of Art's "Related Artworks", the Städel Museum's "Similar Artworks", The Art Institute of Chicago's "Explore Further", as well as Europeana's "Discover Related Items" and Google Arts and Culture's "Where Next? Explore Related Content". These recommendation features typically appear as a bar on individual artwork pages below the work's semantic data. This bar displays a small selection of keyword-related artworks to the one on view, narrowed down from the full range of related items through a combination of parameters, including historic pageview data and curatorial-managed lists (ibid.). When weighed against other navigational tools (search boxes and generous interfaces), these recommendation features emerge as a more efficient way to facilitate non-expert access to collection content without overdetermining the choice of works, or their interpretation. Much like generous interfaces, they expediently convey basic contextual information about the work on view (in more or less explicit/transparent ways[6]) through the suggestion of similar items: e.g., works by the same artist, created in the same medium or style, or dating from the same period. Yet, unlike generous interfaces that comprehensively display all the related artworks of a given class, which can lead to an overwhelming and counterproductive discovery process, these recommendation features offer the added advantage of providing a more visually granular display, closer to in-gallery experience (Windhager et al. 2019: 2316), by proposing a more manageable, personally filtered selection of artworks that helps both maintain engagement and facilitate choice. As Ruotsalo et al. (2013) observe, recommender systems "return a fairly compact set of results, instead of a list of arbitrary length" (61), which is key because "users often prefer the first 20–30 results: if these do not satisfy the user's information need, she tends to abandon the system" (ibid.). What is more, these features also enable users to compare and contrast varying selections of related artworks across different filtering categories, which facilitates non-verbal (visual), user-led understandings of the works. For example, in the case of the Städel Museum, its "Similar

[5] Unlimited access (not universal access) is here used in the sense that online collections can be accessed as often times as desired 24–7 from anywhere in the world provided a desktop computer or mobile device and decent internet connection.

[6] For instance, Google Arts and Culture's "Explore Related Content" feature labels recommendations with textual captions that indicate how each suggested work relates to the initial work (e.g., "uses same medium", "created around the same time", "from related movement", "visually similar work", "from same artist", "from same collection", "depicts same object"). By contrast, Tate's recommendation feature is fairly opaque: the rationale behind the suggestions is often unclear and there are no textual indications explaining the connection between the works.

Works" feature presents different selections of related artworks across 5 categories: "motif", "picture elements", "association", "atmosphere" and "emotion".

Overall, what this suggests is that well-designed recommender systems can assist towards balancing institutional authority and user agency in the context of online digitized art collections, by providing users with the tools and information that they need to explore the collection on their own terms, while also supporting their engagement and understanding of the works. Simply put, these systems offer a promising solution to curating's narrative paradox. Yet, as the following section will examine, recommendation engines' beneficial impact on user-driven choice is not so cut and dry. While these systems are still widely seen as tools that facilitate decision-making and affirm individual taste by mathematically predicting personal preferences with increasing accuracy (Schrage 2020), there has been mounting criticism to the effect that, in reality, these algorithms actually interfere with users' ability to make aesthetic judgements and personally indicative choices, thus jeopardizing the participatory objectives outlined above.

20.4 Curating Versus Personalization Towards Individual Aesthetic Choice

Beyond the cultural domain, the turn from consumerism to prosumerism leads to a significant expansion and redefinition of curating's scope and function in mainstream culture from expert gatekeeping to individualized amateur curating. Outside art world circles, the meaning of curation effectively shifts from collection care—from the Latin "curare"—to the creation of value through acts of selection and arrangement (Bhaskar 2017) in which everyone can ostensibly partake, given the right tools and access. In his book Curation Nation, filmmaker and entrepreneur Steven Rosenbaum (2011) declares that "even someone who is passively consuming is effectively curating" (138). Echoing this view, Stephen Dale (2014) asserts that "technology has enabled anyone with an Internet connection to become a curator" (200). Likewise, Michael Bhaskar (2017) states that "today the word curation means personal choice" (73), equally citing the "behavioral change in Internet users from consumers to curators" (75). Notwithstanding, as all three authors make abundantly clear, users' ability to curate, viz. make personal choices, is conditional on a certain amount of pre-curation: that is, computational aggregation and filtering, given the new post-digital era's overabundance of information and products. In other words, curating nowadays does not only mean "personal choice"; it also denotes personalized pre-filtering (curated for). Simply put, everyone can be a curator today, but only insofar as one is provided with the right pre-selection of items to choose from, which is its own form of curation. In the digital cultural domain, the need for some degree of pre-filtering to assist personal choice is evident from "citizen curation" models that enable users to curate their own online galleries by selecting and arranging collection content (Daga et al. 2022). Far from reflecting users' idiosyncratic preferences, as might be assumed, these user-generated galleries are often dominated by the same recurring motifs: e.g., food, flowers, eyes (Engberg 2016), indicating that even though art perception, interpretation and appreciation are derived from each person's unique memories, experiences, cultural background and knowledge, users are relying heavily on "aesthetic heuristics" (shortcuts) to make artistic choices when faced with an overwhelming profusion of artworks.

As previously observed, recommender systems are precisely designed to help users navigate choice (Schrage 2020). They do so by narrowing down the range of possible options, which decreases complexity and unreliability: that is, facilitates and expediates users' access to relevant options while also helping to reduce the biases that skew their decision-making by simplifying the decisional process (Thaler and Sunstein 2022). Minimizing bias is key when trying to accurately capture users' unique perspective towards establishing a viable power sharing model for art institutions. In fact, broadly speaking, it is an essential pre-condition for any model aiming to recruit collective intelligence on a mass scale (Suran et al. 2020). In the case of online collections, there are multiple, external sources of influence that affect both aesthetic judgment and online endorsements, including expert taste, the media, the entertainment industry and social influence (Bertrand 2023; Salganik et al. 2006; Van de Rijt et al. 2014), complicating the task of accurately seizing individuals' unique outlook. In this respect, online collection pageviews offer a case in point. As reported by the Art Institute of Chicago and the Städel Museum, the "most viewed" artworks on their website correspond almost exclusively to the museum's core highlights, indicating significant art expert influence on users' so-called personal preferences (Bertrand 2023).[7]

Nevertheless, even while having fewer options to choose from makes selecting the most personally relevant item from a group much easier, it is not enough in and of itself to offset these different sources of influences. This requires additional "nudging". Take, for instance, the case of a recommended selection containing several minor and obscure artworks and one famous Van Gogh or Picasso painting: even though the selection's manageable size is sure to help users better weigh the merits of each work, the well-known masterpiece is still likely be favored over the other works given its familiarity and status. To be clear, accurately capturing individual users' unique perspective does not mean overcoming their innate biases, it means seizing their worldview, "warts and all", by minimizing the biasing effects of outside influences. Successfully doing so essentially boils down to presenting users with the right pre-selection—understood here as the selection most liable to aid them make the best aesthetic choice, viz. the choice most aligned with their unique worldview (Klein and Chayka 2024).

Indeed, when it comes to establishing the right pre-selection, size is not enough; content matters, especially since recommender systems are by no means neutral. As choice engines, they are also a source of influence on users' decision-making,

[7] For a more detailed discussions of these different spheres of influence and their impacts, see Bertrand 2023.

ultimately affecting their preference profile (Adomavicius et al. 2013). As Nobel-prize winning behavioral scientist Richard H. Thaler and behavioral economist and legal scholar Cass R. Sunstein (2022) remark: "there is no such thing as a 'neutral' design. (…) A good rule of thumb is to assume that everything matters" (4)—that is, even the smallest detail focuses people's attention in a particular direction (ibid.). Accordingly, Frost et al. (2019) aptly warn, building on Eli Pariser's (2011) work, that personalization in online collections can lead to aesthetic isolation or "filter bubbles" since these algorithms predominantly suggest content similar to "previously viewed content and content viewed by similar users" (n.p.), thereby minimizing exposure to conflicting artworks and perspectives. To counter this tendency, they propose an anti-recommender system for online art collections called "Art I Don't Like" that is programmed to return the most dissimilar artwork to the user's choices so as to promote "serendipity and exploration". In a similar vein, Carnovalini et al. (2023) argue in favor of an unconventional recommender system to promote art discovery—only in this case, within the context of the physical museum. They contend that recommender systems for art museums should be programmed to overcome the popularity bias driving museum visitors towards the institution's main attractions by recommending lesser-known works matching the user's personal preferences, thereby strategically using these systems to influence users towards a particular agenda—albeit one fully aligned with the participatory turn. Indeed, Carnovalini et al. (2023) explicitly promote this approach as a means to redress canonical inequities by giving "more fair visibility to artists that have been neglected in the past, possibly for reasons not directly connected to the quality of their works" (2). Notwithstanding, even while such "anti-recommender" systems may reduce aesthetic isolation and promote discovery, merely exposing users to a greater diversity of options, as argued above, is not enough to offset the impact of the different spheres of influence affecting users' judgement.

Overall, when it comes to determining the right pre-selection of artworks, existing recommendation engines are essentially caught between two conflicting goals: relevance at one extreme versus serendipity at the other, neither of which is adequately suited to the task of capturing user's unique perspective. This impasse is what Keller and Viennet (2015) describe as recommender systems' "necessary trade-off between accuracy and originality" (70)—two conflicting recommendation goals that turn on a lesser or greater degree of novelty, resulting in more similar or dissimilar ("serendipitous") content suggestions. Simply put, current recommender systems can either propose similar items, which are more likely to appeal to users and elicit clicks—i.e., accurately predict preference—owing to the content's familiarity, thereby sustaining more user engagement and trust. However, this approach proves problematic as it can lead, in the long-run, to cultural isolation by creating aesthetic filter bubbles (Frost et al. 2019), thus gradually skewing users' preferences towards familiar content unlikely to provide telling indications of their unique perspective and worldview (e.g., repeatedly choosing artworks by the same artist or in the same style or color palette reveals very little of the user's personal experiences, memories, beliefs, etc.). Alternatively, these systems can be programmed to make more serendipitous suggestions that expose users to novel (unfamiliar) content, thus fostering more discovery, but at the considerable risk of losing users' trust and engagement. Indeed, increasing novelty to promote discovery—either through the introduction of calculatingly dissimilar or purely randomized content suggestions—is an imperfect solution given that serendipity does not occur through mere exposure to new content. Serendipity is, in effect, highly contingent on the user's skill set and mindset (McCay-Peet and Toms 2015). It depends on the user's ability to make a useful (personally meaningful) connection between new content and personal interests, which is not something that is given to everyone; nor, for that matter, to adequately skilled individuals at all times (ibid.). The bottom line is that serendipitous recommendations are not an efficient way to sustain discovery.

So the question is: how can this similarity-serendipity dichotomy be overcome? Moreover, if every content suggestion inevitably influences (biases) choice, how can recommendation features be leveraged to accurately capture users' unique perspective towards fostering more inclusion, diversity and equality in the art museum? As the following section will argue, this is where certain physical curatorial practices can actually provide a solution to recommender systems rather than the other way around.

20.5 Creative Curating and Associative Theory

Contrary to the widespread view that recommendation engines facilitate choice and personal expression, journalist Ezra Klein and culture and technology writer Kyle Chayka (2024) recently advanced the opposite view: namely, that algorithmic curation actually prevents individuals from developing their own sense of taste by interfering with their capacity to identify things that resonate with their unique worldview. Their claim is based on a particular understanding of taste, not as a mark of social standing, viz. "good taste" (Bourdieu 1984), but rather as an external reflection of one's innate worldview and sense of self—an aesthetic theory that has been empirically validated and that explains the huge variation (80–90%) in aesthetic response from one person to the next (Vessel et al. 2023). In this sense, Chayka defines taste as "knowing who you are and knowing what you like, and then being able to look outside of yourself, see the world around you, and then pick out the one thing from around you that does resonate with you, that makes you feel like you are who you are or that you can incorporate into your mindset and worldview" (Klein and Chayka 2024). In line with this understanding, Klein asserts that the decade-old shift from an "internet of curation" characterized by the unique voices of connoisseurs to an "internet of algorithms" dominated by recommender systems has made it difficult to be an individual on the Web. It has dulled "our ability to know what we like" by encouraging "everything to look more the same" (ibid.). In response to this debate, our take is that it is not an either-or scenario: current recommender systems both help users make aesthetic choices and interfere with this process. Still, we believe that it is possible to minimize this interference as well as the interference of external influences on aesthetic judgment by converting the right kind of curation into a recommendation algorithm in order to generate the right pre-selection of artworks. But first, this entails disambiguating curating from personalization.

Although the shift from consumerism to prosumerism effectively blurs the line between curating and personalization, there remains one fundamental difference between these two filtering practices: whereas personalization is user-centered, curating—irrespectively of its audience-centered paradigm shift—is still primarily object-centered. As anthropologist Nicholas Thomas (2010) affirms, museum (curatorial) practices "start from, and stop with, the object" (7). Unlike personalization, curating's fundamental goal is not to predict preference (or crowd-please!): that is, identify items of potential relevance to specific users, even if it always has the public in mind. Its fundamental goal is to create "associative knowledge" through the selection and juxtaposition of often-disparate objects, artworks and artifacts (Boon 2021). This crucial distinction between curating and personalization has important consequences for practice. Among other, curating—as an object-centered rather than user-centered practice—has recourse to a third associative approach beyond similarity and serendipity: i.e., another way of establishing relevant connections between remote items, thus opening up an avenue to resolve recommender systems' accuracy-originality trade-off in the context of online digitized art collections.

Before delving into this solution, however, it is crucial to acknowledge that the vast majority of contemporary curatorial practices today are governed by the same similarity-serendipity logic as recommender systems. Indeed, contemporary curating' main format, the thematic group show, for instance, brings together artworks on the basis of one or several common features, viz. similarity (Bertrand 2022a). Nevertheless, there are a few, distinct, contemporary exhibition making practices that operate according to a different logic. Taken as a whole, these rare and isolated approaches can be characterized as "creative curating", a term borrowed from curator Katerina Gregos (2011) who aptly uses it to describe curatorial "methods that highlight or enhance the practice of an artist and relationships between the works" (46) by making "new relationships visible" (47). Simply put, creative curating judiciously selects and juxtaposes remote (very different) artworks to create rich (complex) semantic associations.

To understand creative curating's particular methodology, it is useful to turn to associative theory, a well-established psychological model of creative thinking first advanced by psychologist Sarnoff A. Mednick in the early 1960s and still used today. Pre-empting Gregos' conception of creative curating as a methodology that makes new relationships between different artworks visible, Mednick (1962) defines the creative thinking process as: "the forming of associative elements into new combinations which either meet specified requirements or are in some way useful" (221). He further clarifies that "the more mutually remote the elements of the new combination, the more creative the process or solution" (ibid.). In other words, highly creative associations are less common and stereotypical (Mednick 1962: 223); they are more difficult to conceive and, by extension, predict—hence, are of greater potential value for recommender systems qua prediction engines. This being said, the chief interest of this model is that it determines that there are three ways to create viable associations between remote elements (meaning, for our purposes, three possible ways to facilitate discovery): similarity, serendipity, and mediation through an implicit term (Mednick 1962: 220).

Linguistic cases offer the most straightforward examples to elucidate the distinctions between these three associative methods. Take the words "table" and "cable", for instance. These words pick out remote things—remote in the sense that they are not usually paired together. When thinking of a table, the first things that comes to mind might be chairs or a tablecloth, but not a wire. Yet, the fact that these two words are homonyms, viz. that they rhyme, instantly creates an association based on similarity (the same sound). By comparison, the words "honeycomb" and "electricity" share no apparent connection, at least to most people; but, to a physicist working on conductive materials, they might inspire a new formula or design, thereby creating a serendipitous association. Meanwhile, the words "wheel", "electric" and "high" form an unlikely triad (Mednick 1962: 227). On the face of it, these three words have nothing in common; and yet, it might seem as though they are somehow related. That is because they are; simply add the word "chair" and they immediately connect: "wheelchair", "electric chair", "high chair". The association created between these three remote words is contingent on mediation by a fourth, implicit (unspoken) term. Naturally, only people with knowledge of this implicit term and how it relates to the three given words will be able to grasp the connection. As follows, this type of remote association is not universally given. Nonetheless, it is more widely available than serendipity, which depends on a specific skill set and mental disposition. In fact, it has been demonstrated that even when individuals cannot consciously identify the precise connection between seemingly unrelated words, they still often recognize that a connection exists if they have pre-existing knowledge of the implicit mediating term (Kahneman 2012). The point is that contrary to conventional exhibition practices and recommender systems, creative curating approaches establish associations between often-radically different artworks by way of mediation, as opposed to similarity or serendipity. These creative exhibition making approaches compellingly juxtapose artworks that are seemingly at odds with one another through an implicit, mediating idea.

Turning back to online art collections, applications that put into practice these different approaches become apparent in light of the examples above. Much like linguistic homonymity, for instance, several advanced collection interfaces (e.g., The Art Institute of Chicago, Google Art and Culture) feature a color palette filter designed to bring together diverse artworks that share the same color scheme. In this respect, Dominguez et al. (2019) describe three corresponding recommender systems for online contemporary art databases that are programmed to suggest artworks based on similar "brightness, saturation, sharpness, colorfulness, naturalness, entropy, and RGB contrast" levels (410). Meanwhile, much like the serendipitous "honeycomb-electricity" connection described above, Frost et al.'s (2019) anti-recommendation engine demonstrates how serendipitous connections between remote artworks can be provoked, at least in some users, through the strategic introduction of forceful novelty. By contrast to these two conventionally-exploited associative methods (similarity and serendipity), take the following artworks: Michelangelo Pistoletto's Venus of the rags (1967)[8] and Barbara Krueger's Untitled (I shop therefore I am) (1987)[9]. Paired together, these two highly diverse artworks offer an example of creative curating akin to the "wheel-electric-high" triad cited above. On the surface, these two pieces have little in common: they were created by different artists (an Italian male artist versus American female artist) using different media (sculpture with found materials versus photographic silkscreen on vinyl) and artistic techniques (representation versus text art). It is therefore highly unlikely that they would appear together in a search result or browsable category. Nevertheless, these two artworks strongly connect by way of a mediating idea: namely, a nuanced critique of consumer culture and its entanglement with feminine identity.

This being said, it is worth noting that art's semantic complexity and ambiguity make it so that remote artworks often share multiple, parallel connections—created through similarity, serendipity or mediation—that are more or less available (perceptible) to different users according to their personal background and knowledge. For instance, in the example above, the classical, white marble figure in Pistoletto's work shares formal affinities (similarities) with the black and white hand in Krueger's piece. As a matter of fact, creative curating practices often exploit formal connections (i.e., juxtapose works that look good together or create a visually-stimulating contrast) to initially capture visitors' wandering attention and direct it towards a more complex mediated association. While eye-catching, formal similarities tend to be quite shallow connections that cannot maintain engagement for very long without at least one other, richer ideological connection, such as the ones established through mediation—or through serendipity for the right user under the right circumstances. It is ultimately these richer semantic connections that sustain attention and lead to rewarding aesthetic experiences. Indeed, aesthetic experience has been shown to depend on interpretive challenge (complexity) and an equivalent capacity for meaning extraction, or processing fluency: the greater the challenge (i.e., emotional and informational density), the greater the aesthetic reward, so long as it is met by an adequately-equipped audience (Lindell and Mueller 2011). Accordingly, these types of semantic connections emerge as the key to sustained engagement online, particularly when it comes to image-based collections that lack the phenomenological quality of in-gallery and immersive digital experiences.

In sum, creative curating approaches can be used to resolve recommender systems' originality-accuracy trade-off and in so doing, both increase non-expert engagement with online collections and facilitate discovery by proposing rich, meaningful connections that do not depend on the users' skill set and mind set, but instead on their tacit knowledge. The question left is: how can this approach sustain a different model of digital cultural participation: i.e., one capable of accurately recruiting users' unique perspective towards fostering more inclusion, diversity and equality in art museums?

[8] An image of this work can be found in Tate's online collection and accessed via the following link: https://www.tate.org.uk/art/artworks/pistoletto-venus-of-the-rags-t12200.

[9] An image of this work can be found on The Pinault Collection's website and accessed via the following link: https://lesoeuvres.pinaultcollection.com/en/artwork/untitled-i-shop-therefore-i-am.

20.6 A New Model of Digital Cultural Participation

To clarify how implementing this approach by means of a novel, interactive recommender system for online art collections can sustain a different model of digital cultural participation, it is first necessary to reiterate two art truisms (one pertaining to the art object, the other to the viewer/user). The first truism is that owing to art's semantic complexity and general ambiguity, the meaning of a work changes depending on the display context (Bertrand 2022a; Chaffee 2010): i.e., how, where, when and next to what it is shown. This is even truer of art digitizations (digital reproductions) (Berger 2008), and can easily be demonstrated using the Pistoletto-Krueger example above. Merely swapping Krueger's work for Ed Ruscha's painting Molten Polyester (2005)[10] or a still from Tejal Shah's video Between the Waves Channel II Landfill Dance (2012)[11] is enough to completely alter the reading of Pistoletto's sculpture. This is because Ruscha and Shah's distinct pieces both connect with Pistoletto's work by way of an altogether different mediating idea from the one connecting it to Krueger's piece: namely, the environmental impact of the fashion industry.

The second truism is that, aside from context, art perception, interpretation and appreciation are largely determined by each individual's unique memories, experiences, cultural background and knowledge (Darda and Chatterjee 2023; De Duve 1996; Falk 2016; Vessel et al. 2023; Weil 2002). The problem, as underscored throughout this chapter, is that this intuitive process is notoriously hard to express (put into words) and even harder to accurately capture by means of digital technology on account of the outside influences and design modalities biasing aesthetic perception and judgement (Bertrand 2023).

This is precisely where creative curating approaches come in. According to Thaler and Sunstein (2022), the right "choice architecture" or "choice engine" can nudge people towards making the best possible choice for them at any given time (e.g., travel websites that help users find the best available flight, which might mean the fastest, most convenient or cheapest flight depending on the user's needs). Correspondingly, we propose that an interactive recommender system for online art collections based on creative curating approaches could, in theory, nudge users towards making the "best" aesthetic choice: meaning, in this case, the choice most aligned with, and indicative of, their unique, evolving perspective and worldview. By recommending a selection of artworks that creates different mediated associations with a given work, we speculate that such an engine would compel users to intuitively choose the association that makes the most sense—that is the most meaningful—to them given their unique worldview (values, beliefs, memories, etc.). For instance, the choice between the Krueger or Ruscha piece in relation to Pistoletto's work, indicating a greater concern for consumer culture's impact on women, or the environmental cost

[10] An image of this work can be found in the Denver Art Museum's online collection and accessed via the following link: https://www.denverartmuseum.org/en/edu/object/molten-polyester.

[11] A still of this video work can be found in the Lenbachhaus's online collection and accessed via the following link: https://www.lenbachhaus.de/en/discover/collection-online/detail/between-the-waves-30059051.

of fast-fashion waste.[12] Moreover, to further nudge users towards making the most personally indicative aesthetic choice, certain display features could also be leveraged. For instance, instead of displaying the recommended works in a bar far below the initial artwork, they could be presented next to it (e.g., initial work on the left and recommended works on the right of the screen) and accompanied by a simple prompt such as: "Which of these artworks makes the most sense to you in relation to this work?", thus adding a further gamification dimension to the experience inciting users to engage. In fact, a similar display is already being exploited by Google Arts and Culture. By clicking on the button "Where Next? Explore Related Content" below the artwork on display, users open up a vertical bar on the righthand side of the screen, which presents suggestions of variously related artworks underneath the simple prompt: "Still looking for more?" In sum, we believe that such an interactive recommendation approach would be compelling enough to overcome external influences given the nature of aesthetic judgments without itself biasing user's choices (viz. continuously reinforcing past preferences).

Because mediated associations hinge on tacit knowledge, these kinds of recommendations, in turn, would provide art institutions with more telling user data than their counterparts. Indeed, similarity-driven choices often convey superficial color/style preferences that say very little about the individual. At the other extreme, serendipity-driven choices are often so idiosyncratic that it is almost impossible for anyone other than the user to grasp the nature of the connection, thus making the data virtually unexploitable. By contrast, choices between mediated associations speak to the person's background. As suggested above, even if users are not immediately able to identify the nature of the connection (viz. why a pair of artworks in meaningful to them), which is frequently the case, they will still be drawn to it. Over time, through repeat engagement, we theorize that such a recommender system could gradually refine its suggestions based on prior choices to draw a more nuanced portrait of the user's personal inclinations. This could be done, for instance, by proposing to a user demonstrating strong ecological leanings different environmentally-based associations to probe more fine-grained memory- and experience-driven preferences and sense-making proclivities. For instance, a user worried about fashion waste might be more drawn to the Ruscha painting because of its clean design aesthetics, or alternatively, to the Shah work because of its raw, earthy look or its group dance sequence.

In sum, our claim is that an interactive recommender system exploiting creative curating's mediation strategy could facilitate non-expert users' discovery of online art collections by providing tailored context for lesser-known artworks, and, at the same time, capture valuable user data towards diversifying art institutions' programs and priorities. What is more, we surmise that such a system would substantially increase engagement with online collections by offering users an added incentive to keep exploring. As Schrage (2020) observes: "recommendations are engines of

[12] It may be necessary to program the recommender system to make conflicting mediated recommendations that share similar contrast and brightness levels, for example, to ensure that visual salience does not bias aesthetic choice.

introspection and self-discovery" (37). They encourage self-awareness by inciting users to reflect on the logic behind the proposed recommendations and the personal reasons driving their ultimate choice. This suggests that our proposed recommender system could also aid users become more aware of their intuitive patterns of perception and meaning-making tendencies as they navigate and choose between different recommendations, especially if they are provided with appropriate feedback and data analytics comparing their choices to that of others. Simply put, through their interactions with the system, users could learn about themselves while they learn about art, thus incentivizing them to stay engaged.

Naturally, there are a number of technical challenges to designing such a recommender system, including the fact that it cannot easily be programmed using currently available keywords, nor conventional semantic relationships (e.g., artist, place, date, etc.). Moreover, it would require the involvement of very diverse curators to create multiple, mediated connections capable of speaking to a plurality of users with different backgrounds and cultural references. Notwithstanding, we believe that the proposed approach offers a new solution to automatically capture users' unique perspective towards establishing a more robust and sustainable power sharing model within art institutions.

20.7 Conclusion

This chapter has argued that altering how online collections are curated can substantially change the extent and the manner in which users interact with art digitizations online, and in turn provide art institutions with valuable data on users' unique perspective towards a new power sharing model on a mass scale. The chapter began by discussing the importance of digital participation for art institutions' continued relevance, and why prevailing access tools (search boxes and generous interfaces) and participatory models limit public engagement, arguing that consensual data tracking via an interactive experience enabling users to discover online collection content on their own terms might offer a more viable and scalable approach, provided adequate content curation. The chapter went on to explore the advantages of personalizing content by means of recommender systems to facilitate public access and engagement, and outlined these systems' current applications in the cultural domain. It discussed the numerous parallels that have been drawn between curation and personalization, emphasizing the need for a certain amount of pre-filtering to support user-driven choice. Nevertheless, it subsequently explored recommender systems' drawbacks, including their limited ability to sustain discovery as well as their negative effects on individual judgements of taste, which it traced to these engine's conflicting recommendation goals (relevance versus serendipity), also known as the accuracy-originality trade-off. In addition, it emphasized the importance of providing users with the right pre-selection of artworks to offset the biasing effects of various outside influences on aesthetic appraisals and online endorsements in order to accurately capture users' unique perspective. To resolve these different issues towards the creation of a new interactive recommender system for online collections, the chapter ultimately turned to a rare physical exhibition making approach, which it coined "creative curating", as an alternative model for algorithmic curation. Drawing on associative theory, it described how creative curating diverges from current algorithmic methodologies, which essentially rely on principles of similarity and serendipity, exploiting instead a third associative principle, mediation, to create complex semantic relationships between different artworks. The chapter concluded by speculating how converting this curatorial approach into an interactive recommender system for online art collections could be used to nudge users into making personally indicative choices as they intuitively explore these collections. In doing so, it ultimately proposed a new digital cultural participation model based on an unprecedented method to reverse-engineering aesthetic judgment. In terms of future research, as the proposed model is currently theoretical, prospective work will involve building a working prototype to test and verify this model's capacity to sustain non-expert engagement and accurately capture diverse users' unique worldview.

Acknowledgements This article is part of a wider research project that has received funding from the European Union's Horizon 2020 research and innovation programme under the Marie Sklodowska-Curie grant agreement No 893454.

References

Adomavicius G, Bockstedt JC, Curley SP, Zhang J (2013) Do recommender systems manipulate consumer preferences? A study of anchoring effects. Inf Syst Res 24(4):956–975. https://doi.org/10.1287/isre.2013.0497

Aggarwal CC (2016) Recommender systems: the texbook. Springer, Heidelberg

Andrews J (2023) Email to one of the authors. 12 April 2023 (permission granted 26 March 2024)

Aoki PM, Grinter RE, Hurst A, Szymanski MH, Thornton JD, Woodruff A (2002) Sotto voce: exploring the interplay of conversation and mobile audio spaces. In: Proceedings of the SIGCHI conference on human factors in computing systems, pp 431–438. ACM. https://dl.acm.org/doi/10.1145/503376.503454

Bennett T (1996) The exhibitionary complex. In: Greenberg R, Ferguson BW, Nairne S (eds) Thinking about exhibitions. Routledge, London, pp 81–112

Benouaret I, Lenne D (2015) Personalizing the museum experience through context-aware recommendations. In: IEEE international conference on systems, man, and cybernetics, Hong Kong, pp 743–748. ACM. https://doi.org/10.1109/SMC.2015.139

Berger J (2008) Ways of seeing. Penguin Books, London

Bertrand S (2022a) Contemporary curating, artistic reference and public reception: reconsidering inclusion, transparency and mediation in exhibition making practice. Routledge, London and New York

Bertrand S (2022b) Curating online collections: towards an authentically digital, mediation protocol for art digitizations. J Curat Stud 11(1):26–51

Bertrand S (2023) Recruiting collective intelligence to level art world stratification: how virtual museums of contemporary art can impact the actual art system. DAHJ-Digit Art Hist J 9:5:14–5:24. https://doi.org/10.11588/dah.2023.9.89264

Bhaskar M (2017) Curation: the power of selection in a world of excess. Piatkus, London

Boltanski L (2011) On critique: a sociology of emancipation (trans: Elliott G). Polity Press, Cambridge

Bonet L, Négrier E (2018) The participative turn in cultural policy: paradigms, models, contexts. Poetics 66:64–73. https://doi.org/10.1016/j.poetic.2018.02.006

Boon T (2021) Curatorial reflections [Online webinar]. Towards a national collection. https://www.youtube.com/watch?v=M7n-jOfkzuk

Bourdieu P (1984) Distinction: a social critique of the judgement of taste (trans: Nice R). Harvard University Press, Cambridge, MA

Cameron F (2019) Theorising heritage collection digitisations in global computational infrastructures. In: Lewi H Smith W, vom Lehn D and Cooke S (eds) The Routledge international handbook of new digital practices in galleries, libraries, archives, museums and heritage sites, pp 55–67. Routledge, London

Carnovalini F, Rodà A, Pretto N, Canazza S (2023) We have other paintings as well! Recommending non-popular cultural heritage in museum visits. ExICE23. Bologna, 15 March 2023. https://zenodo.org/records/7973666

Cardoso PJS, Rodrigues JMF, Pereira JAR, Sardo JDP (2017) An object visit recommender supported in multiple visitors and museums. In: Antona M, Stephanidis C (eds) Universal access in human–computer interaction. Design and development approaches and methods. UAHCI 2017. Lecture Notes in Computer Science 10277. Springer, Cham. https://doi.org/10.1007/978-3-319-58706-6_24

Chaffee C (2010) Situating Marcel Broodthaers's final exhibitions. Manifesta J 7:40–49

Chayka K (2024) Filterworld: how algorithms flattened culture. Doubleday, New York

Colace F, De Santo M, Lombardi M, Santaniello D (2019) CHARS: a cultural heritage adaptive recommender system. In: Proceedings of TESCA '19, New York. https://doi.org/10.1145/3364544.3364830

Daga E, Asprino L, Damiano R, Agudo BD, Gangemi A, Kuflik T, Lieto A, Marras AM, Pandiani DM, Mulholland P, Peroni S, Pescarin S, Wecker A (2022) Integrating citizen experiences in cultural heritage archives: requirements, state of the art, and challenges. JOCCH 15(1):1–35. https://doi.org/10.1145/3477599

Dale S (2014) Content curation: the future of relevance. Bus Inf Rev 31(4):199–205. https://doi.org/10.1177/0266382114564267

Darda K M, Chatterjee A (2023) The impact of contextual information on aesthetic engagement of artworks. Sci Rep 13(4273). https://doi.org/10.1038/s41598-023-30768-9

De Duve T (1996) Kant after Duchamp. MIT Press, Cambridge MA

Dominguez V, Messina P, Donoso-Guzmán I, Parra D (2019) The effect of explanations and algorithmic accuracy on visual recommender systems of artistic images. In: Proceedings of the 24th international conference on intelligent user interfaces, pp 408–416. ACM. https://doi.org/10.1145/3301275.3302274

Engberg M (2016) Digital archives, the museum and the culture snacker. Medium. https://medium.com/the-politics-practices-and-poetics-of-openness/digital-archives-the-museum-and-the-culture-snacker-3103b767bce7

Falk JH (2016) Identity and the museum visitor experience. Routledge, New York

Frost S, Thomas MM, Forbes AG (2019) Art I don't like: an anti-recommender system for visual art. In: Proceedings of MW19: MW 2019, Boston. https://mw19.mwconf.org/paper/art-i-dont-like-an-anti-recommender-system-for-visual-art/

Gielen P, Elkhuizen S, van den Hoogen Q, Lijster T, Otte H (2015) Chapter 1: Culture: the substructure for a European common. Culture: the substructure for a European common [Research Report] Felix De Clerck, Brussel, pp 6–50

Gregos K (2011) The sovereign and its servants: on the ethics of curating. Manifesta J 12:44–50

Hashemi SH, Kamps J (2017) Where to go next? Exploiting behavioral user models in smart environments. In: UMAP '17: Proceedings of the 25th conference on user modeling, adaptation and personalization, pp 50–58. ACM. https://doi.org/10.1145/3079628.3079687
He C, Parra D, Verbert K (2016) Interactive recommender systems: a survey of the state of the art and future research challenges and opportunities. Expert Syst Appl 56:9–27. https://doi.org/10.1016/j.eswa.2016.02.013
Huvila I, Johnston J, Roued-Cunliffe H (2022) LAMs and the participatory turn. In: Rasmussen CH, Rydbeck K, Larsen H (eds) Libraries, archives, and museums in transition changes, challenges, and convergence in a Scandinavian perspective, pp 158–172. Routledge, London. https://doi.org/10.4324/9781003188834-15
Iaquinta L, de Gemmis M, Lops P, Semeraro G, Molino P (2010) Can a recommender system induce serendipitous encounters? In: Kang K (ed) E-Commerce. https://doi.org/10.5772/8905
Kahneman D (2012) Thinking fast and slow. Penguin Books, London
Keller I, Viennet E (2015) Recommender systems for museums: evaluation on a real dataset. In: Proceedings of IMMM 2015: the 5th international conference on advances in information mining and management, Brussels
Klein E, Chayka K (2024) Transcript: Ezra Klein interviews Kyle Chayka. The New York Times. https://www.nytimes.com/2024/01/09/podcasts/transcript-ezra-klein-interviews-kyle-chayka.html?auth=linked-google1tap&referringSource=articleShare&smid=nytcore-ios-share
Konstantakis M, Alexandridis G, Caridakis G (2020) A personalized heritage-oriented recommender system based on extended cultural tourist typologies. Big Data Cogn Comput 4(12). https://doi.org/10.3390/bdcc4020012
Kontiza K, Loboda O, Deladiennee L, Castagnos S, Naudet Y (2018) A museum app to trigger users' reflection. CEUR Workshop Proc 2176(10)
Lindell AK, Mueller J (2011) Can science account for taste? psychological insights into art appreciation. J Cogn Psychol 23(4):453–475. https://doi.org/10.1080/20445911.2011.539556
Margetis G, Apostolakis KC, Ntoa S, Papagiannakis G, Stephanidis C (2021) X-Reality museums: unifying the virtual and real world towards realistic virtual museums. Appl Sci 11(1):338. https://doi.org/10.3390/app11010338
McCay-Peet L, Toms EG (2015) Investigating serendipity: how it unfolds and what may influence it. J Am Soc Inf Sci 66(7):1463–1476. https://doi.org/10.1002/asi.23273
Mednick SA (1962) The associative basis of the creative process. Psychol Rev 69(3):220–232
Noehrer L, Carlton J, Jay C (2021) Machine learning and museum collections: a data conundrum. In: Shehade M, Stylianou-Lambert T (eds) RISE IMET 2021, CCIS 1432, pp 19–31. https://doi.org/10.1007/978-3-030-83647-4_2
Oppermann R, Specht M (1999) A nomadic information system for adaptive exhibition guidance. Arch Museum Inf 13(2):127–138
Pasnak E (2013) Conservation within the multicultural context. CeROArt HS Conserv Cult Connect. https://doi.org/10.4000/ceroart.3635
Pariser E (2011) The filter bubble: what the internet is hiding from you. Penguin UK, London
Pavilidis G (2019) Recommender systems, cultural heritage applications, and the way forward. J Cult Herit 35:183–196
Ricci F, Rokach L, Shapira B, Kantor PB (2011) Recommender systems handbook. Springer, New York
Ridge M, Blickhan S, Ferriter M, Prytz YB, Brumfield B, Brumfield S, Burgher S, Casey J, Coleman S, Cybulska D, Goldman MH, Luther K, Mast A, White N, Wilkins B, Willcox P (2021) The collective wisdom handbook: perspectives on crowdsourcing in cultural heritage. British Library, London. https://doi.org/10.21428/a5d7554f.1b80974b
Riggs S (2019) The end of storytelling: the future of narrative in the storyplex. Beat Media Group, London
Rocchi C, Stock O, Zancanaro M, Kruppa M, Krüger A (2004) The museum visit: generating seamless personalized presentations on multiple devices. In: Proceedings of the 9th international

conference on intelligent user interfaces, pp 316–318. ACM. https://doi.org/10.1145/964442.964517
Rosenbaum S (2011) Curation nation: how to win in a world where consumers are creators. McGraw-Hill, New York
Roued-Cunliffe H (2020) Open heritage data: an introduction to research, publishing and programming with open data in the heritage sector. Facet Publishing, London
Roued-Cunliffe H (2021) The record has left the building. Keynote speech presented at SIC2021: Virtual. sharing is caring. https://www.youtube.com/watch?v=XrHP_VDpGiw&list=PLEGQxIeZnUn0hu8ZBmCG0TirqopH738bi&index=4
Ruotsalo T, Haav K, Stoyanov A, Roche S, Fani E, Deliai R, Mäkelä E, Kauppinen T, Hyvönen E (2013) SMARTMUSEUM: a mobile recommender system for the web of data. J Web Semant 20:50–67. https://doi.org/10.1016/j.websem.2013.03.001
Sacco PL (2021) Cultural participation, digital technologies and transformational social change. Keynote speech presented at Europeana 2021. https://pro.europeana.eu/event/cultural-participation-digital-technologies-and-transformational-social-change
Salganik MJ, Dodds PS, Watts DJ (2006) Experimental study of inequality and unpredictability in an artificial cultural market. Science 311(5762):854–856. https://doi.org/10.1126/science.1121066
Samis P, Michaelson M (2017) Creating the visitor-centered museum. Routledge, New York
Sanchez M (2013) 2011: art and transmission. Artforum 51(10):294–301
Schrage M (2020) Recommendation engines. MIT Press, Cambridge, MA
Suran S, Pattanaik V, Draheim D (2020) Frameworks for collective intelligence: a systematic literature review. ACM Comput Surv 53(1). https://doi.org/10.1145/3368986
Stoneman A, Carvalho J, Daga E, Maguire M, Mulholland P (2021) Uncomfortable revelations: can citizen curation widen access to museums? Museum Ireland 28:64–71
Thaler RH, Sunstein CR (2022) Nudge. Penguin Random House, London
Thomas N (2010) The museum as method. Mus Anthropol 33(1):6–10. https://doi.org/10.1111/j.1548-1379.2010.01070.x
UNESCO Institute for Statistics (2009) 2009 UNESCO Framework for Cultural Statistics. Montreal: UNESCO Institute for Statistics. https://uis.unesco.org/en/files/unesco-framework-cultural-statistics-2009-en-pdf
Van de Rijt A, Kangc SM, Restivod M, Patile A (2014) Field experiments of success-breeds-success dynamics. Proc Nat Acad Sci (PNAS) 111(19):6934–6939. https://doi.org/10.1073/pnas.1316836111
Verwayen H, Kennisland M A, Kaufman P B (2011) The problem of the yellow milkmaid: a business model perspective on open metadata. Europeana White Paper 2. Europeana. https://pro.europeana.eu/post/the-problem-of-the-yellow-milkmaid
Vessel EA, Pasqualette L, Uran C, Koldehoff S, Bignardi G, Vinck M (2023) Self-relevance predicts the aesthetic appeal of real and synthetic artworks generated via neural style transfer. Psychol Sci 34(9):1007–1023. https://doi.org/10.1177/09567976231188107
Villeneuve P, Love AR (eds) (2017) Visitor-centered exhibitions and edu-curation in art museums. Rowman & Littlefield, Lanham, MD
Weil SE (2002) Making museums matter. Smithsonian Press, Washington, DC
Windhager F, Frederico P, Schreder G, Glinka K, Dörk M, Miksch S, Mayr S (2019) Visualization of cultural heritage collection data: state of the art and future challenges. IEEE Trans Vis Comput Graph 25(6). https://doi.org/10.1109/TVCG.2018.2830759
Winesmith K, Lewi H, Smith W (2019) Interview with Keir Winesmith. In: Lewi H, Smith W, vom Lehn D, Cooke S (eds) The Routledge international handbook of new digital practices in galleries, libraries, archives, museums and heritage sites. Routledge, London and New York, pp 42–51

Chapter 21
Designing and Developing Interactive Kiosks for Cultural Heritage: Best Practices and Common Issues

Marco Potenziani, Marco Callieri, and Paolo Cignoni

Abstract Interactive kiosks are a smart way to engage museum visitors and complement their visiting experience with another layer of engagement and interaction with the artworks. Kiosks are also a perfect complement to an integrated Cultural Heritage project that applies digital technologies for the study, the documentation, and the conservation of works of art, as it might help in adding a new dimension of dissemination and public outreach to the project. The design and development of an interactive kiosk for Cultural Heritage involves very different knowledge, skills, and tools. However, it is possible to find various software components that can be used, with a reasonable effort and a sound strategy, to set up an interactive kiosk able to display complex 2D+ and 3D data and implement advanced interaction paradigms. The aim of this work is to help possible developers, by discussing some working strategies and approaches, highlighting possible tools, and analyzing past activities of kiosk development and deployment.

Keywords Kiosk · Interactive · Museum · Media · Cultural heritage

21.1 Introduction

Using interaction in museums is a great way to foster more meaningful engagement with visitors, which facilitates a deeper connection with the exhibits and enriches the overall visiting experience (Allen and Gutwill 2004) (Marty and Jones 2007). As a result, traditional museum exhibitions have evolved from passive presentations of

---

M. Potenziani (✉) · M. Callieri · P. Cignoni
ISTI, CNR, Pisa, Italy
e-mail: marco.potenziani@isti.cnr.it

M. Callieri
e-mail: marco.callieri@isti.cnr.it

P. Cignoni
e-mail: paolo.cignoni@isti.cnr.it

F. Liarokapis et al. (eds.), *Interactive Media for Cultural Heritage*, Springer Series on Cultural Computing, https://doi.org/10.1007/978-3-031-61018-9_21

artifacts to interactive displays (Liarokapis et al. 2008), created to let users directly drive exploration in different ways (Sylaiou et al. 2009).

Multimedia kiosks have proven to be an excellent way to bring interactivity to museum itineraries, since they can present information exploiting various elements (videos, audio, images, 3D models), captivating visitors with dynamic and immersive content presentations. But they are also useful to complement traditional exhibits and guided tours, offering supplementary information, in-depth explanations, and personalized learning (Burmistrov 2015).

While early approaches to multimedia kiosks mainly resulted in informative stands providing historical, artistic, and other information through static visual presentations (e.g., image or video collections) (Vlahakis et al. 2002), modern kiosk installations are now able to offer much more (Umezu et al. 2023).

The available resources for developing a kiosk have increased over the years, and, nowadays, there is a variety of off-the-shelf software and hardware components that can be used to create an interactive installation able to handle complex digital data and implement advanced interaction paradigms, and all of this running over web-based technologies (Fanini et al. 2021a, b; Petroff 2019; Ponchio et al. 2019; Potenziani et al. 2015; Schütz 2016). These web-enabled tools have expanded the range of publishing possibilities for kiosks, with the result that hybrid solutions with a dedicated kiosk machine + an online version are now a prevalent trend for numerous Cultural Heritage (CH) institutions, also prompted by the COVID emergency and the induced need to increase their online offer (Gaballo 2021).

This work presents a discussion on web-based interactive kiosks, from design possibilities to development results. It is aimed at researchers and experts involved in integrated Digital Heritage projects focused on study, diagnostics, and conservation. In this kind of project, it is fairly common to feel the need to reach out to the public through an interactive multimedia kiosk. However, in similar scenarios, it is also fairly common for the people involved in the project to lack the specific skills needed for the creation of such a product. We believe this work can help in approaching the design and development of interactive kiosks from a direction that is sustainable and practical, unveiling the potential of these powerful tools in sharing research data with the community.

To this aim, first, in the Methods section, we will detail some strategies, suggestions, and approaches that we have found relevant in our experience, and that we think can help in the process of designing and implementing an interactive kiosk in a sustainable and practical way. Then, in the results section, we will describe some of our past experiences in the creation and deployment of interactive museum kiosks, with the idea of detailing the choices and the strategies employed in relation to their main CH project.

21.2 Methods

Even if the activity of designing and developing an interactive kiosk can be seen as agnostic, this discussion is still focused on carrying out this task in the context of a scientific project. For this reason, we would like to approach this work from a perspective characterized by sharing and reuse of the data used, openness and sustainability of the technologies introduced, replicability and transparency of the processes covered, following the FAIR principles (Wilkinson et al. 2016) as much as possible.

Thus, this section will focus mostly on open solutions, as they are more sustainable for the project, as well as more interoperable and in line with the idea of the sharing of knowledge. At the same time, particular attention will be paid to data reuse, since allowing data reuse is in line with the modern scientific approach, drives research efficiency, and reduces duplication of effort.

The first point to make is about the actual hardware setup of a multimedia interactive kiosk. Again, following the idea of a cost-effective and sustainable process, we will concentrate on the class of kiosks based on a PC controlled by a touch interface, which is also the most widely used and versatile configuration to use (Apollonio et al. 2021; Micoli et al. 2020; Origlia et al. 2023; Siotto et al. 2017).

The new generation of AR/VR devices has brought new opportunities in the entertainment and communication world, and their use in the creation of interactive museum installations is certainly possible (Gonizzi Barsanti et al. 2015; O'dwyer et al. 2021), also when basing the kiosk on web technology (through the WebXR component) (Fanini et al. 2021a, b). Although more appealing and trendier, they generally require a more cumbersome development, more powerful hardware, a specific design process, and the logistics of their use in a museum are questionable.

A similar argument can be made for specialized hardware components, like 3D input devices (the Kinect controller and the Wiimote sprouted numerous museum installations (Kalarat and Rattanarungrot 2020) (Schaller et al. 2015), a few years ago) and other controllers, stereoscopic and autostereoscopic monitors, touch-enabled physical objects, haptics, and force-feedback devices (Bruno et al. 2010; Palma et al. 2021). They certainly result in a more engaging and impressive experience, but with some drawbacks (Carrozzino and Bergamasco 2010): they add cost, require specific development, are more fragile and susceptible to suddenly becoming unsupported (by drivers and libraries, and sometimes discontinued by their own manufacturers).

21.2.1 Using Web Technology for Kiosks

An approach that has proven valid through the years is to base the interactive kiosk on web technologies. A website contains, more or less, all the components that might be needed in an interactive kiosk: text, images, videos and other media, graphics, interactive elements, and application logic (through JavaScript or similar programming languages). The new components introduced in HTML5 (W3C—World Wide Web Consortium 2008) have further expanded the kind of media that can be effectively used on the web platform.

Almost all of the final users of the kiosk are familiar with navigating the web, especially through the use of a touch interface (like in mobile devices). A kiosk based on the same technologies will provide a familiar experience to the users, increasing its usability and appeal.

The development of a web-based kiosk is also made easier and more cost-efficient, thanks to the availability of ready-made components and libraries. The presence of such components will also increase the sense of familiarity for the final users.

The use of web technologies can also provide a small advantage in terms of maintenance and longevity to the kiosk with respect to custom, stand-alone software. Although the web is indeed volatile, most, if not all, of the content will still be usable and accessible in the future.

Additionally, the use of web technologies makes it possible to deploy the kiosk on multiple platforms: on dedicated machines in a museum, and online. This double-targeting is not completely free, as it is necessary to make the pages responsive and not just hardcoded toward the resolution of the kiosk machine, but the advantage in terms of public outreach is clear.

21.2.2 Data Reuse

When involved in a study, documentation, or conservation project, it is pretty normal to accumulate a corpus of scientific data, like 3D models and other 2D+ images (panoramas, multispectral, RTI, HDR, ...). This data has been generated through measurement and careful processing, resulting in a precise, metric digital representation of the whole artwork or of some specific aspects of interest.

Exploiting for the kiosks this very same scientific data is a great way to both make communication more affordable and more correct (Canevese and De Gottardo 2017). The creation of digital 3D models and 2D+ data is a cumbersome and costly task; being able to reuse it also for the communication stage of the project makes the entire project more cost-effective. At the same time, using data that has been generated to be accurate and metric makes the communication more scientifically correct and honest to the final user. The kiosk will be using what is a digital twin of the object of interest, and not a hand-modeled replica that just "looks like" the original.

Obviously, this data is generally more complex to manage with respect to 3D assets and images that are purposely created for communication. However, there are various ready-made software components that are able to display complex 3D and 2D+ datasets in an interactive way. In most cases, these software are the same tools that are used to visualize and interact with the data in the rest of the project. Most of these viewers are based on web technologies, which makes them usable in a web-based kiosk architecture.

21.2.2.1 3D Viewers

The introduction of HTML5 and its WebGL (Khronos Group Inc. 2011) component has revolutionized the idea of visualizing 3D data inside a web browser. To create an interactive visualization of 3D data for the kiosk, it is possible to use one of the many developer libraries such as the lower level X3DOM (Behr et al. 2009) or Three.js (Cabello 2010), or the higher level frameworks BabylonJS (Catuhe and Rousset 2013), A-Frame (Marcos et al. 2015), and PlayCanvas (Eastcott et al. 2014). By developing the viewer from scratch, there is complete freedom in terms of interaction and behavior, but clearly, it requires much more programming work.

There also exists a plethora of web viewers (like Google Model-Viewer (Google Inc. 2018)) that can be directly used to build an interactive kiosk, without having to develop a viewer from scratch. Solutions like these, however, are generally targeted at displaying and managing game-oriented low-resolution 3D assets and hand-modeled geometries, and sometimes require a live network connection.

3D data coming from measurement (3D scanning and photogrammetry), which is the kind of data used in documentation, diagnostic, and study of CH, is generally high-resolution and unstructured, and requires specific tools to be managed and interacted with.

3DHOP (Potenziani et al. 2015) is a framework for the creation of interactive web presentations of high-resolution 3D models. Developed by ISTI-CNR, it has been designed to cope with the needs of the CH field, and can be used for a range of applications that go from a simple single-object viewer to more complex web apps aimed at technical use, or interactive kiosks. Thanks to a streaming-friendly multiresolution scheme, 3DHOP can manage and effectively render huge geometries and point clouds. 3DHOP offers a strong interconnection with the rest of the webpage DOM, and it is possible to completely customize the 3D scene, the interaction, and the interface, starting from a series of configurable components and helper functions. These features are extremely useful when building a kiosk, even though more complex interaction schemes require some programming.

Potree (Schütz 2016) is a web-based, open-source visualization tool for large 3D point clouds, developed by the University of Wien. Even though point clouds lack the surface representation of triangulated models, they can still be effectively used to present 3D environments to non-experts, and are a very common output of surveys of buildings and terrains via laser scanner or photogrammetry. Potree offers a very fast and efficient visualization and provides simple navigation, and the advanced shading options can make the dataset extremely legible also for the general public. However, the basic Potree viewer comes with an integrated interface that is too technically oriented to be directly usable in a kiosk: it is then necessary to strip the basic interface and build a new one, and this task requires programming and specific knowledge of the tool.

Smithsonian Voyager (The Smithsonian Institution 2018) is another open-source 3D viewer, designed and developed by the Smithsonian Institution as an outreach tool for its 3D digitization program. The tool can be heavily configured to adapt to the characteristics of the displayed model with minimal programming. It provides easy navigation of the 3D models and good rendering options, and it can be connected with the rest of the webpage DOM. As it is developed by museum experts, it provides specific functionalities for dissemination, like annotations, narrative interactive elements, and an authoring tool. This makes it a good choice for a kiosk. However, it remains mostly a "single-object viewer", and more complex scene setups are difficult to achieve.

Aton (Fanini et al. 2021a, b) is an open-source framework based on Node.js and Three.js designed to create Web3D/WebXR applications. Developed by ISPC-CNR, it can be adapted to different scenarios and uses, going from the technical to the dissemination (Gonizzi Barsanti et al. 2018). It is quite flexible in terms of the kind of geometries it can manage, from hand-modeled game-like assets to more complex 3D data generated with 3D scanning and photogrammetry. Aton is also able to deploy to XR and VR devices, to provide an immersive environment; this could open up the possibility of using these devices to build museum installations. Also in this case, a certain degree of programming is necessary to setup the viewer according to the need of the project, and define the interaction with the 3D scene.

Going beyond the open software, there are various commercial solutions for web-based visualization of complex 3D data; this is especially true in the architectural/BIM field, where various companies (like Autodesk and Trimble) are offering integrated environments called Common Data Environments (CDE), with specific web-based viewers and virtual visit components. These tools can effectively be used to show complex 3D data to the general public, but they are tricky to integrate into a kiosk because they have been designed to act as stand-alone tools, they are less customizable (fixed interface/interaction), and often require a live Internet connection.

For example, **Matterport** (Matterport Inc. 2011) is a commercial solution for the capture, interactive exploration, and technical use of 3D environments. Matterport provides an interesting web-based exploration tool based on a hybrid 2D-360 panorama-3D environment representation. This tool is perfectly suited to let an inexperienced user explore a complex environment, and would be a nice addition to a kiosk. However, its integration would not be straightforward, as it is designed to act as a stand-alone web application, and requires network access as the data is streamed from a server.

21.2.2.2 2D+ Viewers

Images, photos, and videos can be directly managed using the built-in elements of HTML5. On top of this basic embedding, it is possible to find ready-made components to add more dynamic image elements in a kiosk. Components like carousels, cover-flow, image grids, before/after sliders, and zoomable images have become extremely common on the web, and the user will expect similar interactions in a kiosk.

More interesting, however, is the integration of more advanced visual data in the kiosk, especially the technical scientific data produced in the CH project.

Most digital heritage projects rely on high-resolution and multi-layer images, like the ones produced by multispectral cameras. Another class of "technical" images is Reflectance Transformation Imaging (RTI): computational images where it is possible to change the illumination interactively at visualization time. RTI images work very well for the study and conservation of mostly flat objects like coins, carvings, fossils, and paintings, and are particularly useful in dissemination, as they are simple to use and understand by the general public.

OpenLIME (Ponchio et al. 2019) is an open-source JavaScript library for the efficient display of high-resolution images (gigapixel), multi-layer (e.g., multispectral), and relightable images (RTI). OpenLIME provides a set of ready-to-use components for web apps and kiosk applications, a responsive user interface, and support for multi-touch input. The viewer can be configured and extended to cope with the specific needs of the project, altering its interface and interaction parameters.

Panoramas/spherical images are another great way to convey a sense of presence in an environment, and are quite common to have as a result of a survey activity. Among the many available viewers for panoramic images, **Pannellum** (Petroff 2019) is a good choice for a kiosk because it is lightweight and simple to use, but provides all the basic features that can be needed in a kiosk, like controlling the viewer from other entities/scripts in the webpage, and creating linked panorama tours.

Maps are another useful ingredient for a kiosk. There are many map viewer widgets available for web development. These components can be customized to add layers of information and clickable elements, and their functionalities can be controlled with scripts from the rest of the webpage, making it possible to integrate them in the kiosk logic.

Leaflet (Agafonkin 2011) is a popular choice for this kind of applications, as it is lightweight, open-source, and easy to setup and use. A more powerful, but also more complex, option is **OpenLayers** (MetaCarta 2006).

The problem of embedding maps into a standalone kiosk is that most of these map widgets require a live Internet connection, to pull the base map data from services like OpenStreetMap (Coast 2004). Creating an offline map is possible, but it might require a deeper knowledge of mapping data and GIS.

21.2.3 Making It Work for a Museum

It is certainly possible to create a website that has the behavior and appearance of an interactive kiosk, but additional care has to be devoted to making it work like a dedicated kiosk application.

It is possible to have the website data stored in a remote server, but it is much more common to have all the data on the kiosk PC and access it through a local web server. Having all the kiosk data locally will also mean faster loading of resources, and this can make a difference when dealing with large datasets. This solution becomes mandatory in those cases where the kiosk will have a poor, or will not have, direct Internet connection (a common situation in many museums). A remote server can be considered when there are specific requirements (the kiosk needs to access complex dynamic data, or some server-side computation is needed), or for those cases where the museum provides a strong infrastructure and multiple kiosk machines have to be used.

In addition to the kiosk content and application logic, it is necessary to implement some essential precautions to make the kiosk installation work smoothly when it is released out in the wild:

- No exit from the kiosk: It is of paramount importance to keep the user inside the kiosk at all times, and not be able to access the rest of the system. Provided that the keyboard is out of reach from the user, it might seem enough to run the browser full-screen with no menu, and disable right-click context. Some operating systems do have a "kiosk mode" that can be activated to restrict operations like context menu, gestures, and application-switching. Most modern browsers have a built-in "kiosk mode", or have add-ons/extensions/plug-ins that provide similar functionalities.
- Startup/shutdown: The kiosk should start automatically when the computer turns on. This is easy to achieve as a startup script, or as a parameter to any of the "kiosk mode" options mentioned in the previous point. Also, the shutdown of the kiosk can be critical to preserving the life extent of HW and SW components: the system should be closed in a safe way, avoiding abrupt disconnections of the power supply (not an uncommon event in museums). As the kiosk is running inside a sandbox, as long as the system shuts down correctly, a safe closing should be guaranteed. However, a forced purge of caches and temporary files at startup can help in keeping the software working. The period of activity of the PC can also be programmed via system BIOS, which is a convenient option since usually the operability of a museum kiosk follows precise and repeatable schedules (such as the opening hours of a museum).
- Timeout and reset: It is fairly common for users to walk away from the kiosk in the middle of a session. To avoid the next user starting the virtual visit from an intermediate/unknown position, the kiosk should be able to automatically return to its initial state after a given inactivity period. As an additional guideline, there should always be, in any page and in every interactive element, a home/reset command, to facilitate the reset in case the next user arrives before the timeout, and to help those users that might be getting lost in the kiosk content. All these functionalities can be easily implemented, e.g., as JavaScript scripts.
- Attract mode: Similar to old arcade video games, it is possible to provide the kiosk with a dedicated page designed to invite users to interact. Even if it may seem trivial, this precaution is of vital importance if the kiosk installation is positioned in a classical visiting path in which museum visitors are typically requested not to touch, or if the kiosk touch screen has been set up between other monitors that simply play video. This special page can also be designed as a semi-transparent overlay component, useful to attract the audience but also to serve as a how-to that can explain the functionality of the kiosk below. Also, in this case, a timeout functionality can be easily implemented in JavaScript, so as to activate the attract

mode after a predefined inactivity period (attract mode that obviously will have to stop as soon as a user begins to interact with the kiosk).

Obviously, these points are relevant only for the dedicated kiosk installation, and can be safely ignored in the online version of the kiosk (even though the suggestion of always having a home/reset button holds true).

Unless the kiosk has to be used for a very short time, like in the case of a temporary exhibition, it is important to think about long-term maintenance and updates. Keeping both the OS and the browser as "stock" as possible helps the maintenance of the kiosk, as future updates can be installed, and in case of a catastrophic event, the entire kiosk might be moved to another machine. Having an up-to-date software environment is important, but, on the other hand, it is better to manually apply updates, keeping the kiosk machine "frozen" on release setup (disabling automatic updates or even keeping the machine offline) to prevent automatic updates from modifying one of the components used by the kiosk (browser, video player, etc.), making it stop working. Finally, it is advisable that kiosk developers leave themselves the possibility of remotely intervening on the system; that is a mandatory option in case it is not possible to physically reach the kiosk installation. Dedicated software solutions (e.g., TeamViewer (TeamViewer SE 2005)) or tools provided by default with some OS installations (e.g., Windows Remote Desktop (Microsoft Corporation 1998)) can serve the purpose.

Besides these software-side concerns, there may also be some hardware-related issues. One example is having the actual power button of the PC in an unreachable position, for instance in those cases where the PC is confined inside a cabinet or another structure that is difficult to reach. In this case, it is possible to buy external power buttons with an extension USB cable to move the control to a reachable position. However, the details to take into consideration about the hardware setup can be numerous (spatial considerations about casework and hardware, ventilation, ergonomic accessibility of components, height, wheelchair access, etc.). Fortunately, most of these duties are the responsibility of the museum staff specifically dedicated to the exhibitions, and, most of the time, kiosk developers are only asked for specifications. This is not the case with the definition of the hardware specification of the PC kiosk, a process in which the content developer is called to be an active part. Delving into the technicalities of this choice is beyond the scope of this discussion. However, it is sufficient to say that good "gaming" PC configurations are usually more than enough for running a multimedia kiosk based on web technologies.

21.2.3.1 Progressive Web App

As said, one of the advantages of working with web technologies is the possibility of deploying the kiosk on both dedicated machines in the museum, but also online. By exploiting a recent addition to web standards, it is also possible to provide a third way. Progressive Web Apps (PWAs) are a type of web application that can behave like a native mobile app, and can be installed on a mobile device without the need to go through an app store (Biørn-Hansen et al. 2017; Steiner 2018). PWAs are sometimes used to create companion apps/audioguides for museums and could be used to provide a mobile kiosk experience. The downside of this strategy is that the development of PWAs is much more complex than a standard web-based kiosk, requiring specific libraries and development frameworks, and some of the complex media viewers mentioned above might have integration issues.

21.3 Results

This section acts as a post-mortem discussion of some past projects that involved the creation and deployment of interactive museum kiosks. Its aim is to provide insights on the design process and to highlight specific technical choices that have made these projects possible.

Besides the pure technical consideration, the process of creating a multimedia kiosk has to go through a design that tries to leverage interlocking components: data, tools, and narrative. The ideal design process would start with establishing a narrative idea, and then construct the kiosk gathering the data and configuring the tools. In reality, however, one quickly finds out that the three components work like a game of rock-paper-scissors. The narrative idea is important, but cannot be fulfilled without proper data and tools that support it. Data can be available and interesting, but useless without a tool to present it, and if it does not fit into the chosen narrative. Tools might be available, but the narrative is influenced by how they implement the interaction. A more realistic design process is to start from the available ingredients and bring them together in a cohesive design by simultaneously working on all three components.

The creation of interactive kiosks has been a long-lasting activity in our lab. The first tests, although not unsuccessful, were limited by the available technology. On that side, the situation has improved drastically, and it is now much more mature.

One early work was the interactive kiosk of the Arrigo VII funerary complex, dating back to 2004 (Baracchini et al. 2004). The kiosk presented a virtual reconstruction of the lost monument, using 3D models, images, videos, and interactive elements (timelines). In retrospect, the kiosk had various issues. At the time, web pages could not directly integrate 3D content, especially the complex datasets we had to display. We had to use a local standalone 3D viewer running in background, switching context with the browser every time the user wanted to access the 3D data. As everything was running on a single dedicated PC, the solution worked without major hiccups, but was far from ideal. Another limitation was the graphics of page elements that, as was common at the time, were entirely static, and difficult to update and adapt to changes in screen resolution. Finally, the logistics of the kiosk in the museum proved tricky: starting and shutting down the PC was mostly done by turning on and off the power to the whole room, sometimes resulting in crashes of the OS or of the PC power supply. Notwithstanding all these issues, the kiosk remained in use in the museum of the Opera Primaziale, in Pisa (Italy), for almost 8 years, and was very positively evaluated by the visitors in a survey carried out for the EU project that supported the activity.

21.3.1 Alchemy by Jackson Pollock

In 2014, the painting "Alchemy" by Jackson Pollock was the subject of a series of diagnostic, cleaning, and consolidation actions. The analyses produced a lot of technical data, including a high-resolution 3D model of the whole painting surface. To commemorate the return of the cleaned painting to its museum, the Peggy Guggenheim Collections in Venice (Italy) organized a temporary exhibition that included a multimedia kiosk showing the painting in detail, using the 3D model (Callieri et al. 2015). The kiosk was based on 3DHOP, and used the highest resolution model available: 80 million triangles, a remarkable result for the time. The user can interact with the painting in different ways: exploring in detail its geometry, also by removing the color and going beyond what is possible to see in reality, experimenting with the interaction of the light with the complex surface, or by selecting annotated elements highlighting specific details/materials/techniques used in the painting process. The kiosk runs on a standard PC equipped with a very large touchscreen (60 inches).

A recurring problem in creating a kiosk is adapting the interface to be used on a touch screen. Most touchscreen monitors support multi-touch interaction, and, most people, nowadays, are used to multi-touch mobile displays. Still, it is always a good idea to make as much as possible the kiosk work in "single finger" mode, to simplify the access.

Interacting with a 3D model is a complex task, especially for people not experienced with 3D. For this reason, it is often necessary to simplify the navigation, provide a reference to show what the user is looking at (e.g., a minimap), and always offer a "home" button to restore the viewer to an initial state. In this specific case, to provide both pan and tilt functionalities, we implemented a tap-to-go animated function to glide around the painting, and a smooth, spring-back tilting control to see the painting surface from different angles, but slowly return to the more familiar straight view.

The process of authoring the content of the kiosk (in terms of which details to highlight and make interactive), the explanatory texts, and which visual options to make available was done in close collaboration with the museum curators. This authoring phase is always time-consuming and requires a coordinated effort from both parties.

The technical partner should clearly present to its CH counterpart what the possibilities are of the kiosk: how the user will interact with the data, which interactive elements/animations/visualization parameters can be controlled, and what kind of information layers might be supported by the viewer. This information should act as a guide for the CH partner to propose suitable content, and help them in adapting their narrative and communication approach to an unfamiliar media (Fig. 21.1).

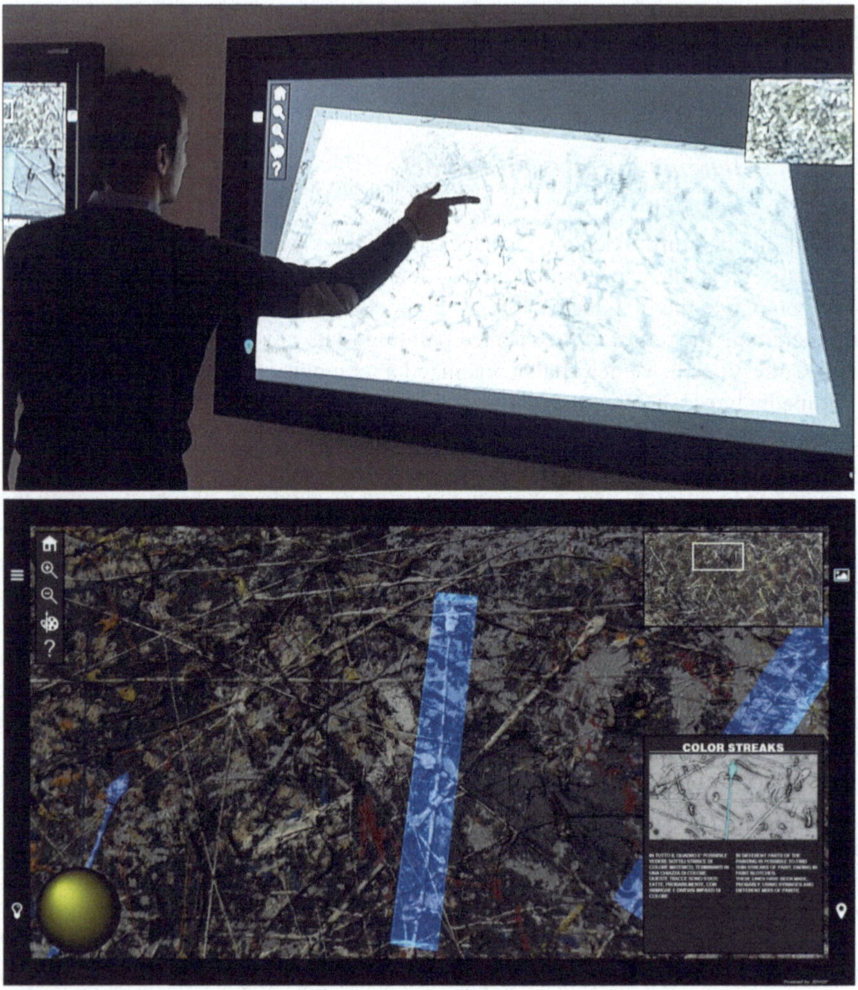

Fig. 21.1 The kiosk for the Alchemy painting. Top: the painting geometry without its color, useful to highlight the intricate layering of the paint. Bottom: screenshot of the 3D viewer showing the interactive hotspots exploited to describe the techniques used by Jackson Pollock

21.3.2 Three Armenian Manuscripts from Tuscany

This kiosk was created for a temporary exhibition at the Matenadaran Museum (Yerevan, Armenia) of some Armenian manuscripts from two historical libraries in Florence (ISTI—CNR, Biblioteca Medicea Laurenziana—MiBAC et al. 2019). This project is slightly different from the other cases presented, as, in this case, the kiosk was the primary objective of the project. However, the data for the kiosk was nevertheless gathered following scientific protocols, to make it usable beyond the scope of the kiosk, for archiving and study.

The kiosk presents, commented by the texts edited by experts, various interactive media elements: 360° panorama images, high-resolution images, and relightable RTI images. The panoramas have been used to convey the space of the libraries (Biblioteca Medicea Laurenziana and Biblioteca San Matteo). The user can browse through the codices using high-resolution, calibrated scans of the manuscript pages. Finally, to convey the micro-geometry and optical properties of the materials, relightable images are used to represent the pages illuminated in gold, and the decorated wooden cover of the codices.

The kiosk uses a familiar "chapter-based" structure, i.e., it is structured as a series of linked pages, grouped by topic in narrative tracks. This narrative structure can be perceived as trivial, but it is still a safe and flexible choice. It is easier to build and manage, as the linked pages exactly match the structure of a website. At the same time, it gives the user more freedom to explore different aspects and themes, following his/her personal interest.

This structure encourages the use of multiple interactive elements, each one focused on a specific aspect of the work, instead of fewer, more complex, all-encompassing interactive viewers. This idea mapped very well on the available data (multiple, non-homogeneous media), and resulted in a more approachable experience for the users (with each viewer simpler and more specialized).

When multiple types of media are used, it is advisable to establish, as much as possible, a uniform interaction across the different elements, even at the cost of restricting possible interactions for the sake of clarity: e.g., use the same graphics for buttons, map the same type of function to the same gesture/interface element, and set the behavior parameters coherent across viewers (Fig. 21.2).

21.3.3 A Kiosk for Coin Collections

In 2012, the San Matteo National Museum (Pisa, Italy) wanted to improve its documentation and the exhibition of its coin collection. This activity involved the digitization of the coins as RTI images and the creation of an interactive kiosk (Palma et al. 2014). The same kiosk code was later re-employed in another museum (Palazzo Blu, Pisa, Italy), on a second coin collection.

For the coins, the kiosks used a web-based RTI viewer (the previous version of the Relight/OpenLIME tool), specifically configured to support the presentation of coins. The viewer implemented a touch interface for zooming/panning, flipping the coin, and changing the light direction. Additionally, it was possible to add hotspots linked to annotations and animate the view to highlight specific details.

These twin projects showcase a class of kiosks that are akin to an "interactive catalog". With respect to the other kiosks presented in this section, these kiosks have a different scope, being focused on a large number of uniform specimens instead of

Fig. 21.2 Screenshots of the Armenian manuscripts' kiosk in action. Top: the homepage showing the "chapter-based" structure of the kiosk. Bottom: one of the interactive pages containing a relightable RTI image

a single "centerpiece" work of art. The narrative is often limited to the context of the collection.

This idea works very well for uniform collections of objects and can be used to complement and expand an exhibition (often, a permanent one) on different levels. It provides additional information on the displayed objects, adds ways to interact with each specimen in ways not possible on the real object, and can also be used to show other specimens not currently in the exhibition, virtually expanding it.

The kiosk is basically composed of two parts: one is narrative and gives context information about the collection/museum/exhibition, and the other is the actual interactive data content. The narrative part relies on usual webpages, maybe enriched with active elements. The data is managed through a single technical solution that provides uniform access to all the specimens.

The development of a similar kiosk is generally easier, as there is one single viewer. This viewer, however, must be customized for a specific class of objects, and be fully parametric. On the other hand, creating the content and assets requires a lot of effort, because of the amount of data to prepare and enrich with annotations.

This kind of kiosk can have a very long lifespan, as their role in a permanent exhibition never runs out, and they require less maintenance being simpler (Fig. 21.3).

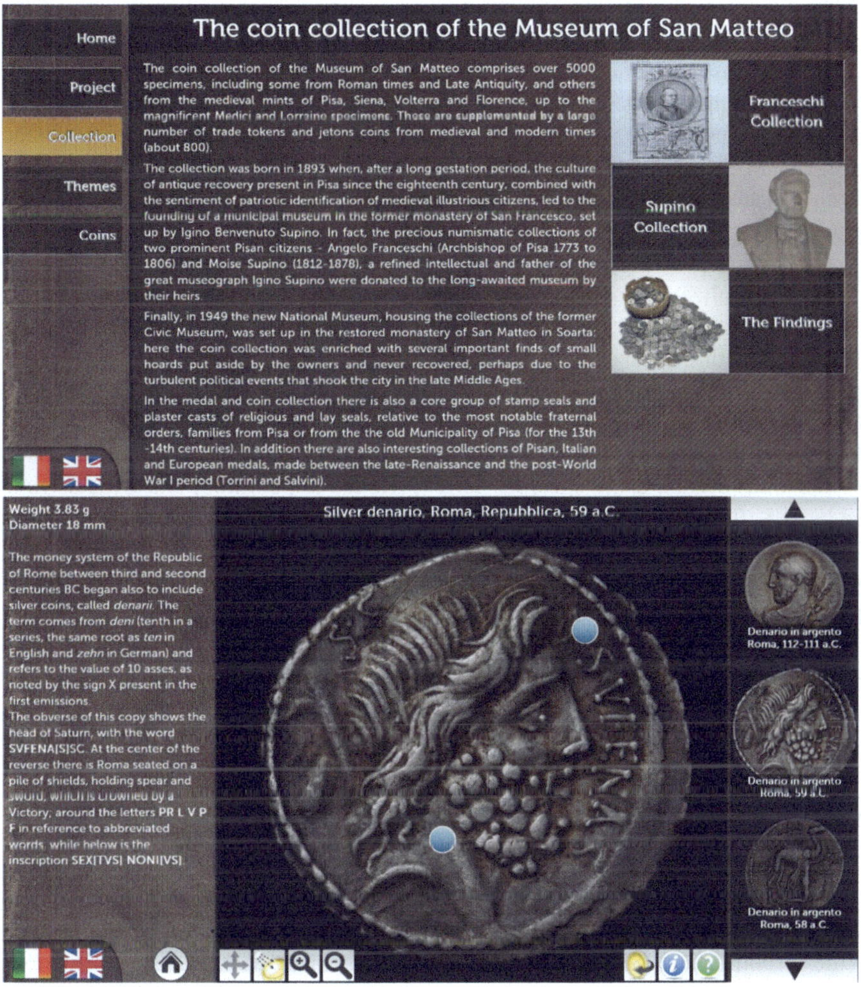

Fig. 21.3 Screenshots of the coin collection kiosk in San Matteo National Museum. Top: the narrative context. Bottom: one of the coins in the RTI viewers, with active hotspots

21.3.4 Ecce Homo

The painting "Ecce Homo" by Antonello da Messina is an artwork of great importance but a precarious state of conservation, from the Collection of the Collegio Alberoni in Piacenza (Italy). In 2017, the artwork was the subject of a campaign of non-invasive investigations, aimed at reaching a deeper understanding of the artwork's conservation conditions and at creating an objective digital twin to support the work of conservators and restorers. As a side-product of this diagnostic activity, the museum wanted to enhance the visit with an interactive kiosk (Albertin et al. 2021).

In this project, the idea of reusing the same data used for the conservation of the work of art was brought one step further. The 3D viewer used in the kiosk is a direct derivation of the very same technical viewer developed for the conservators. The 3DHOP tool has been used to create, for the curators, a technical tool to inspect the geometry of the surface of the painting (from 3D scanning) and the inner volume (from CT scanning) showing the galleries of wood-boring insects and structural issues, to be used as an interactive risk map. This viewer was converted into a viewer for the general public by changing its interface, and selecting just a subset of the available visualization modes, but keeping most of the code and all the data. In this way, the users can experience the same scientific content used by the curators, but still mediated through a design process that makes it accessible.

The rest of the kiosk presents text and visual information organized in different themes/narrative paths. Most of the other physical analyses could be easily displayed as images (single or multi-layered), and it was easy to add interactive elements based on this kind of data, using specific viewers (Relight/OpenLime) and widgets (like the before-after sliding images).

The kiosk was designed to be used on a physical kiosk in the museum (a PC with a touchscreen) or through the web, at home, still on a desktop machine. On a request from the museum, it was later adapted to run also on tablet devices, to be used by tourist guides during organized tours. Having such changes happening in the late development stage (or after deployment) is not uncommon, but in this case it was made easier by the underlying web technology (Fig. 21.4).

21.3.5 Montagnola Tomb Inside and Out

The Montagnola Tomb, in Sesto Fiorentino (Florence, Italy), is a monumental Etruscan mound tomb of remarkable dimension and state of conservation, dating back to the seventh century B.C. A recent restoration was followed by a documentation-oriented terrestrial laser scanner survey that generated high-resolution 3D models of the mound and the inner area of the tomb. As of today, however, the site is not fully open to the public, and the local authorities wanted to have an interactive kiosk in

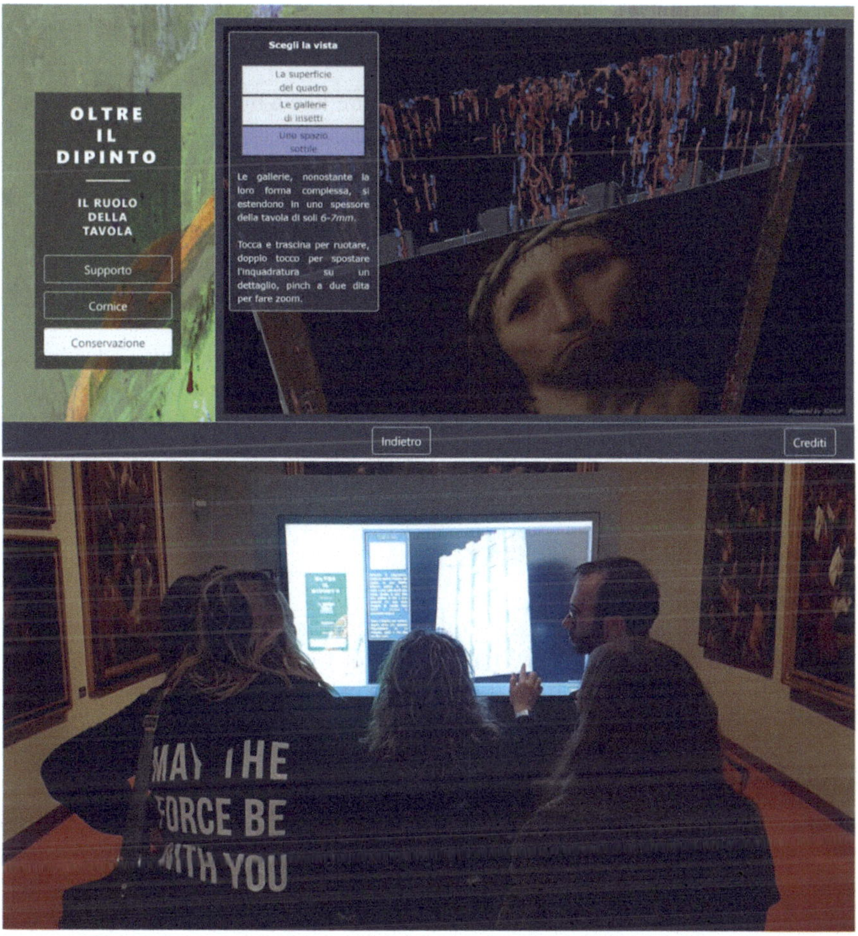

Fig. 21.4 The kiosk for the Antonello da Messina Ecce Homo. Top: screenshot of the 3D viewer showing the woodworm galleries below the painting surface. Bottom: visitors interacting with the kiosk at the Collegio Alberoni (Piacenza, Italy)

the local library, to be used also as a "pre-show" tool for group visits (ISTI—CNR, ISPC—CNR et al. 2020).

In this case, the interesting part of the work was to design the interaction with the 3D models, to achieve the desired narrative, exploiting the available data and tools. We wanted to experience the monument from two different points of view: from outside, to appreciate the structure of the mound and the architectural elements; and from inside, to explore the inner burial chambers in first person. Instead of trying to create an uber-viewer with multiple interaction modes, that would be complex to develop and confusing to use for the user, we decided to split the kiosk in two parts, each one with a specific interaction and focused on one of the two aspects.

Furthermore, the design of each viewer draws inspiration from existing presentation and interaction paradigms to improve the kiosk fruition.

- The external viewer presents the tomb structure like a maquette: museums have always used maquettes and scale models, often with cut-throughs to show inner structures. With specific rendering parameters (e.g., the focal length) and small visual elements (like an underlying base), a 3D model can be made to look like a scale model; and it is possible to digitally slice it into multiple ways, to show the inner structures with much more freedom than a physical maquette.
- The internal viewer implements a videogame-like first-person navigation: this conveys a sense of presence by exploiting a known entertainment media. Normally, first-person games are controlled using a two-stick gamepad or mouse + keyboard; in the kiosk, we implemented an alternative interface to make the navigation more accessible to non-gamers, using a minimap (that also helped the user locate its position) and a drag-to-look function (Fig. 21.5).

21.3.6 The Nivola Experience

In 1954 the Olivetti Showroom opened on 5th Avenue in Manhattan, hosting a monumental semi-abstract frieze by the Italian sculptor Costantino Nivola. In 2022, the Nivola museum, in Sardinia, Italy, organized an exhibition enriched by multimedia elements (Ahsan et al. 2022). The original 24 × 5 m artwork was digitized, and a full-scale physical replica was fabricated and integrated in the exhibition; the 3D model was also used as a base for an interactive kiosk.

The interactive kiosk has been developed by heavily customizing the tools provided by the OpenLIME framework, while the interaction is controlled through a multi-touch interface. As the frieze is mostly a 2.5D object (the depth of the decoration is quite small with respect to the total extent), the kiosk is based on a reduced representation of an orthographic color map plus normal vectors, generated from the high-resolution model. This method greatly reduces the amount of data to manage and the computational cost, while still maintaining a realistic and detailed representation.

The basic mechanism of the kiosk is allowing free navigation of the artwork, progressively presenting additional information spots according to the current view. This kiosk is thus built on top of a single technical solution, which integrates all the interactive and narrative functionalities using the same interaction paradigm. It is also interesting how the information layers are provided to the user following the flow of exploration, with an experience more akin to having a guide explaining things about the artwork following where you are looking. This approach provides a very focused and streamlined experience for the user that can dive in immediately in a way that is more natural than a classic kiosk. We believe this kind of interaction works especially well in a situation where the full artwork (or, in this case, the full-scale replica) is nearby, and the kiosk should augment, rather than fully describe, the object of interest.

Fig. 21.5 Screenshots of the interactive kiosk of the Tomba della Montagnola. First and second from top: the external, digital maquette visualization. Third and fourth from top: the internal, first-person exploration

The amount of authoring needed in this project is considerable, as the kiosk relies on the availability of multiple annotated areas in each part of the artwork to provide a continuous flow of information. Moreover, as the interaction departed from the usual "hotspot", the authoring required more effort and additional time to adjust to its quirks. This is a detail to take into account when working with non-standard

Fig. 21.6 The kiosk for the Nivola frieze in action. Annotations and information layer appear following the exploration of the artwork's surface

interaction paradigms: a more advanced and expressive paradigm may improve the interaction, but it will require more resources to fully exploit its potential (Fig. 21.6).

21.4 Conclusions

Interactive museum kiosks are an interesting opportunity to enrich an integrated CH project, and their creation is now a task that can be safely approached by digital experts, as their development has been made much more sustainable and effective through the evolution of web technologies. With the currently available software components, it is possible to build an advanced web-based kiosk application with a reasonable amount of effort.

The strategy of "developing once, deploying many times" does work: it makes the project more cost-effective, helps in reaching a wider audience, and keeps the product alive longer. While the use of web-based technology does not guarantee an indefinite lifespan, there is a steep improvement with respect to monolithic, custom, standalone software. We have successfully updated all the kiosks to follow the evolution of the browsers and libraries, and often expanded their content during their lifetime. Most of our works, including also the presented examples, are still available online even after their museum incarnation has ceased to exist.

All the presented kiosks are the result of a collaboration between a technical partner and a CH one: in these situations, communication is of paramount importance. The process of designing the interaction and the narrative, and the authoring of the content of the kiosk heavily rely on the mutual knowledge of the object of interest, the available data, and the possibilities offered by the tools.

One critical step in the life cycle of an interactive installation is the evaluation of its effectiveness, ease of use, and user impact. However, a complete evaluation requires following a specific methodology, and on-field activities such as user studies and surveys (Gockel et al. 2013). Unfortunately, these kinds of activities might be difficult to fit into a project with time and resource constraints.

In the case of the kiosk for the Arrigo VII funerary complex (Baracchini et al. 2004), a formal and articulated evaluation was carried out. This included recording the interaction of users, explicit questionnaires, and a third-party evaluation of the kiosk by a company specialized in museum applications. The results were useful for our understanding of the use of these technologies, but it proved to be a cumbersome and costly task. In most of the other cases, it was possible to gather indirect feedback, not from the final user, but from the museums. For example, in the case of the Ecce Homo interactive kiosk (Albertin et al. 2021), the guides that used the kiosk in their tour and museum staff following the visitors provided an extensive feedback on the use of the tool, completed with a list of issues and suggestions: the kiosk was thus updated and perfected to better fit their needs. Concerning the Nivola Experience (Ahsan et al. 2022), even though the kiosk itself was not subject to a formal evaluation, the effectiveness of the interaction paradigm was evaluated through a user study (Bettio et al. 2021).

To simplify the evaluation process, an interesting option that we plan to explore in future work is to instrument the kiosk software, to track information such as how many users have interacted with it, how much of the content has been reached, how much time has been spent in each part, and which functions have been used and how. Instrumenting the kiosk would also help in the development phase, for debugging and tuning the interface and interaction parameters. This process would be entirely possible using the same web-based technologies we have described, and can be done in a completely anonymous way, to satisfy modern privacy concerns.

The design and development strategies outlined in this work are formulated to make the creation of an interactive kiosk more sustainable and approachable.

However, the process still requires a non-trivial effort, mostly due to the lack of integration between the tools and the data. Modern online heritage-science platforms ease data sharing and management, but the support for presentation layers is still limited. The upcoming European Collaborative Cloud for Cultural Heritage (ECCCH) initiative (European Commission et al. 2022) could provide the opportunity to better integrate the presentation and user-oriented technologies with a solid data repository infrastructure, resulting in an easier use of scientific data for user outreach, as described in this work.

References

Agafonkin V (2011) Leaflet—an open-source JavaScript library for mobile-friendly interactive maps. Accessed April 9, 2024. https://leafletjs.com

Ahsan M, Altea G, Bettio F, Callieri M, Camarda A, Cignoni P, Gobbetti E et al (2022) Ebb & flow: uncovering Costantino Nivola's Olivetti Sandcast through 3D fabrication and virtual exploration. In: Eurographics Workshop On Graphics And Cultural Heritage (GCH '22), pp 85–94. The Eurographics Association. https://doi.org/10.2312/gch.20221230

Albertin F, Ruberto C, Cucci C, Callieri M, Potenziani M, Siotto E, Pingi P et al (2021) "Ecce Homo" by Antonello da Messina, from non-invasive investigations to data fusion and dissemination. Sci Rep 15868. https://doi.org/10.1038/s41598-021-95212-2

Allen S, Gutwill J (2004) Designing with multiple interactives: five common pitfalls. Curator Museum J 199–212. https://doi.org/10.1111/j.2151-6952.2004.tb00117.x

Apollonio FI, Foschi R, Gaiani M, Garagnani S (2021) How to analyze, preserve, and communicate Leonardo's drawing? A solution to visualize in RTR fine art graphics established from "the Best Sense". J Comput Cult Herit 30.https://doi.org/10.1145/3433606

Baracchini C, Brogi A, Callieri M, Capitani L, Cignoni P, Fasano A, Montani C et al (2004) Digital reconstruction of the Arrigo VII funerary complex. In: The 5th international symposium on virtual reality, archaeology and cultural heritage (VAST '04), pp 145–154. The Eurographics Association. https://doi.org/10.2312/VAST/VAST04/145-154

Behr J, Eschler P, Jung Y, Zöllner M (2009) X3DOM: a DOM-based HTML5/X3D integration model. In: Proceedings of the 14th international conference on 3D web technology (Web3D '09), pp 127–135. Association for Computing Machinery. https://doi.org/10.1145/1559764.1559784

Bettio F, Ahsan M, Marton F, Gobbetti E (2021) A novel approach for exploring annotated data with interactive lenses. Comput Grap Forum 387–398

Biørn-Hansen A, Majchrzak T, Grønli T (2017) Progressive web apps: the possible web-native unifier for mobile development. In: 13th international conference on web information systems and technologies (WEBIST '17), pp 344–351. SciTePress. https://doi.org/10.5220/0006353703440351

Bruno F, Bruno S, De Sensi G, Luchi M-L, Mancuso S, Muzzupappa M (2010) From 3D reconstruction to virtual reality: a complete methodology for digital archaeological exhibition. J Cult Herit 42–49. https://doi.org/10.1016/j.culher.2009.02.006

Burmistrov I (2015) Touchscreen Kiosks in museums. interUX. Accessed April 9, 2024. https://interux.com/resources-usability-UX.html

Cabello R (2010) Three.js. Accessed April 9, 2024. https://threejs.org/

Callieri M, Pingi P, Potenziani M, Dellepiane M, Pavoni G, Lureau A, Scopigno R (2015) Alchemy in 3D: a digitization for a journey through matter. In: 2015 digital heritage, pp 223–230. IEEE. https://doi.org/10.1109/DigitalHeritage.2015.7413875

Canevese EP, De Gottardo T (2017) Beyond point clouds and virtual reality. Innovative methods and technologies for the protection and promotion of cultural heritage. Int Arch Photogramm Remote Sens Spat Inf Sci 685–691. https://doi.org/10.5194/isprs-archives-XLII-5-W1-685-2017

Carrozzino M, Bergamasco M (2010) Beyond virtual museums: experiencing immersive virtual reality in real museums. J Cult Herit 452–458.https://doi.org/10.1016/j.culher.2010.04.001

Catuhe D, Rousset D (2013) BabylonJS. Accessed April 9, 2024. https://www.babylonjs.com/

Coast S (2004) OpenStreetMap. Accessed April 9, 2024. https://www.openstreetmap.org/

Eastcott W, Evans D, Kalpias-Ilias V, Rooney K, Mihejevs M (2014) PlayCanvas. Accessed April 9, 2024. https://playcanvas.com/

European Commission, Directorate-General for Research and Innovation, Brunet P, De Luca L, Hyvönen E, Joffres A, Plassmeyer P, Pronk M, Scopigno R, Sonkoly G (2022) Report on a European collaborative cloud for cultural heritage: ex—ante impact assessment. Publications Office of the European Union. https://doi.org/10.2777/64014

Fanini B, Ferdani D, Demetrescu E (2021a) Temporal lensing: an interactive and scalable technique for Web3D/WebXR applications in cultural heritage. Heritage 710–724. https://doi.org/10.3390/heritage4020040

Fanini B, Ferdani D, Demetrescu E, Berto S, d'Annibale E (2021b) ATON: an open-source framework for creating immersive, collaborative and liquid web-apps for cultural heritage. Appl Sci 11062.https://doi.org/10.3390/app11221062

Gaballo A (2021) Museums, museum professionals and Covid-19: third survey. In: ICOM—international council of museums. Accessed April 9, 2024. https://icom.museum/en/news/museums-and-covid-19-third-icom-report/

Gockel B, Graf H, Pagano A, Pescarin S, Eriksson J (2013) VMUXE: an approach to user experience evaluation for virtual museums. In: Design, user experience, and usability. design philosophy, methods, and tools (DUXU '13), pp 262–272. Springer. https://doi.org/10.1007/978-3-642-39229-0_29

Gonizzi Barsanti S, Caruso G, Micoli LL, Covarrubias Rodriguez M, Guidi G (2015) 3D visualization of cultural heritage artefacts with virtual reality devices. Int Arch Photogramm Remote Sens Spat Inf Sci 165–172.https://doi.org/10.5194/isprsarchives-XL-5-W7-165-2015

Gonizzi Barsanti S, Malatesta SG, Lella F, Fanini B, Sala F, Dodero E, Petacco L (2018) The Winckelmann300 project: dissemination of culture with virtual reality at the Capito-line Museum in Rome. Int Arch Photogramm Remote Sens Spat Inf Sci 371–378. https://doi.org/10.5194/isprs-archives-XLII-2-371-2018

Google Inc. (2018) *<model-viewer>*. Accessed April 9, 2024. https://modelviewer.dev/

ISTI—CNR, Biblioteca Medicea Laurenziana—MiBAC, Istituto Mesrop Mashtots di manoscritti antichi—MATENADARAN, and Ambasciata d'Italia in Armenia (2019) Three Armenian manuscripts from Tuscany. Accessed April 9, 2024. https://vcg.isti.cnr.it/activities/armenia/

ISTI—CNR, ISPC—CNR, Comune di Sesto Fiorentino, Sesto Fiorentino Associazione Turistica Proloco, and SABAP (2020) La tomba della Montagnola Virtual Tour. Accessed April 9, 2024. https://vcg.isti.cnr.it/activities/montagnola/

Kalarat K, Rattanarungrot S (2020) Natural interaction design for navigation in virtual environment of Sino-Portuguese architecture in museum. Walailak J Sci Technol 17(11).1266–1276. https://doi.org/10.48048/wjst.2021.6493

Khronos Group Inc. (2011) WebGL—OpenGL ES for the web. Accessed Apr 9, 2024. https://www.khronos.org/api/webgl

Liarokapis F, Sylaiou S, Mountain D (2008) Personalizing virtual and augmented reality for cultural heritage indoor and outdoor experiences. In: The 9th international symposium on virtual reality, archaeology and intelligent cultural heritage (VAST '08), pp 55–62. The Eurographics Association. https://doi.org/10.2312/VAST/VAST08/055-062

Marcos D, McCurdy D, Ngo K (2015) A-frame—a web framework for building 3D/AR/VR experiences. Accessed April 9, 2024. https://aframe.io/

Marty PF, Jones K (2007) Museum informatics: people, information, and technology in museums. Routledge, New York. https://doi.org/10.4324/9780203939147

Matterport Inc. (2011) Matterport. Accessed April 9, 2024. https://matterport.com/
MetaCarta (2006) OpenLayers—a high-performance, feature-packed library for all your mapping needs. Accessed April 9, 2024. https://openlayers.org/
Micoli LL, Caruso G, Guidi G (2020) Design of digital interaction for complex museum collections. Multimod Technol Interact 31. https://doi.org/10.3390/mti4020031
Microsoft Corporation (1998) Microsoft remote desktop. Accessed April 9, 2024. https://apps.microsoft.com/detail/9wzdncrfj3ps
O'dwyer N, Zerman E, Young GW, Smolic A, Dunne S, Shenton H (2021) Volumetric video in augmented reality applications for museological narratives: a user study for the long room in the library of Trinity College Dublin. J Comput Cult Herit 20. https://doi.org/10.1145/3425400
Origlia A, Chiacchio ML, Grazioso M, Cutugno F (2023) Increasing visitors attention with introductory portal technology to complex cultural sites. Int J Hum Comput Stud 103135. https://doi.org/10.1016/j.ijhcs.2023.103135
Palma G, Siotto E, Proesmans M, Baldassari M, Baracchini C, Batino S, Scopigno R (2014) Telling the story of ancient coins by means of interactive RTI images visualization. In: Archaeology in the digital era: papers from the 40th annual conference of computer applications and quantitative methods in archaeology (CAA '12), pp 177–185. Amsterdam University Press. https://doi.org/10.1515/9789048519590-019
Palma G, Perry S, Cignoni P (2021) Augmented virtuality using touch-sensitive 3D-printed objects. Remote Sens 2186. https://doi.org/10.3390/rs13112186
Petroff MA (2019) Pannellum: a lightweight web-based panorama viewer. J Open Sour Softw 1628.https://doi.org/10.21105/joss.01628
Ponchio F, Corsini M, Scopigno R (2019) RELIGHT: a compact and accurate RTI representation for the web. Graph Models 101040. https://doi.org/10.1016/j.gmod.2019.101040
Potenziani M, Callieri M, Dellepiane M, Corsini M, Ponchio F, Scopigno R (2015) 3DHOP: 3D heritage online presenter. Comput Graph 129–141. https://doi.org/10.1016/j.cag.2015.07.001
Schaller A, Biedenkapp T, Keil J, Fellner DW, Kuijper A (2015) Immersive interaction paradigms for controlling virtual worlds by customer devices exemplified in a virtual planetarium. In: Universal access in human-computer interaction. Access to the human environment and culture (UAHCI '15), pp 74–86. Springer International Publishing. https://doi.org/10.1007/978-3-319-20687-5_8
Schütz M (2016) Potree: rendering large point clouds in web browsers, Master Thesis. Vienna University of Technology. https://www.cg.tuwien.ac.at/research/publications/2016/SCHUETZ-2016-POT/
Siotto E, Palma G, Scopigno R (2017) Development of the interactive system digital Loggia. In: Sgamellotti A, Caneva G (eds) The loggia of cupid and psyche—Raffaello and Giovanni da Udine—colours of prosperity: fruits from the old and new world, pp 74–77. Bardi Edizioni
Steiner T (2018) What is in a web view: an analysis of progressive web app features when the means of web access is not a web browser. In: Companion proceedings of the the web conference 2018 (WWW '18), pp 789–796. International World Wide Web Conferences Steering Committee. https://doi.org/10.1145/3184558.3188742
Sylaiou S, Liarokapis F, Kotsakis F, Patias P (2009) Virtual museums, a survey and some issues for consideration. J Cult Herit 520–528https://doi.org/10.1016/j.culher.2009.03.003
TeamViewer SE (2005) TeamViewer. Accessed April 9, 2024. https://www.teamviewer.com
The Smithsonian Institution (2018) Smithsonian Voyager. Accessed April 9, 2024. https://smithsonian.github.io/dpo-voyager/
Umezu N, Koizumi S, Nakagawa K, Nishida S (2023) Potential of low-cost light detection and ranging (LiDAR) sensors: case studies for enhancing visitor experience at a science museum. Electronics 3351. https://doi.org/10.3390/electronics12153351
Vlahakis V, Ioannidis M, Karigiannis J, Tsotros M, Gounaris M, Stricker D, Gleue T, Daehne P, Almeida L (2002) Archeoguide: an augmented reality guide for archaeological sites. IEEE Comput Graph Appl 52–60.https://doi.org/10.1109/MCG.2002.1028726

W3C—World Wide Web Consortium (2008) HTML 5 Living Standard. Accessed April 9, 2024. https://html.spec.whatwg.org/

Wilkinson MD, Dumontier M, Aalbersberg I, Appleton G, Axton M, Baak A, Blomberg N et al (2016) The FAIR guiding principles for scientific data management and stewardship. Sci Data 160018.https://doi.org/10.1038/sdata.2016.18

Chapter 22
Interactive Tangible and Intangible Heritage Applications Built on Real-Time Graphics Systems: Heritage Experiences in Desktop CG, Virtual and Augmented Reality

Eike Falk Anderson, Valery Adzhiev, Paul Cheetham, Glyn Hadley, David John, Catja Larsson, Ana-Maria-Cristina Ureche, and Mario Romero

Abstract Modern virtual environment infrastructure, most commonly encountered in the guise of game engines, provide the means for the creation of a wide range of applications across the breadth of the cultural heritage domain, i.e. encompassing both tangible and intangible heritage. This chapter will list and discuss different types of interactive heritage applications, including museum exhibits, games and mobile apps, illustrated with a set of case studies that will highlight aspects of the real-time computer graphics technology of virtual environments that are particularly useful for cultural heritage.

E. F. Anderson (✉) · V. Adzhiev
The National Centre for Computer Animation,Bournemouth University,Poole, UK
e-mail: eanderson@bournemouth.ac.uk

V. Adzhiev
e-mail: vadzhiev@bournemouth.ac.uk

P. Cheetham
Department of Archaeology and Anthropology,Bournemouth University,Poole, UK
e-mail: pcheetham@bournemouth.ac.uk

G. Hadley · D. John
Department of Creative Technology, Bournemouth University, Poole, UK
e-mail: ghadley@bournemouth.ac.uk

D. John
e-mail: djohn@bournemouth.ac.uk

C. Larsson · A.-M.-C. Ureche
Bournemouth University, Poole, UK

M. Romero
Department of Computational Science and Technology, KTH Royal Institute of Technology, Stockholm, Sweden

Department of Science and Technology, Linköping University, Linköping, Sweden
e-mail: mario.romero@liu.se

F. Liarokapis et al. (eds.), *Interactive Media for Cultural Heritage*, Springer Series on Cultural Computing, https://doi.org/10.1007/978-3-031-61018-9_22

22.1 Introduction

Over the past two decades, the technology that allows the creation of interactive computer graphics applications has made massive strides. The exploration of new business models by the developers of game engines, the software systems at the heart of most interactive graphics applications, mean that these software systems are now widely available at low costs. Following in the wake of the advent of smartphones, we have witnessed the appearance of Augmented Reality (AR), as well as the consumer market introduction of Virtual Reality (VR) head-mounted displays (HMDs), making VR accessible to much wider audiences than earlier VR systems. These technologies also allow the development of interactive heritage applications and experiences, with games technologies having established themselves as the preferred infrastructure for interactive heritage experiences. Interactive heritage applications can provide immersive experiences for their users and are therefore not just suitable for visualising tangible heritage, but ideal for conveying intangible cultural heritage.

In this chapter, we first provide a brief overview of the state of the art of interactive heritage experiences built on real-time graphics systems. This is followed by a discussion of different types of applications from the range of interactive heritage experiences, presented in the form of case studies that demonstrate the use of real time graphics systems in the creation of such heritage experiences, spanning both tangible and intangible heritage and highlighting aspects for consideration during the development of such interactive heritage experiences.

22.2 Previous and Related Work

Game engines and related technologies, i.e. the infrastructure for the creation of interactive virtual worlds in computer games, are becoming increasingly popular and relevant for the development of interactive virtual heritage experiences. The proliferation of this type of off-the-shelf software (Anderson et al., 2020) has not only reduced development costs, but has also made the technology for creating virtual worlds more accessible, facilitating the creation of interactive applications in an ever growing number of subject domains. Anderson et al. (2010) provided an early overview of the possibilities offered by these software systems, particularly in the context of cultural heritage serious games, which are a common application of games technology to the cultural heritage domain (Anastasovitis et al., 2017), while, more recently, Buratti and Amoruso (2022), compared several available game engines that are suitable for the development of cultural heritage applications.

One type of heritage application that can make use of this technology are virtual museums and galleries that use the 3D environments facilitated by game engines to create virtual exhibition spaces, as demonstrated by the DynaMus framework (Kiourt et al., 2016). They are prime examples for the public presentation of cultural heritage, which is the main application area for interactive real-time computer graphics systems in the cultural heritage domain. Virtual museums and exhibitions are related to virtual tours, which in turn are frequently used in conjunction with heritage tourism, where they can exist as in situ experiences, sometimes employing VR, or mobile applications in the guise of smartphone or tablet apps. One such mobile app is the game "Travel Tycoon Greece" (Rallis et al., 2022), in which players take on the role of a travel agent, using this as a means to introduce players to these sites and possibly plan their own real-life journeys. A similarly unusual approach was applied by Meier et al. (2020), who experimented with user-created virtual tours, encouraging secondary school students to engage with their cultural heritage by developing their own virtual tours.

Real-time visualisations using games technologies just make up one aspect of interactive heritage experiences, with these technologies also facilitating mixed reality experiences. The use of mobile Augmented Reality (AR) in heritage applications was one of the earliest applications of mixed-reality technologies (Choudary et al., 2009), quickly following the advent of smartphones, and the use of AR has become popular, not only in the context of heritage tourism (Voinea et al., 2019), but also for the creation of other types of interactive applications in the cultural heritage domain (Boboc et al., 2022).

The fairly recent availability of consumer-grade VR equipment, such as HMDs, and the application of these technologies to the cultural heritage domain have in turn led to the development of new methods and techniques to support the creation of applications that employ VR hardware, such as approaches to simulate human-like navigation in VR (Hernández Ibáñez and Naya, 2015) or workflows for the creation of realistic digital reconstructions of cultural heritage sites (Cipriani et al., 2019).

One of the main aims of such applications is to immerse users in the heritage and to create a sense of cultural presence, and modern game engines, such as Unity or Unreal Engine, have been shown to facilitate this (Fredrick, 2014), and they can also greatly simplify the creation of VR experiences (Meegan et al., 2021) or similar applications. For example, a certain degree of immersion can also be achieved by employing a CAVE installation, trying to achieve VR-like immersion without the need for a VR headset, as recently demonstrated by Codina et al. (2017), who created their so-called "immersive room" to present a virtual reconstruction of the ancient Iberian town Ullastret in the Archaeological Museum of Catalonia. Greater immersion can be achieved using HMD based VR applications, such as the one developed by Häkkilä et al. (2019), who created a VR experience to facilitate virtual visits to an otherwise inaccessible heritage site. AlMuraikhi et al. (2021) describe the workflow they employed to develop a VR virtual tour of a heritage site in Quatar, for which they created a detailed digital replica with the aid of 3D photogrammetry, similar to the work by Dhanda et al. (2019), who used photogrammetry for digitising a temple in Bagan for use in a VR environment.

One approach towards maximising immersion was proposed by Duer et al. (2020), who created a mixed-reality exhibition, combining VR with a physical reconstruction of a heritage site, aligned with and mapped to the VR environment to provide a tangible, tactile experience for visitors, as well as physical props—proxy objects—to facilitate passive haptics (Joyce and Robinson, 2017), increasing the immersion of visitors in the virtual heritage experience. More recently, Malý et al. (2023) demonstrated the use of VR in museum education programmes by Prague City Museum, allowing young visitors to virtually recreate the experience of constructing paper model buildings in a similar manner to those displayed in a nineteenth century city model that is on display in the museum. An emerging type of interactive heritage application is related to Computer Art that can be either generated in real time and/or can be experienced in VR/AR environments. There are two main perspectives to Computer Art in that context. First, it can be used as a vehicle to preserve, mimic or reimagine existing, "traditional" artworks. Secondly, Computer Art can be considered as art in its own right in terms of original artistic forms and content different from traditional ones to become "heritage of the future". One of the established directions is so-called "generative art" which means artefacts procedurally generated by a computer program in an automated or even random manner, using mathematical algorithms often related to themes of natural evolution and artificial life and representing dynamic complex systems able to generate endless variations in real-time. Artist and game designer William Latham has been a prominent figure in this kind of art since the late 1980s. An example of his recent work is Mutator VR, which is an art installation mixing "real" and "unreal" visual effects inspired by Surrealist art, creating a highly immersive psychedelic organic experience (Latham et al., 2021).

22.3 Heritage Applications of Interactive Real-Time Graphics Systems

While some form of presentation of heritage content is the main application area for interactive real-time graphics systems in the heritage domain, these technologies are not limited to this, but they can also be used as tools, e.g. to aid archaeologists with testing reconstruction hypotheses (Rua and Alvito, 2011) or to streamline heritage conservation efforts (Ma, 2021).

One of the benefits of presenting heritage using real-time interactive virtual environments is the ability of these systems to fully immerse users in the heritage, allowing them to not only act as passive observers but as active participants. This active participation means that these systems are not only applicable to create experiences of tangible heritage, but their interactive nature means that they are ideal for conveying intangible cultural heritage (Anderson, 2013) to their users, independent of whether the heritage is experienced in a screen-based virtual environment, as AR or as VR. Many modern game engines, such as Unity or Unreal Engine, provide the means for developers to create all of these types of interactive heritage experiences, screen-based, AR or VR, with these modes of interaction either supported natively or facilitated by plug-ins.

The case studies below show the breadth of different heritage experiences that can be created using real-time interactive game engines.

22.3.1 *AR Visualisation of a Roman Villa*

This case study reviews the early stages of the creation of an AR visualisation of Frampton Roman villa in Dorset using off-the-shelf development software. The villa is not a popular tourist destination, and the motivation was not to encourage further visitors, but to create virtual interactive visualisations representing the latest findings from the investigations conducted by Bournemouth University between 2018 and 2021.

22.3.1.1 The Roman Villa at Frampton, Dorset

Frampton Roman villa was located within a water meadow near the River Frome in central Dorset. The site was first excavated in the 1790 s after several Roman mosaics were discovered. The mosaics were remarkable for the inclusion of early Christian imagery alongside depictions of earlier Roman mythology (Perring, 2003). Samuel Lysons (1813) carefully recorded the appearance of the mosaics, but not the overall structure of the parts of the building that did not contain mosaics. For many years, the location was presumed lost until a geophysical survey and exploratory excavations were undertaken by Bournemouth University to re-establish the precise location (Cheetham et al., 2018; Russell et al., 2022). The results of the investigations found parts of the mosaics still intact and demonstrated that there were two distinct phases of development of the villa. The earliest phase is undated but consisted of a villa with a central range facing the south east, with two side ranges forming a conventional courtyard villa layout. By the fourth century, the valley had silted, raising the ground level and presumably causing flooding, and so in the second phase a new villa was built up on top of the original central range. Today there is little sign of the villa above ground except for a protective mound of soil and flints where the buildings with mosaics once stood.

22.3.1.2 Requirements for the AR App

An AR app was proposed that would allow users to explore both phases of Frampton Roman villa at life size (Fig. 22.1). The app would be implemented using off-the-shelf development software (Anderson et al., 2020). Many early examples of the use of AR at Cultural Heritage sites were relatively small, ranging from a few centimetres to a few metres (Boboc et al., 2022; Silva and Teixeira, 2022). More recently the representation of larger models has become more common, such as the mosaic floors displayed inside the museum at Modena (Gherardini et al., 2019). Larger objects, such as the AR visualisation of Maiden Castle (Anderson, 2021), are often displayed at a reduced scale. Examples of large life-size AR overlays include the visualisation of Sheffield Castle (Leach et al., 2018) the old town of Chania, Crete (Panou et al., 2018), the Forum at Conimbriga (Marto and Gonçalves, 2019), designed to be viewed at a distance, and Caistor Roman market place that uses GPS to display a visualisation

Fig. 22.1 Visualisations from different iterations of the Frampton Roman villa AR and VR apps (Top left, the AR app tested on Bournemouth Beach; top right, at Nunnery Mead; bottom right, the interior mosaics; bottom left, the VR version of the two phases of the villa)

of a market square surrounded by buildings, over what is now a featureless field (Bowden et al., 2023). The AR app of Frampton Roman villa contributes to this activity by investigating the ability of AR to represent buildings with a length of about 50 metres and allow users to explore inside without losing tracking.

The development software was selected by comparing alternative AR frameworks (Bekele et al., 2018; González Vargas et al., 2020; Midya and Maity, 2021). Low cost off-the-shelf software were considered that supported both marker and markerless tracking methods (Bekele et al., 2018; Kolivand et al., 2018). Unity with Vuforia were chosen.

22.3.1.3 Development of the AR App

Separate 3D models of the villa were created for the two stages of the villa, using the drawings made in the 1790 s as textures for the mosaics. The app has three operation modes: firstly, field (for outdoor use in large empty open spaces), secondly, home (which can be operated using on screen controls) and thirdly desktop (which allows the user to view the villa at a smaller scale). It was decided not to restrict the AR experience to the original location at Frampton as it was anticipated that few users would have the opportunity to use the app at this location. Nunnery Mead Nature Reserve is not fully accessible to the public except for a path that runs along the side of the river (Dorset Wildlife Trust, 2023). The ground level has continued to change since the Roman era, and the overgrown mound that runs along the central range would prevent users of the AR app having access to the main part of the villa. A major development decision was how to place the villa on the screen, with the three main options being the use of marker-based, markerless or location-based

(GPS) technologies (Cheng et al., 2017; Siriwardhana et al., 2021). As the AR app was to be used in remote locations it was not appropriate to use GPS technology. Similarly, it was not possible to use markers as the user needed to move their phone to navigate around the villa and could not constantly keep their phone pointing at a marker. Historically, registration and tracking was a major problem for markerless AR, and even in 2018 Panou et al. (2018) still reported significant challenges. The situation has eased with the increased computing power of modern mobile phones, and the Frampton Roman villa app was able to make use of the Vuforia markerless Ground Plane tool to place the AR content (Vuforia, 2023). Using the field mode, the user can select the phase and place the corresponding villa model on the screen by pointing their phone at the ground until the ground plane is detected, then tapping on the screen at the desired location. The user can then move their phone freely. The home mode can be explored using an on-screen joystick and a teleport system. In both the field and home modes two types of hotspot can be selected by the user, one to view a display of information and the second to view individual 3D models using a handheld marker. The first two modes present the visualisations at life size, while the desktop mode displays the villa resized to fit on top of a desk which can be explored by walking around the presentation and pointing the camera. This mode allows the model to be examined from different angles that are not possible using the other two modes.

22.3.1.4 Initial Evaluation

A mid-range mobile phone (a two year old Huawei p20 Pro mobile phone running Android 10) was chosen to perform the testing. Three contrasting open spaces that were wide enough to place the full sized visualisation of the villa were chosen in the centre of Bournemouth to test the app. The surfaces included a sandy beach, a grass and tarmac area and an open area with paving tiles. The Ground Plane technology worked well enough to detect the ground and allow the user to place the model in each location. The dimensions appeared correct, and the app was able to keep tracking consistently as the tester walked through the virtual villas. Although the chosen open spaces appeared to be on level ground at first sight, there were variations in the ground level that affected the perception of movement through the building. The profile of the beach was not flat but sloped down towards the sea which means that the user can experience a sensation of flying when physically walking up or down hill. The ground level of the grass and tarmac area similarly slopes down to a road which resulted in the display of the far end of the building floating above the road. This effect can become more exaggerated the further the user is away from the villa, which can lead to the whole virtual building appearing to float in mid-air. The paving tiles were in a large flat area that matched the floor level of the villa and no height issues were detected, however there were more obstacles in this environment which could cause obstruction hazards. The location of the 3D models can be adjusted to match the changes in ground level in a number of ways. The models could be automatically raised or lowered to match the current distance of the mobile phone from the ground, however that would be sensitive to the user lifting or lowering their mobile phone during their exploration of the environment. If the 3D model of the building was made in a more modular manner and content is streamed, it may be possible to calibrate the height of the room relative to the current ground level as new modules are streamed. Alternatively, the user could be provided with controls to manually lower the model if they choose. The issue of physical obstacles needs to be further investigated, and if there is a potential health and safety problem, solutions will have to be found, such as making the virtual overlay more transparent to make the user more aware of the real-world obstacles. Using default lighting settings made the exterior of the virtual villa appear flat when overlayed on the real-world environment. The interior rooms have point lights applied which contribute to a more lifelike appearance. The home mode version also worked well. The users are able to navigate around the virtual environment using an on-screen joystick control and teleport options. The villas have relatively straightforward designs but the environment is approaching the size where users could feel disoriented, especially if they have used the teleport system. It would be useful to provide users with some additional navigational support, such as an overhead map indicating their current location. An additional problem in home mode is that users are still able to walk through walls, which spoils the immersive experience. The desktop version uses markerless AR to display a smaller scale version of the villa that can fit on a desktop. A slider is provided for the user to set the scale. Best results in the testing have been achieved by placing the virtual model on the floor rather than on top of a desk.

22.3.2 Romanian Easter Egg Decoration: Using AR to Convey Intangible Heritage

This case study is concerned with a different application area of AR, employing this in the context of conveying intangible heritage, namely the Romanian tradition of Easter Egg Decoration using a mobile app, making use of a 3D printed AR marker (Ureche et al., 2022) to provide a tactile interactive heritage experience.

22.3.2.1 The Tradition of Easter Egg Decoration

The Romanian tradition of Easter egg decoration is deeply rooted in the Christian Orthodox belief of the majority of the country's population. The most common and widespread method of decorating eggs is by dyeing them red. The origin of this tradition is uncertain, as symbols and traditions involving decorated eggs have been observed even before Christianity. The egg, chosen as a symbol by many cultures, represents the potential for life despite its initial lifelessness. In Romanian Orthodox belief, the egg is associated with the triumph of good over evil. By dyeing the eggs red, Romanians believe they are protected from evil, and the eggs were often used as lucky charms or protectors in households. They were also buried in the land to enhance its fertility and carried around by individuals.

The exact origins of the Romanian tradition of dyeing eggs are not documented, but written mentions of the tradition date back to the late seventeenth century. Different regions had their own variations of the tradition, but most of them involved decorating the eggs during the week of Easter Sunday, a significant period for Orthodox Christians commemorating the events leading to the crucifixion.

There are four main types of Romanian Easter eggs:

- Monochrome eggs: These eggs are dyed in a single colour, with red being the most common. Other colours, e.g. yellow, green, blue and black, were also used.
- Monochrome eggs with ornaments: These eggs feature additional decorative elements.
- Polychrome eggs with ornaments: These eggs require great skill and patience. The decorative motifs are created layer by layer using beeswax as a mask before dipping the egg into dye. The wax is applied selectively to block areas for each colour, creating intricate patterns. After the final stage, the wax is melted off to reveal the completed design.
- Eggs with 3D ornaments: Popular in the Vrancea region, these eggs are adorned with layered colourful wax, creating a three-dimensional effect resembling sculptures.

In the creation of ornamental eggs, artists traditionally used a wooden stick with a metal nib to apply melted wax in intricate patterns on the eggs. This method required precision and attention to detail. The motifs and patterns used on the eggs are diverse and often rooted in religious symbolism (such as crosses), nature (flowers, fruits, cereals, clover), animals (roosters, duck feet) and other cultural elements (such as chariot wheels or ploughs). The choice of colours can also provide clues about the regional origin of a design (Glăveanu, 2013). The art of egg decoration, known as "ouă încondeiate", has been practised for generations, and intricate techniques, motifs, and symbolism are passed down from one artisan to another (Gorovei, 1937). Overall, the Romanian tradition of Easter egg decoration reflects the religious beliefs, cultural heritage and artistic craftsmanship of the Romanian Orthodox population, with various techniques and styles passed down through generations (Murgoci, 1909).

22.3.2.2 An Immersive Experience for the New Generation

We have developed a prototype for a mobile Augmented Reality (AR) app that aims to preserve the folk art of decorating Easter eggs (Fig. 22.2a), which is an essential part of Romania's intangible cultural heritage. Our app allows users to virtually decorate eggs using a 3D printed egg as a physical AR marker. This approach enables tangible interaction with the egg, simulating the traditional decorating process. In order to create an authentic and immersive experience we studied the expertise and artwork of Ileana Hotopila, a renowned Romanian folk artist, whose exceptional mastery in

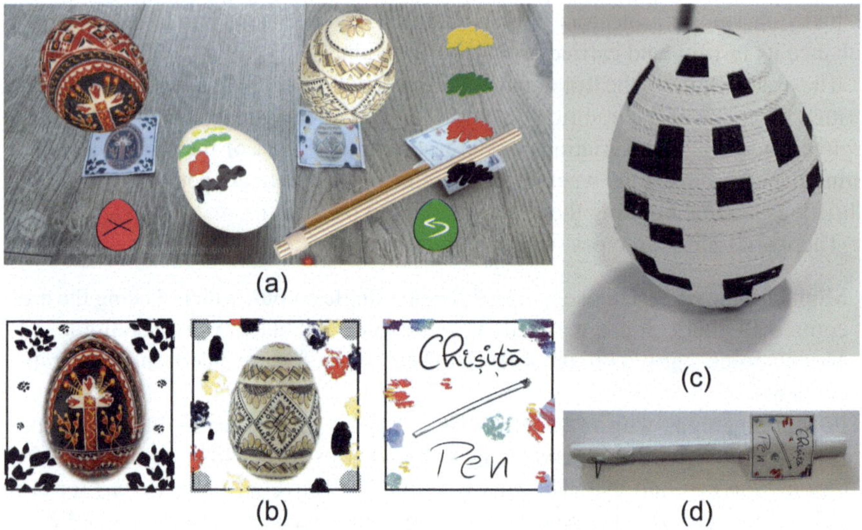

Fig. 22.2 Romanian Easter Egg decoration AR app: **a** screenshot of the app; **b** AR markers for the stylus (right) and two example decorated eggs; **c** 3D printed AR target (3D egg model); **d** Stylus (with AR marker) for drawing on the AR egg

traditional egg decoration served as a valuable reference for the development of the AR app.

The tradition of Easter egg decoration in Romania, as well as in other Eastern European countries, is an example of threatened intangible heritage and folk art. It is a fading tradition due to the skills and patience required for the intricate process. Decorating a single egg can take several hours, deterring the younger generation, particularly those born and raised in the era of instant gratification provided by social media and on-demand entertainment. To bridge the gap between the younger generation and traditional activities, our project utilises interactive digital media and mobile apps. By integrating the heritage craft into an AR application, we aim to attract younger demographic groups and revitalise interest in this traditional art form. Our AR app recreates the experience of Easter egg decoration with wax in an entertaining and interactive manner, introducing traditional Romanian egg decorating patterns to both children and adults.

Unlike traditional 2D markers used in AR applications, we use 3D markers in the form of egg-shaped, 3D printed models (Fig. 22.2c) with a black-and-white pattern (Mann and Fryazinov, 2019). These markers, created through 3D printing technology, enhance the user's experience by providing a tactile feel and mimicking the weight of real eggs. The app requires a smartphone, the 3D printed egg marker and a 2D marker for the pen/brush (Fig. 22.2b, d). Users can freely paint on the egg by moving the pen (with the attached 2D marker) while looking through their smartphone's screen. Our solution for preserving the Romanian folk art of Easter egg decoration is a game-like AR app that utilises a 3D printed egg as an AR marker. To inspire users, the app also showcases digitised hand-decorated Easter eggs by Ileana Hotopila, providing authentic examples of traditional decoration patterns.

We developed the core application using the Unity game engine and integrated AR through the Vuforia plugin. The assets, including 3D models and textures, were created using standard software such as Autodesk Maya for 3D modelling, Adobe Photoshop for textures and Meshroom for generating egg models from photogrammetry. While our prototype has limitations regarding the AR tracking of the 3D printed egg, it offers users a unique experience of freely drawing/painting on the egg. The app allows for tactile and visual interactions, with users physically holding the egg and pen while observing the results through their smartphone's screen.

22.3.3 Virtual and Augmented Reality Interactive Exhibit at the Mediterranean Museum of Stockholm

This case study presents the design process, evaluation and deployment of a mixed reality exhibit at the Mediterranean Museum of Stockholm, Sweden. The exhibit included virtual and augmented reality (VR, AR) interactive experiences of geographical, historical and cultural contextualization. The project deployed off-the-shelf hardware and the Unity game engine as the development and deployment platforms. We focused on the 7000-year-old exhibit of the Cyprus collection, the largest assemblage of Cypriot statuettes in the world outside of Cyprus. Researchers from KTH Royal Institute of Technology and the Mediterranean Museum collaborated on the project from its inception in October 2016, through its development and testing cycles, until its public opening in April 2018, as well as its temporary exhibit between April 2018 and February 2019, and concluding with its analysis and publication into a Master thesis report in April 2019 (Mataruga, 2019). The project was funded by BFUF, the hospitality industry's research and development fund in Sweden.

22.3.3.1 The Cyprus Collection at Medelhavsmuséet (the Museum of Mediterranean and Near Eastern Antiquities)

The Mediterranean Museum of Stockholm (Medelhavsmuséet) houses the largest and most important collection of Cypriot statuettes outside of Cyprus (Winbladh, 2003). The collection is the result of the Swedish Cyprus Expedition (1927–1931) to methodically investigate archaeological sites including Agia Eirini, Lapithos and Marion. The expedition recovered over 10,000 objects from 295 graves at 30 excavation sites. The objects consist mainly of pottery sculptures as well as some metal, ivory and glass objects. The leaders of the expedition were archaeologists Einar Gjerstad, Erik Sjöqvist, and Alfred Westholm and architect John Lindros.

The main physical Cyprus exhibition consists of over 1000 clay statuettes excavated from the Agia Irini sanctuary located at the northern coast of Cyprus (see Fig. 22.3). The small rural sanctuary at Agia Irini lies at Morphou Bay on the north

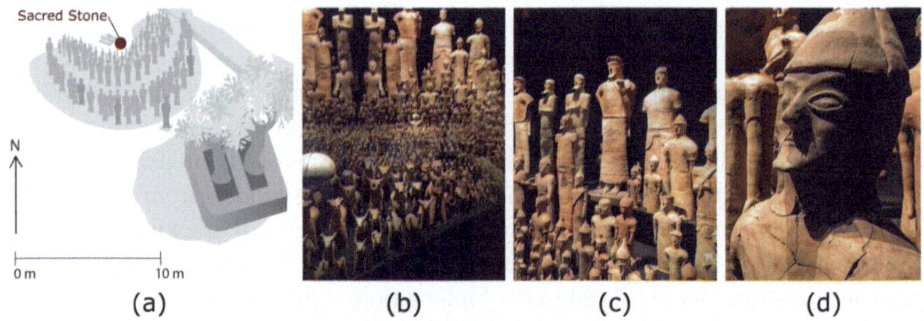

Fig. 22.3 The Cyprus collection at the Mediterranean Museum of Stockholm: **a** a model of the excavation site with the sacred stone highlighted; **b** the exhibit at the museum of more than a thousand figurines and a model of the sacred stone in the foreground; **c** detail of full-body figures; **d** detail of a head

coast of the island between the ancient cities of Soli and Lapithos. It was in use from 1200-100 BC. About 2000 terracotta statuettes were discovered in their original position facing an altar and a cultic stone. Today one half of these figurines are displayed in Stockholm and the other half at the Cyprus Museum in Nicosia.

The busiest period of the sanctuary was 700–500 BC, when most of the terracotta figures were placed as a dedication. The cult centred on sacred trees, an old altar and a holy shelter. In front of the altar stood an egg-shaped stone, called a "Baetylus", a sacred symbol endowing its worshipers life and fertility (see Fig. 22.3).

The terracotta figures were gifts to the gods which served as substitutes for the worshipers, whose social status was expressed by the features of the figure. The attributes include the figurine's size, facial characteristics, hats and clothing, and colour patterns. While colours have faded, through microscopic analysis we know the figures were painted in patterns of bright reds and blacks. Almost all of the human figures depicted men, including priests, soldiers, musicians and farmers. The male figures stood in a semicircle around the altar. The main exceptions include a series of bulls, a group of dual-sexed centaurs and a goddess seated on a throne flanked by sphinxes. These were separated from the human figures, confined to two areas: in a circle next to the altar and on a table east of the ramp leading towards the holy shelter.

22.3.3.2 Design of the VR and AR Experiences

The museum's goal for the mixed reality extension was to increase the immersion and interaction between the visitors and the exhibit. The curators wanted to contextualise the exhibit to its geographical, historical and cultural dimensions through immersive experiences. Through participatory design discussions, KTH researchers and museum curators designed a three-step experience for visitors. The first step of the experience was to design your own statuette using AR interacting directly with the 3D object through the touchscreen of a smartphone provided by the museum. The second step places visitors on the island using VR with a smartphone on a heads-up

Fig. 22.4 The three steps of the mixed reality Cyprus collection experience: (1) users create their own statuettes in AR using the exhibit poster as a tracking image; (2) the user places the statuette on the virtual island through immersive VR interaction by tapping the headset; and (3) the user can view their statuette offering from the air using AR. In this image, the children discovered they could stack statuettes into a tower. A back-lit photograph of the 1917 excavation is the image tracked. The users in the AR and VR Explorers can see each other in the virtual environment

display (HUD) case. There, users place their statuette in the location of their choice around the altar. Finally, users can return to AR and view the island from above, see where they placed their statuette, and interact with users in VR (see Fig. 22.4).

The experience starts with a short onboarding video that explains the historical and geographical context of the exhibit as well as the cultural function of the statuettes, as explained above. The video plays on a mobile phone where the AR experience will take place. Then, visitors are asked to point the phone's camera to a large poster in the exhibit space which we use as an image-based tracking surface. Visitors can chose from a range of three types of bodies, three types of heads and three types of colour patterns. Then they name their statuette and place it on the island. This personalising step is designed to convey the first-person experience of creating the statuette and why people did this in the past.

Next, the visitor places the statuette on the virtual island of Cyprus. We aimed at a simple representation of the island, yet geographically correct. The island consists of landscapes, houses, stables and the altar with the sacred stone. The visitors in VR go to the place where their statuette is delivered from the AR design and take the figure to place it at the altar. Figures are relatively unique, as there are 27 combinations and the island is regularly cleared of older statuettes. While in VR, users can explore freely. Also, they can see the AR visitor that views the island from above, the next step of the experience.

Finally, users can return to the island from above using a second AR phone, hover over it, and view details and layouts from different perspectives. The AR visitor can also see and interact with the VR user on the virtual island and vice-versa.

22.3.3.3 Development and Testing of the VR and AR Applications

The mixed reality exhibition consists of two parts: the VR Agia Irini sanctuary Android application and the AR statuette creator/Island Explorer Android application.

The AR exhibit was installed on three Samsung Galaxy S8+ smartphones featuring a 15.75 cm screen with a resolution of 1440 × 2960 pixels. The operating system of the smartphone was Android v7.0 (Nougat). The device is powered by an Octa core (2.3 GHz, Quad core, M2 Mongoose +1.7 GHz, Quad core, Cortex A53) processor paired with 4 GB of RAM. The built-in rear camera is a 12 MP Exmor-RS CMOS Sensor camera supporting a resolution of 4000 × 3000 pixels. Other sensors include a light sensor, proximity sensor, accelerometer, barometer, compass and gyroscope. We used one phone per stage of the experience, the AR design, the VR island explorer and the AR island explorer.

The AR exhibit was developed using Unity 2018.1.0f2 and Vuforia Engine 7.5 on a Windows 10 PC. The tracking technology used was fiducial marker tracking provided by the AR SDK of the Vuforia Engine. The magic lens metaphor is used to track the fiducial markers. The SDK provides fiducial caching and persistent tracking. This results in robust tracking that persists through partial fiducial occlusion and if parts of the fiducial is outside the field of view of the magic lens. The models of the statuettes, island, buildings and artefacts were created in Blender (see Fig. 22.4).

The museum fiducial is a 2 × 1.5 m back-lit high-contrast mainly black and white description image installed at the museum (see Fig. 22.4).

22.3.3.4 Formative, Summative and Longitudinal Evaluations of the Museum Experience

The KTH researchers and the museum staff collaborated closely towards the opening of the exhibit. We tested early prototypes at KTH with master students and at a local high school with target age students. We ran formal tests logging usage data for statistical analysis of virtual position and interaction with the devices. We collected usage data through surveys and semi-structured interviews. For details on the formative and summative evaluations please refer to (Mataruga, 2019). We focused our evaluations on usability and on affordance adoptions. We observed whether users took advantage of AR's mobility range for the creator tool in AR, e.g. rather than rotating the figure on the screen, users would walk around the figure.

After we determined that the experience was usable, we ran pilot tests at the museum. We collected think aloud data from volunteers in the target age group of 8 to 12 year old children. The goal was to determine how accessible and independent the usage of the application was for children without instruction or prompting. We ran the first test with four volunteers, three boys and one girl, ages 8–11. We ran a second pilot with over 20 children who were visiting the museum. There we only observed and did not interact with the users. With consent from their guardians, we asked participants to summarise the experience and relate what they have learned. After a week of successful trials we deployed the system two weeks before the official opening. The exhibit remained open from April 2018 until February 2019.

For the exhibit, we designed robust phone cases and cables to hold the phones in place. We also installed the application on a second set of phones for charging and swapping. The goal for the museum was to have a robust exhibit that would require as little maintenance and guidance as possible from staff.

After the temporary exhibit ended we debriefed with museum staff to synthesise lessons learned during the project. The main lesson learned is what we call "Museum-Strength" exhibits. The goal is to have exhibits that do not require maintenance or guidance from museum staff. These are self-explaining and robust projects that have resilient software and sturdy hardware. The main problem with the installation was the battery life of the mobile phones. They had to be constantly charged and swapped three or four times per day. VR and AR applications are power-hungry technologies. We considered running a power cord down the holding cable, but decided against it due to safety concerns for the visitors. Powered devices emit higher electromagnetic fields. We considered providing a QR code and wireless network to allow visitors to download and instal the app on their devices, but early tests showed that this was a high barrier to participation.

22.3.3.5 Reflections

The collaboration between curators, communicators, engineers and researchers is a strong mechanisms to building coherent and accurate museum experiences that are technically challenging. Curators and communicators know the content and the pedagogical methods to deliver it. Engineers and researchers know about the technology and its interaction affordances and limitations. It is critical to have ongoing dialogue in the creation of technical experiences for cultural heritage museums. Participatory design and research through design methods are essential for the success of the project. Furthermore, early prototyping and continuous formative evaluations within and outside the development group are indispensable. Early pilot tests with museum beta testers is the next crucial step. Yet, even through all these steps, the longitudinal deployment of an exhibit is a significant challenge for mobile devices. In hindsight, if we are to design long-lasting technical experiences for museums, they need to be continuously powered. Smartphones running AR and VR consume their batteries rapidly and produce waste heat which, when worn on the face, can make the experience uncomfortable. We need greater thought to increase the museum-strength of the devices that go live in the gallery.

22.3.4 *A Virtual Archetypal Japanese Tea House*

At the intersection of tangible and intangible heritage lie archetypal heritage objects, such as descriptions of archetypal architecture, e.g. the description of the architectural style of traditional Malay long-roof type houses (Said and Embi, 2008), which by themselves can serve as educational aids, but these archetypal heritage object depictions can also be expanded into extensive virtual heritage experiences. A prime example for this is the Virtual Egyptian Temple (Troche and Jacobson, 2010) that was developed as an archetypal building representation, showcasing the typical architectural elements of New Kingdom Egyptian temples, or the "Egyptian Oracle" mixed reality virtual heritage experience that was built on top of this (Gillam and Jacobson, 2015). In this case study we describe the Virtual Tea House application, which has similar aims, showcasing the typical architectural elements found in a traditional Japanese tea house in a—functionally limited—virtual environment.

22.3.4.1 Japanese Tea Houses and Their Relation to the Tea Ceremony

The way of tea and the tea ceremony itself are deeply linked to Buddhism, and the ceremony is viewed as a form of meditation. The placement of the tea house within the tea garden emphasises this, the rationale being both practical and symbolic as the separate, almost isolated placement of the tea house helps guests to relieve themselves of the burdens of daily life.

Tea houses are elevated post and beam structures (Fig. 22.5a, e, g), where each post is set on top of an individual foundation stone (Holl, 2020). Their walls are simple, with the building frame holding a thin, clay-covered bamboo lattice and incorporate different types of windows, usually as a loose bamboo lattice covered by translucent rice paper screens, some with exterior bamboo grilles (Handa, 2013) and some with horizontally sliding panels within frames allowing them to be opened (Holl, 2020). Tea houses are built using natural or reclaimed building materials, e.g. their construction might reuse beams from old buildings that have been demolished or suitable logs and branches from nearby trees (Fehrer, 2019), which can often be seen directly in their central tree-like natural log column ('naka-bashira'), making every tea house a unique specimen.

Tea houses often have unique and distinctive irregularities, such as irregular roof beams, and tea houses frequently have more than one roof, with different roofs also having different orientations (Holl, 2020). To ground the tea house in its environment, its roofs have deep overhangs, purposefully covering a larger area than the footprint of the house. The sliding door through which guests enter, called the 'nijiriguchi', is a low square with a size of ca. 66cm by 66cm (Fehrer, 2019), located at a corner of the tea house (Fig. 22.5f, g). This forces guests to crawl into the tea house, the rationale being that as guests have to bow to enter they are humbled (Knight, 1981), symbolically leaving their ranks outside.

Tea houses use tatami mats, woven, padded mats that are twice as long as they are wide (approximately 180 cm by 90 cm in size) as their base unit of measure (Hein, 2016), and the main floor area of the tea room is laid out by combining several tatami mats, the smallest using only $1^1/_2$ mats, with the largest possible ideal area being created by combining $4^1/_2$ tatami mats (Handa, 2013). This $4^1/_2$ tatami-mat-sized room can be arranged into what is known as a magic square, which is one of the most popular lay-outs for tea houses (Fig. 22.5b). In the centre of the room, where the $^1/_2$ size tatami mat is located, there is a sunken hearth called a 'furo', for which part of the tatami mat has been cut out (Holl, 2020). This is where a fire is lit and the water

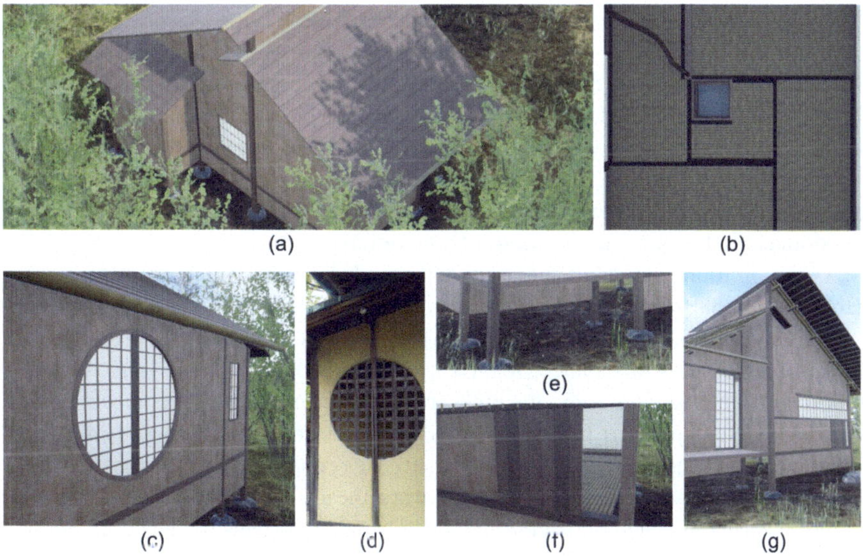

Fig. 22.5 **a** a view of the archetypal Japanese tea house; **b** 4$^{1}/_{2}$ tatami mat floor layout with 'furo' hearth in the central $^{1}/_{2}$ tatami mat area; **c** a round window to the left and the window to the tokonoma on the right side of the wall; **d** photo of a round tea house window; **e** posts on individual foundation stones; **f** square crawling entrance with sliding door 'nijiriguchi'; **g** side view of the tea house (with 'nijiriguchi' entrance on the right)

for the tea is boiled (during summer months this is covered by tatami, and a movable 'furo' is used instead).

Traditionally, a tea house is kept empty and unadorned with only the utensils used for the tea ceremony being kept within the house, where they are stowed away when not in use. The exception is the 'tokonoma', an alcove on one side of the room that is typically located across the room from the 'nijiriguchi', usually south-facing and receiving light from the right, often through a small window (Fehrer, 2019). The tokonoma is elevated from the rest of the room where a hanging scroll or an 'ikebana' (flower arrangement), is displayed. The size of the tokonoma can vary from tearoom to tearoom. It is the only place with decorations in the room, which is changed according to season, time of day and need. Next to the tokonoma is where the main guest, chosen before the guests enter the tea garden, will sit.

An area separate from the guests, the 'mizuya', i.e. water room, is where the utensils for the tea ceremony are kept, where food and sweets are prepared, and where the utensils are cleaned after the tea ceremony. While the guests enter through the 'nijiriguchi', the host enters through a backdoor into the water room and after the guests have seated themselves, the host enters the main tea room from the water room. In smaller tea houses the water room, instead of being a separate room, might instead take the guise of a small alcove or simply shelves on a side of the room, where the utensils for the ceremony can be stored.

22.3.4.2 Virtual Tea House Proof of Concept

Our Virtual Tea House is not based on an existing tea house, but instead is a hypothetical building, designed according to the typical architectural principles and styles found in traditional Japanese tea houses. Its design embodies the most common elements of tea house architecture, incorporating the frequently used square, 4½ tatami mat floor layout and other typical elements such as the 'nijiriguchi' opposite the tokonoma and the 'furo' in the central ½ tatami mat.

A less common but nonetheless frequently used element found in many tea houses (Holl, 2020) that our design integrates is a round window (Fig. 22.5c, d), which was included in our design as the softer shape of the round window aligns with the Buddhist notion of balance, related to the concept of yin and yang, which is important to the tea ceremony: the eight trigrams of yin and yang represent natural phenomena/elements (Art Institute of Chicago, 2000) and five of these (fire, wood, water, metal and earth) are directly related to the tea ceremony (wood is used to make fire, fire is used to boil water in a metal teapot and the tea bowls and ashes from the fire represent earth). As all eight trigrams can be placed in the cells on the periphery of a square that has been divided into nine smaller squares—the magic square mentioned above—with the central square left empty, they are the philosophical basis for the 4½ tatami mat floor layout in tea houses (Fehrer, 2019). For the implementation of our prototype virtual heritage application we used off-the-shelf software (Anderson et al., 2020), namely Unreal Engine as the virtual environment infrastructure, Autodesk Maya for the construction of the 3D models and Adobe Substance 3D Designer in combination with Quixel Mixer to create textures. The tea house was created using straight-forward polygonal modelling to keep the geometry as lightweight as possible, the idea being to potentially facilitate the use of a mobile phone based HMD for experiencing the Virtual Tea House in VR.

The current version of the application presents an archetypal Japanese tea house in a 3D interactive virtual environment, allowing users to examine the architecture of the virtual building model. On the basis of this, extensions are possible, and scenarios that we are considering—both screen-based and/or in VR—include a non-interactive virtual tea ceremony, where the user will be taken along a predetermined path, possibly with narration to explain what is being shown, and possibly an interactive mode to allow users to immerse themselves in the intangible heritage of the Japanese tea ceremony by participating in an interactive virtual tea ceremony.

22.3.5 Exploring Norse Mythology Using a Game Inspired by Viking History

Serious games for cultural heritage (Anderson et al., 2010) are not the only type of interactive virtual heritage experience. Zyda identified "entertainment" as one of the most important factors when games are meant to convey knowledge, demanding that "the entertainment component comes first" (Zyda, 2005), and this wisdom also holds when one aims to convey cultural heritage, and this is what our final case study aims to achieve. "SAGA–Rise of a Valkyrie" (Fig. 22.6) is a screen-based game in development (Larsson and Anderson, 2022), in which the player takes on the role of a young woman who wakes up after the events of Ragnarök (Encyclopaedia Britannica Editors, 2022), the apocalypse in Norse Mythology, and then finds that all people in the world have disappeared. She then takes on the role of a Valkyrie to help the souls of the disappeared to return from the afterlife to repopulate the world.

22.3.5.1 Embedding Intangible Heritage in Fantasy Gameplay

The focus for Project SAGA is on exploring the mythological aspects of the world of the Vikings, and how their beliefs would have influenced their daily lives. Unlike heritage experiences that focus on conveying real historical events and tangible aspects, such as archaeological finds, the focus on the intangible mythology in SAGA allowed the taking of artistic liberties. Set in an environment informed by archaeological surveys and employing real historical information, SAGA incorporates this in the gameplay and combines it with the mythology (Larsson and Anderson, 2022), introducing the player to Viking age beliefs and customs without compromising on either knowledge or entertainment.

A unique advantage of game technology is the ability to not only display the physical aspects of a given topic, but also provide insight into the intangible. In the case of Project SAGA this gives the player the chance to partake in the cultural practices and religious rituals of the Viking society. By allowing the player's actions to influence the world and the characters in it, and by letting the player's curiosity lead, the world provides them with motivation to engage with the information they discover and the knowledge they gain through playing the game.

A game world can provide aspects that cannot be replicated in real life, e.g. magical elements, or creatures and gods, such as those presented in the Völuspá, the first poem of the Poetic Edda (Larrington, 2014), and SAGA's design builds on this.

In Project SAGA the first interaction with the supernatural that the player experiences are glowing stones (Fig. 22.6d), based on painted stones found on Gotland (Oehrl, 2017), an island off the Swedish east coast. The stones hold two purposes, the first is to explain the world in which the game takes place. There is a tradition in Scandinavia to raise stones often inscribed with short tales about a person who had passed away. The stones in SAGA use the same idea of telling a short story, however, in contrast to rune stones (Roesdahl and Wilson, 1992), they tell the different verses of the Völuspá, rather than a person's life and they also use the illustrative image language that is found on the Gotlandic picture stones, rather than runic inscriptions. The second purpose for the stones is a much more active role in the mechanics of the game. When first finding the stones, they are broken, and the player will have to search for the missing pieces. Once restored, the stones' paintings will begin to glow, and the stones will turn into gateways, allowing souls to return to the world.

The picture stones on Gotland that inspired the design for the stones in SAGA, share a similar shape with the north portal of Urnes Stavkirke (UNESCO World

Fig. 22.6 SAGA game world (clockwise): **a** ramparts and entrance to the Viking settlement; **b** deserted houses in the village; **c** exit from the settlement (towards the woods); **d** a picture stone portal in the woods outside of the Viking settlement

Heritage Centre, 1979), one of the oldest stave churches in Norway, dating as far back as the twelfth century. There can also be drawn parallels between the Gotlandic picture stones and doorways when looking at their placement in the landscape. The picture stones are often found at the boundaries of the land, much like how doorways are placed in the walls of a building. There are multiple sources in which a door or doorway is used in Viking rituals to see or contact another realm, this often being the realm of the dead (Eriksen, 2013).

22.3.5.2 Combining Tangible Heritage and Intangible Beliefs and Practices

While the main focus of SAGA is on the storytelling and fantasy elements, to be relevant as an illustration of cultural heritage it is important that the historical knowledge is reflected in the less mythological aspects of the world as well. Knowledge of how architecture and societies were shaped during the Viking age is limited, partially because contemporary written sources are scarce, and all known sources were written by people from other countries and cultures. Archaeological finds are often only simple objects or traces in the earth, so very little is known about the buildings other than placement and general shape. This is most likely due to the majority being built in organic materials which have decomposed during the past millennium. Information about style, decorative elements and height has mostly been lost. This means, however, that opportunities for developers exist where there is little historical or archaeological knowledge, as the design choices made could be more creative. During archaeological excavations it has been found that houses and other buildings rarely were placed in regular angles to each other, likely due to them being added or removed as needed over longer periods of time. In SAGA, this is used to create natural paths for the player to follow. Another aspect that has been found during excavations of some Viking settlements, such as the settlement of Birka near Stockholm (UNESCO World Heritage Centre, 1993), is that the Vikings used earthen ramparts to protect their settlements. In level design such an element can be used to control what the player can or cannot see.

At the beginning of SAGA the player wakes up just outside a small village (Fig. 22.6a). The village entrance is framed by an opening in the earthen rampart, which creates a focal point for the player. The rampart also obscures much of the village, which helps urge the player to explore the areas which are hidden. It is important, especially in open world games, to use techniques to guide players to areas where one wants them to go without limiting their curiosity (Fig. 22.6c).

When developing a game such as SAGA, the greatest challenge lies in creating content that is both unique and engaging the players' creativity, without losing the ability to convey the cultural heritage to the player. However, if one does not push at the boundaries of what is known and realistic, it would be impossible to utilise the capabilities of the technology, identical to those of entertainment games, to their fullest. SAGA is a story-driven exploration game with a focus on not only the Vikings of history, but also the mythological world of the Vikings. By basing design decisions on the historical context where real archaeological and historical information can be found, and simultaneously taking artistic liberties where it cannot, SAGA aims to find a balance between knowledge and entertainment without sacrificing either.

22.4 Conclusions

The case studies we have presented here provide but a sample of the different types of interactive heritage applications, demonstrating the range of different types of such applications that can be built by using the infrastructure for real-time interactive virtual environments, suggesting various combinations of technologies and approaches that would be suitable for different types of interactive heritage experiences and highlighting numerous aspects for consideration for the development of these different types of interactive heritage applications.

These software systems, found at the heart of real-time interactive virtual environments and most commonly encountered in the guise of game engines, allow the creation of virtual heritage experiences that allow users to act not merely as passive observers but instead as active participants in the heritage, fully immersing them in the experience. This provision of immersive interactive experiences for users is key to their ability to not only visualise tangible heritage, but also for conveying intangible cultural heritage.

Their interactivity is the main reason why game-engine based real-time graphics systems provide an ideal infrastructure for interactive virtual heritage experiences, independent of whether they employ screen-based desktop CG, VR or AR.

Acknowledgements For the AR Visualisation of the Roman villa at Frampton, Dorset (Sect. 22.3.1), the authors acknowledge the significant contribution to development by Bournemouth University student research assistant Laura Jenkins. For the Romanian Easter Egg Decoration AR application (Sect. 22.3.2), the authors acknowledge the help of Oleg Fryazinov of the National Centre for Computer Animation at Bournemouth University, whose expertise in digital fabrication and related techniques made the use of the 3D printed AR marker possible. For the VR/AR interactive exhibit at the Mediterranean Museum of Stockholm (Sect. 22.3.3) we acknowledge the following groups: The two developers of the AR and VR apps were master students at KTH: Yinglai Xu and Dani Mataruga. The museum team included curators, researchers and communication staff: Elin Örnberg, Fredrik Helander, Christian Muhlenbock and Johanna Berg. From KTH the researchers who participated were Mario Romero, Björn Thuresson and Mattias Höger. We also want to thank the museum staff who maintained our exhibit and the visitors who tested our prototypes. Finally, for the SAGA game, exploring Norse Mythology and Viking History (Sect. 22.3.5), we extend our gratitude to Joachim Coppens, Senior Level Artist at Rare Ltd, and archaeologist Mattias Frisk from Bohusläns museum for their help and feedback during the SAGA project. We also need to mention Jens Heimdahl and Britt-Marie Birgander, who kindly shared their expertise. The development of SAGA has been partially funded by Orust Sparbank's Culture Grant.

References

AlMuraikhi N, AlMalki F, AlDahnim F, Halabi O (2021) Virtual reality for rich interaction with cultural heritage sites. In: HCI in games: serious and immersive games, pp 319–328

Anastasovitis E, Ververidis D, Nikolopoulos S, Kompatsiaris I (2017) Digiart: building new 3D cultural heritage worlds. In: 2017 3DTV conference: the true vision—capture, transmission and display of 3D video (3DTV-CON), pp 1–4

Anderson EF (2013) Computer games technology and serious games for the preservation of cultural heritage. In: 3rd international conference of young folklorists: vernacular expressions and analytic categories—abstracts. University of Tartu, pp 11–21. http://www.digar.ee/id/nlib-digar:131664

Anderson EF (2021) Reconstructing the past: outstanding student-created virtual heritage experiences. In: Eurographics 2021—education papers

Anderson EF, McLoughlin L, Liarokapis F, Peters C, Petridis P, de Freitas S (2010) tartuDeveloping serious games for cultural heritage: a state-of-the-art review. Virtual Real 14(4):255–275

Anderson EF, John D, Mikulski R, Redford A, Romero M (2020) Preserving and presenting cultural heritage using off-the-shelf software. Springer, pp 423–444

Art Institute of Chicago T (2000) Trigrams. Taoism and the Arts of China Web Site. https://archive.artic.edu/taoism/diag-trigram.php

Bekele MK, Pierdicca R, Frontoni E, Malinverni ES, Gain J (2018) A survey of augmented, virtual, and mixed reality for cultural heritage. J Comput Cult Herit 11(2)

Boboc RG, Băutu E, Gîrbacia F, Popovici N, Popovici DM (2022) Augmented reality in cultural heritage: an overview of the last decade of applications. Appl Sci 12(19)

Bowden W, Brundell P, Harlow N, Martin-Jones A, Mullen A (2023) Developing immersive experience at Caistor Roman Town: final report on AHRC Next Generation of Immersive Experiences Project (2018). Tech rep, AHRC

Buratti G, Amoruso G (2022) Game engine applications overview and comparative analysis for the enhancement of cultural heritage. DN v.9:103–119

Cheetham P, Russell M, Stewart D (2018) The temple or room? The interpretation of Frampton Roman temple/villa site in the light of recent geophysical survey results. In: Recent work in archaeological geophysics
Cheng JC, Chen K, Chen W (2017) Comparison of marker-based AR and markerless AR: a case study on indoor decoration system. In: Lean and computing in construction congress (LC3): proceedings of the joint conference on computing in construction (JC3), pp 483–490
Choudary O, Charvillat V, Grigoras R, Gurdjos P (2009) MARCH: mobile augmented reality for cultural heritage. In: Proceedings of the 17th ACM international conference on multimedia, pp 1023–1024
Cipriani L, Bertacchi S, Bertacchi G (2019) An optimised workflow for the interactive experience with cultural heritage through reality-based 3d models: cases study in archaeological and urban complexes. Int Arch Photogramm Remote Sens Spatial Inf Sci XLII-2/W11:427–434
Codina F, de Prado G, Ruiz I, Sierra A (2017) The Iberian town of Ullastret (Catalonia). An Iron Age urban agglomeration reconstructed virtually. Archeologia e Calcolatori 28(2):311–320
Dhanda A, Reina Ortiz M, Weigert A, Paladini A, Min A, Gyi M, Su S, Fai S, Santana Quintero M (2019) Recreating cultural heritage environments for VR using photogrammetry. Int Arch Photogramm Remote Sens Spatial Inf Sci XLII-2/W9:305–310
Dorset Wildlife Trust (2023) Nunnery Mead
Duer Z, Ogle T, Hicks D, Fralin S, Tucker T, Yu R (2020) Making the invisible visible: illuminating the hidden histories of the world war I tunnels at vauquois through a hybridized virtual reality exhibition. IEEE Comput Graph Appl 40(4):39–50
Encyclopaedia Britannica Editors (2022) Ragnarök. In: Encyclopædia Britannica
Eriksen MH (2013) Doors to the dead. The power of doorways and thresholds in Viking Age Scandinavia. Archaeol Dialogues 20(2):187–214
Fehrer W (2019) The Japanese Teahouse. Niggli Verlag
Fredrick D (2014) TimeDeltaTime: the vicissitudes of presence in visualizing Roman houses with game engine technology. AI Soc 29(4):461–472
Gherardini F, Santachiara M, Leali F (2019) Enhancing heritage fruition through 3D virtual models and augmented reality: an application to Roman artefacts. Virtual Archaeol Rev 10(21):67–79
Gillam R, Jacobson J (eds) (2015) The Egyptian oracle project: ancient ceremony in augmented reality. Bloomsbury Academic
Glăveanu VP (2013) Creativity development in community contexts: the case of folk art. Think Ski Creat 9:152–164
González Vargas JC, Fabregat R, Carrillo-Ramos A, Jové T (2020) Survey: using augmented reality to improve learning motivation in cultural heritage studies. Appl Sci 10(3)
Gorovei A (1937) Ouăle de Paşti : studiu de folklor, Academia Română. Studii şi cercetări, vol XXX. Monitorul Oficial şi Imprimeriile Statului. Imprimeria Naţională Bucureşti
Häkkilä J, Hannula P, Luiro E, Launne E, Mustonen S, Westerlund T, Colley A (2019) Visiting a virtual graveyard: designing virtual reality cultural heritage experiences. In: Proceedings of the 18th international conference on mobile and ubiquitous multimedia
Handa R (2013) Sen no Rikyū and the Japanese way of tea: ethics and aesthetics of the everyday. Interiors 4(3):229–247
Hein C (2016) Tatami. In: Kyoto Design Lab: The tangible and the intangible of the Machiya House. Delft University of Technology, pp 9–12
Hernández Ibáñez LA, Naya VB (2015) An enhanced navigation kit for virtual heritage exploration using a game engine. In: 2015 Digital Heritage, vol 2, pp 755–756
Holl M (2020) Architectural principles of traditional Japanese teahouses. Master's thesis, Technische Universität Wien
Joyce RD, Robinson S (2017) Passive haptics to enhance virtual reality simulations. In: AIAA modeling and simulation technologies conference
Kiourt C, Koutsoudis A, Pavlidis G (2016) DynaMus: a fully dynamic 3D virtual museum framework. J Cult Heritage 22:984–991
Knight TW (1981) The forty-one steps. Environ Plann B: Urban Anal City Sci 8(1):97–114

Kolivand H, Rhalibi AE, Tajdini M, Abdulazeez S, Praiwattana P (2018) Cultural heritage in markerless augmented reality: a survey. In: Advanced methods and new materials for cultural heritage preservation, IntechOpen
Larrington C (ed) (2014) The Poetic Edda, revised edn. Oxford University Press
Larsson C, Anderson EF (2022) Project SAGA: towards bridging the gap between serious and entertainment games. In: Eurographics Workshop on Graphics and Cultural Heritage
Latham W, Todd S, Todd P, Putnam L (2021) Exhibiting Mutator VR: procedural art evolves to virtual reality. Leonardo 54(3):274–281
Leach M, Maddock S, Hadley D, Butterworth C, Moreland J, Dean G, Mackinder R, Pach K, Bax N, Mckone M, Fleetwood D (2018) Recreating Sheffield's Medieval castle in situ using outdoor augmented reality. In: Virtual reality and augmented reality, pp 213–229
Lysons S (1813) Reliquiae Britannico-Romanae: containing figures of Roman antiquities discovered in various parts of England. Printed by T, Bensley
Ma YP (2021) Extending 3D-GIS district models and BIM-Based building models into computer gaming environment for better workflow of cultural heritage conservation. Appl Sci 11(5)
Malý I, Vachková I, Sedlácek D (2023) Draw-Cut-Glue: comparison of paper house model creation in VR and on paper in a museum education programme—pilot study. In: Eurographics 2023—Education Papers
Mann L, Fryazinov O (2019) 3D Printing for mixed reality hands-on museum exhibit interaction. In: ACM SIGGRAPH 2019 Posters
Marto A, Gonçalves A (2019) Mobile AR: user evaluation in a cultural heritage context. Appl Sci 9(24)
Mataruga D (2019) Statistical analysis and evaluation of the 6DOF-utilization of a handheld augmented reality museum application. Master's thesis, KTH
Meegan E, Murphy M, Keenaghan G, Corns A, Shaw R, Fai S, Scandura S, Chenaux A (2021) Virtual heritage learning environments. In: Digital heritage. Progress in cultural heritage: documentation, preservation, and protection. Springer, pp 427–437
Meier C, Saorín J, de León AB, Cobos AG (2020) Using the Roblox Video Game engine for creating virtual tours and learning about the sculptural heritage. Int J Emerg Technol Learn 15(20):268–280
Midya M, Maity R (2021) Preserving cultural heritage with mobile augmented reality–a survey. In: Proceedings of intelligent computing and technologies conference, pp 11–24
Murgoei A (1909) Roumanian Easter Eggs. Folklore 20(3):295–303
Oehrl S (2017) Documenting and interpreting the picture stones of Gotland: old problems and new approaches. Curr Swed Archaeol 25(1):87–122
Panou C, Ragia L, Dimelli D, Mania K (2018) An architecture for mobile outdoors augmented reality for cultural heritage. ISPRS Int J Geo-Inf 7(12)
Perring D (2003) 'Gnosticism' in Fourth-Century Britain: the Frampton Mosaics Reconsidered. Britannia 34:97–127
Rallis I, Kopsiaftis G, Kalisperakis I, Stentoumis C, Koutsomitsos D, Riga V (2022) A mobile game for enhancing Tourism and Cultural Heritage. Procedia Comput Sci 204:513–518
Roesdahl E, Wilson DM (1992) Indleding. In: Viking og Hvidekrist : Norden og Europa 800-1200, Nordisk Ministerråd, pp 24–29
Rua H, Alvito P (2011) Living the past: 3D models, virtual reality and game engines as tools for supporting archaeology and the reconstruction of cultural heritage—the case-study of the Roman villa of Casal de Freiria. J Archaeol Sci 38(12):3296–3308
Russell M, Stewart D, Cheetham P, Manley H (2022) Artistic Lysons? New work on the 'lost' mosaics of Frampton Roman villa, Dorset. Mosaic 49:19–31
Said S, Embi MR (2008) A parametric shape grammar of the traditional malay long-roof type houses. Int J Archit Comput 6(2):121–144
Silva M, Teixeira L (2022) eXtended Reality (XR) Experiences in Museums for cultural heritage: a systematic review. In: Intelligent technologies for interactive entertainment, pp 58–79

Siriwardhana Y, Porambage P, Liyanage M, Ylianttila M (2021) A survey on mobile augmented reality with 5G mobile edge computing: architectures, applications, and technical aspects. IEEE Commun Surv Tutor 23(2):1160–1192

Troche J, Jacobson J (2010) An exemplar of Ptolemaic Egyptian temples. In: CAA'10: computer applications in archaeology 2010

UNESCO World Heritage Centre (1979) Urnes Stave Church. World Heritage List

UNESCO World Heritage Centre (1993) Birka and Hovgården. World Heritage List

Ureche AMC, Fryazinov O, Anderson EF (2022) Traditional Romanian Egg decoration in augmented reality with 3D printing. In: Eurographics workshop on graphics and cultural heritage

Voinea GD, Girbacia F, Postelnicu CC, Marto A (2019) Exploring cultural heritage using augmented reality through Google's Project Tango and ARCore. In: VR technologies in cultural heritage, pp 93–106

Vuforia (2023) Ground Plane. https://library.vuforia.com/environments/ground-plane

Winbladh ML (2003) The Cyprus collections in the Medelhavsmuseet. In: The Cyprus collections in the Medelhavsmuseet, AG Leventis Foundation and Medelhavsmuseet, pp 13–23

Zyda M (2005) From visual simulation to virtual reality to games. Computer 38(9):25–32

The manufacturer's authorised representative in the EU is Springer Nature Customer Service Centre GmbH, Europaplatz 3, 69115 Heidelberg, Germany. If you have any concerns regarding our products, please contact ProductSafety@springernature.com

Printed and bound by CPI Group (UK) Ltd, Croydon, CR0 4YY
23/09/2026
02221532-0016